D0699432

Fundamentals of
CORPORATE
FINANCE

FIRST CANADIAN EDITION

Fundamentals of
CORPORATE
FINANCE

FIRST CANADIAN EDITION

Ronald M. Giammarino
University of British Columbia

Elizabeth M. Maynes
York University

Richard A. Brealey
London Business School

Stewart C. Myers
Massachusetts Institute of Technology

Alan J. Marcus
Boston College

McGraw-Hill Ryerson Limited
Toronto New York Auckland Bogotá Caracas Lisbon
London Madrid Mexico Milan New Delhi San Juan
Singapore Sydney Tokyo

FUNDAMENTALS OF CORPORATE FINANCE
First Canadian Edition

Copyright © McGraw-Hill Ryerson Limited, 1996. Copyright © McGraw-Hill, Inc., 1995. All rights reserved. No part of this publication may be reproduced or transmitted in any form or by any means, or stored in a data base or retrieval system, without the prior written permission of McGraw-Hill Ryerson Limited, or in the case of photocopying or other reprographic copying, a licence from CANCOPY (the Canadian Copyright Licensing Agency), 6 Adelaide Street East, Suite 900, Toronto, Ontario, M5C 1H6.

Any request for photocopying, recording, or taping of any part of this publication shall be directed in writing to CANCOPY.

ISBN: 0-07-551799-X

1 2 3 4 5 6 7 8 9 10   BBM   5 4 3 2 1 0 9 8 7 6

Printed and bound in Canada

Care has been taken to trace ownership of copyright material contained in this text. The publisher will gladly take any information that will enable them to rectify any reference or credit in subsequent editions.

Sponsoring Editor: Jennifer Mix
Developmental Editor: Daphne Scriabin
Production Editor: Gail Marsden
Production Co-ordinator: Nicla Dattolico
Designer: Dianna Little
Cover Design: Dianna Little
Cover Illustration/Photo: T. Heneghan/The Stock Library, Toronto
Typesetter: Bookman Typesetting Co.
Typeface: Times Roman
Printer: Best Book Manufacturers

Canadian Cataloguing in Publication Data
Main entry under title:

Fundamentals of corporate finance

1st Canadian ed.
Includes index.
ISBN 0-07-551799-X

1. Corporations - Finance.   2. Financial statements.
I. Giammarino, Ronald M. (Ronald Mark), 1955-

HG4026.F86 1995   658.15   C95-932309-0

To Bruce and to Stephanie, Matt, Jessy, Jacob, and Mark

About the Authors

RONALD M. GIAMMARINO
Associate Professor at the Faculty of Commerce, University of British Columbia. He is a member of the editorial board of the *Review of Financial Studies* and past chair of the Program Committee of the Northern Finance Association. His research deals with strategic aspects of corporate financial policy, bankruptcy law, and financial regulation. Formerly with the Finance Department at Bell Canada and currently active as a financial consultant.

ELIZABETH M. MAYNES
Associate Professor of Finance and Finance Area Coordinator at the Faculty of Administrative Studies, York University. She is Co-Director of the Joint MBA/LLB Program of York University. She received her Ph.D. degree in Economics from Queen's University, Kingston. Her research interests include the role and value of voting rights of shareholders, initial public offerings, takeovers, and experimental economics and finance.

RICHARD A. BREALEY
London Business School, Tokai Bank Professor of Finance. Past President of European Finance Association and Director of the American Finance Association. Current research interests include portfolio theory and international finance. Member of editorial board of *Journal of Applied Corporate Finance*. Other books include *Introduction to Risk and Return from Common Stocks*. Formerly with Sun Life Assurance Company of Canada and Keystone Custodian Funds of Boston.

STEWART C. MYERS
Gordon Y. Billard Professor of Finance at the Massachusetts Institute of Technology's Sloan School of Management. Director of MIT's International Financial Services Research Center. He is past President and Director of the American Finance Association and co-author of the leading graduate-level textbook on corporate finance. His research is primarily concerned with the valuation of real and financial assets, corporate financial policy, and financial aspects of government regulation of business. He is currently a Research Associate of the National Bureau of Economic Research and is active as a financial consultant.

ALAN J. MARCUS
Professor of Finance at Boston College's Wallace E. Carroll School of Management. His main research interests are in asset valuation, particularly in futures and options markets. Other books include *Investments*. Formerly with the Financial Research department at the Federal Home Loan Mortgage Corporation (Freddie Mac).

Contents in Brief

Contents

Finance in Action

Preface

This book is about corporate finance. It focuses on how companies raise capital and how they invest it.

Financial management is important, interesting, and challenging. It is important because today's capital investment decisions may determine the businesses the firm is in 10, 20, or more years ahead. A firm's success or failure depends in large part on its financial decisions and planning.

Finance is interesting for several reasons. The financial community is international and fast moving, with some colourful heroes and (unfortunately) a sprinkling of unpleasant villains. Financial decisions often involve huge sums of money. For example, large investments or acquisitions may involve billions of dollars.

Finance is challenging. Financial decisions are rarely cut and dried, and the financial markets in which companies operate are changing rapidly. Good managers can cope with routine problems; the best managers can also respond to change. You need to know why companies and financial markets behave as they do and when common practice may not be the best practice. Once you have a consistent framework for making financial decisions, complex problems become more manageable.

This book seeks to provide that framework. It is not an encyclopedia of finance. It focuses instead on setting out the basic *principles* of financial management and applying them to the main decisions faced by the Canadian financial manager. It explains why value maximization provides a coherent framework for making financial decisions, and it looks at how companies can make investment and financing decisions that add value. It also describes the main features of financial markets and the various securities that companies may issue.

Since this text is intended for use in a first course in corporate finance, we assume little in the way of background knowledge. While most users will have had an introductory accounting course, we review the concepts from accounting that are important to the financial manager in Chapter Two.

Fundamentals and Principles of Corporate Finance

This book is derived in part from its sister text *Principles of Corporate Finance*. The spirit of the two books is similar. Both apply modern finance — that is, finance organized by the principal of value maximization — to give students a working ability to make complex and interesting financial decisions. However, there are also substantial differences between the two books.

Fundamentals is geared more toward the finance novice. We envision the typical reader as an undergraduate with little or no business experience, and therefore we simplify the discussion along several dimensions. First, we provide a much more detailed discussion of the principles and mechanics of the time value of money. This material underlies almost all of the rest of the text, and we spend two lengthy chapters providing extensive practice with this key concept. Since most readers will be more familiar with their own financial affairs than with the big leagues of finance, we motivate our discussion of the time value of money by looking first at some personal finance decisions.

Second, we use numerical examples in this text to a greater degree than in *Principles*. Each chapter presents several detailed numerical examples to help the reader become familiar and comfortable with the material.

Third, we streamlined the treatment of most topics. Whereas *Principles* has 36 chapters, *Fundamentals* has only 25. The relative brevity of *Fundamentals* necessitates a broad-brush coverage of some topics, but we feel that this is an advantage for a beginning audience.

Principles is known for its relaxed and informal writing style, and we continue this tradition in *Fundamentals*. In addition, we use as little mathematical notation as possible. Even when we present an equation, we usually write it using words rather than mathematical notation. This approach has two advantages. First, it is less intimidating. Second, it focuses attention on the underlying concepts rather than the formula.

In-Text Study Aids

To aid learning, each chapter contains the following features:

1. *Goals of the chapter.* The introduction to each chapter sets out the aims of the chapter and what it will enable the reader to do.

2. *Self-test questions.* Throughout the chapter, we intersperse questions on the immediately preceding material. These questions do not simply require the student to regurgitate facts; they are designed to test understanding. We have placed these questions in the body of the chapter because we believe that it is useful to pause occasionally for reflection before moving on to new material.

3. *Examples.* Each chapter contains several numbered examples that give the reader an opportunity to see how general principles may be applied to concrete problems.

4. *Finance in Action.* In addition to examples, many chapters have a more detailed application of finance to a real business problem. The Finance in Action boxes are selected to give the reader a taste for the excitement and challenges of making financial decisions.

5. *Chapter summary.* The conclusion of each chapter consists of a numbered summary of the major points. These summaries provide a further opportunity for readers to test their understanding, and they are useful when reviewing the material.

6. *End-of-chapter problems.* We believe in learning by doing. The more than 400 end-of-chapter problems provide plenty of opportunity for practice. The solutions to these problems may be found in the Instructor's Manual that accompanies the text.

Organization of the Text and Possible Alternatives

In the course of writing this book, we have spoken with many instructors. We recognize that there are several effective ways to organize a course in corporate finance. For this reason, we have designed the text to be extremely modular, so that the topics may be introduced in different sequences. Here we will describe our rationale for the text's organization and present some feasible alternative strategies for using the book.

Part One is an introduction. Chapter One lays out the issues that are addressed in the rest of the text. It discusses business organization, the goals of the firm, agency and ethical issues, and the role of the financial manager. Chapter Two reviews the accounting principles necessary for the financial manager. It describes the major financial statements and stresses the distinctions between cash flows and profits and between market and book values.

Part Two, on Value, explains the time value of money. We apply this concept to show how securities are valued and how to make capital investment decisions.

We believe that it is useful to discuss the principles of valuation *before* plunging into detailed financial statement analysis or issues of financial planning. Nevertheless, we recognize that many instructors will prefer to move directly from Chapter Two to Chapter Seventeen, Financial Statement Analysis, because this order provides a gentler transition from the typical prerequisite accounting course. There is no reason that one cannot use the text in this order: Part Six (Financial Planning) can easily follow Part One.

When we discuss project appraisal in Part Two, we frequently stress that the opportunity cost of capital for a project depends on project risk. But we do not discuss how to measure risk or how return and risk are linked until **Part Three**. This ordering can easily be modified. The chapters on risk and return can be introduced before, after, or midway through the material on project valuation (for example, immediately following the chapters on the time value of money).

Part Three includes Chapter Eleven on the cost of capital and the weighted average cost of capital. We believe that the discussion of the distinction between equity risk and project risk follows naturally from the introduction to the cost of equity in Chapter Ten. We review and develop the weighted cost of capital more fully in the later chapter on debt policy (Chapter Fifteen).

Whereas Parts Two (Value) and Three (Risk) focus on the asset side of the firm's balance sheet, Parts Four and Five focus on the liability side. **Part Four** presents an overview of corporate financing, discusses the features of a wide variety of debt and equity instruments, and describes how firms issue securities. This part starts with a chapter on market efficiency. Few other introductory texts offer a full chapter on this topic. We believe that this is a mistake. Without a solid understanding of market efficiency, it is difficult to think through the issues that arise when firms issue securities or when they make capital structure and dividend decisions.

Part Five covers debt and dividend policy. We use the MM propositions to identify the issues that should *not* matter to these decisions, then examine the real-world complications that do influence optimal policy.

As noted above, **Part Six** covers financial planning. We start with financial statement analysis, then move on to long-term and short-term planning models. We emphasize in each chapter both the uses and limitations of these plans.

Part Seven discusses the management of short-term assets and liabilities. We cover working capital management, including inventory and cash management, as well as credit and receivable policies. An attractive and unusual feature of our coverage is the integrated treatment of cash and inventory management. We emphasize the essential similarity between the two tasks. This enables us both to highlight the general principles involved and to cover the material more succinctly and with far less repetition than most other texts. We like to discuss working capital with students familiar with the basics of valuation and corporate finance, but we recognize that many instructors prefer to reverse our order, and there should be no difficulty in taking Part Seven out of sequence.

Part Eight covers several important but somewhat more advanced topics — mergers and acquisitions; international finance; options; and risk management. This is not the first time that we have visited some of these issues. For example, we introduce the idea of options in Chapter Eight when we show how companies build flexibility into capital projects and again in Chapter Thirteen when we describe warrants, convertible bonds, and other financing options. However, Chapter Twenty-Four generalizes this material and explains at a fairly elementary level how options are valued. International finance is not confined to Chapter Twenty-Three. Throughout the book we have taken examples from other countries and financial systems. However, there are some specific problems that arise when a corporation is confronted by different currencies, and we tackle these problems in Chapter Twenty-Three.

Supplements

The text is accompanied by a full ancillary program with items designed to complement your teaching efforts and your students' learning process. The Study Guide, prepared by the authors, includes chapter summaries and many solved problems. The Instructor's Manual, also prepared by the authors, provides chapter summaries and detailed solutions to the end-of-chapter problems. A set of overhead transparencies of various figures and tables is useful for in-class use. Also available is a fully computerized test bank with both multiple-choice questions and longer problems that provide instructors with a full range of test questions.

Acknowledgments

We are indebted to our many colleagues for insightful comments on earlier drafts of this work. Their suggestions have greatly enhanced our final product. Among those who gave us the benefit of their time and advice are:

B. Amoako-Adu	*Wilfrid Laurier University*
D. Connelly	*St. Mary's University*
C. Fabiilli	*Algonquin College*
L. Gallant	*St. Francis Xavier University*
P. Molgat	*Red Deer College*
C. Mossman	*University of Manitoba*
D. Patterson	*Grant MacEwan Community College*
A. Saaltink	*Mohawk College*
K. Vandezande	*Simon Fraser University*

We owe much to our colleagues at the University of British Columbia and York University. Special thanks to Professors John Friedlan, Chris Robinson, and Savita Verma, York University, and Steve Alisharan, University of British Columbia, for their willingness to share their expertise and ideas.

We wish to thank Bruce Rhodes and Samson Hui for their assistance with data analysis and presentation.

We also wish to acknowledge the support of the editorial office at McGraw-Hill Ryerson Limited. We are grateful to our development team: Developmental Editor Daphne Scriabin and Susan Calvert, Manager, Editorial Services. We would also like to thank our sponsoring editor, Jennifer Mix, for her commitment to make this the best book possible.

Finally, we cannot overstate the thanks due to our spouses, Diana, Maureen, Sheryl, Stephanie, and Bruce, who struggled with us throughout the project.

Ronald M. Giammarino
Elizabeth M. Maynes
Richard A. Brealey
Stewart C. Myers
Alan J. Marcus

PART ONE

Introduction

CHAPTER ONE
The Firm and the Financial Manager

CHAPTER TWO
Accounting and Finance

CHAPTER ONE

The Firm and the Financial Manager

This book introduces you to the field of corporate finance. By reading the following chapters you will learn about the various responsibilities of the corporation's financial managers and how to approach many of the problems that such managers are expected to solve. We set the stage in this chapter with a discussion of the corporation, the financial decisions it needs to make, and why they are important.

Corporate managers face many challenges in trying to make their firm successful. To survive and prosper, a company must satisfy its customers. It must also produce and sell products and services at a profit. In order to produce it needs many assets — plant, equipment, offices, computers, technology, and so on. The company has to decide (1) which assets to buy and (2) how to pay for them. The financial manager plays a key role in both these decisions. The *investment decision*, that is, the decision to invest in assets like plant, equipment, and know-how, is in large part a responsibility of the financial manager. So is the *financing decision*, the choice of how to pay for such investments.

We start this chapter by explaining how businesses are organized. We then provide a brief introduction to the role of the financial manager and show you why corporate managers need a sophisticated understanding of financial markets. Next we turn to the goals of the firm and ask what makes for a good financial decision. Is the firm's aim to maximize profits? To avoid bankruptcy? To be a good citizen? We consider some conflicts of interest that arise in large organizations and review some mechanisms that align the interests of the firm's managers with the interests of its owners. Finally, we provide an overview of what is to come in the rest of the text.

After studying this chapter you should be able to

- Explain the advantages and disadvantages of the most common forms of business organization and determine which forms are most suitable to different types of businesses.
- Cite the major business functions and decisions that are the responsibility of the firm's financial managers.
- Explain why it makes sense for corporations to maximize their market values.
- Show why conflicts of interest may arise in large organizations and discuss how corporations can provide incentives for everyone to work toward a common end.

ORGANIZING A BUSINESS

Sole Proprietorships

sole proprietor: The sole owner of a business that has no partners and no shareholders.

In the year 1882 George Weston, then 16 years old, bought two bread routes from his employer. Today, with over 60,000 employees, the company has assets worth around $4 billion and, with sales of around $12 billion, George Weston Ltd. is number 4 on the *Financial Post*'s list of Canada's largest companies. If, like George Weston, you start on your own with no partners or stockholders, you are said to be a **sole proprietor.** You bear all of the costs and keep all of the profits after Revenue Canada has taken its cut.

As a sole proprietor, you are responsible for all the business's debts and other liabilities. If the business borrows from the bank and subsequently cannot repay the loan, the bank will have a claim against your personal belongings. It could force you into personal bankruptcy if the business debts are big enough. Thus as sole proprietor you have *unlimited liability*.

Partnerships

partnership: A business owned by two or more persons who are personally responsible for all its liabilities.

Instead of starting on your own, you may wish to pool money and expertise with friends or business associates. If so, a sole proprietorship is obviously inappropriate. Instead, you can form a **partnership**. Your *partnership agreement* will set out how management decisions are to be made and the proportion of the profits to which each partner is entitled. The partners then pay personal income tax on their share of these profits.

Partners, like sole proprietors, have the disadvantage of unlimited liability. If the business runs into financial heavy weather, each partner has unlimited liability for *all* the business's debts, not just his or her share.[1] The moral is clear and simple: "Know thy partner."

Many professional businesses are organized as partnerships. They include the large accounting, legal, and management consulting firms. Many investment dealers such as Wood Gundy and McLeod Young Weir started life as partnerships. So did some well-known industrial companies. For instance, some of the companies that amalgamated to form Stelco were partnerships. So too were such international giants as Apple Computers and Microsoft. But eventually, these companies and their financing requirements grew too large for them to continue as partnerships.

Corporations

corporation: A business owned by stockholders who have limited liability.

As your firm grows, you may decide to *incorporate*. Unlike a proprietorship or partnership, a **corporation** is legally distinct from its owners. It is established by *articles of incorporation* that set out the purpose of the business, how many shares can be issued, the number of directors to be appointed, and so on. The articles that apply to your company have to conform to Canadian laws. Which laws are relevant will depend on whether you incorporate provincially, in which case the corporate statute for the province that you pick will apply, or federally, in which case the Canadian Business Corporations Act will apply. A corporation is sometimes referred to as a legal fiction because, although it is not human, it legally has many of the characteristics of a person: it can enter into contracts, borrow or lend money, sue or be sued. And it pays its own taxes (but it cannot vote!).

limited liability: The owners of the corporation are not personally responsible for its obligations.

The corporation is owned by its stockholders and they get to vote on important matters. Unlike proprietorships or partnerships, corporations have **limited liability**, which means that the stockholders cannot be held personally responsible for the obligations of the firm. If, say, Canadian Pacific were to fail, no one could demand that its shareholders put up more money to pay off the debts. The most a stockholder can lose is the amount invested in the stock.

While the stockholders of a corporation own the firm, they do not usually manage it. Instead, they elect a *board of directors*, that in turn appoints the top managers. The board is the representative of shareholders and is supposed to ensure that management is acting in their best interests.

This *separation of ownership and management* is one distinctive feature of most corporations. In other forms of business organization, such as proprietorships and partnerships, the owners are the managers.

---

[1] Larger businesses can be set up as limited partnerships. In this case partners are classified as general or limited. General partners manage the business and have unlimited personal liability for the business's debts. The liability of limited partners, however, is limited to the money they contribute to the business. They can lose everything they put in, but no more. Limited partners usually have a restricted role in the management.

The separation between management and ownership gives a corporation more flexibility and permanence than a partnership. Even if managers of a corporation quit or are dismissed and replaced by others, the corporation can survive. Similarly, today's shareholders may sell all their shares to new investors without affecting the business. In contrast, ownership of a proprietorship cannot be transferred without selling the *entire* business to another owner-manager.

By organizing as a corporation, a business may be able to attract a wide variety of investors. The shareholders may include individuals who hold only a single share worth a few dollars, receive only a single vote, and are entitled to only a tiny proportion of the profits. Shareholders may also include giant pension funds and insurance companies whose investment in the firm may run into the millions of shares and who are entitled to a correspondingly large number of votes and proportion of the profits.

Given these advantages, you might be wondering why anyone forms a partnership. One reason is the time and cost required to manage a corporation's legal machinery. There can also be tax reasons. Because the corporation is a separate entity, it is also taxed separately. So corporations pay taxes on their profits, and, in addition, shareholders pay tax on dividends that they receive from the company. The Canadian tax system has features designed to reduce the "double taxation" but it usually doesn't eliminate it. By contrast, income received by partners and sole proprietors is taxed only once as personal income.

When you first establish a corporation, the shares may all be held by a small group; perhaps the company's managers and a small number of backers who believe the business will grow into a profitable investment. Your shares are not offered to the general public and are not publicly traded so your company is said to be *closely held*. Eventually, when the firm grows and new shares are issued to raise additional capital, the shares will be widely traded. Such corporations are known as *public companies*. Most well-known corporations are public companies.[2]

The financial managers of a corporation are responsible, by way of top management and the board of directors, to the corporation's shareholders. Financial managers are supposed to make financial decisions that serve shareholders' interests. Let's now take a closer look at those decisions.

SELF-TEST 1.1

Which form of business organization might best suit the following?
a. A consulting firm with several senior consultants and support staff.
b. A house painting company owned and operated by a college student who hires some friends for occasional help.
c. A paper goods company with sales of $100 million and 2000 employees.

 ## 1.2 THE ROLE OF THE FINANCIAL MANAGER

real asset: Asset used to produce goods and services.

To carry on business, companies may need an almost endless variety of **real assets**. Many of these assets are tangible, such as machinery, factories, and offices; others are intangible, such as technical expertise, trademarks, and patents. All of them must be paid for.

---

[2] For example, when Microsoft was initially established as a corporation, its shares were closely held by a small number of employees and backers. Microsoft shares were issued to the public in 1986. In contrast, the T. Eaton Company is still closely held despite being one of Canada's largest retailers.

financial assets: Claims to the income generated by real assets. Also called *securities*.

To obtain the necessary money, the company sells **financial assets**, or *securities*.[3] These pieces of paper have value because they are claims on the firm's real assets and the cash that those assets will produce. For example, if the company borrows money from the bank, the bank has a financial asset. That financial asset gives it a claim to a stream of interest payments and to repayment of the loan. The bank will only make the loan in the first place if the company's real assets are expected to produce enough cash to satisfy these claims.

financial markets: Markets in which financial assets are traded.

Financial managers stand between the firm's real assets and the **financial markets** in which the firm raises cash. The financial manager's role is shown in Figure 1.1, which traces how cash flows from investors to the firm and back to investors again. The flow starts when financial assets are sold to raise cash (arrow 1 in the figure). The investors give cash to the company, which in turn uses the funds to purchase the real assets used in the firm's operations (arrow 2). So, the investors are investing in the firm as a whole and the firm is investing in specific assets. Later, if the firm does well, the real assets generate enough cash inflow to more than repay the initial investment (arrow 3). Finally, the cash is either reinvested (arrow 4*a*) or returned to the investors who contributed the money in the first place (arrow 4*b*). Of course the choice between arrows 4*a* and 4*b* is not a completely free one. For example, if a bank lends the firm money at stage 1, the bank has to be repaid this money plus interest at stage 4*b*.

FIGURE 1.1
Flow of cash between capital markets and the firm's operations. Key: (1) Cash raised by selling financial assets to investors; (2) cash invested in the firm's operations; (3) cash generated by the firm's operations; (4*a*) cash reinvested; (4*b*) cash returned to investors.

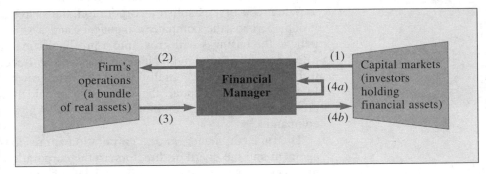

capital budgeting decision: Decision as to which real assets the firm should acquire.

This flow chart suggests that the financial manager faces two basic problems. First, how much should the firm invest, and what specific assets should the firm invest in? This is the firm's *investment*, or **capital budgeting, decision**. Second, how should the cash required for an investment be raised? This is the **financing decision**.

The Capital Budgeting Decision

financing decision: Decision as to how to raise the money to pay for a firm's investments in real assets.

Capital budgeting decisions are central to the company's success or failure. For example, in 1955 the Ford Motor Company decided to launch a new model, the Edsel. It was powerful, stylish, and packed with gadgets. By the time the new car was launched in September 1957, Ford had spent a quarter of a billion dollars, then a record capital investment for any consumer product. Yet the Edsel was dogged by problems. Not only did it have a tendency to rattle or stop, but its chrome, power, and gadgetry attracted more attention than customers. Just over 2 years after its introduction, the Edsel was withdrawn. It was one of the largest capital

---

[3] For present purposes we are using *financial assets* and *securities* interchangeably, though "securities" usually refers to financial assets that are widely held, like the shares of Canadian Pacific. An IOU ("I owe you") from your brother-in-law, which you might have trouble selling outside of the family, is also a financial asset, but most people would not think of it as a security.

budgeting mistakes in history. On top of its initial investment, Ford lost a further $200 million during production — nearly $2000 for each car sold.

Contrast that with Boeing's decision to "bet the company" by developing the 757 and 767 jets. Boeing's investment in these planes was $3 billion, more than double the total value of stockholders' investment as shown in the company's accounts at the time. By 1992, estimated cumulative profits from this investment exceeded $6 billion, and the planes were still selling well.

Ford's decision to invest in the Edsel and Boeing's decision to invest in a new generation of airliners are both examples of capital budgeting decisions. The success of such decisions is usually judged in terms of value. Good investment projects are worth more than they cost. Adopting such projects increases the value of the firm and therefore the wealth of its shareholders. For example, Boeing's investment produced a stream of cash flows that were worth much more than its $3 billion outlay.

Today's investments provide benefits in the future. Thus the financial manager is concerned not solely with the size of the benefits but also with how long the firm must wait for them. The sooner an investment pays off, the better. In addition, these benefits are rarely certain; a new project may be a great success — but then again it could be a dismal failure. The financial manager needs a way to place a value on these uncertain future benefits.

We will spend a considerable time in later chapters on project evaluation. While no one can guarantee that you will avoid disasters like the Edsel or that you will be blessed with successes like the 757 and 767, a disciplined, analytical approach to project proposals will weight the odds in your favour.

The Financing Decision

capital structure: Firm's mix of long-term financing.

capital markets: Markets for long-term financing.

The financial manager's second responsibility is to raise the money to pay for the investment in real assets. This is the financing decision.

When a company needs financing, it can invite investors to put up cash in return for a share of profits or it can promise investors a series of fixed payments. In the first case, the investor receives newly issued shares of stock and becomes a shareholder, a part-owner of the firm. In the second, the investor becomes a lender whom the corporation is obligated to repay. The choice of the long-term financing mix is often called the **capital structure** decision, since *capital* refers to the firm's sources of long-term financing, and the markets for long-term financing are called **capital markets**.[4]

Within the basic distinction — issuing new shares of stock versus borrowing money — there are endless variations. Suppose the company decides to borrow. Should it go to capital markets for long-term debt financing or should it borrow from a bank? Should it borrow in Paris, receiving and promising to repay French francs, or should it borrow dollars in Toronto? Should it demand the right to pay off the debt early if future interest rates fall? We will look at these and other choices in later chapters.

The decision to invest in a new factory or to issue new shares of stock has long-term consequences. But the financial manager is also involved in some important short-term decisions. For example, she needs to make sure that the company has enough cash on hand to pay next week's bills and that any spare cash is put to work to earn interest. Such short-term financial decisions involve both investment (how to invest spare cash) and financing (how to raise cash to meet a short-term need).

---

[4] *Money markets* are used for short-term financing.

SELF-TEST 1.2

Are the following capital budgeting or financing decisions?
a. Intel decides to spend $500 million to develop a new microprocessor.
b. Volkswagen decides to raise 350 million deutschemarks through a bank loan.
c. Alliance Communications Corp. purchases 75 percent of the shares of Partisan Music Productions.
d. Westcoast Energy sells $150 million of new debt to pay for capital expenditures.
e. Glaxo buys a licence to produce and sell a new drug developed by a biotech company.
f. Eurotunnel, owner of the Chunnel, convinces Bombardier Inc. to accept 25 million of its shares as partial payment for the cost of rail cars.

Understanding Financial Markets

Good capital budgeting and financing decisions both require an understanding of the financial markets. For example, suppose a firm chooses to finance a major expansion program by borrowing money. The financial manager must have asked whether the value of the firm would be increased more by an issue of debt rather than an issue of shares. That required a view of how the choice of financing affects value. Also, the financial manager must have considered the interest rate on the loan and concluded that it was not too high. That required an understanding of how interest rates are set and loans are priced.

The investment decision cannot be separated from financial markets either. We have said that a successful investment is one that increases firm value. But to know if something will increase value we have to know how investors value a firm. This has been a subject of much research over the last two decades. New theories have been developed to explain the prices of bonds and stocks. And, when put to the test, these theories have worked well. We therefore devote a large part of this book to explaining these ideas and their implications.

1.3 FINANCIAL MARKETS

We have seen that financial markets allow companies to raise money by selling new financial assets. For example, if Air Canada needs to raise funds to purchase new aircraft, it might hire an investment banking firm such as RBC Dominion or Scotia Macleod to sell $500 million of Air Canada stock to investors. Some of this stock may be bought directly by individuals; the remainder will be bought by financial institutions such as pension funds and insurance companies.

primary market: Market for the sale of new securities by corporations.

A new issue of securities increases both the amount of cash held by the company and the amount of stocks or bonds held by the public. Such an issue is known as a *primary issue* and it is sold in the **primary market**. But in addition to helping companies to raise new cash, financial markets also allow investors to trade stocks or bonds between themselves. For example, Smith might decide to raise some cash by selling her Alcan stock at the same time that Jones invests his spare cash in Alcan. The result is simply a transfer of ownership from Smith to Jones, which has no effect on the company itself. Such purchases and sales of existing securities are known as *secondary transactions* and they take place in the **secondary market**.

secondary market: Market in which already-issued securities are traded among investors.

Some financial assets have no secondary market. For example, when a small company borrows money from the bank, it gives the bank an IOU promising to repay the money with interest. The bank will keep the IOU and will not sell it to another bank. Other financial assets are regularly traded. Thus, when a large public company raises cash by selling new shares to investors, it knows that many of these investors may subsequently decide to sell their shares to others.

Most trading in the shares of large Canadian corporations takes place on stock exchanges such as the Toronto Stock Exchange (TSE) or the Montreal Stock Exchange (MSE). There is also a thriving over-the-counter (OTC) market in securities. The over-the-counter market is not a centralized exchange like the TSE but a network of security dealers who use an electronic system to quote prices at which they will buy and sell shares. While shares of stock are mainly traded on exchanges, almost all short-term debt is traded over-the-counter, if it is traded at all.

SELF-TEST 1.3

Do you understand the following distinctions? Briefly explain in each case.
a. Real versus financial assets.
b. Investment versus financing decisions.
c. Primary versus secondary markets.
d. Capital budgeting versus capital structure decisions.

GOALS OF THE CORPORATION

Shareholders Want Managers to Maximize Market Value

For small firms, shareholders and management may be one and the same. But for large companies, separation of ownership and management is a practical necessity. For example, BCE, the company that owns Bell Canada and Northern Telecom, has over 240,000 shareholders. There is no way that these shareholders can be actively involved in management; it would be like trying to run Montreal by town meetings. Authority has to be delegated.

How can shareholders decide how to delegate decision making when they all have different tastes, wealth, time horizons, and personal opportunities? Delegation can work only if the shareholders have a common objective. Fortunately there is a natural financial objective on which almost all shareholders can agree. This is to maximize the current value of their investment.

A smart and effective management team, led by the financial manager, makes decisions that increase the current value of the company's shares and the wealth of its stockholders. That increased wealth can then be put to whatever purposes the shareholders want. They can give their money to charity or spend it in glitzy night clubs; they can save it or spend it now. Whatever their personal tastes or objectives, they can all do more when their shares are worth more.

Sometimes you hear managers speak as if the corporation has other goals. For example, they may say that their job is to "maximize profits." That sounds reasonable. After all, don't shareholders want their company to be profitable? But taken literally, profit maximization is not a well-defined corporate objective. Here are four reasons:

1. "Maximizing profits" leaves open the question of "which year's profits?" Shareholders might not want a manager to increase next year's profits if that will be at the expense of profits in later years.

2. A company may be able to increase future profits by cutting this year's dividend and investing the freed-up cash in the firm. That is not in the shareholders' best interest if the company earns only a very low rate of return on the extra investment.

3. Different accountants may calculate profits in different ways. So you may find that a decision that improves profits using one set of accounting rules may reduce them using another.

4. Some decisions involve more risk than others even when both of them are expected to increase profits. The higher profit alternative may not be as attractive to shareholders if it also involves higher risk.

In a free economy a firm is unlikely to survive if it pursues goals that reduce the firm's value. Suppose, for example, that a firm's only goal is to increase its market share. It aggressively reduces prices to capture new customers, even when the price discounts cause continuing losses. What would happen to such a firm? As losses mount, it will find it more and more difficult to borrow money, and it may not even have sufficient profits to repay existing debts. Sooner or later, however, outside investors would see an opportunity for easy money. They could offer to buy the firm from its current shareholders and, once they tossed out existing management, could increase the firm's value by changing its policies. They would profit by the difference between the price paid for the firm and the higher value it would have under new management. Managers who pursue goals that destroy value often land in early retirement.

Ethics and Management Objectives

We have suggested that managers should try to maximize market value. But some idealists say that managers should not be obliged to act in the selfish interests of their stockholders. Some realists argue that, regardless of what managers ought to do, they in fact look after themselves rather than their shareholders.

Let us respond to the idealists first. Does a focus on value mean that managers must act as greedy mercenaries riding roughshod over the weak and helpless? Most of this book is devoted to financial policies that increase firm value. None of these policies require galloping over the weak and helpless. In most instances there is little conflict between doing well (maximizing value) and doing good.

The first step in doing well is doing good by your customers. Here is how Adam Smith put the case in 1776:

It is not from the benevolence of the butcher, the brewer, or the baker, that we expect our dinner, but from their regard to their own interest. We address ourselves, not to their humanity but to their self-love, and never talk to them of our own necessities but of their advantages.[5]

By striving to enrich themselves and their shareholders, businesspeople have to provide their customers with the products and services they truly desire.

Of course ethical issues do arise in business as in other walks of life. For example, the objective in football is to score points, but that doesn't mean you should try to maim the opposition. Likewise, when we say that the objective of the firm is to maximize shareholder wealth, we do not mean that anything goes.

In football there are written rules that specify what players may and may not do. In the same way, the law limits what managers may do. Without doubt, there are business managers who are out-and-out crooks, but most of us have no problem in recognizing and avoiding obvious crooked behaviour. It is not the blatantly illegal action but the gray areas that pose the hardest dilemmas for the average manager. In the clarity of hindsight it may be easy to spot these gray areas, but

---

[5] Adam Smith. *An Inquiry into the Nature and Causes of the Wealth of Nations* (New York: Random House, 1937; first published 1776), p. 14.

when the stakes are high, competition is intense, and a deadline is looming, it's easy to blunder. In such cases managers are tempted not to inquire as deeply as they should about the legality or morality of their actions.

Written rules and laws can help only so much. In addition to the written rules of football, there are also unwritten agreements as to what constitutes fair play. Players observe these unwritten rules partly because they know that it is in everybody's interests to abide by them and partly because they know that it is not in their selfish interests to get a reputation for dirty play.

Good managers likewise are not simply concerned to keep on the right side of the law or to keep to written contracts. In business dealings as in our other day-to-day dealings, there are also unwritten or implicit contracts. These work partly because everyone knows that such unwritten rules are in the general interest. But they are reinforced by the fact that good managers know that their firm's reputation is one of its most important assets and therefore playing fair and keeping one's word are simply good business practices. Thus huge deals are regularly completed on a handshake and each side knows that the other will not renege later if things turn sour.[6]

Johnson and Johnson is an example of a firm that places a very high value on its reputation. When it discovered in 1986 that capsules of Tylenol had been tampered with, it withdrew all bottles immediately from the shops. This move cost $140 million, but the company knew that it would be more costly in the end to downplay the risk or to cover it up.

If you buy a well-known brand of goods in a store, you can be fairly sure what you are getting. But in financial transactions the other party often has more information than you and it is less easy to be sure of the quality of the service that you are buying. This opens up plenty of opportunities for sharp practice and outright fraud, and, because the activities of rogues are more entertaining than those of honest people, bookshelves are packed with accounts of financial fraudsters.

What is the reaction of honest financial firms? It is to build long-term relationships with their customers and establish a name for fair dealing and financial integrity. Major banks and securities firms know that their most valuable asset is their reputation and they emphasize their long history and their responsible behaviour when seeking new customers. When something happens to undermine that reputation the costs can be enormous.

Consider the case of Yorkton Securities of Toronto. In 1994 it agreed to pay $575,000 to the Ontario Securities Commission as a fine for inadequately supervising the activities of one of its salespeople. Another, more dramatic example involved the American Investment Banking firm Salomon Brothers and the bidding scandal it became involved in during 1991.[7] A Salomon trader tried to evade rules limiting its allowed participation in auctions of U. S. Treasury bonds by submitting bids in the names of the company's customers without the customers' knowledge. When this was discovered, Salomon settled the case by paying almost $200 million in fines and establishing a $100 million fund for payments of claims from civil lawsuits. Yet the value of Salomon Brothers stock fell by far more than $300 million. In fact, the price dropped by about a third, representing a $1.5 billion decline in market value.

---

[6] For example, the motto of the London Stock Exchange is "My word is my bond."
[7] This discussion is based on Clifford W. Smith, Jr., "Economics and Ethics: The Case of Salomon Brothers," *Journal of Applied Corporate Finance* 5 (Summer 1992), pp. 23–28.

Why did the value of the firm drop so dramatically? Largely because investors were worried that Salomon would lose business from customers that now distrusted the company. The damage to Salomon's reputation was far greater than the explicit costs of the scandal, and hundreds or thousands of times as costly as the potential gains it could have reaped from the illegal trades.

SELF-TEST 1.4
••••••••••••••

Without knowing anything about the personal ethics of the owners, which company would you better trust to keep its word in a business deal?
a. Harry's Hardware has been in business for 50 years. Harry's grandchildren, now almost adults, plan to take over and operate the business. Hardware stores require considerable investment in customer relations to become established.
b. Victor's Videos just opened for business. It rents a storefront in a strip mall and has financed its inventory with a bank loan. Victor has little of his own money invested in the business. Video shops usually command little customer loyalty.

••••••••••••••••••••
Do Managers Really Maximize Firm Value?

Owner-managers have no conflicts of interest in their management of the business. They work for themselves, reaping the rewards of good work and suffering the penalties of bad work. Their personal well-being is tied to the value of the firm.

In most large companies the managers are not the owners and they might be tempted to act in ways that are not in the best interests of the owners. For example, they might buy luxurious corporate jets for their travel, or overindulge in expense-account dinners. They might shy away from attractive but risky projects because they are worried more about the safety of their jobs than the potential for superior profits. They might engage in empire building, adding unnecessary capacity or employees. Such problems can arise because the managers of the firm, who are hired as *agents* of the owners, may have their own axes to grind. Therefore they are called **agency problems**.

agency problem: Conflict of interest between the firm's owners and managers.

Think of the company's net revenue as a pie that is divided among a number of claimants. These include the management and the work force as well as the lenders and shareholders who put up the money to establish and maintain the business. The government is a claimant, too, since it gets to tax the profits of the enterprise. It is common to hear these claimants called **stakeholders** in the firm. Each has a stake in the firm and their interests may not coincide.

stakeholder: Anyone with a financial interest in the firm.

All these stakeholders are bound together in a complex web of contracts and understandings. For example, when banks lend money to the firm, they insist on a formal contract stating the rate of interest and repayment dates. They may also place restrictions on dividends, the extent to which additional borrowing is allowed, and so on. Similarly, large companies have carefully worked out personnel policies that establish employees' rights and responsibilities. But you can't devise written rules to cover every possible future event. So the written contracts are supplemented by understandings. For example, managers understand that in return for a fat salary they are expected to work hard and not spend the firm's money on unwarranted personal luxuries.

What enforces these understandings? Is it realistic to expect managers always to act on behalf of the shareholders? The shareholders can't spend their lives watching through binoculars to check that managers are not shirking or dissipating company funds on the latest executive jet.

A closer look reveals several arrangements that help to ensure that the shareholders and managers are working toward common goals.

Compensation Plans. Managers are spurred on by incentive schemes that provide big returns if shareholders gain but are valueless if they do not. For example, when Michael Eisner was hired as chief executive officer (CEO) by the Walt Disney Company his compensation package had three main components: a base annual salary of $750,000; an annual bonus of 2 percent of Disney's net income above a threshold of "normal" profitability; and a 10-year option to purchase 2 million shares of stock for $14 per share, which was about the price of Disney stock at the time. Those options would be worthless if Disney's shares were selling for below $14 but highly valuable if the shares were worth more. This gave Eisner a huge personal stake in the success of the firm.

As it turned out, by the end of Eisner's 6-year contract the value of Disney shares had increased by $12 billion, more than sixfold. Eisner's compensation over the period was $190 million.[8] Was he overpaid? We don't know (and we suspect nobody else knows) how much Disney's success was due to Michael Eisner or how hard Eisner would have worked with a different compensation scheme. Our point is that managers often have a strong financial interest in increasing firm value.

The Board of Directors. Boards of directors are sometimes portrayed as passive supporters of top management. But when company performance starts to slide, and managers don't offer a credible recovery plan, boards do act. For example, in 1994 the Chief Executives of Greyhound and Domtar were forced out.

If shareholders believe that the corporation is underperforming and that the board of directors is not sufficiently aggressive in holding the managers to task, they can try to replace the board in the next election to the board of directors. The dissident shareholders will attempt to convince other shareholders to vote for their slate of candidates to the board. If they succeed, a new board will be elected and it can replace the current management team.

Takeovers. Poorly performing companies are also more likely to be taken over by another firm. After the takeover, the old management team may find itself out on the street. Sometimes, even when takeovers are unsuccessful, they alert shareholders to potential problems with management. For instance, Michael Eisner was brought in to run Disney after two unsuccessful takeover bids. We discuss takeovers in Chapter 22.

Specialist Monitoring. Finally, managers are subject to the scrutiny of specialists. Their actions are monitored by the security analysts who advise investors to buy, hold or sell the company's shares. They are also reviewed by banks, pension fund trustees, and other institutional investors who keep an eagle eye on the progress of firms receiving their loans.

Of course, this raises another question: "Who monitors the directors, bankers, trustees, and security analysts to make sure that they are doing their jobs?" The problem is rather like that faced by the citizens of Hawtch-Hawtch as described by Dr. Seuss:

OH, THE JOBS people work at!
Out west, near Hawtch-Hawtch,
There's a Hawtch-Hawtch Bee Watcher,

---

[8] This discussion is based on Stephen F. O'Byrne, "What Pay for Performance Looks Like: The Case of Michael Eisner," *Journal of Applied Corporate Finance* 5 (Summer 1992), pp. 135–136.

His job is to watch ...
Is to keep both his eyes on the lazy town bee,
A bee that is watched will work harder, you see
Well ... he watched and he watched.
But in spite of his watch,
that bee didn't work any harder. Not mawtch.
So then somebody said,
"Our old bee-watching man
just isn't bee-watching as hard as he can.
He ought to be watched by another Hawtch-Hawtcher.
The thing that we need
is a Bee-Watcher-Watcher."

WELL ...

The Bee-Watcher-Watcher watched the Bee Watcher.
He didn't watch well. So another Hawtch-Hawtcher
had to come in as a Watch-Watcher-Watcher.
And today all the Hawtchers who live in Hawtch-Hawtch
are watching on Watch-Watcher-Watchering-Watch,
Watch-Watching the Watcher who's watching that bee.
You're not a Hawtch-Hawtcher. You're lucky, you see.[9]

We do not want to leave the impression that corporate life is a series of squabbles and management-watcher-watching. It isn't, because practical corporate finance has evolved to reconcile personal and corporate interests — to keep everyone working together to increase the value of the whole pie, not merely the size of each person's slice.

SELF-TEST 1.5

Corporations are now required to make public the amount and form of compensation (e.g., stock options versus salary versus performance bonuses) received by their top executives. Of what use would that information be to a potential investor in the firm?

1.5 WHO IS THE FINANCIAL MANAGER?

In this book we will use the term *financial manager* to refer to anyone responsible for a significant corporate investment or financing decision. But except in the smallest firms, no *single* person is responsible for all the decisions discussed in this book. Responsibility is dispersed throughout the firm. Top management is of course constantly involved in financial decisions. But the engineer who designs a new production facility is also involved: the design determines the kind of asset the firm will invest in. Likewise the marketing manager who undertakes a major advertising campaign is making an investment decision: the campaign is an investment in an intangible asset that the manager expects will pay off in future sales and earnings.

---

[9] From *Did I Ever Tell You How Lucky You Are?* by Dr. Seuss. TM and copyright © 1973 by Dr. Seuss Enterprises, L. P. Reprinted by permission of Random House, Inc.

treasurer: Manager responsible for financing, cash management, and relationships with financial markets and institutions.

Nevertheless, there are managers who specialize in finance. The **treasurer** is usually the person most directly responsible for obtaining financing, managing the firm's cash account and its relationships with banks and other financial institutions, and making sure the firm meets its obligations to the investors holding its securities. Typical responsibilities of the treasurer are listed in the left-hand column of Table 1.1.

TABLE 1.1
Some typical responsibilities of the treasurer and controller

Treasurer	Controller
Banking relationships	Preparation of financial statements
Cash management	Internal auditing
Obtaining financing	Accounting
Credit management	Payroll
Dividend disbursement	Custody of records
Insurance	Preparing budgets
Pensions management	Taxes

Note: This table is not an exhaustive list of tasks treasurers and controllers may undertake.

controller: Officer responsible for budgeting, accounting, and auditing.

For small firms, the treasurer is likely to be the only financial executive. Larger corporations usually also have a **controller**. The right-hand column of Table 1.1 lists the typical controller's responsibilities. Notice that there is a conceptual difference between the two jobs. The treasurer's main task is to obtain and manage the company's capital. By contrast, the controller's function is to check that the money is used efficiently. The controller manages budgeting, accounting, and auditing.

chief financial officer (CFO): Officer who oversees the treasurer and controller and sets overall financial strategy.

The largest firms usually appoint a **chief financial officer (CFO)** to oversee both the treasurer's and the controller's work. The CFO is deeply involved in financial policymaking and corporate planning. Often he or she will have general managerial responsibilities beyond strictly financial issues.

Usually the treasurer, controller, or CFO is responsible for organizing and supervising the capital budgeting process. However, major capital investment projects are so closely tied to plans for product development, production, and marketing that managers from these other areas are inevitably drawn into planning and analyzing the projects. If the firm has staff members specializing in corporate planning, they are naturally involved in capital budgeting too.

Because of the importance of many financial issues, ultimate decisions often rest by law or by custom with the board of directors.[10] For example, only the board has the legal power to declare a dividend or to sanction a public issue of securities. Boards usually delegate decision-making authority for small- or medium-sized investment outlays, but the authority to approve large investments is almost never delegated.

SELF-TEST 1.6

Sal and Sally went to business school together 10 years ago. They have just been hired by a midsized corporation that wants to bring in new financial managers. Sal studied finance, with an emphasis on financial markets and institutions. Sally majored in accounting and became a CA five years ago. Who is more suited to be treasurer and who controller? Briefly explain.

---

[10] Often the firm's chief financial officer is also a member of its board of directors.

Finance in Action

The Role of the CFO

Abitibi-Price is one of the world's largest manufacturers and marketers of newsprint and uncoated groundwood papers. Abitibi-Price produces over 2 million tonnes of paper each year at its 10 mills located in Canada and the southeastern United States. It employs approximately 6400 people and net sales in 1994 were $2.1 billion.

Ms. Eileen Mercier, former Senior Vice-President and Chief Financial Officer (CFO) of Abitibi-Price talked with us about her job as CFO. We asked Ms. Mercier to tell us about her responsibilities as CFO for this large company. She told us that her job has two parts. One part has been the traditional CFO's responsibility for many years. In this role, the CFO has been responsible for financial reporting and control, management of the firm's capital structure (for instance, how much

debt the company carries), and the management of its financial risks. Thus the CFO raises and manages the firm's capital and monitors how the money is spent.

In addition to the traditional treasury and control activities, she is a key player in Abitibi-Price's strategic planning team. The team is responsible for formulating and implementing Abitibi-Price's mission. Strategic planning activities include the assessment of merger and acquisition opportunities and the development of Abitibi-Price's financing strategy.

As CFO, Ms. Mercier must ensure that proper analytical rigour and discipline are followed in evaluating various options faced by Abitibi-Price. Her focus is on the cash flows associated with the projects being evaluated. She adds that, "measuring cash flow is the only meaningful way of assessing the rate of return on the funds we invest in the project."

Ms. Mercier's job has an added degree of complexity because Abitibi-Price is publicly owned. The CFO must interact with the shareholders, especially the large institutional investors, and with the financial analysts who follow the company and provide investment advice to clients. She told us, "This job is for a communicator. The CFO is an extremely important communicator for the company, second only to the chief executive officer (CEO). A lot rides on the way the investment community perceives you as a representative of the company. You must be a credible spokesperson. The investment community must be able to believe what you tell them.

The Role of the CFO *(continued)*

Honesty and straightforward dealing are very important. You cannot make statements that you cannot live up to."

In addition, Ms. Mercier encouraged students not to limit their studies to business courses. Successful financial managers have a broad range of skills and interests. The ability to interact with people is equally important to having the analytical skills.

Finally, she advised students to learn to handle rejection and to bounce back from setbacks. Keeping healthy and thick skinned at times are key to handling the stresses of the job.

Ms. Mercier told us that she really enjoys her job. She is continually learning and conquering new challenges. She travels extensively and meets interesting people. All in all, it's a very rewarding career.

1.6 TOPICS COVERED IN THIS BOOK

This book covers investment decisions first, then financing decisions, and then a variety of planning issues that require understanding of both investments and financing.

In Parts Two and Three we look at different aspects of the investment decision. The first is the problem of how to value assets, and the second is the link between risk and value. Our discussion of these topics occupies Chapters 3 through 11.

Nine chapters devoted to the simple problem of finding real assets that are worth more than they cost may seem excessive, but that problem is not so simple in practice. We will require a theory of how long-lived, risky assets are valued, and that requirement will lead us to basic questions about capital markets. For example:

- How are corporate bonds and stocks valued in capital markets?
- What risks are borne by investors in corporate securities? How can these risks be measured?
- What compensation do investors expect for bearing risk?
- What rate of return can investors in common stocks reasonably expect to receive?

Intelligent capital budgeting and financing decisions require answers to these and other questions about how capital markets work.

Financing decisions occupy Parts Four and Five. We begin in Chapter 12 with another basic question about capital markets: Do security prices reflect the fair value of the underlying assets? This question is crucially important because the financial manager must know whether securities can be issued at a fair price. The remaining chapters in Part Four describe the kinds of securities corporations use to raise money and explain how and when they are issued.

Part Five continues the analysis of the financing decision, covering dividend policy and debt policy. We will also describe what happens when firms find themselves in financial distress because of poor operating performance, excessive borrowing, or both.

Part Six covers financial planning. Decisions about investment, dividend policy, debt policy, and other financial issues cannot be reached independently. They have to add up to a sensible overall financial plan for the firm, one which increases the value of the shareholders' investment yet still retains enough flexibility for the firm to avoid financial distress and to pursue unexpected new opportunities.

Part Seven is devoted to decisions about the firm's short-term assets and liabilities. We discuss channels for short-term borrowing or investment, management of liquid assets (cash and marketable securities), and management of accounts receivable (money lent by the firm to its customers) and inventories.

Part Eight covers three important problems that require decisions about both investment and financing. First we look at mergers and acquisitions. Then we consider international financial management. All the financial problems of doing business at home are present overseas, but the international financial manager faces the additional complications created by multiple currencies, different tax systems, and special regulations imposed by foreign institutions and governments. Finally, we look at risk management and the specialized securities, including futures and options, that managers can use to hedge or lay off risks.

Snippets of History

Now let's lighten up a little. In this book we are going to describe how financial decisions are made today. But financial markets also have an interesting history. Look at the accompanying box, which lays out bits of this history, starting in prehistoric times, when the growth of bacteria anticipated the mathematics of compound interest, and continuing nearly to the present. We have keyed each of these episodes to the chapter of the book that discusses it.

Finance Through the Ages

Date unknown   *Compound Growth*
Bacteria start to propagate by subdividing. They thereby demonstrate the power of compound growth. (*Chapter 3*)

c. 1800 b.c.   *Interest Rates*
In Babylonia Hammurabi's Code established maximum interest rates on loans. Borrowers often mortgaged their property and sometimes their spouses but in these cases the lender was obliged to return the spouse in good condition within 3 years. (*Chapter 4*)

c. 1000 b.c.   *Options*
One of the earliest recorded options is described by Aristotle. The philosopher Thales knew by the stars that there would be a great olive harvest, so, having a little money, he bought options for the use of olive presses. When the harvest came Thales was able to rent the presses at great profit. Today financial managers need to be able to evaluate options to buy or sell a wide variety of assets. (*Chapter 24*)

15th century   *International Banking*
Modern international banking has its origins in the great Florentine banking houses. But the entire European network of the Medici empire employed only 57 people in eight offices. Today the Royal Bank has 52,000 employees, 1731 branches, and operates in 33 different countries. (*Chapter 13*)

1650   *Futures*
Futures markets allow companies to protect themselves against fluctuations in commodity prices. During the Tokugawa era in Japan feudal lords collected rents in the form of rice but often they wished to trade their future rice deliveries.

Finance Through the Ages *(continued)*

Rice futures therefore came to be traded on what was later known as the Dojima Rice Market. Rice futures are still traded but now companies can also trade in futures on a range of items from pork bellies to stock market indexes. *(Chapter 25)*

17th century   *Joint Stock Corporations*

Although investors have for a long time combined together as joint owners of an enterprise, the modern corporation with a large number of stockholders originates with the formation in England of the great trading firms like the East India Company (est. 1599). Another early trading firm, Hudson's Bay (est. 1670), still survives and is one of Canada's largest companies. *(Chapter 14)*

17th century   *Money*

Prior to 1685 the governor of New France received annual shipments of coin from France with which to finance his garrison. For some reason, the shipment did not arrive in 1685 and the governor was forced to devise a method for meeting his bills. His solution was to use ordinary playing cards as paper money. Each playing card promised to pay the bearer a fixed amount of coin when the gold arrived from France and was signed by three colonial officials. He cut the playing cards into a different shape for each denomination and threatened to fine anyone who refused to accept the cards in settlement of bills. The experiment was so successful that the governor issued playing card money almost every year until 1719. In the 1800s banks, including the Bank of Montreal and the Bank of Nova Scotia, began issuing private money. This form of money was augmented with provincial and federal government notes until 1935 when the Bank of Canada was given monopoly power in printing money. *(Chapter 20)*

1720   *New Issue Speculation*

From time to time investors have been tempted by speculative new issues. During the South Sea Bubble in England one company was launched to develop perpetual motion. Another enterprising individual announced a company "for carrying on an undertaking of great advantage but nobody to know what it is." Within 5 hours he had raised £2000; within 6 hours he was on his way out of the country. *(Chapter 14)*

1792   *Formation of the New York Stock Exchange*

The New York Stock Exchange (NYSE) was founded in 1792 when a group of brokers met under a buttonwood tree and arranged to trade shares with one another at agreed rates of commission. Today the NYSE is the largest stock exchange in the world, trading on average 200 million shares a day. In 1852 the Toronto Stock Exchange was founded. Today an average of about 59 million shares worth $583 million are traded on the TSE each day. *(Chapter 5)*

1920   *Financial Swindles*

Bad financial deals are often difficult for the unsophisticated to spot and this helps financial fraudsters. In 1920 Charles Ponzi raised about $15 million from 40,000 investors by promising to double their money in 90 days. Unfortunately, Ponzi was playing a financial chain letter game; new investors' money was used to pay off the old investors. When the rate of new investment stopped, Ponzi's scheme collapsed and he was convicted and sent to prison. *(Chapter 1)*

Finance Through the Ages (*continued*)

1929   *Stock Market Crashes*

Common stocks are risky investments. In September 1929 stock prices in North America reached an all-time high and the economist Irving Fisher forecast that they were at "a permanently high plateau." Some 3 years later stock prices were almost 90 percent lower and it was to be a quarter of a century before the prices of September 1929 were seen again. Contrary to popular impression, no Wall Street broker jumped out the window. (*Chapter 9*)

1960s   *Eurodollar Market*

In the 1950s the Soviet Union transferred its dollar holdings from the United States to a Russian-owned bank in Paris. This bank was best known by its telex address, EUROBANK, and consequently dollars held outside the United States came to be known as eurodollars. In the 1960s U.S. taxes and regulation made it much cheaper to borrow and lend dollars in Europe rather than in the United States and a huge market in eurodollars grew. (*Chapter 13*)

1972   *Financial Futures*

Financial futures allow companies to protect themselves against fluctuations in interest rates, exchange rates, and so on. It is said that they originated from a remark by the economist Milton Friedman that he was unable to profit from his view that sterling was overpriced. The Chicago Mercantile Exchange founded the first financial futures market. However, it wasn't until 1981 that the Winnipeg Commodity Exchange first introduced financial futures on Canadian Government securities. (*Chapter 25*)

1986   *Capital Investment Decisions*

The largest investment project undertaken by private companies was the construction of the tunnel under the English Channel. This started in 1986 and was completed in 1994 at a total cost of $15 billion. (*Chapter 6*)

1988   *Mergers*

The 1980s saw a wave of takeovers. These include the takeover of Federated and Allied department stores in the U.S. by the Canadian real estate developer, Robert Campeau. The wave culminated in the $25 billion takeover of RJR Nabisco. Over a period of 6 weeks three groups battled for control of the company. As one of the contestants put it, "We were charging through the rice paddies, not stopping for anything and taking no prisoners." The takeover was the largest in history and generated almost $1 billion in fees for the banks and advisers. (*Chapter 22*)

1995   *Inflation*

Financial managers need to recognize the effect of inflation on interest rates and on the profitability of the firm's investments. In Canada, after a battle fought with high interest rates, inflation has been brought down to a relatively modest level. But at various times in history, some countries have suffered from hyperinflation. In Hungary after World War II the government issued banknotes worth 1000 trillion pengoes. In Yugoslavia in October 1993 prices rose by nearly 2000 percent and a dollar bought 105 million dinars. (*Chapter 4*)

1995   *Derivatives*

After 233 years of operations one of the oldest banks in the world, Barings PLC, collapsed after losing more than $1.4 billion on derivatives. (*Chapters 24 and 25*)

 **SUMMARY**

1. Businesses may be organized as proprietorships, partnerships, or corporations. A corporation is legally distinct from its owners. Therefore, the shareholders who own a corporation enjoy limited liability for its obligations. Corporations also are distinctive for the separation of ownership and management.

2. The overall task of financial management can be broken down into (1) the investment, or capital budgeting, decision and (2) the financing decision. In other words, the firm has to decide (1) how much to invest and what assets to invest in and (2) how to raise the necessary cash. The objective is to increase the value of the shareholders' stake in the firm.

3. The financial manager acts as the intermediary between the firm and financial markets. In small companies there is often only one financial executive. However, the larger corporation usually has both a treasurer and a controller. The treasurer's job is to obtain and manage the company's financing. By contrast, the controller's job is one of inspecting to see that the money is used correctly. Large firms may also appoint a chief financial officer, or CFO.

4. Value maximization is usually taken to be the goal of the firm. Such a strategy maximizes shareholders' wealth, thereby enabling them to pursue their personal goals. However, value maximization does not imply a disregard for ethical decision making, in part because the firm's reputation as an employer and business partner depends on its past actions.

5. Agency problems imply that managers may have interests that differ from those of the firm. These problems are kept in check by compensation plans that link the well-being of employees to that of the firm, by monitoring of management by the board of directors, securityholders, and creditors, and by the threat of takeover.

KEY TERMS

sole proprietor
partnership
corporation
limited liability
real asset
financial assets
financial markets

investment or capital
   budgeting decision
financing decision
capital structure
capital markets
primary market
secondary market

agency problem
stakeholder
treasurer
controller
chief financial officer
   (CFO)

PROBLEMS

1. Fit each of the following terms into the most appropriate space: *financing, real, stock, investment, executive airplanes, financial, capital budgeting, brand names.*

   "Companies usually buy _____ assets. These include both tangible assets such as _____ and intangible assets such as _____. In order to pay for these assets, they sell _____ assets such as _____. The decision regarding which assets to buy is usually termed the _____ or _____ decision. The decision regarding how to raise the money is usually termed the _____ decision."

2. Which of the following statements more accurately describes the treasurer than the controller?
   a. Likely to be the only financial executive in small firms
   b. Monitors capital expenditures to make sure that they are not mis-appropriated
   c. Responsible for investing the firm's spare cash
   d. Responsible for arranging any issue of common stock
   e. Responsible for the company's tax affairs

3. Which of the following are real assets, and which are financial?
   a. A share of stock
   b. A personal IOU
   c. A trademark
   d. A truck
   e. Undeveloped land
   f. The balance in the firm's chequing account
   g. An experienced and hardworking sales force
   h. A bank loan agreement

4. Is there a conflict between "doing well" and "doing good"? In other words, are policies that increase the value of the firm (doing well) necessarily at odds with socially responsible policies (doing good)? When there are conflicts, how might government regulations or laws tilt the firm toward doing good? For example, how do taxes or fees charged on pollutants affect the firm's decision to pollute? Can you cite other examples of "incentives" used by governments to align private interests with public ones?

5. Sometimes lawyers work on a contingency basis. They collect a percentage of their client's settlement instead of receiving a fixed fee. Why might clients prefer this arrangement? Would this sort of arrangement be more appropriate for clients that use lawyers regularly or infrequently?

6. As you drive down a deserted highway you are overcome with a sudden desire for a hamburger. Fortunately, just ahead are two hamburger outlets; one is owned by a national brand, the other appears to be owned by "Joe." Which outlet has the greater incentive to serve you catmeat? Why?

7. In some countries, such as Japan and Germany, corporations develop close long-term relationships with one bank and rely on that bank for a large part of their financing needs. In Canada companies are more likely to shop around for the best deal. Do you think that this practice is more or less likely to encourage ethical behaviour on the part of the corporation?

8. Discuss which of the following forms of compensation is most likely to align the interests of managers and shareholders:
   a. A fixed salary
   b. A salary linked to company profits
   c. A salary that is paid partly in the form of the company's shares
   d. An option to buy the company's shares at an attractive price

9. When a company's stock is widely held, it may not pay an individual shareholder to spend time monitoring the managers' performance and trying to replace poor management. Explain why. Do you think that a bank that has made a large loan to the company is in a different position?

10. Explain why each of the following may not be appropriate corporate goals:
    a. Increase market share
    b. Minimize costs
    c. Underprice any competitors
    d. Expand profits

11. What are the advantages and disadvantages of setting up business as
    a. a sole proprietor
    b. a partnership
    c. a corporation

SOLUTIONS TO SELF-TEST QUESTIONS

1.1

a. The consulting firm is most suited to a partnership. Each senior consultant might be a partner, with partial responsibility for managing the firm and its clients.
b. The college student would set up the business as a sole proprietorship. He or she is the only manager, and has little need for partners to contribute capital.
c. The large firm would be set up as a corporation. It requires great amounts of capital and with the budgetary, payroll, and management issues that arise with such a large number of employees, it probably needs a professional management team.

1.2

a. The development of a microprocessor is a capital budgeting decision. The investment of $500 million will purchase a real asset, the microprocessor.
b. The bank loan is a financing decision. This is how Volkswagen will raise money for its investment.
c. Capital budgeting.
d. Financing.
e. Capital budgeting. Though intangible, the licence is a real asset that is expected to produce future sales and profits.
f. Financing.

1.3

a. Real assets support the operations of the business. They are necessary to produce future profits and cash inflows. Financial assets or securities are claims on the profits and cash inflows generated by the firm's real assets and operations.
b. A company invests in real assets to support its operations. It finances the investment by raising money from banks, shareholders, or other investors.
c. When a company raises money from investors, it sells financial assets or securities in the primary market. Later trades among investors occur in the secondary market.
d. Capital budgeting deals with investment decisions. Capital structure is the composition of the company's sources of financing.

1.4 Harry's has a far bigger stake in the reputation of the business than Victor's. The store has been in business for a long time. The owners have spent years establishing customer loyalty. In contrast, Victor's has just been established. The owner has little of his own money tied up in the firm, and so has little to lose if the business fails. In addition, the nature of the business results in little customer loyalty. Harry's is probably more reliable.

1.5   An investor would like top management to be compensated according to the fortunes of the firm. If management is willing to bet its own compensation on the success of the firm, that is good news, first because it shows management has confidence in the firm, and second because it gives managers greater incentives to work hard to make the firm succeed.

1.6   Sal would more likely be the treasurer and Sally the controller. The treasurer raises money from the credit and financial markets and requires background in financial institutions. The controller is more of an overseer who requires background in accounting.

CHAPTER TWO

Accounting and Finance

In Chapter 1 we pointed out that a large corporation is a team effort. All the players — the shareholders, lenders, directors, management, and employees — have a stake in the company's success and all therefore need to monitor its progress. For this reason the company prepares regular financial accounts and arranges for an independent firm of auditors to examine them. If all looks well the auditors certify that, in their opinion, the accounts present a "true and fair view."

Until the mid-nineteenth century most businesses were owner-managed and seldom used outside capital beyond personal loans to the proprietor. When businesses were small and there were few outside stakeholders in the firm, accounting could be less formal. But with the industrial revolution and the creation of large railroad and canal companies, the shareholders and bankers demanded information that would help them gauge a firm's financial strength. That was when the accounting profession began to come of age.

We don't want to discuss the details of accounting practice. But because we will be referring to financial statements throughout this book, it may be useful to review briefly their main features. In this chapter we introduce the major financial statements, the balance sheet, the income statement, and the statement of cash flow. We discuss the important differences between income and cash flow and between book values and market values. We also discuss the tax system.

After studying this chapter you should be able to

- Interpret the information contained in the balance sheet, income statement, and statement of cash flows.
- Distinguish between market and book value.
- Explain why income differs from cash flow.
- Understand the essential features of the taxation of corporate and personal income.

THE BALANCE SHEET

balance sheet: Financial statement that shows the value of the firm's assets and liabilities at a particular time.

We will look first at the **balance sheet**, which presents a snapshot of the firm's assets and the source of the money to buy those assets. The assets are listed on the left-hand side of the balance sheet. Some assets can be turned more easily into cash than others; these are known as *liquid* assets. The accountant puts the most liquid assets at the top of the list and works down to the least liquid.

Look, for example, at the left-hand column of Table 2.1, the balance sheet for Hudson's Bay Company (HBC), at the end of 1993.[1] The principal assets owned by HBC are the Bay and Zellers retail department store chains and this balance sheet reflects the consolidated position of the whole company. You can see that HBC had $17 million of cash and marketable securities.

In addition it had sold but had not yet received payment for $1232 million worth of merchandise. Payments for these items are expected soon and therefore the balance sheet shows the uncollected customer bills or *accounts receivable* (or sim-

---

[1] Actually, the Hudson's Bay Company, unlike most companies, has chosen January 31 as its fiscal year-end. So the year-end 1993 numbers are actually end of January 1994 numbers.

TABLE 2.1

BALANCE SHEET FOR HUDSON'S BAY COMPANY (HBC)
As of January 31 (Figures are in millions of dollars)

Assets	1994	1993	Liabilities and Shareholders' Equity	1994	1993
Current assets			Current liabilities		
Cash and marketable			Debt due for		
securities	$ 17	$ 15	repayment	$ 179	$ 427
Accounts receivable	1232	1080	Accounts payable	713	581
Inventories	1160	1033	Other current liabilities	1	0
Other current assets	44	43	Total current liabilities	893	1007
Total current assets	2453	2171	Long-term debt	1084	875
Fixed assets			Other long-term liabilities	83	82
Property, plant, and			Shareholders' equity		
equipment	1381	1254	Common stock and		
Less accumulated			other paid in capital	1046	851
depreciation	608	549	Retained earnings	568	465
Net fixed assets	773	706	Total shareholder's		
Other assets	449	404	equity	1614	1316
			Total liabilities and		
Total assets	3675	3280	shareholders' equity	3675	3280

Note: Columns may not add because of rounding.
Source: Hudson's Bay Company, 1993 Annual Report.

ply *receivables*) as an asset. The next asset consists of $1160 million of goods held in inventories. These are made up primarily of merchandise in the Bay and Zellers stores. Of course there are always some items that don't fit into neat categories. So the current assets include a fourth entry, *other current assets* that for HBC consist of prepaid expenses.

Up to this point all the assets in HBC's balance sheet are likely to be used or turned into cash within a year. They are therefore described as *current assets*. The other assets in the balance sheet are known as *fixed assets*. For HBC these consist of buildings, equipment, vehicles, and securities held as investments. The balance sheet shows that the gross value of HBC's fixed assets is $1381 million. This is what the assets originally cost. But they are unlikely to be worth that now. For example, suppose it bought a delivery van 2 years ago; that van may be worth far less now than HBC paid for it. It might in principle be possible for the accountant to estimate separately the value of the van today, but this would be costly and somewhat subjective. Accountants rely instead on rules of thumb to estimate the depreciation in the value of assets and with rare exceptions they stick to these rules. For example, in the case of that delivery van the accountant may deduct a third of the original cost each year to reflect its declining value. So if HBC bought the van 2 years ago for $15,000, the balance sheet would show that accumulated depreciation is 2 × $5000 = $10,000. Net of depreciation the value is only $5000. Table 2.1 shows that HBC's total accumulated depreciation on fixed assets is $608 million. So while the assets cost $1381 million, their net value in the accounts is only 1381 − 608 = $773 million.

Don't be misled, however, by the balance sheet into thinking that these are its only fixed assets. Some of the most valuable assets may not be recorded on its books, such as the status that comes from being the second oldest company on the face of the earth, trademarks, reputation, a skilled management, and a well-trained labour force. Accountants are generally reluctant to record these intangible assets in the balance sheet unless they can be readily identified and valued.

Now look at the right-hand portion of HBC's balance sheet, which shows where the money to buy the assets came from. The accountant starts by looking at the company's liabilities — that is, the money owed by the company. First come those liabilities that are likely to be paid off most rapidly. For example, HBC has borrowed $179 million, due to be repaid within a year. It also owes its suppliers $713 million for goods that have been delivered but not yet paid for. These unpaid bills are shown as *accounts payable* (or *payables*). Both the borrowings and the payables are debts that HBC must repay within the year. They are therefore classified as *current liabilities*.

HBC's current assets total $2453 million; its current liabilities amount to $893 million. Therefore the difference between the value of HBC's current assets and its current liabilities is 2453 − 893 = $1560 million. This figure is known as HBC's *net current assets* or *net working capital*. It roughly measures the company's potential reservoir of cash.

Below the current liabilities HBC's accountants have listed the firm's long-term liabilities — that is, debts that come due after the end of a year. You can see that banks and other investors have made long-term loans to HBC of $1167 million.

HBC's liabilities are financial obligations to various parties. For example, when HBC buys goods from its suppliers, it has a liability to pay for them; when it borrows from the bank, it has a liability to repay the loan. Thus the suppliers and the bank have first claim on the firm's assets. What is left over after the liabilities have been paid off belongs to the shareholders. This figure is known as the shareholders' equity. For HBC the total value of shareholders' equity amounts to $1614 million. A large part of this sum ($1046 million) has resulted from the sale of shares to investors. The remainder ($568 million) has come from earnings that HBC has retained and invested on shareholders' behalf.

Figure 2.1 shows how the separate items in the balance sheet link together. There are two classes of asset — current assets, which will soon be used or turned into cash, and long-term or "fixed" assets, which may be either tangible or intangible. There are also two classes of liability — current liabilities, which are due for payment shortly, and long-term liabilities. The difference between the assets and the liabilities represents the amount of the shareholders' equity.

FIGURE 2.1

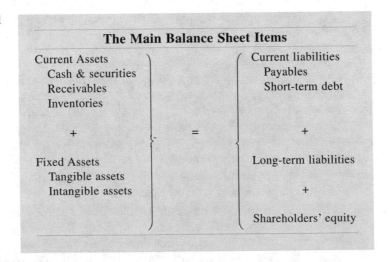

The Main Balance Sheet Items

Current Assets
  Cash & securities
  Receivables
  Inventories

+

Fixed Assets
  Tangible assets
  Intangible assets

=

Current liabilities
  Payables
  Short-term debt

+

Long-term liabilities

+

Shareholders' equity

SELF-TEST 2.1

Suppose that HBC borrows $50 million by issuing new long-term bonds. It places $10 million of the proceeds in the bank and uses $40 million to buy new machinery. What items of the balance sheet would change? Would shareholders' equity change?

Book Values and Market Values

generally accepted accounting principles (GAAP): Procedures for preparing financial statements.

book value: Net worth of the firm according to the balance sheet.

Throughout this book we will frequently make a distinction between the *book values* of the assets shown in the balance sheet and their market values.

Items in the financial statements are valued according to **generally accepted accounting principles**, commonly called **GAAP**. These state that assets must be shown in the balance sheet at their *historical cost* adjusted for depreciation. These **book values** are therefore "backward-looking" measures of value. They are based on the past cost of the asset, not its current market price or value to the firm. For example, suppose that a printing press cost Best Book Manufacturers $1 million 2 years ago, but that in today's market such presses sell for $1. 3 million. The book value of the press would be less than its market value and the balance sheet would understate the value of Best Book Manufacturers' assets.

Or consider the case of the ANIk E-2 satellite put into space by Telesat Canada at a cost of $300 million. In January 1994 the satellite was disabled by an electrical storm. Plans to repair the satellite were expensive and uncertain and experts felt that even if successful, the life of the satellite had been shortened. In this case it is likely that market value would be less than book level. Moreover, the drop in value would be very difficult to estimate.

The difference between book value and market value is greater for some assets than for others. It is zero in the case of cash but potentially very large for fixed assets where the accountant starts with the initial cost of the fixed assets and then depreciates that figure according to a prespecified schedule. The purpose of depreciation is to allocate the original cost of the asset over its life, and the rules governing the depreciation of asset values do not reflect actual loss of market value. As a result, the book value of fixed assets often is much higher than the market value, but sometimes it is less.

The same goes for the right-hand side of the balance sheet. In the case of liabilities the accountant simply records the amount of money that the company has promised to pay. For short-term liabilities this figure is generally close to the market value of that promise. For example, if you owe the bank $1 million tomorrow, the accounts show a book liability of $1 million. As long as you are not bankrupt, that $1 million is also roughly the value to the bank of your promise. But now suppose that the $1 million that was borrowed is not due to be repaid for several years. The accounts still show a liability of $1 million, but how much your debt is worth depends on what happens to interest rates. If interest rates rise after you have issued the debt, lenders may not be prepared to pay as much as $1 million for your debt; if interest rates fall, they may be prepared to pay more than $1 million.[2] Thus the market value of a long-term liability may be higher or lower than the book value.

The differences between book value and market value are likely to be greatest for shareholders' equity. The book value of equity measures the assets that shareholders have contributed in the past plus the profits that the company has retained and reinvested in the business on their behalf. But this often bears little resemblance to the total market value that investors place on the shares.

---

[2] We will show you how changing interest rates affect the market value of debt in Chapter 4.

If the market price of the firm's shares falls through the floor, don't try telling the shareholders that the book value is satisfactory — they won't want to hear. For instance, in June of 1993 HBC sold 5 million new common shares to the public at a price of $36.25. By the end of 1994 these shares were trading at a price of around $25 per share. If you had bought some of the new issue in June and sold at the end of 1994, I don't think you would be any happier to know that the book value of your shares had increased by over $3 per share: the book value increase can't be converted into cash and covers none of your loss. You can see that managers who want to keep their shareholders happy will focus on maximizing the market value of the shares.

We will often find it useful to think about the firm in terms of a *market-value balance sheet*. Like a conventional balance sheet, a market-value balance sheet lists the firm's assets, but it records each asset at its current market value rather than at historical cost less depreciation. Similarly, each liability is shown at its market value. Therefore, the difference between the market values of assets and liabilities is the market value of the shareholders' equity claim. The stock price is simply the market value of shareholders' equity divided by the number of outstanding shares. In Chapter 5 we look into the determination of market value in more detail but the following example illustrates some of the basic ideas.

● EXAMPLE 2.1 Market- versus Book-Value Balance Sheets

Jupiter has developed a revolutionary auto production process that enables it to produce cars 20 percent more efficiently than any rival. It has invested $10 billion in producing its new plant. To finance the investment, Jupiter borrowed $4 billion and raised the remaining funds by selling new shares of stock in the firm. There are currently 100 million shares of stock outstanding. Investors are very excited about Jupiter's prospects. They believe that the flow of profits from the new plant justifies a stock price of $75.

If these are Jupiter's only assets, the book-value balance sheet immediately after it has made the investment is as follows:

BOOK-VALUE BALANCE SHEET FOR JUPITER MOTORS
(Figures in billions of dollars)

Assets		Liabilities and Shareholders' Equity	
Auto plant	$10	Debt	$4
		Shareholders' equity	6

Investors are placing a *market value* on Jupiter's equity of $7.5 billion ($75 per share times 100 million shares). We assume that the debt outstanding is worth $4 billion.[3] Therefore, if you owned all Jupiter's shares and all its debt, the value of your investment would be 7.5 + 4 = $11.5 billion. In this case you would own the company lock, stock, and barrel and would be entitled to all its cash flows. Because you can buy the entire company for $11.5 billion, the total value of Jupiter's assets must also be $11.5 billion. In other words, the market value of the assets must be equal to the market value of the liabilities plus the market value of the shareholders' equity.

We can now draw up the market-value balance sheet as follows:

---

[3] Jupiter has borrowed $4 billion to finance its investment, but if the interest rate has changed in the meantime, the debt could be worth more or less than $4 billion.

MARKET-VALUE BALANCE SHEET FOR JUPITER MOTORS
(Figures in billions of dollars)

Assets		Liabilities and Shareholders' Equity	
Auto plant	$11.5	Debt	$4.0
		Shareholders' equity	7.5

Notice that the market value of Jupiter's plant is $1.5 billion more than the plant cost to produce. The difference is due to the superior profits that investors expect the plant to earn. Thus in contrast to the balance sheet shown in the company's books, the market-value balance sheet is forward-looking. It depends on the benefits that investors expect the assets to provide.

Is it surprising that market value exceeds book value? It shouldn't be. Firms find it attractive to raise money to invest in various projects because they believe the projects will be worth more than they cost. Otherwise, why bother? You will often find that shares of stock sell for more than the value shown in the company's books.

SELF-TEST 2.2

a. What would be Jupiter's price per share if the auto plant had a market value of $14 million?
b. How would you reassess the value of the auto plant as a going concern if the value of outstanding stock were $8 billion?

2.2 THE INCOME STATEMENT

income statement: Financial statement that shows the revenues, expenses, and net income of a firm over a period of time.

If HBC's balance sheet resembles a snapshot of the firm at a particular time, its **income statement** is like a video. It shows how profitable the firm has been during the past year.

Look at the summary income statement in Table 2.2. You can see that during 1993 HBC sold goods worth $5442 million and that the expenses it incurred in producing and selling goods was $5019 million. These expenses consisted of the cost of the goods they purchased for resale, the raw materials, labour, and so on that were needed to run their retail operation. In addition, there are administrative expenses such as head office costs, advertising, and distribution.

In addition to these out-of-pocket expenses, HBC also made a deduction for the value of the stores, warehouses, and equipment used up in selling goods. In 1993 this charge for depreciation was $59 million. Thus HBC's total *earnings before interest and taxes* (EBIT) were

$$EBIT = total\ revenues - costs - depreciation$$

$$= 5442 - 5019 - 59$$

$$= \$364\ million$$

The remainder of the income statement shows where these earnings went. As we saw earlier, HBC has partly financed its investment in stores and equipment by borrowing. In 1993 it paid $97 million of interest on this borrowing. A further slice of the profit went to the government in the form of taxes. This amounted in 1993 to $119 million. The $148 million that was left over after paying interest and taxes belonged to the shareholders. Of this sum HBC paid out $44 million in

TABLE 2.2

INCOME STATEMENT FOR HUDSON'S BAY COMPANY (HBC), 1993
(Figures are in millions of dollars)

Sales and revenue	
The Bay	$2183
Zellers	3160
Others	99
	5442
Cost of goods sold and administrative expenses	5019
Depreciation	59
Earnings before interest and taxes (EBIT)	364
Interest expense	97
Income taxes	119
Net earnings	148
Allocation of new income	
Addition to retained earnings	104
Dividends	44

Note: Numbers may not add because of rounding.
Source: Hudson's Bay Company 1993 Annual Report.

dividends and reinvested the remaining $104 million in the business. Presumably, these reinvested funds made the company more valuable.

....

**Profits versus
Cash Flow**

It is important to distinguish between HBC's profits and the cash that the company generates. Here are three reasons why profits and cash are not the same:

1. When HBC's accountants prepare the income statement, they do not simply count the cash coming in and the cash going out. Instead the accountant starts by recording revenues when they are "earned," even if the firm did not receive any cash at the time because they sold on credit. To illustrate, consider the following stages in a manufacturing business. In period 1 the firm produces the goods; it sells them in period 2 for $100; and it gets paid for them in period 3. Although the cash does not arrive until period 3, the sale shows up in the income statement for period 2. The figure for accounts receivable in the balance sheet for period 2 shows that the company's customers owe an extra $100 in unpaid bills. Next period, after the customers have paid their bills, the receivables decline by $100. Therefore, the cash that the company receives is equal to the sales shown in the income statement less the increase in unpaid bills:

Period:	2	3
Sales	100	0
– Change in receivables	100	(100)
= Cash received	0	+100

2. The accountant also tries to match the costs of producing the goods with the revenues from the sale. For example, suppose that it costs $60 in period 1 to produce the goods that are then sold in period 2 for $100. It would be misleading to say that the business made a loss in period 1 (when it produced the goods) and was very profitable in period 2 (when it sold them). Therefore, to provide a fairer measure of the firm's profitability, the income

statement will not show the $60 as an expense of producing the goods until they are sold in period 2. This practice is known as accrual accounting. The accountant gathers together all expenses that are associated with a sale and deducts them from the revenues to calculate profit, even though the expenses may have occurred in an earlier period.

Of course the accountant cannot ignore the fact that the firm spent money on producing the goods in period 1. So the expenditure will be shown in period 1 as an investment in inventories. Subsequently in period 2, when the goods are sold, the inventories would decline again.

In our example, the cash is paid out when the goods are manufactured in period 1 but this expense is not recognized until period 2 when the goods are sold. Therefore, the cash outflow is equal to the cost of goods sold, which is shown in the income statement, plus the change in inventories:

Period:	1	2
Costs of goods sold	0	60
+ Change in inventories	60	(60)
= Cash paid out	+60	0

3. Although the matching principle outlined above applies to many of the expenses incurred by the firm, not all expenses are treated this way. In particular, the accountant divides expenses into two groups — current expenditures (such as wages) and capital expenditures (such as the purchase of a new store). Current expenditures are deducted from current profits in the manner outlined above. However, rather than deducting the cost of a new store in the year it is purchased, the accountant makes an annual charge for depreciation. Thus the cost of the new store is spread over its forecast life.

When calculating profits, the accountant does not deduct the expenditure on the new store that year, even if cash is paid out. However, the accountant does deduct depreciation on assets previously purchased, even when no cash is currently paid out. Therefore, to calculate the cash produced by the business it is necessary to add back the depreciation charge (which is not a cash payment) and to subtract the expenditure on new capital equipment (which is a cash payment).

SELF-TEST 2.3

A firm pays $100 in period 1 to produce some goods. It sells those goods for $150 in period 2 but does not collect payment from its customers until period 3. Calculate the cash flows to the firm in each period by completing the following table. Do the resulting values for net cash flow in each period make sense?

Period:	1	2	3
Sales			
Change in accounts receivable			
Cost of goods sold			
Change in inventories			
Net cash flow			

2.3 THE STATEMENT OF CASH FLOWS

The firm requires *cash* when it buys new plant and machinery or when it pays interest and principal to the bank and dividends to the shareholders. Therefore, the financial manager needs to keep track of the cash that is coming in and going out.

We have seen that the firm's cash flow can be quite different from its net income. These differences can arise for at least two reasons:

1. The income statement does not recognize capital expenditures as expenses in the year that the capital goods are paid for. Instead, it spreads those expenses over time in the form of an annual deduction for depreciation.
2. The income statement uses the accrual method of accounting, which means that revenues are recognized as they are earned and expenses are matched to revenues independent of when the cash is received or paid out.

statement of cash flows: Financial statement that shows the firm's cash receipts and cash payments over a period of time.

The **statement of cash flows** shows the firm's cash inflows and outflows from operations as well as from its investments and financing activities. Table 2.3 is the cash-flow statement for HBC. It contains three sections. The first shows the cash flow from operations. This is the cash flow generated from HBC's normal business activity. Next comes the cash that HBC has invested in new plant and equipment as well as the cash received from the sale of old plant and equipment. The final section reports cash flows from financing activities such as the sale of new bonds or stocks and the repayment of principal on debt. We will look at these three sections in turn.

The first section, cash flow from operations, starts with net income but adjusts that figure for those parts of the income statement that do not involve cash coming in or going out. For example, it adds back the allowance for depreciation because depreciation is not a cash flow even though it is treated as an expense in the income statement. It also adds back income tax that the firm deducted from profits but did not pay.

Any additions to current assets need to be subtracted from net income, since these absorb cash but do not show up in the income statement. Conversely, any additions to current liabilities need to be added to net income because these release cash. For example, you can see that the increase of $152 million in accounts receivable is subtracted from net income, because this represents sales that HBC shows in its income statement though it has not yet received payment. On the other hand, HBC increased its accounts payable by $132 million. The goods bought on account were either sold or added to inventory though there was no cash payment involved. Thus the $132 million increase in accounts payable must be added back to calculate the cash flow from operations.

The second section of the cash-flow statement shows cash expenditures on fixed assets. We have pointed out that depreciation is not a cash payment; it is simply the accountant's allocation to the current year of the original cost of the capital equipment. Cash of course does flow out the door when the firm actually buys and pays for new capital equipment. This is therefore recorded in the cash-flow statement. You can see that HBC spent $127 million on new capital equipment in 1993 and $45 million on other noncurrent assets, for a total of $172 million.

Finally, the third section of the cash-flow statement shows the cash flow from financing activities. For example, HBC spent $39 million by repaying debt and it

TABLE 2.3

HUDSON'S BAY COMPANY STATEMENT OF CASH FLOWS, 1993
(Figures in millions of dollars)

Cash provided by operations	
Net income	$ 148
Noncash expenses	
Depreciation	59
Deferred income taxes	1
Changes in working capital	
Decrease (increase) in inventories	(127)
Decrease (increase) in accounts receivable	(152)
Decrease (increase) in other current assets	(1)
Increase (decrease) in accounts payable	132
Increase (decrease) in other current liabilities	1
Cash provided by operations	61
Cash provided (used) by investments	
Additions to property, plant, and equipment	(127)
Additions to other noncurrent assets	(45)
Cash provided (used) by investments	(172)
Cash provided (used) by financing	
Additions (reductions) to debt	(39)
Dividends	(44)
Sale of common stock	195
Cash provided (used) by financing	112
Net increase in cash and marketable securities	$ 2

Note: Numbers may not add because of rounding.
Source: Hudson's Bay Company, 1993 Annual Report.

spent a further $44 million on dividends for its shareholders.[4] On the other hand, it raised $195 million by selling new shares to the public.

The cash-flow statement tells us that HBC generated $61 million from operations, it spent $172 million on new investments, and raised enough money by issuing new equity to provide it with $112 million as well as the cash it needed to repay some of its debts and pay dividends to its shareholders. Overall, HBC generated slightly more cash than it spent; its cash balance increased by $2 million during the year. To calculate the change in cash balance, we subtract the uses of cash from the sources:

	In millions
Cash flow from operations	$ 61
− Cash flow for new investment	−172
+ Cash raised by new financing	+112
= Change in cash balance	$ 2

---

[4] You might think that interest payments also ought to be listed in this section. However, it is usual to include interest in the first section with cash flow from operations. This is because, unlike dividends, interest payments are not discretionary. The firm must pay interest when a payment comes due, so these payments are treated as a business expense rather than as a financing decision.

SELF-TEST 2.4

Would the following activities increase or decrease the firm's cash balance?
a. Inventories are increased
b. The firm reduces its accounts payable
c. The firm issues additional common stock
d. The firm buys new equipment

2.4 ACCOUNTING FOR DIFFERENCES

While generally accepted accounting principles go a long way to standardize accounting practice in Canada, accountants still have some leeway in reporting earnings and book values. Financial analysts have even more leeway in how to use those reports; for example, some analysts will include profits or losses from extraordinary or nonrecurring events when they report net income, but others will not. Similarly, accountants have discretion concerning the treatment of intangible assets such as patents, trademarks, or franchises. Some believe that including these intangibles on the balance sheet provides the best measure of the company's value as an ongoing concern. Others take a more conservative approach, and they exclude intangible assets. This approach is better suited for measuring the liquidation value of the firm.

Another source of imprecision arises from the fact that firms are not required to include all their liabilities on the balance sheet. For example, firms are not always required to include as liabilities on the balance sheet the value of their lease obligations.[5] They likewise are not required to include the value of several potential obligations such as warrants[6] sold to investors or issued to employees.

Even bigger differences can arise in international comparisons. Accounting practices can vary greatly from one country to another. For example, most countries do not follow the Canadian practice of allowing firms to maintain separate sets of accounting statements for tax versus reporting purposes. In Canada, firms typically use accelerated depreciation for tax purposes and straight-line depreciation for reporting purposes. On the other hand, Canadian standards are relatively stringent in most other regards. For example, German firms have far greater leeway than Canadian firms to tuck money away in hidden reserve accounts.

Daimler-Benz AG, producer of the Mercedes-Benz automobile, provides a nice illustration of how important international differences in accounting standards can be. When Daimler-Benz decided to list its shares on the New York Stock Exchange in 1993, it was required to revise its accounting practices to conform to United States standards. While it reported a modest profit using German accounting rules in the first half of 1993, it reported a loss of $592 million under the much more revealing United States rules, primarily because of differences in the treatment of reserves.

The lesson here is clear. While accounting values are often the starting point for the financial analyst, it is usually necessary to probe more deeply. The financial manager needs to know how the values on the statements were computed and whether there are important assets or liabilities missing altogether.

---

[5] Some airlines at times actually have not had any aircraft on their balance sheets because their aircraft were all leased. In contrast, General Electric owns the world's largest private airfleet because of its leasing business.
[6] A warrant is the right to purchase a share of stock from the corporation for a specified price, called the *exercise price*.

The trend today is toward greater recognition of the market values of various assets and liabilities. Firms are now required to acknowledge on the balance sheet the value of unfunded pension liabilities and other postemployment benefits, such as medical benefits.[7] In addition, a growing (although still controversial) trend toward "market-value accounting" would have them record many assets at market value rather than at historical book cost minus accumulated depreciation.

2.5　TAXES

Taxes often have a major effect on financial decisions. Therefore, we should explain how corporations and investors are taxed.

Corporate Tax　Companies pay taxes on their income to both the federal and provincial governments. The basic federal tax rate is 38 percent. However, many companies qualify for a small business deduction that allows a lower rate of 22 percent on the first $200,000 of taxable income. In addition, companies that qualify as manufacturing and processing companies are eligible for a tax rate of 22 percent. If the company pays provincial taxes, the federal tax rate is reduced by 10 percent and the provincial tax rate is added. For instance, the corporate tax rate in Alberta in 1994 is 15.5 percent. So a company in Alberta would pay:

$$38\% \quad - \quad 10\% \quad + \quad 15.5\% \quad = \quad 43.5\%$$

(basic federal rate) (provincial tax abatement) (Alberta tax rate) (total tax rate)

If the company qualified for the small business deduction, then the rate on the first $200,000 of taxable income would be:

$$22\% \quad - \quad 10\% \quad + \quad 6\% \quad = \quad 18\%$$

(basic federal rate) (provincial tax allowance) (Alberta tax rate) (total tax rate)

Table 2.4 on page 38 provides a summary of corporate tax rates in Canada as of October, 1994.

When firms calculate taxable income they are allowed to deduct expenses. These expenses include an allowance for depreciation. However, Revenue Canada specifies the rates of depreciation that the company can use for different types of equipment.[8] The rates of depreciation that are used to calculate taxes may differ from the rates that are used when the firm reports its profits to shareholders. The company is also allowed to deduct interest paid to debtholders when calculating its taxable income, but dividends paid to shareholders are not deductible. These dividends are therefore paid out of after-tax income.

The bad news about taxes is that each extra dollar of revenue increases taxable income by $1 and results in 38 cents of extra taxes. The good news is that each extra dollar of expense reduces taxable income by $1 and therefore reduces taxes by 38 cents. For example, if the firm borrows money, every dollar of interest it pays on the loan reduces taxes by 38 cents. Therefore, after-tax income is reduced by only 62 cents.

---

[7] The Hudson's Bay Company put $702 million aside to cover its future pension obligations. It estimates that this is substantially more than it will need and reports the excess as an asset of the company. Although there are some other postemployment benefits that HBC is responsible for, these tend to be small. In contrast, when General Motors in the United States recognized the value of its postemployment obligations to GM employees, it resulted in the largest quarterly loss in United States history.

[8] We will tell you more about these allowances in Chapter 7.

TABLE 2.4
Corporate income tax
rates in Canada

	Small Business Rate (%)	Manufacturing & Processing Rate (%)	General Rate (%)
British Columbia	10.0	—	16.5
Alberta	6.0	14.5	15.5
Saskatchewan	8.0	—	17.0
Manitoba	9.0	—	17.0
Ontario	9.5	13.5	15.5
Quebec	5.75	—	8.9/16.25
New Brunswick	9.0	—	17.0
Nova Scotia	5.0	—	16.0
P.E.I.	7.5	7.5	15.0
Newfoundland	5.0	5.0	14.0

Source: Arthur Andersen & Co. Tax Forum, volume 6, No. 9, November, 1994

Personal Tax

marginal tax rate: Additional taxes owed per dollar of additional income.

Table 2.5 shows the Canadian rates of personal tax. As with corporate tax, personal taxes are paid at both the provincial and federal level. Notice that as income increases the tax rate also increases. These rates are **marginal tax rates**. The marginal tax rate is the tax that the individual pays on each *extra* dollar of income. For example, an individual would pay an extra 17 cents on every dollar earned below $29,590 and then pays 26 cents on each additional dollar earned up to $59,180. If your taxable income was $50,000, your total tax bill would be 17 percent of the first $29,590 plus 26 percent of the remaining $20,410:

$$\text{Tax} = (.17 \times 29,590) + (.26 \times 20,410) = 10,336.60$$

average tax rate: Total taxes owed divided by total taxable income.

The **average tax rate** is simply the total tax bill divided by total income. In this example it is $10,336.60/$50,000 = 20.67%. Notice that the average tax rate is below the marginal tax rate. This is because of the lower rate on the first $29,590 of income.

dividend tax credit: A credit given by Revenue Canada to any individual receiving dividends from a Canadian company. The credit reflects part of the taxes already paid by the company on the dividend.

Interest received by individuals is subject to tax at the rates shown in Table 2.5. Dividend income is more complicated due to something called the **dividend tax credit**. To illustrate how dividend income is taxed, suppose that you received a $100 dividend and that your combined provincial and federal marginal tax rate is 43 percent. When you fill in your tax return, you would report a "grossed up" dividend of 125 percent of the actual dividend or $125. So you report 25 percent more in dividend income than you actually receive and you owe taxes on this income of 43% × $125 = $53.75. However, you also get to claim a tax credit equal to 13.33 percent of the grossed up dividend, or in this case $16.67. So the net amount of tax that you pay is $53.75 − 16.67 = 37.08. Notice that the taxes paid will depend on your personal tax rate.

Remember that each dollar of income that the company earns is taxed at the corporate tax rate. If the company then pays a dividend out of this after-tax income, the shareholder also pays personal income tax on the dividend. Thus income that is paid out as dividends is taxed twice, once in the hands of the firm and once in the hands of the shareholder. The dividend tax credit is intended to help offset this double taxation by recognizing the pretax corporate earnings (through the dividend gross up) and the taxes paid by the corporation on behalf of the shareholders (through the dividend tax credit).

TABLE 2.5
Personal tax rates, 1994

Taxable Income	Federal Tax
$0–29,590	17%
$29,591–$59,180	$5,030 + 26% on next $29,590
$59,181+	$12,724 + 29% on remainder

Provincial Tax as % of Federal Tax	
British Columbia	52.5
Alberta	45.5
Saskatchewan	50.0
Manitoba	52.0
Ontario	58.0
New Brunswick	64.0
Nova Scotia	59.5
P.E.I.	59.5
Newfoundland	69.0

Source: Arthur Andersen & Co. Tax Forum, volume 6, No. 9, November, 1994
Note: Quebec administers its own tax regime.

Capital gains are also taxed, but only 75 percent of the capital gain is taxable and taxes are only paid when the capital gains are realized. For example, suppose that you bought Bio-technics stock when it was selling for 10 cents a share. Its market price is now $1 a share. As long as you hold onto your stock, there is no tax to pay on your gain. But if you sell, 75 percent of the 90 cents of capital gain is taxed with the rest of your income.

The tax rates in Table 2.5 apply to individuals. But financial institutions are major investors in shares and bonds. These institutions often have special rates of tax. For example, pension funds, which hold huge numbers of shares, are not taxed on either dividend income or capital gains.

 **SUMMARY**

1. Investors and other stakeholders in the firm need regular financial information to help them monitor the firm's progress. Accountants summarize this information in a balance sheet, income statement, and statement of cash flows.

2. The balance sheet provides a snapshot of the firm's assets and liabilities. The assets consist of current assets that can be rapidly turned into cash and fixed assets such as plant and machinery. The liabilities consist of current liabilities that are due for payment shortly and long-term debts. The difference between the assets and the liabilities represents the amount of the shareholders' equity.

3. It is important to distinguish between the book values that are shown in the company accounts and the market values of the assets and liabilities. Book values are historical measures. For example, the assets in the balance sheet are shown at their historical cost less an allowance for depreciation. Similarly, the figure for shareholders' equity measures the cash that shareholders have contributed in the past or that the company has contributed on their behalf.

4. The income statement measures the profitability of the company during the year. Income is not the same as cash flow. There are two reasons for this: (a) the accountant records revenues when the sale is made rather than when

the customer actually pays the bill and at the same time deducts the production costs even though those costs may have been incurred earlier, and (b) investment in fixed assets is not deducted immediately from income but is instead spread over the expected life of the equipment.

5. The statement of cash flows measures the sources and uses of cash. The change in the company's cash balance is the difference between sources and uses.

6. For large companies the basic rate of tax on income is 38 percent. In calculating taxable income the company deducts an allowance for depreciation and interest payments. It cannot deduct dividend payments to the shareholders.

7. Individuals are also taxed on their income, which includes dividends and interest on their investments. Capital gains are taxed, but only when the investment is sold and the gain realized.

KEY TERMS

balance sheet	**book value**	**marginal tax rate**
generally accepted	**income statement**	**average tax rate**
accounting principles	**statement of cash flows**	**dividend tax credit**
(GAAP)		

SUGGESTED READINGS

A good introduction to financial statements may be found in
  Belverd E. Needles, Jr. *Financial Accounting*, 4th ed. Boston: Houghton Mifflin, 1992.

PROBLEMS

1. Construct a balance sheet for Sophie's Sofas given the following data. What is shareholders' equity?
   Cash balances = $10,000
   Inventory of sofas = $200,000
   Store and property = $100,000
   Accounts receivable = $20,000
   Accounts payable = $15,000
   Long-term debt = $170,000

2. Can cash flow from operations be positive if net income is negative? Can operating cash flow be negative if net income is positive? Give examples.

3. Sheryl's Shingles had sales of $10,000 in 1994. The cost of goods sold was $6000, general and administrative expenses were $1000, interest expenses were $500, and depreciation was $1000. The firm's combined federal and provincial tax rate is 35 percent.
   a. What is earnings before interest and taxes?
   b. What is net income?
   c. What is cash flow from operations?

4. Ponzi Products produced 100 chain letter kits this quarter, resulting in a total cash outlay of $10 per unit. It will sell 50 of the kits next quarter at a

price of $11, and the other 50 kits in two quarters at a price of $12. It takes a full quarter for it to collect its bills from its customers.

   a. Prepare an income statement for Ponzi for today and for each of the next three quarters. Ignore taxes.

   b. What are the cash flows for the company today and in each of the next three quarters?

   c. What is Ponzi's net working capital in each quarter?

5. You live in Nova Scotia and have set up your tax preparation firm as an incorporated business. You took $70,000 from the firm as your salary. The firm qualifies for the small business tax rate and has taxable income for the year (net of your salary) of $30,000. How much taxes must be paid to the federal government, including both your personal taxes and the firm's taxes? By how much will you reduce the total tax bill by reducing your salary to $50,000, thereby leaving the firm with taxable income of $50,000? Use the tax rates presented in Tables 2.4 and 2.5.

6. This is harder. Reconsider the data in problem 5 which imply that you have $100,000 of total pretax income to allocate between your salary and your firm's profits. What allocation will minimize the total tax bill? *Hint*: Think about marginal tax rates and the ability to shift income from a higher marginal bracket to a lower one.

7. South Sea Baubles has the following (incomplete) balance sheet and income statement.

BALANCE SHEET, AS OF END OF YEAR
(Figures in millions of dollars)

Assets	1994	1995	Liabilities and Shareholders' Equity	1994	1995
Current assets	$100	$150	Current liabilities	$ 60	$ 70
Net fixed assets	800	900	Long-term debt	600	750

INCOME STATEMENT, 1995
(Figures in millions of dollars)

Revenue	$1950
Cost of goods sold	1030
Depreciation	350
Interest expense	240

   a. What is shareholders' equity in 1994 and 1995?

   b. What is net working capital in 1994 and 1995?

   c. What is taxable income and taxes paid in 1995? Assume the firm pays taxes equal to 35 percent of taxable income.

   d. What is cash provided by operations during 1995? Pay attention to changes in net working capital, using Table 2.3 as a guide.

   e. Net fixed assets increased from $800 to $900 during 1995. What must have been South Sea's gross investment in fixed assets during 1995?

   f. If South Sea reduced its outstanding accounts payable by $40 during the year, what must have happened to its other current liabilities?

Here are some data on Fincorp, Inc., that you should use for problems 8–14. The balance sheet items correspond to values at year-end of 1994 and 1995, while the income statement items correspond to revenues or expenses during the year ending in either 1994 or 1995. All values are in thousands of dollars.

	1994	1995
Revenue	4000	4100
Cost of goods sold	1600	1700
Depreciation	500	520
Inventories	300	350
Administrative expenses	500	550
Interest expense	150	150
Federal and provincial taxes[a]	400	420
Accounts payable	300	350
Accounts receivable	400	450
Net fixed assets[b]	5000	5800
Long-term debt	2000	2400
Notes payable	1000	600
Dividends paid	410	410
Cash and marketable securities	800	300

[a] Taxes are paid in their entirety in the year that the tax obligation is incurred.
[b] Net fixed assets are fixed assets net of accumulated depreciation since the asset was installed.

8. Construct a balance sheet for Fincorp for 1994 and 1995. What is shareholders' equity?

9. What happened to net working capital during the year?

10. Construct an income statement for Fincorp for 1994 and 1995. What were retained earnings for 1995? How does that compare to the increase in shareholders' equity between the two years?

11. Suppose that Fincorp has 500,000 shares outstanding. What were earnings per share?

12. Examine the values for depreciation in 1995 and net fixed assets in 1994 and 1995. What was Fincorp's *gross* investment in plant and equipment during 1995?

13. Construct a statement of cash flows for Fincorp for 1995.

14. Now suppose that the market value (in thousands of dollars) of Fincorp's fixed assets in 1995 is $6000, and that the value of its long-term debt is only $2200. In addition, the consensus among investors is that Fincorp's past investments in developing the skills of its employees are worth $3000. This investment of course does not show up on the balance sheet. What will be the price per share of Fincorp stock?

SOLUTIONS TO SELF-TEST QUESTIONS

2.1 Cash and equivalents would increase by $10 million. Property, plant, and equipment would increase by $40 million. Long-term debt would increase by $50 million. Shareholders' equity would not increase: assets and liabilities have increased equally, leaving net worth unchanged.

2.2

a. If the auto plant were worth $14 billion, the equity in the firm would be worth $14–$4 = $10 billion. With 100 million shares outstanding, each share would be worth $100.

b. If the outstanding stock were worth $8 billion, we would infer that the market values the auto plant at 8 + 4 = $12 billion.

Period:	1	2	3
Sales	0	150	0
– Change in accounts receivable	0	150	(150)
– Cost of goods sold	0	100	0
– Change in inventories	100	(100)	0
Net cash flow	–100	0	+150

2.3

The net cash flow pattern does make sense. The firm expends $100 in period 1 to produce the product, but it is not paid its $150 sales price until period 3. In period 2 no cash is exchanged.

2.4

a. An increase in inventories uses cash, reducing the firm's net cash balance.

b. A reduction in accounts payable uses cash, reducing the firm's net cash balance.

c. An issue of common stock is a source of cash.

d. The purchase of new equipment is a use of cash, and it reduces the firm's net cash balance.

PART TWO

Value

CHAPTER THREE
The Time Value of Money

CHAPTER FOUR
More Time Value: Bonds and Inflation

CHAPTER FIVE
How Common Stocks Are Valued

CHAPTER SIX
Investment Criteria

CHAPTER SEVEN
Discounted Cash-Flow Analysis

CHAPTER EIGHT
Project Analysis

CHAPTER THREE

The Time Value of Money

Companies invest in lots of things. Some are *tangible assets* — that is, assets you can kick, like factories, machinery, and offices. Others are *intangible assets*, such as patents or trademarks. In each case the company lays out some money now in the hope of receiving even more money later.

Individuals also make investments. For example, your college education may cost you $20,000. That is an investment you hope will pay off in the form of a higher salary and/or a more satisfying job later in life. You are sowing now and expecting to reap later.

Companies pay for their investments by raising money and assuming liabilities. For example, they may borrow money from a bank and promise to repay it with interest later. You also may have financed your investment in a college education by borrowing money that you plan to pay back out of that fat salary.

All these financial decisions require comparisons of cash payments at different dates. Will your future salary be sufficient to justify the current expenditure on college tuition? How much will you have to repay the bank if you borrow to finance your education?

In this chapter we take the first steps toward understanding the relationship between the value of dollars today and that of dollars in the future. We start by looking at how funds invested at a specific interest rate will grow over time. We then ask how much you would need to invest today to produce a specified future sum of money. Next we describe some shortcuts for working out the value of a series of cash payments. Finally, we show how to evaluate a simple investment opportunity.

After studying this chapter you should be able to

- Calculate the future value to which an investment at a given interest rate will grow.
- Compare interest rates quoted over different time intervals — for example, monthly versus annual rates.
- Calculate the present value of future cash flows.
- Calculate present and future values of streams of cash payments.
- Calculate the net present value of a simple investment.

There is nothing complicated about these calculations but if they are to become second nature, you should read the chapter thoroughly, work carefully through the examples (we have provided plenty), and make sure you tackle the self-test questions. We are asking you to make an investment now in return for a payoff later.

3.1 FUTURE VALUES AND COMPOUND INTEREST

It is 1995 and you have $100 to invest in a bank account. Suppose banks are currently paying an interest rate of 6 percent per year on deposits. So after a year, your account will earn interest of $6:

$$\text{Interest} = \text{interest rate} \times \text{initial investment}$$

$$= .06 \times \$100 = \$6$$

You start the year with $100 and you earn interest of $6, so the value of your investment will grow to $106 by the end of the year:

$$\text{Value of investment after 1 year} = \$100 + \$6 = \$106$$

Notice that the $100 invested grows by the factor $(1 + .06) = (1.06)$. In general, for any interest rate r, the value of the investment at the end of 1 year is $(1 + r)$ times the initial investment:

$$\text{Value after 1 year} = \text{initial investment} \times (1 + r)$$

$$= \$100 \times (1.06) = \$106$$

What if you leave your money in the bank for a second year? Your balance, now $106, will continue to earn interest of 6 percent. So

$$\text{Interest in Year 2} = .06 \times \$106 = \$6.36$$

You start the second year with $106 on which you earn interest of $6.36. So by the end of the year the value of your account will grow to $106 + $6.36 = $112.36.

In the first year your investment of $100 increases by a factor of 1.06 to $106; in the second year the $106 again increases by a factor of 1.06 to $112.36. Thus the initial $100 investment grows twice by a factor 1.06:

$$\text{Value of account after 2 years} = \$100 \times 1.06 \times 1.06$$

$$= \$100 \times (1.06)^2 = \$112.36$$

If you keep your money invested for a third year, your investment multiplies by 1.06 each year for 3 years. By the end of the third year it will total $100 × $(1.06)^3 = \$119.10$, scarcely enough to put you in the millionaire class but even millionaires have to start somewhere.

So in general, if your money is invested for a total of t years, the original $100 investment will grow to $\$100 \times (1.06)^t$. For an interest rate of r and a horizon of t years, the **future value** of your investment will be

$$\text{Future value of } \$100 = \$100 \times (1 + r)^t$$

Notice in our example that your interest income in the first year is $6 (6 percent of $100), and in the second year it is $6.36 (6 percent of $106). Your income in the second year is higher because you now earn interest on *both* the original $100 investment and the $6 of interest earned in the previous year. Earning interest on interest is called *compounding* or **compound interest**. In contrast, if the bank calculated the interest it paid you each year by multiplying the rate times your original investment, you would be paid **simple interest**.

Table 3.1 and Figure 3.1 illustrate the mechanics of compound interest. Table 3.1 shows that in each year, you start with a greater balance in your account — your savings have been increased by the previous year's interest. As a result, your interest income also is higher.

future value: Amount to which an investment will grow after earning interest.

compound interest: Interest earned on interest.

simple interest: Interest earned only on the original investment; no interest is earned on interest.

TABLE 3.1
Compound interest

Year	Balance at Start of Year	Interest Earned during Year	Balance at End of Year
1	$100.00	.06 × $100.00 = $6.00	$106.00
2	$106.00	.06 × $106.00 = $6.36	$112.36
3	$112.36	.06 × $112.36 = $6.74	$119.10
4	$119.10	.06 × $119.10 = $7.15	$126.25
5	$126.25	.06 × $126.25 = $7.57	$133.82

FIGURE 3.1
Compound interest.

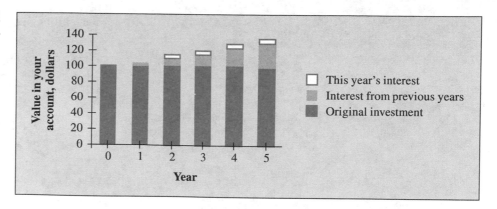

Obviously, the higher the rate of interest, the faster your savings will grow. Figure 3.2 shows that a few percentage points added to the (compound) interest rate can dramatically affect the future balance of your savings account. For example, after 10 years $1000 invested at 10 percent will grow to $1000 \times (1.10)^{10} = \$2594$. If invested at 5 percent, it will grow to only $1000 \times (1.05)^{10} = \$1629$.

FIGURE 3.2
Future values with compound interest.

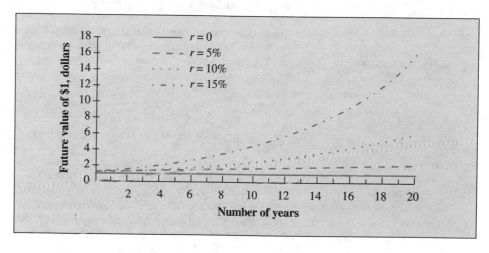

Calculating future values is easy using most any calculator. If you have the patience, you can multiply your initial investment by $1 + r$ (1.06 in our example) once for each year of your investment. A simpler procedure is to use the power key (the y^x key) on your calculator. For example, to compute 1.06^{10}, enter 1.06, press the y^x key, enter 10, press = and discover that the answer is 1.791. (Try this!)

If you don't have a calculator, you can use a table of future values such as Table 3.2. Check that you can use it to work out the future value of a 10-year investment at 6 percent. First find the row corresponding to 10 years. Now work along that row until you reach the column for a 6 percent interest rate. The entry shows that $1 invested for 10 years at 6 percent grows to $1.791.

Now try one more example. If you invest $1 for 20 years at 10 percent, what will you have at the end? Your answer should be $6.727.

Table 3.2 gives futures values for only a small selection of years and interest rates. Table A.1 at the end of the book is a bigger version of Table 3.2. It presents the future value of a $1 investment for a wide range of time periods and interest rates.

TABLE 3.2 Future value of $1	**Number of Years**	**Interest Rate per Year**					
		5%	**6%**	**7%**	**8%**	**9%**	**10%**
	1	1.050	1.060	1.070	1.080	1.090	1.100
	2	1.103	1.124	1.145	1.166	1.188	1.210
	3	1.158	1.1191	1.225	1.260	1.295	1.331
	4	1.216	1.262	1.311	1.360	1.412	1.464
	5	1.276	1.338	1.403	1.469	1.539	1.611
	10	1.629	1.791	1.967	2.159	2.367	2.594
	20	2.653	3.207	3.870	4.661	5.604	6.727
	30	4.322	5.743	7.612	10.063	13.268	17.449

Future value tables are tedious, and as Table 3.2 demonstrates, they show future values only for a limited set of interest rates and time periods. For example, suppose that you want to calculate future values using an interest rate of 7.835 percent. The power key on your calculator will be faster and easier than future value tables. A third alternative is to use a financial calculator. These are discussed in a box on pages 64 and 65.

● Example 3.1 Manhattan Island

Almost everyone's favourite example of the power of compound interest is the sale of Manhattan Island for $24 in 1626 to Peter Minuit. Based on New York real estate prices today, it seems that Minuit got a great deal. But consider the future value of that $24 if it had been invested for 369 years (1995 minus 1626) at an interest rate of 8 percent per year:

$$\$24 \times (1.08)^{369} = \$51,710,000,000,000$$

$$= \$51,710 \text{ billion}$$

Perhaps the deal wasn't as good as it appeared. The total value of land on Manhattan today is probably about $51 billion.

Though entertaining, this analysis is actually somewhat misleading. First, the 8 percent interest rate we've used to compute future values is quite high by historical standards. At a 3.5 percent interest rate, more consistent with historical experience, the future value of the $24 would be dramatically lower, only $24 \times (1.035)^{369} = \$7,819,884$! Second, we have understated the returns to Mr. Minuit and his successors: we have ignored all the rental income that the island's land has generated over the last three or four centuries.

All things considered, if we had been around in 1626, we would have gladly paid $24 for the island.

The power of compounding is not restricted to money. Foresters try to forecast the compound growth rate of trees, demographers the compound growth rate of population. One American social commentator has observed that the number of lawyers is increasing at a higher compound rate than the population as a whole (3.6 vs. 0.9 percent in the 1980s) and calculated that in about two centuries there will be more lawyers than people.

SELF-TEST 3.1
• • • • • • • • • • •

Suppose that Peter Minuit did not become the first New York real estate tycoon, but instead had invested his $24 at a 5 percent interest rate in New Amsterdam Saving Bank. What would have been the balance in his account after 5 years? 50 years?

● Example 3.2 Credit Cards

As a saver, you may be understandably enthusiastic about compound interest. As a borrower, however, it works against you. Consider your credit card as an example. Suppose you have to pay interest on unpaid balances at the rate of 1.5 percent per *month*. What is it going to cost you if you don't pay off a $1000 balance for a year? How much would you save if you instead took out a one-year bank loan at 13% to pay off your credit card balance?

Don't be put off because the credit card interest rate is quoted per month rather than per year. The important thing is to maintain consistency between the interest rate and the number of periods. If the interest rate is quoted as percent per month, then we must define the number of periods in our future value calculation as the number of months. So if you borrow $1000 from the credit card company at 1.5 percent per month for 12 months, you will need to repay $1000 $\times (1.015)^{12} = \$1195.62$.

Because the interest is calculated monthly and added to your unpaid balance, you are paying interest on interest. Thus your $1000 debt grows after 1 year to $1195.62. Using simple interest, you would pay interest only on the original $1000 borrowed, and therefore you would owe $1000 + $180 = $1180 after 1 year.

If you take out a $1000 loan at a rate of 13% to pay off your credit card balance, you would only owe $1000 + 130 = $1130, a savings of about $65.

SELF-TEST 3.2

Bacteria grow by division: one bacterium becomes two, the two become four, and so on. In other words, a population of bacteria can grow by 100 percent per period. Start with one bacterium. How many bacteria will there be after 1 week if division occurs every 12 hours? Assume none die. Use your calculator for this one.

3.2 ANNUALLY COMPOUNDED INTEREST RATES VERSUS ANNUAL PERCENTAGE RATES

Interest rates may be quoted for days, months, years, or any convenient interval. For example, when calculating your credit card payment, we used a monthly interest rate. When working out the value of Peter Minuit's investments, we used an annual rate. How should we compare rates when they are quoted for different periods, such as monthly versus annually?

effective annual interest rate: The rate of interest that would apply if interest was compounded once per year.

Our analysis of the finance charges on your credit card in Example 3.2 suggests how to convert a monthly rate to an **effective annual interest rate**. We saw that a year's interest at 1.5 percent per month increases your unpaid balance after a year by a factor of $(1.015)^{12} = 1.1956$. The balance increases by 19.56 percent. Therefore, we say that the *effective annual rate of interest*, or, equivalently, the *annually compounded rate* on the loan, is 19.56 percent.

In general, the effective annual interest rate is defined as the annual growth rate of funds allowing for the effects of compounding. Therefore,

$$(1 + \text{annual rate}) = (1 + \text{monthly rate})^{12}$$

When comparing interest rates, it is best to use effective annual rates, because this compares the growth of funds over a common period allowing for possible compounding during the period. Unfortunately, common practice annualizes short-term rates using simple interest by multiplying the rate per period by the number of periods in a year. In fact, Canada's Bank Act *requires* that rates

annual percentage rate (APR): Interest rate that is annualized using simple interest.

annualized in this manner be disclosed to borrowers. Such rates are called **annual percentage rates (APRs)**.[1] Thus our 1.5 percent a month credit card loan has an annually compounded rate of 19.56 percent but an APR of 18 percent.

If rates are quoted on an APR basis, how can we find the effective annual rate? The solution is simple. First take the quoted APR and divide by the number of compounding periods in a year to recover the original rate per period actually charged on the loan. Then calculate the equivalent annually compounded interest rate. For example, interest on the credit card loan will be quoted as an APR of 18 percent. Because the interest is calculated monthly, there are 12 compounding periods in a year. So we first divide by 18 to obtain the rate of interest per month, 1.5 percent. Then we convert to an annually compounded rate:

$$(1 + \text{annual rate}) = (1 + \text{monthly rate})^{12} = (1 + .015)^{12} = 1.1956$$

The annual interest rate is .1956 = 19.56 percent.

In general, suppose interest is paid on the loan m times per year. If interest is compounded monthly, $m = 12$; if it is compounded semiannually, $m = 2$. The interest charged *per period* equals the APR divided by m. After one period an investment of \$1 appreciates to $1 + \text{APR}/m$. After a year the same investment appreciates to $(1 + \text{APR}/m)^m$. Thus the equivalent annually compounded rate is $(1 + \text{APR}/m)^m - 1$.

● **Example 3.3 The Effective Interest Rates on Bank Accounts**

Back in the 1960s and 1970s U. S. banking regulations limited the (APR) interest rate that banks could pay on savings accounts in the U.S. Banks were hungry for depositors, and they searched for ways to increase the effective rate of interest that could be paid within the rules. Their solution was to keep the same APR but to calculate the interest on deposits more frequently. As interest is calculated at shorter and shorter intervals, less time passes before interest can be earned on interest. Therefore, the effective annually compounded rate of interest increases. Table 3.3 shows the calculations assuming that the maximum APR that banks could pay was 6 percent. (Actually, it was a bit less than this, but 6 percent is a nice round number to use for illustration.)

TABLE 3.3
Compounding frequency and effective annual interest rate (APR = 6%)

Compounding Period	Periods per Year	Per Period Interest Rate (%)	Growth Factor of Invested Funds	Effective Annual Rate (%)
1 year	1	6	1.06	6.0000
Semiannual	2	3	$1.03^2 = 1.0609$	6.0900
Quarterly	4	1.5	$1.015^4 = 1.061364$	6.1364
Monthly	12	0.5	$1.005^{12} = 1.061678$	6.1678
Weekly	52	0.11538	$1.0011538^{52} = 1.061800$	6.1800
Daily	365	0.0001644	$1.0001644^{365} = 1.061831$	6.1831

You can see from Table 3.3 how banks were able to increase the effective interest rate simply by calculating interest at more frequent intervals.

The ultimate step was to assume that interest was paid in a continuous stream rather than at fixed intervals. With one year's continuous compounding,

---

[1] Although the APR must be disclosed in the loan document, financial institutions typically (though not always) advertise effective rates when selling their products. APRs are not commonly used or quoted for securities used in the big leagues of finance.

$1 grows to $e^{(APR)}$, where $e = 2.718$ (a figure that may be familiar to you from an introductory calculus class). Thus if you deposited $1 with a bank that offered a continuously compounded rate of 6 percent, your investment would grow by the end of the year to $2.718^{.06} = \$1.061837$, just a hair's breadth more than if interest were compounded daily.

SELF-TEST 3.3 A car loan requiring quarterly payments carries an APR of 8 percent and interest is calculated quarterly. What is the annually compounded rate of interest?

3.3 PRESENT VALUES

Money can be invested to earn interest. If you are offered the choice between $100,000 now and $100,000 at the end of the year, you naturally take the money now to get a year's interest. Financial managers make the same point when they say that money in hand today has a *time value* or when they quote perhaps the most basic financial principle: *a dollar today is worth more than a dollar tomorrow*.

present value (PV): Value today of a future cash flow.

We have seen that $100 invested for 1 year at 6 percent will grow to a future value of $100 \times 1.06 = \$106$. Let's turn this around: How much do we need to invest now in order to produce $106 at the end of the year? Financial managers refer to this as the **present value** (or **PV**) of the $106 payoff.

Future value is calculated by multiplying present investment by 1 plus the interest rate, .06, or 1.06. To calculate present value, we simply reverse the process and divide the future value by 1.06:

$$\text{Present Value} = \text{PV} = \frac{\text{future value}}{1.06} = \frac{\$106}{1.06} = \$100$$

What is the present value of, say, $112.36 to be received 2 years from now? Again we ask, "How much would we need to invest now?" The answer is obviously $100; we've already calculated that at 6 percent $100 grows to $112.36:

$$\$100 \times (1.06)^2 = 112.36$$

However, if we don't know, or forgot the answer, we just divide future value by $(1.06)^2$:

$$\text{Present value} = \text{PV} = \frac{\$112.36}{(1.06)^2} = 100$$

In general, for a future value or payment t periods away, present value is

$$\text{Present value} = \frac{\text{future value after } t \text{ periods}}{(1 + r)^t}$$

discount rate: Interest rate used to compute present values of future cash flows.

In this context the interest rate r is known as the **discount rate** and the present value is often called the *discounted value* of the future payment. To calculate present value, we discounted the future value at the interest r.

● Example 3.4 Saving to Buy a New Computer

Suppose you need $3000 next year to buy a new computer. The interest rate is 8 percent per year. How much money should you set aside now in order to pay for the purchase? Just calculate the present value at an 8 percent interest rate of a $3000 payment at the end of one year. This value is

$$PV = \frac{\$3000}{1.08} = \$2777.77$$

Notice that $2777.77 invested for 1 year at 8 percent will prove just enough to buy your computer:

$$\text{Future value} = \$2777.77 \times 1.08 = \$3000$$

The longer the time before you must make a payment, the less you need to invest today. For example, suppose that you can postpone buying that computer until the end of 2 years. In this case we calculate the present value of the future payment by dividing $3000 by $(1.08)^2$:

$$PV = \frac{\$3000}{(1.08)^2} = \$2572.02$$

Thus you need to invest $2777.77 today to provide $3000 in 1 year, but only $2572.02 to provide the same $3000 in 2 years.

We repeat the basic procedure. To work out how much you will have in the future if you invest for t years at an interest rate r, multiply the initial investment by $(1 + r)^t$. To find the present value of a future payment, run the process in reverse and divide by $(1 + r)^t$.

Present values are always calculated using compound interest. Whereas the ascending lines in Figure 3.2 showed the future value of $100 invested with compound interest, when we calculate present values we move back along the lines from future to present. Present values fall with longer horizons, as in Figure 3.3.

FIGURE 3.3
Present value of a future cash flow of $1.

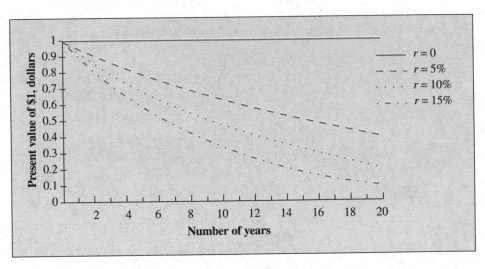

Thus present values decline, other things equal, when future cash payments are delayed. The longer you have to wait for money, the less it's worth.

● **Example 3.5 Calculating PV**

The interest rate is 9 percent. What is the present value of $10 million to be received in 30 years?

$$\text{Present value} = PV = \frac{\$10 \text{ million}}{(1.09)^{30}} = \$753,711$$

Note that $753,711 invested at 9 percent compound interest for 30 years grows to $10 million:

$$\$753{,}711 \times (1.09)^{30} = \$10{,}000{,}000$$

The present value formula is sometimes written differently. Instead of dividing the future payment by $(1 + r)^t$ we could equally well multiply it by $1/(1 + r)^t$:

$$PV = \frac{\text{future payment}}{(1 + r)^t}$$

$$= \text{future payment} \times \frac{1}{(1 + r)^t}$$

discount factor: Present value of a $1 future payment.

The expression $1/(1 + r)^t$ is called the **discount factor**. It measures the present value of $1 received in year t.

The simplest way to find the discount factor is to use a calculator, but financial managers sometimes find it convenient to use tables of discount factors. For example, Table 3.4 shows discount factors for a small range of years and interest rates. Table A.2 at the end of the book provides a set of discount factors for a wide range of years and interest rates.

Try using Table 3.4 to check our calculations of how much to put aside for that $3000 computer purchase. If the interest rate is 8 percent, the present value of $1 paid at the end of 1 year is $.926. So the present value of $3000 is

$$PV = \$3000 \times \frac{1}{(1.08)} = \$3000 \times .926 = \$2778$$

which except for rounding error matches the value we obtained in Example 3.4.

What if the computer purchase is postponed until the end of 2 years? Table 3.4 shows that the present value of $1 paid at the end of 2 years is .857. So the present value of $3000 is

$$PV = \$3000 \times \frac{1}{(1.08)^2} = \$3000 \times .857 = \$2571$$

which again differs from the calculation in Example 3.4 only because of rounding error.

TABLE 3.4
Present value of $1

Number of Years	Interest Rate per Year					
	5%	**6%**	**7%**	**8%**	**9%**	**10%**
1	.952	.943	.935	.926	.917	.909
2	.907	.890	.873	.857	.842	.826
3	.864	.840	.816	.794	.772	.751
4	.823	.792	.763	.735	.708	.683
5	.784	.747	.713	.681	.650	.621
10	.614	.558	.508	.463	.422	.386
20	.377	.312	.258	.215	.178	.149
30	.231	.174	.131	.099	.075	.057

Notice that as you move along the rows in Table 3.4, moving to higher interest rates, present values decline. As you move down the columns, moving to longer discounting periods, present values again decline. (Why does this make sense?)

● Example 3.6 The Italian Government Borrows $48 Million

In February 1992 the Italian government needed to borrow $48 million for 6 years. It did so by selling IOUs, each of which simply promised to pay the holder $1000 at the end of 6 years.[2] The market interest rate at the time was 7.5 percent. How much would you have been prepared to pay for one of the Italian government's IOUs?

To calculate this value we multiply the $1000 future payment by the 6-year discount factor:

$$PV = \$1000 \times \frac{1}{(1.075)^6}$$

$$= \$1000 \times .648 = \$648$$

Instead of using a calculator to find the discount factor, we could use Table A.2 at the end of the book. You can see that the 6-year discount factor is .666 if the interest rate is 7 percent and it is .630 if the rate is 8 percent. For an interest rate of 7.5 percent the discount factor is roughly halfway between at .648 — accurate in this case to three figures.

SELF-TEST 3.4

At the time it borrowed money for 6 years, the Italian government borrowed a further $48 million for 5 years. If the market interest rate was 7.5 percent, how much would you have been prepared to pay for a 5-year IOU of $1000?

● Example 3.7 Finding the Value of Free Credit

Kangaroo Autos is offering free credit on a $10,000 car. You pay $4000 down and then the balance at the end of 2 years. Turtle Motors next door does not offer free credit but will give you $500 off the list price. If the interest rate is 10 percent[3], which company is offering the better deal?

Notice that you pay more in total by buying through Kangaroo, but, since part of the payment is postponed, you can keep this money in the bank where it will continue to earn interest. To compare the two offers, you need to calculate the present value of the payments to Kangaroo:

$$PV = \$4000 + \$6000 \times \frac{1}{(1.10)^2} = \$4000 + (\$6000 \times .826)$$

$$= \$4000 + \$4958.68 = \$8958.68$$

If you pay $4000 down and put aside $4958.68 in a bank account, you will have just enough to pay Kangaroo Autos. The total cost of $8958.68 is a better deal than the $9500 charged by Turtle Motors.

These calculations illustrate how important it is to use present values when comparing alternative patterns of cash payment. You should never compare cash flows occurring at different times without first discounting them to a common date. By calculating present values, we see how much cash must be set aside today to pay future bills.

Finding the Interest Rate

When we looked at the Italian government's IOUs in the previous section, we used the interest rate to compute a fair market price for each IOU. Sometimes you are given the price and have to calculate the interest rate that is being offered.

---

[2] These IOUs are known as *bonds*. Usually, bond investors receive a regular interest or coupon payment. The Italian government bond will make only a single payment at the end of Year 6. It was therefore known as a *zero-coupon bond*. More on this in Chapter 4.
[3] We assume annual compounding, so there's no need to distinguish APRs from effective annual rates.

For example, when the Italian government borrowed money, it did not announce an interest rate; it simply offered to sell each IOU for $648. Thus we know that

$$PV = \$1000 \times \frac{1}{(1 + r)^6} = \$648$$

What is the interest rate?

There are several ways to approach this. First, you might use a table of discount factors. You need to find the interest rate for which the 6-year discount factor = .648. Look at Table A.2 at the end of the book and run your finger along the row corresponding to 6 years. You can see that an interest rate of 7 percent gives too high a discount factor and a rate of 8 percent gives too low a discount factor. The interest rate on the Italian government loan was about halfway between at 7.5 percent.

Second, you can rearrange the equation and use your calculator to show that

$$\$648 \times (1 + r)^6 = \$1000$$

$$(1 + r)^6 = \frac{\$1000}{\$648} = 1.543$$

$$(1 + r) = (1.543)^{1/6} = 1.075$$

$$r = .075, \text{ or } 7.5\%$$

In general this is more accurate. You can also use a financial calculator (see the box on pages 64 and 65).

SELF-TEST 3.5
. . . .

> What is the interest rate if the Italian government can sell its IOU for $705? Before doing the calculation, can you say whether *r* must be more or less than 7.5 percent?

 ## 3.4 MULTIPLE CASH PAYMENTS

One of the nice things about present values is that they are all expressed in current dollars — so that you can add them up. Thus when there are several future cash payments, we simply value each one separately and sum the present values.

● Example 3.8 Installment Payments on a Car Purchase

Kangaroo Autos has revised its offer. It's now $2000 down, $3000 at the end of 1 year, and $5000 at the end of 2 years. How does this compare with the previous offer?

To value the 1-year payment we multiply by the 1-year discount factor; to value the 2-year payment, we multiply by the 2-year discount factor. The total value of the payments is

$$PV = \$2000 + \left(\$3000 \times \frac{1}{(1.1)}\right) + \left[\$5000 \times \frac{1}{(1.1)^2}\right]$$

$$= \$2000 + (\$3000 \times .909) + (\$5000 \times .826)$$

$$= \$2000 + \$2727.27 + \$4132.23$$

$$= \$8859.50$$

Kangaroo has cut its effective asking price by about $100.

When there are many payments, you'll hear businesspeople refer to a *stream of cash flows*. They calculate the present value of the stream by first calculating the present value of each period's cash payment and then summing up.

Sometimes there are shortcuts that make it easy to calculate the present value of an asset that pays off in several different periods. Let us look at some examples.

Perpetuities

perpetuity: Stream of level cash payments that never ends.

Occasionally you come across investments that make a regular payment forever. For instance, some time ago the British government borrowed by issuing **perpetuities**. Instead of repaying these loans, the British government pays the investors holding these securities a fixed annual payment in perpetuity (forever).

The rate of interest on a perpetuity is equal to the promised annual payment C divided by the present value. For example, if a perpetuity pays $10 per year and you can buy it for $100, you will earn 10 percent interest each year on your investment. In general,

$$\text{Interest rate on a perpetuity} = \frac{\text{cash payment}}{\text{present value}}$$

$$r = \frac{C}{PV}$$

We can rearrange this relationship to derive the present value of a perpetuity, given the interest rate r and the cash payment C:

$$\text{PV of perpetuity} = \frac{C}{r} = \frac{\text{cash payment}}{\text{interest rate}}$$

Suppose some worthy person wishes to endow a chair in finance at your university. If the rate of interest is 10 percent and the aim is to provide $100,000 a year forever, the amount that must be set aside today is

$$\text{Present value of perpetuity} = \frac{C}{r} = \frac{\$100,000}{.10} = \$1,000,000$$

Two warnings about the perpetuity formula. First, at a quick glance you can easily confuse the formula with the present value of a single cash payment. A payment of $1 at the end of 1 year has a present value $1/(1 + r)$. The perpetuity has a value of $1/r$. These are quite different.

Second, the perpetuity formula tells us the value of a regular stream of payments starting one period from now. Thus our endowment of $1 million would provide the university with its first payment of $100,000 one year hence. If the worthy donor wants to provide the university with an additional payment of $100,000 up front, he or she would need to put aside $1,100,000.

SELF-TEST 3.6

A British government perpetuity pays £4 a year forever and in June 1993 was priced at £48. What was the interest rate?

How to Value Annuities

annuity: Equally spaced level stream of cash flows.

An **annuity** is an investment that pays a fixed sum each period for a specified number of periods. For example, a home mortgage might call on the homeowner to make equal monthly payments over the life of the loan. For a 25-year loan, this would result in 300 equal payments. Four-year car loans require 48 equal monthly payments.

There are two ways to value an annuity. The slow way is to value each payment and add up the values. The quick way is to take advantage of the following simple trick. Figure 3.4 shows the cash payments and values of three investments.

FIGURE 3.4
Valuing an annuity.

	Year:	1	2	3	4	5	6 ...	Present Value
				Cash Flow				
1.	Perpetuity A	$1	$1	$1	$1	$1	$1	$\dfrac{1}{r}$
2.	Perpetuity B				$1	$1	$1	$\dfrac{1}{r(1+r)^3}$
3.	Three-year annuity	$1	$1	$1				$\dfrac{1}{r} - \dfrac{1}{r(1+r)^3}$

Row 1. The investment shown in the first row provides a perpetual stream of $1 payments starting in Year 1. We have already seen that this perpetuity has a present value of $1/r$.

Row 2. Now look at the investment shown in the second row of Figure 3.4. It also shows a perpetual stream of $1 payments, but these payments don't start until Year 4. We know that it will have a value of $1/r$ in Year 3 (because at that time, it will be an ordinary perpetuity with payments starting at the end of 1 year), but it is not worth that much now. To find *today's* value we need to multiply $1/r$ by the 3-year discount factor. Thus the "delayed" perpetuity is worth

$$\frac{1}{r} \times \frac{1}{(1+r)^3} = \frac{1}{r(1+r)^3}$$

Row 3. Finally, look at the investment shown in the third row of Figure 3.4. This provides a level payment of $1 a year for each of 3 years. In other words, it is a 3-year annuity. You can also see that, taken together, the investments in rows 2 and 3 provide exactly the same cash payments as the investment in row 1. Thus the value of our annuity (row 3) must be equal to the value of the row 1 perpetuity less the value of the delayed row 2 perpetuity:

$$\text{Present value of 3-year \$1 annuity} = \frac{1}{r} - \frac{1}{r(1+r)^3}$$

The general formula for the value of an annuity that pays C dollars a year for each of t years is

$$\text{Present value of } t\text{-year annuity} = C\left[\frac{1}{r} - \frac{1}{r(1+r)^t}\right]$$

annuity factor: Present value of a $1 annuity.

The expression in square brackets shows the present value of a t-year annuity of $1 a year. It is generally known as the t-year **annuity factor**. Therefore, another way to write the value of an annuity is

$$\text{Present value of } t\text{-year annuity} = \text{payment} \times \text{annuity factor}$$

Remembering formulas is about as difficult as remembering other people's birthdays. But as long as you bear in mind that an annuity is equivalent to the difference between an immediate and a delayed perpetuity, you shouldn't have any difficulty.

● **Example 3.9 Back to Kangaroo Autos**

Let us return to Kangaroo Autos for (almost) the last time. Most installment plans call for level streams of payments. So let us suppose that this time Kangaroo offers an "easy payment" scheme of $4000 a year for each of the next

3 years payable at the end of the year. First let's do the calculations the slow way to show that the present value of the three payments is $9947.41:

	Present Value
First payment	$4000/1.10 = $3636.36
Second payment	$4000/1.10^2 = 3305.79
Third payment	$4000/1.10^3 = 3005.26
Total present value	$9947.41

The annuity formula is much quicker:

$$\text{Present value} = \$4000 \times \left[\frac{1}{.10} - \frac{1}{.10(1.10)^3}\right]$$

$$= \$4000 \times 2.487 = \$9947.41$$

You can use a calculator to work out annuity factors or you can use a set of annuity tables. Table 3.5 is an abridged annuity table (an extended version is shown in Table A.3 at the end of the book). Check that you can find the 3-year annuity factor for an interest rate of 10 percent.

A present value calculation shows you how much you have to invest today to generate a stream of future cash payments. For example, if you put aside $9947.41 today, you will have enough money to pay the future installments to Kangaroo Autos. Let's check that this works. Invested at 10 percent, your savings would grow by the end of the first year to $9947.41 × 1.10 = $10,942.15. Out of this you would need to pay the first $4000 installment, leaving you with $6942.15. By the end of the second year, your savings would grow with interest to $6942.15 × 1.10 = $7636.37. You then would make the second $4000 payment and be left with $3636.37. This sum left in the bank would grow in the last year to $3636.37 × 1.10 = $4000, just enough to make the last payment.

TABLE 3.5

Annuity table: present value of $1 a year for each of *t* years

Number of Years	Interest Rate per Year					
	5%	**6%**	**7%**	**8%**	**9%**	**10%**
1	.952	.943	.935	.926	.917	.909
2	1.859	1.833	1.808	1.783	1.759	1.736
3	2.723	2.673	2.624	2.577	2.531	2.487
4	3.546	3.465	3.387	3.312	3.240	3.170
5	4.329	4.212	4.100	3.993	3.890	3.791
10	7.722	7.360	7.024	6.710	6.418	6.145
20	12.462	11.470	10.594	9.818	9.129	8.514
30	15.372	13.765	12.409	11.258	10.274	9.427

SELF-TEST 3.7

If the interest rate is 8 percent, what is the 4-year discount factor? What is the 4-year annuity factor? What is the relationship between these two numbers? Explain.

Warning: The perpetuity and annuity formulas assume that the first payment occurs at the end of the period. They tell you the value of a stream of cash payments starting one period hence.

Installment loans often require the first payment to be made immediately.[4] For example, Kangaroo might have required three annual payments of $4000 starting immediately. In this case

$$\text{Present value} = \$4000 + \text{PV(2-year annuity)}$$

At 10 percent the 2-year annuity factor is 1.736. So present value is

$$\text{PV} = \$4000 + \$4000(1.736) = \$10,944$$

● Example 3.10 Winning Big at a Slot Machine

In May 1992, a 60-year-old nurse plunked down $12 in a Reno casino and walked away with the biggest jackpot in history — $9.3 million. We suspect she received unsolicited congratulations, good wishes, and requests for money from dozens of more or less worthy charities, relatives, and newly devoted friends. In response she could fairly point out that her prize wasn't really worth $9.3 million. That sum was to be paid in 20 annual installments of $465,000 each. What is the present value of the jackpot? Assume an interest rate of 8 percent.

The present value of these payments is simply the sum of the present values of each payment. But rather than valuing each payment separately, it is much easier to treat the cash payments as a 20-year annuity. To value this annuity we simply multiply $465,000 by the 20-year annuity factor:

$$\text{PV} = \$465,000 \times \text{20-year annuity factor}$$

$$= \$465,000 \times \left[\frac{1}{r} - \frac{1}{r(1+r)^{20}} \right]$$

At an interest rate of 8 percent, the annuity factor is

$$\left[\frac{1}{.08} - \frac{1}{.08(1.08)^{20}} \right] = 9.818$$

(We also could look up the annuity factor in Table A.3.) The present value of the $465,000 annuity is $465,000 × 9.818 = $4,565,000. That "$9.3 million prize" has a true value of about $4.6 million.

This present value is the price that investors would be prepared to offer for the series of cash flows. For example, the gambling casino might arrange for an insurance company to actually make the payments to the lucky winner. In this case, the company would charge a bit under $4.6 million to take over the obligation. With this amount in hand today, it could generate enough interest income to make the 20 payments before running its "account" down to zero.

SELF-TEST 3.8
· · · · · · · · · · · · · · ·

When calculating the value of the slot machine winnings, we assumed that the first of the 20 payments occurs at the end of 1 year. However, the first payment was probably made immediately, with the remaining payments spread over the following 19 years. What is the present value of the $9.3 million prize?

● Example 3.11 Home Mortgages

Sometimes you may need to find the series of cash payments that would provide a given value today. For example, home purchasers typically borrow the

---

[4] A level stream of payments starting immediately is usually known as an annuity due.

bulk of the house price from a lender. The most common loan arrangement is a 25-year loan that is repaid in equal monthly installments. Suppose that a house costs $125,000, and that the buyer puts down 20 percent of the purchase price, or $25,000, in cash, borrowing the remaining $100,000 from a mortgage lender such as the local trust company or bank. What is the appropriate monthly mortgage payment?

The borrower repays the loan by making monthly payments over the next 25 years (300 months). The savings bank needs to set these monthly payments so that they have a present value of $100,000. Thus

$$\text{Present value} = \text{mortgage payment} \times \text{300-month annuity factor}$$

$$= \$100,000$$

$$\text{Mortgage payment} = \frac{\$100,000}{\text{300-month annuity factor}}$$

Suppose that the interest rate is 1 percent a month.[5] Then

$$\text{Mortgage payment} = \frac{\$100,000}{\frac{1}{.01} - \frac{1}{.01(1.01)^{300}}}$$

$$= \frac{\$100,000}{94.947}$$

$$= 1053.22$$

This type of loan, in which the monthly payment is fixed over the life of the mortgage, is called an *amortizing loan*. "Amortizing" means that part of the monthly payment is used to pay interest on the loan and part is used to reduce the amount of the loan. For example, the interest that accrues after 1 month on this loan will be 1 percent of $100,000, or $1000. So $1000 of your first monthly payment is used to pay interest on the loan and the balance of $53.22 is used to reduce the amount of the loan to $99,946.78. The $53.22 is called the *amortization* on the loan in that month.

Next month, there will be an interest charge of 1 percent of $99,946.78 = $999.47. So $999.47 of your second monthly payment is absorbed by the interest charge and the remaining $53.75 of your monthly payment ($1053.22 − 999.47 = $53.75) is used to reduce the amount of your loan. Amortization in the second month is higher than in the first month because the amount of the loan has declined, and therefore less of the payment is taken up in interest. This procedure continues each month until the last month, when the amortization is just enough to reduce the outstanding amount on the loan to zero, and the loan is paid off.

Because the loan is steadily paid off, the fraction of the monthly payment devoted to interest steadily falls, while the fraction used to reduce the loan (the amortization) steadily increases. Thus the reduction in the size of the loan is much more rapid in the later years of the mortgage. Figure 3.5 illustrates how in the early years almost all of the mortgage payment is for interest. Even after 15 years, the bulk of the monthly payment is interest.

SELF-TEST 3.9   What will the monthly payment be if you take out a $100,000 fifteen-year mortgage at an interest rate of 1 percent per month?

---
[5] The effective annual rate is $(1.01)^{12}-1 = .1268$, or 12.68 percent.

FIGURE 3.5
Mortgage amortization.

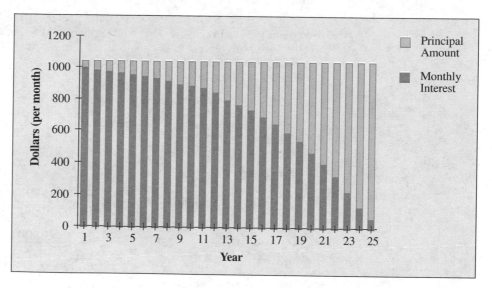

● **Example 3.12 How Much Luxury and Excitement Can $37 Billion Buy?**

The Sultan of Brunei is reputedly the world's richest person, with wealth estimated at $37 billion. We haven't yet met the Sultan, and so cannot fill you in on his plans for allocating the $37 billion between charitable good works and the cost of a life of luxury and excitement (L&E). So to keep things simple, we will just ask the following entirely hypothetical question: How much could the Sultan spend yearly on 40 more years of L&E if he were to devote the entire $37 billion to those purposes? Assume that his money is invested at 9 percent interest.

The 40-year, 9 percent annuity factor is 10.76. Thus

$$\text{Present value} = \text{annual spending} \times \text{annuity factor}$$

$$\$37,000,000,000 = \text{annual spending} \times 10.76$$

$$\text{Annual spending} = \$3,439,000,000$$

Warning to the Sultan: We haven't considered inflation. The cost of buying L&E will increase, so $3.4 billion won't buy as much L&E in 2010 as it will today. More on that in the next chapter.

SELF-TEST 3.10

Suppose you retire at age 70, with a life expectancy of 20 more years, and you expect to spend $55,000 a year during your retirement. How much money do you need to save by age 70 to support this consumption plan? Assume an interest rate of 7 percent.

● **Example 3.13 The Low-Interest-Rate Car Loan**

Low-interest-rate financing is a popular promotional tool in the auto industry. For example, a dealer selling a $12,000 car might offer to lend the purchase price to the buyer at an interest rate of .5 percent per month[6] even if the going market rate is 1 percent per month. How much does this subsidized loan reduce the cost of the car?

---

[6] This would be quoted as a 6 percent APR. The effective annual rate would be $(1.005)^{12} - 1 = .0617$, or 6.17 percent.

If you take up the dealer's offer, the dealer will lend you $12,000 and calculate the loan repayment schedule as though the interest rate is .5 percent. If the loan is to be repaid in equal installments over a 3-year period, the present value of the 36 monthly payments using a .5 percent interest rate will have to equal $12,000. Thus

Present value of payments at .5 percent interest rate

= monthly payment × 36-month annuity factor

= $12,000

Therefore,

$$\text{Monthly payment} = \frac{\$12,000}{36\text{-month annuity factor}}$$

$$= \frac{\$12,000}{\dfrac{1}{.005} - \dfrac{1}{.005(1.005)^{36}}}$$

$$= \frac{\$12,000}{32.87} = 365.06$$

But the interest rate at which you can actually invest is not .5 percent; it is 1 percent. Therefore, 1 percent is the rate that you should use to calculate the true present value of these payments. The rate at which you can invest determines how much money you need to set aside now to cover the monthly payments. Therefore, the present value of your payment stream is

$$\$365.06 \times 36\text{-month annuity factor} = \$365.06 \times \left[\frac{1}{.01} - \frac{1}{.01(1.01)^{36}}\right]$$

$$= \$365.06 \times 30.11$$

$$= \$10,991$$

The subsidized loan therefore reduces the cost of the car from $12,000 to $10,991.

FINANCIAL CALCULATORS

Most financial calculators are designed to solve problems involving single cash flows, level annuities, or both. Look at your calculator. It has five financial keys labeled: *n* (for number of periods), *i* (for interest rate), *PV* (for present value), *FV* (for future value), and *PMT* (for payment, or the amount of a level annuity). Given four of these variables, the calculator can solve for the fifth.

We will explain how to use the calculator by referring to some of the examples in this chapter.

1. Future Values

Recall Example 3.2, where we calculated the future value of your $100 credit card balance. Enter 100 in the *PV* register. We assumed an interest rate of 1 percent per month, so enter 1 in the *i* register, and because the $100 had 12 months to compound, enter 12 in the *n* register. Enter 0 into the *PMT* register because there is no annuity involved in the calculation. Now ask the calculator to compute future value (*FV*). Enter *COMP FV*, and obtain 112.68. (On some brands of calculators, the *COMP* or "compute" key may have a different label.)

> **FINANCIAL CALCULATORS** *(continued)*
>
> **2. Present Values**
> In Example 3.6 we calculated the present value of a $1000 payment to be made in 6 years when the interest rate was 7.5 percent. In this problem, we are given a future payment and need to compute its present value. Again, there is no annuity involved. Enter *n* = 6; *i* = 7.5; *FV* = 1000; *PMT* = 0. Then compute *PV*. You should get a present value of $648.
>
> **3. Finding the Interest Rate**
> Suppose a $1000 payment in Year X̃ is worth $648 today (as in Example 3.6). We can obtain the interest rate by entering *n* = 7, *FV* = 1000, *PV* = 648, *PMT* = 0. Compute *i* as 7.5 percent.
>
> **4. Present Value of an Annuity**
> In Example 3.11 we considered a 25-year mortgage with monthly payments of $1053.22 and an interest rate of 1 percent. Suppose we didn't know the amount of the mortgage. Enter *n* = 300 (months), *PMT* = 1053.22, *i* = 1, *FV* = 0 (the mortgage is wholly paid off after 3̶0̶ years). Then compute *PV*. You should get $100,000.

3.5 NET PRESENT VALUE: A FIRST LOOK

You should now be familiar with the basic principles of discounting future cash payments to find their present value. We conclude this chapter by applying these ideas to evaluating a simple investment decision.

Suppose that you are in the real estate business. You are considering the construction of an office block. The land would cost $50,000 and construction would cost a further $300,000. You foresee a shortage of office space and predict that a year from now you will be able to sell the building for $400,000. Thus you would be investing $350,000 now in the expectation of realizing $400,000 at the end of the year. You should go ahead if the present value of the $400,000 payoff is greater than the investment of $350,000.

Assume for the moment that the $400,000 payoff is a sure thing. The office building is not the only way to obtain $400,000 a year from now. You could invest in a 1-year Canadian government IOU. Suppose the IOU offers interest of 7 percent. How much would you have to invest in order to receive $400,000 at the end of the year? That's easy: you would have to invest

$$\$400,000 \times \frac{1}{1.07} = \$400,000 \times .935 = \$373,832$$

Therefore, at an interest rate of 7 percent, the present value of $400,000 is $373,832.

Let's assume that as soon as you have purchased the land and begun construction, you decide to cash in on your project. How much could you sell it for? Since the property will be worth $400,000 in a year, investors would be willing to pay at most $373,832 for it now. That's all it would cost them to get the same $400,000 payoff by investing in a government security. Of course you could always sell your property for less, but why sell for less than the market will bear?

The $373,832 present value is the only price that satisfies both buyer and seller. In general, the present value is the only feasible price, and the present value of the property is also its *market price* or *market value*.

opportunity cost of capital: Expected rate of return given up by investing in a project.

To calculate present value, we discounted the expected future payoff by the rate of return offered by comparable investment alternatives. The discount rate — 7 percent in our example — is often known as the **opportunity cost of capital**. It is called the opportunity cost because it is the return that is being given up by investing in the project.

Net Present Value

net present value (NPV): Present value of project cash flows minus initial investment.

The building is worth $373,832, but this does not mean that you are $373,832 better off. You committed $350,000, and therefore your **net present value (NPV)** is $23,832. Net present value is found by subtracting the required investment:

$$NPV = PV - required\ investment$$

$$= \$373,832 - \$350,000 = \$23,832$$

In other words, your office development is worth more than it costs — it makes a net contribution to value.

A Comment on Risk and Present Value

In our discussion of the office development we assumed we knew the value of the completed project. Of course, you will never be certain about future values of office buildings. The $400,000 represents the best forecast, but it is not a sure thing.

Therefore, our conclusion about how much investors would pay for the building is wrong. Since they could achieve $400,000 risklessly by investing in $373,832 worth of Canadian government loans, they would not buy your building for that amount. You would have to cut your asking price to attract investors' interest.

Here we can invoke a basic financial principle: *A risky dollar is worth less than a safe one.* Most investors avoid risk when they can do so without sacrificing return. However, the concepts of present value and the opportunity cost of capital still apply to risky investments. It is still proper to discount the payoff by the rate of return offered by a comparable investment. But we have to think of expected payoffs and the expected rates of return on other investments.

Not all investments are equally risky. The office development is riskier than a government loan but is probably less risky than drilling an oil well. Suppose you believe the project is as risky as an investment in the stock market and that you forecast a 12 percent rate of return for stock market investments. Then 12 percent becomes the appropriate opportunity cost of capital. That is what you are giving up by not investing in comparable securities. You can now recompute NPV:

$$PV = \$400,000 \times \frac{1}{1.12} = \$400,000 \times .893 = \$357,143$$

$$NPV = PV - \$350,000 = \$7143$$

If other investors agree with your forecast of a $400,000 payoff and with your assessment of a 12 percent opportunity cost of capital, then your property ought to be worth $357,143 once construction is under way. If you tried to sell for more than that, there would be no takers, because the property would then offer a lower expected rate of return than the 12 percent available in the stock market. The office building still makes a net contribution to value, but it is much smaller than our earlier calculations indicated.

Present Value by Another Name...

Present value, like most important concepts, has several names. Financial managers may say

Present value, or just PV
Discounted value

Investment needed to generate specified future payment(s)
Market price
Market value

and mean exactly the same thing.

3.6 SUMMARY

1. An investment of $1 earning an interest rate of r will increase in value each period by the factor $(1 + r)$. After t periods its value will grow to $(1 + r)^t$. This is the future value of the $1 investment with compound interest.

2. Interest rates for short time periods are often quoted as annual rates by multiplying the per-period rate by the number of periods in a year. These annual percentage rates (APRs) do not recognize the effect of compound interest.

3. The present value of a future cash payment is the amount that you would need to invest today to match that future payment. To calculate present value we divide the cash payment by $(1 + r)^t$ or, equivalently, multiply by the discount factor $1/(1 + r)^t$. The discount factor measures the value today of $1 received in period t.

4. A level stream of cash payments that continues indefinitely is known as a perpetuity; one that continues for a limited number of years is called an annuity. Shortcut formulas make valuing perpetuities and annuities easy. The value of a perpetuity is the annuity payment, C, divided by r while the value of an annuity is the annuity payment multiplied by the annuity factor

$$\left[\frac{1}{r} - \frac{1}{r(1 + r)^t} \right]$$

5. The present value of an investment is a measure of how much it is worth. The difference between the present value of an investment and the required investment is known as the net present value. Net present value measures how much better off you would be by undertaking the investment.

6. A risky dollar is worth more than a safe one. As a result, the rate used to discount expected cash flows should be higher for risky cash flows than for safe ones.

KEY TERMS

future value	annual percentage	perpetuity
compound interest	rate (APR)	annuity
simple interest	present value (PV)	annuity factor
effective annual	discount rate	opportunity cost of capital
interest rate	discount factor	net present value (NPV)

SUGGESTED READINGS

The material in this chapter should cover all you need to know about the mathematics of present and future values, but if you wish to dig deeper, there are a number of books on the subject. Try, for example:

R. Cissell, H. Cissell, and D. C. Flaspohler. *The Mathematics of Finance*, 6th ed. Boston: Houghton Mifflin, 1982.

PROBLEMS

1. Compute the present value of a $100 cash flow for the following combinations of discount rates and times:
   a. $r = 10$ percent, $t = 10$ years
   b. $r = 10$ percent, $t = 20$ years
   c. $r = 15$ percent, $t = 10$ years
   d. $r = 15$ percent, $t = 20$ years

2. Compute the future value of a $100 cash flow for the same combinations of rates and times as in problem 1.

3. In 1880 five aboriginal trackers were each promised the equivalent of 100 Australian dollars for helping to capture the notorious outlaw Ned Kelley. In 1993 the granddaughters of two of the trackers claimed that this reward had not been paid. The Victorian prime minister stated that if this was true, the government would be happy to pay the $100. However, the granddaughters also claimed that they were entitled to compound interest. How much was each entitled to if the interest rate was 5 percent? What if it was 10 percent?

4. You deposit $1000 in your bank account. If the bank pays 10 percent simple interest, how much will you accumulate in your account after 10 years? What if the bank pays compound interest? How much of your earnings will be interest on interest?

5. You will require $700 in 5 years. If you earn 6 percent interest on your funds, how much will you need to invest today in order to reach your savings goal?

6. Find the equivalent annual rate of interest.

Stated Interest Annual Rate (APR)	Compounding Period
10%	3 months
8%	6 months
4%	1 month

7. Would you rather receive $100 a year for 10 years or $80 a year for 15 years if
   a. the interest rate is 5 percent
   b. the interest rate is 20 percent
   c. Why do your answers to (a) and (b) differ?

8. Find the annual interest rate.

Present Value	Future Value	Time Period
100	115.76	3 years
200	262.16	4 years
100	110.41	5 years

9. If you earn 6 percent per year on your bank account, how long will it take an account with $100 to double to $200?

10. Suppose you can borrow money at 8.6 percent per year (APR) compounded semiannually or 8.4 percent per year (APR) compounded monthly. Which is the better deal?

11. What is the present value of the following cash-flow stream if the discount rate is 5 percent?

Year	Cash Flow
1	$200
2	400
3	300

12. a. What is the present value of a 3-year annuity of $100 if the discount rate is 10 percent?
    b. What is the present value of the annuity in (a) if you have to wait 2 years for the payment stream to start instead of 1 year?

13. A famous quarterback just signed a $15 million contract providing $3 million a year for 5 years. A less famous receiver signed a $14 million 5-year contract providing $4 million now and $2 million a year for 5 years. Who is better paid? The interest rate is 10 percent.

14. If you take out an $8000 car loan that calls for 48 monthly payments at an APR of 10 percent, what is your monthly payment? What is the effective annual interest rate on the loan?

15. If you take out an $8000 car loan that calls for 48 monthly payments of $225 each, what is the APR of the loan? What is the effective annual interest rate on the loan?

16. Reconsider the car loan in the previous question. What if the payments are made in four annual year-end installments? What annual payment would have the same present value as the monthly payment you calculated? Use the same effective annual interest rate as in the previous question. Why is your answer not simply 12 times the monthly payment?

17. A local bank will pay you $100 a year for your lifetime if you deposit $2500 in the bank today. If you plan to live forever, what interest rate is the bank paying?

18. A local bank advertises the following deal: "Pay us $100 a year for 10 years and we will pay you (or your beneficiaries) $100 a year forever." Is this a good deal if the interest rate available on other deposits is 8 percent?

19. You can buy property today for $3 million and sell it in 5 years for $4 million. (You earn no rental income on the property.)
    a. If the interest rate is 8 percent, what is the net present value of the project?
    b. Why is NPV negative although the profit on the project is positive?
    c. Suppose you also earn rent of $200,000 per year on the property. How does the net present value of the property change?

20. A property will provide $10,000 a year forever. If its value is $125,000, what must be the opportunity cost of capital?

21. You invest $1000 at a 6 percent annual interest rate, stated as an APR. Interest is compounded monthly. How much will you have in 1 year? In 1.5 years?

22. You invest $1000 today and expect to sell your investment for $2000 in 10 years.
    a. Is this a good deal if the opportunity cost of capital is 5 percent?
    b. What if the opportunity cost of capital is 10 percent?

23. If a bank pays 10 percent interest with continuous compounding, what is the effective annual rate?

24. A store offers two payment plans. Under the installment plan, you pay 25 percent down and 25 percent of the purchase price in each of the next 3 years. If you pay the entire bill immediately, you can take a 10 percent discount from the purchase price. Which is a better deal if you can borrow or lend funds at a 6 percent interest rate?

25. Reconsider the previous question. How will your answer change if the payments on the 4-year installment plan do not start for a full year?

26. a. If you borrow $1000 and agree to repay the loan in five equal annual payments at an interest rate of 10 percent, what will your payment be?
    b. What if you make the first payment on the loan immediately instead of at the end of the first year?

27. You believe you will need to have saved $500,000 by the time you retire in 40 years in order to live comfortably. If the interest rate is 4 percent per year, how much must you save each year to meet your retirement goal?

28. How much would you need in problem 27 if you believe that you will inherit $100,000 in 10 years?

29. You believe you will spend $40,000 a year for 20 years once you retire in 40 years. If the interest rate is 4 percent per year, how much must you save each year until retirement to meet your retirement goal?

30. You borrow $10,000, and you repay the loan by making total payments of $12,000: $1000 a month for 12 months. The lender argues that since the loan is for 1 year and the total amount of interest paid is $2000, the interest rate on the loan is 20 percent. What is the APR and the effective annual rate on this loan? Is either rate as low as 20 percent? Why is the 20 percent rate quoted on this loan deceptive?

31. You take out a 25-year $100,000 mortgage loan with an APR of 8 percent compounded monthly and with monthly payments. In 10 years you decide to sell your house and pay off the mortgage.
    a. What is the effective monthly rate on the mortgage?
    b. What is the principal balance on the loan?

32. British government 4 percent perpetuities pay £4 interest each year forever. Another bond, 2 1/2% perpetuities, pays £2.50 a year forever. What is the value of 4 percent perpetuities, if the long-term interest rate is 6 percent? What is the value of 2 1/2 percent perpetuities?

33. Your wealthy uncle established a $1000 bank account for you when you were born. For the first 8 years of your life, the interest rate earned on the account was 8 percent. Since then, rates have been only 6 percent. Now you are 21 years old and ready to cash in. How much is in your account?

34. A factory costs $400,000. You forecast that it will produce cash inflows of $100,000 in Year 1, $200,000 in Year 2, and $300,000 in Year 3. The opportunity cost of capital is 12 percent. What is the net present value of the factory?

35. How much will $100 grow to if invested at a continuously compounded interest rate of 8 percent for 6 years? What if it is invested for 6 years at 8 percent?

36. You can buy a car that is advertised for $12,000 on the following terms: (a) pay $12,000 and receive a $1000 rebate from the manufacturer; (b) pay $250 a month for 4 years for total payments of $12,000, implying zero percent financing. Which is the better deal if the interest rate is 1 percent per month?

37. I now have $20,000 in the bank earning interest of .5 percent per month. I need $30,000 to make a down payment on a house. I can save an additional $100 per month. How long will it take me to accumulate the $30,000?

SOLUTIONS TO SELF-TEST QUESTIONS

3.1 Value after 5 years will be $24 \times (1.05)^5 = \$30.63$; after 50 years, $24 \times (1.05)^{50} = \$275.22$.

3.2 The growth rate is 100 percent per period. After the first 12 hours, 1 bacterium becomes 2 bacteria. After the first day, the 2 become 4, and so on. This is just like earning interest on money at 100 percent per period. If r is the growth rate, $(1 + r) = (1 + 1) = 2$. There are 14 twelve-hour periods in 1 week. Thus the bacteria count at the end of the week will be

$$1 \times (1 + r)^{14} = 1 \times 2^{14} = 16,384$$

3.3 The quarterly rate is $8/4 = 2$ percent. The effective annual rate is $(1.02)^4 - 1 = .0824$, or 8.24 percent.

3.4 Multiply the $1000 payment by the 5-year discount factor:

$$PV = 1000 \times \frac{1}{(1.075)^5} = \$696.56$$

3.5 $705 \times (1 + r)^6 = 1000$ implies that $r = .06$, or 6 percent. You knew that the rate had to be less than 7.5 percent because the present value of the loan at 7.5 percent was $648. Since PV is higher in this example, the interest rate must be lower.

3.6 The rate is $4/48 = .0833$, about 8.3 percent.

3.7 The 4-year discount factor is $1/(1.08)^4 = .735$. The 4-year annuity factor is $[1/.08 - 1/(.08 \times 1.08^4)] = 3.312$. This is the difference between the present value of a $1 perpetuity starting next year and of a $1 perpetuity starting in Year 5:

$$PV \text{ (perpetuity starting next year)} = \frac{1}{.08} = 12.50$$

$$- PV \text{ (perpetuity starting in Year 5)} = \frac{1}{.08} \times \frac{1}{(1.08)^4}$$

$$= 12.50 \times .735 = 9.188$$

$$= PV \text{ (4-year annuity)} \qquad = 12.50 - 9.188 = 3.312$$

3.8   Calculate the value of a 19-year annuity, then add the immediate $465,000 payment:

$$\text{19-year annuity factor} = \frac{1}{r} - \frac{1}{r(1 + r)^{19}}$$

$$= \frac{1}{.08} - \frac{1}{.08(1.08)^{19}}$$

$$= 9.604$$

$$PV = \$465,000 \times 9.604 = \$4,466,000$$

$$\text{Total value} = \$4,466,000 + \$465,000$$

$$= \$4,931,000$$

Starting the 20-year cash flow stream immediately, rather than waiting 1 year, increases value by nearly $400,000.

3.9   Fifteen years means 180 months. Then

$$\text{Mortgage payment} = \frac{100,000}{\text{180-month annuity factor}}$$

$$= \frac{100,000}{83.32}$$

$$= \$1200.17 \text{ per month}$$

3.10   You will need the present value at 7 percent of a 20-year annuity of $55,000:

$$\text{Present value} = \text{annual spending} \times \text{annuity factor}$$

The annuity factor is $[1/.07 - 1/(.07 \times 1.07^{20}] = 10.594$. Thus you need $55,000 \times 10.594 = \$582,670$.

CHAPTER FOUR

More Time Value: Bonds and Inflation

In Chapter 3 we showed that a dollar today is worth more than a dollar tomorrow, because the dollar today can be invested to start earning interest immediately. To value a future dollar payment we ask, "How much do we need to invest today to produce that future cash?" The answer to this question is the present value of that payment.

In this chapter we extend our analysis of the time value of money in two directions. We look first at corporate and government bonds and then at the impact of inflation on cash flows, interest rates, and present values. You will find that the chapter gives you plenty of extra practice in discounting and valuation.

After studying this chapter you should be able to

● Find the market price of a bond given its yield to maturity.
● Find the bond's yield given its price.
● Demonstrate why prices and yields move in opposite directions.
● Calculate inflation-adjusted values of cash flows.
● Calculate and use real interest rates.

 4.1 BOND PRICES AND YIELDS

Bond Pricing

bond: Security that obligates the issuer to make specified payments to the bondholder.

coupon: The interest payments paid to the bondholder.

face value: Payment at the maturity of the bond. Also called par value or maturity value.

coupon rate: Annual interest payment as a percentage of face value.

A **bond** is simply a long-term debt. Governments and corporations borrow money by selling bonds to investors. When you own a bond, you receive a fixed interest payment each year until the bond matures. This payment is known as the **coupon** because most bonds used to have coupons that the investors clipped off and mailed to the bond issuer to claim interest. At maturity the debt is repaid. The amount that is repaid is known as the bond's **face value**, *par value*, or *maturity value*.[1] In Canada most bonds issued by corporations have a face value of $1000.

How do bonds work? Consider a Canadian government bond as an example. In 1993 the Canadian government raised money by selling 6.5 percent coupon, 1998 maturity bonds. Each bond has a face value of $1000 and the **coupon rate** is 6.5 percent of this face value. So each year until 1998 the government is obliged to make a coupon payment of 6.5 percent of $1000, or $65. Then in 1998 the government must also pay the face value of the bond, $1000.

Suppose that in 1994 you decided to buy the 6.5s of 1998, that is, the 6.5 percent coupon bonds maturing in 1998. You could then look forward to the following cash payments:

1995	1996	1997	1998
$65	$65	$65	$1065

What is the market value of this stream of cash flows? To answer, we need to look at the return provided by similar securities. In 1994 Canada bonds with similar maturities offered a return of about 9 percent. This interest rate is what investors could have earned on alternative investments of comparable risk.

---

[1] Occasionally, you come across zero-coupon bonds. In this case you receive the $1000 face value at maturity but don't get any interest payments. In the last chapter you learned how to value a zero-coupon bond issued by the Italian government. Sometimes you encounter bonds that only pay interest and never mature. The British government perpetuity that we valued in the last chapter is an example. The Canadian government also issued a perpetual bond in 1936 but then changed its mind in 1975 when it announced that these bonds would be retired in 1996. See "Finance in Action," on page 81.

Therefore, to value these bonds, we need to discount the prospective stream of cash flows at 9 percent:

$$PV = \frac{\$65}{(1+r)} + \frac{\$65}{(1+r)^2} + \frac{\$65}{(1+r)^3} + \frac{\$1065}{(1+r)^4}$$

$$= \frac{\$65}{(1.09)} + \frac{\$65}{(1.09)^2} + \frac{\$65}{(1.09)^3} + \frac{\$1065}{(1.09)^4}$$

$$= \$919.00$$

Bond prices are usually expressed as a percentage of their face value. Thus we can say that our 6.5 percent Canada bond is worth 91.9 percent of face value, and its price commonly would be quoted simply as 91.9.

● **EXAMPLE 4.1 Bond Prices and Interest Rates**

Investors will pay $919 for a 6.5 percent, 4-year Government of Canada bond, when the interest rate is 9 percent. Suppose that the interest rate suddenly becomes much higher — 15 percent, say. Now what is the value of the bond? Simple! We just repeat our initial calculation with $r = .15$:

$$PV = \frac{\$65}{(1.15)} + \frac{\$65}{(1.15)^2} + \frac{\$65}{(1.15)^3} + \frac{\$1065}{(1.15)^4}$$

$$= \$757.33$$

Did you notice that the coupon payments on the bond are an annuity? In other words, the bondholder receives a level stream of coupon payments of $65 a year for each of 4 years. At maturity the bondholder gets an additional payment of $1000. Therefore, you can use the annuity formula to value the coupon payments and then add on the present value of the final payment:

PV = PV(coupons) + PV(final payment)

= (coupon × annuity factor) + (face value × discount factor)

$$= \$65 \times 1 \left[\frac{1}{.09} - \frac{1}{.09(1.09)^4} \right] + \$1000 \times \frac{1}{(1.09)^4}$$

$$= \$919.00$$

If you need to value a bond with many years to run before maturity, it is usually easiest to value the coupon payments as an annuity and then add on the present value of the final payment.

SELF-TEST 4.1

Calculate the present value of a 6-year bond with a 9 percent coupon. The interest rate is 12 percent.

Thus far we've assumed that interest payments occur annually. This is the case for bonds in many European countries but most bonds in Canada and the United States make coupon payments *semiannually*. Instead of receiving $65 each year from the 6.5 percent bonds, you would receive $32.5 every *half* year. To value semiannual payment bonds we must discount a series of semiannual payments by the semiannual rate of interest. But since this would just add to the arithmetic, we will stick to our approximation and assume annual interest payments.

The Yield to Maturity

Suppose you are considering purchase of a bond. Your investment adviser quotes a current price. How do you calculate the rate of return the bond offers?

For bonds purchased at face value the answer is easy. The rate of return is the coupon rate. Consider the following 1-, 2-, and 3-year maturity 20 percent coupon bonds. In each case, suppose you can buy the bond for $1000, the face value.

Bond Maturity	You Pay	Cash Paid to You in Year 1	2	3	Rate of Return
1 year	$1000	$1200			20%
2 years	1000	200	$1200		20
3 years	1000	200	200	$1200	20

In each year you get 20 percent on your money ($200/$1000) and in the final year you get your $1000 back.

That 20 percent coupon is pretty attractive compared with the return offered by other bonds, so you might actually have to pay more than $1000 for the bonds. Suppose the market price of the 3-year bond is $1248.69. Your cash flows are then as follows:

You Pay	Cash Paid to You in Year 1	2	3	Rate of Return
$1248.69	$200	$200	$1200	?

current yield: Annual coupon payments divided by current price.

What's the rate of return now? Not $200/$1248.69 = .16, or 16 percent; that would measure only the first year's immediate or **current yield** in cash. Sixteen percent overstates the true rate of return, because you're paying $1248.69 for a bond that will pay only $1000 when it matures in Year 3.

We need a measure of rate of return that takes account of both current yield and the appreciation or depreciation of a bond's value over its life. The standard measure is called **yield to maturity** or *internal rate of return*. This is *the discount rate that makes the present value of a bond's payments equal to its price.*

yield to maturity: Interest rate for which the present value of the bond's payments equals the price.

If you can buy the 1-, 2-, and 3-year bonds at face value, the yield to maturity is 20 percent. Discounting at 20 percent gives face value in each case:

$$PV(\text{1-year bond}) = \frac{\$1200}{1.20} = \$1000$$

$$PV(\text{2-year bond}) = \frac{\$200}{1.20} + \frac{\$1200}{(1.20)^2} = \$1000$$

$$PV(\text{3-year bond}) = \frac{\$200}{1.20} + \frac{\$200}{(1.20)^2} + \frac{\$1200}{(1.20)^3} = \$1000$$

But if you have to buy the 3-year bond for $1248.69, the yield to maturity is 10 percent. At that discount rate, the bond's present value equals its actual market price, $1248.69:

$$PV \text{ at } 10\% = \frac{\$200}{1.10} + \frac{\$200}{(1.10)^2} + \frac{\$1200}{(1.10)^3} = \$1000$$

● EXAMPLE 4.2 Calculating Yield to Maturity for the Treasury Bond

We found the value of the 6.5 percent coupon Canada bond by discounting at a 9 percent interest rate. We could have phrased the question the other way around: If the price of the bond is $919, what return do investors expect? We need to find the yield to maturity, in other words, the discount rate r that solves the following equation:

$$PV = \frac{\$65}{(1 + r)} + \frac{\$65}{(1 + r)^2} + \frac{\$65}{(1 + r)^3} + \frac{\$1065}{(1 + r)^4}$$

$$= \$919.00$$

To find the yield to maturity, you can use a book of bond tables that show values of r for different coupons and maturities. You can also use a financial calculator. For our Canada bond you would enter a PV of 919.00. The bond provides a regular payment of $65, entered as PMT = 65. The bond has a future value of $1000, so FV = 1000. The bond life is 4 years, so n = 4. Now compute the interest rate, and you will find that the yield to maturity is 9 percent.

The yield to maturity depends on the coupon payments that you receive each year ($65) and the final repayment of face value ($1000). Thus it is a measure of the total return on this bond.

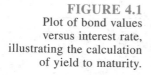

SELF-TEST 4.2

A 4-year bond with a 14 percent coupon can be bought for $1200. What is the yield to maturity? You will need a bit of trial and error to answer this question.

The only *general* procedure for calculating yield to maturity is trial and error. In fact, when you use a calculator to compute yield to maturity, you will notice that it takes the calculator a few moments to compute the interest rate. This is because it must perform a series of trial-and-error calculations.

Figure 4.1 offers a graphical view of yield to maturity. It shows the present value of the bond for different interest rates. The actual bond price, $919.00, is marked on the vertical axis. A line is drawn from this price over to the present value curve and then down to the interest rate, 9.0 percent. If we picked a higher or lower figure for the interest rate, then we would not obtain a bond price of $919.00. Thus we know that the yield to maturity on the bond must be 9.0 percent.

Figure 4.1 also illustrates a fundamental relationship between interest rates and bond prices: *As interest rates rise, bond prices fall (and vice versa).*

FIGURE 4.1
Plot of bond values versus interest rate, illustrating the calculation of yield to maturity.

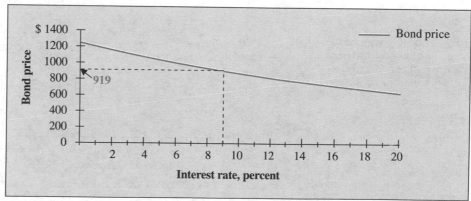

A gentle warning! People sometimes confuse the *interest rate* — that is, the return that investors require — with the *interest*, or *coupon payment* on the bond. Although interest rates change from day to day, the coupon payments on our Canada bond are fixed at $65. Changes in interest rates affect the *present value* of the payments on the bond but not the payments themselves.

SELF-TEST 4.3
• • • • • • • • • • • • • •

Figure 4.1 illustrates another general point. If the interest rate (yield to maturity) is equal to the coupon payment — 6.5 percent in our case — the bond is worth exactly $1000. Show that this is the case with the 6.5 percent bond.

• • • • • • • • • • • • • • • • • •
Interest Rate Risk

We have just seen that bond prices fluctuate as interest rates change. If you buy a bond and the interest rate rises, the value of your investment will fall.

But all bonds are not equally affected by changing interest rates. Compare the two curves in Figure 4.2. The solid line shows how the value of the 5-year, 9 percent coupon bond varies with the level of the interest rate. The broken line shows how the price of a 1-year, 9 percent bond varies with the level of interest rates. You can see that it is less sensitive to interest rate fluctuations than the 5-year bond. This should not surprise you. If you buy a 1-year bond when the interest rate is 5 percent and rates then rise, you will be stuck with a bad deal — you have just loaned your money at a lower interest rate than if you had waited a little. However, think how much worse it would be if the loan had been for 5 years rather than 1 year. The longer the loan, the more income you have lost by accepting what turns out to be a low interest rate. This shows up in a bigger decline in the price of the longer-term bond. Of course, there is a flip side to this effect, which you can also see from Figure 4.2. When interest rates fall, the longer-term bond responds with a greater increase in price.

rate of return: Earnings per period per dollar invested.

The **rate of return** on an investment equals the dollars earned per period for every dollar invested. For investments in bonds, earnings come from the payment of coupons as well as from any price change in the bond. For example, if you buy the 6.5 percent Canada bond today for a price of $919.00 and sell it next year at a price of $1100, your total income is the $65 coupon payment plus the price change of ($1100 – $919) = $181.00. Your rate of return over the year therefore equals

$$\text{Rate of return} = \frac{\text{total income}}{\text{investment}}$$

$$= \frac{\$65 + \$181}{\$919} = .268 = 26.8\%$$

FIGURE 4.2
Plot of bond prices versus interest rates for different maturity, illustrating greater exposure of long bonds.

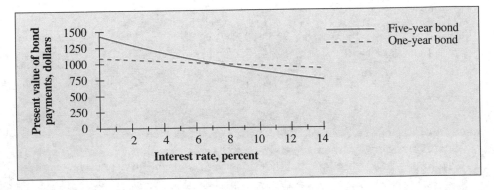

Five-year bond
One-year bond

Because bond prices fall when market interest rates rise and rise when market rates fall, the rate of return that you earn on a bond also will fluctuate with market interest rates. This is why we say bonds are subject to interest rate risk.

Do not confuse the bond's rate of return over a particular investment period with its yield to maturity. The yield to maturity is defined as the discount rate that equates the bond's price to its present value. It is a measure of the average rate of return you will earn over the bond's life if you hold it to maturity. The rate of return, in contrast, can be calculated for any holding period and is based on the actual income generated by the bond over that period.

● EXAMPLE 4.3 The Rate of Return on the Canada Bond

What will happen to the price of our 6.5 percent Canada bond if interest rates do not change? In 1995, the bond has only 3 years to maturity. If investors still demand an interest rate of 9 percent, the value of the bond will be

$$PV = \frac{\$65}{(1.09)} + \frac{\$65}{(1.09)^2} + \frac{\$1065}{(1.09)^3}$$

$$= \$936.72$$

You invested $919.00. At the end of the year you receive a coupon payment of $65 and have a bond worth $936.72, slightly more than you paid for it. Your total profit is $65 + ($936.72 − $919.00) = $82.72. You have invested $919.00 for a profit of $82.72. The return on your $919.00 investment is therefore $82.72/$919.00 = .09, or 9 percent. When interest rates do not change, the bond price changes with time so that the total return on the bond is equal to the yield to maturity.

SELF-TEST 4.4

Suppose that you buy the 6.5 percent Canada bond for $936.72 in 1995 and sell it 1 year later (that is, 2 years before maturity). If the interest rate is still 9 percent when you sell, what return will you earn on your investment? Demonstrate your answer.

Reading the Financial Pages

The prices at which you can buy and sell bonds are shown each day in the financial press. Figure 4.3 is an excerpt from the bond quotation page of *The Globe and Mail* and shows the prices of bonds that have been issued by the Government of Canada, various provinces and provincial agencies (such as Hydro Quebec) and corporations. The entry for the 6.5 percent bonds is highlighted. You can see that they are due to mature in September 1998.

The prices quoted are calculated by taking the sum of something called the *bid price* and the *asked price* and dividing the sum by 2. The bid price is the price investors receive if they sell the bond. The asked price is the price investors would have to pay if they wanted to buy the bond. Just as the used car dealer earns his living by reselling cars at higher prices than he paid for them, so the bond dealer needs to charge a spread between the bid and asked price. Thus for the 6.5 percent bond the quoted price is 92.545[2] which is half way between the bid and the ask price set for this bond. Now skip to the final column. It shows the change in

---

[2] The price that we worked out in illustrating bond pricing was 91.9. The difference is due to rounding and to the fact that for simplicity we assumed that the bond had four years to maturity when in fact on December 22, 1994, it had three years and eight months to maturity. We also ignored the semiannual nature of the coupon payments.

FIGURE 4.3
Government and corporate
bond quotes taken from
The Globe and Mail.

CANADIAN BONDS

Selected quotations, with changes since the previous day, on actively traded bond issues, provided by RBC Dominion Securities. Yields are calculated to full maturity, unless marked C to indicate callable date. Price is the midpoint between final bid and ask quotations Dec. 22, 1994.

Issuer	Coupon	Maturity	Price	Yield	$ Chg	Issuer	Coupon	Maturity	Price	Yield	$ Chg
GOVERNMENT OF CANADA						NEWFOUNDLAND	10.13	22 NOV 14	100.425	10.073	−0.450
CANADA	6.50	1 AUG 96	96.925	8.597	−0.350	NOVA SCOTIA	9.60	30 JAN 22	96.625	9.743	−0.450
CANADA	7.75	15 SEP 96	98.765	8.528	−0.380	ONTARIO HYD	10.88	8 JAN 96	102.303	8.453	−0.307
CANADA	8.00	15 MAR 97	98.793	8.600	−0.424	ONTARIO HYD	7.25	31 MAR 98	95.075	9.030	−0.450
CANADA	7.50	1 JUL 97	97.175	8.777	−0.500	ONTARIO HYD	9.63	3 AUG 99	101.600	9.185	−0.500
CANADA	6.25	1 FEB 98	93.095	8.858	−0.360	ONTARIO HYD	8.63	6 FEB 02	95.725	9.463	−0.350
CANADA	6.50	1 SEP 98	92.545	8.929	−0.410	ONTARIO HYD	9.00	24 JUN 02	97.475	9.478	−0.400
CANADA	5.75	1 MAR 99	89.140	8.930	−0.370	ONTARIO	8.75	16 APR 97	99.675	8.899	−0.500
CANADA	7.75	1 SEP 99	95.550	8.934	−0.450	ONTARIO	9.00	15 SEP 04	96.675	9.529	−0.400
CANADA	9.25	1 DEC 99	101.100	8.964	−0.500	ONTARIO	7.50	7 FEB 24	79.225	9.640	−0.400
CANADA	8.50	1 MAR 00	98.360	8.898	−0.490	PEI	9.75	30 APR 02	100.275	9.692	−0.400
CANADA	9.75	1 JUN 01	103.550	9.006	−0.450	PEI	11.00	19 SEP 11	109.600	9.816	−0.550
CANADA	9.50	1 OCT 01	102.425	9.007	−0.400	QUEBEC	8.00	30 MAR 98	96.750	9.175	−0.425
CANADA	9.75	1 DEC 01	103.650	9.025	−0.450	QUEBEC	10.25	7 APR 98	102.925	9.181	−0.450
CANADA	8.50	1 APR 02	97.200	9.031	−0.400	QUEBEC	10.25	15 OCT 01	102.475	9.737	−0.425
CANADA	7.25	1 JUN 03	89.475	9.063	−0.341	QUEBEC	9.38	16 JAN 23	93.575	10.065	−0.400
CANADA	7.50	1 DEC 03	90.550	9.067	−0.360	SASKATCHEWAN	9.88	6 JUL 99	102.275	9.246	−0.500
CANADA	10.25	1 FEB 04	107.050	9.090	−0.450	SASKATCHEWAN	9.50	16 AUG 04	99.425	9.590	−0.400
CANADA	6.50	1 JUN 04	84.000	9.061	−0.350	SASKATCHEWAN	9.60	4 FEB 22	98.850	9.719	−0.500
CANADA	9.00	1 DEC 04	99.728	9.040	−0.418	TORONTO -MET	10.38	4 SEP 01	104.875	9.370	−0.450
CANADA	10.00	1 JUN 08	106.700	9.122	−0.450	**CORPORATE**					
CANADA	9.50	1 JUN 10	102.950	9.138	−0.450	AGT LIMITED	9.50	24 AUG 04	99.875	9.516	−0.375
CANADA	9.00	1 MAR 11	98.800	9.141	−0.450	AVCO FIN	8.50	8 SEP 97	98.125	9.298	−0.625
CANADA	10.25	15 MAR 14	109.900	9.143	−0.450	BELL CANADA	9.20	1 JUN 99	99.750	9.266	−0.375
CANADA	9.75	1 JUN 21	105.850	9.157	−0.550	BELL CANADA	9.50	15 JUN 02	99.750	9.546	−0.375
CANADA	8.00	1 JUN 23	88.500	9.140	−0.450	BELL CANADA	9.70	15 DEC 32	99.625	9.736	−0.625
CMHC	8.80	1 MAR 00	98.979	9.047	−0.491	BC TELEPHONE	9.65	8 APR 22	99.750	9.673	−0.500
REAL RETURNS	4.25	1 DEC 21	89.750	4.943	NC	CDN IMP BANK	7.10	10 MAR 04	85.250	9.544	−0.375
PROVINCIAL						CDN IMP BANK	9.65	31 OCT 14	99.000	9.762	−0.625
ALBERTA	7.00	20 AUG 97	95.850	8.795	−0.550	CDN UTIL	9.40	1 MAY 23	97.625	9.644	−0.500
ALBERTA	8.50	1 SEP 99	97.975	9.037	−0.450	FINNING LTD	8.35	22 MAR 04	90.375	9.966	−0.250
ALBERTA	6.38	1 JUN 04	82.425	9.206	−0.350	IMASCO LTD	8.38	23 JUN 03	92.500	9.692	−0.250
BC	7.00	9 JUN 99	92.800	9.004	−0.400	INTERPRV PIP	8.20	15 FEB 24	85.125	9.745	−0.500
BC	9.00	9 JAN 02	98.650	9.265	−0.350	MOLSON BREW	8.20	11 MAR 03	91.625	9.702	−0.375
BC	9.00	21 JUN 04	98.000	9.322	−0.400	MOLSON BREW	8.40	7 DEC 18	86.625	9.864	−0.500
BC	8.50	23 AUG 13	91.600	9.465	−0.400	NVA SCOT PWR	6.50	15 DEC 98	91.000	9.272	−0.500
BC	8.00	8 SEP 23	85.625	9.461	−0.450	NVA SCOT PWR	9.75	2 AUG 19	99.375	9.816	−0.375
HYDRO QUEBEC	9.25	2 DEC 96	100.725	8.821	−0.400	NOVA GAS	8.30	15 JUL 03	92.000	9.699	−0.250
HYDRO QUEBEC	10.88	25 JUL 01	105.525	9.714	−0.450	NOVA GAS	9.90	16 DEC 24	100.500	9.847	−0.500
HYDRO QUEBEC	11.00	15 AUG 20	108.725	10.044	−0.450	ROYAL BANK	10.50	1 MAR 02	105.125	9.492	−0.375
HYDRO QUEBEC	9.63	15 JUL 22	95.925	10.064	−0.400	TALISMAN	9.45	22 DEC 99	99.625	9.545	−0.500
MANITOBA	6.75	24 AUG 95	99.365	7.763	NC	TALISMAN	9.80	22 DEC 04	99.750	9.839	−0.500
MANITOBA	7.00	19 APR 99	92.750	9.072	−0.400	THOMSON CORP	9.15	6 JUL 04	96.625	9.701	−0.375
MANITOBA	7.88	7 APR 03	91.300	9.410	−0.300	TRANSCDA PIP	9.45	20 MAR 18	96.625	9.818	−0.500
MANITOBA	10.50	5 MAR 31	109.750	9.535	−0.600	UNION GAS	9.75	13 DEC 04	100.625	9.649	−4.625
NEW BRUNSWIC	7.00	17 MAR 98	94.475	9.018	−0.450	WSTCOAST ENE	9.50	10 JAN 00	100.375	9.404	−0.500
NEW BRUNSWIC	8.38	26 AUG 02	94.350	9.425	−0.400	WSTCOAST ENE	9.70	15 NOV 04	100.125	9.676	−0.375
NEW BRUNSWIC	8.50	28 JUN 13	90.625	9.592	−0.400	WSTCOAST ENE	9.90	10 JAN 20	100.375	9.859	−0.625

Source: The Globe and Mail, December 23, 1994.

price since the previous day. The 6.5 percent bonds have declined by 41 cents. If you had bought the bond yesterday, you would have bought when the quoted price was $92.955.

The next column in the table shows the *yield to maturity* that the bond provides. Some bond quotes report something called the current yield which is the annual interest income that the bond provides as a percentage of the bond price. This should not be confused with the yield to maturity as it only tells us part of the story. The current yield measures only how much regular interest income you will receive for each dollar you invest, but ignores the fact that you need only pay $925.45 to get back $1,000 at maturity. The yield to maturity reflects both the interest income and the appreciation in price.

Sometimes investors speak loosely of the "yield" on a bond without specifying which measure of yield they are talking about; in the case of professional investors it is a good bet that they mean yield to maturity.

Elsewhere in the table of bond quotes you will find the prices of bonds issued by provincial governments, government agencies, municipalities, and companies. Notice that companies like Bell Canada, Westcoast Energy, and Molsons Brewers have issued several different bonds.

SELF-TEST 4.5

Calculate the *current yield* on the 6.5 percent Canada bonds in 1994. Why is it less than the yield to maturity? Will current yield necessarily be less than yield to maturity for all bonds?

Finance in Action

The Up and Down Life of Canada's Perpetual Bonds

Like the British, whose perpetuals were discussed in Chapter 3, Canadians have some experience with their own perpetual bonds. The saga of the only Canadian perpetuity issued is one of agony and ecstasy, of huge losses and huge gains. It is a story of politics and of finance. And it illustrates the valuation techniques presented in this chapter.

The Government of Canada issued $55 million worth of 3% perpetual bonds on September 15, 1936. Under the terms of the bond, the government kept for itself the option of buying back the bonds at the par value of $1000 anytime after the bond's 30th anniversary. Technically, this meant that the bonds would become "callable at par" in September 1966.

Only thirty years worth of interest coupons were attached to the bonds upon issue. (Apparently it was not considered convenient to print up the infinite number of coupons that would be required over the contractual life of the bonds.)

Investors who purchased the bonds in 1936 and held them into the 1950s found that rising interest rates pushed the market values of the bonds down. In June 1958, when yields on long-term government bonds were roughly 3.5%, the formula for finding the present value of a perpetuity suggests that these securities should have traded for about $30.00/.035 = $857.14. Prices published in *The Financial Post* for June were between $847.50 and $857.50.

In early 1963, when yields of long-term Canadian government bonds were approximately 5.05%, the perpetual bonds could be purchased for $630 — about $36 above their theoretical value as perpetuities (30.00/.0505 = $594.06). As the bonds began to approach their thirtieth birthday their market value began climbing, possibly fuelled by hopes of redemption. By September 1965 they traded near $770 — roughly $200 above their theoretical worth as perpetuities. (Since market yields had risen to about 5.34%, the theoretical value of the perpetual bonds had fallen to $30/.0534 = $561.80).

The announcement that the government would not exercise its right to call the bonds, and was mailing out coupons for the thirty-year period ending 1996, caused considerable disappointment to some investors, who had hoped that the bonds would have been bought back at par. These bondholders were outraged. Government officials, on the other hand, expressed surprise that anyone would expect the government to spend $55 million of taxpayer's money to buy bonds worth less than $40 million on the open market at September 1966 prices.

Owners of the perpetuities decided to take political action, eventually

The Up and Down Life of Canada's Perpetual Bonds
(*continued*)

forming a "Perpetual Bond Association" to represent their interests with the government. Ultimately they had some success. In March 1975 Finance Minister John Turner — apparently swayed by the arguments of the society, or by the belief that the perpetuities were more trouble than they were worth — announced that the issue would be redeemed in 1996. Not surprisingly, prices of the bonds immediately rocketed from about $390.00 to about $470.00 as they now came to be valued as "ordinary" government bonds.

The Term Structure of Interest Rates

term structure of interest rates: Relationship between time to maturity and yield to maturity.

yield curve: Graph of the term structure.

Look back for a moment to Figure 4.3. The Government of Canada bonds are arranged in order of their maturity. Notice that in general, the longer the maturity, the higher the yield. (Sometimes, however, long-term bonds offer lower yields.) Financial managers refer to the differences in yields on bonds of different maturities as the **term structure of interest rates**.

In addition to showing the yields on individual bonds, each week *The Globe and Mail* also shows a plot of the relationship between bond yields and maturity. This is known as the **yield curve**. You can see from the yield curve in Figure 4.4 that bonds with 1 year to maturity offered a yield of just under 8 percent; those with 10 years to maturity offered a yield of over 9 percent.

Why didn't everyone buy long-maturity bonds and earn an extra 1 percent? Who were those (stupid?) investors who put their money into short-term Canadas at only 8 percent? You see from the yield curve that the situation was even more dramatic five weeks earlier when the difference between short-term and long-term rates was closer to 3 percent.

FIGURE 4.4
Yield curve from *The Globe and Mail.*

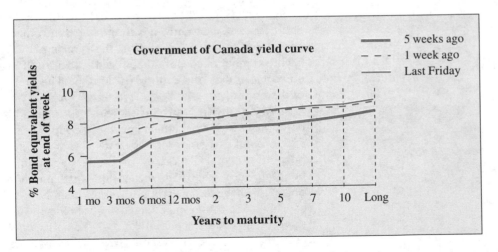

Source: The Globe and Mail, January 23, 1995.

Even when the yield curve is upward-sloping, investors might rationally stay away from long-term bonds for two reasons. First, the prices of long-term bonds fluctuate much more than prices of short-term bonds. Figure 4.2 illustrates that long-term bond prices are more sensitive to shifting interest rates. A sharp increase in interest rates could easily knock 20 or 30 percent off long-term bond prices. If investors don't like price fluctuations, they will invest their funds in short-term bonds unless they receive a higher yield to maturity on long-term bonds.

Second, short-term investors can profit if interest rates rise. Suppose you hold a 1-year bond. A year from now when the bond matures you can reinvest the proceeds and enjoy whatever rates the bond market offers then. Rates then may be high enough to offset the first year's relatively low yield on the 1-year bond. Thus you often see an upward-sloping yield curve when future interest rates are expected to rise. We return to this issue in Chapter 12.

Defaults

National governments don't go bankrupt — they just print more money.[3] So investors don't worry that the Government of Canada will *default* on its bonds. But a corporation may not be able to find enough cash to pay the bondholders all that they have been promised. Thus payments promised to corporate bondholders represent a best-case scenario: The firm will never pay more than these payments, but it may pay less.

When we calculate the yield to maturity on a bond, we assume that all payments will be made as promised. Therefore, the yield to maturity also represents a best-case calculation; if things go wrong and the company runs out of cash, the eventual yield may be much less than originally promised.

For example, in December 1994 some investment houses were offering to pay only 45% of face value for various types of Dylex debt. These prices imply huge yields to maturity on Dylex bonds. Of course, investors did not expect to earn these high annual rates of return. Dylex was in bankruptcy at the time, and investors recognized that it was highly unlikely that the bondholders would receive all the promised payments.

It should be no surprise that investors demand compensation for the risk that the debt may not be repaid. So we find that Finning Ltd. needs to promise a higher rate of interest than, say, Bell Canada when it borrows money.

default premium: Difference in promised yields between a default-free bond and a riskier bond.

The difference between the promised yield on a corporate bond and the yield on a government bond with the same coupon and maturity is called the **default premium**. The higher the chance that the company will get into trouble, the higher the default premium that is required to attract investors.

Bond Ratings

The safety of most traded bonds can be judged from *bond ratings* provided by Canada Bond Rating Service (CBRS), Dominion Bond Rating Service (DBRS), and Moody's. For example, the bonds that receive the highest Canada Bond Service rating are known as A++ bonds. Then come A+ , A, B++ bonds, and so on. Bonds rated B++ and above are called *investment grade*, while those with a rating of B+ or below are known as *speculative grade*, or **junk bonds**.

junk bond: Bond with a rating below B+.

Figure 4.5 presents the yields on default-free long-term Government of Canada bonds and corporate bonds. You can see that promised yields go up as safety falls. However, it is also clear that yields on the two groups of bonds track each other closely. So financial managers are often content to talk about "the" interest rate moving up or down, although there are in fact a myriad of interest rates, depending on default risk, maturity, and other things that we will get to in Chapter 13.

---

[3] But they can't print money of other governments. When the Italian government issued dollar-denominated bonds, investors contemplated the (small) probability of some future crisis in which Italy could not come up with enough dollars to pay off the country's dollar debts. Here's a more dramatic example. In 1992 Turkey issued dollar-denominated bonds that offered yields to maturity 2.6 percentage points higher than similar United States Treasury issues. This spread reflected investors' worries that Turkey might have difficulty obtaining the dollars to pay off on these bonds.

FIGURE 4.5
Time series for yields on
long-term government and
corporate bonds.

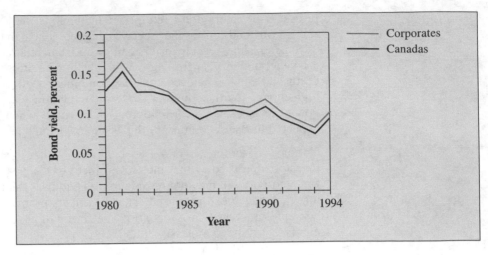

4.2   INFLATION AND THE TIME VALUE OF MONEY

When the Canadian government issued its 6.5 percent bond, it promised to pay interest of $65 a year. When a bank offers to pay 6 percent on a savings account, it promises to pay interest of $60 for every $1000 you deposit. Both the Government of Canada and the bank fix the number of dollars that they pay you, but they don't provide any assurance of how much those dollars will buy. If the value of your investment increases by 50 percent, while the prices of goods and services increase by 60 percent, you have actually lost ground in terms of the goods you can buy.

....

**Real versus
Nominal Cash
Flows**

inflation: Rate at which prices as a whole are increasing.

Prices of goods and services continually change. Textbooks may become more expensive (sorry) while calculators become cheaper. An overall general rise in prices is known as **inflation**. If the inflation rate is 5 percent per year, then goods that cost $1.00 a year ago typically cost $1.05 this year. The increase in the general level of prices means that the purchasing power of money has eroded. If a dollar bill bought one loaf of bread last year, the same dollar this year buys only part of a loaf.

Economists track the general level of prices using several different price indexes. The best known of these is the *Consumer Price Index*, or *CPI*. This measures the number of dollars that it takes to buy a specified basket of goods and services that is supposed to represent the typical family's purchases[4]. Thus the percentage increase in the CPI from one year to the next measures the rate of inflation.

Figure 4.6 graphs the CPI since 1945. We have set the index for the beginning of 1945 to 100, so the graph shows the price level in each year as a percentage of 1945 prices. For example, the index in 1946 was 103. This means that on average $103 in 1946 would have bought the same quantity of goods and services as $100 in 1945. The inflation rate between 1945 and 1946 was therefore 3 percent. By the start of 1994, the index was 940 meaning that 1994 prices were 9.4 times as high as 1945 prices.[5]

---

[4] Don't ask how you buy a "basket" of services.
[5] The choice of 100 for the index in 1945 is arbitrary. For example, we could have set the index at 50 in 1945. In this case the index in 1946 would have been 3 percent higher at 51.50 (that is, $50 in 1945 and $51.50 in 1946 would have bought the same basket of goods).

FIGURE 4.6
Consumer Price Index,
1945–1993.

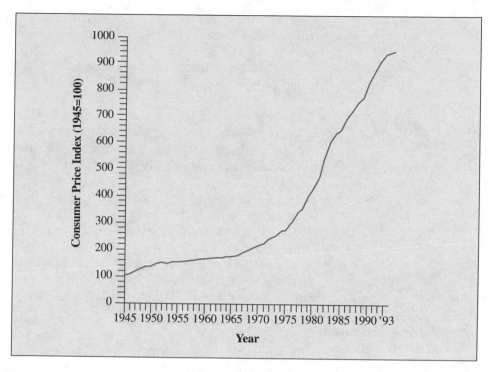

The purchasing power of money fell by a factor of 9.4 between 1945 and 1994. A dollar in 1994 would buy only 11 percent of the goods it could buy in 1945 (1/9.4 = .11). In this case, we would say that the **real value of $1** declined by 100 − 11 = 89 percent from 1945 to 1994.

real value of $1: Purchasing power-adjusted value of a dollar

● EXAMPLE 4.4 British Inflation

Charles Dickens's character Mr. Micawber summed up his financial situation as follows: "Annual income twenty pounds, annual expenditure nineteen and six, result happiness. Annual income twenty pounds, annual expenditure twenty pounds ought and six, result misery."

How much did Mr. Micawber need to invest to escape misery? In 1850 the yield on perpetual British government bonds was 3.1 percent. So if Mr. Micawber invested £645 in these bonds, he would have just teetered on the edge:

Annual income = yield on bond × amount invested

£20 = .031 × £645

By investing in perpetual government bonds Mr. Micawber and his heirs could have been assured of £20 a year forever.[6] Unfortunately, they could not have been assured of what that money would buy — the income on the bonds is fixed in money but not in purchasing power. Between 1850 and 1992 retail prices in Britain increased by a factor of 51. So an annual income of £20 would nearly have bought happiness in 1850 but certainly not in 1992. In real terms (that is, measured in 1850 pounds), the income on the bonds would have fallen from £20 in 1850 to £20/51 = £.39 in 1992.

---

[6] We oversimplify. Although the British government was not obliged ever to repay the bonds, it had the right to do so. When interest rates fell in 1888 and again in 1902, it bought back the existing bonds and replaced them with new perpetual bonds offering a lower annual income.

Economists sometimes talk about current or nominal dollars versus constant or real dollars. Current or nominal dollars refers to the actual number of dollars of the day; Mr. Micawber's income was unchanged in current pounds at £20 a year. Constant or real dollars refers to the amount of purchasing power; in constant pounds, Mr. Micawber's income fell from £20 to £.39.

SELF-TEST 4.6

The price index in 1980 was 483. If a family spent $250 a week on their typical purchases in 1945, how much would those purchases have cost in 1980? If your salary in 1980 was $30,000 a year, what would be the real value of that salary in terms of 1945 dollars?

Some expenditures are fixed in nominal terms, and therefore *decline* in real terms. Suppose you took out a 25-year house mortgage in 1983. The monthly payment was $800. It was still $800 in 1994, even though the CPI increased by a factor of 1.41 over those years.

What's the monthly payment for 1994 expressed in real 1983 dollars? The answer is $800/1.41, or $565.96 per month. The real burden of paying the mortgage was much less in 1993 than in 1983.

Inflation and Interest Rates

Whenever you see an interest rate quoted in Canada, you can be fairly sure that it is a *nominal*, not a *real* rate. It sets the actual number of dollars you will be paid with no offset for future inflation.

If you deposit $1000 in the bank at a **nominal interest rate** of 6 percent, you will have $1060 at the end of the year. But this does not mean you are 6 percent better off. Suppose that the inflation rate during the year is also 6 percent. Then the goods that cost $1000 last year will now cost $1000 × 1.06 = $1060, so you've gained nothing:

nominal interest rate: Rate at which money invested grows.

$$\text{Real future value of investment} = \$1000 \times \frac{(1 + \text{nominal interest rate})}{(1 + \text{inflation rate})}$$

$$= \frac{\$1000 \times 1.06}{1.06} = \$1000$$

real interest rate: Rate at which the purchasing power of an investment increases.

In this example, the nominal rate of interest is 6 percent, but the **real interest rate** is zero.

The real rate of interest is calculated by

$$1 + \text{real interest rate} = \frac{1 + \text{nominal interest rate}}{1 + \text{inflation rate}}$$

In our example both the nominal interest rate and the inflation rate were 6 percent. So

$$1 + \text{real interest rate} = \frac{1.06}{1.06} = 1$$

$$\text{real interest rate} = 0$$

What if the nominal interest rate is 6 percent but the inflation rate is only 2 percent? In that case the real interest rate is 1.06/1.02 − 1 = .039, or 3.9 percent. Imagine that the price of a loaf of bread is $1, so that $1000 would buy 1000 loaves today. If you invest that $1000 at a nominal interest rate of 6 percent, you will have $1060 at the end of the year. However, if the price of loaves has risen in the meantime to $1.02, then your money will buy you only $1060/1.02 = 1039 loaves. The real rate of interest is 3.9 percent.

SELF-TEST 4.7

a. Suppose that you invest your funds at an interest rate of 8 percent. What will be your real rate of interest if the inflation rate is zero? What if it is 5 percent?

b. Suppose that you demand a real rate of interest of 3 percent on your investments. What nominal interest rate do you need to earn if the inflation rate is zero? If it is 5 percent?

Here is a useful approximation. The real rate approximately equals the difference between the nominal rate and the inflation rate:[7]

$$\text{real interest rate} \approx \text{nominal interest rate} - \text{inflation rate}$$

Our example used a nominal interest rate of 6 percent, an inflation rate of 2 percent, and a real rate of 3.9 percent. If we round to 4 percent, the approximation gives the same answer:

$$\text{real interest rate} \approx \text{nominal interest rate} - \text{inflation rate}$$

$$\approx 6 - 2 = 4\%$$

The approximation works best when both the inflation rate and the real rate are small.[8] When they are not small, throw the approximation away and do it right.

● **EXAMPLE 4.5 Real and Nominal Rates**

In Canada in 1992, the interest rate on a 1-year Treasury bill was about 7 percent. The inflation rate was about 2 percent. Therefore, the real rate on these bonds can be found by computing

$$1 + \text{real interest rate} = \frac{1 + \text{nominal interest rate}}{1 + \text{inflation rate}}$$

$$= \frac{1.07}{1.02} = 1.049$$

$$\text{real interest rate} = .049, \text{ or } 4.9\%$$

The approximation rule gives a similar value of $7.0 - 2.0 = 5.0$ percent. But the approximation would not have worked in the German hyperinflation of 1922–1923, when the inflation rate was well over 100 percent per *month* (at one point you needed 1 million marks to mail a letter) or in Peru in 1990, when prices increased by nearly 7500 percent.

Suppose you try to invest in Treasury bonds issued by the remote Republic of Costaguana. The good news is that you get an interest rate of 70 percent per month. Bad news? The inflation rate of pulgas, the Costaguanan currency, is 60 percent per month. Your real interest rate is

$$1 + \text{real interest rate} = \frac{1 + \text{nominal interest rate}}{1 + \text{inflation rate}}$$

$$= \frac{1.70}{1.60} = 1.0625$$

$$\text{real interest rate} = .0625, \text{ or } 6 \ 1/4\% \text{ per month}$$

---

[7] The squiggle ($\approx$) means "approximately equal to."

[8] When the interest and inflation rates are expressed as decimals (rather than percentages), the approximation error equals the product (real interest rate $\times$ inflation rate).

In this case, the approximation isn't very accurate: it would give a real rate of 70 − 60 = 10 percent.

What Fluctuates: Real or Nominal Rates?

Suppose that the expected inflation rate rises by one percentage point. What moves? Does the real interest rate go down or the nominal rate go up?

Investors are most concerned about the purchasing power of their money and the real rates of interest. We would therefore expect them to demand higher nominal interest rates when the rate of inflation increases.

Suppose the real rate of interest is 5 percent, the inflation rate 10 percent, and the nominal interest rate 15.5 percent. If the rate of inflation goes to 11 percent, then the nominal rate should climb to roughly 16.5 percent. At this inflation rate, investors need 16.5 percent before inflation to maintain a 5 percent gain in actual purchasing power.

Real interest rates depend on the supply of savings and the demand for new investment. This supply-demand balance changes from year to year and country to country, so fluctuations in nominal interest rates cannot be due entirely to changes in expected inflation. Nevertheless, countries with high inflation almost always have high nominal interest rates. In Canada periods of high inflation and high nominal rates generally go together, as illustrated in Figure 4.7.

FIGURE 4.7
Nominal and real interest rates since 1969. Interest rates are those paid on Treasury bills.

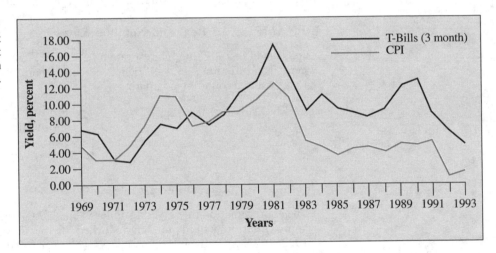

Valuing Real Cash Payments

Think again about how to value future cash payments. In Chapter 3 you learned how to value payments in current dollars by discounting at the nominal interest rate. For example, suppose that the nominal interest rate is 10 percent. How much do you need to invest now to produce $100 in a year's time? Easy! Calculate the present value of $100 by discounting by 10 percent:

$$PV = \frac{\$100}{1.10} = \$90.91$$

You get exactly the same result if you discount the real payment by the real interest rate. For example, assume that you expect inflation of 7 percent over the next year. The real value of that $100 is therefore only $100/1.07 = $93.46. In one year's time your $100 will buy only as much as $93.46 today. Also with a 7 percent inflation rate the real rate of interest is only about 3 percent. We can calculate it exactly from the formula

$$(1 + \text{real interest rate}) = \frac{1 + \text{nominal interest rate}}{1 + \text{inflation rate}}$$

$$= \frac{1.10}{1.07} = 1.028$$

$$\text{real interest rate} = .028, \text{ or } 2.8\%$$

If we now discount the $93.46 real payment by the 2.8 percent real interest rate, we have a present value of $90.91, just as before:

$$PV = \frac{\$93.46}{1.028} = \$90.91$$

The two methods should always give the same answer.[9]

Remember: Current dollar cash flows must be discounted by the nominal interest rate; real cash flows must be discounted by the real interest rate. Mixing up nominal cash flows and real discount rates (or real rates and nominal flows) is an unforgivable sin. It is surprising how many sinners one finds.

SELF-TEST 4.8

You are owed $5000 by a relative who will pay back in 1 year. The nominal interest rate is 8 percent and the inflation rate is 5 percent. What is the present value of your relative's IOU? Show that you get the same answer (a) discounting the nominal payment at the nominal rate and (b) discounting the real payment at the real rate.

Providing for Retirement

Sooner or later most of us will be called on to advise elderly relatives who worry about their long-run financial security. The tools you've learned in Chapters 3 and 4 can really help — in fact they're essential.

Assume your retired 70-year-old uncle, a widower, asks for your help. You spend an afternoon talking through his situation and establish the following facts:

- Your uncle owns his home, now worth $120,000, and does not want to move. He wants to bequeath the house, and any remaining assets, to his daughter.
- He has accumulated savings of $180,000, conservatively invested in long-term bonds yielding 9 percent. He has planned to draw down these savings over the rest of his life.
- He receives $10,000 a year in Old Age Security payments. This is indexed to the cost of living and will increase in line with inflation.
- Your uncle's living expenses are now $24,000 per year.

You also survey various financial publications and find that economists are forecasting long-run inflation of about 5 percent per year.

---

[9] If they don't there must be an error in your calculations. All we have done in the second calculation is to divide both the numerator (the cash payment) and the denominator (one plus the nominal interest rate) by the same number (one plus the inflation rate):

$$PV = \frac{\text{payment in current dollars}}{1 + \text{nominal interest rate}}$$

$$= \frac{\text{payment in current dollars}/(1 + \text{inflation rate})}{(1 + \text{nominal interest rate})/(1 + \text{inflation rate})}$$

$$= \frac{\text{payment in constant dollars}}{1 + \text{real interest rate}}$$

We have tried to make this example realistic. Except for a bit of rounding we have used actual interest rates, inflation rates, Old Age Security benefits[10], and so on, in late 1994. However, we do simplify by assuming your uncle will live for exactly 20 years more. We won't consider what happens if he lives more or less than another 20 years.

How much can your uncle spend each year if he is willing to run down his savings? We need to find the 20-year annuity with present value equal to his savings:

Present value = annual payment × 20-year annuity factor at 9% interest rate

$180,000 = annual payment × 9.129

$$\text{Annual payment} = \frac{\$180,000}{9.129} = \$19,717$$

So if your uncle is prepared to use up *all* his savings, he can draw $19,717 a year from his investment account. With Old Age Security, his total income would be $10,000 + $19,717 = $29,717, comfortably above his current living expenses.

The problem of course is inflation. We have sinned; we have mixed up real and nominal flows. The social security payments are tied to the consumer price index and therefore are level in *real* terms. But the annuity of $19,717 a year from your uncle's savings is fixed in *nominal* terms and therefore its purchasing power will steadily decline.

Figure 4.8 shows what happens if your uncle spends all his social security plus the $19,717 from his savings. The real value of his income declines steadily as inflation bites. For example, let's look out 15 years. At 5 percent inflation prices will increase by a factor of $1.05^{15} = 2.08$. His income in 15 years will therefore be as follows:

FIGURE 4.8
Real income provided by the level *nominal* annuity from savings and the *real* annuity from old age security. If your uncle spends a level nominal amount out of his savings, the real value of his expenditures decreases.

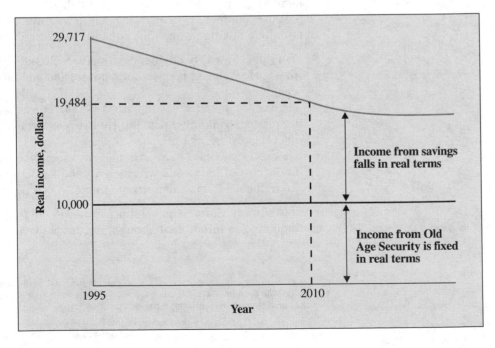

[10] Actually Old Age Security by itself only provides about $4600 a year in benefits. However, a Guaranteed Income Supplement for those who would have no other source of income brings total income up to $10,000.

Income Source	Nominal Income	Real Income
Social security (indexed to CPI; fixed in real terms at $7800)	$20,800	$10,000
Savings (fixed nominal annuity)	19,717	9,484
Total income	40,517	19,484

Once we recognize inflation, we see that the income from your uncle's savings will buy less than half the goods that it buys today.

Obviously your uncle needs to spend less today and put more aside for the future. Rather than spending a constant *nominal amount* out of his savings, he would probably be better off spending a constant *real* amount.

Since we are interested in level real expenditures, we must use the real interest rate to calculate the 20-year annuity that can be provided by $180,000. The real interest rate is 3.8 percent (because 1 + real interest rate = 1.09/1.05 = 1.038). We therefore calculate the real sum that your uncle can spend out of his savings as follows:

$$\text{Present value} = \text{annual real payment} \times \text{20-year annuity factor at } 3.8\% \text{ real interest rate}$$

$$\$180,000 = \text{annual real payment} \times 13.834$$

$$\text{Annual real payment} = \$13,011$$

Thus your uncle's savings can generate a real income of over $13,000 a year. To keep pace with inflation your uncle will need to spend 5 percent more of his savings each year. In 1996, after 1 year of inflation, he will spend $1.05 \times \$13,011 = \$13,622$; after 2 years he will spend $(1.05)^2 \times \$13,011 = \$14,345$, and so on. The picture 15 years out looks like this:

Income Source	Nominal Income	Real Income
Social security (indexed to CPI; fixed in real terms at $7800)	$20,800	$10,000
Savings (uncle now draws a fixed *real* annuity)	27,049	13,011
Total income	47,849	23,011

Your uncle's income and expenditure will roughly double in 15 years but his real income and expenditure are unchanged at $23,011.

This may be bad news for your uncle since this doesn't quite cover his living expenses of $24,000. Do you advise him to prune his living expenses? Perhaps he should put part of his nest egg in junk bonds, which offer higher *promised* interest rates, or into the stock market, which has generated higher returns on average than investment in bonds.[11] These higher returns might support a higher real annuity — but is your uncle prepared to bear the extra risks?

Should your uncle consume more today and risk having to sell his house if his savings are run down late in life? Of course that would disappoint your uncle and his daughter. Remember, too, that elderly people often face heavy medical expenses late in life. Your uncle may wish to keep the value of the house, or some other assets, in reserve for this sort of rainy day. These issues make the planning

---

[11] We'll give you the evidence on stock market risks and returns in Chapter 9.

problem even more difficult. It is clear, however, that one cannot plan for retirement without considering inflation.

● **EXAMPLE 4.6 How Inflation Might Affect the Sultan of Brunei**

In the last chapter (Example 3.12), we demonstrated that at an interest rate of 9 percent the Sultan of Brunei could, if he wished, turn his $37 billion wealth into a 40-year annuity of $3.4 billion per year of luxury and excitement (L&E). Unfortunately L&E expenses inflate just like gasoline and groceries. Thus the Sultan would find the purchasing power of that $3.4 billion steadily declining. If he wants the same luxuries in 2020 as in 1995, he'll have to spend less in 1995, and then increase expenditures in line with inflation. How much should he spend in 1995? Assume the long-run inflation rate is 5 percent.

The Sultan needs to calculate a 40-year real annuity. The real interest rate is a little less than 4 percent:

$$1 + \text{real interest rate} = \frac{1 + \text{nominal interest rate}}{1 + \text{inflation rate}}$$

$$= \frac{1.09}{1.05} = 1.038$$

so the real rate is 3.8 percent. The 40-year annuity factor at 3.8 percent is 20.4. Therefore, annual spending (in 1995 dollars) should be chosen so that

$$\$37,000,000,000 = \text{annual spending} \times 20.4$$

$$\text{annual spending} = \$1,814,000,000$$

The Sultan could spend that amount on L&E in 1995 and 5 percent more (in line with inflation) in each subsequent year. This is only about half the value we calculated when we ignored inflation. Life has many disappointments, even for sultans.

SELF-TEST 4.9

You have reached age 60 with a modest fortune of $3 million and are considering early retirement. How much can you spend each year for the next 30 years? Assume that spending is stable in real terms. The nominal interest rate is 10 percent and the inflation rate is 5 percent.

Real or Nominal?

Any present value calculation done in nominal terms can also be done in real terms, and vice versa. Most financial analysts forecast in nominal terms and discount at nominal rates. However, in some cases real cash flows are easier to deal with.

In the retirement planning problem the cash flows increase with the general level of prices, so that real cash flows are fixed. In this case, it was easiest to use real quantities. On the other hand, if the cash-flow stream is fixed in nominal terms (for example, the coupons on a bond), it is easiest to use all nominal quantities.

4.3 SUMMARY

1. A bond is a long-term debt of a government or corporation. When you own a bond, you receive a fixed interest payment each year until the bond matures. This payment is known as the coupon. At maturity the bond's face value is repaid. In Canada most corporate bonds have a face value of $1000.

2. Bonds are valued by discounting the coupon payments and the final repayment by the rate of interest on comparable bonds. Bond prices are subject to interest rate risk, rising when market interest rates fall and falling when market rates rise. The interest rate risk is generally greater for long-term bonds than for short-term bonds.

3. You may also start with the bond price and ask what interest rate the bond offers. This interest rate is known as the yield to maturity, the rate that equates the present value of bond payments to the bond price.

4. Long-term and short-term bond yields usually are different. The differences are called the term structure of interest rates. Investors also demand higher promised yields if there is a high probability that the company will run into trouble and default.

5. A dollar is a dollar but the amount of goods that a dollar can buy is eroded by inflation. If prices double, the real value of the dollar halves. Financial managers and economists often find it helpful to re-express future cash flows in terms of real dollars — that is, dollars of constant purchasing power.

6. Bonds promise a fixed nominal interest rate, but they make no promises about inflation. Be careful to distinguish the promised nominal rate and the real interest rate — that is, the rate at which the real value of the investment grows.

7. Discount nominal cash flows (that is, cash flows measured in current dollars) at nominal interest rates. Discount real cash flows (cash flows measured in constant dollars) at real interest rates. Never mix and match nominal and real.

KEY TERMS

bond	**yield to maturity**	**junk bond**
coupon	**rate of return**	**inflation**
par value, face value, maturity value	**term structure of interest rates**	**real value of $1**
coupon rate	**yield curve**	**nominal interest rate**
current yield	**default premium**	**real interest rate**

SUGGESTED READINGS

There are a number of discussions of the valuation of bonds in investment texts. We suggest:

G. J. Alexander and W. F. Sharpe, *Fundamentals of Investments*. Englewood Cliffs, N.J.: Prentice-Hall, 1989.

J.E. Hatch and M. J. Robinson, *Investment Management in Canada*, 2nd Edition, Scarborough: Prentice-Hall, 1989.

PROBLEMS

1. A 6-year Circular File bond pays interest of $90 annually and sells for $950. What is its coupon rate, current yield, and yield to maturity?

2. If Circular File (see question 1) wants to issue a new 6-year bond at face value, what coupon rate must the bond offer?

3. A Westcoast Energy bond carries a coupon rate of 9.5 percent, has 5 years until maturity, and sells at a yield to maturity of 9 percent.
   a. What interest payments do bondholders receive each year?
   b. At what price does the bond sell? (Assume annual interest payments.)
   c. What will happen to the bond price if the yield to maturity falls to 7 percent?

4. A Canadian Imperial Bank of Commerce bond has 10 years until maturity, a coupon rate of 7 percent, and sells for $872.00.
   a. What is the current yield on the bond?
   b. What is the yield to maturity?

5. a. If the Canadian Imperial Bank of Commerce bond in problem 4 has a yield to maturity of 7 percent 1 year from now, what will its price be?
   b. What will be the rate of return on the bond?
   c. If the inflation rate during the year is 3 percent, what is the real rate of return on the bond?

6. Large Industries bonds sell for $1065.15. The bond life is 9 years, and the yield to maturity is 7 percent. What must be the coupon rate on the bonds?

7. a. Several years ago, Castles in the Sand, Inc., issued bonds at face value at a yield to maturity of 8 percent. Now, with 8 years left until the maturity of the bonds, the company has run into hard times and the yield to maturity on the bonds has increased to 12 percent. What has happened to the price of the bond?
   b. Suppose that investors believe that Castles can make good on the promised coupon payments, but that the company will go bankrupt when the bond matures and the principal comes due. The expectation is that investors will receive only 80 percent of face value at maturity. If they buy the bond today, what yield to maturity do they expect to receive?

8. Consider three bonds with 8 percent coupon rates, all selling at face value. The short-term bond has a maturity of 2 years, the intermediate-term bond has a maturity of 8 years, and the long-term bond has a maturity of 20 years.
   a. What will happen to the price of each bond if their yields increase to 9 percent?
   b. What will happen to the price of each bond if their yields decrease to 7 percent?
   c. What do you conclude about the relationship between time to maturity and the sensitivity of bond prices to interest rates?

9. You buy an 8 percent coupon, 10-year maturity bond for $980. A year later, the bond price is $1020.
   a. What is the new yield to maturity on the bond?
   b. What is your rate of return over the year?

10. You buy an 8 percent coupon, 10-year maturity bond when its yield to maturity is 9 percent. A year later, the yield to maturity is 10 percent. What is your rate of return over the year?

11. Long-term bonds rated A+ currently offer yields to maturity of 8.5 percent. A-rated bonds sell at yields of 8.8 percent. If a 10-year bond with a coupon rate of 8 percent is downgraded by Canadian Bond Rating Service from A+ to A rating, what is the likely effect on the bond price?

12. An engineer in 1950 was earning $6000 a year. Today she earns $60,000 a year. However, on average, goods today cost 6.9 times what they did in 1950. What is her real income today in terms of constant 1950 dollars?

13. If investors are to earn a 3 percent real interest rate, what nominal interest rate must they earn if the inflation rate is:
    a. zero
    b. 3 percent
    c. 6 percent

14. If investors receive an 8 percent interest rate on their bank deposits, what real interest rate will they earn if the inflation rate over the year is:
    a. zero
    b. 3 percent
    c. 6 percent

15. You will receive $100 from a savings bond in 3 years. The nominal interest rate is 8 percent.
    a. What is the present value of the proceeds from the bond?
    b. If the inflation rate over the next few years is expected to be 5 percent, what will the real value of the $100 payoff be in terms of today's dollars?
    c. What is the real interest rate?
    d. Show that the real payoff from the bond (from part b) discounted at the real interest rate (from part c) gives the same present value for the bond as you found in part a.

16. Your consulting firm will produce cash flows of $100,000 this year, and you expect cash flow to keep pace with any increase in the general level of prices. The interest rate currently is 8 percent, and you anticipate inflation of about 3 percent.
    a. What is the present value of your firm's cash flows for years 1 through 5?
    b. How would your answer to (a) change if you anticipated no growth in cash flow?

17. Good news: You will almost certainly be a millionaire by the time you retire in 50 years. Bad news: The inflation rate over your lifetime will average about 3 percent.
    a. What will be the real value of $1 million by the time you retire in terms of today's dollars?
    b. What real annuity (in today's dollars) will $1 million support if the real interest rate at retirement is 2 percent and the annuity must last for 20 years?

18. A retiree wants level consumption in real terms over a 30-year retirement. If the inflation rate equals the interest rate she earns on her $450,000 of savings, how much can she spend in real terms each year over the rest of her life?

19. Inflation in Brazil in 1992 averaged about 23 percent per month. What was the annual inflation rate?

20. a. You plan to retire in 30 years and want to accumulate enough by then to provide yourself with $30,000 a year for 15 years. If the interest rate is 10 percent, how much must you accumulate by the time you retire?
    b. How much must you save each year until retirement in order to finance your retirement consumption?

c. Now you remember that the annual inflation rate is 6 percent. If a loaf of bread costs $1.00 today, what will it cost by the time you retire?

d. You really want to consume $30,000 a year in real dollars during retirement and wish to save a constant real amount each year until then. What is the real amount of savings that you need to accumulate by the time you retire?

e. Calculate the required preretirement real annual savings necessary to meet your consumption goals. Compare to your answer to (b). Why is there a difference?

f. What is the nominal value of the amount you need to save during the first year? (Assume the savings are put aside at the end of each year.) The thirtieth year?

SOLUTIONS TO SELF-TEST QUESTIONS

4.1 The coupon is 9 percent of $1000, or $90 per year. First value the 6-year annuity of coupons:

$$PV = \$90 \times (\text{6-year annuity factor})$$

$$= \$90 \times \left[\frac{1}{.12} - \frac{1}{.12(1.12^6)} \right]$$

$$= \$90 \times 4.11 = \$370.03$$

Then value the final payment and add up:

$$PV = \frac{\$1000}{(1.12)^6} = \$506.63$$

$$PV \text{ of bond} = \$370.03 + \$506.63 = \$876.66$$

4.2 The yield to maturity is about 8 percent, because the present value of the bond's cash returns is $1199 when discounted at 8 percent:

$$PV = PV \text{ (coupons)} + PV \text{ (final payment)}$$

$$= (\text{coupon} \times \text{annuity factor}) + (\text{face value} \times \text{discount factor})$$

$$= \$140 \times \left[\frac{1}{.08} - \frac{1}{.08(1.08^4)} \right] + \$1000 \times \frac{1}{1.08^4}$$

$$= \$463.70 + \$735.03 = \$1199$$

4.3 Calculate PV with a discount rate of 6.5 percent:

$$PV = \$65 \times \left[\frac{1}{.065} - \frac{1}{.065(1.065^4)} \right] + \$1000 \times \frac{1}{1.065^4}$$

$$= \$222.68 + \$777.32 = \$1000$$

4.4 You'll earn 9.0 percent. To show this, calculate the value of the bond 1 year hence, when maturity is 2 years:

$$PV = \$65 \times \left[\frac{1}{.09} - \frac{1}{.09(1.09^2)} \right] + \$1000 \times \frac{1}{1.09^2}$$

$$= \$114.34 + \$841.68 = \$956.02$$

Your total return is the coupon, $65, plus a gain of $956.02 – $936.72 = $19.30, for a total of $84.30. The rate of return is $84.30/$936.72 = .090, exactly 9.0 percent.

4.5 Current yield = $65/$925.45 = .07 , or 7.0 percent. The low current yield (lower than the 9.0 percent interest rate and overall return) is compensated for by the rise in the bond's value, from $925.45 in 1994 to $1000 at maturity. Current yield need not always be below yield to maturity. For bonds selling above face value, yield to maturity will be less than current yield, since yield to maturity accounts for the built-in price depreciation of the bond, which is bought for more than face value and eventually will be redeemed for face value.

4.6 The weekly cost in 1980 is $250 × (483/100) = $1207. The real value of a 1980 salary of $30,000, expressed in real 1945 dollars, is $30,000 × (100/483) = $6211.18.

4.7
a. If there's no inflation, real and nominal rates are equal at 8 percent. With 5 percent inflation, the real rate is (1.08/1.05) – 1 = .02857, a bit less than 3 percent.
b. If you want a 3 percent *real* interest rate, you need a 3 percent nominal rate if inflation is zero and 8.15 percent if inflation is 5 percent. Note 1.03 × 1.05 = 1.0815.

4.8 The present value is

$$PV = \frac{\$5000}{1.08} = \$4629.63$$

The real interest rate is 2.857 percent (see Self-Test 4.7). The real cash payment is $5000/(1.05) = $4761.90. Thus

$$PV = \frac{\$4761.90}{1.02857} = \$4629.63$$

4.9 Calculate the real annuity. The real interest rate is 1.10/1.05 – 1 = .0476. We'll round to 4.8 percent. The real annuity is

$$annual\ payment = \frac{\$3,000,000}{30\text{-year annuity factor}}$$

$$= \frac{\$3,000,000}{\dfrac{1}{.048} - \dfrac{1}{.048(1.048^{30})}}$$

$$= \frac{\$3,000,000}{15.73} = \$190,728$$

You can spend this much each year in dollars of constant purchasing power. The purchasing power of each dollar will decline at 5 percent per year so you'll need to spend more in nominal dollars — $190,728 × 1.05 = $200,264 in the second year, $190,728 × 1.05^2 = $210,278 in the third year, and so on.

CHAPTER FIVE

How Common Stocks Are Valued

Investment in new plant and equipment requires money — often a lot of money. Sometimes firms may be able to save enough money out of previous earnings to cover the cost of investments but often they need to raise cash from investors. In broad terms, we can think of two ways to raise new money from investors: borrow the cash or sell additional shares of common stock.

When companies borrow, they promise to make a series of fixed interest payments and then to repay the debt. As long as the company generates sufficient cash, the payments on a bond are certain. In the case of common stock, however, dividends fluctuate. Investors hope profits will expand, enabling the firm to increase dividends, but that is not something anyone can forecast with certainty. Also, unlike bonds, common stocks do not have a date at which they must be repaid; barring such corporate hazards as bankruptcy or acquisition, they are immortal.

Because the payments to the shareholder are more closely tied to the fortunes of the company, common stock investments are riskier than bond investments. To compensate for this risk, investors will demand higher expected rates of return to invest in stocks. We will have more to say about the *risk premium* on stocks in later chapters. For now, however, just remember that there is a difference in required returns.

In Chapter 4 we looked at how bonds are valued. Now we move on to common stocks. We start by looking at how stocks are bought and sold. Then we look at what determines stock prices and how stock valuation formulas can be used to infer the return that investors are expecting. We will see how the firm's investment opportunities are reflected in the stock price, and why stock market analysts focus so much attention on the price-earnings or P/E ratio of the company. As you work through the chapter, you will find many opportunities to brush up on your skill in discounting future cash payments.

After studying this chapter you should be able to

- Understand the stock trading reports in newspaper financial pages.
- Calculate the present value of a stock given forecasts of future dividends and future stock price.
- Use stock valuation formulas to infer the expected rate of return on a common stock.
- Interpret price-earnings ratios.

5.1 STOCKS AND THE STOCK MARKET

common stock: Ownership shares in a publicly held corporation.

primary market: Market for the sale of new securities by corporations.

When a firm needs more cash to pay for its investments, it can either borrow the money or sell new shares of **common stock** to investors.[1] Sales of new stock by the firm are said to occur in the **primary market**.

Shares of stock are risky investments. For example, in late 1993, shares of Cott beverages were trading for over $40. A year later, after a number of stock analysts

---

[1] We use the terms "shares," "stock," and "common stock" interchangeably, as we do "shareholders" and "stockholders."

capital gain (loss): The amount by which the selling price of an asset exceeds (is less than) the price at which the asset was bought.

began predicting lower than expected earnings, they were selling for less than $14 per share. Had you purchased at $40 and sold at $14 you would have had a **capital loss** of $26 on your investment.

You can understand why investors would be unhappy if forced to tie the knot with a particular company and hold its shares for better or worse, for richer or poorer. So large companies usually arrange for their stocks to be listed on a stock exchange. Stock exchanges allow investors to trade existing stocks among themselves. Exchanges are really markets for secondhand stocks, but they prefer to describe themselves as **secondary markets**, which sounds better.

How Stock Exchanges Work

secondary market: Market in which already-issued securities are traded among investors.

Aunt Hermione has bequeathed to you her Van Gogh, which you decide to convert into cash.[2] There are two ways that you can do so. One is to put the painting up for auction at Christie's, Sotheby's, or one of the other large auction houses. In this case the auctioneer accepts bids for the painting, which is then sold to the museum or collector who posts the highest bid. The alternative is to sell the painting directly to an art dealer, who buys it in the hope of reselling at a profit. Thus there are two types of markets for paintings — an *auction market* and a *dealer market*.

Similarly, stock exchanges may operate as auction markets or as dealer markets. For example, suppose that your aunt has also bequeathed to you 1000 shares of Air Canada stock, which you would like to sell. Air Canada shares are traded on the Toronto Stock Exchange (TSE). To sell your Air Canada stock, you give an order to a stockbroker, who then transmits that order to the floor of the exchange by computer or telephone. A floor trader receives the order and proceeds to the area on the floor of the exchange where the share trades. Here they will, through open outcry, make known the price at which you are willing to sell the stock — known as the *asked price*. If instead you were buying, the floor trader would make known the price you are willing to pay for the stock — known as the *bid price*. If another floor trader is interested in trading at these prices, a transaction takes place.

Each company that is listed on the exchange is assigned by the exchange to a special floor trader, known as a *pro*. The exchange requires that the pro stand ready to "make the market" in the stocks they are assigned by always quoting bid prices and asked prices. So if you need to sell in a hurry, your broker will either sell to another investor who has submitted a buy order that is in your range, or will sell to the pro who is always willing to buy or sell. In addition to making the market, the pro keeps track of the activity in the stock that she is responsible for and may decide to change her prices to satisfy some of the orders by either buying the stock to add to her inventory or selling out of her inventory.

When your order to sell Air Canada stock arrives, the floor trader will identify the buyer who is prepared to pay the highest price. That buyer may be an investor whose order is recorded but not yet filled, or it may be one of the other brokers gathered around the pro with orders to buy or sell. Or it may be the pro herself. If nobody is prepared to pay the price that you demand, you can leave your order on the computer display and it will be executed as soon as the price reaches your limit. Alternatively, you may enter a "market order," directing your broker to sell at the best price available, whatever that is.

---

[2] For details of how Aunt Hermione made her fortune, see Section 3-1 of R. A. Brealey, S. C. Myers, G. Sick and R. Giammarino: *Principles of Corporate Finance*, 2nd Canadian Edition. (Toronto: McGraw-Hill Ryerson, 1992).

The Toronto Stock Exchange, like Sotheby's, is an auction market. Some other stock exchanges are dealer markets. For example, there is an active and growing *over-the-counter* market (OTC) for shares that are not listed on other Canadian exchanges. The OTC is a network of dealers who trade from their offices by computer. The dealers enter prices at which they are prepared to buy and sell into a system called the Canadian Dealing Network (CDN). These prices are then displayed on computer screens in the offices of stockbrokers and large investment firms. Any broker or dealer wishing to trade simply picks up the telephone, calls a dealer, and strikes a deal.

....
Reading the Stock Market Listings

When you read the stock market pages in the newspaper, you are looking at the secondary market. Figure 5.1 is an excerpt from *The Financial Post* of TSE trading on January 24, 1995. The first white bar in the figure highlights the listing for BC Gas.[3] The two numbers to the left of BC Gas are the highest and lowest prices at which the stock has traded in the last 52 weeks, $17 and $13 1/8, respectively. That's another reminder of just how much stock prices fluctuate.

Skip to the four columns on the right, and you will see the prices at which the stock traded on January 24. The highest price at which the stock traded that day was $13 1/2 per share, the lowest was $13 1/4, and the closing price was $13 1/2, which was 1/4 dollar higher than the previous day's close. When there is no trading in a stock the prices in these columns reflect the bid and the ask.

dividends: Periodic cash distributions from the firm to its shareholders.

The 0.90 value to the right of the ticker symbol indicates the annual **dividend** per share paid by the company.[4] In other words, investors holding BC Gas shares currently receive an annual income of $0.90 on each share. Of course BC Gas is not bound to keep that level of dividend in the future. You hope earnings and dividends will rise, but it's possible that profits will slump and BC Gas will cut its dividend.

The dividend yield in the next column tells you how much dividend income you receive for each $100 that you invest in the stock. For BC Gas, the yield is $0.90/$13.50 = .067, or 6.7 percent. Therefore, for every $100 invested in the stock, you would receive annual dividend income of $6.70. The dividend yield on the stock is like the current yield on a bond. Both look at the current income as a percentage of price. Both ignore prospective capital gains or losses and therefore do not correspond to total rates of return.

If you scan Figure 5.1, you will see that dividend yields vary widely across companies. While Ballard Power (BallrdPwr) doesn't even pay a dividend and therefore has zero yield, BC Gas has a relatively high 6.7 percent yield. Investors are content with a low or zero current yield as long as they can look to higher *future* dividends and/or rising share prices.

price-earnings (P/E) multiple: Ratio of stock price to earnings per share.

The **price-earnings (P/E) multiple** for BC Gas is reported as 14.1. This is the ratio of the share price to earnings per share. The P/E ratio is a key tool of stock market analysts. For example, low P/E stocks are sometimes touted as good buys for investors. We will have more to say about P/E later in the chapter.

The column headed "Vol 100s" shows that the trading volume in BC Gas was 126 *round lots*. Each round lot is 100 shares, so 12,600 shares of BC Gas traded on this day. A trade of less than 100 shares is an *odd lot*.

---

[3] The table shows not only the company's name, usually abbreviated, but also the symbol, or ticker, which is used to identify the company on the TSE price screens. The symbol for BC Gas is "BCG."

[4] Actually, it's the last quarterly dividend multiplied by 4 or (if the symbol 'p' is beside the number) the dividends actually paid over the past 12 months.

FIGURE 5.1

Toronto Tues., Jan. 24, 1995

Figures supplied by Star Data Systems Inc.

	52W high	52W low	Stock	Ticker	Div	Yield %	P/E	Vol 100s	High /ask	Low /bid	Cla/ last	Net chg
	5 3/8	315	A Buck Two	BUC	p0.08			nt	3.36	3.10	3.15	
	7 3/4	1.26	ABL Cdst	ABL				67	1.70	1.60	1.60	−0.15
	11	2.50	ACCTel	ACL				37	3.75	3.75	3.75	+0.05
	0.48	0.15	ADEX‡	AMG				415	0.21	0.20	0.20	−0.01
n	8 1/2	7 7/8	AFM Hosp‡	AFM				nt	8 1/2	7 7/8	8	
	21	14	AGFpB♦	AGF	0.60	3.9	7.9	90	16	15 1/2	15 1/2	−1/2
	10 1/8	5 7/8	AGRA A	AGR	0.14			nt	6 1/2	6	6	
	10 1/4	5 1/2	AGRA B♦		0.16	2.8		40	5 3/4	5 3/4	5 3/4	
	12 3/4	3.30	AJMStty‡	AJM				51	11	10 1/2	10 3/4	
	15 1/8	8 1/2	AIT Advd	AIV			13.3	450	8 7/8	8 1/2	8 1/2	−1/2
	0.225	0.105	AJPerron‡	AJP				195	0.125	0.12	0.125	
n	1.00	0.86	APEX A	AXD				nt	0.89	0.86	0.86	
n	1.50	1.00	ARC Resint	ASR				nt	1.25	1.05	1.05	
n	12 1/4	6 1/2	AT Plastics	ATP	0.18	1.6	10.4	37	11 1/2	11 1/8	11 3/8	−1/8
	16 1/4	12	ATCO I♦	ACD	0.28	2.0	9.5	25	14 1/8	13 7/8	14 1/8	−1/8
	16 1/4	12 1/2	ATCO II		0.28			nt	14 1/4	13 3/4	14 3/8	
	4.85	2.35	ATCOR A♦	AKR			12.9	15	2.50	2.45	2.45	−0.10
	4.75	2.40	ATCOR B					nt	2.65	2.45	2.50	
	19 3/8	4.50	ATI Tech	ATY				1.32	6 7/8	6 3/4	6 7/8	+1/8
	12 3/4	6 5/8	ATS Auto	ATA			13.2	86	7	6 3/4	7	+1/4
	0.40	0.21	AbbeyWd‡	AWD				nt	0.40	0.25	0.28	
n	14 5/8	3.95	AberRest	ABZ				317	6 3/4	6 1/2	6 3/4	+1/8
	20 5/8	15 5/8	Abitibi	A				776	19 3/8	19 1/8	19 3/8	+1/8
n	11	6 3/4	Abitibi rcpt					3526	9 5/8	9 3/8	9 1/2	
	145	123	Abitibi db					nt	141	135	137	
	2.50	1.75	Accordfn	ACD	0.06			nt	2.20	2.10	2.20	
	6 5/8	1.50	AccugrphA‡	ACU			16.1	1550	6 1/2	6	6 3/8	+3/8
	14 7/8	10 7/8	Acklands	ACK			8.1	20	11	11	11	
n	34 1/8	21 1/4	AcmeMd	AMK				nt	26 1/4	26	26 1/4	
n	5 1/4	2.70	Adrian‡	ADL				201	3.65	3.50	3.55	+0.05
	3.45	1.10	AdvdGrav‡	AED				24	1.35	1.30	1.35	+0.05
n	0.60	0.60	AdvdMat‡	AMR				nt	0.60	0.58	0.60	
n	1.10	0.30	Advantex‡	ADX				nt	0.35	0.30	0.35	
	7 1/4	5	AdvntrBtr	AVN	p0.14	2.6	9.0	10	5 3/8	5 3/8	5 3/8	
n	1.16	0.33	AdvtBtrwt					nt	0.50	0.35	0.45	
	19 3/4	11 1/4	AgnicoEag	AGE	u0.10	1.0	31.4	1.39	14 1/8	13 7/8	14 1/8	+1/8
	18 7/8	11	AinswrthL	ANS			7.4	76	12	11 3/4	12	+1/4
	8 7/8	5 1/2	AirCda	AC				9354	8	7 1/4	7 7/8	
	3.15	1.58	AirCda wt					2383	2.40	2.30	2.40	
	1.05	0.38	Airboss‡	BOS				nt	0.48	0.41	0.47	
	5 1/4	3.10	AkitaDrA♦‡	AKT			5.4	12	3.30	3.25	3.25	−0.15
	5 1/4	3.40	AkitaDrB					nt	3.40	3.20	3.75	
	22 3/4	16 3/8	AltaEn	AEC	0.40	2.2	11.3	3282	18 3/8	18	18 1/8	+3/8
	17 5/8	13 1/4	AltaNGas	ANG	0.68	4.5	12.3	175	15 1/4	15	15 1/4	
	38 5/8	27 3/8	Alcan	AL	u0.30	1.2	74.1	5515	35 7/8	35 1/2	35 5/8	−7/8
	24 3/8	21 5/8	AlcanOpf*		0.81	8.3		48	21 7/8	21 3/4	21 3/4	+1/8
	21	17 1/4	AlcanEpf		0.36	7.5		17	18 1/4	18 1/8	18 1/8	
	26 3/8	23 5/8	AlcanOpf*		u1.87	7.9		28	24 1/8	23 5/8	23 5/8	−1/2
	2.45	0.60	AlgoA♦	AO				nt	0.65	0.55	0.60	
	23	13	AlgomCent	ALC				nt	22 7/8	22	22 1/2	
	23	19 3/4	AlgomFn pf	AFC	1.37	6.5		15	21 1/4	21 1/4	21 1/4	
	4.15	3.00	AlgonMerc	AM	p0.30			nt	3.75	3.50	3.50	
	8 5/8	5 1/8	AlxBio	AXB				nt	7 3/8	7 1/8	7	
	18 1/4	12 3/8	AllncCom	AAC			14.9	1640	15 5/8	15 1/2	15 1/2	−1/8
n	25	16 1/4	AllnceFor	ALP			9.2	219	23 3/4	23 3/8	23 3/4	
	14 1/2	6 1/2	AlphaNet	FAX				92	9	7 3/4	8 1/2	−5/8
n	2.45	1.15	AlpineOil	ASL			9.2	20	1.40	1.40	1.40	+0.05
	7	4.10	AltaGene	AGI				nt	4.75	4.60	4.75	
	3.50	0.53	AltaRs‡	ATI				235	0.67	0.62	0.63	−0.03
	11 5/8	7	AmaxGld	AXG				nt	...	7	7	
	1.30	0.20	AmaxGldwt					nt	...	0.15	0.20	
	6 1/2	3.05	Amer ECO	ECX				nt	3.50	3.30	3.35	
s	5 5/8	3.00	Amer Gem‡	GBM				3	4.00	4.00	4.00	+0.50
	0.48	0.25	AmerLeduc	ARL				z400	0.26	0.26	0.26	
n	25 1/4	17	Am Sensor	ASZ				141	22 3/4	22 3/8	22 3/8	−1/2
	122	110	Amoco db*	AMN				nt	114	112	113	
	8 1/8	4.75	AnchorLam	AKC	0.12	2.2	9.8	29	5 3/8	5 3/8	5 3/8	
s	18	10 3/4	AndersnEx	AXL			29.7	307	13 3/8	12 3/4	13 3/8	+3/4
	12 1/2	10	AndresA♦	ADW	0.59			nt	11 1/2	11	11 1/4	
	12 1/8	10 5/8	AndresB		0.52			nt	11 5/8	10 5/8	11	
n	9 1/2	7	Andyne	ADV			29.0	77	7 1/4	7 1/4	7 1/4	
	34 1/2	29 3/4	AnCdnApf	ACT	2.25			nt	30	29 5/8	29 3/4	
	40	35 1/2	AnCdnBpf		2.65			nt	36	34 1/2	36	
	43	39	AnCdnOpf		2.90			nt	40	36 1/2	39	
	46	40 1/2	AnCdnDpf		3.15			nt	42	40 7/8	40 7/8	
	1.35	0.60	Antares	ANZ				11	0.68	0.68	0.68	+0.03
n	6 3/4	5 3/4	AnvilRng‡	ARO				nt	5 3/4	5 1/4	5 3/4	
	1.30	0.06	ApldCarb‡	APN				120	0.12	0.11	0.12	+0.01
	19 1/4	12 1/2	ArborMemA	ABO	p0.07			nt	18	17	17 1/4	
	19 1/4	12 3/4	ArborMemB♦		p0.07	0.4	17.6	16	16	15 7/8	15 7/8	−1/8
	23 1/4	10	ArcherRs	ARC			17.5	947	10 1/2	10 1/8	10 1/2	+3/8
	49 5/8	42 1/8	Argus$2.50pf	AR	2.50			nt	47	44	45 3/8	
	38	32	Argus$2.70pf		2.70			nt	34 1/2	33 1/2	33 1/2	
	41 3/8	35 1/2	Argus$2.60pf		2.60			nt	45	39	39	
n	2.55	1.31	ArielRs‡	AU				1792	2.40	2.26	2.30	−0.11
	2.20	0.98	Arimetco‡	ARX				262	116	113	113	−0.02
	2.70	0.80	Armbro	ARE				nt	1.25	1.22	1.23	
	2.18	0.18	Arrowlink‡	ARK				1100	0.20	0.20	0.20	
n	4.45	2.40	ArtisanDrl	ADR			4.7	20	2.50	2.50	2.50	−0.10
	51	6	Asbestos	AB				nt	8 1/2	6	7	
	1.00	0.70	AscentexEn‡	AEN			70.0	101	0.70	0.70	0.70	
↓	3.20	0.62	Ashton	ACA				202	0.65	0.62	0.65	
	1.60	0.04	Ashton wt					20	0.10	0.10	0.10	
	19 1/2	12	AstralA♦	ACM	0.30	2.1	17.5	1	14 1/2	14 1/2	14 1/2	−1/8
	19	12	AstralB♦		0.30			nt	15	14 1/2	15 1/4	
	1.85	0.61	AthabskGld‡	AHB				715	1.08	0.94	1.08	+0.14
	1.55	0.75	AtlantaGld‡	AAG				400	0.83	0.81	0.81	+0.01
	5	3.10	AtlntcCoast	ATC				nt	3.30	3.05	3.10	
	25 3/4	24 5/8	AtlanticSh pf	ATS	2.31	9.3		2	25	25	25	
	16 1/2	7 3/4	AttntsCom♦	ATV			9.6	6	8 1/2	8 1/2	8 1/2	
n	0.75	0.25	Atlantiswt					nt	0.50	0.25	0.50	
	1.57	1.05	AudreyRs	AUY				10	1.41	1.38	1.40	−0.03
	19 1/2	14 3/4	AultFds	AUL	0.66	3.6	15.4	241	18 3/8	18 1/8	18 1/8	−3/8
	7 7/8	3.60	AurRs‡	AUR				102	4.20	4.05	4.05	−0.15
n	1.49	0.95	AurexRs‡	AXR				nt	1.00	0.90	0.96	
n	0.22	0.05	Aurex wt					nt	0.08	0.06	0.08	
	1.13	0.70	Aurizon‡	ARZ			19.0	38	0.80	0.76	0.76	+0.01
n	5 1/8	4.55	Autostck	OTO	0.14			nt	5 1/8	5	5	
	1.30	0.86	AutrexA♦	AUT				nt	1.08	0.84	0.86	
	1.30	1.00	AutrexB					nt	1.20	...	1.00	
	30 1/8	19 1/2	Avenor	AVR				2092	29 1/4	28 5/8	29	+3/8
n	23 3/4	17 5/8	Avenor rcp					2276	23	22 3/8	22 7/8	+3/8
n	155	114 1/2	Avenor deb					3	150	149	150	+3
	3.85	2.45	Azco‡	AZC				45	2.70	2.60	2.70	−0.05
n	3.30	2.10	AztecRs	AZL			9.8	164	2.38	2.36	2.36	−0.04

B

	52W high	52W low	Stock	Ticker	Div	Yield %	P/E	Vol 100s	High /ask	Low /bid	Cla/ last	Net chg
s	11	9 3/8	BAA	BAA	p0.21			nt	10 1/2	10	10 1/8	
	1.35	0.57	BC Banc	BBC				14	0.66	0.66	0.66	
	17	13 1/8	BC Gas	BCG	0.90	6.7	14.1	126	13 1/2	13 1/4	13 1/2	+1/4
n	25 3/8	24 5/8	BCGasUrpfB	BGU	1.77	7.2		25	24 5/8	24 5/8	24 5/8	
	11 1/8	7 1/2	BC SugarA	BCS	0.40	5.0	18.2	221	8	7 7/8	8	+1/8
	16 1/8	16	BC Sugr pf		1.00			nt	17	16	16	
	27 3/8	21 1/2	BC TELECOM	BCT	1.24	5.5	11.8	833	22 5/8	22 1/4	22 1/2	+1/4
	66	62	BC TelApf	BT	4.38			nt	64	60	65	
	68	62	BC TelBpf		4.50			nt	64	60	64	
	73	66	BC TelCpf		4.75			nt	68	64	66	
	73	62	BC TelDpf		4.75			nt	64	60	62	
	21 1/2	19	BC TelEpf		1.21			nt	19 1/2	19	19	
	79	71	BC TelFpf		5.15			nt	78 1/2	77	77	
	89	83 1/2	BC TelGpf		5.75			nt	89	86	86	
	102	84 1/2	BC TelHpf		6.00			nt	86	82	86	
	52 7/8	41 1/8	BCE	B	2.72	6.5	12.6	11077	42 1/4	41 3/8	42	+5/8
	27 1/8	24 1/2	BCE Mpf		1.95	7.7		1	25 1/4	25 1/4	25 1/4	+1/4
	44	41 1/4	BCE Opf		v2.72	6.5		14	41 3	41 3/4	41 3	
	8 3/8	0.26	BCE wt					1963	0.47	0.35	0.44	+0.10
	48 5/8	35	BCE Mob	BCX			88.7	51	47	46	47	+1 1/2
	17 1/4	12 3/4	BGR A	BPT			5.9	85	13 1/4	13	13 1/4	+1/4
n	4.70	3.25	BGR wt					25	3.50	3.40	3.40	−0.20
	3.60	0.40	BMB Comp	BMB				7	3.15	3.15	3.15	
	0.56	0.16	BMR Gld‡	BGL				210	0.18	0.18	0.18	+0.02
	23 5/8	14 5/8	BNT cap	XBN				nt	15	13 7/8	15	
	30	27 1/2	BNT eq		v2.72			nt	27 7/8	27 1/2	27 5/8	
n	2.50	1.45	BPI Fn	BPF	0.04	2.0	18.6	474	1.99	1.95	1.99	+0.04
	4.45	3.15	BRL Ent	BRL				nt	3.95	3.70	3.95	
n	2.50	0.70	BT Cda call	BTA				15	0.90	0.90	0.90	+0.10
n	2.86	0.82	BT Cda put					nt	0.93	0.81	0.90	
n	3.90	0.85	BT Cda rcpt					nt	1.15	1.05	1.20	
n	0.95	0.85	BackerP‡	BCM				105	0.90	0.90	0.90	−0.05
	3.00	1.40	BajaGld‡	BGJ				16	2.35	2.27	2.35	+0.05
	10 3/4	5 3/8	BallrdPwr	BLD				1437	8 1/2	8	8 1/2	+1/2
	3.50	1.50	BallrdPwr wt					15	2.40	2.40	2.40	−0.10
	10 3/8	4.75	BallisticEn‡	BAL			14.6	32	5 1/8	5	5	−1/8
	20 3/4	13 1/4	Banister	BAC			11.2	1	14 1/4	14 1/4	14 1/4	
	30 3/4	22	BkofMtl	BMO	1.32	5.3	8.3	7245	25 1/8	24 5/8	25	+3/8
	29 3/4	26 5/8	BkofMtl4pf		v2.25	8.3		10	27	26 7/8	27	
	32 1/4	27 1/2	BkofMtl1pf		2.25	8.1		4	27 5/8	27 5/8	27 5/8	
	28 3/8	24 1/2	BkofMtl2pf*		u1.68	6.8		36	25	24 5/8	25	
	32 3/4	23 1/8	BkofNS	BNS	1.24	4.9	14.3	4505	25 1/8	24 3/4	25 1/8	
	24 1/4	21 5/8	BkofNS1pf		0.26	5.7		33	22 1/8	22 1/8	22 1/8	
	27 1/2	25 1/4	BkofNS4pf		v2.25	8.7		44	26 3/8	26	26	
	29 1/2	26 3/8	BkofNS5pf		2.31	8.8		25	26 3/8	26 3/8	26 3/8	
	28 7/8	24 1/4	BkofNS6pf		1.78			nt	24 7/8	24 5/8	24 5/8	
n	25 1/4	24 3/8	BkofNS7pf		1.77	7.2		5	24 1/2	24 1/2	24 1/2	
	38 3/4	27 1/4	BarrickGld	ABX	u0.10	0.5	26.4	3647	30 5/8	30 1/8	30 1/4	
	7 1/4	3.85	Barrington	BPL			17.1	22	4.10	4.10	4.10	
	8 3/4	6	Baton	BNB				nt	8 1/4	7 7/8	7 7/8	
n	3.45	2.60	BaytexA‡	BTE			33.8	30	2.70	2.70	2.70	
n	0.50	0.31	BaytexB♦					50	0.38	0.38	0.38	
	14 1/2	9 1/4	Beamscope	BSP			17.2	39	13	12 3/4	12 3/4	
↓	1.25	0.50	BearingPwr	BPO			8.3	20	0.50	0.50	0.50	
	2.59	1.65	BeauCda	BAU			17.0	97	1.70	1.70	1.70	
	13 1/4	7 1/4	BeckerB♦	BEK				20	8	8	8	
n	2.45	1.80	Bedford B♦‡	BED				nt	2.00	1.85	2.00	
	28 1/2	25 1/4	Bell8pf	BC	1.94			nt	25 1/2	25 1/4	25 1/4	

Source: The Financial Post, January 25, 1995.

SELF-TEST 5.1 Explain the entries for Bank of Montreal (BkofMtl) in Figure 5.1.

 BOOK VALUES, LIQUIDATION VALUES, AND MARKET VALUES

Why is BC Gas selling at $13 1/2 per share when the stock of BC Sugar, listed below BC Gas , is priced at $8? And why does it cost $14.10 to buy one dollar of BC Gas earnings, while one dollar of BC Sugar earnings costs $18.20? Do these numbers imply that one stock is a better buy than the other?

Finding the value of BC Gas stock may sound like a simple problem. Each year BC Gas publishes a balance sheet that shows the value of the firm's assets and liabilities. The simplified balance sheet in Table 5.1 shows that the book value of all BC Gas' assets — plant and machinery, inventories of materials, cash in the bank, and so on — was $2033 million at the end of 1993. BC Gas's liabilities — money that it owes the banks, taxes that are due to be paid, and the like — amounted to $1548 million. The difference between the value of the assets and the liabilities was $485 million. This was the **book value** of the firm's equity.[5] Book value records all the money that BC Gas has raised from its shareholders plus all the earnings that have been plowed back on their behalf.

> **book value:** Net worth of the firm according to the balance sheet.

TABLE 5.1

BALANCE SHEET FOR BC GAS, DECEMBER 31, 1993
(Figures in millions of dollars)

Assets		Liabilities and Shareholders' Equity	
Plant, equipment, and other assets	$2033	Liabilities	$1548
		Equity	485

Note: Share of stock outstanding: 35.5 million. Book value of equity (per share) $13.66

Book value is a reassuringly definite number. KPMG Peat Marwick Thorne, one of Canada's largest accounting firms, tells us:

> *In our opinion, these consolidated financial statements present fairly in all material respects, the financial position of the Company as of December 31, 1993 and 1992, and the results of its operations and the changes in its financial position for the years then ended in accordance with generally accepted accounting principles.*

But does stock value equal book value? Let's see. BC Gas has issued 35.5 million shares, so the balance sheet suggests that each BC Gas share was worth $485/35.5 = $13.66 on December 31, 1993.

But BC Gas shares actually were selling at $16.63 on December 31, 1993. This and the other cases shown in Table 5.2 tell us that investors in the stock market do not just buy and sell at book value per share. In fact, the relationship of market value to book value is one of the more widely studied measures of how a company is performing. If book value is a good measure of the replacement cost of a firm's assets, the excess of market over book value gives some idea of the wealth added to the firm through such factors as managerial expertise or market power.

Investors know that accountants don't even try to estimate true current values. The value of the assets reported on the firm's balance sheet is equal to their original (or "historical") cost less an allowance for depreciation. But that may not be

---

[5] "Equity" is still another word for stock. Thus stockholders are often referred to as "equity investors."

TABLE 5.2

Market versus book values, December, 1993

Firm	Stock Price	Book Value Per Share	Ratio: Price/ Book Value
Bank of Nova Scotia	29.00	21.79	1.33
BC Gas	16.63	13.66	1.22
Imperial Oil Limited	29.00	21.79	1.33
Interprovincial Pipe	32.25	11.60	2.78
Northern Telecom	40.88	12.01	3.40
Poco Petroleums	8.88	5.51	1.61
George Weston Ltd.	39.00	27.42	1.42

a good guide to what the firm would need to pay to buy the same assets today. For example, Canadian Airlines depreciates jets over a twenty-year period. Thus the book value of each addition to the fleet is never more than the purchase value. But the market value of their fleet changes rapidly. As with many other airlines, Canadian buys and sells jets in response to market conditions and when they do so they discover what the market value is. For instance, in 1993 they made a $10 million gain on the sale of just one Boeing 767, suggesting that the value of the fleet that they kept was well above book value. However, 3 years earlier they recorded a loss of $51 million on the sale of several jets. Given the volatile market for commercial aircraft, book value is a poor measure of market value.

liquidation value: Net proceeds that would be realized by selling the firm's assets and paying off its creditors.

Well, maybe stock price equals **liquidation value** per share, that is, the amount of cash per share a company could raise if it sold off all its assets in secondhand markets and paid off all its debts. Wrong again. A successful company ought to be worth more than liquidation value. That's the goal of bringing all those assets together in the first place.

The difference between a company's actual value and its book or liquidation value is often attributed to *going-concern value*. We can trace *going-concern value* to three things.

1. *Extra earning power*. A company may have the ability to earn more than an adequate rate of return on assets. For example, the new "open skies" policy provides companies like Canadian Airlines opportunities to mesh its domestic and international routes. But they know that it gives the same opportunities to American and United. If Canadian can make better use of its planes than American and United make of theirs, it will earn a higher rate of return. In this case the value of the planes to the more efficient operator will be higher than their book value or secondhand value.

2. *Intangible assets*. There are many assets that accountants don't put on the balance sheet. Some of these assets are extremely valuable to the companies owning or using them but would be difficult to sell intact to other firms. Take Northern Telecom. As you can see from Table 5.2, it sells at over three times book value per share. Where did all that extra value come from? Largely from the cash flow generated by the technology that it has developed, patented, and marketed. These telecommunications products are the fruits of a research and development (R&D) program that required expenditures of $2.7 billion over the preceding 3 years. Successful R&D does show up in stock prices, however.

3. *Value of future investments*. If investors believe a company will have the opportunity to make exceedingly profitable investments in the future, they will pay more for the company's stock today. When Microsoft, the computer software company, sold its stock to investors in 1986, its tangible assets and

working capital added up to $73 million. Yet the prices investors paid for Microsoft's stock gave a total company value of $519 million. In part this reflected an intangible asset, the MS-DOS operating system for computers. In addition, Microsoft was a *growth* company. Investors were betting that it had the know-how that would enable it to devise successful *follow-on* products.

It is not surprising that stocks virtually never sell at book or liquidation values. Investors buy shares based on present and *future* earning power. Two key features determine the profits the firm will be able to produce: first, the earnings that can be generated by the firm's current tangible and intangible assets, and, second, the opportunities the firm has to invest in lucrative projects that will increase future earnings.

● **EXAMPLE 5.1 BC Gas and Northern Telecom**

BC Gas isn't a growth company. Its market is limited and it is expanding capacity at a very deliberate pace. More important, it is largely a regulated utility, so its profits on present and future investments are limited. It is legally entitled only to a "fair and adequate" rate of return. It is no surprise that BC Gas sells for only 22 percent above book value (see Table 5.2) and that investors value the company based mostly on current earnings and dividends.

We pointed out that Northern Telecom relies heavily on the success of its R&D effort. At the end of 1993 the market seems to have expressed confidence in the company's new products and market development: At the end of a year in which the company reported an $878 million loss, Northern Telecom stock was selling at 3.4 times its book value. The very next year provided some justification for this confidence as Northern Telecom reported a profit of $408 million. The 1994 profits reflected Northern Telecom's development of new markets in China and Latin America. We can see that the market value of Northern Telecom depends heavily on intangible assets: the ability of the company to develop and market innovative products and services.

market-value balance sheet: Financial statement that uses the market value of all assets and liabilities.

Managers and investors are not bound by generally accepted accounting principles, and they sometimes construct a **market-value balance sheet**. Take a look at Table 5.3. A market-value balance sheet contains two classes of assets: (1) assets already in place, (a) tangible and (b) intangible; and (2) opportunities to invest in attractive future ventures. BC Gas's stock market value is dominated by tangible assets in place; Northern Telecom's reflects the value of future investment opportunities.

TABLE 5.3

A MARKET-VALUE BALANCE SHEET

Assets	Liabilities and Shareholders' Equity
Plant, equipment, and other assets	Market value of liabilities
Investment opportunities	Market value of equity

Other firms, like McDonald's, have it all. McDonald's earns plenty from its current franchises. These earnings are part of what makes the stock attractive to investors. In addition, investors are willing to pay for the company's ability to invest profitably in new outlets that will increase future earnings.

Let's summarize. Just remember:

● *Book value* records what a company has paid for its assets, with a simple, and often unrealistic, deduction for depreciation and no adjustment for inflation. It does not capture the true value of a business.

● *Liquidation value* is what the company could net by selling its assets and repaying its debts. It does not capture the value of a successful going concern.
● *True value* is market value, that is, the amount that investors are willing to pay for the firm. This depends on the earning power of today's assets and the profitability of *future* investments.

The next question is: What determines market value?

SELF-TEST 5.2

In the 1970s, the computer industry was dominated by IBM and was growing rapidly. In the 1980s, many new competitors entered the market, and computer prices fell. Computer makers in the 1990s, including IBM, have struggled with thinning profit margins and intense competition. How has IBM's market-value balance sheet changed over time? Have assets in place become proportionately more or less important? Do you think this progression is unique to the computer industry?

 ## VALUING COMMON STOCKS

Today's Price and Tomorrow's Price

The cash payoff to owners of common stocks comes in two forms: (1) cash dividends and (2) capital gains or losses. Usually investors expect to get some of each. Suppose that the current price of a share is P_0, that the expected price a year from now is P_1, and that the expected dividend per share is DIV_1. The subscript on P_0 denotes time zero, which is today; the subscript on P_1 denotes time 1, which is 1 year hence. We simplify by assuming that dividends are paid only once a year and that the next dividend will come in 1 year. The rate of return that investors expect from this share over the next year is the expected dividend per share DIV_1 plus the expected increase in price $P_1 - P_0$, all divided by the price at the start of the year P_0:

$$\text{Expected return} = r = \frac{DIV_1 + P_1 - P_0}{P_0}$$

Let us now look at how our formula works. Suppose Blue Skies stock is selling for $75 a share ($P_0 = 75). Investors expect a $3 cash dividend over the next year ($DIV_1 = 3). They also expect the stock to sell for $81 a year hence ($P_1 = 81). Then the expected return to stockholders is 12 percent:

$$r = \frac{\$3 + \$81 - \$75}{\$75} = .12, \text{ or } 12\%$$

Notice that this expected return comes in two parts, the dividend yield and the capital appreciation:

$$\text{Expected return} = \begin{matrix}\text{expected} \\ \text{dividend} \\ \text{yield}\end{matrix} + \begin{matrix}\text{expected} \\ \text{capital} \\ \text{appreciation}\end{matrix}$$

$$= \frac{DIV_1}{P_0} + \frac{P_1 - P_0}{P_0}$$

$$= \frac{\$3}{\$75} + \frac{\$81 - \$75}{\$75}$$

$$= .04 + .08 = .12, \text{ or } 12\%$$

Of course, the *actual* return for Blue Skies may turn out to be more or less than investors expect. For example, one of the biggest winners on the Toronto Stock Exchange in 1994 was Caledonia Mining Corporation with a realized return of 1,150%. This figure was almost certainly well in excess of investor expectations. At the other extreme is Bramalea, which spent much of 1994 trying to restructure its debt. It provided its shareholders an actual return of -98 percent. Never confuse the actual outcome with the expected outcome.

We saw how to work out the expected return on Blue Skies stock given today's stock price and forecasts of next year's stock price and dividends. You can also explain the market value of the stock in terms of investors' forecasts of dividends and price and the expected return offered by other equally risky stocks. This is just the present value of the cash flows the stock will provide to its owner:

$$\text{Price today} = P_0 = \frac{DIV_1 + P_1}{1 + r}$$

For Blue Skies $DIV_1 = 3$ and $P_1 = 81$. If stocks of similar risk offer an expected return of $r = 12$ percent, then today's price for Blue Skies should be $75:

$$P_0 = \frac{\$3 + \$81}{1.12} = \$75$$

How do we know that $75 is the right price? Because no other price could survive in competitive markets. What if P_0 were above $75? Then the expected rate of return on Blue Skies stock would be *lower* than on other securities of equivalent risk. (*Check this!*) Investors would bail out of Blue Skies stock and substitute the other securities. In the process they would force down the price of Blue Skies stock. If P_0 were less than $75, Blue Skies stock would offer a *higher* expected rate of return than equivalent-risk securities. (*Check this too.*) Everyone would rush to buy, forcing the price up to $75. When the stock is priced correctly (that is, price equals present value), the *expected* rate of return on Blue Skies stock is also the rate of return that investors *require* to hold the stock.

At each point in time *all securities of the same risk are priced to offer the same expected rate of return.* This is a fundamental characteristic of prices in well-functioning markets. It is also common sense.

SELF-TEST 5.3

Androscoggin Copper is increasing next year's dividend to $5.00 per share. The forecast stock price next year is $105. Equally risky stocks of other companies offer expected rates of return of 10 percent. What should Androscoggin common stock sell for?

The Dividend Discount Model

dividend discount model: Computation of today's stock price which states that share value equals the present value of all expected future dividends.

We have managed to explain today's stock price P_0 in terms of the dividend DIV_1 and the expected stock price next year P_1. But future stock prices are not easy to forecast directly, though you may encounter individuals who claim to be able to do so. A formula that requires tomorrow's stock price to explain today's stock price is not generally helpful.

As it turns out, we can express a stock's value as the present value of all the forecast future dividends paid by the company to its shareholders without referring to the future stock price. This is the **dividend discount model:**

$$P_0 = \text{present value of } (DIV_1, DIV_2, DIV_3, \ldots, DIV_t \ldots)$$

$$= \frac{DIV_1}{1 + r} + \frac{DIV_2}{(1 + r)^2} + \frac{DIV_3}{(1 + r)^3} + \ldots + \frac{DIV_t}{(1 + r)^t} + \ldots$$

How far out in the future could we look? In principle for 40, 60, or 100 years or more — corporations are potentially immortal. However, far-distant dividends will not have significant present values. Most of the value of established companies comes from dividends to be paid within a person's working lifetime.

How do we get from the one-period formula $P_0 = (\text{DIV}_1 + P_1)/(1 + r)$ to the dividend discount model? We look at longer and longer investment horizons.

Let's start with a 1-year horizon:

$$P_0 = \frac{\text{DIV}_1 + P_1}{1 + r}$$

If this price formula holds now, it ought to hold next year as well:

$$\text{Price at year-end} = P_1 = \frac{\text{DIV}_2 + P_2}{1 + r}$$

That is, a year from now investors will be looking out at dividends in Year 2 and price at the end of Year 2. Thus we can forecast P_1 by forecasting DIV_2 and P_2. We can then substitute for P_1 and turn the one-period stock valuation model

$$P_0 = \frac{\text{DIV}_1 + P_1}{1 + r}$$

and

$$P_1 = \frac{\text{DIV}_2 + P_2}{1 + r}$$

into a two-period model:

$$P_0 = \frac{\text{DIV}_1}{1 + r} + \frac{\text{DIV}_2 + P_2}{(1 + r)^2}$$

We have succeeded in relating today's price to the forecast dividends for the next 2 years (DIV_1 and DIV_2) plus the forecast price at the end of the *second* year (P_2). You will probably not be surprised to learn that we could go on to replace P_2 by ($\text{DIV}_3 + P_3/(1 + r)$) and relate today's price to the forecast dividends for 3 years (DIV_1, DIV_2, and DIV_3) plus the forecast price at the end of the *third* year (P_3). In fact we can look as far out into the future as we like, removing P's as we go. Suppose we call our horizon date H. This gives us a general formula for the intrinsic value of the stock:

$$P_0 = \frac{\text{DIV}_1}{1 + r} + \frac{\text{DIV}_2}{(1 + r)^2} + \ldots + \frac{\text{DIV}_H + P_H}{(1 + r)^H}$$

Regardless of the investment horizon, the stock value will be the same. This is because the stock price at the horizon date is determined by expectations of dividends from that date forward. Let's confirm this with an example.

● EXAMPLE 5.2 Valuing Blue Skies Stock

Take Blue Skies. The firm is growing steadily and investors expect both the stock price and the dividend to increase at 8 percent per year. Now consider three investors, Erste, Zweiter, and Dritter. Erste plans to hold Blue Skies for 1 year, Zweiter for 2, and Dritter for 3. Compare their payoffs:

	Year 1	Year 2	Year 3
Erste	$DIV_1 = 3$ $P_1 = 81$		
Zweiter	$DIV_1 = 3$	$DIV_2 = 3.24$ $P_2 = 87.48$	
Dritter	$DIV_1 = 3$	$DIV_2 = 3.24$	$DIV_3 = 3.50$ $P_3 = 94.48$

Remember, we assumed that dividends and stock prices for Blue Skies are expected to grow at a steady 8 percent. Thus $DIV_2 = \$3 \times 1.08 = \$3.24$, $DIV_3 = \$3.24 \times 1.08 = \$3.50$, and so on.

Erste, Zweiter, and Dritter all require the same 12 percent expected return. So we can calculate present value over Erste's 1-year horizon:

$$PV = \frac{DIV_1 + P_1}{1 + r} = \frac{\$3 + \$81}{1.12} = \$75$$

or Zweiter's 2-year horizon:

$$PV = \frac{DIV_1}{1 + r} + \frac{DIV_2 + P_2}{(1 + r)^2}$$

$$= \frac{\$3.00}{1.12} + \frac{\$3.24 + \$87.48}{(1.12)^2}$$

$$= \$2.68 + \$72.32 = \$75$$

or Dritter's 3-year horizon:

$$PV = \frac{DIV_1}{1 + r} + \frac{DIV_2}{(1 + r)^2} + \frac{DIV_3 + P_3}{(1 + r)^3}$$

$$= \frac{\$3}{1.12} + \frac{\$3.24}{(1.12)^2} + \frac{\$3.50 + \$94.48}{(1.12)^3}$$

$$= \$2.68 + \$2.58 + \$69.74 = \$75$$

All agree it's worth $75 per share. This illustrates our basic principle: The value of a common stock equals the present value of dividends received out to the investment horizon, plus the present value of the forecast stock price at the horizon. Moreover, when you move the horizon date, the stock's present value should not change. The principle holds for horizons of 1, 3, 10, 20, or 50 years or more.

SELF-TEST 5.4

Refer to Self-Test 5.3. Assume that Androscoggin Copper's dividend and share price are expected to grow at a constant 5 percent per year. Calculate the current value of Androscoggin stock with the dividend discount model using a 3-year horizon. You should get the same answer as in Self-Test 5.3.

Look at Table 5.4, which continues the Blue Skies example for various time horizons, still assuming that the dividends are expected to increase at a steady 8 percent compound rate. The expected price increases at the same 8 percent rate. Each row in the table represents a present value calculation for a different horizon year. Note that present value does not depend on the investment horizon. Figure 5.2 presents the same data in a graph. Each column shows the present value of the dividends up to the horizon and the present value of the price at the horizon. As the horizon recedes, the dividend stream accounts for an increasing proportion of present value but the *total* present value of dividends plus terminal price always equals $75.

TABLE 5.4
Value of Blue Skies

Horizon	PV(Dividends)	+	PV (Terminal Price)	=	Value Per Share
1	$ 2.68		$72.32		$75.00
2	5.26		69.74		75.00
3	7.75		67.25		75.00
10	22.87		52.13		75.00
20	38.76		36.24		75.00
30	49.81		25.19		75.00
50	62.83		12.17		75.00
100	73.02		1.98		75.00

If the horizon is infinitely far away, then we can forget about the final horizon price — it has almost no present value — and simply say

Stock price = PV (all future dividends per share)

This is the dividend discount model.

FIGURE 5.2
Value of Blue Skies for different horizons.

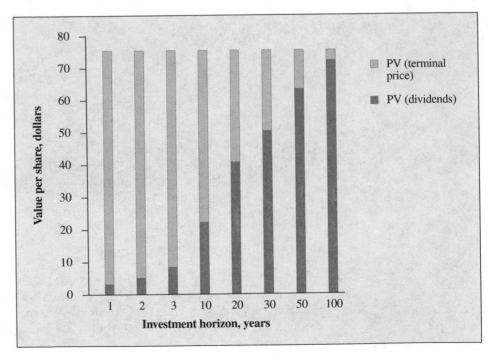

SELF-TEST 5.5   How can we say that price equals the present value of all future dividends when many actual investors may be seeking capital gains and planning to hold for only a year or two? Explain.

SIMPLIFYING THE DIVIDEND DISCOUNT MODEL

The Dividend Discount Model with No Growth

Consider a company that pays out all its earnings to its common shareholders. Such a company could not grow because it could not reinvest.[6] Stockholders might enjoy a generous immediate dividend, but they could forecast no increase in future dividends. The company's stock would offer a perpetual stream of equal cash payments, $DIV_1 = DIV_2 = \ldots = DIV_t = \ldots$.

The dividend discount model says that these no-growth shares should sell for the present value of a constant, perpetual stream of dividends. We learned how to do that calculation when we valued perpetuities in Chapter 3. Just divide the annual cash payment by the discount rate. The discount rate is the rate of return demanded by investors in other stocks of the same risk:

$$P_0 = \frac{DIV_1}{r}$$

Since our company pays out all its earnings as dividends, dividends and earnings are the same, and we could just as well calculate stock value by

$$\text{Value of a no-growth stock} = P_0 = \frac{EPS_1}{r}$$

where EPS_1 represents next year's earnings per share of stock. Thus some people loosely say, "Stock price is the present value of future earnings" and calculate value by this formula. Be careful — this is a special case. We'll return to the formula later in this chapter.

SELF-TEST 5.6

Moonshine Industries has produced a barrel per week for the past 20 years but cannot grow because of certain legal hazards. It earns $25 per share per year and pays it all out to stockholders. The stockholders have alternative, equivalent-risk ventures yielding 20 percent per year on average. How much is one share of Moonshine worth? Assume the company can keep going indefinitely.

The Constant-Growth Dividend Discount Model

The dividend discount model requires a forecast of dividends for every year into the future, which poses a bit of a problem for stocks with potentially infinite lives. Unless we want to spend a lifetime forecasting dividends, we must use simplifying assumptions to reduce the number of estimates. The simplest simplification assumes a no-growth perpetuity that works for no-growth common shares.

Here's another simplification that finds a good deal of practical use. Suppose forecast dividends grow at a constant rate into the indefinite future. If dividends grow at a steady rate, then instead of forecasting an infinite number of dividends, we need to forecast only the next dividend and the dividend growth rate.

Recall Blue Skies Inc. It will pay a $3 dividend in 1 year. If the dividend grows at a constant rate of $g = .08$ (8 percent) thereafter, then dividends in future years will be

$$DIV_1 = \$3 \qquad\qquad = \$3.00$$

$$DIV_2 = \$3 \times (1 + g) = \$3 \times 108 \quad = \$3.24$$

$$DIV_3 = \$3 \times (1 + g)^2 = \$3 \times 1.08^2 = \$3.50$$

$$\ldots$$

---

[6] We assume it does not raise money by issuing new shares.

Plug these forecasts of future dividends into the dividend discount model:

$$P_0 = \frac{D_1}{1+r} + \frac{D_1(1+g)}{(1+r)^2} + \frac{D_1(1+g)^2}{(1+r)^3} + \frac{D_1(1+g)^3}{(1+r)^4} + \cdots$$

$$= \frac{\$3}{1.12} + \frac{\$3.24}{1.12^2} + \frac{\$3.50}{1.12^3} + \frac{\$3.78}{1.12^4} + \cdots$$

$$= \$2.68 + \$2.58 + \$2.49 + \$2.40 + \cdots$$

Although there is an infinite number of terms, each term is proportionately smaller than the preceding one as long as the dividend growth rate g is less than the discount rate r. Because the present value of far-distant dividends will be ever-closer to zero, the sum of all of these terms is finite despite the fact that an infinite number of dividends will be paid. The sum can be shown to equal

$$P_0 = \frac{DIV_1}{r-g}$$

constant-growth dividend discount model: Version of the dividend discount model in which dividends grow at a constant rate. Also called the Gordon growth model.

This equation is called the **constant-growth dividend discount model** or the *Gordon growth model* after Myron Gordon, who did much to popularize it.

Notice that the first dividend, DIV_1, is assumed to come at the end of the first period and is discounted for a full period. If there's an immediate dividend DIV_0, we have to add it in:

$$\text{Including immediate dividend: } P_0 = DIV_0 + \frac{DIV_1}{r-g}$$

We could also base DIV_1 on the immediate dividend adjusted for a year's growth: $DIV_1 = DIV_0(1+g)$, so

$$\text{Including immediate dividend: } P_0 = DIV_0 + \frac{DIV_0(1+g)}{r-g}$$

If DIV_0 has already been paid out, we obviously can't include its value in the stock price. However, we could still observe what it was and write

$$P_0 = \frac{DIV_1}{r-g} = \frac{DIV_0(1+g)}{r-g}$$

● EXAMPLE 5.3 Blue Skies Valued by the Constant-Growth Model

Let's apply the constant-growth model to Blue Skies. Assume a dividend has just been paid. The next dividend, to be paid in a year, is forecast at $DIV_1 = \$3$, the growth rate of dividends is $g = 8$ percent, and the discount rate is $r = 12$ percent. Therefore, we solve for the stock value as

$$P_0 = \frac{DIV_1}{r-g} = \frac{\$3}{.12 - .08} = \$75$$

The constant-growth formula is close to the formula for the present value of a perpetuity. Suppose you forecast no growth in dividends ($g = 0$). Then the dividend stream is a simple perpetuity, and the valuation formula is $P_0 = DIV_1/r$. This is precisely the formula you used in Self-Test 5.6 to value Moonshine, a no-growth common stock.

The constant-growth model generalizes the perpetuity formula to allow for constant growth in dividends. Notice that as g increases, the stock price also rises.

However, the constant-growth formula is valid only when g is less than r. If some-one forecasts perpetual dividend growth at a rate greater than investors' required return r, then two things happen:

1. The formula explodes. It gives nutty answers. (Try a numerical example.)
2. You know the forecast is wrong, because far-distant dividends would have incredibly high present values. (Again, try a numerical example. Calculate the present value of a dividend paid after 100 years, assuming $DIV_1 = \$3$, $r = .12$, but $g = .20$.)

....

Estimating Expected Rates of Return

We argued in Chapter 4 that fairly priced bonds will earn expected rates of return equal to those available on competitive investments. In this chapter we argued that the same property should be true of stock prices. But how do you figure out what that expected rate of return is?

It's not easy. Consensus estimates of future dividends, stock prices, or overall rates of return are not published in *The Financial Post* or reported by TV news-casters. Economists argue about which statistical models give the best estimates. There are nevertheless some useful rules of thumb that can give sensible numbers.

One rule of thumb is based on the constant-growth dividend discount model. Remember that it forecasts a constant growth rate g in both future dividends and stock prices. That means forecast capital gains equal g percent per year.

We can calculate the expected rate of return by rearranging the constant-growth formula as

$$r = \frac{DIV_1}{P_0} + g$$

$$= \text{dividend yield} + \text{growth rate}$$

For Blue Skies, the expected first-year dividend is \$3 and the growth rate 8 percent. With an initial stock price of \$75, the expected rate of return is

$$r = \frac{DIV_1}{P_0} + g$$

$$= \frac{\$3}{\$75} + .08$$

$$= .04 + .08 = .12, \text{ or } 12\%$$

Suppose we found another stock with the same risk as Blue Skies. It ought to offer the same expected rate of return even if its immediate dividend or expected growth rate is very different. The required rate of return is not the unique property of Blue Skies or any other company; it is set in the worldwide market for common stocks. Blue Skies cannot change its value of r by paying higher or lower dividends or by growing faster or slower, unless these changes also affect the risk of the stock. When we use the rule of thumb formula

$$r = \frac{DIV_1}{P_0} + g$$

we are *not* saying that r, the expected rate of return, is *determined* by DIV_1 or g. It is determined by the rate of return offered by other equally risky stocks. That return determines how much investors are willing to pay today for Blue Skies' forecast future dividends:

$$\frac{DIV_1}{P_0} + g = r = \begin{array}{l} \text{expected rate of return offered} \\ \text{by other, equally risky stocks} \end{array}$$

Given DIV_1 and g, investors set the stock price

so that Blue Skies offers an adequate expected rate of return r

● **EXAMPLE 5.4   Blue Skies Gets a Windfall**

Blue Skies has won a lawsuit against its archrival, Nasty Manufacturing. The award amounts to $5 per share, which Blue Skies decides to pay out as an immediate one-time special dividend. Will this change r, the expected *future* rate of return to investors? No, the stock price will go up by $5, to $P_0 = \$80$, as soon as investors hear of the award, and it will fall again to $75 right after the dividend is paid. The expected future rate of return stays at $r = 12$ percent.

Suppose the lawsuit does not generate a cash award for Blue Skies, but instead forces Nasty Manufacturing to withdraw as a competitor in a key market. As a result Blue Skies is able to generate 9 percent per year future growth without sacrificing immediate dividends. Will that increase r, the expected rate of return?

This is very good news for Blue Skies stockholders. The stock price will jump to

$$P_0 = \frac{DIV_1}{r - g} = \frac{\$3}{.12 - .09} = \$100$$

But at the new price Blue Skies will offer the same 12 percent return:

$$r = \frac{DIV_1}{P_0} + g$$

$$= \frac{\$3}{\$100} + .09 = .12, \text{ or } 12\%$$

SELF-TEST 5.7

Androscoggin Copper can grow at 5 percent per year for the indefinite future. It's selling at $100 and next year's dividend is $5.00. What is the expected rate of return from investing in Carrabasset Mining common stock? Carrabasset and Androscoggin shares are equally risky.

Few real companies grow in such a regular and convenient way as Blue Skies or Androscoggin Copper. Nevertheless, in some mature industries, growth is reasonably stable and the constant-growth model approximately valid. In such cases the model can be turned around to infer the rate of return expected by investors.

This procedure can be especially useful in public utility regulation. For example, one task of the Canadian Radio-television and Telecommunications Commission (CRTC) is to set prices for telephone services in a number of provinces. The price is supposed to provide the seller with a "reasonable" profit. But what is reasonable? The usual interpretation is that a fair profit should provide a rate of return on the company's investment in plant and equipment equal to the return required from investments with the same risk as the company's stock. Therefore, to determine the fair profit, CRTC must determine the return investors believe is appropriate for the risk of the stock. CRTC uses the turned around constant-growth model to help determine a benchmark r for the telephone companies that it regulates.

Many companies grow at rapid or irregular rates for several years before finally settling down. Obviously we can't use the constant-growth dividend discount model in such cases. However, we have already looked at an alternative approach. Set the *investment horizon* (year *H*) at the future year by which you expect the company's growth to settle down. Calculate the present value of dividends from now to the horizon year. Forecast the stock price in that year and discount it also to present value. Then add up to get the total present value of dividends plus the ending stock price. The formula is

$$P_0 = \underbrace{\frac{DIV_1}{1 + r} + \frac{DIV_2}{(1 + r)^2} + \ldots + \frac{DIV_H}{(1 + r)^H}}_{\text{PV of dividends from Year 1 to horizon}} + \underbrace{\frac{P_H}{(1 + r)^H}}_{\substack{\text{PV of stock} \\ \text{price at} \\ \text{horizon}}}$$

The stock price in the horizon year is often called *terminal value*.

● EXAMPLE 5.5 Estimating the Value of United Bird Seed's Stock

Ms. Dawn Chorus, founder and president of United Bird Seed, is wondering whether the company should make its first public sale of common stock and if so at what price.

The company's financial plan envisages rapid growth over the next 8 years but only moderate growth afterwards. Forecast earnings and dividends are as follows:

Year:	1	2	3	4	5	6	7	8	
Earnings per share	$10.24	12.80	16.00	20.00	25.00	27.50	30.25	31.75	
Dividends per share	$ 5.00	6.00	7.20	8.64	9.50	10.45	11.50	12.07	13.00.

Thus you have a forecast of the dividend stream for the next 8 years. The tricky part is to estimate the price in the horizon Year 8. Ms. Chorus could look at stock prices for mature pet food companies whose scale, risk, and growth prospects today roughly match those projected for United Bird Seed in Year 8. Suppose further that these companies tend to sell at price-earnings ratios of about 8. Then you could reasonably guess that the P/E ratio of United will likewise be 8. That implies

$$P_8 = 8 \times \$31.75 = \$254.$$

You are now in a position to determine the value of shares in United. If investors demand a return of $r = 10$ percent, then price today should be

$$P_0 = \text{PV(dividends from Years 1 to 8)} + \text{PV(forecast stock price in Year 8)}$$

$$\text{PV(dividends)} = \frac{\$5.00}{1.10} + \frac{\$6.00}{1.10^2} + \frac{\$7.20}{1.10^3} + \frac{\$8.64}{1.10^4} + \frac{\$9.50}{1.10^5}$$

$$+ \frac{\$10.45}{1.10^6} + \frac{\$11.50}{1.10^7} + \frac{\$12.07}{1.10^8} = \$44.15$$

$$\text{PV}(P_8) = \frac{\$254}{(1.10)^8} = \$118.49$$

$$P_0 = \$44.15 + \$118.49 = \$162.64$$

Thus price today should be about $160 per share.

United Bird Seed is looking forward to several years of very rapid growth, so you could not use the constant-growth formula to value United's stock today. But the formula may help you check your estimate of the terminal price in Year 8 when the company has settled down to a steady rate of growth. Suppose that from then on dividends are forecast to grow at a constant rate of $g = .05$ (5 percent). Thus the expected dividend in Year 9 is

$$DIV_9 = 1.05 \times DIV_8 = 1.05 \times \$12.07 = \$12.68$$

and the expected terminal price in Year 8 is

$$P_8 = \frac{DIV_9}{r - g} = \frac{\$12.68}{.10 - .05} = \$254$$

the same value we found when we used the P/E ratio to predict P_8. In this case our two approaches give the same estimate of P_8, though you shouldn't bet on that always being the case in practice.

SELF-TEST 5.8
• • • • • • • • • • • • • • •

Suppose that another stock market analyst predicts that United Bird Seed will not settle down to a constant 5 percent growth rate in dividends until after Year 9, and that dividends in Year 9 will be $13.00 per share. What is the fair price for the stock according to this analyst?

• •
Valuing a Business

Investors routinely buy and sell shares of common stock. Companies often buy and sell entire businesses. For example, when Loblaws agreed to sell its U.S. based National Tea Company to Schnuck Markets for $300 million, you can be sure that both companies burned a lot of midnight oil to make sure that the deal was fairly priced.

Could our formula for valuing a share of stock also be used to value National Tea? Sure, as long as you could forecast the dividends paid by National. It may seem odd to talk about the dividends paid by Loblaws' U.S. operations since that business had only one shareholder — Loblaws — which received all the division's profits and paid for all its new investments. But remember that dividends are simply the profits available for owners to spend after deducting profits that are plowed back into new investment. The dividends Loblaws received on its U.S. operations were therefore equal to National's *free cash flow*, that is, profits less the money reinvested. This was the amount of cash that the company took out of its operation each year.

To value National Tea, you would need to forecast the free cash flow that would be paid to the owner up to a horizon date together with the terminal value of the business. These could then be discounted back to today to give current value.

 ## 5.5 GROWTH STOCKS AND INCOME STOCKS

We often hear investors speak of *growth stocks* and *income stocks*. They seem to buy growth stocks primarily in the expectation of capital gains, and they are interested in the future growth of earnings rather than in next year's dividends. On the other hand, they buy income stocks principally for the cash dividends. Let us see whether these distinctions make sense.

Think back once more to Blue Skies. It is expected to pay a dividend next year of $3 ($DIV_1 = 3$), and this dividend is expected to grow at a steady rate of 8 percent a year ($g = .08$). If investors require a return of 12 percent ($r = .12$), then the price of Blue Skies should be $DIV_1/(r - g) = \$3/(.12 - .08) = \$75$.

Finance in Action

Wrongly Valuing a Business

The story of what Fortune *magazine called "the biggest looniest deal ever" illustrates both the difficulty and the importance of business valuation.*

In January, 1988, colourful Canadian real-estate entrepreneur Robert Campeau launched a takeover bid for the huge American retailing operation Federated Department Stores. Using what many consider to be extremely optimistic forcasts of the free cash flows that the target could generate, Campeau eventually paid $8.17 billion for Federated. In a carefully-worked analysis, Steven Kaplan* estimated that

Federated's real value at the time of Campeau's takeover bid was approximately $4.25 billion — about half of what Campeau paid.

Kaplan also estimated that decisions and business events that took place after the acquisition increased Federated's value by $1.6 billion. Unfortunately, the total value was still below what was owed to creditors, and Campeau went bankrupt during 1989.

*"Campeau's acquisition of Federated," published in the *Journal of Financial Economics* 25, no. 2 (December 1989).

---

payout ratio: Fraction of earnings paid out as dividends.

Suppose that Blue Skies' existing assets generate earnings per share of $5.00. It pays out 60 percent of these earnings as a dividend. This **payout ratio** results in a dividend of $.60 \times \$5.00 = \$3.00$. The remaining 40 percent of earnings, the **plowback ratio**, is retained by the firm and plowed back into new plant and equipment. On this new equity investment Blue Skies earns a return of 20 percent.

plowback ratio: Fraction of earnings retained by the firm.

If *all* of these earnings were plowed back into the firm, Blue Skies would grow at 20 percent per year. Because a portion of earnings is not reinvested in the firm, the growth rate will be less than 20 percent. The higher the fraction of earnings plowed back into the company, the higher the growth rate. So assets, earnings, and dividends all grow by

$$g = \text{return on equity} \times \text{plowback ratio}$$

$$= 20\% \times .40 = 8\%$$

What if Blue Skies did not plow back any of its earnings into new plant and equipment? In that case it would pay out all its earnings as dividends but would forgo any growth in dividends. So we could recalculate value with $\text{DIV}_1 = \$5.00$ and $g = 0$:

$$P_0 = \frac{\$5.00}{.12 - 0} = \$41.67$$

Thus if Blue Skies did not reinvest any of its earnings, its stock price would not be $75 but $41.67. The $41.67 represents the value of earnings from the assets that are already in place. The rest of the stock price ($75 − $41.67 = $33.33) is the net present value of the future investments that Blue Skies is expected to make. This is reflected in the market-value balance sheet, Table 5.5.

TABLE 5.5

MARKET-VALUE BALANCE SHEET FOR BLUE SKIES
(all quantities on a per-share basis)

Assets		Liabilities and Shareholders' Equity	
Assets in place	$41.67	Shareholders' equity	$75
Investment opportunities	33.33		

What if Blue Skies kept to its policy of reinvesting 40 percent of its profits but the forecast return on this new investment was only 12 percent? In that case the expected growth in dividends would also be lower:

$$g = \text{return on equity} \times \text{plowback ratio}$$

$$= 12\% \times .40 = 4.8\%$$

If we plug this new value for g into our valuation formula, we come up again with a value of $41.67 for Blue Skies stock:

$$P_0 = \frac{DIV_1}{r - g} = \frac{\$3.00}{.12 - .048} = \$41.67$$

Plowing earnings back into new investments may result in growth in earnings and dividends but it does not add to the current stock price if that money is expected to earn only the return that investors require. Plowing earnings back *does* add to value if investors believe that the reinvested earnings will earn a higher rate of return. (Remember that investors expected Blue Skies to earn 20 percent on its new investments, well above the 12 percent expected return necessary to attract investors.)

To repeat, if Blue Skies did not plow back earnings or if it earned only the return that investors required on the new investment, its stock price would be $41.67. The total value of Blue Skies stock is $75. Of this figure, $41.67 is the value of the assets already in place, and the remaining $33.33 is the present value of the superior returns on assets to be acquired in the future. The latter is called the **present value of growth opportunities**, or **PVGO**. It is the extra value that comes from the expectation that Blue Skies will be able to reinvest earnings to earn a higher return than investors require. What makes Blue Skies a growth stock is not that its earnings and dividends are expected to grow but that it has the opportunity to add to share value by reinvesting to earn a superior return.

By the way, growth rates calculated as

$$g = \text{return on equity} \times \text{plowback ratio}$$

are often referred to as **sustainable growth rates.**

present value of growth opportunities (PVGO): Net present value of a firm's future investments.

sustainable growth rate: Steady rate at which firm can grow; plowback ratio × return on equity.

SELF-TEST 5.9

Suppose that instead of plowing money back into lucrative ventures, Blue Skies' management is investing at an expected return on equity of 10 percent, which is below the return of 12 percent that investors could expect to get from comparable securities.
a. Find the sustainable growth rate of dividends and earnings in these circumstances. Assume a 60 percent payout ratio.
b. Find the new value of its investment opportunities. Explain why this value is negative despite the positive growth rate of earnings and dividends.
c. If you were a corporate raider, would Blue Skies be a good candidate for an attempted takeover?

The Price-Earnings Ratio

The superior prospects of Blue Skies are reflected in its price-earnings ratio. With a stock price of $75.00 and earnings of $5.00, the P/E ratio is $75/$5 = 15. If Blue Skies had no growth opportunities, its stock price would be only $41.67 and its P/E would be $41.67/$5 = 8.33. The P/E ratio, therefore, is an indicator of the prospects of the firm. To justify a high P/E, one must believe the firm is endowed with ample growth opportunities.

Turn the price-earnings ratio upside down and you get the earnings-price ratio. There is a relationship between this ratio and the return that investors require (r = .12). For Blue Skies the earnings-price ratio is $5/$75 = 0.67 — *lower* than the required return. However, if Blue Skies had no growth opportunities, the earnings-price ratio would be $5/$41.67 = .12, *exactly equal* to the required return. This is a general result. If PVGO = 0, then the required return equals the sustainable level of earnings per share divided by share price. If PVGO is positive, then the required return is higher than the earnings-price ratio.

What Do Earnings Mean?

Be careful when you look at price-earnings ratios. In our discussion, "expected future earnings" refers to average predicted cash flow less the true depreciation in the value of the assets. This is the amount a company could pay out if it did not reinvest earnings. But the earnings reported in the company's income statement are determined using arbitrary methods to measure the depreciation in the value of the firm's assets. A switch in the depreciation method that the company uses to calculate earnings can dramatically change the earnings that it reports without affecting the true profitability of the firm. Other accounting choices that can change reported earnings are the method for valuing inventories, the decision to treat research and development as a current expense rather than as an investment, and the way that tax liabilities are reported.

 SUMMARY

1. Firms that wish to raise new capital may either borrow money or bring new "partners" into the business by selling shares of common stock. Unlike the fixed interest payments that the firm promises to bondholders, the dividends that are paid to stockholders depend on the fortunes of the firm. That's why a company's common stock is riskier than its debt.

2. Large companies usually arrange for their stocks to be traded on a stock exchange.

3. Stockholders generally expect to receive (a) cash dividends and (b) capital gains or losses. The rate of return that they expect over the next year is defined as the expected dividend per share DIV_1 plus the expected increase in price $P_1 - P_0$ all divided by the price at the start of the year P_0:

$$\text{Expected return} = r = \frac{DIV_1 + P_1 - P_0}{P_0}$$

The return that investors expect on any one stock is also the return that they demand on all stocks subject to the same degree of risk.

4. The present value of a share is equal to the stream of expected dividends per share up to some horizon date plus the expected price at this date, all discounted at the return that investors require. If the horizon date is far away, we simply say that stock price equals the present value of all future dividends per share.

5. If dividends are expected to grow forever at a constant rate g, then the expected return on the stock is equal to the dividend yield (DIV_1/P_0) plus the expected rate of dividend growth. The value of the stock is equal to $P_0 = DIV_1/(r - g)$.

6. You can think of a share's value as the sum of two parts — the value of the assets in place and the value of the future opportunities for the firm to invest in high-return projects. The price-earnings (P/E) ratio reflects the market's assessment of the firm's growth opportunities. Firms with no growth opportunities should have a P/E ratio that is just the reciprocal of the return that investors demand, r. As growth opportunities become more important, the price-earnings ratio increases and the earnings-price ratio falls below r.

KEY TERMS

common stock	book value	payout ratio
primary market	liquidation value	plowback ratio
capital gain (loss)	market-value	present value of
secondary markets	balance sheet	growth opportunities
dividend	dividend discount model	(PVGO)
price-earnings (P/E)	constant-growth	sustainable growth rate
multiple	discount model	

SUGGESTED READINGS

There are a number of discussions of the valuation of common stocks in investment texts. We suggest:

> J.E. Hatch and M. J. Robinson. *Investment Management in Canada*, 2nd Edition, Toronto: Prentice-Hall, 1989.

> Z. Bodie, A. Kane, and A. J. Marcus. *Essentials of Investments*, 2nd ed. Homewood, Ill.: Richard D. Irwin, 1994.

> G. J. Alexander and W. F. Sharpe. *Fundamentals of Investments*. Englewood Cliffs, N.J.: Prentice-Hall, 1989.

A very readable classic work on equity valuation is:

> J. B. Williams. *The Theory of Investment Value*. Cambridge, Mass.: Harvard University Press, 1938.

PROBLEMS

1. Integrated Potato Chips paid a $1 per share dividend *yesterday*. You expect the dividend to grow steadily at a rate of 4 percent per year.
   a. What is the expected dividend in each of the next 3 years?
   b. If the discount rate for the stock is 12 percent, at what price will the stock sell?
   c. What is the expected stock price 3 years from now?
   d. If you buy the stock and plan to hold it for 3 years, what payments will you receive? What is the present value of those payments? Compare your answer to (b).

2. Grandiose Growth has a dividend growth rate of 20 percent. The discount rate is 10 percent. The end-of-year dividend will be $2 per share.

    a. What is the present value of the dividend to be paid in Year 1? Year 2? Year 3?

    b. Could anyone rationally expect this growth rate to continue indefinitely?

3. Gentleman Gym just paid its annual dividend of $2 per share, and it is widely expected that the dividend will increase by 5 percent per year indefinitely.

    a. What price should the stock sell at? The discount rate is 15 percent.

    b. How would your answer change if the discount rate were only 12 percent? Why does the answer change?

4. Arts and Crafts, Inc., will pay a dividend of $5 per share in 1 year. It sells at $50 a share, and firms in the same industry provide an expected rate of return of 14 percent. What must be the expected growth rate of the company's dividends?

5. A share of preferred stock sells for $80. If it pays a $4 dividend, what must be the discount rate?

6. BCE currently pays a dividend of about $2.72 per share and sells for $42.50 a share.

    a. If investors believe the growth rate of dividends is 4 percent per year, what rate of return do they expect to earn on the stock?

    b. If investors' required rate of return is 11 percent, what must be the growth rate they expect of the firm?

    c. If the sustainable growth rate is 5 percent, and the plowback ratio is .4, what must be the rate of return earned by the firm on its new investments?

7. You believe that the Non-stick Gum Factory will pay a dividend of $2 on its common stock next year. Thereafter, you expect dividends to grow at a rate of 4 percent a year in perpetuity. If you require a return of 12 percent on your investment, how much should you be prepared to pay for the stock?

8. Horse and Buggy Inc. is in a declining industry. Sales, earnings, and dividends are all shrinking at a rate of 10 percent per year.

    a. If $r = 15$ percent and $DIV_1 = \$3$, what is the value of a share?

    b. What price do you forecast for the stock next year?

    c. If you held the stock for one year, and then sold it, what rate of return would you receive?

    d. Can you distinguish between "bad stocks" and "bad companies"? Does the fact that the industry is declining mean that the stock is a bad buy?

9. You expect a share of stock to pay dividends of $1.00, $1.25, and $1.50 in each of the next 3 years. You believe the stock will sell for $20 at the end of the third year.

    a. What is the stock price if the discount rate for the stock is 10 percent?

    b. What is the dividend yield?

10. Computer Corp. reinvests 60 percent of its earnings in the firm. The stock sells for $50, and the next dividend will be $2.50 per share. The discount rate is 15 percent. What is the rate of return on the company's reinvested funds?

11. No-Growth Industries pays out all of its earnings as dividends. It will pay its next $4 per share dividend in a year. The discount rate is 10 percent.

    a. What is the price-earnings ratio of the company?

    b. What would the P/E ratio be if the discount rate were 12 percent?

12. A stock sells for $40. The next dividend will be $4 per share. If the rate of return earned on reinvested funds is 15 percent and the company reinvests 40 percent of earnings in the firm, what must be the discount rate?

13. Start-up Industries is a new firm, which has raised $100 million by selling shares of stock. Management plans to earn a 20 percent rate of return on equity, which is more than the 15 percent rate of return available on comparable-risk investments. Half of all earnings will be reinvested in the firm.
    a. What will be Start-up's ratio of market value to book value?
    b. How would that ratio change if the firm can earn only a 10 percent rate of return on its investments?

14. Stormy Weather has no attractive investment opportunities. Its return on equity equals the discount rate, which is 10 percent. Its expected earnings this year are $3 per share. Find the stock price, P/E ratio, and growth rate of dividends for plowback ratios of
    a. zero
    b. .30
    c. .80

15. Trend-line Inc. has been growing at a rate of 6 percent per year and is expected to continue to do so indefinitely. The next dividend is expected to be $5 per share.
    a. If the market expects a 10 percent rate of return on Trend-line, at what price must it be selling?
    b. If Trend-line's earnings per share will be $8, what part of Trend-line's value is due to assets in place, and what part to growth opportunities?

16. Castles in the Sand generates a rate of return of 20 percent on its investments and maintains a plowback ratio of .40. Its earnings this year will be $2 per share. Investors expect a 12 percent rate of return on the stock.
    a. Find the price and P/E ratio of the firm.
    b. What happens to the P/E ratio if the plowback ratio is reduced to .30? Why?
    c. Show that if plowback equals zero, the earnings-price ratio E/P falls to the expected rate of return on the stock.

17. Better Mousetraps has come out with an improved product, and the world is beating a path to its door. As a result, the firm projects growth of 20 percent per year for 4 years. By then, other firms will have copycat technology, competition will drive down profit margins, and the sustainable growth rate will fall to 5 percent. The most recent annual dividend was $DIV_0 =$ $1.00 per share.
    a. What are the expected values of DIV_1, DIV_2, DIV_3, and DIV_4?
    b. What is the expected stock price 4 years from now? The discount rate is 10 percent.
    c. What is the stock price today?
    d. Find the dividend yield, DIV_1/P_0.
    e. What will next year's stock price, P_1, be?
    f. What is the expected rate of return to an investor who buys the stock now and sells it in 1 year?

18. A company will pay a $1 per share dividend in 1 year. The dividend in 2 years will be $2 per share, and it is expected that dividends will grow at

5 percent per year thereafter. The expected rate of return on the stock is 12 percent.

   a. What is the current price of the stock?

   b. What is the expected price of the stock in a year?

   c. Show that the expected return, 12 percent, equals dividend yield plus capital gains yield.

19. Moose Jaw Industries has pulled off a miraculous recovery. Four years ago it was near bankruptcy. Today, it announced a $1 per share dividend to be paid a year from now, the first dividend since the crisis. Analysts expect dividends to increase by $1 a year for another 2 years. After the third year (in which dividends are $3 per share) dividend growth is expected to settle down to a more moderate long-term growth rate of 6 percent. If the firm's investors expect to earn a return of 14 percent on this stock, what must be its price?

20. Compost Science, Inc. (CSI), is in the business of converting Vancouver's sewage sludge into fertilizer. The business is not in itself very profitable. However, to induce CSI to remain in business, the Greater Vancouver Regional District (GVRD) has agreed to pay whatever amount is necessary to yield CSI a 10 percent return on investment. At the end of the year, CSI is expected to pay a $4 dividend. It has been reinvesting 40 percent of earnings and growing at 4 percent a year.

   a. Suppose CSI continues on this growth trend. What is the expected rate of return from purchasing the stock at $100?

   b. What part of the $100 price is attributable to the present value of growth opportunities?

   c. Now the GVRD announces a plan for CSI to treat Richmond's sewage. CSI's plant will therefore be expanded gradually over 5 years. This means that CSI will have to reinvest 80 percent of its earnings for 5 years. Starting in Year 6, however, it will again be able to pay out 60 percent of earnings. What will be CSI's stock price once this announcement is made and its consequences for CSI are known?

SOLUTIONS TO SELF-TEST QUESTIONS

5.1 Bank of Montreal's high and low prices over the past 52 weeks have been $30.75 and $22 per share. Its annual dividend was $1.32 per share and its dividend yield (annual dividend as a percentage of stock price) 5.3 percent. The ratio of stock price to earnings per share, the P/E ratio, is 8.3. Trading volume was 724,500 shares. The highest price at which the shares traded during the day was $25 1/8, the lowest price was $24 5/8, and the closing price was $25, which was $3/8 higher than the previous day's closing price.

5.2 IBM's forecast future profitability has fallen. Thus the value of future investment opportunities has fallen relative to the value of assets in place. This happens in all growth industries sooner or later, as competition increases and profitable new investment opportunities shrink.

5.3

$$P_0 = \frac{DIV_1 + P_1}{1 + r} = \frac{\$5 + \$105}{1.10} = \$100$$

5.4 Since dividends and share price grow at 5 percent,

$$\text{DIV}_2 = \$5 \times 1.05 = \$5.25, \quad \text{DIV}_3 = \$5 \times 1.05^2 = \$5.51$$

$$P_3 = \$100 \times 1.05^3 = \$115.76$$

$$P_0 = \frac{\text{DIV}_1}{1 + r} + \frac{\text{DIV}_2}{(1 + r)^2} + \frac{\text{DIV}_3 + P_3}{(1 + r)^3}$$

$$= \frac{\$5.00}{1.10} + \frac{\$5.25}{1.10^2} + \frac{\$5.51 + \$115.76}{1.10^3} = \$100$$

5.5 An investor holding the shares for only 1 year must sell to someone else at the start of Year 2. The stock price at that time will incorporate the present value of dividends in Year 2, and beyond. If the investor holding the shares in Year 2 wants to sell at the end of the year, the stock price he or she gets will capture the present value of dividends in Year 3 and beyond. The argument clearly repeats for investors in Years 3, 4, and so on. Thus stock price today equals the present value of all future dividends. Investors as a group get only dividends; one investor's capital gain is offset by the higher price paid by the next owner of the shares.

5.6

$$P_0 = \frac{\text{DIV}}{r} = \frac{\$25}{.20} = \$125$$

5.7 The two firms have equal risk, so we can use the data for Androscoggin to find the expected return on either stock:

$$r = \frac{\text{DIV}_1}{P_0} + g = \frac{\$5}{\$100} + .05 = .10, \text{ or } 10\%$$

5.8 We've already calculated the present value of dividends through Year 8 as $44.15. We can also forecast stock price in Year 9 as

$$P_9 = \frac{\$13(1.05)}{.10 - .05} = 273$$

$$P_0 = \text{PV(dividends through Year 8)} + \text{PV(DIV}_9\text{)} + \text{PV}(P_9)$$

$$= \$44.15 + \frac{\$13.00}{1.10^9} + \frac{\$273}{1.10^9}$$

$$= \$44.15 + \$5.51 + \$115.78 = \$165.44$$

5.9
a. The sustainable growth rate is

$$g = \text{return on equity} \times \text{plowback ratio}$$

$$= 10\% \times .40 = 4\%$$

b. First value the company. At a 60 percent payout ratio, $\text{DIV}_1 = \$3.00$ as before. Using the constant-growth model,

$$P_0 = \frac{\$3}{.12 - .04} = \$37.50$$

which is $4.17 per share less than the company's no-growth value of $41.67. In this example Blue Skies is throwing away $4.17 of potential value by investing in projects with unattractive rates of return.
c. Sure. A raider could take over the company and generate a profit of $4.17 per share just by halting all investments offering less than the 12 percent rate of return demanded by investors. This assumes the raider could buy the shares for $37.50.

CHAPTER SIX

Investment Criteria

The investment decision, also known as *capital budgeting*, is central to the success of the company. We have already seen that capital investments sometimes absorb substantial amounts of cash; they also have very long-term consequences. The assets you buy today may determine the business you are in many years hence.

For some investment projects "substantial" is an understatement. Consider the following examples:

- Production costs for the hit dinosaur movie *Jurassic Park* were about $60 million.
- The cost of bringing one new prescription drug to market was estimated at about $200 million in 1992.
- The development cost of Ford's "world car," the Mondeo, was about $6 billion.
- The future development cost of a super-jumbo jet airliner, seating 600 to 800 passengers, has been estimated at over $10 billion.
- Construction of the Channel Tunnel linking England and France cost about $15 billion from 1986 to 1994.

Some of these are "bet-the-company" projects — projects big enough and important enough that failure would cripple the companies undertaking them.

We begin our discussion of capital budgeting by looking at the criteria that companies use for selecting projects. Shareholders prefer to be rich rather than poor. Therefore, they want companies to invest in projects that make a net contribution to company value. Net present value measures each project's contribution to shareholder wealth.

Instead of calculating net present value, companies sometimes compare the expected rate of return from a project with the expected return that shareholders could earn on other equivalent-risk investments. The rate of return rule generally gives the same answers as net present value but, as we shall see, it has some pitfalls.

Other criteria — notably, payback and rate of return on book — are little better than rules of thumb. Although there is a place for rules of thumb in this world, an engineer will need something more accurate when designing a 100-storey building, and a financial manager needs more than a rule of thumb when making a substantial capital investment decision.

Notice from our examples of big capital projects that many projects require heavy investment in intangible assets. The costs of drug development are almost all research and testing, for example, and much of the development cost of Ford's Mondeo went into design and testing. Any program of cash outlays made in the hope of generating more cash later can be called a *capital investment project*, regardless of whether cash outlays go to tangible or intangible assets. As we recognized in Chapter 1, assets can be real even when they are not physical.

After studying this chapter you should be able to

- Calculate the net present value of an investment.
- Calculate the internal rate of return of a project and know what to look out for when using the internal rate of return rule.

● Show why the payback rule and book rate of return rule don't always increase shareholder wealth.

6.1 NET PRESENT VALUE

A Review of the Basics

capital budgeting decision: Choice of investment projects.

In Chapter 3 you learned how to evaluate a simple investment proposal — that is, how to make a **capital budgeting decision**. The proposal, you may remember, is to invest $350,000 now in the construction of an office block. You tackled the problem in four steps.

Step 1. Forecast the project cash flows. You estimate that you can sell the office block at the end of the year for $400,000. So if you go ahead with the project, you would be investing $350,000 now in the expectation of realizing $400,000 at the end of the year.

There is a negative cash flow of $350,000 in Year 0 ($C_0 = -\$350,000$) and a positive cash flow of $400,000 in Year 1 ($C_1 = +\$400,000$).

Step 2. Estimate the opportunity cost of capital. Suppose that the $400,000 payoff is a sure thing. That's great, because sure things in business are very rare. However, the office building is not the only way to obtain a sure-fire $400,000 a year from now. You could instead invest in a 1-year Canadian Treasury bill — that is, a 1-year loan to the Canadian government. Suppose T-bills offer an interest rate of 7 percent. By investing in the office building rather than the T-bill you are forgoing the chance to earn 7 percent on your capital. You are not actually losing the interest on the T-bill, but you are missing out on the chance of earning it. That is why the 7 percent rate is described as the **opportunity cost of capital** for investing in the project.

opportunity cost of capital: Expected rate of return given up by investing in a project.

In practice office blocks are not sure-fire investments. But the principle behind determining the opportunity cost of capital is the same. You need to determine the expected return that you would forgo by investing in the project rather than in an equally risky investment in the capital market. So when we use the term "the opportunity cost of capital" we mean an expected rate of return that includes an adjustment for taking on the risk of the project.

Step 3. Use the opportunity cost of capital to discount the future cash flows. To calculate the present value (PV) of the future payoff you need to discount the cash flow (C_1) by the opportunity cost of capital (r). For the office block

$$PV = \frac{C_1}{1 + r} = \frac{\$400,000}{1.07} = \$373,832$$

Investors are prepared to pay $373,832 for a government loan that produces a payoff of $400,000 ($373,832 \times 1.07 = 400,000$). So they would be prepared to pay you the same amount for an office block that gives a payoff of $400,000.

Step 4. Go ahead with the project if the present value of the payoff is greater than the investment. Your office block is worth $373,832 but you are not $373,832 better off. You committed $350,000, and therefore the **net present value (NPV)** is $23,832. Net present value is found by subtracting the required investment:

net present value (NPV): Present value of project cash flows minus initial investment.

$$NPV = PV - \text{required investment}$$

$$= \$373,832 - \$350,000 = \$23,832$$

In other words, your office development is worth more than it costs — it makes a *net* contribution to value.

The net present value *rule* states that managers increase shareholders' wealth by accepting all projects that are worth more than they cost. Therefore, they should accept all projects with a positive net present value.

SELF-TEST 6.1

Suppose that the opportunity cost of capital for your office project is 16 percent rather than 7 percent. Is the project still attractive? Explain why a higher discount rate can turn a previously attractive project into a loser.

Valuing Long-Lived Projects

The net present value rule works for projects of any length. For example, suppose that you have identified a possible tenant who would be prepared to rent your office block for 3 years at a fixed annual rent of $16,000. You forecast that after you have collected the third year's rent the building could be sold for $450,000. We will again assume that these cash flows are certain and that the opportunity cost of capital is 7 percent.

The revised cash flows are as follows:

Year	0	1	2	3
Cash flows	−$350,000	+$16,000	+$16,000	+$466,000

To find the present value of the office block, you discount the future cash flows at the 7 percent opportunity cost of capital r:

$$PV = \frac{C_1}{1 + r} + \frac{C_2}{(1 + r)^2} + \frac{C_3}{(1 + r)^3}$$

$$= \frac{\$16,000}{1.07} + \frac{\$16,000}{(1.07)^2} + \frac{\$466,000}{(1.07)^3} = \$409,323$$

The net present value of the revised project is NPV = $409,323 − $350,000 = $59,323. Constructing the office block and renting it for 3 years makes a greater addition to your wealth than selling the office block at the end of the first year.

Of course, rather than subtracting the initial investment from the project's present value, you could calculate NPV directly:

$$NPV = C_0 + \frac{C_1}{1 + r} + \frac{C_2}{(1 + r)^2} + \frac{C_3}{(1 + r)^3}$$

$$= -\$350,000 + \frac{\$16,000}{1.07} + \frac{\$16,000}{(1.07)^2} + \frac{\$466,000}{(1.07)^3} = \$59,323$$

Let's check that the owners of this project really are better off. Suppose you put up $350,000 of your own money, commit to build the office building, and sign a lease that will bring $16,000 a year for 3 years. Now you can cash in by selling the project to someone else.

Suppose you sell 1000 shares in the project. Each share represents a claim to 1/1000 of the future cash flows. Since the cash flows are sure things, and the interest rate offered by other sure things is 7 percent, investors will value the shares for

$$\text{Price per share} = P = \frac{\$16}{1.07} + \frac{\$16}{(1.07)^2} + \frac{\$466}{(1.07)^3} = \$40.93$$

Thus you can sell the project to outside investors for 1000 × $40.93 = $409,300, which, save for rounding, is exactly the present value we calculated earlier. Your net gain is

Net gain = $409,300 - $350,000 = +$59,300

which is the project's NPV. This equivalence should be no surprise, since the present value calculation is *designed* to calculate the value today of future cash flows to investors in the capital markets.

Notice that in principle there could be a different opportunity cost of capital for each period's cash flow. In that case we would discount C_1 by r_1, the discount rate for 1-year cash flows; C_2 would be discounted by r_2; and so on. Here we assume that the cost of capital is the same regardless of the date of the cash flow. We do this for one reason only — simplicity. But we are in good company: with only rare exceptions firms decide on an appropriate discount rate and then use it to discount all project cash flows.

● Example 6.1 Calculating NPV for a Long-Lived Project

The Weightsnatchers Company wants to drill a new well to obtain naturally carbonated diet water. The well will cost $14 million, and annual production, shipping, and marketing costs will be $500,000. Annual revenues of $2 million will last 15 years before the well clogs and has to be abandoned. Is the project worth pursuing? The cost of capital is 10 percent.

The annual net cash flow is $2,000,000 - $500,000 = $1,500,000. This is a 15-year annuity worth

$$PV \text{ (15-year annuity at 10\%)} = \$1,500,000 \times 7.606$$

$$= \$11,409,000$$

The net present value is

$$NPV = -\$14,000,000 + \$11,409,000 = -\$2,591,000$$

The project has a negative NPV of about $2.6 million. Undertaking it would reduce the value of Weightsnatchers by that amount.

SELF-TEST 6.2

Suppose Weightsnatchers drills the well anyway and sets up a separate company to bottle and market the well's diet water. The company issues 1 million shares. How much will each share sell for? Show that Weightsnatchers cashes in at a loss of $2.6 million when it sells shares in the new company to outside investors.

The first two steps in calculating NPVs — forecasting the cash flows and estimating the opportunity cost of capital — are tricky, and we will have a lot more to say about them in later chapters. But once you have assembled the data, the calculation of present value and net present value should be routine. Here is one more example.

● Example 6.2 Calculating Eurotunnel's NPV

One of the world's largest commercial investment projects is construction of the Channel Tunnel by the Anglo-French company Eurotunnel. Here is a chance to put yourself in the shoes of Eurotunnel's financial manager and find out whether the project looked like a good deal for shareholders. The figures in the column headed Cash Flow in Table 6.1 are based on the forecasts of construction costs and revenues that the company provided to investors in 1986.

The Channel Tunnel project was not a safe investment. Indeed the prospectus to the Channel Tunnel share issue cautioned investors that the project "involves significant risk and should be regarded at this stage as speculative. If for any reason the Project is abandoned or Eurotunnel is unable to raise the necessary finance, it is likely that equity investors will lose some or all of their money."

To induce them to invest in the project, investors needed a higher prospective rate of return than they could get on safe government bonds. Suppose investors expected a return of 13 percent from other investments that had a degree of risk similar to that of the Channel Tunnel. That was what investors were giving up when they provided the capital for the tunnel. To find the project's NPV we therefore discount the cash flows in Table 6.1 at 13 percent.

Don't be put off by the several years of negative cash flows in Table 6.1. To calculate NPV you just discount all the cash flows, positive and negative, at 13 percent and sum the results. Call 1986 Year 0, call 1987 Year 1, and so on. Then

$$NPV = C_0 + \frac{C_1}{1 + r} + \frac{C_2}{(1 + r)^2} + \cdots$$

$$= -£457 + \frac{-£476}{1.13} + \frac{-£497}{(1.13)^2} + \cdots = £251 \text{ million}$$

TABLE 6.1

Forecast cash flows and present values in 1986 for the Channel Tunnel. The investment apparently had a small positive NPV of £251 million (figures in millions of pounds).

Year	Cash Flow	PV at 13 Percent
1986	–£457	–£457
1987	– 476	– 421
1988	– 497	– 389
1989	– 522	– 362
1990	– 551	– 338
1991	– 584	– 317
1992	– 619	– 297
1993	211	90
1994	489	184
1995	455	152
1996	502	148
1997	530	138
1998	544	126
1999	636	130
2000	594	107
2001	689	110
2002	729	103
2003	796	100
2004	859	95
2005	923	90
2006	983	86
2007	1,050	81
2008	1,113	76
2009	1,177	71
2010	17,781	946
Total		+£251

NPV – total = +£251

Note: Cash flow for 2010 includes the value in 2010 of forecast cash flows in all subsequent years.
Source: Eurotunnel Equity II Prospectus, October 1986. Some of these figures involve guesswork because the prospectus reported accumulated construction costs including interest expenses.

Net present value of the cash flows is £251 million, making the tunnel a worthwhile project, though not by a wide margin, considering the planned investment of nearly £4 billion.[1]

Of course, NPV calculations are only as good as the underlying cash flow forecasts. The well-known Pentagon Law of Large Projects states that anything big takes longer and costs more than you're originally led to believe. As the law predicted, the tunnel has proved much more expensive to build than anticipated in 1986, and in mid-1993, when the ChannelTunnel should have been generating cash inflows, Eurotunnel announced that it would have to seek extra funds from investors to complete construction. Unless the revenues also turn out to be much higher than anticipated, the tunnel will prove with hindsight to be a negative-NPV venture.

6.2 THE RATE OF RETURN RULE

Think back to your initial proposal to build the office block. You are investing $350,000 to make $400,000. Your profit on the venture is therefore the final cash inflow, $C_1 = 400,000$, plus the initial cash flow, $C_0 = -\$350,000$, or $50,000.[2] The rate of return on your initial outlay is the profit as a proportion of the investment:

$$\text{Rate of return} = \frac{\text{profit}}{\text{investment}} = \frac{C_1 + C_0}{-C_0} = \frac{\$400,000 - \$350,000}{\$350,000}$$

$$= .1429, \text{ or about } 14.3\%$$

The alternative of investing in a government loan would provide a return of only 7 percent. Thus the return on your office building is higher than the opportunity cost of capital.[3]

This suggests that there are two rules for deciding whether to go ahead with an investment project:

1. *The NPV rule.* Invest in any project that has a positive NPV when its cash flows are discounted at the opportunity cost of capital.
2. *The rate of return rule.* Invest in any project offering a rate of return that is higher than the opportunity cost of capital.

Both rules set the same cutoff point. An investment that is on the knife edge with an NPV of zero will also have a rate of return that is equal to the cost of capital.

Suppose that the rate of interest on Treasury bills is not 7 percent but 14.3 percent. Since your office project also offers a return of 14.3 percent, the rate of return rule suggests that there is now nothing to choose between taking the project and leaving your money in Treasury bills.

The NPV rule also tells you that if the interest rate is 14.3 percent, the project is evenly balanced with an NPV of zero:

$$\text{NPV} = C_0 + \frac{C_1}{1 + r} = -\$350,000 + \frac{\$400,000}{1.143} = 0$$

---

[1] Instead of calculating NPV in one fell swoop, we could first calculate the present value of the income stream that begins in 1993 and then subtract the present value of the earlier construction costs from 1986 to 1992. The result is of course the same.

[2] Notice that the initial cash flow C_0 is negative. The investment in the project is therefore $-C_0 = -(-\$350,000)$, or $350,000.

[3] Recall that we are assuming the profit on the office building is risk-free. Therefore, the opportunity cost of capital is the rate of return on other risk-free investments.

The project would make you neither richer nor poorer; it is worth what it costs. Thus the NPV rule and the rate of return rule both give the same decision on accepting the project.

•••••••••••••••••••••••••
**A Closer Look
at the Rate of
Return Rule**

We know that if the office project's cash flows are discounted at a rate of 7 percent, the project has a net present value of $23,832. If they are discounted at a rate of 14.3 percent, it has an NPV of zero. In Figure 6.1 the project's NPV for a variety of discount rates is plotted. A graph of this sort is referred to as a *present value profile*. Notice two important things about Figure 6.1:

FIGURE 6.1
The value of the office project is lower when the discount rate is higher. The project has a positive NPV if the discount rate is less than 14.3 percent.

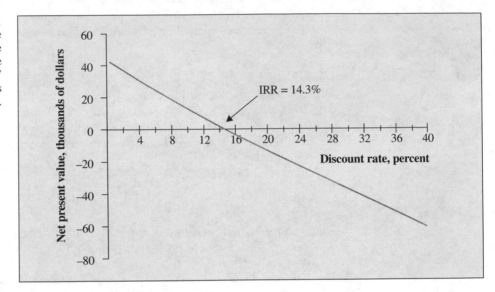

1. The project rate of return (in our example, 14.3 percent) is also the discount rate that would give the project a zero NPV. This gives us a useful definition: *the rate of return is the discount rate at which NPV equals zero*.[4]

2. If the opportunity cost of capital is less than the project rate of return, then the NPV of your project is positive. If the cost of capital is greater than the project rate of return, then NPV is negative. Thus the rate of return rule and the NPV rule are equivalent.

•••••••••••••••••••••••••
**Calculating the
Rate of Return for
Long-Lived Projects**

There is no ambiguity in calculating the rate of return for an investment that generates a single payoff after one period. Remember that C_0, the time 0 cash flow corresponding to the initial investment, is negative. Thus

$$\text{Rate of return} = \frac{\text{profit}}{\text{investment}} = \frac{C_1 + C_0}{-C_0}$$

But how do we calculate return when the project generates cash flows in several periods? Go back to the definition that we just introduced — *the project rate of return is also the discount rate that gives the project a zero NPV*. Managers usually refer to this figure as the project's **internal rate of return**, or **IRR**. It is also known as the *discounted cash flow (DCF) rate of return*.

**internal rate of return
(IRR):** Discount rate at
which project NPV = 0.

Let's calculate the IRR for the revised office project. If you rent out the office block for 3 years, the cash flows are as follows:

---

[4] Check it for yourself. If NPV = $C_0 + C_1/(1 + r) = 0$, then the rate of return = $(C_1 + C_0)/-C_0 = r$.

Year	0	1	2	3
Cash flows	−$350,000	+16,000	+16,000	+466,000

The IRR is the discount rate at which these cash flows would have zero NPV. Thus

$$NPV = -\$350,000 + \frac{\$16,000}{1 + IRR} + \frac{\$16,000}{(1 + IRR)^2} + \frac{\$466,000}{(1 + IRR)^3} = 0$$

There is no simple general method for solving this equation. You have to rely on a little trial and error. Let us arbitrarily try a zero discount rate. This gives an NPV of $148,000:

$$NPV = -\$350,000 + \frac{\$16,000}{1.0} + \frac{\$16,000}{(1.0)^2} + \frac{\$466,000}{(1.0)^3} = \$148,000$$

With a zero discount rate the NPV is positive. So the IRR must be greater than zero.

The next step might be to try a discount rate of 50 percent. In this case NPV is −$194,000:

$$NPV = -\$350,000 + \frac{\$16,000}{1.50} + \frac{\$16,000}{(1.50)^2} + \frac{\$466,000}{(1.50)^3} = -\$194,000$$

NPV is now negative. So the IRR must lie somewhere between zero and 50 percent. In Figure 6.2 we have plotted the net present values for a range of discount rates. You can see that a discount rate of 12.96 percent gives an NPV of zero. Therefore, the IRR is 12.96 percent. You can always find the IRR by plotting a graph like Figure 6.2, but it is quicker and more accurate to let a computer or specially programmed calculator do the trial and error for you.

FIGURE 6.2
The internal rate of return is the discount rate for which NPV equals zero.

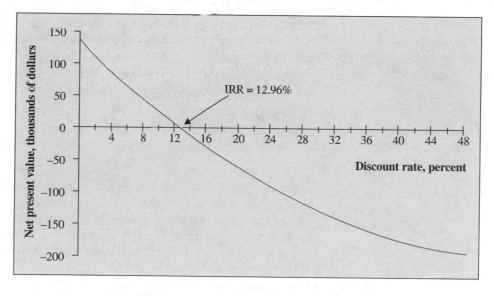

The rate of return rule tells you to accept a project if the rate of return exceeds the opportunity cost of capital. You can see from Figure 6.2 why this makes sense. As long as the opportunity cost of capital is less than the project's 12.96 percent IRR, the project has a positive NPV. If the opportunity cost of capital is higher than the 12.96 percent IRR, NPV is negative. Therefore, when we compare the project IRR with the opportunity cost of capital, we are effectively asking whether the project has a positive NPV. This was true for our one-period office project. It is also true for our three-period office project. In fact the rate of return rule will give the same answer as the NPV rule *as long as the NPV of a project declines smoothly as the discount rate increases.*

SELF-TEST 6.3

Suppose the cash flow in Year 3 is only $416,000. Redraw Figure 6.2. How would the IRR change?

A Word of Caution

Some people confuse the internal rate of return on a project with the opportunity cost of capital. Remember that the project IRR measures the profitability of the project. It is an *internal* rate of return in the sense that it depends only on the project's own cash flows. The return available in the capital market on equivalent risk investments — the opportunity cost of capital — is the standard for deciding whether to accept the project.

Pitfalls of the Rate of Return Rule

Many firms prefer to calculate the IRR rather than the net present value when deciding whether to go ahead with an investment. They seem to find it an easier shorthand to describe the profitability of an investment. A return of 30 percent when the opportunity cost of capital is 12 percent is clearly attractive. In contrast, an NPV of $1000 is not obviously large or small. If the initial investment is $500, such an NPV would be outstanding, whereas if the project requires an investment of $1 million, the project is barely viable, since a small percentage error in the cash-flow forecasts would put the project underwater.

While we understand why companies like to look at a project's rate of return, our advice is always to base the final decision on the project's net present value. The reason is that the IRR rule has a number of pitfalls. Here are some of the ways that it can lead you astray.

Pitfall 1: Lending or Borrowing? Remember our condition for the IRR rule to work: the project's NPV must fall as the discount rate increases. Now consider the following projects:

| Project | Cash Flows, Dollars | | IRR, % | NPV at 10% |
	C_0	C_1		
A	−100	+150	+50	+$36.4
B	+100	−150	+50	−$36.4

Each project has an IRR of 50 percent. In other words, if you discount the cash flows at 50 percent both of them would have zero NPV.

Does this mean that the two projects are equally attractive? Clearly not. In the case of A we are paying out $100 now and getting $150 back at the end of the year. That is better than any bank account. But what about B? Here we are getting paid $100 now but we have to pay out $150 at the end of the year. That is equivalent to borrowing money at 50 percent.

If someone asked you whether 50 percent was a good rate of interest, you could not answer unless you also knew whether that person was proposing to lend or borrow at that rate. Lending money at 50 percent is great (as long as the borrower does not flee the country), but borrowing at 50 percent is not usually a good deal (unless of course you plan to flee the country). When you lend money, you want a *high* rate of return; when you borrow, you want a *low* rate of return.

If you plot a graph like Figure 6.1 or 6.2 for project B, you will find that NPV increases as the discount rate increases. (*Try it!*) Obviously, the rate of return rule will not work in this case; you have to look for an IRR less than the opportunity cost of capital.

Project B is a fairly obvious trap, but if you want to make sure you don't fall into it, calculate the project's NPV. For example, suppose that the cost of capital is 10 percent. Then the NPV of project A is +$36.4 and the NPV of project B is −$36.4. The NPV rule correctly warns us away from a project that is equivalent to borrowing money at 50 percent.

Pitfall 2: Multiple Rates of Return. Here is a trickier problem. Project C costs $4000 and brings you in $25,000 in the first year. Then in Year 2 you have to pay out $25,000. There are many projects like this. For example, if you strip mine coal, you may incur substantial costs in reclaiming the land after the coal is mined. Similarly, a nuclear power plant is expensive to decommission when it has reached the end of its useful life.

| | **Cash Flows, Dollars** | | | | |
Project	C_0	C_1	C_2	IRR, %	NPV at 10%
C	−4,000	+25,000	−25,000	25 and 400	−$1,934

To find the IRR of project C, we have calculated the NPV for various discount rates and plotted the results in Figure 6.3. You can see that there are *two* discount rates at which NPV = 0. That is, *each* of the following statements holds:

$$\text{NPV} = -\$4000 + \frac{\$25,000}{1.25} - \frac{\$25,000}{(1.25)^2} = 0$$

and

$$\text{NPV} = -\$4000 + \frac{\$25,000}{1 + 4} - \frac{\$25,000}{(1 + 4)^2} = 0$$

In other words, the investment has an IRR of both 25 *and* 400 percent. The reason for this is the double change in the sign of the cash flows. There can be as many different internal rates of return as there are changes in the sign of the cash-flow stream.[5]

Is the project worth accepting? The simple IRR rule — accept if the IRR is greater than the cost of capital — won't help. For example, you can see from Figure 6.3 on page 136 that with a low cost of capital (less than 25 percent) the project has a negative NPV. It has a positive NPV only if the cost of capital is between 25 percent and 400 percent.

When there are multiple changes in the sign of the cash flows, the IRR rule does not work. But the NPV rule always does. The obvious solution is to calculate NPV.

Pitfall 3: Mutually Exclusive Projects. Firms are seldom faced with take-it-or-leave-it projects. Usually they need to choose between a number of alternatives. For example, an electric utility might build an oil-fired power plant or a coal-fired plant, but it will not build both. The two projects are therefore **mutually exclusive.**

Given a choice between two competing projects, you should accept the one that adds the most to shareholder wealth. This is the one with the higher NPV.

mutually exclusive projects: Two or more projects that cannot be pursued simultaneously.

---

[5] There may be fewer IRRs than the number of sign changes. You may even encounter projects for which there is no IRR. For example, there is no IRR for a project that has cash flows of +$1000 in Year 1, −$3000 in Year 2, and +$2500 in Year 3. If you don't believe us, try plotting NPV for different discount rates. Can such a project ever have a zero NPV?

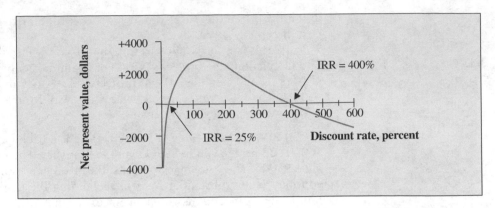

FIGURE 6.3
Project C has two internal rates of return. NPV = 0 when the discount rate is 25 percent and when it is 400 percent.

However, it won't necessarily be the project with the higher internal rate of return. So the IRR rule can lead you astray when choosing between projects.

Suppose that project E is a manually controlled machine and project F is the same tool with the addition of computer control. This computer control adds to the initial cost but increases efficiency and thereby improves the subsequent cash flow.

Project	Cash Flows, Dollars C_0	C_1	IRR, %	NPV at 10%
E	−10,000	+13,000	+30	+$1,818
F	−20,000	+25,000	+25	+$2,727

Both projects are good investments, offering a positive NPV. But F has the higher net present value and therefore is the better choice.

Unfortunately, project F's superiority doesn't show up as a higher rate of return. The IRR rule seems to say you should go for E because it has the higher IRR. If you follow the IRR rule, you have the satisfaction of earning a 30 percent rate of return; if you use NPV, you are $2727 richer.

Figure 6.4 shows why the IRR rule gives the wrong signal. The NPV's of the two projects are different for every discount rate except 20 percent, their "crossover" point. If the opportunity cost of capital is higher than 20 percent, project E is the superior investment. If the cost of capital is lower than 20 percent (we assume that it is 10 percent), then project F dominates. The higher IRR of project E has no bearing on the relative merits of the two projects.

You can salvage the IRR rule in these cases by looking at the IRR on the incremental cash flows. Here is how to do it. First, consider the smaller project (E in our example). It has an IRR of 30 percent, well in excess of the 10 percent cost of capital. You know therefore that project E is acceptable. Now consider the *extra* cash flows from adding on computer control. Project F requires an extra investment of $10,000 and produces an extra income of $12,000 in Year 1. So the rate of return on the additional investment is 20 percent, also well in excess of the 10 percent opportunity cost of capital. Not only is it worth buying the basic machine tool but it is worth the extra investment in computer control.

Whenever you are using the rate of return rule to choose between mutually exclusive projects (such as E and F), you need to calculate the IRR on the incremental cash flows.It is easy to do; it is also easy to forget.

Pitfall 3a: Mutually Exclusive Projects with Different Lives. We just compared mutually exclusive projects with different investment outlays, and we saw that the

FIGURE 6.4
Project E has a higher internal rate of return than Project F, but its NPV is lower if the discount rate is less than 20 percent.

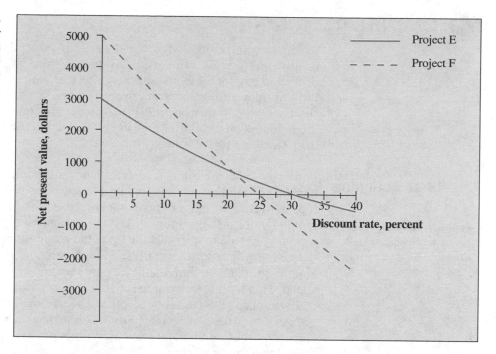

SELF-TEST 6.4

A rich, friendly, and probably slightly unbalanced benefactor offers you the choice of two opportunities:

- Invest $1000 today and quadruple your money — a 300 percent return — in 1 year with no risk.
- Invest $1 million for 1 year at a guaranteed 50 percent return.

You can't take both, so the choices are mutually exclusive. Which will you take? Do you want to earn a wonderful rate of return (300 percent) or do you want to be rich? By the way, if you really had the second investment opportunity, you'd have no trouble borrowing the money to undertake it.

IRR rule can mistakenly favour small projects with high percentage rates of return but low NPVs. A similar misranking also occurs when comparing short- and long-lived projects, even where the initial outlay is the same. The IRR rule can mistakenly favour quick payback projects with high percentage returns but low NPVs.

Remember, a high IRR is not an end in itself. You want projects that increase the value of the firm. Projects that earn a good rate of return for a long time often have higher NPVs than projects that offer high percentage rates of return but die in a year or two.

SELF-TEST 6.5

Your wacky benefactor now offers you the opportunity to invest $1 million in two mutually exclusive ways. The payoffs are

- $2 million after 1 year, a 100 percent return.
- $300,000 a year forever, a 30 percent rate of return.

Neither investment is risky, and safe securities are yielding 7.5 percent. Which investment will you take? Do you want to earn a high percentage return or do you want to be rich? (You're already well off, having made the right choice on Self-Test 6.4.)

6.3 CAPITAL RATIONING

A firm maximizes its shareholders' wealth by accepting every project that has a positive net present value. But this assumes that the firm can raise the funds needed to pay for these investments. This is usually a good assumption, particularly for major firms that can raise very large sums of money on fair terms and short notice. Why then does top management sometimes tell subordinates that capital is limited and that they may not exceed a specified amount of capital spending? There are two reasons.

Soft Rationing

capital rationing: Limit set on the amount of funds available for investment.

For many firms the limits on capital funds are "soft." By this we mean that the **capital rationing** is not imposed by investors. Instead the limits are imposed by top management. For example, suppose that you are an ambitious, upwardly mobile junior manager. You are keen to expand your part of the business and as a result you tend to overstate the investment opportunities. Rather than trying to determine which projects really are worthwhile, upper management may find it simpler to impose a limit on the amount that you and other junior managers can spend. This limit forces you to set your own priorities.

Even if capital is not rationed, other resources may be. For example, very rapid growth can place considerable strains on management and the organization. A somewhat rough-and-ready response to this problem is to ration the amount of capital that the firm spends.

Finance in Action

Capital Rationing Costs Jobs

While in theory soft capital rationing shouldn't reduce the value of a firm, sometimes in practice things don't seem to work out that way.

In the early 1980s, Lawson and Jones (L&J), an Ontario-based packaging manufacturer, found that approvals for capital spending were being delayed and denied by their corporate parent in the United Kingdom. While L&J had been founded in London, Ontario in 1882 as an independent Canadian firm, its owners had in 1953 "joined forces" with a British packaging firm. And so 75% of L&J's shares came to be owned by Mardon Packaging International, which decided from its head office in the U.K. how much the managers at L&J would have available to invest and which projects could go forward.

Larry Tapp, the then president of L&J, found the restrictions on investment hampered the ability of L&J management to properly operate the business. "Our competitors were putting in equipment that ran at twice or three times the speed of ours, and we were losing market share." Tapp told a class of business students during a discussion of the situation, "There were some fairly key areas where we could have gone in and gotten our margins up."

The capital restrictions had a definite effect on employment. When Tapp and his team determined that they

Capital Rationing Costs Jobs *(continued)*
••

could do a better job running the business without the interference of head office, they organized a successful takeover bid that gave them control over Mardon Packaging! As Tapp and his team began to manage the resul-

tant company, which they renamed The Lawson-Mardon Group, they made significant changes to operating and budgeting procedures. As a result, the services of some staff at the U.K. head office were no longer required.

Source: Based on case materials published in Mark C. Baetz and Paul W. Beamish, *Strategic Management* 3rd ed. (Illinois: Richard D. Irwin, Inc., 1994).

Hard Rationing

If properly implemented, soft rationing should not cost the firm anything. If the limits on investment become so tight that truly good projects are being passed up, then upper management should raise more money and relax the limits it has imposed on capital spending.

But what if there is "hard rationing," meaning that the firm actually cannot raise the money it needs? In that case, it may be forced to pass up positive-NPV projects.

With hard rationing you may still be interested in net present value, but you now need to select the package of projects that is within the company's resources and yet gives the highest net present value.

Let us illustrate. Suppose that the opportunity cost of capital is 10 percent, that the company has total resources of $20 million, and that it is presented with the following project proposals:

	Cash Flows, Millions of Dollars				
Project	C_0	C_1	C_2	PV at 10%	NPV
I	−3	+2.2	+2.42	$ 4	$1
J	−5	+2.2	+4.84	6	1
K	−7	+6.6	+4.84	10	3
L	−6	+3.3	+6.05	8	2
M	−4	+1.1	+4.84	5	1

All five projects have a positive NPV. Therefore, if there were no shortage of capital, the firm would like to accept all five proposals. But with only $20 million available, the firm needs to find the package that gives the highest possible NPV within the budget.

The solution is to pick the projects that give the highest present value *per dollar of investment*. The ratio of a present value to initial investment is known as the **profitability index**.[6]

profitability index: Ratio of present value to initial investment.

$$\text{Profitability index} = \frac{\text{Present value}}{\text{Initial investment}}$$

---

[6] Sometimes the profitability index is defined as the ratio of net present value to required investment. By this definition, all the profitability indexes calculated below are reduced by 1.0. For example, project I's index would be NPV/investment = 1/3 = .33. Note that project rankings under either definition are identical.

For our five projects the profitability index is calculated as follows:

Project	PV	Investment	Profitability Index
I	$ 4	$3	4/3 = 1.33
J	6	5	6/5 = 1.20
K	10	7	10/7 = 1.43
L	8	6	8/6 = 1.33
M	5	4	5/4 = 1.25

Project K offers the highest ratio of present value to investment (1.43) and therefore K is picked first. Next come projects I and L, which tie with a ratio of 1.33, and after them comes M. These four projects exactly use up the $20 million budget. Between them they offer shareholders the highest attainable gain in wealth.

Unfortunately, when capital is rationed in more than one period, or when personnel, production capacity, or other resources are rationed in addition to capital, it isn't always possible to get the NPV-maximizing package just by ranking projects on their profitability index. Tedious trial and error may be called for, or linear programming methods may be used.

SELF-TEST 6.6

Which projects should the firm accept if its capital budget is only $10 million?

Pitfalls of the Profitability Index

The profitability index is sometimes used to rank projects even when there is no soft or hard capital rationing. In this case it can generate the same kinds of mistaken rankings as the IRR rule: the unwary user may be led to favour small projects over larger projects with higher NPVs or short-lived projects over long-lived projects with higher NPVs.

The profitability index was designed to select the projects with the most bang per buck — the greatest NPV per dollar spent. That's the right objective when bucks are limited. When they are not, a bigger bang is always better than a smaller one, even when more bucks are spent. Self-Test 6.7 will serve as a numerical example.

SELF-TEST 6.7

Calculate the profitability indexes of the two pairs of mutually exclusive investments in Self-Tests 6.4 and 6.5. Use a 7.5 percent discount rate. Does the profitability index give the right ranking in each case?

6.4 OTHER INVESTMENT CRITERIA

Net present value, internal rate of return, and profitability index are all *discounted cash flow* methods of choosing between projects. Indeed the three rules are usually equivalent, though we have seen that the rate of return and profitability index rules have some pitfalls for the unwary.

The three rules are concerned with identifying those projects that make shareholders better off. They recognize that companies always have a choice: they can invest in a project or they can give the money back to shareholders and let them invest it for themselves in the capital market.

These days almost all large companies use discounted cash flow in some form, but sometimes they use it in combination with other theoretically inappropriate techniques. You should be aware of these techniques and of how they can get you into trouble.

Payback

payback period: Time until cash flows recover the initial investment of the project.

We suspect that you have often heard conversations that go something like this: "A washing machine costs about $400. But we are currently spending $3 a week, or around $150 a year, at the laundromat. So the washing machine should pay for itself in less than 3 years." You have just encountered the payback rule.

A project's **payback period** is the length of time before you recover your initial investment. For the washing machine the payback period was just under 3 years. The *payback rule* states that a project should be accepted if its payback period is less than a specified cutoff period. For example, if the cutoff period is 4 years, the washing machine makes the grade; if the cutoff is 2 years, it doesn't.

As a rough rule of thumb the payback rule may be adequate, but it is easy to see that it can lead to nonsensical decisions. For example, compare projects N and O. Project N has a 2-year payback and a large positive NPV. Project O also has a 2-year payback but a negative NPV. Project N is clearly superior, but the payback rule ranks both equally. This is because payback does not consider any cash flows that arrive after the payback period. A firm that uses the payback criterion with a cutoff of two or more years would accept both N and O despite the fact that only N would increase shareholder wealth.

Project	**Cash Flow, Dollars**				Payback Period, Years	NPV at 10%
	C_0	C_1	C_2	C_3		
N	−2,000	+1,000	+1,000	+10,000	2	$7,249
O	−2,000	+1,000	+1,000	0	2	−264
P	−2,000	0	+2,000	0	2	−347

A second problem with payback is that it gives equal weight to all cash flows arriving *before* the cutoff period, despite the fact that the more distant flows are less valuable. For example, look at project P. It also has a payback period of 2 years but it has an even lower NPV than project O. Why? Because its cash flows arrive later within the payback period.

To use the payback rule a firm has to decide on an appropriate cutoff period. If it uses the same cutoff regardless of project life, it will tend to accept too many short-lived projects and reject too many long-lived ones. The payback rule will bias the firm against accepting long-term projects because cash flows that arrive after the payback period are ignored.

Earlier in the chapter we evaluated the Channel Tunnel project. Large construction projects of this kind inevitably have long payback periods. The cash flows that we presented in Table 6.1 implied a payback period of just over 14 years. But most firms that employ the payback rule use a much shorter cutoff period than this. If they used the payback rule mechanically, long-lived projects like the Channel Tunnel wouldn't have a chance.

The primary attraction of the payback criterion is its simplicity. But remember that the hard part of project evaluation is forecasting the cash flows, not doing the arithmetic. Today's spreadsheets make discounting a trivial exercise. Therefore, the payback rule saves you only the easy part of the analysis.[7]

We have had little good to say about payback. So why do many large companies continue to use it? Senior managers don't truly believe that all cash flows after the payback period are irrelevant. It seems more likely (and more charitable to those managers) that payback survives because the deficiencies are relatively unimportant or because there are some offsetting benefits. Thus managers may point out that payback is the simplest way to *communicate* an idea of project desirability. Investment decisions require discussion and negotiation between people from all parts of the firm and it is important to have a measure that everyone can understand.

In practice payback is most commonly used when the capital investment is small or when the merits of the project are so obvious that more formal analysis is unnecessary. For example, if a project is expected to produce constant cash flows for 10 years and the payback period is only 2 years, the project in all likelihood has a positive NPV.

SELF-TEST 6.8
• • • • • • • • • • • • • •

A project costs $5000 and will generate cash flows of $55 per month for 20 years. What is the payback period? If the interest rate is .5 percent per month, what is the project NPV? Should the project be accepted?

• • • • • • • • • • • • • • • • • •

Book Rate of Return

book rate of return: Average income divided by average book value over project life. Also called accounting rate of return.

In addition to calculating a project's internal rate of return, some companies also consider its **book rate of return** (also called the *accounting rate of return*).

Any rate of return measures income as a proportion of the money invested. In the case of book rate of return, *income* and *money invested* are taken from the company's financial statements. Thus a project's average book rate of return is defined as

$$\text{Average book rate of return} = \frac{\text{average annual income}}{\text{average annual book assets}}$$

Here's an example. A company invests $60,000 in project Q and depreciates this investment straight-line over 3 years.[8] Thus each year depreciation is $60,000/3 = $20,000. The book value of the asset starts at $60,000 and runs down to zero over 3 years. So average book assets are $30,000:

---

[7] Sometimes managers calculate the *discounted payback period*. This is the number of periods before the present value of prospective cash flows equals or exceeds the initial investment. Therefore, this rule asks, "How long must the project last in order to offer a positive net present value?" This surmounts the objection that equal weight is given to all cash flows before the cutoff date. However, the discounted payback rule still takes no account of any cash flows after the cutoff date.

The discounted payback does offer one important advantage over the normal payback criterion. If a project meets a discounted payback cutoff, it must have a positive NPV, because the cash flows that accrue up to the discounted payback period are (by definition) just sufficient to provide a present value equal to the initial investment. Any cash flows that come after that date tip the balance and ensure positive NPV.

Despite this advantage, the discounted payback has little to recommend it. It still ignores all cash flows occurring after the arbitrary cutoff date and therefore will incorrectly reject some positive NPV opportunities. It is no easier to use than the NPV rule, because it requires determination of both project cash flows and an appropriate discount rate. The best that can be said about it is that it is a better criterion than the even more unsatisfactory ordinary payback rule.

[8] Straight-line depreciation means a constant proportion of the investment is depreciated each year over the accounting life.

Year:	0	1	2	3
Gross book value of asset	$60,000	$60,000	$60,000	$60,000
Cumulative depreciation	0	20,000	40,000	60,000
Net book value of asset	60,000	40,000	20,000	0

Average = $30,000

Table 6.2 shows projected income statements for project Q over its 3-year life, assuming for simplicity that there are no taxes. Average income over the life of the project is $10,000. Putting together the book assets and average forecast income gives

$$\text{Average book rate of return} = \frac{\$10,000}{\$30,000} = .33, \text{ or } 33\%$$

TABLE 6.2

Forecast income from asset Q

Year:	1	2	3
Revenues	$40,000	$60,000	$80,000
Expenses	20,000	30,000	40,000
Cash flow	20,000	30,000	40,000
Depreciation	20,000	20,000	20,000
Net income	0	$10,000	$20,000

Average = $10,000

If this figure is higher than the firm's cutoff rate of return, the rule tells the firm to go ahead with the project.

A return of 33.3 percent is higher than the book rate of return earned by most firms; it is also likely to be higher than the opportunity cost of capital. Notice, however, that the *IRR* for the project is only 20.6 percent, much lower than the return on book. It is quite possible that the return on book is higher than the cost of capital but the IRR is lower.

There are several problems with book rate of return. First, because it is based on *average* income, there is no allowance for the fact that immediate cash flows are more valuable than distant ones. In our example, cash flows rose from $20,000 in Year 1 to $40,000 in Year 3. Suppose instead that the cash-flow pattern was reversed, so that cash flow was $40,000 in Year 1 and $20,000 in Year 3. The IRR would be higher, but the average rate of return on book would be the same.

Second, the average rate of return on book is based on accounting data rather than the project's cash flows. We have already seen that cash flows and accounting income may be very different. For example, the accountant labels some cash outflows *capital investment* and others *operating expenses*. The operating expenses are deducted immediately from each year's income, while the capital investment is depreciated over a number of years. Thus the average rate of return on book depends on which items the accountant chooses to treat as capital investments and how rapidly they are depreciated.

Finally, a firm that uses average return on book must decide on a yardstick for judging a project. Sometimes the firm uses its current book rate of return as a cutoff. In this case companies with high rates of return on their existing business have high thresholds and may be led to reject good projects. Companies with low rates of return have low thresholds and may be led to accept bad projects.

SELF-TEST 6.9

Suppose the firm uses accelerated depreciation instead of straight-line.[9] The depreciation charges are now $30,000, $20,000, and $10,000 in Years 1, 2, and 3. What is the average book rate of return? Is the project any better or worse than before?

 **SUMMARY**

1. The net present value of a project measures the difference between its value and cost. NPV is therefore the amount that the project will add to shareholder wealth. A company maximizes shareholder wealth by accepting all projects that have a positive NPV.

2. Instead of asking whether projects have a positive NPV, many businesses prefer to ask whether they offer a higher return than shareholders could expect to get elsewhere by investing in the capital market. Return is usually defined as the discount rate that would result in a zero NPV. This is known as the internal rate of return, or IRR. There are some pitfalls in using the internal rate of return rule. Be careful about using the IRR when (a) the early cash flows are positive, (b) there is more than one change in the sign of the cash flows, or (c) you need to choose between two mutually exclusive projects.

3. The net present value rule and the rate of return rule both properly reflect the time value of money. But companies also use rules of thumb to judge projects. One is the payback rule, which states that a project is acceptable if you get your money back within a specified period. The payback rule takes no account of any cash flows that arrive after the payback period and fails to discount cash flows within the payback period.

4. Book (or accounting) rate of return is the average net income of a project divided by the average book value. It does not recognize that income received early in the project's life is more valuable than income received late.

KEY TERMS

capital budgeting
 decision
opportunity cost of
 capital
net present value
 (NPV)

internal rate of return
 (IRR)
mutually exclusive
 projects
capital rationing

profitability index
payback period
book rate of return
 (accounting rate
 of return)

SUGGESTED READINGS

An extensive discussion of various capital budgeting techniques may be found in:

   H. Bierman and S. Smidt. *The Capital Budgeting Decision*, 7th ed. New
      York: Macmillan, 1988.

---

[9] Accelerated depreciation means that depreciation charges are higher in early years rather than being distributed evenly over the accounting life of the project.

PROBLEMS

Problems 1–9 refer to two projects with the following cash flows:

Year	Project A	Project B
0	–$100	–$100
1	40	50
2	40	50
3	40	50
4	40	

1. If the opportunity cost of capital is 12 percent, which of these projects is worth pursuing?

2. Suppose that you can choose only one of these projects. Which would you choose? The discount rate is still 12 percent.

3. Which project would you choose if the opportunity cost of capital were 16 percent?

4. What are the internal rates of return on projects A and B?

5. In light of your answers to problems 2–4, is there any reason to believe that the project with the higher IRR is the better project?

6. If the opportunity cost of capital is 12 percent, what is the profitability index for each project? Does the profitability index rank the projects correctly?

7. What is the payback period of each project?

8. Considering your answers to problems 2, 3, and 7, is there any reason to believe that the project with the lower payback period is the better project?

9. Accountants have set up the following depreciation schedules for the two projects:

Year:	1	2	3	4
Project A	$25	$25	$25	$25
Project B	33.33	33.33	33.34	

Calculate each project's average book rate of return. Do these figures rank the projects correctly?

10. If you insulate your office for $1000, you will save $100 a year in heating expenses. These savings will last forever.
    a. What is the NPV of the investment when the cost of capital is 5 percent? 10 percent?
    b. What is the IRR of the investment?
    c. What is the payback period on this investment?

11. A project requires an initial investment of $10,000, and over its 5-year life it will generate annual cash revenues of $5000 and cash expenses of $2000. The firm will use straight-line depreciation on its investment, but it does not pay taxes.
    a. Find the average book rate of return on the project.
    b. What does the project add to or take away from the value of the firm's shares if the opportunity cost of capital is 8 percent?

c. What would happen to the book rate of return if half the initial $10,000 outlay were treated as an expense instead of a capital investment? *Hint*: Instead of depreciating all of the $10,000, treat $5000 as an expense in the first year.

d. Does NPV change as a result of the different accounting treatment proposed in (c)?

12. Consider projects E and F:

	Cash Flows, Dollars		
Project	C_0	C_1	C_2
E	−30,000	21,000	21,000
F	−50,000	33,000	33,000

Calculate IRRs for E and F. Which project does the IRR rule suggest is best? Calculate the NPV at 10% for each investment and for the incremental investment in F over E. Which project is really best?

13. You are a manager with an investment budget of $8 million. You may invest in the following projects. Investment and cash-flow figures are in millions of dollars.

Project	Discount Rate, %	Investment	Cash Flow	Project Life, Years
A	10	3	1	5
B	12	4	1	8
C	8	5	2	4
D	8	3	1.5	3
E	12	3	1	6

a. Why might these projects have different discount rates?
b. Which projects should the manager choose?
c. Which projects will be chosen if there is no capital rationing?

14. You have the chance to participate in a project that produces the following cash flows:

C_0	C_1	C_2
+$5000	+$4000	−$11,000

The internal rate of return is 13.6 percent. If the opportunity cost of capital is 10 percent, would you accept the offer?

15. A machine costs $8000 and is expected to produce profit before depreciation of $2500 in each of Years 1 and 2 and $3500 in each of Years 3 and 4. Assuming that the machine is depreciated at a constant rate of $2000 a year and that there are no taxes, what is the average return on book?

16. a. Calculate the net present value of the following project for discount rates of 0, 50, and 100 percent:

C_0	C_1	C_2
−$6750	+$4500	+$18,000

b. What is the IRR of the project?

17. Consider the following projects:

	Cash Flows, Dollars		
Project	C_0	C_1	C_2
A	−$1600	+$1200	+$1440
B	− 2100	+ 1440	+ 1728

   a. Calculate the profitability index for A and B assuming a 20 percent opportunity cost of capital.

   b. Use the profitability index rule to determine which project(s) you should accept (i) if you could undertake both and (ii) if you could undertake only one.

18. A project has a life of 10 years and a payback period of 10 years. What must be true of project NPV?

19. Consider these data on a proposed project:
     Original investment = $200
     Straight-line depreciation of $50 a year for 4 years
     Project life = 4 years

Year:	0	1	2	3	4
Book value	$200	___	___	___	___
Sales		100	110	120	130
Costs		30	35	40	45
Depreciation		___	___	___	___
Net income		___	___	___	___

   a. Fill in the blanks in the table.

   b. Find the book rate of return of this project.

   c. Find project NPV if the discount rate is 20 percent.

20. Here are the cash flow forecasts for two *mutually exclusive* projects:

	Cash Flow in Dollars	
Year	Project A	Project B
0	−$100	−$100
1	30	49
2	50	49
3	70	49

   a. Which project would you choose if the opportunity cost of capital is 1 percent?

   b. Which would you choose if the opportunity cost of capital is 12 percent?

   c. Why does your answer change?

21. Consider this project with an internal rate of return of 13.1 percent. Should you accept or reject the project if the discount rate is 12 percent?

Year	Cash Flow
0	+$100
1	−60
2	−60

22. **a.** What is the payback period on each of the following projects?

Project	Cash Flows, Dollars				
	Time: 0	1	2	3	4
A	−5000	+1000	+1000	+3000	0
B	−1000	0	+1000	+2000	+3000
C	−5000	+1000	+1000	+3000	+5000

b. Given that you wish to use the payback rule with a cutoff period of 2 years, which projects would you accept?

c. If you use a cutoff period of 3 years, which projects would you accept?

d. If the opportunity cost of capital is 10 percent, which projects have positive NPVs?

e. "Payback gives too much weight to cash flows that occur after the cutoff date." True or false?

SOLUTIONS TO SELF-TEST QUESTIONS

6.1   The project is not attractive. It has a negative NPV at a 16 percent discount rate:

$$\text{NPV} = \frac{\$400,000}{1.16} - \$350,000 = -\$5172$$

Investors with an opportunity to invest at 16 percent, rather than 7 percent, will place a lower value on a fixed future cash inflow.

6.2   The project generates a cash flow of $1.50 per share for 15 years. Then

Price per share = P = PV of a $1.50 annuity for 15 years at 10%

$$P = \$11.41$$

Thus 1 million shares could be sold for only $11.41 million. Weightsnatchers would absorb a loss of $14 million − $11.41 million = $2.59 million.

6.3   The IRR is now about 8.9 percent because

$$\text{NPV} = -\$350,000 + \frac{\$16,000}{1.089} + \frac{\$16,000}{(1.089)^2} + \frac{\$416,000}{(1.089)^3} = 0$$

Note in Figure 6.5 that NPV falls to zero as the discount rate reaches 8.9 percent.

6.4   You want to be rich. The second alternative generates greater value at any reasonable discount rate. For example, suppose other risk-free investments offer 8 percent. Then

$$\text{NPV} = -\$1000 + \frac{\$4000}{1.08} = +\$2703$$

$$\text{NPV} = -\$1,000,000 + \frac{\$1,500,000}{1.08} = +\$388,888$$

6.5   You want to be richer. The NPV of the long-lived investment is much larger.

Short: $\text{NPV} = -\$1 + \dfrac{\$2}{1.075} = +\$.860$ million

Long: NPV = $-\$1 + \dfrac{\$.3}{.075} = +\$3$ million

FIGURE 6.5
NPV falls to zero at an
interest rate of 8.9 percent.

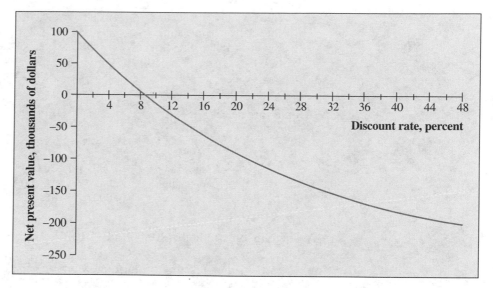

6.6 Rank each project in order of profitability index as in the following table:

Project	Profitability Index	Investment
K	1.43	$7
I	1.33	3
L	1.33	6
M	1.25	4
J	1.20	5

Starting from the top, we run out of funds after accepting projects K and I. While I and L have equal profitability indexes, project L could not be chosen because it would force total investment above the limit of $10 million.

6.7 The profitability index gives the wrong ranking for the first pair, correct ranking for the second:

Project	NPV	PV	Investment	Profitability Index (PV/investment)
Small	2,703	$ 3,703	$ 1,000	3.7
Large	388,888	1,388,888	1,000,000	1.39
Short	860,000	1,860,000	1,000,000	1.86
Long	3,000,000	4,000,000	1,000,000	4.0

6.8 The payback period is about 91 months or 7.6 years. Calculate NPV as follows. The present value of a $55 annuity for 240 months at .5 percent per month is

$$\text{PV annuity} = \$7677$$

$$\text{NPV} = -\$5000 + \$7677 = +\$2677$$

The project should be accepted.

6.9   Now book values are

Year:	0	1	2	3
Gross book value	$60,000	$60,000	$60,000	$60,000
Cumulative depreciation	0	30,000	50,000	60,000
Net book value	60,000	30,000	10,000	0

Average = $25,000

Income forecast is

Year:	1	2	3
Cash flow	$20,000	$30,000	$40,000
Depreciation	30,000	20,000	10,000
Net income	–10,000	10,000	30,000

Average income remains $10,000.

$$\text{Average rate of return on book} = \frac{10,000}{25,000} = .4, \text{ or } 40\%$$

The project is no better or worse than before, since cash flows are the same.

CHAPTER SEVEN

Discounted Cash-Flow Analysis

We hope by now you are convinced that wise investment decisions are based on the net present value rule. In this chapter we will show how to apply that rule to practical investment problems. The first step is to decide what to discount. We know the answer in principle: discount cash flows. This is why capital budgeting is often referred to as *discounted cash flow,* or *DCF,* analysis. But useful forecasts of cash flows do not arrive on a silver platter. Often the financial manager has to make do with raw data supplied by specialists in product design, production, marketing, and so on, and must adjust such data before they are useful. In addition, most financial forecasts are prepared in accordance with accounting principles that do not necessarily recognize cash flows when they occur. These data must also be adjusted.

We start this chapter with a discussion of the principles governing the cash flows that are relevant for discounting. We then present an example designed to show how standard accounting information can be used to compute those cash flows and why cash flows and accounting income usually differ. Next we introduce more complex considerations that enter most real-world capital budgeting problems. Finally, we discuss how DCF analysis can be used when there are project interactions. These occur when a decision about one project cannot be separated from a decision about another. Project interactions can get a bit complicated. We will work through three important cases.

After studying this chapter you should be able to

- Identify the cash flows properly attributable to a proposed new project.
- Calculate the cash flows of a project from standard financial statements.
- Understand how the company's tax bill is affected by depreciation and how this affects project value.
- Analyze three common problems that involve project interactions: (a) when to postpone an investment expenditure, (b) how to choose between projects with unequal lives, and (c) when to replace equipment.

7.1 DISCOUNT CASH FLOWS, NOT PROFITS

Up to this point we have been concerned mainly with the mechanics of discounting and with the various methods of project appraisal. We have had almost nothing to say about the problem of *what* you should discount. The first and most important point is this: To calculate net present value you need to discount cash flows, *not* accounting profits.

We stressed the difference between cash flows and profits in Chapter 2. Here we stress it again. Income statements are intended to show how well the firm has performed. They do not track cash flows.

If the firm lays out a large amount of money on a big capital project, you would not conclude that the firm performed poorly that year, even though a lot of cash is going out the door. Therefore, the accountant does not immediately deduct the entire amount spent when calculating the year's income but instead depreciates the capital expenditure over several years.

That is fine for computing year-by-year profits, but it could get you into trouble when working out net present value. For example, suppose that you are analyzing an investment proposal. It costs $2000 and is expected to bring in a cash flow of $1500 in the first year and $500 in the second. You think that the opportunity cost of capital is 10 percent and so calculate the present value of the cash flows as follows:

$$PV = \frac{\$1500}{1.10} + \frac{\$500}{(1.10)^2} = \$1776.86$$

The project is worth less than it costs; it has a negative NPV:

$$NPV = \$1776.86 - \$2000 = -\$223.14$$

But now suppose that someone comes along and tells you that the project does not *really* cost $2000 today. Instead you should depreciate that $2000 over 2 years and deduct the depreciation from the cash flow to obtain accounting income:

	Year 1	Year 2
Cash inflow	+$1500	+$ 500
Less depreciation	– 1000	– 1000
Accounting income	+ 500	– 500

Thus an accountant would forecast income of $500 in Year 1 and an accounting loss of $500 in Year 2.

Suppose you were given this forecast income and loss and naively discounted them. Now NPV *looks* positive:

$$\text{Apparent NPV} = \frac{\$500}{1.10} + \frac{-\$500}{(1.10)^2} = \$41.32$$

Of course we know that this is nonsense. The project is obviously a loser; we are spending money today ($2000 cash outflow) and we are simply getting our money back ($1500 in Year 1 and $500 in Year 2). We are earning a zero return when we could get a 10 percent return by investing our money in the capital market.

The message of the example is this: When calculating NPV, recognize investment expenditures when they occur, not later when they show up as depreciation. Projects are financially attractive because of the cash they generate, either for distribution to shareholders or for reinvestment in the firm. Therefore, the focus of capital budgeting must be on cash flow, not profits.

Here is another example of the distinction between cash flow and accounting profits. Accountants try to show profit as it is earned, rather than when the company and the customer get around to paying their bills. For example, an income statement will recognize revenue when the sale is made, even if the bill is not paid for months. This practice also results in a difference between accounting profits and cash flow.

● **Example 7.1 Sales before Cash**

Reggie Hotspur, ace computer salesman, closed a $500,000 sale on December 15, just in time to count it toward his annual bonus. How did he do it? Well, for one thing he gave the customer 180 days to pay. The income statement will recognize Hotspur's sale in December, even though cash will not arrive until June. But a financial analyst tracking cash flows would concentrate on the latter event.

The accountant takes care of the timing difference by adding $500,000 to accounts receivable in December, then reducing accounts receivable when the money arrives in June. (The total of accounts receivable is just the sum of all cash due from customers.)

You can think of the increase in accounts receivable as an investment — it's effectively a 180-day loan to the customer — and a cash outflow. That investment is recovered when the customer pays. Thus financial analysts often find it convenient to calculate cash flow as follows:

December		June	
Sales	$500,000	Sales	0
Less investment in accounts receivable	−500,000	Plus recovery of accounts receivable	+$500,000
Cash flow	0	Cash flow	$500,000

Note that this procedure gives the correct cash flow of $500,000 in June.

SELF-TEST 7.1

A regional supermarket chain is deciding whether to install a tewgit machine in each of its stores. Each machine costs $250,000. Projected income per machine is as follows:

Year:	1	2	3	4	5
Sales	$250,000	$300,000	$300,000	$250,000	$250,000
Operating expenses	200,000	200,000	200,000	200,000	200,000
Depreciation	50,000	50,000	50,000	50,000	50,000
Accounting income	0	50,000	50,000	0	0

Why would the stores continue to operate a machine in Years 4 and 5 if it produces no profits? What are the cash flows from investing in a machine? Assume each tewgit machine is completely depreciated and has no salvage value at the end of its 5-year life.

It is not always easy to translate accounting data back into actual dollars. If you are in doubt about what is a cash flow, simply count the dollars coming in and take away the dollars going out.

 DISCOUNT *INCREMENTAL* CASH FLOWS

A project's present value depends on the *extra* cash flows that it produces. Forecast first the firm's cash flows if you go ahead with the project. Then forecast the cash flows if you *don't* accept the project. Take the difference and you have the extra (or *incremental*) cash flows produced by the project:

$$\frac{\text{Incremental}}{\text{cash flow}} = \frac{\text{cash flow}}{\text{with project}} - \frac{\text{cash flow}}{\text{without project}}$$

● **Example 7.2 A New Model for Honda**

One of Honda's successful models, the Accord, sells about 1.7 million a year and at a rough guess each additional car sold earns Honda about 200,000 yen. Suppose that Honda is considering a proposal to bring out a new model to replace the Accord. It estimates that it will sell 2 million of the new models a year and that it will earn 210,000 yen on each car sold.

Does this mean that the incremental cash flows from the project are 2 million × 210,000 yen = 420,000 million yen? Not at all. Our with-versus-without principle tells us to think about what the cash flows would be without the new model. If Honda goes ahead, it will earn revenues from the new model but will cease to produce the Accord; if it does not go ahead, it will continue to produce the Accord. The incremental cash flows are

Cash flow with project – cash flow without project
(produce new model)   (continue to produce Accord)

= 420,000 – 340,000
= 80,000 million yen

The trick in capital budgeting is to trace all the incremental flows from a proposed project. Here are some things to look out for.

Include All Incidental Effects

Honda's new model illustrates a common incidental effect. New products often damage sales of an existing product. Of course, companies frequently introduce new products anyway, usually because they believe that their existing product line is under threat from competition. If you don't go ahead with a new product, there is no guarantee that sales of the existing product line will continue at their present level. Sooner or later they probably will decline.

Sometimes a new project will *help* the firm's existing business. Suppose that you are the financial manager of an airline that is considering opening a new short-haul route from Medicine Hat to Calgary's International Airport. When considered in isolation, the new route may have a negative NPV. But once you allow for the additional business that the new route brings to your other traffic out of Calgary, it may be a very worthwhile investment.

Some capital investments have very long lives once all incidental effects are recognized. Consider the introduction of a new jet engine. Engine manufacturers often offer attractive pricing to achieve early sales, because once an engine is installed, 15 years' sales of replacement parts is almost assured. Also, since airlines prefer to reduce the number of different engines in their fleet, selling jet engines today improves sales tomorrow as well.

Later sales will generate further demands for replacement parts. Thus the string of incremental effects from the first sales of a new model engine can run out 20 years or more.

Forget Sunk Costs

Sunk costs are like spilled milk: they are past and irreversible outflows. Sunk costs will remain the same whether or not you accept the project. Unfortunately, managers often are influenced by sunk costs. For example, in 1971 Lockheed sought a federal guarantee for a bank loan to continue development of the Tristar airplane. Lockheed and its supporters argued that it would be foolish to abandon a project on which nearly $1 billion had already been spent. This was a poor argument, however, because the $1 billion was sunk. The relevant questions were how much more needed to be invested and whether the finished product warranted the *incremental* investment.

Lockheed's supporters were not the only ones to appeal to sunk costs. Some of its critics claimed that it would be foolish to continue with a project that offered no prospect of a satisfactory return on that $1 billion. This argument too was faulty. The $1 billion was gone, and the decision to continue with the project should have depended only on the return on the incremental investment.

Include Opportunity Costs

Resources are almost never free, even when no cash changes hands. For example, suppose a new manufacturing operation uses land that could otherwise be sold for $100,000. This resource is costly; by using the land you pass up the opportunity

opportunity cost: Benefit or cash flow forgone as a result of an action.

to sell it. There is no out-of-pocket cost but there is an **opportunity cost**, that is, the value of the forgone alternative use of the land.

This example prompts us to warn you against judging projects "before versus after" rather than "with versus without." A manager comparing before versus after might not assign any value to the land because the firm owns it both before and after:

Before	Take Project	After	Cash Flow, Before versus After
Firm owns land	———→	Firm still owns land	0

The proper comparison, with versus without, is as follows:

Before	Take Project	After	Cash Flow with Project
Firm owns land	———→	Firm still owns land	0
	Do Not Take Project	**After**	**Cash Flow, without Project**
	———→	Firm sells land for $100,000	$100,000

Comparing the cash flows with and without the project, we see that $100,000 is given up by undertaking the project. The original cost of purchasing the land is irrelevant — that cost is sunk. The opportunity cost equals the cash that could be realized from selling the land now.

When the resource can be freely traded, its opportunity cost is simply the market price.[1] However, sometimes opportunity costs are difficult to estimate. Suppose that you can go ahead with a project to develop Computer Nouveau, pulling your software team off their work on a new operating system that some existing customers are not-so-patiently awaiting. The exact cost of infuriating those customers may be impossible to calculate, but you'd be wise to think twice about the opportunity cost of moving the software team to Computer Nouveau.

Remember Working Capital

net working capital: Current assets minus current liabilities.

Net working capital (often referred to simply as *working capital*) is the difference between a company's short-term assets and liabilities. The principal short-term assets are cash, accounts receivable (customers' unpaid bills), and inventories of raw materials and finished goods. The principal short-term liabilities are accounts payable (bills that *you* have not paid), notes payable, and accruals (liabilities for items such as wages or taxes that have recently been incurred but have not yet been paid).

Most projects entail an additional investment in working capital. For example, before you can start production, you need to invest in inventories of raw materials. Then, when you deliver the finished product, customers may be slow to pay and accounts receivable will increase. (Remember Reggie Hotspur's computer sale, described in Example 7.1. It required a $500,000, six-month investment in accounts receivable.) Next year, as business builds up, you may need a larger stock of raw materials and you may have even more unpaid bills. These investments

---

[1] If the value of the land to the firm were less than the market price, the firm would sell it. On the other hand, the opportunity cost of using land in a particular project cannot exceed the cost of buying an equivalent parcel to replace it.

in working capital, just like investments in plant and equipment, result in a cash outflow.[2]

We find that working capital is one of the most common sources of confusion in forecasting project cash flows. Here are the most common mistakes:

1. *Forgetting about working capital entirely.* We hope that you never fall into that trap.

2. *Forgetting that working capital may change during the life of the project.* Imagine that you sell $100,000 of goods per year and customers pay on average 6 months late. You will therefore have $50,000 of unpaid bills. Now you increase prices by 10 percent, so that revenues increase to $110,000. If customers continue to pay 6 months late, unpaid bills increase to $55,000, and therefore you need to make an *additional* investment in working capital of $5000.

3. *Forgetting that working capital is recovered at the end of the project.* When the project comes to an end, inventories are run down, any unpaid bills are (you hope) paid off, and you can recover your investment in working capital. This generates a cash *inflow*.

Beware of Allocated Overhead Costs

We have already mentioned that the accountant's objective in gathering data is not always the same as the investment analyst's. A case in point is the allocation of overhead costs such as rent, heat, or electricity. These overhead costs may not be related to a particular project, but they must be paid for nevertheless. Therefore, when the accountant assigns costs to the firm's projects, a charge for overhead is usually made. But our principle of incremental cash flows says that in investment appraisal we should include only the extra expenses that would result from the project. A project may generate extra overhead costs, but then again, it may not. We should be cautious about assuming that the accountant's allocation of overhead costs represents the incremental costs that would be incurred by accepting the project.

SELF-TEST 7.2

A firm is considering an investment in a new manufacturing plant. The site already is owned by the company, but existing buildings would need to be demolished. Which of the following should be treated as incremental cash flows?
a. The market value of the site.
b. The market value of the existing buildings.
c. Demolition costs and site clearance.
d. The cost of a new access road put in last year.
e. Lost cash flows on other projects due to executive time spent on the new facility.
f. Future depreciation of the new plant.

7.3 DISCOUNT NOMINAL CASH FLOWS BY THE NOMINAL COST OF CAPITAL

The distinction between nominal and real cash flows and interest rates is crucial in capital budgeting. Interest rates are usually quoted in *nominal* terms. If you

---

[2] If you are not clear *why* working capital affects cash flow, look back to Chapter 2, where we gave a primer on working capital and a couple of simple examples.

invest $100 in a bank deposit offering 6 percent interest, then the bank promises to pay you $106 at the end of the year. It makes no promises about what that $106 will buy. The real rate of interest on the bank deposit depends on inflation. If inflation is 2 percent, that $106 will buy you only 4 percent more goods at the end of the year than your $100 could buy today. The *real* rate of interest is therefore about 4 percent.[3]

If the discount rate is nominal, consistency requires that cash flows be estimated in nominal terms as well, taking account of trends in selling price, labour and materials costs, and so on. This calls for more than simply applying a single assumed inflation rate to all components of cash flow. Some costs or prices increase faster than inflation, some slower. For example, perhaps you have entered into a 5-year fixed-price contract with a supplier. No matter what happens to inflation over this period, this part of your costs is fixed in nominal terms.

Of course, there is nothing wrong with discounting real cash flows at the real interest rate, although this is not commonly done. We saw in Chapter 4 that real cash flows discounted at the real discount rate give exactly the same present values as nominal cash flows discounted at the nominal rate.

It should go without saying that you cannot mix and match real and nominal quantities: discounting real cash flows at a nominal interest rate is a big mistake. While it may seem like an obvious point, analysts sometimes forget to account for the effects of inflation when forecasting future cash flows. As a result, they end up discounting real cash flows at a nominal interest rate. This can grossly understate project values.

SELF-TEST 7.3

> Nasty Industries is closing down an outmoded factory and throwing all of its workers out on the street. Nasty's CEO, Cruella deLuxe, is enraged to learn that she must continue to pay for workers' dental insurance for 4 years. The cost per worker next year will be $2400 per year, but the inflation rate is 4 percent, and dental costs have been increasing at three percentage points faster than inflation. What is the present value of this obligation? The (nominal) discount rate is 10 percent.

7.4 SEPARATE INVESTMENT AND FINANCING DECISIONS

When we calculate the cash flows from a project, we ignore how that project is financed. The company may decide to finance partly by debt but, even if it did, we would neither subtract the debt proceeds from the required investment nor recognize the interest and principal payments as cash outflows. Regardless of the actual financing, we should view the project as if it were all equity-financed, treating all cash outflows required for the project as coming from stockholders and all cash inflows as going to them.

---

[3] Remember from Chapter 4,

$$\text{Real rate of interest} \approx \text{nominal rate of interest} - \text{inflation rate}$$

The exact formula is

$$1 + \text{real rate of interest} = \frac{1 + \text{nominal rate of interest}}{1 + \text{inflation rate}}$$

$$= \frac{1.06}{1.02} = 1.0392$$

Therefore, the real interest rate is .039, or 3.9 percent.

The reason we do this is to separate the analysis of the investment decision from the financing decision. We first measure the project's present value. Then we can undertake a separate analysis of the financing decision. We discuss financing decisions later in the book.

 ## 7.5 CORPORATE TAXES IN CANADA AND THE CAPITAL BUDGETING DECISION

Businesses have many dealings with governments. They pay out money in the form of income taxes, property taxes, licence fees, and stumpage charges, and in return they get services, grants, and subsidies. Usually, the most important of these cash flows are the corporate income taxes. We don't want to describe these taxes in great detail but it is important that you understand the basics of how they are calculated and, in particular, how they enter the capital budgeting decision.

As we mentioned in Chapter 2, corporate income tax is paid to both the federal and the provincial government. While each province sets its own tax laws, they are generally similar to the federal law,[4] so we will concentrate on the federal law.

We saw in Chapter 2 that the combined federal and provincial tax rate varies from province to province and is also affected by whether the firm is in manufacturing and processing or some other area. To illustrate the calculation of taxes, we will assume that the company pays a total of 36 percent of its taxable income to the federal and provincial government.

capital cost allowance: The depreciation charge against taxable income allowed by Revenue Canada.

When calculating taxable income, the firm is allowed to make a deduction for depreciation. In Canada the allowed deduction is called the **capital cost allowance** (or **CCA**). That is

$$\text{Taxable income} = \text{revenues} - \text{expenses} - \text{CCA}$$

$$\text{Tax} = .36 \times \text{taxable income}$$

Since CCA is taken after the initial investment is made, it is not a cash flow itself, though it does affect the cash flow by reducing the tax paid by $0.36 \times \text{CCA}$. This tax saving is sometimes called the **CCA tax shield** or **depreciation tax shield**.

CCA tax shield or depreciation tax shield: Reduction in taxes attributable to the capital cost allowance.

A gentle warning: CCA is not necessarily the same as the depreciation figure shown in the company's profit statement: Revenue Canada allows the company to keep one set of books for the tax collector and a different set for shareholders. Cash flows will be determined only by the CCA since CCA determines the company's tax bill. So if a number other than CCA is being reported, remember to check that it is not being used to determine the company's tax bill.

The Asset Class System

asset classes: Each depreciable asset is assigned to an asset class for tax purposes. The definition as well as the maximum allowable depreciation rate for each category is set by Revenue Canada.

A few assets, such as land and securities, cannot be depreciated at all. The others are divided by Revenue Canada into different CCA **asset classes,** and a different depreciation rate, referred to as the CCA rate, applies to each asset class. For instance, buildings acquired after 1987 fall into Class 1. A firm is allowed to take a CCA equal to 4 percent of the value of the balance of the asset Class 1. At the other extreme, chinaware and most computer software falls into asset Class 12, which has an allowance of 100 percent.

To illustrate how the asset class system works, suppose that you started a business by investing $10 million in a new factory. This would be a Class 1 asset

---

[4] The province of Quebec deviates most sharply from the federal tax law.

so at the end of the year you could claim CCA of 4 percent of the cost of the factory.[5]

$$CCA = 0.04 \times 10 = \$0.4 \text{ million.}$$

So you would reduce your taxable income in the first year by $0.4 million. You begin the next year with an undepreciated balance (known as the **undepreciated capital cost** or **UCC**) of $10 - 0.4 = 9.6$ million. In the second year you would be entitled to a CCA deduction of $0.04 \times 9.6 = .384$ and so on.

An important feature of the asset class system is that for tax purposes, all assets within a particular CCA class are depreciated as if they were a single asset. For example suppose that after the first year you acquired a second factory for $10 million. Your UCC for Class 1 would rise to $9.6 + 10 = 19.6$ and your CCA deduction for that year would be $0.04 \times 19.6 = .784$.

> **undepreciated capital cost (UCC):** The amount of an asset class that has not been depreciated for tax purposes.

A company is entitled to a CCA as long as it owns at least one asset in the asset class. The tax laws provide a complex set of rules that arise when an asset is sold. The procedure is as follows:

Disposition of Assets

A. When a depreciable asset is sold, the lower of the sale price or the initial cost is deducted from the undepreciated capital cost of its asset class.

B. If Step A leaves a negative balance, this amount is called **recaptured depreciation** and is added back to taxable income. The undepreciated capital cost of the asset class is then set to zero.

> **recaptured depreciation:** When the sale of an asset would result in an asset class with a negative balance, the amount of the negative balance is referred to as recaptured depreciation and is included in taxable income.

C. If Step A leaves a positive balance and *there are no other assets remaining* in the class, this remaining balance is called a **terminal loss** and is deducted from taxable income. Also, the undepreciated capital cost is then set to zero, so that the class ceases to generate CCA tax shields. But if Step A leaves a positive balance and *there are other assets remaining* in the asset class, this balance becomes the UCC of the class and it continues to generate CCA tax shields.

> **terminal loss:** When the last asset in an asset class is sold and the asset class has a positive balance, the balance is treated as a loss for tax purposes and referred to as a terminal loss. Recognizing a terminal loss will result in the UCC being set to zero.

D. When an asset is sold for more than its initial cost, the difference between the sale price and initial cost is called a **capital gain**.[6] Three-quarters of the capital gain is taxable and therefore is added to the year's taxable income.

> **capital gain:** The size of the gain that is realized when an asset is sold for more than it cost to purchase.

● Example 7.3

Suppose that you start a business by purchasing $10 million worth of machinery that falls into asset Class 8 and assume that you have other assets in this asset class. Asset Class 8 is eligible for a 20 percent CCA rate. After taking two years of CCA, the undepreciated capital cost of that machine is $6.4 million ($10 million minus $.2 \times \$10$ million minus $.2 \times \$8$ million). At that point you sell the machine for $12 million. Because the sale price is higher than the asset cost, the machine has appreciated in value, not depreciated. Thus the tax authorities calculate that you have taken $10 - \$6.4 = \$3.6$ million depreciation that did not reflect the economic depreciation. This $3.6 million is then "recaptured" and added to your income. In addition, you have also made a capital gain

---

[5] We are simplifying here. In fact, a firm is only allowed to include one-half of the purchase in the asset class in the year it is purchased and must then add the second half the following year. We ignore this complication in the body of the text but show you, in Appendix 7.1, how recognizing the so-called "half-year rule" changes our calculations. You will see that our simplification does not make much of a difference.
[6] Capital gains or losses also arise from the sale of non-depreciable assets such as land and financial securities. However, you never get a capital loss with a depreciable asset: Steps A, B, and C apply instead.

of $12 – $10 = $ 2 million. Three-quarters of this gain is taxable and is added to your taxable income.

Now, we have assumed that the machine is your only Class 8 asset. Suppose instead that there are other items in Class 8, and just before you dispose of the machine, Class 8 has a UCC greater than $10 million. Then there is no recaptured depreciation, but there is still the $2 million capital gain and a reduction of the UCC of Class 8 by $10 million.

SELF-TEST 7.4

Think again about Example 7.3. Suppose that instead of selling it for $12 million, the asset is sold for $4 million. What are the tax consequences of this transaction assuming first that the firm has no other assets in Asset Class 8 and then that it does?

Present Values of CCA Tax Shields

Our example illustrates a peculiar feature of the asset class system embodied in Canadian tax law: an asset can still generate CCA tax shields for the firm even after it is sold, provided there are other assets remaining in its class. Furthermore, since we are always deducting a fraction of the remaining UCC balance, the depreciation tax shield from a capital investment can have an infinite life. This means that to calculate the PV of a project requires that we compute the PV of a perpetual tax shield.

Suppose you start a new asset class by buying an asset. We'll use the following notation to describe the asset and your firm:

C = Capital cost of an asset acquired in year 0
d = CCA rate for the asset class to which the asset belongs
T_c = corporate tax rate
r = discount rate
UCC_t = undepreciated capital cost in year t after deducting CCA for the year.

For simplicity, we'll assume that you get your first CCA tax shield from the asset in Year 1.[7] The UCC of the class starts out at $\text{UCC}_0 = C$, so the CCA you get in Year 1 is $d \times \text{UCC}_0 = Cd$.

After deducting the CCA, the UCC for Year 1 becomes:

$$\text{UCC}_1 = \text{UCC}_0 - \text{CCA}$$

$$= C - Cd$$

$$= C(1 - d)$$

In example 7.3, C is $10 million, and d is 20 percent, so UCC_1 is $(1 - .2) \times 10 = $8 million. Similarly, the CCA taken for Year 2 is

$$d \times \text{UCC}_1 = Cd(1 - d),$$

which, for our example is

$$.2 \times \$8 \text{ million} = 8 \times .2 \times (1 - .2) = \$1.6 \text{ million}.$$

In year t, you will have taken $t - 1$ previous CCA tax shields, so the UCC at the start of the year is $\text{UCC}_{t-1} = C(1 - d)^{t-1}$. So, the CCA for the year t will be

$$d \times \text{UCC}_{t-1} = Cd(1 - d)^{t-1}.$$

---

[7] As noted earlier, this ignores the "half-year rule." See footnote 5.

If the asset class in example 7.3 stays open for 10 years, then the UCC balance in Year ten will be

$$10 \times .2 \times (1 - .2)^{10} = 214,748$$

So far all we have is an expression for the CCA for any particular year. But given the way CCA is computed, each asset in a declining balance class will generate a stream of CCA's that stretches forward hundreds of years and, in theory, will continue to the end of time! As a result, there is a similar number of tax savings. In order to figure out the value added to an investment project by the CCA we need to determine the present value of this infinite stream of tax savings. This amount can then be added to PV of the "after-tax" revenues and expenses to get the over-all PV of the project.

To illustrate this, let ATCF stand for the annual after-tax cash flow and Rev and Exp stand for revenues and expenses, respectively. Taxable operating cash prof-its are simply

$$\text{Taxable operating profits} = \text{Rev} - \text{Expense} - \text{CCA}$$

and after-tax profits are

$$\text{After-tax profits} = (1 - T_c) \times (\text{Rev} - \text{Expense} - \text{CCA})$$

To obtain ATCF we add back the CCA because it is a noncash expense. Then the ATCF equals after-tax revenues net of expenses plus the CCA tax shield:

$$\text{ATCF} = (1 - T_c) \times (\text{Rev} - \text{Exp} - \text{CCA}) + \text{CCA}$$

$$= (1 - T_c) \times (\text{Rev} - \text{Exp}) + (T_c \times \text{CCA})$$

Because present values are additive, the PV of the after-tax cash flows equals the PV of the after-tax revenues net of expenses plus the PV of the CCA tax shield:

$$\text{PV(ATCF)} = \text{PV}((1 - T_c) \times (\text{Rev} - \text{Exp})) + \text{PV}(T_c \times \text{CCA})$$

Let's see how to calculate the PV of the CCA tax shield. First, let's suppose you never sell the asset. The project generates the following CCA tax shields:

Year:	1	2	3	—	t	—
CCA tax shield	CdT_c	$CdT_c(1 - d)$	$CdT_c(1 - d)^2$	—	$CdT_c(1 - d)^{t-1}$	—

We can see that this forms a perpetuity that is growing (really declining) at the rate $-d$. The CCA tax shield is like the growing dividend we looked at in Section 5.4. And, similar to the stock value, the CCA tax shield has the follow-ing present value:

$$\text{PV of perpetual tax shield} = \frac{CdT_c}{(r + d)}$$

What happens if you sell the asset after using it for a few years? We use the same type of trick you saw in Section 3.4: we combine the present value of two declining perpetuities to calculate the present value of the declining annuity. Let's look at some examples that show how to combine tax principles and present value principles to get the PV of the tax shields. You can sharpen your understanding of these principles by doing some of the problems at the end of the chapter.

While going through these problems, remember that we always want to analyze the incremental cash flows created by the project in order to calculate its present value. In particular, we are looking for incremental changes in CCA and UCC that arise because of the purchase (or sale) of assets for the project.

● EXAMPLE 7.4

Suppose that you buy a metal stamping machine for C ($1 million) in Year 0 (CCA rate $d = 0.10$). You will sell the machine in Year 10 for S ($200,000), at which time you will still have other assets in the class and a UCC in excess of $200,000. Your tax rate is 36 percent and your discount rate is 15 percent. You want to know the present value of the incremental tax shields generated by the ownership and sale of the asset. Since you have other assets in the class and a UCC in excess of the sale price, you will have neither recaptured depreciation nor a terminal loss. The only tax effect of the sale of the asset will arise from the reduction of the UCC of Class 6 by $200,000 in Year 10. You have

$$\text{PV of CCA tax shields} = \begin{array}{c} \text{PV of perpetual tax} \\ \text{shield on \$1 million} \\ \text{in Year 0} \end{array} - \begin{array}{c} \text{PV of perpetual tax} \\ \text{shield on \$200,000} \\ \text{in Year 10} \end{array}$$

$$= \frac{CdT_c}{(r + d)} - \frac{1}{(1 + r)^{10}} \times \frac{SdT_c}{(r + d)}$$

$$= \frac{1,000,000 \times 0.1 \times 0.36}{0.15 + 0.1} - \frac{1}{(1.15)^{10}} \times \frac{200,000 \times 0.1 \times .036}{0.15 + 0.1}$$

$$= \$136,886$$

straight-line depreciation: Depreciation method in which a constant proportion of the cost is depreciated each year over the accounting life.

Note that the UCC generated by the machine after ten years of CCA tax shields is $\text{UCC}_{10} = (1 - 0.1)^{10} \times \$1,000,000 = \$348,678$. Even *after* selling the machine in Year 10, you will continue to depreciate $348,678 - \$200,000 = \$148,678$ of it because of the special features of Canadian tax law. The PV of the tax shield calculated above includes the value of this continuing tax deduction.

Some Asset Classes Give Straight-Line Depreciation

Not all asset classes in Canada's tax system have the declining balance feature you have just seen. For example, a "two-year write-off" (that is, **straight-line depreciation** over two years) is allowed for some pollution control and energy conservation equipment. Also, patents, franchises, and improvements to leasehold interests (for example, redecoration of a store you have leased) generate straight-line capital cost allowances. The CCA tax shield is just an annuity in these cases.

7.6 EXAMPLE: BLOOPER INDUSTRIES

The best way to understand how to track a project's cash flows is to work through an example. As the newly appointed financial manager of Blooper Industries, you are about to analyze a proposal for mining and selling a small deposit of high-grade magnoosium.[8] You are given the forecasts shown in Table 7.1. We will walk through the lines in the table.

---

[8] Readers have inquired whether magnoosium is a real substance. Here, now, for the first time, are the facts. Magnoosium was created in the early days of TV, when a splendid-sounding announcer closed a variety show by saying, "This program has been brought to you by Blooper Industries, proud producer of aleemium, magnoosium, and stool." We forget the company, but the blooper really happened.

TABLE 7.1

Financial projections for Blooper's magnoosium mine (figures in thousands of dollars)

Year:	0	1	2	3	4	5	6
1. Capital investment	10,000						
2. Working capital	1,500	4,075	4,279	4,493	4,717	3,039	0
3. Change in working capital	1,500	2,575	204	214	225	−1,678	−3,039
4. Revenues		15,000	15,750	16,538	17,364	18,233	
5. Expenses		10,000	10,500	11,025	11,576	12,155	
6. CCA of mining equipment (asset Class 38, $d = 30\%$)		3,000	2,100	1,470	1,029	720	504 ...
6a. Undepreciated capital cost	10,000	7,000	4,900	3,430	2,401	1,681	1,177 ...
7. Pretax profit		2,000	3,150	4,043	4,759	5,358	− 504
8. Tax (36%)		720	1,134	1,455	1,713	1,929	− 181
9. Profit after tax		1,280	2,016	2,588	3,046	3,429	− 323

Capital Investment (line 1). The project requires an investment of $10 million in mining machinery. At the end of 5 years the machinery has no further value. The machinery falls into asset Class 38, which has a CCA rate of 30 percent. We assume that the company owns many other assets that fall into this asset class.

Working Capital (lines 2 and 3). Line 2 shows the level of working capital. This increases in the initial years, but the working capital is recovered at the end of the project's life. We will look soon at where these figures came from, but for now you can take them on trust.

Line 3 shows the *change* in working capital from year to year. Notice that in Years 1–4 the change is positive; in these years the project requires a continuing investment in working capital. Starting in Year 5 the change is negative; there is a *disinvestment* as working capital is recovered.

Revenues (line 4). The company expects to be able to sell 750,000 kilograms of magnoosium a year at a price of $20 per kilogram in Year 1. That points to initial revenues of $750,000 \times 20 = \$15,000,000$. But be careful; inflation is running at about 5 percent a year. If magnoosium prices keep pace with inflation, you should up your forecast of the second-year revenues by 5 percent. Third-year revenues should increase by a further 5 percent, and so on. Line 4 in Table 7.1 shows revenues rising in line with inflation.

The sales forecasts in Table 7.1 are cut off after 5 years. That makes sense if the ore deposit will run out at that time. But if Blooper could make sales for Year 6, you should include them in your forecasts. We have sometimes encountered financial managers who assume a project life of (say) 5 years, even when they confidently expect revenues for 10 years or more. When asked the reason, they explain that forecasting beyond 5 years is just too hazardous. We sympathize, but you can't *avoid* making a forecast. If you value a long-lived project using cash flows for only 5 years, you have implicitly made a forecast of zero cash flows thereafter. Do not arbitrarily truncate a project's life.

Expenses (line 5). We assume that the expenses of mining and refining also increase in line with inflation at 5 percent a year.

CCA (lines 6 and 6a). The company depreciates mining equipment using a declining balance system described in the previous section. The equipment is in asset Class 38, which allows a CCA rate of 30 percent. We can see that the declining balance system makes the profit calculation a bit difficult. Even though the magnoosium mine stops producing in Year 6, line 6a indicates that the initial investment has not been completely depreciated. In fact, it will continue to provide an infinite depreciation allowance that declines in value each year. Although the magnoosium mine will not be generating income against which the depreciation can apply, we assume the company has other income against which the allowance can be charged. Fortunately, we have a convenient method for dealing with the CCA related tax shield that we will demonstrate below.

Pretax Profits (line 7). Profit after depreciation is equal to (revenues − expenses − depreciation).

Tax (line 8). Company taxes are 36 percent of pretax profits. For example, in Year 1,

$$\text{Tax} = .36 \times 2000 = 1280 \text{ or } \$1,280,000$$

Profit after Tax (line 9). Profit after tax is simply equal to pretax profit less taxes.

Calculating Blooper's Project Cash Flows

Table 7.1 provides all the information you need to figure out the cash flows on the magnoosium project. Project cash flows are the sum of four components: investment in plant and equipment, investment in working capital, cash flow from operations assuming no depreciation, and the depreciation tax shield:

Cash flow from investments in plant and equipment
+ Cash flow from investments in working capital
+ Cash flow from operations assuming no depreciation
+ Depreciation tax shield
= Total project cash flow

In Table 7.2 we have set out the project cash flows. Now let's see where these figures came from.

Capital Investment. Investment in plant and equipment is taken from line 1 of Table 7.1. Blooper's initial investment is a negative cash flow of −$10 million.

Investment in Working Capital. When the company builds up inventories of refined magnoosium, the company's cash is reduced; when customers are slow to pay their bills, cash is reduced. Thus investment in working capital, just like investment in plant and equipment, produces a negative cash flow. The numbers required for these calculations come from the section of Table 7.1 shaded in ▓.

Suppose that Blooper makes an initial (Year 0) investment of $1,500,000 in inventories of magnoosium. Then in Year 1 it accumulates an additional $75,000. The *total* level of inventories is now $1,500,000 + $75,000 = $1,575,000, but the cash expenditure in Year 1 is simply the $75,000 addition to inventory. Thus the $75,000 investment in additional inventory results in a cash flow of −$75,000.

The investment in working capital shown in Table 7.2 is simply taken from line 3 of Table 7.1. Notice

- The cash flow is measured by the *change* in working capital, not the level of working capital.
- An increase in working capital implies a negative cash flow; a decrease implies a positive cash flow.

TABLE 7.2

Cash flows for Blooper's magnoosium mine (figures in thousands of dollars)

Year:	0	1	2	3	4	5	6
1. Capital investment	−10,000						
2. Investment in working capital	− 1,500	−2,575	− 204	− 214	− 225	1,678	3,039
3. Cash flow from operations		3,200	3,360	3,528	3,704	3,890	
4. Depreciation tax shield		1,080	756	529	370	259	181...

Cash Flow from Operations Assuming No Depreciation. The third component of project cash flow is cash flow from operations. The necessary data for these calculations comes from the portion of Table 7.1 shaded in ▨. The calculation of the first year's cash flow from operations is:

Revenues	15,000
− Expenses	10,000
= Profit before tax	5,000
− Tax at 36%	1,800
= Cash flow from operations	3,200

Depreciation Tax Shield. Depreciation is important only because tax is calculated on profits after depreciation. Depreciation provides a *tax shield* because it reduces taxable income. For example, if the firm's tax bracket is 36 percent, each additional dollar of depreciation reduces taxable income by $1 and taxes owed by 36 cents. Therefore, the total depreciation tax shield equals the product of depreciation and the tax rate:

$$\text{Depreciation tax shield} = \text{depreciation} \times \text{tax rate}$$

An investment in new equipment creates a series of depreciation tax shields. When Blooper purchased the machine, the asset class balance was increased by the initial investment and then decreased in subsequent years by 30 percent of the declining undepreciated capital cost. In Year one, the asset class is reduced by the depreciation of $10,000 \times .3 = \$3000$. The depreciation tax shield for the year is:

$$\$3000 \times .36 = 1080$$

When we worked out the cash flow from operations we took tax as a percentage of profit before tax, ignoring the depreciation tax shield. So, to obtain the correct cash flow number we add back this tax savings as a cash inflow.

SELF-TEST 7.5

A project requires an investment of $1000, generates revenues of $600, expenses of $300, and depreciation charges based on a declining balance with a CCA rate of .25. The project will last for 5 years at which time the machinery will be worthless and the firm will no longer produce cash flows. The firm's tax bracket is 36 percent.
a Find the relevant cash flows for the first five years.
b Assume that depreciation is on a straight-line basis over five years (i.e., the company can depreciate $200 per year for 5 years). How would this change the cash flows for the first five years?

Calculating the
NPV of Blooper's
Project

You have now derived (in Table 7.2) the forecast cash flows from Blooper's mag-noosium mine. Assume that investors expect a return of 12 percent from invest-ments in the capital market with the same risk as the magnoosium project. This is the opportunity cost of the shareholders' money that Blooper is proposing to invest in the project. Therefore, to calculate NPV you need to discount the cash flows at 12 percent.

Table 7.3 sets out the calculations. Remember that to calculate the value of a cash flow in Year t you can divide the cash flow by $(1 + r)^t$ or you can multiply by a discount factor which is equal to $1/(1 + r)^t$.

TABLE 7.3

Cash flows and total present value of Blooper's project (figures in thousands of dollars)

Year:	0	1	2	3	4	5	6
Total cash flow excluding tax shields	−11,500	625	3156	3314	3479	5568	3039
Discount factor	1.0	.8929	.7972	.7118	.6355	.5674	.5066
Present value	−11,500	558	2,515	2,359	2,211	3,519	1,540
Total present value	1,202						

The total present value in Table 7.3 is not the net present value of the project because we still have to deal with the depreciation tax shield. The reason we deal with tax shields separately is that doing so allows us to use the formula introduced when we looked at the present value of a growing perpetuity to value the tax sav-ings stream[9]:

$$\text{PV of CCA tax shield} = \frac{CdT_c}{(r + d)} - \frac{1}{(1 + r)^5}\frac{SdT_c}{(r + d)}$$

$$= \frac{10{,}000 \times .3 \times .36}{(.12 + .3)} - \frac{1}{(1.12)^{10}} \times \frac{0 \times .3 \times .36}{(.12 + .3)}$$

$$= 2{,}571$$

Now we can bring all of this information together to determine the net present value: It is the total present value in Table 7.3 (i.e., 1202) plus the PV of the CCA tax shield. When all cash flows are discounted and added up, the magnoosium pro-ject is seen to offer a positive net present value of about $3.8 million.

Now here is a small point that often causes confusion. To calculate the value of the first year's cash flow, we divide by $(1 + r) = 1.12$. But this makes sense only if all the sales and all the costs occur exactly 365 days, zero hours, and zero min-utes from now. But of course the year's sales don't all take place on the stroke of midnight on December 31. However, when making capital budgeting decisions, companies are usually happy to pretend that all cash flows occur at 1-year inter-vals. They pretend this for one reason only — simplicity. When sales forecasts are sometimes little more than intelligent guesses, it may be pointless to inquire how the sales are likely to be spread out during the year.[10]

---

[9] Notice that the assumption that the investment will be worthless in five years is reflected in the PV of the CCA tax shield by setting S, the salvage value, equal to zero. Below we consider the alternative case where the asset has a salvage value that is not zero.

[10] Financial managers sometimes assume cash flows arrive in the middle of the calendar year, that is, at the end of June. This makes NPV also a midyear number. If you needed to move NPV back to the start of a year (January), another half year's compounding would be required.

   This midyear convention is roughly equivalent to assuming cash flows are distributed evenly through-out the year. This is a bad assumption for some industries. In retailing, for example, most of the cash flow comes late in the year, as the holiday season approaches.

....

Further Notes and Wrinkles Arising from Blooper's Project

Before we leave Blooper and its magnoosium project, we should cover a few extra wrinkles.

A Further Note on Depreciation. We have seen that depreciation provides a tax shield that is equal to the product of depreciation and the tax rate. We warned you earlier not to assume that all cash flows are likely to increase with inflation. The depreciation tax shield is a case in point, because Revenue Canada lets companies depreciate only the amount of the original investment. It is no good, for example, going back to Revenue Canada and saying that there has been a lot of inflation since you made the investment and you should be allowed to depreciate more. They won't listen. The *nominal* amount of depreciation is fixed, and therefore the higher the rate of inflation, the lower the *real* value of the depreciation that you can claim.

SELF-TEST 7.6
....

> Suppose that Blooper's mining equipment could be depreciated on a 5-year, straight-line basis. What is the present value of the depreciation tax shield?

What to Do about Salvage Value. We assumed earlier that the mining equipment would be worthless when the magnoosium mine closed. But suppose that it can be sold for $2 million in Year 6. (The $2 million forecast salvage value recognizes inflation.) Remember that we have assumed that Blooper has lots of other machines in this asset class so the sale will not close out the asset class.

You recorded the initial $10 million investment as a negative cash flow. Now in Year 6 you have a forecast return of $2 million of that investment. That is a positive cash flow with a present value of:

$$\frac{S}{(1 + r)^6} = \frac{2}{(1.12)^6} = 1.013$$

However, we also have to recognize that when we computed the present value of the tax shield we assumed that the salvage value was zero. Now with a positive salvage value, *S*, the present value of the tax shield will have to be reduced by :

$$\frac{1}{(1 + r)^6} \frac{SdT_c}{(r + d)} = \frac{1}{(1.12)^6} \times \frac{2 \times .3 \times .36}{(.12 + .3)} = .261$$

So the ability to sell the equipment will increase the net present value of the project by the present value of the sales price, $1,013,000, minus the present value of the lost tax shield, $261,000, for a net increase of $752,000.

A Further Note on Working Capital. The figures for Blooper's working capital appeared to come out of the air. Table 7.4 shows where they in fact came from.

An important component of working capital is inventories of raw materials, work in process, and finished goods awaiting sale. In this example, we will just look at inventories of refined magnoosium. You estimate that Blooper needs to keep a 5-week supply of refined magnoosium ready for shipment. So each year inventories are about 10 percent of next year's revenues (since 5 weeks is about one-tenth of a year). For example, the initial inventory is .10 × 15,000 = 1500, or $1.5 million, and by Year 1 you need an inventory of .10 × 15,750 = 1575, or $1.575 million. This is inserted in the second line of Table 7.4.

The other component of Blooper's working capital is accounts receivable. You estimate that customers will on average pay with a delay of 2 months.[11] Thus you

---

[11] For convenience we assume that Blooper pays all its bills immediately and therefore accounts payable equals zero. If it didn't, working capital would be reduced by the amount of the payables.

can see from Table 7.4 that at the end of Year 1 you will have accumulated unpaid bills of $2/12 \times 15{,}000 = \$2500$.

One can refine forecasts of working capital further. But we will defer such refinements until Chapter 19.

TABLE 7.4

Working capital for Blooper's project (figures in thousands of dollars)

Year:	0	1	2	3	4	5
1. Revenues		15,000	15,750	16,538	17,364	18,233
2. Inventory of refined magnoosium (10% of *next year*'s revenues)	1,500	1,575	1,654	1,736	1,823	0
3. Accounts receivable (2/12 of this year's revenues)		2,500	2,625	2,756	2,894	3,309
4. Working capital (lines 2 + 3)	1,500	4,075	4,279	4,493	4,717	3,309

Note: Column sums subject to rounding error

PROJECT INTERACTIONS

Almost all decisions about capital expenditures involve either–or choices. The firm can build either a 90,000 square metre warehouse or a 100,000 square metre warehouse. It can build the warehouse in Kingston or Halifax. It can heat it with oil or with natural gas. These are all choices between mutually exclusive alternatives. Mutually exclusive projects are the simplest project interaction: Taking project A forecloses project B. The decision rule is simple too. Even if both choices have a positive NPV, we must choose the option with the *higher* NPV. Other project interactions are trickier. For example,

- Should the company build that warehouse now or wait and think again next year? (Here today's investment is competing with possible future investments.)
- Should the company save money by installing cheaper machinery that will not last as long? (Here today's decision would accelerate a later investment in machine replacement.)
- When should existing machinery be replaced? (Using it another year could delay investment in machine replacement.)

We will now tackle these three cases.

Investment Timing

Obsolete Technologies knows that it could enhance efficiency by installing a new computer system. The efficiency gains would easily justify the expense of the system. But the firm sees that the price of computers is continually falling and therefore decides to postpone the purchase, arguing that the NPV of the system will be even higher if it waits until the following year. Unfortunately, it has been making this argument since 1976, and it is steadily losing business to competitors with more efficient systems. Is there a flaw in its reasoning?

This is a problem in investment timing. When is it best to commit to positive-NPV investment?

Table 7.5 lays out the basic data for Obsolete. You can see that the cost of the computer is expected to decline from $50,000 today to $45,000 next year, and so on. The value of the savings that the computer will produce is expected to stay at $70,000. (This is not an annual figure; it is the present value of the savings at the time you buy the computer.) Thus if Obsolete invests today, it achieves an NPV of $70,000 - $50,000 = $20,000; if it invests next year, it will have an NPV of $70,000 - $45,000 = $25,000.

TABLE 7.5

Obsolete Technologies: The gain from purchase of a computer is rising, but the NPV today is highest if the computer is purchased in Year 3 (figures in thousands of dollars)

Year of Purchase	Cost of Computer	PV of Savings	NPV at Year of Purchase ($r = 10\%$)	NPV Today	
0	$50	$70	$20	$20.0	
1	45	70	25	22.7	
2	40	70	30	24.8	optimal
3	36	70	34	25.5	← purchase
4	33	70	37	25.3	date
5	31	70	39	24.2	

Isn't a gain of $25,000 better than one of $20,000? Well, not necessarily — you may prefer to be $20,000 richer today rather than $25,000 richer next year. The answer depends on the cost of capital. The fourth column of Table 7.5 shows the value today (Year 0) of those gains assuming a 10 percent cost of capital. For example, you can see that the discounted value of that $25,000 gain is 25/1.10 = 22.7, or $22,700. It is therefore worth postponing investment in the computer but not indefinitely. You maximize net present value today by buying the computer in Year 3.

Notice that you are involved in a trade-off. The sooner you can capture the $70,000 savings the better, but if it costs you less to realize those savings by postponing investment, it may pay to do so. If you postpone purchase by 1 year, the gain from buying a computer rises from $20,000 to $25,000, an increase of 25 percent. Since the cost of capital is only 10 percent, it pays to postpone at least until Year 1. If you postpone purchase from Year 3 to Year 4, the gain rises from $34,000 to $37,000, a rise of just under 9 percent. Since this is less than the cost of capital, it is not worth waiting any longer.

SELF-TEST 7.7

Unfortunately Obsolete Technology's business is shrinking as the company dithers and dawdles. Its senior managers realize that the savings from installing the new computer will likewise shrink by $4000 per year, from a present value of $70,000 now, to $66,000 next year, then to $62,000, and so on. Redo Table 7.5 with this new information. When should Obsolete buy the new computer?

Long- versus Short-Lived Equipment

Suppose the firm is forced to choose between two machines, A and B. The two machines are designed differently but have identical capacity and do exactly the same job. Machine A costs $15,000 and will last 3 years. It costs $4000 per year to run. Machine B is an "economy" model, costing only $10,000, but it will last only 2 years and cost $6000 per year to run.

Because the two machines produce exactly the same product, the only way to choose between them is on the basis of cost. Suppose we compute the present value of the costs:

	Costs, Thousands of Dollars				
Year:	0	1	2	3	PV at 6%
Machine A	15	4	4	4	25.69
Machine B	10	6	6	—	21.00

Should we take machine B, the one with the lower present value of costs? Not necessarily. All we have shown is that machine B offers 2 years of service for a lower cost than 3 years of service from machine A. But is the annual cost of using B lower than that of A?

Suppose the financial manager agrees to buy machine A and pay for its operating costs out of her budget. She then charges the plant manager an annual amount for use of the machine. There will be three equal payments starting in Year 1. Obviously, the financial manager has to make sure that the present value of these payments equals the present value of the costs of machine A, $25,690. The payment stream with such a present value turns out to be $9610 a year. In other words, the cost of buying and operating machine A is equivalent to an annual charge of $9610 a year for 3 years. This figure is therefore termed the **equivalent annual cost** of machine A.

equivalent annual cost: The cost per period with the same present value as the cost of buying and operating a machine.

	Costs, Thousands of Dollars				
Year:	**0**	**1**	**2**	**3**	**PV at 6%**
Machine A	15	4	4	4	25.69
Equivalent annual cost		9.61	9.61	9.61	25.69

How did we know that an annual charge of $9610 has a present value of $25,690? The annual charge is a 3-year annuity. So we calculate the value of this annuity and set it equal to $25,690:

Equivalent annual cost × 3-year annuity factor = PV costs of A = $25,690

If the cost of capital is 6 percent, the 3-year annuity factor is 2.673. So

$$\text{Equivalent annual cost} = \frac{\text{Present value of costs}}{\text{3-year annuity factor}} = \frac{\$25,690}{2.673} = \$9,610$$

If we make a similar calculation of costs for machine B, we get:

	Costs, Thousands of Dollars			
Year:	**0**	**1**	**2**	**PV at 6%**
Machine B	$10	6	6	$21.00
Equivalent 2-year annuity		11.45	11.45	$21.00

We see now that machine A is better, because its equivalent annual cost is less ($9,610 for A versus $11,450 for B). In other words, the financial manager could afford to set a lower *annual* charge for the use of A.

We thus have a rule for comparing assets of different lives: *Select the machine that has the lowest equivalent annual cost.*

Think of the equivalent annual cost as the level annual charge[12] necessary to recover the present value of investment outlays and operating costs. The annual rental charge continues for the life of the equipment. Calculate equivalent annual cost by dividing the appropriate present value by the annuity factor.

● **Example 7.5 Equivalent Annual Cost**

You need a new car. You can either purchase one outright for $15,000 or lease one for 7 years for $3000 a year. If you buy the car, it will be worth $500 to

---

[12] This introduction to equivalent annual cost is somewhat simplified. For example, equivalent annual costs should be escalated with inflation when inflation is significant and the equipment long-lived. This would require us to equate equipment cost to the present value of a *growing* annuity.

you in 7 years. The discount rate is 10 percent. Should you buy or lease? What is the maximum lease you would be willing to pay?

The present value of the cost of purchasing is

$$PV = \$15,000 - \frac{500}{(1.10)^7} = \$14,743$$

The equivalent annual cost of the car is therefore the annuity with this present value:

$$\text{Equivalent annual cost} \times \frac{\text{7-year annuity}}{\text{factor at 10\%}} = \frac{\text{PV costs}}{\text{of buying}} = \$14,743$$

$$\text{Equivalent annual cost} = \frac{\$14,743}{\text{7-year annuity factor}} = \frac{\$14,743}{4.8684} = \$3028$$

Therefore, the annual lease payment of $3000 is less than the equivalent annual cost of buying the car. You should be willing to pay up to $3028 annually to lease.

Replacing an Old Machine

The previous example took the life of each machine as fixed. In practice, the point at which equipment is replaced reflects economics, not physical collapse. We usually decide when to replace. The machine will rarely decide for us.

Here is a common problem. You are operating an old machine that will last 2 more years before it gives up the ghost. It costs $12,000 per year to operate. You can replace it now with a new machine, which costs $25,000 but is much more efficient ($8000 per year in operating costs) and will last for 5 years. Should you replace now or wait a year? The opportunity cost of capital is 6 percent.

We can calculate the NPV of the new machine and its equivalent annual cash flow, that is, the 5-year annuity that has the same present value.

| | Costs, Thousands of Dollars | | | | | | |
Year:	0	1	2	3	4	5	PV at 6%
New machine	25	8	8	8	8	8	58.70
Equivalent 5-year annuity		13.93	13.93	13.93	13.93	13.93	58.70

The cash flows of the new machine are equivalent to an annuity of $13,930 per year. So we can equally well ask at what point we would want to replace our old machine, which costs $12,000 a year to run, with a new one costing $13,930 a year. When the question is posed this way, the answer is obvious. As long as your old machine costs only $12,000 a year, why replace it with a new machine that costs $1930 more?

SELF-TEST 7.8

Machines A and B are mutually exclusive and have the following investment and operating costs. Note that machine A lasts for only 2 years:

Year:	0	1	2	3
A	10,000	1,100	1,200	—
B	12,000	1,100	1,200	1,300

Calculate the equivalent annual cost of each investment using a discount rate of 10 percent. Which machine is the better buy?

Now suppose you have an existing machine. You can keep it going for 1 more year only, but it will cost $2500 in repairs and $1800 in operating costs. Is it worth replacing now with either A or B?

 **SUMMARY**

1. Here is a checklist to bear in mind when forecasting a project's cash flows:

- Discount cash flows, not profits.
- Estimate the project's incremental cash flows — that is, the difference between the cash flows with the project and those without the project.
- Include all incidental effects of the project, such as its impact on the sales of the firm's other products.
- Forget sunk costs.
- Include opportunity costs, such as the realizable market value of land that you could otherwise sell.
- Beware of allocated overhead charges for heat, light, and so on. Adjust them to reflect the true incremental costs caused by the project.
- Remember the investment in working capital. As sales increase, the firm may need to make additional investments in working capital and, as the project finally comes to an end, it will recover its earlier investment in working capital.
- Do not include debt interest or the cost of repaying a loan. When calculating NPV, assume that the project is financed entirely by the shareholders and that they receive all the cash flows. This isolates the investment decision from the financing decision.

2. If you use a nominal cost of capital, consistency requires that you forecast nominal cash flows — that is, cash flows that recognize the effect of inflation.

3. Capital cost allowance is not a cash flow. However, because depreciation reduces taxable income, it reduces taxes. This tax reduction is called the depreciation tax shield. Because of the declining balance system used in Canada, most investments provide depreciation tax shields that extend for hundreds of years into the future. For this reason, it is easiest to compute the present value of the tax shield separately from the present value of the other cash flows produced by the project.

4. Investment decisions are rarely take-it-or-leave-it decisions. Usually they involve a choice of alternatives. We looked at three common choices:

- Sometimes a project may have a positive NPV if undertaken today but an even higher NPV if the investment is delayed. Choose between these alternatives by comparing their NPVs today.
- When you have to choose between projects with different lives, put them on an equal footing by comparing the equivalent annual cost or benefit of the two projects.
- When you are considering whether to replace an aging machine with a new one, you should compare the cost of operating the old one with the equivalent annual cost of the new one.

KEY TERMS

opportunity cost	**asset class**	**capital gain**
net working capital	**undepreciated capital**	**straight-line**
capital cost allowance	**cost (UCC)**	**depreciation**
(CCA)	**recaptured depreciation**	**equivalent annual cost**
depreciation tax shield	**terminal loss**	

SUGGESTED READINGS

There are several good general texts on capital budgeting. See, for example:

H. Bierman and S. Smidt. *The Capital Budgeting Decision*, 7th ed. New York: Macmillan, 1988.

PROBLEMS

1. The owner of a bicycle repair shop forecasts revenues of $150,000 a year. Variable costs will be $40,000, and rental costs for the shop are $30,000 a year. Depreciation on the repair tools will be $10,000 per year. Prepare an income statement for the shop based on these estimates. The tax rate is 36 percent.

2. Calculate the after-tax operating cash flow for the repair shop in problem 1.

3. A house painting business had revenues of $16,000 and expenses of $9000. There were no depreciation expenses. However, the business reported the following changes in various components of working capital:

	Beginning	End
Accounts receivable	$1200	$4400
Accounts payable	500	200

   Calculate net cash flow for the business for this period.

4. A corporation donates a valuable painting from its private collection to an art museum. Which of the following are incremental cash flows associated with the donation?
   a. The price the firm paid for the painting.
   b. The current market value of the painting.
   c. The deduction from income that it declares for its charitable gift.
   d. The reduction in taxes due to its declared tax deduction.

5. Laurel's Lawn Care, Ltd. has a new mower line that can generate revenues of $120,000 per year. Direct production costs are $40,000 and the fixed costs of maintaining the lawn mower factory are $15,000 a year. The factory originally cost $1 million and is included in asset Class 1 with a CCA rate of 4 percent. Calculate the cash flows of the project for the next 5 years if the firm's tax bracket is 36 percent.

6. A firm had net income last year of $1.2 million. Its depreciation expenses were $.4 million, and its total cash flow was $1.2 million. What happened to net working capital during the year?

7. Talia's Tutus bought a new sewing machine for $40,000 that will be depreciated in an asset class that has a CCA rate of 25 percent. There are no other assets in this asset class and the firm's tax bracket is 36 percent.
   a. Find the depreciation charge for each of the next 5 years.
   b. If the sewing machine is sold after 3 years for $20,000, what will be the after-tax proceeds on the sale ?

8. A firm's balance sheets for 1995 and 1996 contain the following data. What happened to investment in net working capital during 1995? All items are in millions of dollars.

	Dec. 31, 1995	**Dec. 31, 1996**
Accounts receivable	30	35
Inventories	25	28
Accounts payable	12	23

9. Bottoms Up Diaper Service is considering the purchase of a new industrial washer. It can purchase the washer for $6000 and sell its old washer for $2000. If it keeps its old washer it will last for 6 more years and then be worthless. The new washer will also last for 6 years but will save $1500 a year in expenses. It too will be worthless at the end of 6 years. The washing machines fall into an asset class that has a CCA rate of 30 percent and Bottoms Up has many other machines in this asset class. The opportunity cost of capital is 15 percent, and the firm's tax rate is 40 percent.
   a. If the salvage value of the machine is expected to be zero at the end of its 6-year life, what are the cash flows of the project in Years 0–6?
   b. What is project NPV?
   c. What will NPV be if the firm were required to use straight-line depreciation with a 6-year tax life?

10. What is the equivalent annual cost of the washer in problem 9 if the firm uses straight-line depreciation?

11. Revenues generated by a new fad product in each of the next 5 years are forecast as follows:

Year	Revenues
1	$40,000
2	30,000
3	20,000
4	10,000
Thereafter	0

   Expenses are expected to be 40 percent of revenues, and working capital required in each year is expected to be 20 percent of revenues in the following year. The product requires an immediate investment of $50,000 in plant and equipment.
   a. What is the initial investment in the product? Remember working capital.
   b. If the plant and equipment are put into an asset class with a CCA rate of 20 percent, and the firm's tax rate is 40 percent, what are the project cash flows in each of the next 4 years?
   c. If the opportunity cost of capital is 12 percent, what is project NPV?
   d. What is project IRR?

12. You can buy a car for $20,000 and sell it in 5 years for $5000. Or you can lease the car for 5 years for $4000 a year. The discount rate is 10 percent per year.
   a. Which option do you prefer?
   b. What is the maximum amount you should be willing to pay to lease rather than buy the car?

13. You are operating an old machine that is expected to produce a cash inflow of $5000 in each of the next 3 years before it fails and becomes worthless.

You can replace it now with a new machine, which costs $20,000 but is much more efficient and will provide a cash flow of $10,000 a year for 4 years. The new machine will be worthless at the end of 4 years. Should you replace your equipment now? The discount rate is 15 percent.

14. The following table presents sales forecasts for Golden Gelt Giftware. The unit price is $40. The unit cost of the giftware is $25.

Year	Unit Sales
1	22,000
2	30,000
3	14,000
4	5,000
Thereafter	0

It is expected that net working capital will amount to 25 percent of the following year's sales. For example, the store will need an initial (Year 0) investment in working capital of .25 × 22,000 × $40 = $220,000. Plant and equipment necessary to establish the Giftware business will require an additional investment of $200,000. This investment will be in an asset class with a CCA rate of 20 percent. After 4 years, the equipment will have an economic value of zero, but, since the asset class will have other assets in it, the depreciation tax shield will continue indefinitely. The firm's tax rate is 36 percent. What is the net present value of the project? The discount rate is 20 percent.

15. Ilana Industries, Inc., needs a new lathe. It can buy a new high-speed lathe for $1 million. The lathe will cost $30,000 to run, will save the firm $120,000 in labour costs, and will be useful for 10 years. The lathe will be one of many assets in an asset class with a CCA rate of 20 percent. The lathe will have a life of 10 years and a salvage value in 10 years of $100,000. The actual market value of the lathe at that time also will be $100,000. The discount rate is 10 percent and the corporate tax rate is 36 percent. What is the NPV of buying the new lathe?

16. The efficiency gains resulting from a just-in-time inventory management system will allow a firm to reduce its level of inventories permanently by $200,000. What is the most the firm should be willing to pay for installing the system?

17. Econo-cool air conditioners cost $300 to purchase, result in electricity bills of $150 per year, and last for 5 years. Luxury Air models cost $500, result in electricity bills of $100 per year, and last for 8 years. The discount rate is 21 percent.
    a. What are the equivalent annual costs of the Econo-cool and Luxury Air models?
    b. Which model is the more cost-effective?
    c. Now you remember that the inflation rate is expected to be 10 percent per year for the foreseeable future. Redo parts a and b.

18. You can purchase an optical scanner today for $400. The scanner provides benefits worth $60 a year. The expected life of the scanner is 10 years. Scanners are expected to decrease in price by 20 percent per year. Suppose

the discount rate is 10 percent. Should you purchase the scanner today or wait to purchase? When is the best purchase time?

19. A forklift will last for only 2 more years. It costs $5000 a year to maintain. For $20,000 you can buy a new lift that can last for 10 years and should require maintenance costs of only $2000 a year.
    a. If the discount rate is 5 percent per year, should you replace the forklift?
    b. What if the discount rate is 10 percent per year? Why does your answer change?

20. The New York Livery Service[13]:

    Angelo, a friend of your family, hearing that you are taking a course in Finance asks for your advice about whether he should trade in his current limo. The current limousine is a stretched 1956 Chrysler New Yorker, with "push-button" transmission, tons of steel and chrome, and a 440 cubic inch engine to power it. A new limousine could be purchased for $30,000 cash from a dealer, or $5,000 after the trade-in. Angelo is finding that it keeps getting more and more difficult to get parts for the Chrysler, and that the gas and insurance bills just keep getting higher. He expects to save $4800 per year in operating expenses by switching to the newer machine. By the time he retires in 4 years, this savings will have amounted to almost $20,000. Angelo's main concerns about going to the new limo are tax effects and the resale value of the cars. He paid $50,000 for the New Yorker in 1990, during the economic boom. He believes that its value will rise back to that level in 4 years, and the experts agree — the car is becoming more "collectable" each year. On the other hand, the newer model limo will probably depreciate to a market value of only $16,000.

    Angelo is in a 45 percent tax bracket; limos are in a 30 percent CCA class; assume that Angelo will sell the business as a going concern, so that there will always be assets in the pool, and use a 16 percent discount rate.

    What should Angelo do?

SOLUTIONS TO SELF-TEST QUESTIONS

7.1 Remember, discount cash flows, not profits. Each tewgit machine costs $250,000 right away. Recognize that outlay, but forget accounting depreciation. Cash flows per machine are:

Year:	0	1	2	3	4	5
Investment (outflow)	−250,000					
Sales		250,000	300,000	300,000	250,000	250,000
Operating expenses		−200,000	−200,000	−200,000	−200,000	−200,000
Cash flow	−250,000	+ 50,000	+100,000	+100,000	+ 50,000	+ 50,000

Each machine is forecast to generate $50,000 of cash flow in Years 4 and 5. Thus it makes sense to keep operating for 5 years.

---

[13] We thank Guus Saaltink for providing us with this problem.

7.2

a, b. The site and buildings could have been sold or put to another use. Their values are opportunity costs, which should be treated as incremental cash outflows.

c. Demolition costs are incremental cash outflows.

d. The cost of the access road is sunk and not incremental.

e. Lost cash flows from other projects are incremental cash outflows.

f. Depreciation is not a cash expense and should not be included, except as it affects taxes. (Taxes are discussed later in this chapter.)

7.3 Actual dental costs will be increasing at about 7 percent a year.

Year	1	2	3	4
Cost per worker	$2400	$2568	$2748	$2940

The present value at 10 percent is $9214 if the first payment is made immediately. If it is delayed a year, present value falls to $8377.

7.4 If the firm has no other assets in the asset class, then UCC is reduced to zero. The sale reduces the UCC by 4 million to 2.4 million. The company treats the 2.4 million as a terminal loss bringing the UCC to zero.

7.5

a. The cash flows consist of the following three components:

i) The capital investment which requires a cash disbursement of $1000 in year zero.

ii) The operating cash flows, assuming no depreciation, are

$$(600 - 300)(1 - T_c) = 192$$

per year.

iii) Depreciation tax shield: With a CCA rate of .25, the CCA for the first year is

$$.25 \times 1000 = 250.$$

The UCC will be

$$1000 - 250 = 750,$$

and the depreciation tax shield is

$$.36 \times 250 = 90$$

A similar calculation for each year leads to the figures in the following table.

Year:	0	1	2	3	4	5	6
i). Capital investment	−1,000						
ii). Cash flow from operations		192	192	192	192	192	0
iii). UCC	1,000	750	562	421	316	237	178
CCA		250	188	141	105	79	59
Depreciation tax shield		90	68	51	38	28	21...

b. The only change would be to the depreciation tax shield, which would become

$$200 \times .36 = 72$$

in each of the five years.

7.6   The annual depreciation tax shield would be

$$\frac{10,000}{5} \times .36 = 720$$

The present value of this tax shield is the value of a 5-year annuity with annual level cash flows of 720: that is

$$720 \times \left(\frac{1}{.12} - \frac{1}{.12(1.12)^5}\right) = 2595.44.$$

This is $25 more than the present value of the tax shield under a declining balance system.

7.7

Year of Purchase	Cost of Computer	PV Savings	NPV at Year of Purchase	NPV Today
0	50	70	20	20
1	45	66	21	19.1
2	40	62	22	18.2
3	36	58	22	16.5
4	33	54	21	14.3
5	31	50	19	11.8

Purchase the new computer now.

7.8

Year:	0	1	2	3	PV
A. Cash flows	10,000	1,100	1,200		11,992
Equivalent annual cost		6,910	6,910		11,992
B. Cash flows	12,000	1,100	1,200	1,300	14,968
Equivalent annual cost		6,019	6,019	6,019	14,968

Machine B is the better buy. However, it's still better to keep the old machine going one more year. That costs $4300, which is less than B's equivalent annual cost, $6019.

APPENDIX 7.1   THE HALF-YEAR RULE FOR CAPITAL COST ALLOWANCE

We made two simplifying assumptions in our analysis of the CCA tax shields in Section 7.5. Fortunately, the formula we gave there for the PV of CCA tax shields is quite accurate because the two simplifications generally create errors that offset each other. The first simplification was to ignore a feature of tax law called "the half-year rule." This rule requires that, when depreciable assets are purchased, only half of the value of the asset purchases are added to the asset class balance. The other half is added in the next year. The second simplification was in the way that we treated the timing of asset purchases: we assumed that assets are purchased on the first day of the tax year. Because these simplifications can cause some confusion, we want to discuss them in more detail.

Let's use the same notation as in Section 7.5:

C = capital cost of an asset
d = CCA rate
T_c = corporate tax rate
r = discount rate
UCC_t = undepreciated capital cost after deducting CCA tax shield for year t.

The incremental effect of purchasing the asset is to start depreciating half of it in Year 0 and the other half in Year 1 as follows:

Year:	0	1	2	...	t	...
CCA on first half of asset	$Cd/2$	$Cd(1-d)/2$	$Cd(1-d)^2/2$	...	$Cd(1-d)^t/2$	...
CCA on second half of asset	0	$Cd/2$	$Cd(1-d)/2$	...	$Cd(1-d)^{t-1}/2$	

If we multiply by T_c and add these up we get:

$$\text{PV of perpetual CCA tax shields} = \frac{1}{2}\left(CdT_c + \frac{CdT_c(1-d)}{1+r} + \frac{CdT_c(1-d)}{(1+r)^2} + \ldots\right)$$

$$+ \frac{1}{2}\left(\frac{CdT_c}{1+r} + \frac{CdT_c(1-d)}{(1+r)^2} + \ldots\right)$$

$$= \frac{1}{2}\frac{CdT_c}{(r+d)}(1+r) + \frac{1}{2}\frac{CdT_c}{(r+d)}$$

$$= \frac{CdT_c}{(r+d)}(1+r/2)$$

Compared to the formula in Section 7.5, this formula gives a PV of the perpetual CCA tax shield that is larger by a half year of interest. This is usually not a significant difference, although it may be large in some applications.

CHAPTER EIGHT

Project Analysis

It helps to use discounted cash flow techniques to value new projects but good investment decisions also require good data. Therefore, we start this chapter by thinking about how firms organize the capital budgeting operation to get the kind of information they need. In addition, we look at how they try to ensure that everyone involved works together toward a common goal.

Project evaluation should never be a mechanical exercise in which the financial manager takes a set of cash flow forecasts and cranks out a net present value. Cash flow estimates are just that — estimates. Financial managers need to look behind the forecasts to try to understand what makes the project tick and what could go wrong with it. A number of techniques have been developed to help managers identify the key assumptions in their analysis. These techniques involve asking a number of "what-if" questions. What if your market share turns out to be higher or lower than you forecast? What if interest rates rise during the life of the project? In the second part of this chapter we show how managers use the techniques of sensitivity analysis, scenario analysis, and break-even analysis to help answer these what-if questions.

Books about capital budgeting sometimes create the impression that once the manager has made an investment decision, there is nothing to do but sit back and watch the cash flows develop. But since cash flows rarely proceed as anticipated, companies constantly need to modify their operations. If cash flows are better than anticipated, the project may be expanded; if they are worse, it may be scaled back or abandoned altogether. In the third section of this chapter we describe how good managers take account of these options when they analyze a project and why they are willing to pay money today to build in future flexibility. In summary, this chapter is a triple-decker.

After studying this chapter you should be able to

- Appreciate the practical problems of capital budgeting in large corporations.
- Use sensitivity, scenario, and break-even analysis to see how project profitability would be affected by an error in your forecasts and understand why an overestimate of sales is more serious for projects with high operating leverage.
- Recognize the importance of managerial flexibility in capital budgeting.

8.1   CAPITAL BUDGETING IN LARGE CORPORATIONS

For most sizable firms, there are two separate stages in the investment process.

Stage 1: The Capital Budget

Once a year, the head office generally asks each of its divisions and plants to provide a list of the investments that they would like to make.[1] These are gathered together into a proposed **capital budget**.

This budget is then reviewed and pruned by senior management and staff specializing in planning and financial analysis. Usually there are negotiations

capital budget: List of planned investment projects.

---

[1] Large firms may be divided into several divisions or operating groups. For example, BC Gas has a division that specializes in delivering gas to customers, another that runs an oil pipeline, and a third that runs an independent electric power plant and various other smaller investments.

between the firm's senior management and its divisional management, and there may also be special analyses of major outlays or ventures into new areas. Once the budget has been approved, it generally remains the basis for operating over the ensuing year.

Many investment proposals bubble up from the bottom of the organization. But the managers of plants A and B cannot be expected to see the potential economies of scale of closing their plants and consolidating production at a new plant C. We expect divisional management to propose plant C. Similarly, divisions 1 and 2 may not be eager to give up their own data processing operations to a standardized corporate data management system. That proposal would come from senior management.

Senior management's concern is to see that the capital budget matches the firm's strategic plans. It needs to ensure that the firm is concentrating its efforts in areas where it has a real competitive advantage. As part of this effort, management must also identify declining businesses that should be sold or allowed to run down.

The firm's capital investment choices should be based on a strategic view that reflects both "bottom-up" and "top-down" processes. The two processes should complement each other. Plant and division managers, who do most of the work in bottom-up capital budgeting, may not see the forest for the trees. Strategic planners who ignore the details in the bottom-up view may have a mistaken picture of the forest because they do not look at the trees.

Stage 2: Project Authorizations

The annual budget is important because it allows everybody to exchange ideas before attitudes have hardened and personal commitments have been made. However, the fact that your pet project has been included in the annual budget doesn't mean you have permission to go ahead with it. At a later stage you will need to draw up a detailed proposal describing particulars of the project, engineering analyses, cash-flow forecasts, and present value calculations. If your project is large, this proposal may have to pass a number of hurdles before it is finally approved.

The type of backup information that you need to provide depends on the project category. For example, some firms use a fourfold breakdown:

1. Outlays required by law or company policy, for example, for pollution control equipment. These outlays do not need to be justified on financial grounds. The main issue is whether requirements are satisfied at the lowest possible cost. The decision is therefore likely to hinge on engineering analyses of alternative technologies.

2. Maintenance or cost reduction, such as machine replacement. Engineering analysis is also important in machine replacement, but new machines have to pay their own way. In this category of proposal the firm faces the classical capital budgeting problems described in Chapter 7.

3. Capacity expansion in existing businesses. Projects in this category are less straightforward; these decisions may hinge on forecasts of demand, possible shifts in technology, and the reactions of competitors.

4. Investment for new products. Projects in this category are most likely to depend on intangibles. The first projects in a new area may not have positive NPVs if considered in isolation, but they may give the firm a valuable option to undertake follow-on projects. More about this later in this chapter.

······················
**Problems and
Some Solutions**

Valuing capital investment opportunities is hard enough when you can do the entire job yourself. In most firms, however, capital budgeting is a cooperative effort, and this brings with it some challenges.

Ensuring that Forecasts Are Consistent. Inconsistent assumptions often creep into investment proposals. For example, suppose that the manager of the furniture division is bullish (optimistic) on housing starts but the manager of the appliance division is bearish (pessimistic). This inconsistency makes the projects proposed by the furniture division look more attractive than those of the appliance division.

To ensure consistency, many firms begin the capital budgeting process by establishing forecasts of economic indicators, such as inflation and the growth in national income, as well as forecasts of particular items that are important to the firm's business, such as housing starts or the price of raw materials. These forecasts can then be used as the basis for all project analyses.

Eliminating Conflicts of Interest. Plant and divisional managers want to do a good job, but they must also be concerned about their own futures. Sometimes their interests conflict with those of stockholders, leading to poor investment decisions. For example, new plant managers naturally want to demonstrate good performance right away. To this end, they might propose quick-payback projects even if NPV is sacrificed. In addition, many firms measure performance and reward managers in such a way as to encourage this behaviour. If the firm always demands quick results, it is unlikely that plant managers will concentrate on NPV.

Reducing Forecast Bias. Someone who is keen to get a project proposal accepted is also likely to look on the bright side when forecasting the project's cash flows. Such overoptimism seems to be a common feature in financial forecasts. For example, think of large public expenditure proposals. How often have you heard of a new stadium, dam, or highway that actually cost less than was originally forecast? Think back to the Eurotunnel project introduced in Chapter 6. The final cost of the project will be about 50 percent higher than initial forecasts. It is probably impossible to ever eliminate bias completely, but if senior management is aware of why bias occurs, it is at least partway to solving the problem.

Project sponsors are likely to overstate their case deliberately only if the head office encourages them to do so. For example, if middle managers believe that success depends on having the largest division rather than the most profitable one, they will propose large expansion projects that they do not believe have the largest possible net present value. Or if divisions must compete for limited resources, they will try to outbid each other for those resources. The fault in such cases is top management's — if lower level managers are not rewarded based on net present value and contribution to firm value, it should not be surprising that they focus their efforts elsewhere.

Other problems stem from sponsors' eagerness to obtain approval for their favourite projects. As the proposal travels up the organization, alliances are formed. Thus once a division has screened its own plants' proposals, the plants in that division unite in competing against outsiders. The result is that the head office may receive several thousand investment proposals each year. All are essentially sales documents presented by united fronts and designed to persuade. The forecasts have been doctored to ensure that NPV appears positive.

Since it is difficult for senior management to evaluate each specific assumption in an investment proposal, capital investment decisions are effectively decentralized whatever the rules say. Some firms accept this; others rely on head office staff to check capital investment proposals.

Sorting the Wheat from the Chaff. Senior managers are continually bombarded with requests for funds for capital expenditures. All these requests are supported with detailed analyses showing that the projects have positive NPVs. How then can managers ensure that only worthwhile projects make the grade? One response of senior managers to the problem of poor information is to impose rigid expenditure limits on individual plants or divisions. These limits force the subunits to choose among projects. The firm ends up using capital rationing not because capital is unobtainable but as a way of decentralizing decisions.[2]

Senior managers might also ask some searching questions about why the project has a positive NPV. After all, if the project is so attractive, why hasn't someone already undertaken it? Will others copy your idea if it is so profitable? Positive NPVs are plausible only if your company has some competitive advantage.

Such an advantage can arise in several ways. You may be smart or lucky enough to be the first to the market with a new or improved product for which customers will pay premium prices. Your competitors eventually will enter the market and squeeze out excess profits, but it may take them several years to do so. Or you may have a proprietary technology or production cost advantage that competitors cannot easily match. You may have a contractual advantage such as the distributorship for a particular region. Or your advantage may be as simple as a good reputation and an established customer list.

Analyzing competitive advantage can also help ferret out projects that incorrectly appear to have a negative NPV. If you are the lowest cost producer of a profitable product in a growing market, then you should invest to expand along with the market. If your calculations show a negative NPV for such an expansion, then you probably have made a mistake.

The important point to emphasize is that careful managers will always look beyond NPV calculations. They make sure they understand the economic nature of the opportunity being considered.

8.2 SOME "WHAT-IF" QUESTIONS

Sensitivity Analysis

sensitivity analysis: Analysis of the effects of changes in sales, costs, and so on, on project profitability.

Uncertainty means that more things *can* happen than *will* happen. Therefore, whenever managers are given a cash-flow forecast, they try to determine what else might happen and the implications of those possible events. This is called **sensitivity analysis**.

Put yourself in the well-heeled shoes of the financial manager of the Finefodder supermarket chain. Finefodder is considering opening a new superstore in Ecum Secum and your staff members have prepared the figures shown in Table 8.1. The figures are fairly typical for a new supermarket except that to keep the example simple we have assumed no inflation. We have also assumed that the entire investment can be depreciated straight-line for tax purposes and we have ignored the fact that at the end of the 12 years you could sell off the land and buildings.

As an experienced financial manager, you recognize immediately that these cash flows constitute an annuity and therefore you calculate present value by multiplying the $780,000 cash flow by the 12-year annuity factor. If the cost of capital is 8 percent, present value is

$$PV = \$780,000 \times \text{12-year annuity factor}$$

$$= \$780,000 \times 7.536 = \$5.878 \text{ million}$$

---

[2] We discussed capital rationing in Chapter 6.

Subtract the initial investment of $5.4 million and you obtain a net present value of $478,000:

$$NPV = PV - \text{investment}$$

$$= \$5.878 \text{ million} - \$5.4 \text{ million} = \$478,000$$

TABLE 8.1

Cash flow forecasts for Finefodder's new superstore (all forecasts are in thousands of dollars)

	Year 0	Years 1–12
Investment	−$5,400	
1. Sales		$16,000
2. Variable costs		13,000
3. Fixed costs		2,000
4. Depreciation		450
5. Pretax profit (1 − 2 − 3 − 4)		550
6. Taxes (at 40%)		220
7. Profit after tax		330
8. Cash flow from operations (4 + 7)		780
Net cash flow	−$5,400	$ 780

Before you agree to accept the project, however, you want to delve behind these forecasts and identify the key variables that will determine whether the project succeeds or fails.

Some of the costs of running a supermarket are fixed. For example, regardless of the level of output, you still have to heat and light the store and pay the store manager. These fixed costs are forecast to be $2 million per year.

Other costs vary with the level of sales. In particular, the lower the sales, the less food you need to buy. Also, if sales are lower than forecast, you can operate a lower number of checkouts and reduce the staff needed to restock the shelves. The new superstore's variable costs are estimated at 81.25 percent of sales. Thus variable costs = .8125 × $16 million = $13 million.

The initial investment of $5.4 million will be depreciated on a straight-line basis over the 12-year period, resulting in annual depreciation of $450,000. Profits are taxed at a rate of 40 percent.

These seem to be the important things you need to know, but look out for things that may have been forgotten. Perhaps there will be delays in obtaining planning permission, or perhaps you will need to undertake costly landscaping. The greatest dangers often lie in these *unknown* unknowns, or "unk-unks," as scientists call them.

Having found no unk-unks (no doubt you'll find them later), you look at how far NPV may be affected if you have made a wrong forecast of sales, costs, and so on. To do this, you first obtain optimistic and pessimistic estimates for the underlying variables. These are set out in the left-hand columns of Table 8.2.

TABLE 8.2

Sensitivity analysis for the superstore project

Variable	Range			NPV, Thousands of Dollars		
	Pessimistic	Expected	Optimistic	Pessimistic	Expected	Optimistic
Investment ($000)	6,200	5,400	5,000	−121	+478	+778
Sales ($000)	14,000	16,000	18,000	−1218	+478	+2,174
Variable costs as percent of sales	83	81.25	80	−788	+478	+1,382
Fixed Costs ($000)	2,100	2,000	1,900	+26	+478	+930

Next you see what happens to NPV under the optimistic or pessimistic fore-casts for each of these variables. The right-hand side of Table 8.2 shows the project's net present value if the variables are set *one at a time* to their optimistic and pessimistic values. For example, if fixed costs are $1.9 million rather than the fore-cast $2.0 million, annual cash flows are increased by (1 – tax rate) × ($2.0 mil-lion – $1.9 million) = .6 × $100,000 = $60,000. An extra $60,000 a year for 12 years adds 7.536 × $60,000 = $452,000 to the project's value. Therefore, NPV increases from $478,000 to $930,000.

Your project appears to be by no means a sure thing. The principal uncertain-ties appear to be sales and variable costs. For example, if sales are only $14 mil-lion rather than the forecast $16 million (and all other forecasts are unchanged), then the project has an NPV of –$1.218 million. If variable costs are 83 percent of sales (and all other forecasts are unchanged), then the project has an NPV of –$788,000.

SELF-TEST 8.1
• • • • • • • • • • • • • • •

Recalculate cash flow as in Table 8.1 and confirm that NPV will be –$788,000 million if variable costs are 83 percent of sales.

Value of Information. Now that you know the project could be thrown badly off course by a poor estimate of sales, you might like to see whether it is possible to resolve some of this uncertainty. Perhaps your worry is that the store will fail to attract sufficient shoppers from neighbouring towns. In that case, additional sur-vey data and more careful analysis of travel times may be worthwhile.

On the other hand, there is less value to gathering additional information about fixed costs. Because the project is marginally profitable even under pessimistic assumptions about fixed costs, you are unlikely to be in trouble if you have mis-estimated that variable.

Limits to Sensitivity Analysis. Your analysis of the forecasts for Finefodder's new superstore is known as a *sensitivity analysis*. Sensitivity analysis expresses cash flows in terms of the variables and then calculates the consequences of misesti-mating those variables. It forces the manager to identify the underlying factors, indicates where additional information would be most useful, and helps to expose confused or inappropriate forecasts.

Of course, there is no law stating which variables you should consider in your sensitivity analysis. For example, you may wish to look separately at labour costs and the costs of the goods sold. Or, if you are concerned about a possible change in the corporate tax rate, you may wish to look at the effect of such a change on the project's NPV.

One drawback to sensitivity analysis is that it gives somewhat ambiguous results. For example, what exactly does *optimistic* or *pessimistic* mean? One department may be interpreting the terms in a different way from another. Ten years from now, after hundreds of projects, hindsight may show that one depart-ment's pessimistic limit was exceeded twice as often as the other's; but hindsight won't help you now while you're making the investment decision.

Another problem with sensitivity analysis is that the underlying variables are likely to be interrelated. For example, if sales exceed expectations, demand will likely be stronger than you anticipated and, if this allows your prices to be increased, your profit margins will be wider. Or, if wages are higher than your forecast, both variable costs and fixed costs are likely to be at the upper end of your range.

Because of these connections, you cannot push *one-at-a-time* sensitivity analysis too far. It is impossible to obtain expected, optimistic, and pessimistic values for total *project* cash flows from the information in Table 8.2. Still, it does give a sense of which variables should be most closely monitored.

Scenario Analysis

scenario analysis: Project analysis given a particular combination of assumptions.

When variables are interrelated, managers often find it helpful to look at how their project would fare under different scenarios. **Scenario analysis** allows them to look at different but *consistent* combinations of variables. Forecasters generally prefer to give an estimate of revenues or costs under a particular scenario rather than giving some absolute optimistic or pessimistic value.

For example, perhaps you are worried that Stop and Scoff may decide to build a new store in nearby Oxford Junction. That would reduce sales in your Ecum Secum store by 15 percent and you might be forced into a price war to keep the remaining business. Prices might be reduced to the point that variable costs equal 82 percent of revenue. Table 8.3 shows that under this scenario of lower sales and smaller margins your new venture would no longer be worthwhile.

TABLE 8.3

Scenario analysis. NPV of Finefodder's Ecum Secum superstore with scenario of new competing store in nearby Oxford Junction (figures in thousands of dollars).

	Cash Flows, Years 1–12	
	Base Case	**Competing Store Scenario**[a]
1. Sales	$16,000	$13,600
2. Variable costs	13,000	11,152
3. Fixed costs	2,000	2,000
4. Depreciation	450	450
5. Pretax profit (1 − 2 − 3 − 4)	550	−2
6. Taxes (at 40%)	220	1
7. Profit after tax	330	−1
8. Cash flow from operations (4 + 7)	780	449
Present value of cash flows	5,878	3,382
NPV	478	−2,018

[a] *Assumptions:* Competing store causes (1) a 15 percent reduction in sales, and (2) variable costs to increase to 82 percent of sales.

An extension of scenario analysis is called *simulation analysis.* Here, instead of specifying a relatively small number of scenarios, a computer generates several hundred or thousand possible combinations of variables according to a probability distribution specified by the analyst. Each combination of variables corresponds to one scenario. Project NPV and other outcomes of interest can be calculated for each combination of variables, and the entire probability distribution of outcomes can be constructed from the simulation results.

Break-Even Analysis

break-even analysis: Analysis of the level of sales at which the company breaks even.

When we undertake a sensitivity analysis of a project or when we look at alternative scenarios, we are asking how serious it would be if we have misestimated sales or costs. Managers sometimes prefer to rephrase this question and ask how far out the estimates could be before the project begins to lose money. This exercise is known as **break-even analysis.**

For many projects, the make-or-break factor is sales volume. Therefore, managers most often focus on the break-even level of sales. However, you might also look at other variables, for example, at how high costs could be before the project goes into the red.

As it turns out, "losing money" can be defined in more than one way. Most often, the break-even condition is defined in terms of accounting profits. More properly, however, it should be defined in terms of net present value. We will start with accounting break-even, show that it can lead you astray, and then show how NPV break-even can be used as an alternative.

Accounting Break-Even Analysis

The *accounting break-even* point is the level of sales at which profits are zero or, equivalently, at which total revenues equal total costs. As we have seen, some costs are fixed regardless of the level of output. Other costs vary with the level of output.

When you first analyzed the superstore project, you came up with the following estimates:

Sales	$16 million
Variable cost	13 million
Fixed costs	2 million
Depreciation	0.45 million

Notice that variable costs are 81.25 percent of sales. So, for each additional dollar of sales, costs increase by only $.8125. We can easily determine how much business the superstore needs to attract to avoid losses. If the store sells nothing, the income statement will show fixed costs of $2 million and depreciation of $450,000. Thus there will be a loss of $2.45 million. Each dollar of sales reduces this loss by $1.00 − $.8125 = $.1875. Therefore, to cover fixed costs plus depreciation, you need sales of 2.45 million/.1875 = $13.067 million. At this sales level, the firm will break even. More generally,

$$\text{Break-even level of revenues} = \frac{\text{fixed costs including depreciation}}{\text{additional profit from each additional dollar of sales}}$$

Table 8.4 shows how the income statement looks with only $13.067 million of sales.

TABLE 8.4
Income statement, break-even sales volume

Item	$ Thousands
Revenues	13,067
Variable costs	10,617 (81.25 percent of sales)
Fixed costs	2,000
Depreciation	450
Pretax profit	0
Taxes	0
Profit after tax	0

Figure 8.1 shows how the break-even point is determined. The 45-degree line shows accounting revenues. The cost line shows how costs vary with sales. If the store doesn't sell a cent, it still incurs fixed costs and depreciation amounting to $2.45 million. Each extra dollar of sales adds $.8125 to these costs. When sales are $13.067 million, the two lines cross, indicating that costs equal revenues. For lower sales, revenues are less than costs and the project is in the red; for higher sales, revenues exceed costs and the project moves into the black.

Is a project that breaks even in accounting terms an acceptable investment? If you are not sure about the answer, here's a possibly easier question. Would you be happy about an investment in a stock that after 5 years gave you a total rate of return of zero? We hope not. You might break even on such a stock but a zero return does not compensate you for the time value of money or the risk that you

FIGURE 8.1
Accounting break-even
analysis.

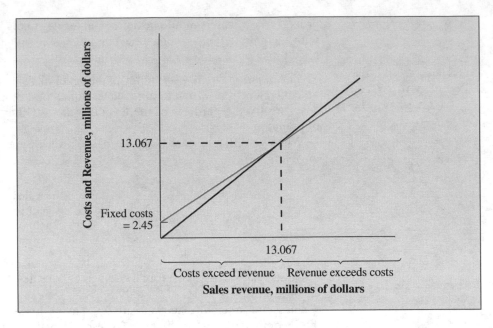

may have taken. In the same way, a project that simply breaks even on an accounting basis gives you your money back but does not cover the opportunity cost of the capital tied up in the project. A project that breaks even in accounting terms will surely have a negative NPV.

Let's check this with the superstore project. Suppose that in each year the store has sales of $13.067 million — just enough to break even on an accounting basis. What would be the cash flow from operations?

$$\text{Cash flow from operations} = \text{profit after tax} + \text{depreciation}$$

$$= 0 + \$450{,}000 = \$450{,}000$$

The initial investment is $5.4 million. In each of the next 12 years, the firm receives a cash flow of $450,000. So the firm gets its money back:

$$\text{Total cash flow from operations} = \text{Initial investment}$$

$$12 \times \$450{,}000 = \$5.4 \text{ million}$$

But revenues are not sufficient to repay the opportunity cost of that $5.4 million investment. NPV is negative.

NPV Break-Even Analysis

Instead of asking how bad sales can get before the project makes an accounting loss, it is more useful to focus on the point at which NPV switches from positive to negative.

The cash flows of the project in each year will depend on sales as follows:

1.	Variable costs	81.25 percent of sales
2.	Fixed costs	$2 million
3.	Depreciation	$450,000
4.	Pretax profit	$(.1875 \times \text{sales}) - \$2.45$ million
5.	Tax (at 40%)	$.40 \times (.1875 \times \text{sales} - \$2.45 \text{ million})$
6.	Profit after tax	$.60 \times (.1875 \times \text{sales} - \$2.45 \text{ million})$
7.	Cash flow (3 + 6)	$\$450{,}000 + .60 \times (.1875 \times \text{sales} - \$2.45 \text{ million})$ $= .1125 \times \text{sales} - \$1.02 \text{ million}$

This cash flow will last for 12 years. So to find its present value we multiply by the 12-year annuity factor. With a discount rate of 8 percent, the present value of $1 a year for each of 12 years is $7.536. Thus the present value of the cash flows is

$$PV(\text{cash flows}) = 7.536 \times (.1125 \times \text{sales} - \$1.02 \text{ million})$$

The project breaks even in present value terms (that is, has a zero NPV) if the present value of these cash flows is equal to the initial $5.4 million investment. Therefore, break-even occurs when

$$PV(\text{cash flows}) = \text{investment}$$

$$7.536 \times (.1125 \times \text{sales} - \$1.02 \text{ million}) = \$5.4 \text{ million}$$

$$-\$7.69 \text{ million} + .8478 \times \text{sales} = \$5.4 \text{ million}$$

$$\text{sales} = \frac{5.4 + 7.69}{.847} = \$15.4 \text{ million}$$

This implies that the store needs sales of just over $15.4 million a year for the investment to have a zero NPV. This is more than 18 percent higher than the point at which the project has zero profit.

Figure 8.2 is a plot of the present value of the inflows and outflows from the superstore as a function of annual sales. The two lines cross when sales are $15.4 million. This is the point at which the project has zero NPV. As long as sales are greater than this, the present value of the inflows exceeds the present value of the outflows and the project has a positive NPV.

FIGURE 8.2
NPV break-even analysis.

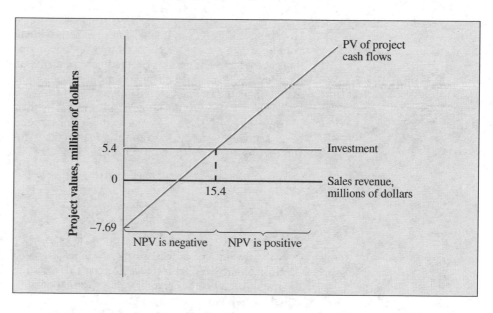

SELF-TEST 8.2   What would be the NPV break-even level of sales if the capital investment was only $5 million?

● **EXAMPLE 8.1 Break-Even Analysis**

We have said that projects that break even on an accounting basis are really making a loss — they are losing the opportunity cost of their investment. Here is a dramatic example. Lophead Aviation is contemplating investment in a new passenger aircraft, code-named the Trinova. Lophead's financial staff has gathered together the following estimates:

1. The cost of developing the Trinova is forecast at $900 million, and this investment can be depreciated in six equal annual amounts.
2. Production of the plane is expected to take place at a steady annual rate over the following 6 years.
3. The average price of the Trinova is expected to be $15.5 million.
4. Fixed costs are forecast at $175 million a year.
5. Variable costs are forecast at $8.5 million a plane.
6. The tax rate is 50 percent.
7. The cost of capital is 10 percent.

TABLE 8.5

Forecast profitability for production of the Trinova airliner (figures in millions of dollars)

	Year 0	Years 1–6
Investment	$900	
1. Sales		15.5 × planes sold
2. Variable costs		8.5 × planes sold
3. Fixed costs		175
4. Depreciation		900/6 = 150
5. Pretax profit (1 − 2 − 3 − 4)		(7 × planes sold) − 325
6. Taxes (at 50%)		(3.5 × planes sold) − 162.5
7. Net profit (5 − 6)		(3.5 × planes sold) − 162.5
8. Net cash flow (4 + 7)	−$900	(3.5 × planes sold) − 12.5

How many aircraft does Lophead need to sell to break even in accounting terms? And how many does it need to sell to break even on the basis of NPV? (Notice that the break-even point is defined here in terms of number of aircraft, rather than revenue. But since revenue is proportional to planes sold, these two break-even concepts are interchangeable.)

To answer the first question we set out the profits from the Trinova program in rows 1 to 7 of Table 8.5 (ignore row 8 for a moment).

In accounting terms the venture breaks even when pretax profit (and therefore net profit) is zero. In this case

$$(7 \times \text{planes sold}) - 325 = 0$$

$$\text{Planes sold} = \frac{325}{7} = 46$$

Thus Lophead needs to sell about 46 planes a year, or a total of about 280 planes over the 6 years to show a profit.

Notice that we obtain the same result if we attack the problem in terms of the break-even level of revenue. The variable cost of each plane is $8.5 million, which is 54.8 percent of the $15.5 million price. Therefore, each dollar of sales increases pretax profits by $1 − $.548 = $.452. So

$$\text{Break-even revenue} = \frac{\text{fixed costs including depreciation}}{\text{additional profit from each additional dollar of sales}}$$

$$= \frac{\$325 \text{ million}}{.452} = \$719 \text{ million}$$

Since each plane cost $15.5 million, this revenue level implies sales of 719/15.5 = 46 planes per year.

Now let us look at what sales are needed before the project has a zero NPV. Development of the Trinova costs $900 million. For each of the next 6 years the company expects a cash flow of $3.5 million × planes sold – $12.5 million (see row 8 of Table 8.5). If the cost of capital is 10 percent, the 6-year annuity factor is 4.355. So

$$NPV = -900 + 4.355(3.5 \times \text{planes sold} - 12.5)$$

$$= 15.24 \times \text{planes sold} - 954.44$$

If the project has a zero NPV,

$$0 = 15.24 \text{ planes sold} - 954.44$$

$$\text{Planes sold} = 63$$

Thus Lophead can recover its initial investment with sales of 46 planes a year (about 280 in total), but it needs to sell 63 a year (or about 375 in total) to earn a return on this investment equal to the opportunity cost of capital.

Our example may seem fanciful but it is based loosely on reality. In 1971 Lockheed was in the middle of a major program to bring out the L-1011 TriStar airliner. This program was to bring Lockheed to the brink of failure and it tipped

Finance in Action

Capital Budgeting in Large Canadian Firms

Responses to a survey sent to Canada's largest corporations paint a surprising picture of capital budgeting in Canada in the 90s.

In their article "Corporate Financial Decision Making in Canada," published in *The Canadian Journal of Administrative Sciences* during 1994, Jog and Srivastava note a variety of disturbing facts about firms that completed the survey. Their overall conclusion is that "significant challenges lie ahead for corporate management in Canada and its ability to be internationally competitive." When evaluating one technical issue the authors suggest that "It appears that we are where the United States was about a decade back"! Some of their findings about capital budgeting in Canada's largest firms—

- When forecasting cash flows, most rely on subjective estimates by managers.
- When determining the attractive-

ness of projects, internal rate of return and payback period measures are used more than the superior NPV approach.

- When it came to factoring in the effects of risk, 31 percent of firms increased their required return and 24 percent shortened their discount period, but only 18 percent explored the probability distribution of cash flows. Less than 60 percent of the firms used sensitivity analysis to analyze risk. (*Note:* Responses totalled more than 100 percent as many firms used multiple approaches.)

Other shortcomings of surveyed firms included a low use of analytical methods, and significant use of inappropriate discount rates.

Rolls-Royce (supplier of the TriStar engine) over the brink. In giving evidence to the U.S. Congress, Lockheed argued that the TriStar program was commercially attractive and that sales would eventually exceed the break-even point of about 200 aircraft. But in calculating this break-even point Lockheed appears to have ignored the opportunity cost of the huge capital investment on the project. Lockheed probably needed to sell about 500 aircraft to reach a zero net present value.[3]

·······················
Operating Leverage

fixed costs: Costs incurred regardless of the level of output.

variable cost: Costs that rise with the level of output.

A project's break-even point depends on both its **fixed costs**, that is, costs that do not vary with sales, and the profit on each extra sale. Managers often face a trade-off between these variables. For example, we typically think of rental expenses as fixed costs. But supermarket companies sometimes rent stores with contingent rent agreements. This means that the amount of rent the company pays is tied to the level of sales from the store. Rent rises and falls along with sales. The store thus replaces a fixed cost with a **variable cost**, that is, a cost that rises along with sales. Because a greater proportion of the company's expenses will fall when its sales fall, its break-even point is reduced.

Of course, a high proportion of fixed costs is not all bad. The firm whose costs are largely fixed fares poorly when demand is low, but it may make a killing during a boom. Let us illustrate.

Finefodder has a policy of hiring long-term employees who will not be laid off except in the most dire circumstances. For all intents and purposes, these salaries are fixed costs. Its rival, Stop and Scoff, has a much smaller permanent labour force and uses expensive temporary help whenever demand for its product requires extra staff. A greater proportion of its labour expenses are therefore variable costs.

Suppose that if Finefodder adopted its rival's policy, fixed costs in its new superstore would fall from $2 million to $1.56 million but variable costs would rise from 81.25 to 84 percent of sales. Table 8.6 shows that with the normal level of sales, the two policies fare equally. In a slump a store that relies on temporary labour does better since its costs fall along with revenue. In a boom the reverse is true and the store with the higher proportion of fixed costs has the advantage.

operating leverage: Degree to which costs are fixed.

If Finefodder follows its normal policy of hiring long-term employees, each extra dollar of sales results in a change of $1.00 - $.8125 = $.1875 in pretax profits. If it uses temporary labour, an extra dollar of sales leads to a change of only $1.00 - $.84 = $.16 in profits. As a result, a store with high fixed costs is said to have high **operating leverage**. High operating leverage magnifies the effect on profits of a fluctuation in sales.

TABLE 8.6

A store with high operating leverage performs relatively badly in a slump but flourishes in a boom (figures in thousands of dollars)

	High Fixed Costs			High Variable Costs		
	Normal	**Slump**	**Boom**	**Normal**	**Slump**	**Boom**
Sales	16,000	13,000	19,000	16,000	13,000	19,000
– Variable costs	13,000	10,563	15,438	13,440	10,920	15,960
– Fixed costs	2,000	2,000	2,000	1,560	1,560	1,560
– Depreciation	450	450	450	450	450	
= Pretax profit	550	–13	1,112	550	70	1,030

---

[3] The true break-even point for the TriStar program is estimated in U. E. Reinhardt, "Break-Even Analysis for Lockheed's TriStar: An Application of Financial Theory," *Journal of Finance* 28 (September 1973), pp. 821–838.

degree of operating leverage (DOL): Percentage change in profits given a 1 percent change in sales.

We can measure a business's operating leverage at a projected level of sales by asking how much profits change for each 1 percent change in sales. The **degree of operating leverage**, often abbreviated as **DOL**, is this measure:

$$DOL = \frac{\text{percentage change in profits}}{\text{percentage change in sales}}$$

For example, Table 8.6 shows that as the store moves from normal conditions to boom, sales increase from $16 million to $19 million, a rise of 18.75 percent. For the policy with high fixed costs, profits increase from $550,000 to $1,112,000, a rise of 102.2 percent. Therefore,

$$DOL = \frac{102.2}{18.75} = 5.45$$

The percentage change in sales is magnified more than fivefold in terms of the percentage impact on profits.

Now look at the operating leverage of the store if it uses the policy with low fixed costs but high variable costs. As the store moves from normal times to boom, profits increase from $550,000 to $1,030,000, a rise of 87.3 percent. Therefore,

$$DOL = \frac{18.75}{87.3} = 4.65$$

Because some costs remain fixed, a change in sales continues to have a magnified effect on profits but the degree of operating leverage is lower.

In fact, one can show that degree of operating leverage depends on fixed charges (including depreciation) in the following manner:

$$DOL = 1 + \frac{\text{fixed costs}}{\text{profits}}$$

This relationship makes it clear that operating leverage increases with fixed costs. For example, using the data from the normal sales scenario, the formula predicts that DOL under the high-fixed-cost policy should be

$$DOL = 1 + \frac{2.00 + .45}{.55} = 5.45$$

This value matches the one we obtained by comparing the actual percentage changes in sales and profits.

You can see from this example that the risk of a project is affected by the degree of operating leverage. If a large proportion of costs is fixed, a shortfall in sales has a magnified effect on profits. We will have more to say about risk in the next three chapters.

SELF-TEST 8.3

Suppose that sales increase by 10 percent from the values in the normal scenario. Compute the percentage change in pretax profits from the normal level for both policies in Table 8.6. Compare your answers to the values predicted by the DOL formula.

 ## 8.3 FLEXIBILITY IN CAPITAL BUDGETING

Sensitivity analysis and break-even analysis help managers understand why a venture might fail. Once you know this you can decide whether it is worth investing more time and effort in trying to resolve the uncertainty.

Of course it is impossible to clear up all doubts about the future. Therefore, managers also try to build flexibility into the project and they value more highly a project that allows them to mitigate the effect of unpleasant surprises and to capitalize on pleasant ones.

Decision Trees

The scientists at MacCaugh have developed a diet whiskey and the firm is ready to go ahead with pilot production and test marketing. The preliminary phase will take a year and cost $200,000. Management feels that there is only a 50–50 chance that the pilot production and market tests will be successful. If they are, then MacCaugh will build a $2 million plant that will generate an expected annual cash flow in perpetuity of $480,000 a year after taxes. Given an opportunity cost of capital of 12 percent, project NPV in this case will be –$2 million + $480,000/.12 = $2 million. If the tests are not successful, MacCaugh will discontinue the project and the cost of the pilot production will be wasted. How can MacCaugh decide whether to spend the money on the pilot program?

Notice that the only decision MacCaugh needs to make now is whether to go ahead with the preliminary phase. Depending on how that works out, it may choose to go ahead with full-scale production.

decision tree: Diagram of alternative sequential decisions and possible outcomes.

When faced with projects like this that involve sequential decisions, it is often helpful to draw a **decision tree**, as in Figure 8.3. You can think of the problem as a game between MacCaugh and fate. The square represents a decision point for MacCaugh and the circle represents a decision point for fate. MacCaugh starts the play at the left-hand box. If MacCaugh decides to test, then fate will cast the enchanted dice and decide the result of the tests. Given the test results, the firm faces a second decision: Should it invest $2 million and start full-scale production?

FIGURE 8.3
Decision tree.

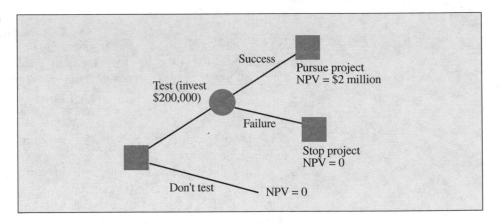

The second-stage decision is obvious: *Invest if the tests indicate that NPV is positive, and stop if they indicate that NPV would be negative.* Now the firm can easily decide between paying for the test program or stopping immediately. The net present value of stopping is zero, so the first-stage decision boils down to a simple problem: Should MacCaugh invest $200,000 now to obtain a 50 percent chance of a project with an NPV of $2 million a year later? If payoffs of zero and $2 million are equally likely, the expected payoff is (.5 × 0) + (.5 × 2 million) = $1 million. Thus the pilot project offers an expected payoff of $1 million on an investment of $200,000. At any reasonable cost of capital this is a good deal.[4]

---

[4] The pilot project is riskier than the later investment. If diet whiskey proves unpopular, the investment of $200,000 in the pilot project will be completely wasted. Thus the company should require a higher return from the pilot project than from the second-stage investment.

Notice that MacCaugh's expenditure on the pilot program buys a valuable managerial option. The firm has the *option* to produce the new product depending on the outcome of the tests. If the pilot program turns up disappointing results, the firm can walk away from the project without incurring additional costs. This option to walk away once the results are revealed introduces a valuable asymmetry. Good outcomes can be exploited, while bad outcomes can be limited by canceling the project.

MacCaugh was not obliged to have a pilot program. Instead, it could have gone directly into full-scale whiskey production. After all, if diet whiskey is a success, the sooner MacCaugh can clean up the market the better. But it is possible that the product will *not* take off; in that case the expenditure on the pilot operation may help the firm avoid a costly mistake. When it proposed a pilot project, MacCaugh's management was simply following the fundamental rule of swimmers: If you know the water temperature, dive in; if you don't, try putting a toe in first.

Here is another example of an apparently unprofitable investment that has value because of the flexibility it gives to make further follow-on investments. Some of the world's largest oil reserves are found in Alberta's Athabasca tar sands. Unfortunately, the cost of extracting oil from the sands is substantially higher than the current market price and almost certainly higher than most people's estimate of the likely price in the future. Yet oil companies have been prepared to pay considerable sums for these tracts of barren land. Why?

The answer is that they give the companies an option. They are not obliged to extract the oil. If oil prices remain below the cost of extraction, the Athabasca sands will remain undeveloped. But if prices do rise above the cost of extraction, those land purchases could prove very profitable.

Notice that flexibility is valuable only because the future is so uncertain. If we *knew* that future oil prices would remain at their current level, nobody would pay a cent for the tar sands. It is the prospect that oil prices may fluctuate sharply around their present level that gives the option value.[5]

You can probably think of many other investments that take on added value because of the further opportunities that they may open up. For example, when designing a factory, it may make sense to provide for the possibility in the future of an additional production line; when building a four-lane highway, it may pay to build six-lane bridges so that the road can be converted later to six lanes if traffic volume turns out to be higher than expected.

If the option to expand has value, what about the option to bail out? Projects don't just go on until the equipment disintegrates. The decision to terminate a project is usually taken by management, not by nature. Once the project is no longer profitable, the company will cut its losses and exercise its option to abandon the project.

Some assets are easier to bail out of than others. Tangible assets are usually easier to sell than intangible ones. It helps to have active secondhand markets, which really exist only for standardized, widely used items. Real estate, airplanes, trucks, and certain machine tools are likely to be relatively easy to sell. On the other hand, the knowledge accumulated by a drug company's research and development program is a specialized intangible asset and probably would not have significant abandonment value. Some assets, such as old mattresses, even have

---

[5] Oil prices sometimes move very sharply. They roughly doubled in 1979; in 1986 they fell by more than 40 percent.

negative abandonment value; you have to pay to get rid of them. It is very costly to decommission nuclear power plants or to reclaim land that has been strip-mined.

Managers recognize the option to abandon when they make the initial investment. For example, suppose that the Wigeon Company must choose between two technologies for the manufacture of a new product, a Wankel engine outboard motor:

1. Technology A uses custom-designed machinery to produce the complex shapes required for Wankel engines at low cost. But if the Wankel engine doesn't sell, this equipment will be worthless.
2. Technology B uses standard machine tools. Labour costs are much higher, but the tools can easily be sold if the motor doesn't sell.

Technology A looks better in a simple NPV analysis of the new product, because it was designed to have the lowest possible cost at the planned production volume. Yet you can sense the advantage of technology B's flexibility if you are unsure whether the new outboard will sink or swim in the marketplace. In such cases managers may choose technology B because it gives them the option to abandon the project at low cost.

SELF-TEST 8.4	Consider a firm operating a copper mine that incurs both variable and fixed costs of production. Suppose the mine can be shut down temporarily if copper prices fall below the variable cost of mining copper. Why is this a valuable operating option? How does it increase the NPV of the mine to the operator?

Flexible Production Facilities

If the firm is uncertain about the future demand for its products, it may build in the option to vary the output mix. For example, many oil refineries are designed to produce a diverse mix of oil products. The refinery can then vary its output to capture the highest profits. Of course such flexibility seldom comes free; it is worth paying for the flexibility only because the future is uncertain and demand is variable.

Companies also try to avoid becoming dependent on a single source of raw materials, and, whenever possible, they build flexibility into their production facilities. For example, a power plant may be designed to operate with either gas or oil. The company can then choose the lower cost alternative. In effect, the company has the option to exchange one asset (a gas-fired station) for another (an oil-fired station).

Investment Timing Options

Suppose that you have a project that might be a big winner or a big loser. The project's upside potential outweighs its downside potential, and it has a positive NPV if undertaken today. However, the project is not "now-or-never." Should you invest right away or wait? It's hard to say. If the project truly is a winner, waiting means loss or deferral of its early cash flows. But if it turns out to be a loser, it may pay to wait and get a better fix on the likely demand.

You can think of any project proposal as giving you the *option* to invest today. You don't have to exercise that option immediately. Instead you need to weigh the value of the cash flows lost by delaying against the possibility that you will pick up some valuable information.

Think again of those tar sands in Athabasca. Suppose that the price of oil rises to 10 cents a barrel above your cost of production. You can extract the oil profitably at this price. But it still might be worth delaying production. After all, if the price dips, you have not lost much. If it rises further, however, you could make a killing.

Flexibility is valued by managers because the future is so uncertain. Ideally, a project will give the firm an option to expand if things go well and to bail out or switch production if they don't. In addition, it may pay the firm to postpone the project.

Some managers treat capital investment decisions as black boxes; they are handed cash-flow forecasts and they churn out present values without looking inside the black box. But successful firms ask not only what could be wrong with the forecasts but whether there are opportunities to respond to surprises. In other words, they recognize the value of flexibility.

 **SUMMARY**

1. For most large corporations there are two stages in the investment process: the preparation of the regular capital budget, which is a list of planned investments, and the detailed approval process for individual projects. This process is usually an effort that involves many individuals, and potential problems must be considered.

2. Good managers realize that the forecasts behind NPV calculations are imperfect. Therefore they explore the consequences of a poor forecast and check whether it is worth doing some more homework. They use two principal tools to answer these what-if questions:

- Sensitivity analysis, where only one variable at a time is changed.
- Scenario analysis, where the manager considers changes to entire groups of variables so as to simulate alternative scenarios.

3. In break-even analysis the focus is on how far sales could fall before the project begins to lose money. Often the phrase "lose money" is defined in terms of accounting losses, but this could destroy shareholder wealth by ignoring the opportunity cost of their invested capital. It makes more sense to define losing money as "failing to cover the opportunity cost of capital" — in other words, as a negative NPV.

4. A project's break-even point will be affected by the extent to which costs can be reduced as sales decline. If costs are largely fixed, the project is said to have high *operating leverage.*

5. Some projects may take on added economic value because they give the firm the option to bail out if things go wrong or to capitalize on success by expanding. We showed how decision trees may be used to analyze such flexibility.

KEY TERMS

capital budget	break-even analysis	operating leverage
sensitivity analysis	fixed costs	degree of operating
scenario analysis	variable costs	leverage
		decision tree

SUGGESTED READINGS

For an excellent case study of break-even analysis, see

U. E. Reinhardt, "Break-Even Analysis for Lockheed's TriStar: An Application of Financial Theory," *Journal of Finance*, 28 (September 1973): 821–838.

The use of decision trees in investment appraisal is discussed in

J. Magee, "How to Use Decision Trees in Capital Investments," *Harvard Business Review*, 43 (September–October 1964): 79–96.

PROBLEMS

1. In a slow year, Wimpy's Burgers will produce 1 million hamburgers at a total cost of $1.5 million. In a good year, it can produce 2 million hamburgers at a total cost of $2 million. What are the fixed and variable costs of hamburger production?

2. Dime a Dozen Diamonds makes synthetic diamonds by treating carbon. Each diamond can be sold for $100. The materials cost for a standard diamond is $30. The fixed costs incurred each year for factory upkeep and administrative expenses are $200,000. The machinery costs $1 million and is depreciated straight-line over 10 years to a salvage value of zero.
   a. What is the accounting break-even level of sales in terms of number of diamonds sold?
   b. What is NPV break-even sales assuming a tax rate of 35 percent, a 10-year project life, and a discount rate of 12 percent?
   c. Would the accounting break-even point in the first year of operation increase or decrease if the machinery were depreciated over a 5-year period?
   d. Would the NPV break-even point increase or decrease if the machinery were depreciated over a 5-year period?

3. You are evaluating a project that will require an investment of $10 million that will be depreciated for tax purposes on a straight-line basis over a period of 7 years. You are concerned that the corporate tax rate will increase during the life of the project. Would such an increase affect the accounting break-even point? Would it affect the NPV break-even point?

4. You estimate that your cattle farm will generate $1 million of profits on sales of $4 million under normal economic conditions, and that the degree of operating leverage is 7.6. What will profits be if sales turn out to be $3.5 million? What if they are $4.5 million?

5. Define the *cash-flow break-even point* as the sales volume (in dollars) at which cash flow equals zero. Is the cash-flow break-even level of sales higher or lower than the zero-profit break-even point?

6. If a project operates at cash-flow break-even for its entire life, what must be true of the project's NPV?

7. A project currently generates sales of $10 million, variable costs equal to 50 percent of sales, and fixed costs of $2 million. The firm's tax rate is 35 percent. What are the effects of the following changes on after-tax profits and cash flow?
   a. Sales increase from $10 million to $11 million.
   b. Variable costs increase to 60 percent of sales.

8. The project in problem 7 will last for 10 years. The discount rate is 12 percent.
   a. What is the effect on project NPV of each of the changes considered in problem 7?

    b. If project NPV under the base-case scenario is $2 million, how much can fixed costs increase before NPV turns negative?

    c. How much can fixed costs increase before accounting profits turn negative?

9. A project has fixed costs of $1000 per year, depreciation charges of $500 a year, revenue of $6000 a year, and variable costs equal to two-thirds of revenues.

    a. If sales increase by 10 percent, what will be the increase in pretax profits?

    b. What is the degree of operating leverage of this project?

    c. Confirm that the percentage change in profits equals DOL times the percentage change in sales.

10. Emperor's Clothes Fashions can invest $5 million in a new plant for producing invisible makeup. The plant has an expected life of 5 years, and expected sales are 6 million jars of makeup a year. Fixed costs are $2 million a year, and variable costs are $1 per jar. The product will be priced at $2 per jar. The plant will be depreciated straight-line over 5 years to a salvage value of zero. The opportunity cost of capital is 12 percent, and the tax rate is 40 percent.

    a. What is project NPV under these base-case assumptions?

    b. What is NPV if variable costs turn out to be $1.20 per jar?

    c. What is NPV if fixed costs turn out to be $1.5 million per year?

    d. At what price per jar would project NPV equal zero?

11. Reconsider Finefodder's new superstore. Suppose that by investing an additional $600,000 initially in more efficient checkout equipment, Finefodder could reduce variable costs to 80 percent of sales.

    a. Using the base-case assumptions (Table 8.1), find the NPV of this alternative scheme. *Hint*: Remember to focus on the *incremental* cash flows from the project.

    b. At what level of sales will accounting profits be unchanged if the firm invests in the new equipment? Assume the equipment receives the same 12-year straight-line depreciation treatment as in the original example. *Hint*: Focus on the project's incremental effects on fixed and variable costs.

    c. What is the NPV break-even point?

12. If the superstore project operates at accounting break-even will net present value be positive or negative?

13. Your midrange guess as to the amount of oil in a prospective field is 10 million barrels, but in fact there is a 50 percent chance that the amount of oil is 15 million barrels, and a 50 percent chance of 5 million barrels. If the actual amount of oil is 15 million barrels, the present value of the cash flows from drilling will be $8 million. If the amount is only 5 million barrels, the present value will be only $2 million. It costs $3 million to drill the well. Suppose that a seismic test that costs $100,000 can verify the amount of oil under the ground. Is it worth paying for the test? Use a decision tree to justify your answer.

14. A silver mine can yield 10,000 ounces of copper at a variable cost of $8 per ounce. The fixed costs of operating the mine are $10,000 per year. In half the years, silver can be sold for $11 per ounce; in the other years, silver can be sold for only $7 per ounce. Ignore taxes.

a. What is the average cash flow you will receive from the mine if it is always kept in operation and the silver always is sold in the year it is mined?

b. Now suppose you can shut down the mine in years of low silver prices. What happens to the average cash flow from the mine?

15. An auto plant that costs $1 million to build can produce a new line of cars that will produce cash flows with a present value of $1.4 million if the line is successful, but only $500,000 if it is unsuccessful. You believe that the probability of success is only about 50 percent.

a. Would you build the plant?

b. Suppose that the plant can be sold for $900,000 to another automaker if the auto line is not successful. Now would you build the plant?

c. Illustrate the option to abandon in (b) using a decision tree.

SOLUTIONS TO SELF-TEST QUESTIONS

8.1 Cash flow forecasts for Finefodder's new superstore (all forecasts in thousands of dollars):

	Year 0	Years 1–12
Investment	−5,400	
1. Sales		16,000
2. Variable costs		13,280
3. Fixed costs		2,000
4. Depreciation		450
5. Pretax profit $(1 - 2 - 3 - 4)$		270
6. Taxes (at 40%)		108
7. Profit after tax		162
8. Cash flow from operations $(4 + 7)$		612
Net cash flow	−5,400	612

$$\text{NPV} = -\$5.4 \text{ million} + (7.536 \times \$612{,}000) = -\$788{,}000$$

8.2 With the lower initial investment, depreciation is also lower; it now equals $417,000 per year. Cash flow is now as follows:

1. Variable costs   81.25 percent of sales
2. Fixed costs $2 million
3. Depreciation $417,000
4. Pretax profit $(.1875 \times \text{sales}) - \$2.417$ million
5. Tax (at 40%) $.4 \times (.1875 \times \text{sales} - \$2.417 \text{ million})$
6. Profit after tax $.6 \times (.1875 \times \text{sales} - \$2.417 \text{ million})$
7. Cash flow $(3 + 6)$ $.6 \times (.1875 \times \text{sales} - \$2.417 \text{ million})$
                            $+\$417{,}000 = .1125 \times \text{sales} - \$1.033 \text{ million}$

Break-even occurs when

$$\text{PV (cash inflows)} = \text{investment}$$

$$7.536 \times (.1125 \times \text{sales} - \$1.033 \text{ million}) = \$5.0 \text{ million}$$

and sales = $15.08 million.

8.3 Reworking Table 8.6 for the normal level of sales and 10 percent higher sales gives the following:

	High Fixed Costs		High Variable Costs	
	Normal	**10% Higher Sales**	**Normal**	**10% Higher Sales**
Sales	16,000	17,600	16,000	17,600
− Variable costs	13,000	14,300	13,440	14,784
− Fixed costs	2,000	2,000	1,560	1,560
− Depreciation	450	450	450	450
= Pretax profit	550	850	550	806

For the high-fixed-cost policy, profits increase by 54.5 percent, from $550,000 to $850,000. For the low-fixed-cost policy, profits increase by 46.5 percent. In both cases the percentage increase in profits equals DOL times the percentage increase in sales. This illustrates that DOL measures the sensitivity of profits to changes in sales.

8.4 The option to shut down is valuable because the mine operator can avoid incurring losses when copper prices are low. If the shut-down option were not available, cash flow in the low-price periods would be negative. With the option, the worst cash flow is zero. By allowing managers to respond to market conditions, the option makes the worst-case cash flow better than it would be otherwise. The average cash flow (that is, averaging over all possible scenarios) therefore must improve, which increases project NPV.

PART THREE

Risk

CHAPTER NINE
Introduction to Risk, Return, and the
Opportunity Cost of Capital

CHAPTER TEN
Risk, Return, and Capital Budgeting

CHAPTER ELEVEN
The Cost of Capital

CHAPTER **NINE**

Introduction to Risk, Return, and the Opportunity Cost of Capital

We have thus far skirted issues concerning project risk; now it is time to confront these issues head-on. We can no longer be satisfied with vague statements like "The opportunity cost of capital depends on the risk of the project." We need to know how to measure risk and we need to understand the relationship between risk and the cost of capital. These are the topics of the next two chapters.

Think for a moment what the cost of capital for a project means. It is the rate of return that shareholders could expect to earn if they invested in equally risky securities. So one way to estimate the cost of capital is to find securities that have the same risk as the project and then estimate the expected rate of return on these securities.

We start our analysis by looking at the rates of return earned in the past from different investments, concentrating on the *extra* return that investors have received for investing in risky rather than safe securities. We then show how to measure the risk of a portfolio by calculating its standard deviation and we look again at past history to find out how risky it is to invest in the stock market.

Finally, we explore the concept of diversification. Most investors do not put all their eggs into one basket — they diversify. Thus investors are not concerned with the risk of each security in isolation; instead they are concerned with how much it contributes to the overall risk of their "basket" of securities — their diversified portfolio. We therefore need to distinguish between the risk that can be eliminated by diversification and the risk that cannot be eliminated.

After studying this chapter you should be able to

- Estimate the opportunity cost of capital for an "average-risk" project.
- Calculate the standard deviation of returns for individual common stocks or for a stock portfolio.
- Understand why diversification reduces risk.
- Distinguish between unique risk, which can be diversified away, and market risk, which cannot.

9.1 RATES OF RETURN: A REVIEW

If you buy a stock or a bond, your return comes in two forms: (1) a dividend or interest payment, and (2) a capital gain or capital loss. For example, suppose you were lucky enough to buy the stock of CanWest Global Communications, a television broadcaster, at the beginning of June, 1993 when its price was $18.75 a share. By the end of one year the price of the stock had appreciated to $34, giving a capital gain of $34 – $18.75 = $15.25 a share. In addition, over the year CanWest paid a dividend of $.35 a share.

The percentage return on your investment was therefore

$$\text{Percentage return} = \frac{\text{capital gain} + \text{dividend}}{\text{initial share price}}$$

$$= \frac{\$15.25 + \$.35}{\$18.75} = .832, \text{ or } 83.2\%$$

Remember that in Chapter 4 we made a distinction between the *nominal* rate of return and the *real* rate of return. The nominal return measures how much more money you will have at the end of the year if you invest today. The return that we have just calculated for CanWest stock is therefore a nominal return. The real rate of return tells you how much more you will be able to buy with your money at the end of the year. To convert from a nominal to a real rate of return, we use the following relationship:

$$1 + \text{real rate of return} = \frac{(1 + \text{nominal rate of return})}{1 + \text{inflation rate}}$$

In 1993 inflation was 1.7 percent. So we calculate the real return for CanWest stock as follows:

$$1 + \text{real rate of return} = \frac{1 + .832}{1 + .017} = 1.801$$

Therefore the real rate of return equals .801, or 80.1 percent.

SELF-TEST 9.1

> Suppose you buy a bond for $1020 with a 15-year maturity paying an annual coupon of $80. A year later interest rates have dropped and the bond's price has increased to $1050. What are your nominal and real rates of return? Assume the inflation rate is 4 percent.

9.2 SEVENTY YEARS OF CAPITAL MARKET HISTORY

When you invest in a stock, you can't be sure that your return is going to be as high as CanWest's in 1993. But by looking back at the history of security returns, you can get some idea of the return that investors might reasonably expect from investments in different types of securities and of the risks that they face. Therefore, we begin with a brief review of the risk–return tradeoff investors have experienced in the past.

Market Indexes

market index: Measure of the investment performance of the overall market.

Investors can choose from an enormous number of different securities. Currently more than 1500 issues of common and preferred stocks issued by about 1200 companies trade on the Toronto Stock Exchange (TSE), 886 issues trade on the Montreal Exchange (ME), almost 1800 securities are traded on the Vancouver Stock Exchange (VSE), more than 800 securities are listed on the Alberta Stock Exchange (ASE), and well over 500 are traded in the over-the-counter market called the Canadian Dealing Network (CDN).[1] In addition to the four Canadian stock exchanges and the over-the-counter market, Canadian investors are free to cross-border shop in U.S. and overseas markets.

Financial analysts can't track every stock, so they rely on **market indexes** to summarize the return on different classes of securities. The best-known stock market index in Canada is the **Toronto Stock Exchange (TSE) 300 Composite Index**.

Toronto Stock Exchange (TSE) 300 Composite Index: Index of the investment performance of a portfolio of 300 major stocks listed on the Toronto Stock Exchange. Also called the *TSE 300*.

The "TSE 300" tracks the performance of a portfolio of 300 stocks selected from the 14 industry subgroups on the TSE. As a broadly based index, the TSE 300 is designed to capture the overall performance of the Toronto Stock Exchange. It is a value-weighted index with weights based on the total number of shares out-

---

[1] The CDN System is a network of dealers linked by computer terminals and telephone. It is a price quotation system, not a trading system. An investor, through his or her broker, can use the CDN system to find out the price that various dealers are willing to trade listed shares. The actual transactions are made via direct negotiations between a trader and the broker. In contrast, shares are sold through open auctions on organized stock exchanges such as the TSE or ME.

standing minus any shares held in control blocks.[2] To calculate the index, the prices of each of the 300 stocks are multiplied by their weight and then are added together. Thus the index measures the current value of a portfolio of 300 stocks. Suppose that the TSE 300 starts the day at a value of 4000 and then rises by 40 points to a new value of 4040. Over the day the portfolio makes a capital gain of 40/4000 = .01 or 1 percent.

Toronto Stock Exchange (TSE) 300 Total Return Index: Index based on the prices plus the dividends paid by the 300 stocks in the TSE 300 Composite Index.

If you want to know the total rate of return (capital gains plus dividends) on the TSE 300, you must use the **TSE 300 Total Return Index**, which includes both the stock prices and all the dividends paid. The TSE 300 Total Return Index is currently around 8000. An increase in the index of 100 points implies a total return of 100/8000 = 0.0125 or 1.25 percent.

When the TSE 300 is reported in the news, typically it is the TSE 300 Composite Index and not the Total Return Index. However, you will want to use the Total Return Index if, for example, you want to see how well a stock did in comparison to the overall market. Dividends are an important part of the payment received as a shareholder. If you use the TSE 300 Composite Index, you will underestimate the return on the market because the dividends have been ignored.

Other Canadian stock exchanges publish market indexes. The Montreal Exchange main index is the Market Portfolio Index and consists of 25 of the largest publicly held corporations in Canada listed on the ME. The Vancouver Stock Exchange Composite Index is based on the prices of 300 of the biggest stocks listed on the VSE.

In today's world with the highly integrated, global financial markets, it is important to monitor trading activity in other countries' financial markets. The four leading stock markets are the American New York Stock Exchange (NYSE), the Japanese Toyko Stock Exchange, the British London Stock Exchange, and the German Frankfurt Stock Exchange. Each of these exchanges has its own stock index. By far the most widely quoted is the **Dow Jones Industrial Average**, generally known as the *Dow*. The Dow tracks the performance of a portfolio that invests one share in each of 30 large firms listed on the NYSE.

Dow Jones Industrial Average: Index of the investment performance of a portfolio of 30 U.S. "blue-chip" stocks.

Although it is widely quoted, the Dow Jones Industrial Average is far from the best measure of the performance of the U.S. stock market. First, with only 30 large industrial stocks, it is not representative of stocks generally. Second, it is an equal weighted index, with each security given equal weight, regardless of the relative number of shares available. The **Standard and Poor's Composite Index**, better known as the *S&P 500*, includes the stocks of 500 major companies and is therefore a more comprehensive index than the Dow. Also, it measures the performance of a portfolio that holds shares in each firm in proportion to the number of shares that have been issued. For example, the S&P portfolio would hold just over five times as many shares in Du Pont as Union Carbide. Thus the S&P 500 shows the average performance of investors in the 500 firms.

Standard and Poor's Composite Index: Index of the investment performance of a portfolio of 500 large U.S. stocks. Also called the *S&P 500*.

Only a small proportion of the thousands of publicly traded companies are represented in the TSE 300 or the S&P 500. However, these firms are among the largest in Canada and the U.S., respectively, and they account for a high percentage of the *value* of stocks traded. The TSE 300 stocks account for over 40 percent of the value of stocks listed on the Toronto Stock Exchange and the S&P 500 accounts for roughly 70 percent of the value of publicly traded stocks in the U.S.

---

[2] The TSE defines a control block as a block of shares representing more than 20 percent of the outstanding shares. Shares in control blocks are not included on the grounds that they tend to trade infrequently.

Therefore, success for professional and institutional investors usually means "beating the TSE 300" or "beating the S&P."

Important indexes from countries outside of North America include the Nikkei 225 Index for Tokyo and the Financial Times–Stock Exchange Index for London, England and the DAX Index for the Frankfurt Stock Exchange. Morgan Stanley Capital International (MSCI) even computes a world stock market index. Dow Jones, Inc., which publishes the Dow, has responded with its own World Stock Index. Some stock market indexes, such as the Wilshire 5000, include an even larger number of stocks, while others focus on special groups of stocks such as the stocks of small companies.

The Historical Record

The historical returns of stock or bond market indexes can give us an idea of the typical performance of different investments. A study by Boyle, Panjer and Sharp, which covers 1924 to 1990, augmented with data from *ScotiaMcLeod's Handbook of Canadian Debt Market Indices* provided information on Canadian market indices.[3] U.S. data was collected from an ongoing study by Ibbotson Associates, which reports the performance of several portfolios of securities since 1926.[4] From the information sources we measure the historical performance of the following portfolios:

1. A portfolio of Treasury bills — Canadian or United States government securities maturing in less than one year.[5]
2. A portfolio of long-term government bonds.
3. A portfolio of long-term corporate bonds.
4. A portfolio of stocks — the Toronto Stock Exchange Composite Index and the Standard and Poor's Composite Index. These are portfolios of the 300 and 500 common stocks, respectively.[6]

These portfolios are not equally risky. Treasury bills are about as safe an investment as you can make. Because they are issued by the government, you can be sure that you will get your money back. Their short-term maturity means that their prices are relatively stable. In fact, investors who wish to lend money for 3 months can achieve a certain payoff by buying 3-month Treasury bills. Of course, they can't be sure what that money will buy: there is still some uncertainty about inflation.

Long-term government bonds are also certain to be repaid when they mature, but the prices of these bonds fluctuate more as interest rates vary. When interest rates fall, the value of a long-term bond portfolio rises; when rates rise, the value of the bond portfolio falls.

An investment in corporate bonds is also subject to the risk of interest rate fluctuations but carries with it the additional risk that a company may become bankrupt and be unable to pay off its debts.

[3] Canadian data was taken from P.P. Boyle, H.H. Panjer and K.P. Sharp, "Report on Canadian Economic Statistics 1924–1990," Canadian Institute of Actuaries, Ottawa, 1991 and *ScotiaMcLeod's Handbook of Canadian Debt Market Indices*, 1947–1993, ScotiaMcLeod, Toronto, February 1994.
[4] U.S. data is taken from *Stocks, Bonds, and Inflation 1993 Yearbook*, Ibbotson Associates, Chicago.
[5] Canada did not have Treasury bills prior to 1933. To get a data series for the whole period, we used Ibbotson Associates Treasury bill data for 1926 to 1933.
[6] Data for the TSE 300 index are only available from 1956. Boyle et al. use the TSE Industrial Index for 1935–1956 and an index by Urquhart and Buckley for 1925–1934. (See Urquhart, M.C. and Buckley, K.A.H., *Historical Statistics of Canada*, Macmillan Company, Toronto, 1965). Naturally this raises questions as to whether these three indexes are really comparable in terms of risk. Of course, the structure of the S&P Index has changed over time, as well.

Common stocks are the riskiest of the four groups of securities. When you invest in common stocks, there is no promise that you will get your money back. As a part-owner of the corporation, you receive whatever is left over after the bonds and any other debts have been repaid.

Figure 9.1 illustrates the investment performance for each asset class since 1925. The figure shows how much one dollar invested in 1925 would have grown to by the end of 1993 assuming that all dividend or interest income had been reinvested in the portfolio.

FIGURE 9.1

The value to which a $1 investment in 1925 would have grown by the end of 1993.

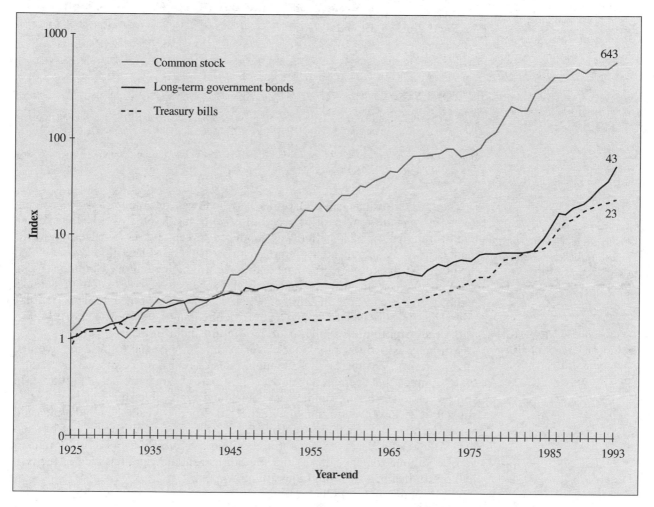

Source: Calculated with data from P.P. Boyle, H.H. Panjer, and K.P. Sharp, "Report on Canadian Economic Statistics 1924–1990," Canadian Institute of Actuaries, Ottawa, 1991; and *ScotiaMcLeod's Handbook of Canadian Debt Market Indices*, 1947–1993.

You can see that the performance of the four portfolios fits with our intuitive risk ranking. Common stocks were the riskiest investment but they also offered the greatest gains. One dollar invested in 1925 in a portfolio of Toronto Stock Exchange listed stocks would have grown to $643 by the end of 1993. At the other end of the spectrum, an investment of $1 in Treasury bills would have accumulated to only $23. A dollar invested in long-term government bonds would have grown to $43 over the 69 years.

With the historical data, the annual rates of return for each of these portfolios is calculated for each year from 1926 to 1992. We picked this period to match the period of the available U.S. data. These rates of return are calculated in the same way as was done for CanWest. In other words, they include (1) dividends or interest and (2) any capital gains or losses. The averages of the 67 annual rates of return are shown in Table 9.1.

TABLE 9.1

Average rates of return on Treasury bills, government bonds, corporate bonds, and common stocks, 1926–1992 (figures in percent per year)

Portfolio	Average Annual Rate of Return (Nominal) (%)		Average Annual Rate of Return (Real) (%)		Average Risk Premium (Extra Return versus Treasury Bills) (%)	
	Canada	U.S.	Canada	U.S.	Canada	U.S.
Treasury bills	4.8	3.8	1.4	0.6		
Government bonds	5.8	5.2	2.5	2.1	1.0	1.4
Corporate bonds	7.2	5.8	2.6	2.7	2.4	2.0
Common stocks	11.4	12.4	7.8	9.0	6.6	8.6

Source: Canadian results are calculated with data provided from P.P. Boyle, H.H. Panjer, and K.P. Sharp, "Report on Canadian Economic Statistics 1924–1990," Canadian Institute of Actuaries, Ottawa, 1991 and *ScotiaMcLeod's Handbook of Canadian Debt Market Indices*, 1947–1993. American results are from © *Stocks, Bonds, and Inflation 1993 Yearbook*™, Ibbotson Associates, Chicago (annual updates work by Roger G. Ibbotson and Rex A. Sinquefield). Used with permission. All rights reserved.

maturity premium: Extra average return from investing in long- versus short-term Treasury securities.

risk premium: Expected return in excess of risk-free return as compensation for risk.

The safest investment, Treasury bills, had the lowest rate of return — 4.8 percent a year in *nominal* terms and 1.4 percent in *real* terms. In other words, the average rate of inflation over this period was about 3.4 percent a year. Long-term government bonds gave slightly higher returns than Treasury bills. This difference is called the **maturity premium**. Corporate bonds gave still higher returns. Common stocks were in a class by themselves. Investors who accepted the risk of common stocks received on average an extra return of 6.6 percent a year over the return on Treasury bills. This compensation for taking on the risk of common stock ownership is known as the **risk premium**. A similar pattern of returns holds for U.S. securities.

You may ask why we look back over such a long period to measure average rates of return. The reason is that annual rates of return for common stocks fluctuate so much that averages taken over short periods are extremely unreliable. In some years investors in common stocks had a disagreeable shock and received a substantially lower return than they expected. In other years they had a pleasant surprise and received a higher return. Our only hope of gaining insights from historical rates of return is to look at a very long period. By averaging the returns across both the rough years and the smooth, we should get a fair idea of the typical return that investors might justifiably expect.

While common stocks have offered the highest average returns, they have also been riskier investments. Figure 9.2 shows the 68 annual rates of return for the four portfolios. The fluctuations in year-to-year stock returns are remarkably wide. There were two years (1933 and 1950) when investors earned a return of more than 50 percent. However, Figure 9.2 shows that you can also lose money by investing in the stock market. The most dramatic case was the stock market crash of 1929–1932. By July 1932 TSE listed common stocks had fallen four years in succession in a series of agonizing slides for a total decline of 88 percent.

Another major market crash, that of Monday, October 19, 1987, does not show up in Figure 9.2. On that day the TSE 300 fell by 11 percent and the S&P 500 fell

Finance in Action

The Fall of Barings Bank

The indexes of stock prices are used for more than just reporting on overall share price movements. As you will see in Chapters 13 and 25, there are a variety of financial instruments that firms and investors can use to take on or offload risk. Some of these instruments are based directly on stock market indexes. Contracts related to the Nikkei-225 stock market average caused many headlines in early 1995.

On February 23, 1995, officials at the Barings Bank found that Nick Leeson, a 28-year-old trader working in the Bank's Singapore branch, had, as part of a multi-billion dollar gamble, bought $7 billion worth of contracts tied to a future level of the Nikkei-225 stock market index. Leeson's buying and selling of futures contracts had apparently been profitable for the Bank in 1994, when Barings profits from futures trading were $12 million. But things went sour in early '95, when Leeson's trading — in the face of a 5 percent drop in the Tokyo stock market index — generated large losses for the Bank. Apparently Leeson then tried a "double or nothing" gamble, hoping that Tokyo's Nikkei would recover from its January plunge before the initial losses were discovered.

The Tokyo market did not improve, and Leeson's attempt to recoup the losses failed. By March 4th, Barings' losses on the Nikkei futures contracts reached $1 billion U.S. This huge loss exceeded the bank's equity, causing the spectacular collapse of the 233-year-old Barings.

by 23 percent, their largest one-day fall in history. However, Black Monday came after a prolonged rise in stock prices, so that over 1987 as a whole investors in common stocks earned a return of 5.2 percent. This was not a terrible return, but many investors who rode the 1987 roller coaster feel that it is not a year they would care to repeat.

SELF-TEST 9.2

Here are the average rates of return calculated for the postwar period 1949–1993:

Stocks	12.71%
Corporate bonds	7.59
Government bonds	6.38
Treasury bills	6.37

What were the risk premium on stocks and the maturity premium on government bonds for this period?

Using Historical Evidence to Estimate Today's Cost of Capital

We now have an idea of the average return an investor might expect to earn from an investment in a portfolio of common stocks. What does this have to do with the cost of capital? Suppose there is an investment project that you *know* — don't ask how — has the same risk as an investment in the portfolio of stocks in the TSE

FIGURE 9.2
Rates of return, 1926–1993.

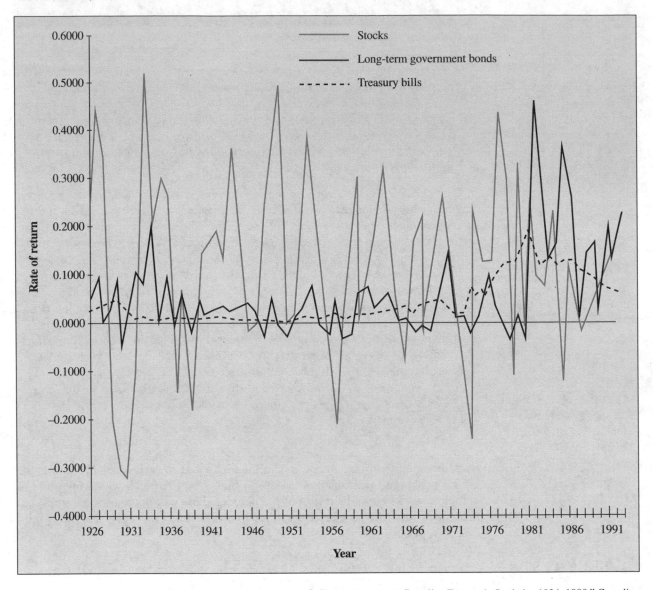

Source: Calculated with data from P.P. Boyle, H.H. Panjer, and K.P. Sharp, "Report on Canadian Economic Statistics 1924–1990," Canadian Institute of Actuaries, Ottawa, 1991; and *ScotiaMcLeod's Handbook of Canadian Debt Market Indices*, 1947–1993.

300 Composite Index. We will say that it has the same degree of risk as the market portfolio of common stocks.[7]

Instead of investing in the project, your shareholders could invest directly in this market portfolio of common stocks. Therefore, the opportunity cost of capital for your project is the return that the shareholders could expect to earn on the market portfolio. This is what they are giving up by investing money in your project.

---

[7] This is speaking a bit loosely, because the TSE 300 does not include all stocks traded in Canada, much less in world markets.

The problem of estimating the project cost of capital boils down to that of estimating the currently expected rate of return on the market portfolio. One way to estimate the expected market return is to assume that the future will be like the past and that today's investors expect to receive the average rates of return shown in Table 9.1. In this case, you would judge that the expected market return today is 11.4 percent, the average of past market returns.

Unfortunately, this is *not* the way to do it. Investors are not likely to demand the same return each year of an investment in common stocks. For example, we know that the interest rate on safe Treasury bills varies over time. At their peak in 1981, Treasury bills offered a return of 18 percent, more than 13 percentage points above the 4.8 percent average return on bills shown in Table 9.1.

What if you were called upon to estimate the expected return on common stocks in 1981? Would you have said 11.4 percent? That doesn't make sense. Who would invest in the risky stock market for an expected return of 11.4 percent when you could get a safe 18 percent from Treasury bills?

A better procedure is to take the *current* interest rate on Treasury bills plus 7 percent, the average *risk premium* shown in Table 9.1. In 1981, when the rate on Treasury bills was 18 percent, that would have given

$$\text{Expected market return (1981)} = \text{interest rate on Treasury bills (1981)} + \text{normal risk premium}$$

$$= 18\% + 7\% = 25\%$$

The first term on the right-hand side tells us the time value of money in 1981; the second term measures the compensation for risk. The sum of the two terms tells us the compensation for both waiting (time value) and worrying (risk).

This calculation assumes that there is a normal, stable risk premium on the market portfolio, so that the expected *future* risk premium can be measured by the average past risk premium. One could quarrel with this assumption, but it does yield estimates of the expected market return that are reasonable.

What about today? As we write this in July 1994, inflation has fallen from its 1981 figure of 12.2 percent to about 1.5 percent. As a result interest rates are also much lower and three month Treasury bills offer a return of only 5.9 percent. This suggests investors in common stocks are looking for a return of almost 13 percent:[8]

$$\text{Expected market return (1994)} = \text{interest rate on Treasury bills (1994)} + \text{normal risk premium}$$

$$= 5.9\% + 7\% = 12.9\%$$

You now have a couple of benchmarks. You know that the opportunity cost of capital for safe projects must be the rate of return offered by safe Treasury bills and you know that the opportunity cost of capital for "average-risk" projects must be the expected rate of return on the market portfolio. But you don't know how to estimate the cost of capital for projects that do not fit these two simple cases. Before you can do this, you need to understand more about investment risk.

---

[8] In practice, things might be a bit more complicated. We've mentioned the term structure of interest rates, the relationship between bond maturity and yield. When firms consider investments in long-lived projects, they usually think about risk premiums relative to long-term bonds. In this case, the risk-free rate would be taken as the current long-term bond yield less the average maturity premium on such bonds.

9.3 MEASURING PORTFOLIO RISK

The average fuse time for army hand grenades is 7.0 seconds, but that average hides a lot of potentially relevant information. If you are in the business of throwing grenades, you need some measure of the variation around the average fuse time.[9] Similarly, if you are in the business of investing in securities, you need some measure of how far the returns may differ from the average.

Figure 9.2 showed the year-by-year returns for several investments over the 1926–1993 period. Another way of presenting these data is by a histogram such as those in Figure 9.3. Each bar shows the number of years that the market return fell within a specific range. For example, you can see that in 8 of the 68 years the return on common stocks was between +10 percent and +15 percent. The risk shows up in the wide spread of outcomes. In 2 years the return was between +50 percent and +60 percent but there were also 2 years in which it was between –30 percent and –35 percent.

Variance and Standard Deviation

variance: Average value of squared deviations from mean. A measure of volatility.

standard deviation: Square root of variance. Another measure of volatility.

One of the histograms in Figure 9.3 illustrates the variation in common stock returns, but we need a simpler way to summarize this variation. Intuitively, we know that risk should be related to the dispersion or spread of possible outcomes. More variable returns imply greater investment risk. This suggests that some measure of dispersion will provide a reasonable measure of risk, and dispersion is precisely what is measured by **variance** and **standard deviation**.

Here is a very simple example showing how variance and standard deviation are calculated. Suppose that you are offered the chance to play the following game. You start by investing $100. Then two coins are flipped. For each head that comes up your starting balance will be *increased* by 20 percent, and for each tail that comes up your starting balance will be *reduced* by 10 percent. Clearly there are four equally likely outcomes:

- Head + head: You make   20 + 20 =   40%
- Head + tail: You make   20 – 10 =   10%
- Tail + head: You make –10 + 20 =   10%
- Tail + tail: You make –10 – 10 = –20%

There is a chance of 1 in 4, or .25, that you will make 40 percent; a chance of 2 in 4, or .5, that you will make 10 percent; and a chance of 1 in 4, or .25, that you will lose 20 percent. The game's expected return is therefore a weighted average of the possible outcomes:

Expected return = Probability-weighted average of possible outcomes

$$= (.25 \times 40) + (.5 + 10) + (.25 \times -20) = +10\%$$

If you play the game a very large number of times, your average return should be 10 percent.

Table 9.2 shows how to calculate the variance and standard deviation of the returns on your game. Column 1 shows the four equally likely outcomes. In column 2 we calculate the difference between each possible outcome and the expected outcome. You can see that at best the return could be 30 percent higher than expected; at worst it could be 30 percent lower.

These deviations in column 2 illustrate the spread of possible returns. But if we want a measure of this spread, it is no use just averaging the deviations in

---

[9] We can reassure you; the variation around the standard fuse time is very small.

FIGURE 9.3
Historical returns on major asset classes, 1926–1993.

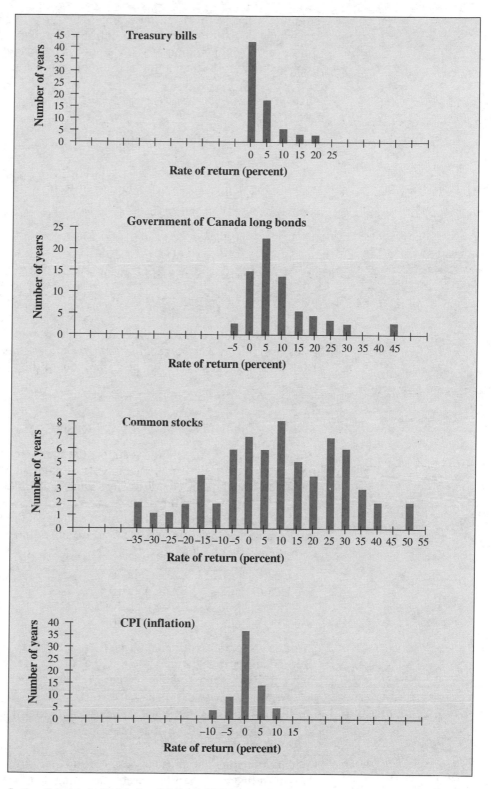

Source: Calculated with data from P.P. Boyle, H.H. Panjer, and K.P. Sharp, "Report on Canadian Economic Statistics 1924–1990," Canadian Institute of Actuaries, Ottawa, 1991; and *ScotiaMcLeod's Handbook of Canadian Debt Market Indices, 1947–1993.*

column 2 because this is always going to be zero. To get round this problem, we square the deviations in column 2 before averaging them. These squared deviations are shown in column 3. The variance is the average of these squared deviations and therefore is a natural measure of dispersion:

Variance = average of squared deviations around the mean

$$= \frac{1800}{4} = 450$$

TABLE 9.2

The coin-tossing game: calculating variance and standard deviation

(1) Percent Rate of Return (%)	(2) Deviation from Expected Return	(3) Squared Deviation
+40	+30	900
+10	0	0
−10	0	0
−20	−30	900

Variance = average of squared deviations = 1800/4 = 450

Standard deviation = square root of variance = $\sqrt{450}$ = 21.2, about 21%.

When we squared the deviations from the expected return, we changed the units of measurement from *percentages* to *percentages squared*. Our last step is to get back to percentages by taking the square root of the variance. This is the standard deviation:

Standard deviation = square root of variance

$$= \sqrt{450} = 21\%$$

Because standard deviation is simply the square root of variance, it too is a natural measure of risk. If the outcome of the game had been certain, the standard deviation would have been zero. The actual standard deviation is positive because we don't know what will happen.

Now think of a second game. It is the same as the first except that each head means a 35 percent gain and each tail means a 25 percent loss. Again there are four equally likely outcomes:

- Head + head: You gain 70%
- Head + tail: You gain 10%
- Tail + head: You gain 10%
- Tail + tail: You lose 50%

For this game, the expected return is 10 percent, the same as that of the first game. But its standard deviation is double that of the first game, 42 percent versus 21 percent. By this measure the second game is twice as risky as the first.

SELF-TEST 9.3

Calculate the variance and standard deviation of this second coin-tossing game in the same format as Table 9.2.

Measuring the Variation in Stock Returns

When estimating the spread of possible outcomes from investing in the stock market, most financial analysts start by assuming that the spread of returns in the past is a reasonable indication of what could happen in the future. Therefore, they calculate the standard deviation of past returns. To illustrate, suppose that you were presented with the data for stock market returns shown in Table 9.3. The average return over the 6 years from 1988 to 1993 was 9.8 percent. This is just the sum of the returns over the 6 years divided by 6 (58.9/6 = 9.8 percent).

TABLE 9.3

The average return and standard deviation of stock market returns, 1988–1993

Year	(1) Rate of Return (%)	(2) Deviation from Average Return	(3) Squared Deviation
1988	11.1	1.3	1.6
1989	21.4	11.6	133.7
1990	−14.8	−24.6	605.6
1991	12.0	2.2	4.8
1992	− 1.4	−11.2	125.6
1993	30.6	20.8	432.3
Total	58.9		1,303.6

Average rate of return = 58.9/6 = 9.8%

Variance = average of squared deviations = 1,303.6/6 = 217.3

Standard deviation = square root of variance = $\sqrt{217.3}$ = 14.7%

Column 2 in Table 9.3 shows the difference between each year's return and the average return. For example, in 1989 the return of 21.4 percent on common stocks exceeded the 6-year average by 11.6 percent (21.4 − 9.8 = 11.6 percent). In column 3 we square these deviations from the average. The variance is then the average of these squared deviations:[10]

$$\text{Variance} = \text{average of squared deviations}$$

$$= \frac{1303}{6} = 217.3$$

Since standard deviation is the square root of the variance,

$$\text{Standard deviation} = \text{square root of variance}$$

$$= \sqrt{217.3} = 14.7\%$$

It is difficult to generalize about the risk of securities on the basis of just six past outcomes. Therefore, Table 9.4 lists the annual standard deviations for our four portfolios of securities over the period 1926–1993. As expected, Treasury bills were the least variable security, and common stocks were the most variable. Long-term government and corporate bonds hold the middle ground.

Of course, there is no reason to believe that the market's variability should stay the same over many years. Indeed many people believe that in recent years the stock market has become more volatile due to irresponsible speculation by (fill in here the name of your preferred guilty party). Table 9.5 provides information on the volatility of the Canadian stock market for 6 periods from 1926 to 1993. We should be cautious about reading too much into standard deviations calculated with ten or so annual returns. However, these figures do not support the wide-

---

[10] Consider this technical point. When we use a series of past returns to predict or generalize about the variability of returns, we need to divide the sum of the squared deviations by the number of observations minus one. We do this to correct for what is known as the loss of a degree of freedom. The corrected variance is 1303.6/5 = 260.7 and the corrected standard deviation is 16.1 percent.

TABLE 9.4
Standard deviation
of rates of return,
1926*–1993

Portfolio	Standard Deviation (%)
Treasury bills	4.5
Long-term government bonds	8.7
Corporate bonds	9.6
Common stocks	19.3

* = All except corporate bonds (1949–1993).
Source: Calculated with data from P.P. Boyle, H.H. Panjer, and K.P. Sharp, "Report on Canadian Economic Statistics 1924–1990," Canadian Institute of Actuaries, Ottawa, 1991, and *ScotiaMcLeod's Handbook of Canadian Debt Market Indices*, 1947–1993.

spread impression of especially volatile stock prices during the 1980s. Overall, the 1980s had below average volatility.

However, the 1980s did experience brief episodes of extreme volatility. On Black Monday, October 19, 1987, the TSE 300 fell 11 percent and the U.S. stock market fell 23 percent *on a single day!* The standard deviation for the U.S. market index for the week surrounding Black Monday was equivalent to 89 percent per week. Fortunately, volatility dropped back to normal levels within a few weeks after the crash.

TABLE 9.5
Stock market standard
deviation

Period	Standard Deviation (%)
1926–1939	27.3
1940–1949	15.2
1950–1959	21.5
1960–1969	14.1
1970–1979	19.7
1980–1993	15.6

Source: Calculated with data from P.P. Boyle, H.H. Panjer, and K.P. Sharp, "Report on Canadian Economic Statistics 1924–1990," Canadian Institute of Actuaries, Ottawa, 1991 and *ScotiaMcLeod's Handbook of Canadian Debt Market Indices*, 1947–1993.

 RISK AND DIVERSIFICATION

Diversification

We can calculate our measures of variability equally well for individual securities and portfolios of securities. Of course, the level of variability over 68 years is less interesting for specific companies than for the market portfolio because it is a rare company that faces the same business risks today as it did in 1926.

Table 9.6 presents estimated standard deviations for 14 well-known common stocks for a recent 5-year period.[11] Do these standard deviations look high to you? They should. Remember that the market portfolio's standard deviation was about 20 percent over the entire 1926–1993 period. None of the 14 individual stocks had standard deviations of less than 20 percent. Most stocks are substantially more variable than the market portfolio; only a handful are less variable.

This raises an important question: The market portfolio is made up of individual stocks, so why isn't its variability equal to the average variability of its components? The answer is that **diversification** reduces variability.

diversification: Strategy designed to reduce risk by spreading the portfolio across many investments.

---

[11] We pointed out earlier that five annual observations are insufficient to give a reliable estimate of variability. Therefore, these estimates are derived from 60 *monthly* rates of return. We converted the monthly variance to an annual variance by multiplying by 12. In other words, the variance of annual returns is 12 times that of monthly returns. The longer you hold a security, the more risk you have to bear.

TABLE 9.6
Standard deviations for
selected common stocks,
1989–1993 (figures in
percent per year)

Stock	Standard Deviation (%)	Stock	Standard Deviation (%)
Alcan Aluminum	68.9	Magna International	217.9
BC Telecom	49.7	Molson Companies	71.8
Bombardier	108.1	Northern Telecom	100.4
Finning Limited	90.1	Royal Bank of Canada	67.1
George Weston	58.2	Shaw Communications	78.2
Greyhound Lines	75.1	SHL Systemhouse	217.1
Inco Limited	97.1	Westcoast Energy	54.4

Source: Calculated with monthly return data from the CFMRC database.

Selling umbrellas is a risky business; you may make a killing when it rains but you are likely to lose your shirt in a heat wave. Selling ice cream is no safer; you do well in the heat wave but business is poor in the rain. Suppose, however, that you invest in both an umbrella shop and an ice cream shop. By diversifying your investment across the two businesses you make an average level of profit come rain or shine.

Portfolio diversification works because prices of different stocks do not move exactly together. Statisticians make the same point when they say that stock price changes are less than perfectly correlated. Diversification works best when the returns are negatively correlated, as is the case for our umbrella and ice cream businesses. When one business does well, the other does badly. Unfortunately, in practice stocks that are negatively correlated are as rare as haggis in Budapest.

Asset versus Portfolio Risk

The history of returns on different asset classes provides compelling evidence of a risk-return trade-off and suggests that the variability of the rates of return on each asset class is a useful measure of risk. However, volatility of returns can be a misleading measure of risk for an individual asset held as part of a portfolio. To see why, consider the following example.

Suppose there are three equally likely outcomes, or scenarios, for the economy: a recession, normal growth, and a boom. An investment in an auto stock will have a rate of return of –8 percent in a recession, 5 percent in a normal period, and 18 percent in a boom. Auto firms are *cyclical*: They do well when the economy does well. In contrast, gold firms are often said to be *countercyclical*, meaning that they do well when other firms do poorly. Suppose that stock in a gold mining firm will provide a rate of return of 20 percent in a recession, 3 percent in a normal period, and –20 percent in a boom. These assumptions are summarized in Table 9.7.

TABLE 9.7
Rate of return
assumptions for
two stocks

Scenario	Probability	Rate of Return (%)	
		Auto stock	Gold stock
Recession	1/3	– 8	+20
Normal	1/3	+ 5	+ 3
Boom	1/3	+18	–20

It appears that gold is the more volatile investment. The difference in return across the boom and bust scenarios is 40 percent (–20 percent in a boom versus +20 percent in a recession), compared to a spread of only 26 percent for the auto stock. In fact, we can confirm the higher volatility by measuring the variance or standard deviation of returns of the two assets. The calculations are set out in Table 9.8.

TABLE 9.8
Expected return and
volatility for two stocks

Scenario	Auto Stock			Gold Stock		
	Rate of Return (%)	Deviation from Expected Return (%)	Squared Deviation	Rate of Return (%)	Deviation from Expected Return (%)	Squared Deviation
Recession	− 8	−13	169	+20	+19	361
Normal	+ 5	0	0	+ 3	+ 2	4
Boom	+18	+13	169	−20	−21	441
Expected return	$\frac{1}{3}(-8 + 5 + 18) = 5\%$			$\frac{1}{3}(+20 + 3 - 20) = 1\%$		
Variance*	$\frac{1}{3}(169 + 0 + 169) = 112.7$			$\frac{1}{3}(361 + 4 + 441) = 268.7$		
Standard deviation (= √variance)	$\sqrt{112.7} = 10.6\%$			$\sqrt{268.7} = 16.4\%$		

*Variance = average of squared deviations from the expected value.

Since all three scenarios are equally likely, the expected return on each stock is simply the average of the three possible outcomes.[12] For the auto stock the expected return is 5 percent; for the gold stock it is 1 percent. The variance is the average of the squared deviations from the expected return and the standard deviation is the square root of the variance.

SELF-TEST 9.4

Suppose the probabilities of the recession or boom are .30, while the probability of a normal period is .40. Would you expect the variance of returns on these two investments to be higher or lower? Why? Confirm by calculating the standard deviation of the auto stock. (Refer back to the coin-toss example if you are unsure of how to do this.)

The gold mining stock offers a lower expected rate of return than the auto stock, and more volatility — a loser on both counts, right? Would anyone be willing to hold gold mining stocks in an investment portfolio? The answer is a resounding yes.

To see why, suppose you do believe that gold is a lousy asset, and therefore hold your entire portfolio in the auto stock. Your expected return is 5 percent and your standard deviation is 10.6 percent. We'll compare that portfolio to a partially diversified one, invested 75 percent in autos and 25 percent in gold. For example, if you have a $10,000 portfolio, you could put $7500 in autos and $2500 in gold.

First, we need to calculate the return on this portfolio in each scenario. The portfolio return is the weighted average of returns on the individual assets with weights equal to the proportion of the portfolio invested in each asset. For example, autos have a weight of .75 and a rate of return of −8 percent in the recession, and gold has a weight of .25 and a return of 20 percent in a recession. Therefore, the portfolio return in the recession is the following weighted average:[13]

---

[12] If the probabilities were not equal, we would need to weight each outcome by its probability in calculating the expected outcome and the variance.

[13] Let's confirm this. Suppose you invest $7500 in autos and $2500 in gold. If the recession hits, the rate of return on autos will be −8 percent, and the value of the auto investment will fall by 8 percent to $6900. The rate of return on gold will be 20 percent, and the value of the gold investment will rise 20 percent to $3000. The value of the total portfolio falls from its original value of $10,000 to $6900 + $3000 = $9900, which is a rate of return of −1 percent. This matches the rate of return given by the formula for the weighted average.

Portfolio return in recession = $[.75 \times (-8\%)] + [.25 \times 20\%] = -1\%$

Table 9.9 expands Table 9.7 to include the portfolio of the auto stock and the gold mining stock. The expected returns and volatility measures are summarized at the bottom of the table. The surprising finding is this: When you shift funds from the auto stock to the more volatile gold mining stock, your portfolio variability actually *decreases*. In fact, the volatility of the auto-plus-gold stock portfolio is considerably less than the volatility of either stock separately. This is the payoff to diversification.

TABLE 9.9

Rate of return for two stocks and a portfolio

Scenario	Probability	Rate of Return (%)		Portfolio* (%)
		Auto Stock	**Gold Stock**	
Recession	1/3	− 8	+20	−1.0
Normal	1/3	+ 5	+ 3	+4.5
Boom	1/3	+18	−20	+8.5
Expected return		5%	1%	4%
Variance		112.7	268.7	15.2
Standard deviation		10.6%	16.4%	3.9%

*Portfolio variance = (.75 × auto stock return) + (.25 × gold stock return)

We can understand this more clearly by focusing on asset returns in the two extreme scenarios, boom and recession. In the boom, when auto stocks do best, the poor return on gold reduces the performance of the overall portfolio. However, when auto stocks are stalling in a recession, gold shines, providing a substantial positive return that boosts portfolio performance. The gold stock offsets the swings in the performance of the auto stock, reducing the best-case return but increasing the worst-case return. The inverse relationship between the returns on the two stocks means that the addition of the gold mining stock to an all-auto portfolio stabilizes returns.

A gold stock is really a *negative risk* asset to an investor starting with an all-auto portfolio. Adding it to the portfolio reduces the volatility of returns. The *incremental* risk of the gold stock (that is, the change in overall risk when gold is added to the portfolio) is *negative* despite the fact that gold returns are highly volatile.

In general, the incremental risk of a stock depends on whether its returns tend to vary with or against the returns of the other assets in the portfolio. Incremental risk does not just depend on a stock's volatility. If returns vary inversely with those of the rest of the portfolio, the stock will reduce the volatility of portfolio returns. We can summarize as follows:

1. Investors care about the expected return and risk of their portfolio of assets. The risk of the overall portfolio can be measured by the volatility of returns, that is, the variance or standard deviation.

2. The risk of an individual security held as part of a portfolio depends on how it affects portfolio volatility. This depends on how the security's returns vary in relation to the rest of the portfolio. The total volatility of individual securities held as parts of a larger portfolio is of little concern.

The Mathematics of Portfolio Diversification

We have given you an intuitive idea of how diversification reduces risk: combining assets in a portfolio reduces portfolio risk because the assets' prices do not move in exact lockstep. When one stock is doing poorly, another will be doing well, helping to offset the negative impact on the portfolio return. To more fully understand how diversification works, we introduce you to a concept from statistics: *correlation*.

correlation coefficient:
Measure of the closeness
of the relationship be-
tween two variables.

Correlation (or **correlation coefficient**) measures the degree to which two variables move together. The correlation coefficient between two variables is a number between −1 and +1. If the correlation is positive, the two variables tend to move in the same direction. If the correlation is negative, the two variables tend to move in the opposite direction. If the correlation is zero, a change in one variable does not tell you anything about the likely change in the other. The closer to 1 (−1) is the correlation, the stronger is the positive (negative) relationship between the two variables. Two variables with a correlation of 1 are said to be perfectly positively correlated. If the correlation is −1, they are perfectly negatively correlated. Two variables with a correlation of zero are said to be uncorrelated.

SELF-TEST 9.5

Are each of the following pairs of variables likely to be positively correlated, negatively correlated, or uncorrelated? Briefly explain why.

a. The number of hours of sunshine per day and average daily air temperature.

b. The number of hours of television you watch per day and your grade on your finance final.

c. The flying time from Vancouver to St. John's and the quality of the inflight movie.

d. The level of interest rates in the United States and the level of interest rates in Canada.

Correlation is a useful concept for measuring how stocks move relative to each other. In the previous example, we said that auto firms were cyclical: they tend to do well when the economy is doing well. In other words, the return on auto stocks is positively correlated with the economy. On the other hand, gold stocks were said to be countercyclical, tending to do well when the economy is doing poorly. Thus the return on gold stocks tends to have low correlation with the economy.

The degree of correlation among assets determines the extent to which risk is reduced through portfolio diversification. To illustrate, we will create a portfolio of two stocks, Steelco (S), manufacturer of construction steel, and Gold Bear (G), a gold mine and refinery. The expected return on Steelco shares is 15 percent and the expected return on Gold Bear shares is 9 percent. The expected return on the portfolio will depend on the fraction of funds invested in the two stocks. Let x_S be the fraction of the total funds invested in shares of Steelco, a manufacturer of construction steel, and x_G be the fraction invested in shares of Gold Bear Mine. The expected return on the portfolio is the weighted average of the expected returns on the two stocks, where the weights equal the fraction invested in each:

$$r_p = x_S(15\%) + x_G(9\%)$$

If 100 percent of the funds are invested in Steelco, $x_S = 1$ and $x_G = 0$, the portfolio expected return is 15 percent, the expected return on Steelco. If 25 percent of the funds are invested in Steelco ($x_S = .25$) and 75 percent is invested in Gold Bear ($x_G = .75$), then the expected portfolio return is:

$$r_p = .25(15\%) + .75(9\%) = 10.5\%$$

We can write the general formula for expected return as

$$r_p = x_S r_S + x_G r_G,$$

where r_S and r_G are the expected returns on Steelco and Gold Bear shares, respectively.

The above mathematical formula shows that the expected return on the portfolio is the weighted average of the expected return on the assets in the portfolio. Is the portfolio standard deviation equal to the weighted average of the standard deviations of assets in the portfolio? The answer depends on the correlation between the assets in the portfolio! If the assets' returns are perfectly positively correlated, then there is no benefit from diversification and the portfolio standard deviation is simply the weighted average of the individual stocks' standard deviations. However, if the stocks are less than perfectly correlated, diversification reduces portfolio risk — the portfolio standard deviation will be less than the simple weighted average of the assets' standard deviations.

To show you how this works, we need a bit of notation. The standard deviation of the return on Steelco is σ_S and the standard deviation of the return on Gold Bear is σ_G. We use the symbol ρ_{SG} to represent the correlation between the return on the two companies' shares. The expression for the standard deviation of the portfolio combining shares of Steelco and Gold Bear is:

$$\sigma_p = \sqrt{x_S^2 \sigma_S^2 + x_G^2 \sigma_G^2 + 2 x_S x_G \rho_{SG} \sigma_S \sigma_G}$$

where σ_p is the standard deviation of the portfolio of stocks S and G. You can see that the correlation coefficient between stocks S and G, ρ_{SG}, is included in the formula for the portfolio standard deviation. Thus the standard deviation of the portfolio depends on the individual stocks' standard deviations and also on their correlation with each other.

To see how different values of the correlation coefficient affect the portfolio standard deviation, look again at the Steelco and Gold Bear portfolio. The portfolio has 25 percent of the funds invested in Steelco ($x_S = .25$) and 75 percent invested in Gold Bear Mine ($x_G = .75$). The standard deviation of return on Steelco is 12 percent ($\sigma_S = .12$) and the standard deviation of return on Gold Bear is 18 percent ($\sigma_G = .18$). If the returns on Steelco and Gold Bear are perfectly positively correlated, $\rho_{SG} = 1$, the porfolio standard deviation is

$$\sigma_p = \sqrt{(.25)^2(.12)^2 + (.75)^2(.18)^2 + 2(.25)(.75)(1)(.12)(.18)} = 0.165$$

This is the weighted average of Steelco's and Gold Bear's standard deviations: $(.25)(.12) + (.75)(.18) = 0.165$. Only if the stocks are perfectly positively correlated, $\rho_{SG} = 1$, will there be no benefit from diversification. The following shows that as the correlation gets lower, the benefit from diversification increases:

Correlation Coefficient	Portfolio Standard Deviation $= \sigma_p = \sqrt{x_S^2 \sigma_S^2 + x_G^2 \sigma_G^2 + 2 x_S x_G \rho_{SG} \sigma_S \sigma_G}$ $= \sqrt{(.25)^2(.12)^2 + (.75)^2(.18)^2 + 2(.25)(.75)\rho_{SG}(.12)(.18)}$
1.0	.165
.8	.160
.2	.144
0	.138
− .3	.129
− .7	.116
−1.0	.105

Can portfolio risk be reduced to zero through diversification? If some assets are negatively correlated with the others, then it is mathematically possible to reduce the portfolio risk to zero. Unfortunately, assets with negative correlation with the economy are hard to find. Although some assets have low correlation with other assets, such as gold, all assets tend to be positively correlated. Portfolio diversification can reduce risk up to a point but cannot remove all risks.

● Example 9.1 Greyhound Lines and Shaw Communications

Let's look at a more realistic example of the effect of diversification. Figure 9.4a shows the monthly returns of Greyhound Lines stock from 1989 to 1993. The average *monthly* return was 0.38 percent but you can see that there was considerable variation around that average. The standard deviation of monthly returns was 6.3 percent. As a rule of thumb, in roughly one-third of the months the return is likely to be more than one standard deviation above or below the average return.[14] The figure shows that the return did indeed differ by more than 6.3 percent from the average on about a third of the occasions.

Figure 9.4b shows the monthly returns of Shaw Communications shares. The average *monthly* return on Shaw was 1.8 percent and the standard deviation was 6.5 percent, about the same as that of Greyhound. Again you can see that in about a third of the cases the return differed from the average by more than one standard deviation.

An investment in either Greyhound or Shaw would have been very variable. But the fortunes of the two stocks were not perfectly related. There were many occasions when a decline in the value of one stock was cancelled by a rise in the price of the other. Because the two stocks did not move in exact lockstep, there was an opportunity to reduce variability by spreading one's investment between them. In fact, the correlation coefficient for the two stocks was only .286.

Figure 9.4c shows the returns on a portfolio that was equally divided between the stocks. The monthly standard deviation of this portfolio would have been only 5.1 percent — that is, 80 percent of the variability of the individual stocks. We can verify that this is correct using the formula for portfolio standard deviation:

$$\sigma_p = \sqrt{(.5)^2(.063)^2 + (.5)^2(.065)^2 + 2(.5)(.5)(.286)(.063)(.065)} = .051 = 5.1\%$$

SELF-TEST 9.6

An investor is currently fully invested in gold mining stocks. Which action would do more to reduce portfolio risk: diversification into silver mining stocks or into automotive stocks? Why?

Market Risk versus Unique Risk

Our examples illustrate that even a little diversification can provide a substantial reduction in variability. Suppose you calculate and compare the standard deviations of randomly chosen one-stock portfolios, two-stock portfolios, five-stock portfolios, and so on. You can see from Figure 9.5 that diversification can cut the variability of returns by about half. But you can get most of this benefit with relatively few stocks: the improvement is slight when the number of stocks is increased beyond, say, 20 or 30.

Figure 9.5 also illustrates that no matter how many securities you hold, you cannot eliminate all risk. There remains the danger that the market — every share, including your portfolio — will plummet.

The risk that can be eliminated by diversification is called **unique risk**. Unique risk stems from the fact that many of the perils that surround an individual company are peculiar to that company and perhaps its direct competitors. The exis-

unique risk: Risk factors affecting only that firm. Also called diversifiable risk.

---

[14] For any normal distribution, approximately one-third of the observations lie more than one standard deviation above or below the average. Over short intervals stock returns are roughly normally distributed.

FIGURE 9.4 (a), (b), (c)
Calculated with monthly return data from the CFMRC database.

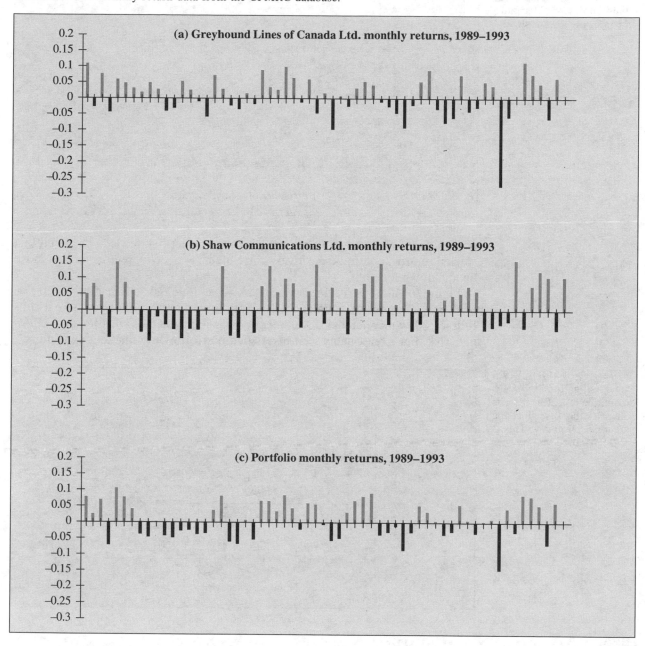

tence of unique risk means that stock returns are less than perfectly positively correlated — some part of a stock's return does not depend on other stocks' returns. For example, a fire at IBM may cause the return on IBM's stock to fall but this variation in return will not be correlated with variations in other stocks' returns.

The risk that you can't avoid regardless of how much you diversify is generally known as **market risk** or *systematic risk*. Market risk stems from the existence of economy-wide perils that threaten all businesses. Market risk explains why stocks have a tendency to move together, so that even well-diversified

market risk: Economy-wide (macroeconomic) sources of risk that affect the overall stock market. Also called *systematic risk*.

FIGURE 9.5
Diversification reduces risk (standard deviation) rapidly at first, then more slowly.

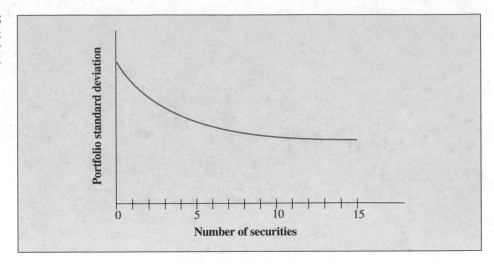

portfolios are exposed to market movements. Market risk leads to the result that stocks' returns tend to be positively correlated — stocks' returns tend to move up and down together.

Figure 9.6 divides risk into its two parts — unique risk and market risk. If you have only a single stock, unique risk is very important; but once you have a portfolio of 20 or more stocks, diversification has done most of what it can to eliminate risk. For a reasonably well-diversified portfolio, only market risk matters.

FIGURE 9.6
Diversification eliminates unique risk. But there is some risk that diversification *cannot* eliminate. This is called *market risk*.

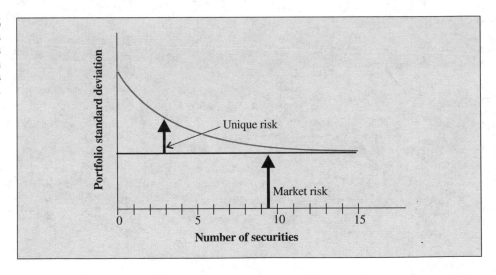

9.5   THINKING ABOUT RISK

How can you tell which risks are unique and diversifiable? Where do market risks come from? Here are three messages to help you think clearly about risk.

Message 1: Some Risks Look Big and Dangerous but Really Are Diversifiable

Managers confront risks "up close and personal." They must make decisions about particular investments. The failure of such an investment could cost a promotion, bonus, or otherwise steady job. Yet that same investment may not seem risky to an investor who can stand back and combine it in a diversified portfolio with many other assets or securities.

● Example 9.2 Wildcat Oil Wells

You have just been promoted to director of exploration, Western Hemisphere, of MPS Oil. The manager of your exploration team in far-off Costaguana has appealed for $20 million extra to drill in an even steamier part of the Costaguanan jungle. The manager thinks there may be an "elephant" field worth $500 million or more hidden there. But the chance of finding it is at best one in ten, and yesterday MPS's CEO sourly commented on the $100 million already "wasted" on Costaguanan exploration.

Is this a risky investment? For you it probably is; you may be a hero if oil is found and a goat otherwise. But MPS drills hundreds of wells worldwide; for the company as a whole, it's the *average* success rate that matters. Geologic risks (is there oil or not?) should average out. The risk of a worldwide drilling program is much less than the apparent risk of any single wildcat well.

Back up one step, and think of the investors who buy MPS stock. The investors may hold other oil companies too, as well as companies producing steel, computers, clothing, cement, and breakfast cereal. They naturally — and realistically — assume that your successes and failures in drilling oil wells will average out with the thousands of independent bets made by the companies in their portfolio.

Therefore, the risks you face in Costaguana do not affect the rate of return investors demand for investing in MPS Oil. Diversified investors in MPS stock will be happy if you find that elephant field, but they probably will not notice if you fail and lose your job. In any case, they will not demand a higher average rate of return for worrying about geologic risks in Costaguana.

● Example 9.3 Fire Insurance

Would you be willing to write a $100,000 fire insurance policy on your neighbour's house? The neighbour is willing to pay you $1000 for a year's protection, and experience shows that the chance of fire damage in a given year is substantially less than one in a thousand. But if your neighbour's house is damaged by fire, you would have to pay up.

Few of us have deep enough pockets to insure our neighbours, even if the odds of fire damage are very low. Insurance seems a risky business if you think policy by policy. But a large insurance company, which may issue a million policies, is concerned only with average losses, which can be predicted with excellent accuracy. The risk of fire on your neighbour's house is not in itself a big deal to the insurance company, providing that the fire insurance premium covers expected losses.

SELF-TEST 9.7

Imagine a laboratory at IBM, late at night. One scientist speaks to another.
"You're right, Watson. I admit this experiment will consume all the rest of this year's budget. I don't know what we'll do if it fails. But if this yttrium–magnoosium alloy superconducts, the patents will be worth millions."
Would this be a good or bad investment for IBM? Can't say. But from the ultimate investors' viewpoint this is *not* a risky investment. Explain why.

Message 2: Market Risks Are Macro Risks

We have seen that diversified portfolios are not exposed to the unique risks of individual stocks but are exposed to the uncertain events that affect the entire securities market and the entire economy. These are macroeconomic, or "macro," factors such as changes in interest rates, industrial production, inflation, foreign exchange rates, and energy costs. These factors affect almost all firms' earnings and stock prices. When the relevant macro risks turn generally favourable, stock prices rise and investors do well; when the same variables go the other way, investors suffer.

You can often assess relative market risks just by thinking through exposures to the business cycle and other macro variables. Consider the following businesses that have substantial macro and market risks:

Airlines. Because business travel falls during a recession, and individuals postpone vacations and other discretionary travel, the airline industry is subject to the swings of the business cycle. On the positive side, airline profits really take off when business is booming and personal incomes are rising.

Machine tool manufacturers. These businesses are especially exposed to the business cycle. Manufacturing companies that have excess capacity rarely buy new machine tools to expand. During recessions, excess capacity can be quite high.

Here, on the other hand, are two industries with less than average macro exposures:

Food companies. Companies selling staples, such as breakfast cereal, flour, and dog food, find that demand for their products is relatively stable in good times and bad.

Electric utilities. Business demand for electric power varies somewhat across the business cycle, but by much less than demand for air travel or machine tools. Also, electric utilities' profits are regulated. Regulation cuts off upside profit potential but also gives the utilities the opportunity to increase prices when demand is slack.

SELF-TEST 9.8

Which company of each of the following pairs would you expect to be more exposed to macro risks?
a. A luxury Montreal restaurant or an established Burger Queen franchise?
b. A paint company that sells through small paint and hardware stores to do-it-yourselfers, or a paint company that sells in large volumes to Ford, GM, and Honda?

Remember, investors holding diversified portfolios are mostly concerned with macroeconomic risks. They do not worry about microeconomic risks peculiar to a particular company or investment project. Micro risks wash out in diversified portfolios. *Managers* worry about both macro and micro risks, but only the former affect the cost of capital.

The risks of writing individual fire insurance policies are almost all micro. So are the geological and technical uncertainties of a wildcat oil well. Of course, the wildcat well may face some macro risks too, for example, changes in future oil prices, which will affect the value of oil *if* you find it.

Message 3: Risk Can Be Measured

Air Canada clearly has more exposure to macro risks than food companies such as McCain Foods or General Mills. These are easy cases. But is IBM stock a riskier investment than Imperial Oil? That's not an easy question to reason through. We can, however, *measure* the risk of IBM and Imperial Oil by looking at how their stock prices fluctuate.

We've already hinted at how to do this. Remember that diversified investors are concerned with market risks. The movements of the stock market sum up the net effects of all relevant macroeconomic uncertainties. If the market portfolio of all traded stocks is up in a particular month, we conclude that the net effect of macroeconomic news is positive. Remember, the performance of the market is barely affected by a firm-specific event. These cancel out across thousands of stocks in the market.

How do we measure the risk of a single stock, like IBM or Imperial Oil? We do not look at the stocks in isolation, because the risks that loom when you're up close to a single company are often diversifiable. Instead we measure the individual stock's sensitivity to the fluctuations of the overall stock market. We will show you how this works in the next chapter.

9.6 SUMMARY

1. The payoff from an investment in stocks or bonds consists of both the dividend or interest payment and any capital gain. The rate of return is equal to the payoff divided by the amount of the initial investment.

2. Over the past 67 years the return on common stocks has averaged about 7 percent a year higher than the return on safe Treasury bills. This is the premium that investors have received for taking on the risk of investing in stocks. Long-term bonds have offered a higher return than Treasury bills but less than stocks.

3. If the risk premium in the past is a guide to the future, we can estimate the expected return on the market today by adding that 7 percent expected risk premium to today's interest rate on Treasury bills.

4. The spread of outcomes on different investments is commonly measured by the standard deviation. The standard deviation of the returns on a market portfolio of common stocks has averaged about 20 percent a year.

5. The standard deviation of returns is generally higher on individual stocks than it is on the market. Because individual stocks do not move in exact lockstep, much of their risk can be diversified away. This diversifiable risk is known as unique risk.

6. Even if you hold a well-diversified portfolio, you will not eliminate all risk. You will still be exposed to macroeconomic changes that affect most stocks and the overall stock market. These macro risks combine to create market risk — that is, the risk that the market as a whole will slump.

7. Stocks are not all equally risky. But what do we mean by a "high-risk stock"? We don't mean a stock that is risky if held in isolation; we mean a stock that makes an above-average contribution to the risk of a diversified portfolio. In other words, investors don't need to worry much about the risk that they can diversify away; they do need to worry about risk that can't be diversified. This depends on the stock's sensitivity to macroeconomic conditions.

KEY TERMS

market index
Toronto Stock
   Exchange (TSE) 300
   Composite Index
Toronto Stock
   Exchange (TSE) 300
   Total Return Index

Dow Jones Industrial
   Average
Standard and Poor's
   Composite Index
maturity premium
risk premium

variance
standard deviation
diversification
correlation coefficient
unique risk
market risk

SUGGESTED READINGS

An empirical study of the effect of diversification on portfolio risk is:

Meir Statman, "How Many Stocks Make a Diversified Portfolio?" *Journal of Financial and Quantitative Analysis*, 22 (September 1987).

PROBLEMS

1. You purchase 100 shares of stock for $40 a share. The stock pays a $2 per share dividend at year-end. What is the rate of return on your investment for these end-of-year stock prices? What is your real (inflation-adjusted) rate of return? Assume an inflation rate of 5 percent.
   a. $35
   b. $40
   c. $45

2. The accompanying table shows the complete history of stock prices on the Polish stock exchange for 12 weeks in 1991. At that time only 6 stocks were traded. Construct two stock market indexes, one using equal weights for each stock, as calculated in the Dow Jones Industrial Average, the other using value-weighted weights as calculated in the TSE 300 Composite and Standard and Poor's Composite Indexes.

Prices (in zlotys) for the first 12 weeks' trading on the Warsaw Stock Exchange, beginning in April 1991. There was one trading session per week. Only five stocks were listed at first; a sixth stock (Swarzedz) was added in week ten.

	Number of Shares Outstanding in Thousands	Stock					
		Tonsil (Electronics) 1500	Prochnik (Garments) 1500	Krosno (Glass) 2200	Exbud (Construction) 1000	Kable (Electronics) 1000	Swarzedz (Furniture) 2500
Week	1	85	56	59.5	149	80	
	2	76.5	51	53.5	164	80	
	3	69	46	49	180	80	
	4	62.5	41.5	47	198	79.5	
	5	56.5	38	51.5	217	80	
	6	56	41.5	56.5	196	80	
	7	61.5	45.5	62	177	80	
	8	67.5	50	60	160	80.5	
	9	61	45.5	54	160	72.5	
	10	60	42	49	145	66	48
	11	66	42	53.5	159	72.5	43
	12	59.5	45.5	48.5	174	65.5	43

Source: We are indebted to Professor Mary M. Cutler for providing these data.

3. Here are the prices of the TSE 300 Composite Total Return Index and Treasury bill returns between 1989 and 1993:

Year	TSE 300 Total Return Index (price)	T-Bill Return (%)
1988	5431.68 *21-37*	9.49
1989	6592.58 *21.37*	12.06
1990	5617.01 *-14.80*	12.77
1991	6291.90 *12.02*	8.70
1992	6201.72 *- 1.43*	6.56
1993	8220.23 *32.55*	4.81

Source: ScotiaMcLeod's Handbook of Canadian Debt Market Indices, 1947–1993.

   a. Calculate the annual rate of return earned on the TSE 300 Composite Total Return Index.

   b. What was the risk premium on the TSE 300 Composite Total Return Index in each year?

   c. What was the average risk premium?

   d. What was the standard deviation of the risk premium?

4. Investments in long-term government bonds produced a negative average return during the period 1977–1981. How should we interpret this? Did bond investors in 1977 expect to earn a negative maturity premium? What do these 5 years' bond returns tell us about the normal future maturity premium?

5. What will happen to the opportunity cost of capital if investors suddenly become especially conservative and less willing to bear investment risk?

6. You believe that a stock with the same market risk as the TSE 300 will sell at year-end at a price of $50. The stock will pay a dividend at year-end of $2. What price will you be willing to pay for the stock today? *Hint:* Start by checking today's 1-year Treasury rates.

7. The common stock of Leaning Tower of Pita, Inc., a restaurant chain, will generate the following payoffs to investors next year:

	Dividend	Stock Price
Boom	$5.00	$195
Normal economy	2.00	100
Recession	0	0

The company goes out of business if a recession hits. Calculate the expected rate of return and standard deviation of return to Leaning Tower of Pita shareholders. Assume for simplicity that the three possible states of the economy are equally likely. The stock is selling today for $90.

8. Consider the following scenario analysis:

Scenario	Probability	Rate of Return (%) Stocks	Rate of Return (%) Bonds
Recession	.20	− 5	+14
Normal economy	.60	15	+ 8
Boom	.20	25	+ 4

a. Is it reasonable to assume that government bonds will provide higher returns in recessions than in booms?

b. Calculate the expected rate of return and standard deviation for each investment.

c. Which investment would you prefer?

9. Use the data in problem 8 and consider a portfolio with weights of .60 in stocks and .40 in bonds.

a. What is the rate of return on the portfolio in each scenario?

b. What is the expected rate of return and standard deviation of the portfolio?

c. Would you prefer to invest in the portfolio, in stocks only, or in bonds only?

10. If the stock market return in 1998 turns out to be –20 percent, what will happen to our estimate of the "normal" risk premium? Does this make sense?

11. In which of the following situations would you get the largest reduction in risk by spreading your portfolio across two stocks?

a. The stock returns vary with each other.

b. The stock returns are independent.

c. The stock returns vary against each other.

12. Who would view the stock of Leaning Tower of Pita (see problem 7) as a risk-reducing investment — the owner of a gambling casino or a successful bankruptcy lawyer? Explain.

13. The common stock of Escapist Films sells for $25 a share and offers the following payoffs next year:

	Dividend	Stock Price
Boom	0	$18
Normal economy	$1.00	26
Recession	3.00	34

Calculate the expected return and standard deviation of Escapist. All three scenarios are equally likely. Then calculate the expected return and standard deviation of a portfolio half-invested in Escapist and half in Leaning Tower of Pita. Show that the portfolio standard deviation is lower than either stock's. Explain why this happens.

14. Which firms of each pair would you expect to have greater market risk:

a. General Steel or General Food Supplies.

b. Club Med or General Cinemas.

15. Your portfolio will provide a rate of return of either –15 percent or +25 percent.

a. If both possibilities are equally likely, calculate the expected return and standard deviation.

b. If Treasury bills yield 5 percent, and investors believe that the portfolio offers a satisfactory expected return, what must the market risk of the portfolio be?

16. Sassafras Oil is staking all its remaining capital on wildcat exploration off the Cóte d'Huile. There is a 10 percent chance of discovering a field with

reserves of 50 million barrels. If it finds oil, it will immediately sell the reserves to Big Oil, at a price depending on the state of the economy. Thus the possible payoffs are as follows:

	Value of Reserves, Per Barrel	Value of Reserves, 50 Million Barrels	Value of Dryholes
Boom	$4.00	$200,000,000	0
Normal economy	$5.00	$250,000,000	0
Recession	$6.00	$300,000,000	0

Is Sassafras Oil a risky investment for a diversified investor in the stock market — compared, say, to the stock of Leaning Tower of Pita, described in problem 7? Explain.

SOLUTIONS TO SELF-TEST QUESTIONS

9.1 The bond price at the end of the year is $1050. Therefore, the capital gain on each bond is $1050 – 1020 = $30. Your dollar return is the sum of the income from the bond, $80, plus the capital gain, $30, or $110. The rate of return is

$$\frac{\text{Income plus capital gain}}{\text{Original price}} = \frac{80 + 30}{1020} = .108, \text{ or } 10.8\%$$

The real rate of return is

$$\frac{1 + \text{nominal return}}{1 + \text{inflation rate}} - 1 = \frac{1.108}{1.04} - 1 = .065, \text{ or } 6.5\%$$

9.2 The risk premium on stocks is the average return in excess of Treasury bills. This was 12.71 – 6.37 = 6.34%. The risk premium on the corporate bonds is the difference between the return on the corporate bond portfolio and the return on Treasury bills. This was 7.59 – 6.37 = 1.22%. The maturity premium is the average return on government bonds minus the return on Treasury bills. It was 6.38 – 6.37 = 0.01%.

9.3

Rate of Return (%)	Deviation	Squared Deviation
+70	+60	3600
+10	0	0
+10	0	0
–50	–60	3600

Variance = average of squared deviations = 7200/4 = 1800

Standard deviation = square root of variance = ($\sqrt{1800}$ = 42.4, about 42%

9.4 The standard deviation should decrease because there is now a lower probability of the more extreme outcomes. The expected rate of return on the auto stock is now

$$[.3 \times (-8\%)] + [.4 \times 5\%] + [.3 \times 18\%] = 5.0\%$$

The variance is

$$[.3 \times (-8 - 5.0)^2] + [.4 \times (5 - 5.0)^2] + [.3 \times (18 - 5.0)^2] = 101.4$$

The standard deviation is $\sqrt{101.4} = 10.07$ percent, which is lower than the previous value assuming equal probabilities of each scenario.

9.5 Since sunshine heats the air, the number of hours of sunshine per day and average daily temperature will be positively correlated. However, they will not be perfectly positively correlated because other factors affect air temperature such as latitude and altitude.

The more television watched, the less time you have to study and the lower will be your grade in finance. Thus these two variables will be negatively correlated.

The quality of the inflight movie has no relationship with the flying time. Thus these two variables are uncorrelated. Of course, if the movie is boring, the trip will seem to take longer!

The integration of the Canadian and U.S. financial markets will give rise to a positive correlation between interest rates in Canada and the U.S.

9.6 The gold mining stock's returns are more highly correlated with the silver mining company than with a car company. As a result, the automotive firm will offer a greater diversification benefit. The power of diversification is lowest when rates of return are highly correlated, performing well or poorly in tandem. Shifting the portfolio from one such firm to another has little impact on overall risk.

9.7 The success of this project depends on the experiment. Success does not depend on the performance of the overall economy. The experiment creates a diversifiable risk. A portfolio of many stocks will embody "bets" on many such unique risks. Some bets will work out and some will fail. Because the outcomes of these risks do not depend on common factors, such as the overall state of the economy, the risks will tend to cancel out in a well-diversified portfolio.

9.8
a. The luxury restaurant will be more sensitive to the state of the economy because expense account meals will be curtailed in a recession. Burger Queen meals should be relatively recession-proof.
b. The paint company that sells to the auto producers will be more sensitive to the state of the economy. In a downturn, auto sales fall dramatically as consumers stretch the lives of their cars. In contrast, in a recession, more people "do it themselves," which makes paint sales through small stores more stable and less sensitive to the economy.

Risk, Return, and Capital Budgeting

In Chapter 9 we distinguished *unique* risk from macro, or *market*, risk. Unique risk arises from events that affect only the individual firm or its immediate competitors; it can be eliminated by diversification. But regardless of how much you diversify, you cannot avoid the macroeconomic events that create market risk. This is why investors do not require a higher rate of return to compensate for unique risk but do need a higher return to persuade them to take on market risk.

How can you measure the market risk of a security or a project? We will see that market risk is usually measured by the sensitivity of the investment's returns to fluctuations in the market. We will also see that the risk premium investors demand should be proportional to this sensitivity. This relationship between risk and return is a useful way to estimate the return that investors expect from investing in the common stock of some well-known companies.

Finally, we will distinguish between the risk of the company's securities and the risk of an individual project. We will also consider what managers should do when the risk of the project is different from that of the company's existing business.

After studying this chapter you should be able to

- Measure and interpret the market risk, or beta, of a security.
- Relate the market risk of a security to the rate of return that investors demand.
- Calculate the opportunity cost of capital for a project.

10.1 MEASURING MARKET RISK

market portfolio: Portfolio of all assets in the economy. In practice a broad stock market index, such as the TSE 300 is used to represent the market.

Changes in interest rates, government spending, monetary policy, oil prices, foreign exchange rates, and other things macroeconomic affect almost all companies and the returns on almost all stocks. We can therefore assess the impact of "macro" news or events by tracking the rate of return on a **market portfolio** of all securities. If the market is up on a particular day, then the net impact of macroeconomic changes must be positive. We know the performance of the market reflects only macro events, because firm-specific events — that is, unique risks — average out when we look at the combined performance of thousands of companies and securities.

In principle the market portfolio should contain all assets in the world economy — not just stocks, but bonds, foreign securities, real estate, and so on. In practice, however, financial analysts make do with indexes of the stock market, such as the TSE 300 or the Standard and Poor's Composite Index.[1]

Our task here is to define and measure the risk of individual common stocks. You can probably see where we are headed. Risk depends on exposure to macroeconomic events and can be measured as the sensitivity of a stock's returns to fluctuations in returns on the market portfolio. This sensitivity is called the stock's **beta**. Beta is often written as the Greek letter ß.

beta: Sensitivity of a stock's return to the return on the market portfolio.

---

[1] We discussed the most popular stock market indexes in Section 9.2.

....
Measuring Beta

In the last chapter we looked at the variability of individual securities. Magna International ("Magna"), an automobile parts manufacturer, had the highest standard deviation and British Columbia Telecom ("BC Tel"), a telephone company, the lowest. If you had held Magna on its own, your returns would have varied four times as much as if you had held BC Tel. But wise investors don't put all their eggs in just one basket: They reduce their risk by diversification. An investor with a diversified portfolio will be interested in the effect each stock has on the risk of the entire portfolio.

Diversification can eliminate the risk that is unique to individual stocks, but not the risk that the market as a whole may decline, carrying your stocks with it.

Some stocks are less affected than others by market fluctuations. Investment managers talk about "defensive" and "aggressive" stocks. Defensive stocks are not very sensitive to market fluctuations. In contrast, aggressive stocks amplify any market movements. If the market goes up, it is good to be in aggressive stocks; if it goes down, it is better to be in defensive stocks (and better still to have your money in the bank).

Aggressive stocks have high betas, betas greater than 1.0, meaning that their returns tend to respond by more than one-for-one to changes in the return of the overall market. Defensive stocks' betas are less than 1.0. The returns of these stocks vary less than one-for-one with market returns. The average beta of all stocks is — no surprises here — 1.0 exactly.

Now we'll show you how betas are measured.

● **Example 10.1 Measuring Beta for Turbot-charged Seafoods**

Suppose we look back at the trading history of Turbot-charged Seafoods and pick out 6 months when the return on the market portfolio was plus or minus 1 percent.

Month	Market Return (%)	Turbot-charged Seafoods' Return (%)	
1	+1	+ .8	
2	+1	+1.8	Average = .8%
3	+1	− .2	
4	−1	−1.8	
5	−1	+ .2	Average = −.8%
6	−1	− .8	

Look at Figure 10.1, where these observations are plotted. We've drawn a line through the average performance of Turbot when the market is up or down by 1 percent. *The slope of this line is Turbot's beta.* You can see right away that the beta is .8, because on average Turbot stock gains or loses .8 percent when the market is up or down by 1 percent. Notice that a 2-percentage-point difference in the market return (−1 to +1) generates on average a 1.6-percentage-point difference for Turbot shareholders (−.8 to +.8). The ratio, 1.6/2 = .8, is beta.

In 4 months, Turbot's returns lie above or below the line in Figure 10.1. The distance from the line shows the response of Turbot's stock returns to news or events that affected Turbot but did *not* affect the overall market. For example, in Month 2, investors in Turbot stock benefited from good macroeconomic news (the market was up 1 percent) and also from some favourable news specific to Turbot. The market rise gave a boost of .8 percent to Turbot stock (beta of .8 times the 1 percent market return). Then firm-specific news gave Turbot stockholders an extra 1 percent return, for a total return that month of 1.8 percent.

FIGURE 10.1
FIGURE 10.1
Each point shows the performance of Turbot-charged Seafoods' stock when the overall market is either up or down by 1 percent. On average Turbot-charged moves in the same direction as the market, but not so far. Therefore Turbot-charged's beta is less than 1.0. We can measure beta by the slope of a line fitted to the points in the figure. In this case it is .8.

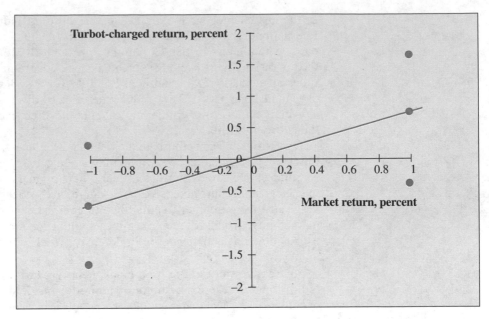

Thus we can break down Turbot's common stock returns into two parts: the part explained by market returns and Turbot's beta, and the part due to Turbot-specific news and events. Fluctuations in the first part come from Turbot's market risk, in the second from its unique risk.

Of course diversification can get rid of the unique risks. That's why wise investors, who don't put all their eggs in one basket, will look to Turbot's less-than-average beta and call its stock "defensive."

SELF-TEST 10.1

Here are 6 months' returns to stockholders in the Anchovy Queen restaurant chain:

Month	Market Return (%)	Anchovy Queen Return (%)
1	+1	+2.0
2	+1	+0.0
3	+1	+1.0
4	−1	−1.0
5	−1	+0.0
6	−1	−2.0

Draw a figure like Figure 10.1 and check the slope of the fitted line. What is Anchovy Queen's beta?

Real life doesn't serve up numbers quite as convenient as those in our examples so far. However, the procedure for measuring real companies' betas is exactly the same:

1. Observe rates of return, usually monthly, for the stock and the market.
2. Plot the observations as in Figure 10.1.
3. Fit a line showing the average return to the stock at different market returns.

Beta is the slope of the fitted line.

This may sound like a lot of work but in practice computers do it for you. Here are two real examples.

Betas for Magna International and BC Telecom

Each point in Figure 10.2a shows the return on Magna stock and the return on the market index in a different month. For example, the circled point shows that in the month of July 1989 Magna stock price fell by 5.6 percent, whereas the market index rose by 5.8 percent. Notice that more often than not Magna outper-formed the market when the index rose and underperformed the market when the index fell. Thus Magna was a relatively aggressive, high-beta stock.

We have drawn a line of best fit through the points in the figure.[2] The slope of this line is 1.64. For each extra 1 percent rise in the market Magna stock price

FIGURE 10.2
(*a*) Magna International monthly return versus market return, 1989–1993. (*b*) BC Telecom monthly return versus market return, 1989–1993.

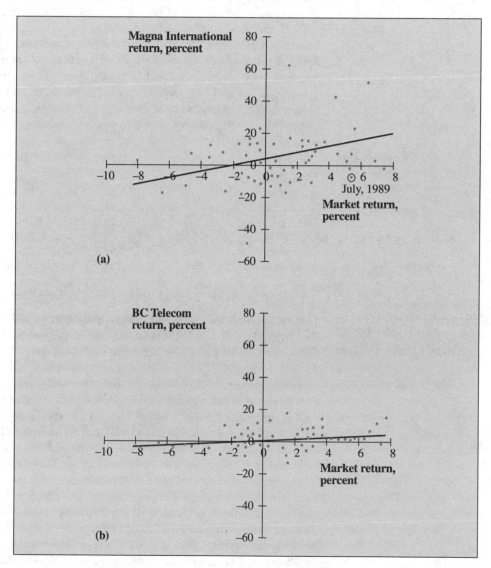

Source: Calculated with monthly return data from CFMRC database.

[2] The line of best fit is usually known as a regression line. The slope of the line can be calculated using ordinary least squares regression. The dependent variable is the return on the stock (Magna). The independent variable is the return on the market index, in this case the return on the TSE 300 Total Return Index (includes both prices and dividends paid to the 300 stocks).

moved on average an extra 1.64 percent. For each extra 1 percent fall Magna stock price fell an extra 1.64 percent. Thus Magna's beta was 1.64.

Of course, Magna's stock returns are not perfectly related to market returns. The company was also subject to unique risk, which shows up in the scatter of points about the line. Sometimes Magna flew south while the market went north (for example, in July 1989), or vice versa.

Figure 10.2b shows a similar plot of the monthly returns for BC Telecom. In contrast to Magna, BC Telecom was a defensive, low-beta stock. It was not highly sensitive to market movements, usually lagging when the market rose and yet doing better (or less badly) when the market fell. The slope of the line of best fit shows that on average an extra 1 percent change in the index resulted in an extra .65 percent change in the price of BC Telecom stock. Thus BC Telecom's beta was .65.

You may find it interesting to look at Table 10.1, which shows how past market movements have affected several well-known stocks. Westcoast Energy, a natural gas processing, transportation, and marketing company, had the lowest beta: its stock return was about half as sensitive as the average stock to market movements. Magna and SHL Systemhouse, a computer and communications systems integration company, were at the other extreme: each one's return was 1.64 times as sensitive as the average stock to market movements.

TABLE 10.1
Betas for selected common stocks, 1989–1993

Stock	Beta	Stock	Beta
Alcan Aluminum	1.06	Magna International	1.64
BC Telecom	0.65	Molson Companies	0.87
Bombardier	1.58	Northern Telecom	0.73
Finning Limited	1.27	Royal Bank of Canada	1.16
George Weston	0.69	Shaw Communications	0.62
Greyhound Lines	0.57	SHL Systemhouse	1.64
Inco Limited	1.42	Westcoast Energy	0.56

Source: Calculated with monthly returns from the CFMRC database.

Portfolio Betas

Diversification decreases variability from unique risk but not from market risk. The beta of a portfolio is just an average of the betas of the securities in the portfolio, weighted by the investment in each security. Thus a portfolio invested 50-50 in Magna and BC Telecom would have a beta of $(.5 \times 1.64) + (.5 \times .65) = 1.15$.

A fully diversified portfolio of stocks all with betas of 1.64, like Magna, would still have a portfolio beta of 1.64. However, most of the individual stocks' unique risk would be diversified away. The market risk would remain, and such a portfolio would end up 1.64 times as variable as the market. For example, if the market has an annual standard deviation of 20 percent (about the historical average reported in Chapter 9), a fully diversified portfolio with beta of 1.64 has a standard deviation of $1.64 \times 20 = 32.8$ percent.

Portfolios with betas between 0 and 1.0 tend to move in the same direction as the market but not as far. A well-diversified portfolio of low-beta stocks like BC Telecom, all with betas of .65, has no unique risk and is relatively unaffected by market movements. Such a portfolio is .65 times as variable as the market.

Of course, on average stocks have a beta of 1.0. A well-diversified portfolio including all kinds of stocks, with an average beta of 1, has the same variability as the market index.

SELF-TEST 10.2

Suppose you invested an equal amount in each of the stocks shown in Table 10.1. Calculate the beta of your portfolio.

● Example 10.2 How Risky Are Mutual Funds?

You don't have to be wealthy to own a diversified portfolio. You can buy shares in one of the more than 600 mutual funds in Canada.

Investors buy shares of the funds, which use the money to buy portfolios of securities. The returns on the portfolios are passed back to the funds' owners in proportion to their shareholdings. Therefore, the funds act like investment cooperatives, offering even the smallest investors diversification and professional management at low cost.

Let's look at the betas of two mutual funds that invest in stocks. Figure 10.3a shows how market movements have affected the returns of Dynamic Precious Metals mutual fund. You can see that the stocks in the Dynamic Precious Metals Fund had below average sensitivity to market changes: they had on average a beta of .74.

If the Dynamic Precious Metals Fund had no unique risk, its portfolio would have been .74 times as variable as the market portfolio. But the fund had not

FIGURE 10.3
(*a*) Dynamic Precious Metals Fund monthly return versus market return, 1989–1993.
(*b*) Green Line Canadian Index Fund monthly return versus market return, 1989–1993.

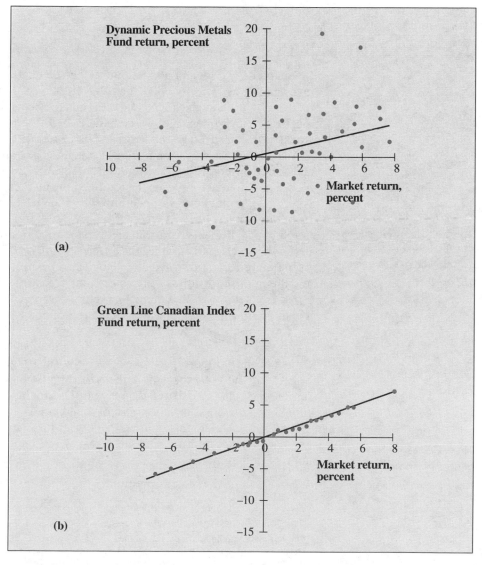

Source: Globe Information Services

diversified away all the unique risk; there is still a lot of scatter about the line in Figure 10.3a. As a result, the variability of the fund was more than .74 times that of the market.

Figure 10.3b shows the same sort of plot for Green Line Canadian Index mutual fund. Notice that this fund has a beta of 1.0 and only a tiny residual of unique risk — the fitted line fits almost exactly because an *index fund* is designed to track the market as closely as possible. The managers of the fund do not attempt to pick good stocks but just work to achieve full diversification at very low cost. (The index fund takes investments of as little as $2000 and manages the fund for an annual fee of less than .80 percent of the fund's assets.) The index fund is *fully diversified*. Investors in this fund buy the market as a whole and don't have to worry at all about unique risk.

SELF-TEST 10.3

Suppose you could achieve full diversification in a portfolio constructed from stocks with an average beta of .5. If the standard deviation of the market is 20 percent per year, what is the standard deviation of the portfolio return?

RISK AND RETURN

In Chapter 9 we looked at past returns on selected investments. The least risky investment was Treasury bills. Since the return on Treasury bills is fixed, it is unaffected by what happens to the market. Thus the beta of Treasury bills is zero. The most risky investment that we considered was the market portfolio of common stocks. This has average market risks: its beta is 1.0.

Wise investors don't run risks just for fun. They are playing with real money, and therefore require a higher return from the market portfolio than from Treasury bills. The difference between the return on the market and the interest rate on bills is termed the **market risk premium**. Over the past 67 years the average market risk premium has been 7 percent a year. We will treat this as the normal risk premium, the additional return that an investor could reasonably expect from investing in the stock market rather than Treasury bills.

In Figure 10.4a we have plotted the risk and expected return from Treasury bills and the market portfolio. You can see that Treasury bills have a beta of zero and a risk-free return; we'll assume that return is 4 percent. The market portfolio has a beta of 1.0 and an assumed expected return of 11 percent.[3]

Now, given these two benchmarks, what expected rate of return should an investor require from a stock or portfolio with a beta of .5? Halfway between, of course. Thus in Figure 10.4b we have drawn a straight line through the Treasury bill return and the expected market return and marked with an X the expected return for a beta of .5, that is, 7.5 percent. This includes a risk premium of 3.5 percent above the Treasury bill return of 4 percent.

You can calculate this return as follows: Start with the difference between the expected market return r_m and the Treasury bill rate r_f. This is the expected market risk premium:

$$\text{Market risk premium} = r_m - r_f = 11\% - 4\% = 7\%$$

market risk premium: Risk premium of market portfolio. Difference between market return and return on risk-free Treasury bills.

---

[3] On past evidence the risk premium on the market is 7 percent. With a 4 percent Treasury bill rate, the expected market return would be 4 + 7 = 11 percent.

FIGURE 10.4
(*a*) Here we begin the plot of expected rate of return against beta. The first benchmarks are Treasury bills (beta = 0) and the market portfolio (beta = 1). We assume a Treasury bill rate of 4 percent and a market return of 11 percent. The market risk premium is 11 − 4 = 7 percent. (*b*) A portfolio split evenly between Treasury bills and the market will have beta = .5 and expected return of 7.5 percent (point *X*). A portfolio 80 percent invested in the market and 20 percent in Treasury bills has beta of .8 and an expected rate of return of 9.6 percent (point *Y*). Note that the expected rate of return on any portfolio mixing Treasury bills and the market lies on a straight line and is proportional to the portfolio beta.

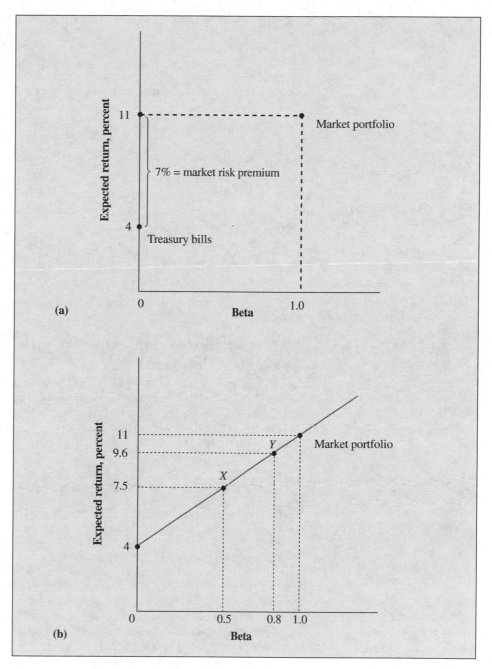

Beta measures risk relative to the market. Therefore, the expected risk premium on any asset equals beta times the market risk premium:

$$\text{Risk premium on any asset} = r - r_f = \beta(r_m - r_f)$$

With a beta of .5 and a market risk premium of 7 percent,

$$\text{Risk premium} = \beta(r_m - r_f) = .5 \times 7\% = 3.5\%$$

The total expected rate of return is the sum of the risk-free rate and the risk premium:

$$\text{Expected return} = \text{risk-free rate} + \text{risk premium}$$

$$r = \quad r_f \quad + \quad ß(r_m - r_f)$$

$$= 4\% + 3.5\% = 7.5\%$$

You could have calculated the expected rate of return in one step from this formula:

$$\text{Expected return} = r = r_f + ß(r_m - r_f)$$

$$= 4\% + (.5 \times 7\%) = 7.5\%$$

capital asset pricing model (CAPM): Theory of the relationship between risk and return which states that the expected risk premium on any security equals its beta times the market risk premium.

This formula states the basic risk-return relationship called the **capital asset pricing model**, or **CAPM**. The CAPM has a simple interpretation. The expected rates of return demanded by investors depend on two things: (1) compensation for the time value of money (the risk-free rate r_f), and (2) a risk premium, which depends on beta and the market risk premium.

Note that the expected rate of return on an asset with ß = 1 is just the market return. With a risk-free rate of 4 percent and market risk premium of 7 percent,

$$r = r_f + ß(r_m - r_f)$$

$$= 4\% + (1 \times 7\%) = 11\%$$

SELF-TEST 10.4

What are the risk premium and expected rate of return on a stock with ß = 1.5? Assume a Treasury bill rate of 6 percent and a market risk premium of 7 percent.

Why the CAPM Works

The CAPM assumes that the stock market is dominated by well-diversified investors who are concerned only with market risk. That makes sense in a stock market where trading is dominated by large institutions and even small fry can diversify at very low cost.

● **Example 10.3 How Would You Invest $1 Million?**

Have you ever daydreamed about receiving a $1 million cheque, no strings attached, from an unknown benefactor? Let's daydream about how you would invest it.

We have two good candidates: Treasury bills, which offer an absolutely safe return, and the market portfolio (possibly via the Green Line Canadian Index Fund discussed earlier in this chapter). The market has generated superior returns on average, but those returns have fluctuated a lot. (Look back to Figure 9.3) So your investment policy is going to depend on your tolerance for risk.

If you're a cautious soul, you may invest only part of your money in the market portfolio and lend the remainder to the government by buying Treasury bills. Suppose that you invest 80 percent of your money in the market portfolio and lend out the other 20 percent to the government by buying Treasury bills. Then the beta of your portfolio will be a mixture of the beta of the market ($ß_{market}$ = 1.0) and the beta of the T-bills ($ß_{T\text{-}bills}$ = 0):

$$\text{Beta of portfolio} = \left(\begin{array}{c}\text{proportion} \\ \text{in market}\end{array} \times \begin{array}{c}\text{beta of} \\ \text{market}\end{array}\right) + \left(\begin{array}{c}\text{proportion} \\ \text{in T-bills}\end{array} \times \begin{array}{c}\text{beta of} \\ \text{T-bills}\end{array}\right)$$

$$ß = \quad (.8 \times ß_{market}) \quad + \quad (.2 \times ß_{T\text{-}bills})$$

$$= \quad (.8 \times 1.0) \quad + \quad (.2 \times 0) = .80$$

The fraction of funds that you invest in the market also affects your return. If you invest your entire million in the market portfolio, you earn the full market risk premium. But if you invest only half your money in the market, you earn only half the risk premium:

$$\begin{array}{l} \text{Expected} \\ \text{risk premium} \\ \text{on portfolio} \end{array} = \left(\begin{array}{c}\text{proportion} \\ \text{in T-bills}\end{array} \times \begin{array}{c}\text{risk premium} \\ \text{on T-bills}\end{array}\right) + \left(\begin{array}{c}\text{proportion in} \\ \text{market}\end{array} \times \begin{array}{c}\text{market risk} \\ \text{premium}\end{array}\right)$$

$$= (.2 \times 0) + (.8 \times \text{expected market risk premium})$$

$$= .8 \times \text{expected market risk premium}$$

$$= .8 \times 7 = 5.6\%$$

The expected return on your portfolio is equal to the risk-free interest rate plus the expected risk premium:

$$\text{Expected portfolio return} = r_{\text{portfolio}} = 4 + 5.6 = 9.6\%$$

In Figure 10.4b we show the beta and expected return on this portfolio by the letter Y.

The Security Market Line

Example 10.3 illustrates a general point: by investing some proportion of your money in the market portfolio and lending (or borrowing)[4] the balance, you can obtain any combination of risk and expected return along the sloping line in Figure 10.5. This line is generally known as the **security market line.**

SELF-TEST 10.5

How would you construct a portfolio with a beta of .25? What is the expected return to this strategy? Assume Treasury bills yield 6 percent and the market risk premium is 7 percent.

security market line: Relationship between expected return and beta.

The security market line describes the expected return and risk from investing a different fraction of your funds in the market. It also sets a standard for other investments. Investors will be willing to hold other investments only if they offer equally good prospects. Thus the required risk premium for any investment is given by the security market line:

$$\text{Risk premium on investment} = \text{beta} \times \text{expected market risk premium}$$

Look back to Figure 10.4b, which asserts that an individual common stock with $\beta = .5$ must offer a 7.5 percent expected rate of return when Treasury bills yield 4 percent and the market risk premium is 7 percent. You can now see why this has to be so. If that stock offered a lower rate of return, nobody would buy even a little of it — they could get 7.5 percent just by investing 50-50 in Treasury bills and the market. And if nobody wants to hold the stock, its price has to drop. A lower price means a better buy for investors, that is, a higher rate of return. The price

---

[4] Notice that the security market line extends above the market return at $\beta = 1$. How would you generate a portfolio with, say, $\beta = 2$? It's easy, but it's risky. Suppose you borrow $1 million and invest the loan plus $1 million in the market portfolio. That gives you $2 million invested and a $1 million liability. Your portfolio now has a beta of 2.0:

$$\beta_{\text{portfolio}} = (\text{proportion in market} \times \text{beta of market}) + (\text{proportion in loan} \times \text{beta of loan})$$

$$\beta_{\text{portfolio}} = (2 \times \beta_{\text{market}}) + (-1 \times \beta_{\text{loan}})$$

$$= (2 \times 1.0) + (-1 \times 0) = 2$$

Notice that the proportion in loan is negative because you are borrowing, not lending money.

By the way, borrowing from a bank or stockbroker would not be difficult or unduly expensive as long as you put up your $2 million stock portfolio as security for the loan.

Can you calculate the risk premium and expected rate of return on this borrow-and-invest strategy?

FIGURE 10.5
The security market line
shows how expected rate of
return depends on beta.
According to the capital
asset pricing model,
expected rates of return for
all securities and all
portfolios lie on this line.

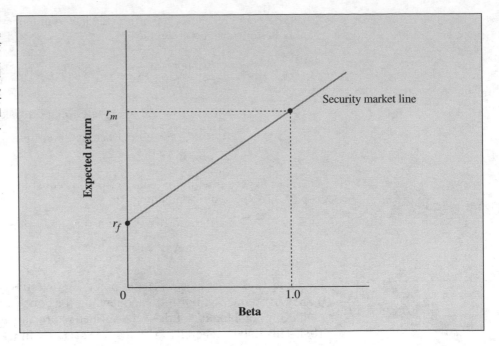

will fall until the stock's expected rate of return is pushed up to 7.5 percent. At that price and expected return the CAPM holds.

If, on the other hand, our favourite stock offered more than 7.5 percent, diversified investors would want to buy more of it. That would push the price up and the expected return down to the levels predicted by the CAPM.

This reasoning holds for stocks with any beta. That's why the CAPM makes sense, and why the expected risk premium on an investment should be proportional to its beta.

SELF-TEST 10.6

Suppose you invest $400,000 in Treasury bills and $600,000 in the market portfolio. What is the return on your portfolio if bills yield 6 percent and the expected return on the market is 14.6 percent? What does the return on this portfolio imply for the expected return on individual stocks with betas of .6?

The basic idea behind the capital asset pricing model is that investors expect a reward for both waiting and worrying. The greater the worry, the greater the expected return. If you invest in a risk-free Treasury bill, you just receive the rate of interest. That's the reward for waiting. When you invest in risky stocks, you can expect an extra return or risk premium for worrying. The capital asset pricing model states that this risk premium is equal to the stock's beta times the market risk premium. Therefore,

Expected return on stock = risk-free interest rate + (beta × market risk premium)

$$r = r_f + \beta(r_m - r_f)$$

How well does the CAPM work in practice? Do the returns on stocks with betas of .5 on average lie halfway between the return on the market portfolio and the interest rate on Treasury bills? Unfortunately, the evidence is conflicting. A study of U.S. stocks found for the period between 1932 and 1982, an increase of .5 in the beta of a portfolio would have brought an average extra return of 4.2 percent

— almost exactly half the 8.6 percent market risk premium estimated for the U.S.[5] That's the good news. However, recent years have not been so kind to the CAPM. If you were to look only at the more recent period 1962–1991, you would find very little relation between a portfolio's beta and its return. We expect that a similar relationship exists in Canada because the Canadian and U.S. stock markets are highly correlated. Has there been a fundamental change in the relation between risk and return in the last 30 years or did high-beta stocks just perform worse during these years than investors expected? It is hard to be sure.

There is little doubt that the CAPM is too simple to capture everything that is going on in the stock market. For example, it appears that stocks of small companies or stocks with low price-earnings ratios have offered higher rates of return than the CAPM predicts. This has prompted headlines like "Is Beta Dead?" in the business press.[6] It is not the first time that beta has been declared dead, but the CAPM is still being used. Only strong theories can have more than one funeral.

This CAPM is not the only model of risk and return. It has several brothers and sisters as well as second cousins. However the CAPM captures in a simple way two fundamental ideas. First, almost everyone agrees that investors require some extra return for taking on risk. Second, investors appear to be concerned principally with the market risk that they cannot eliminate by diversification. That is why financial managers rely on the capital asset pricing model as a good rule of thumb.

Using the CAPM to Estimate Expected Returns

To calculate the returns that investors are expecting from particular stocks, we need three numbers — the risk-free interest rate, the expected market risk premium, and beta. In November 1994, the interest rate on three-month Treasury bills was about 5.6 percent. Assume as before that the market risk premium is 7 percent. Finally, look back to Table 10.1, where we gave you betas of several stocks. Table 10.2 puts these numbers together to give an estimate of the expected return from each stock. Let's take BC Telecom as an example:

$$\text{Expected return on BC Telecom stock} = \text{risk-free interest rate} + \left(\text{beta} \times \text{expected market risk premium}\right)$$

$$r = 5.6\% + (.65 \times 7\%)$$

$$= 10.15\%$$

You can also use the capital asset pricing model to find the discount rate for a new capital investment. For example, suppose you are asked to analyze a proposal

TABLE 10.2
Expected rates of return

Stock	Expected Return (%)	Stock	Expected Return (%)
Alcan Aluminum	13.1	Magna International	17.2
BC Telecom	10.3	Molson Companies	11.8
Bombardier	16.8	Northern Telecom	10.8
Finning Limited	14.6	Royal Bank of Canada	13.8
George Weston	10.5	Shaw Communications	10.0
Greyhound Lines	9.7	SHL Systemhouse	17.2
Inco Limited	15.6	Westcoast Energy	9.6

Note: Expected return is computed as $r = r_f + \beta\,(r_m - r_f) = 5.7\% + \beta\,(7\%)$
Source: Calculated with monthly returns from CFMRC database.

[5] See L. K. C. Chan and J. Lakonishok, "Are the Reports of Beta's Death Premature?" *Journal of Portfolio Management* 19 (Summer 1993):51–62.
[6] A. Wallace, "Is Beta Dead?" *Institutional Investor* 14 (July 1980):22–30.

by Greyhound Lines to expand its operations.[7] At what rate should you discount the forecast cash flows? According to Table 10.2 investors are looking for a return of 9.7 percent from investments with the risk of Greyhound's stock. That is the opportunity cost of capital for Greyhound's expansion project.

In practice, choosing a discount rate is seldom this easy. (After all, you can't expect to become a captain of industry simply by plugging numbers into a formula.) For example, you must learn how to adjust for the extra risk caused by company borrowing and how to estimate the discount rate for projects that do not have the same risk as the company's existing business. We will come to these refinements later.

● Example 10.4 Comparing Project Returns and the Opportunity Cost of Capital

You have forecast the cash flows on a project and calculated that its internal rate of return is 15.0 percent. Treasury bills offer a return of 4 percent and the expected market risk premium is 7 percent. Should you go ahead with the project?

To answer this question you need to figure out the opportunity cost of capital r. This depends on the project's beta. For example, if the project is a sure thing, the beta is zero and the cost of capital equals the interest rate on Treasury bills:

$$r = 4 + (0 \times 7) = 4\%$$

If your project offers a return of 15.0 percent when the cost of capital is 4 percent, you should obviously go ahead.[8]

Sure-fire projects rarely occur outside finance texts. So let's think about the cost of capital if the project has the same risk as the market portfolio. In this case beta is 1.0 and the cost of capital is the expected return on the market:

$$r = 4 + (1.0 \times 7) = 11\%$$

The project appears less attractive than before but still worth doing.

But what if the project has even higher risk? Suppose, for example, that it has a beta of 1.8. What is the cost of capital in this case? To find the answer, we plug a beta of 1.8 into our formula for r:

$$r = 4 + (1.8 \times 7) = 16.6\%$$

A project this risky would need a return of at least 16.6 percent to justify going ahead. The 15 percent project should be rejected.

The security market line provides a standard for project acceptance. If the project's return lies above the security market line, then the return is higher than investors could expect to get by investing their funds in the capital market. For example, you can see in Figure 10.6 that a project with a beta of 1.8 and an expected return of 15 percent would plot below the security market line. Such a project would offer a lower return than investors could get elsewhere, and it would have a negative NPV.

---

[7] We've chosen a company with hardly any debt, so the risk of its assets equals the risk of its stock. This is not true when the company's assets are partly debt-financed. We'll explain how to handle this more general case in Chapter 11.

[8] In Chapter 6 we described some special cases where you should prefer projects that offer a lower internal rate of return than the cost of capital. We assume here that your project is a "normal" one, and that you prefer high IRRs to low ones.

FIGURE 10.6
The expected return of the project is less than the expected return one could earn from stock market investments with the same market risk (beta). Therefore, the project's expected return/risk combination lies below the security market line.

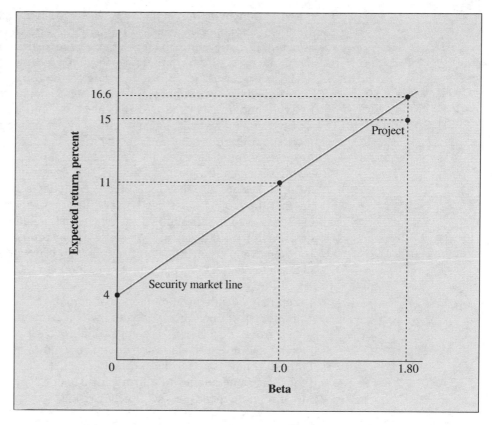

SELF-TEST 10.7

Suppose that Greyhound Line's expansion project is forecast to produce cash flows of $50 million a year for each of 10 years. What would be its present value? What would be the present value if the beta of the investment were 1.2?

 ## 10.3 CAPITAL BUDGETING AND PROJECT RISK

Company versus Project Risk

Long before the development of modern theories linking risk and return, smart financial managers adjusted for risk in capital budgeting. They realized intuitively that, other things equal, risky projects are less desirable than safe ones and must provide higher rates of return.

Many companies estimate the rate of return required by investors on their securities and use this **company cost of capital** to discount the cash flows on all new projects. Since investors require a higher rate of return from a risky company, risky firms will have a higher company cost of capital and will set a higher discount rate for their new investment opportunities. For example, we showed in Table 10.2 that on past evidence Greyhound Lines has a beta of 0.57 and the corresponding expected rate of return is 9.7 percent. According to the company cost of capital rule, Greyhound should use a 9.7 percent cost of capital to calculate project NPVs.

> **company cost of capital:** Expected rate of return demanded by investors in a company, determined by the average risk of the company's assets and operations.

This is a step in the right direction, but this approach can get a firm in trouble if its new projects do not have the same risk as its existing business. Greyhound's beta reflects investors' estimate of the risk of the bus transportation business and its company cost of capital is the return that investors require for taking on this risk. If Greyhound is considering an expansion of its regular business, it makes sense to discount the forecast cash flows by the company cost of capital. But suppose that Greyhound is wondering whether to branch out into air transportation. Its beta tells us nothing about the risk of the airline business or the return that shareholders require from investing in such a business.

project cost of capital: Minimum acceptable expected rate of return on a project given its risk.

The **project cost of capital** depends on the use to which that capital is put. Therefore, it depends on the risk of the *project* and not on the risk of the company. If Greyhound invests in a low-risk project, it should discount the cash flows at a correspondingly low cost of capital. If it invests in a high-risk project, those cash flows should be discounted at a high cost of capital.

The concept of measuring the project's cost of capital on the basis of the project's risk seems straightforward to us. However, sometimes managers make serious mistakes because they focus on the company's cost of capital and ignore the fact that the project's risk can be very different from the firm's overall risk. We don't want you to fall into that trap when making capital budgeting decisions. A good way to avoid it is to ask yourself, "If this project were a mini-firm, separate from our company, what rate of return would investors require to be willing to invest in the project?" By asking the question, you won't be tempted to ignore the risk of the project.

You may already be applying the principal, "Match the project's cost of capital to the risk of the project," to your own investment activities. Suppose you take money from your savings account, which is currently paying 1 percent annual interest, and invest in shares of Inco. You would expect to earn a higher rate of return to compensate for the substantial higher market risk associated with Inco, right? The same applies to a firm's investment decisions: the project's required rate of return depends on the project's risk.

SELF-TEST 10.8

The company cost of capital for Greyhound is 9.7 percent; for SHL Systemhouse it is 17.2 percent. What would be the more reasonable discount rate for Greyhound to use if it was considering entering the computer systems business? Why?

Determinants of Project Risk

We have seen that the company cost of capital is the correct discount rate for projects that have the same risk as the company's existing business, but not for those projects that are safer or riskier than the company's average. How do we know whether a project is unusually risky? Estimating project risk is never going to be an exact science, but here are two things to bear in mind.

Many people intuitively associate risk with the variability of earnings. But much of this variability reflects diversifiable risk. Lone prospectors in search of gold look forward to extremely uncertain future earnings, but whether they strike it rich is not likely to depend on the performance of the rest of the economy. Furthermore, gold has a very low beta. These investments have a high standard deviation but a low beta.

What matters is the strength of the relationship between the firm's earnings and the aggregate earnings of all firms. Thus cyclical businesses, whose revenues and earnings are strongly dependent on the state of the economy, tend to have high betas and a high cost of capital. By contrast, businesses that produce essentials, such as food, beer, and cosmetics, are less affected by the state of the economy. They tend to have low betas and a low cost of capital.

We saw in Chapter 8 that operating leverage increases the risk of a project. When a large fraction of your costs is fixed, any change in revenues can have a dramatic effect on earnings. Therefore, projects that involve high fixed costs tend to have higher betas.

When determining the risk of a project it may also be helpful to look at the risk and required rate of return of a similar risk project outside of the firm. This is precisely the logic behind the analysis in Self-Test 10.8. Greyhound, considering entering the computer systems business, uses the required rate of return of a company already in the business, SHL Systemhouse, in its assessment of the computer systems investment. Using SHL Systemhouse's cost of capital is an application of the **pure play approach** to project risk determination. *Pure play* is a term used by investors to refer to companies exclusively involved in a single line of business. If you wanted a pure play in silver, you would invest in a silver mining company and not in a diversified company that owns a silver mine.

The key to applying the pure play approach is finding the beta and market-required rate of return of a company exclusively involved in the type of project under consideration. If the comparable company is publicly traded, its beta may be available in a "beta book." For example, the *Polymetric Report* is a monthly publication of betas for some of the larger stocks listed on the Toronto and Montreal Stock Exchanges. You can also estimate the beta yourself using the stock's monthly rates of return, like we did for Figure 10.2. If the comparable company is not publicly traded, you may wish to estimate its beta with rates of return based on accounting earnings or cash flow.[9]

It may be difficult to find a suitable pure play for comparison. Many companies are involved in several different businesses and hence their betas reflect the risks of all of the businesses.[10] Even if a comparable company is found, determining the appropriate risk and discount rate may be complicated by a different capital structure. We will have more to say about this in Chapter 11.

You cannot hope to measure the systematic risk of a project with any precision, but good managers examine any project from a variety of angles and look for clues of its riskiness. They know that high market risk is a characteristic of cyclical ventures and of ventures with high fixed costs. They think about the major uncertainties affecting the economy and how projects are affected by these uncertainties. Experience at assessing risks plays an important role too. Regrettably, we have no magic formula for determining a project's risk. On the other hand, if such a formula existed, no one would pay financial managers handsomely for their expertise.

pure play approach: Estimating project cost of capital using the cost of capital of another company involved exclusively in the same type of project.

Don't Add Fudge Factors to Discount Rates

Risk to an investor arises because an investment adds to the spread of possible portfolio returns. But in everyday usage *risk* simply means "bad outcome." People think of the "risks" of a project as the things that can go wrong. For example,

- A geologist looking for oil worries about the risk of a dry hole.
- A pharmaceutical manufacturer worries about the risk that a new drug that reverses balding may not be approved by the Food and Drug Administration.
- The owner of a hotel in a politically unstable part of the world worries about the political risk of expropriation.

Managers sometimes add fudge factors to discount rates to account for worries such as these.

---

[9] For example, see W.H. Beaver and J. Manegold, "The Association Between Market-Determined and Accounting-Determined Measures of Systematic Risk: Some Further Evidence," *Journal of Financial and Quantitative Analysis*, 10:(June 1975):231–284.

[10] By the principal of value additivity, the beta of the company is the sum of the betas of the businesses, each weighted by their fraction of the firm's total value.

This sort of adjustment makes us nervous. First, the bad outcomes we cited appear to reflect diversifiable risks that would not affect the expected rate of return demanded by investors. Second, the need for an adjustment in the discount rate usually arises because managers fail to give bad outcomes their due weight in cash-flow forecasts. They then try to offset that mistake by adding a fudge factor to the discount rate. For example, if a manager is worried about the possibility of a bad outcome such as a dry hole in oil exploration, he or she may reduce the value of the project by using a higher discount rate. This approach is unsound, however. Instead, the possibility of the dry hole should be included in the calculation of the expected cash flows to be derived from the well. Suppose that there is a 50 percent chance of a dry hole and a 50 percent chance that the well will produce oil worth $20 million. Then the expected cash flow is not $20 million but $(.5 \times 0) + (.5 \times 20) = \$10$ million. You should discount the $10 million expected cash flow at the opportunity cost of capital: It does not make sense to discount the $20 million using a fudged discount rate.

Expected cash-flow forecasts should already reflect the probabilities of all possible outcomes, good and bad. If the cash-flow forecasts are prepared properly, the discount rate should reflect only the market risk of the project. It should not be fudged to offset other errors in the cash-flow forecast.

10.4 SUMMARY

1. The contribution of a security to the risk of a diversified portfolio depends on its market risk. But not all securities are equally affected by fluctuations in the market. The sensitivity of a stock to market movements is known as beta. Stocks with a beta greater than 1.0 are particularly sensitive to market fluctuations. Those with a beta of less than 1.0 are not so sensitive to such movements. The average beta of all stocks is 1.0.

2. The extra return that investors require for taking risk is known as the risk premium. The capital asset pricing model states that the expected risk premium of an investment should be proportional to its beta. The expected rate of return from any investment is equal to the risk-free interest rate plus the risk premium, so the CAPM boils down to

$$r = r_f + \beta(r_m - r_f)$$

3. The opportunity cost of capital is the return that investors give up by investing in the project rather than in securities of equivalent risk. Financial managers use the capital asset pricing model to estimate the opportunity cost of capital.

4. The opportunity cost of capital depends on the use to which the capital is put. Therefore, required rates of return are determined by the risk of the project, not by the risk of the firm's existing business.

5. Cash-flow forecasts should already reflect the probabilities of all possible outcomes. Potential bad outcomes should be reflected in the discount rate only to the extent that they affect beta.

KEY TERMS

market portfolio	capital asset pricing	company cost of capital
beta	model (CAPM)	project cost of capital
market risk premium	security market line	pure play approach

SUGGESTED READINGS

A good intuitive introduction to the CAPM is:

B. G. Malkiel. *A Random Walk Down Wall Street*, 5th ed. New York: W. W. Norton, 1990.

A discussion of the use of the CAPM in capital budgeting may be found in:

David Mullins, "Does the Capital Asset Pricing Model Work?" *Harvard Business Review*, (January/February 1982):105–114.

PROBLEMS

1. True or false? Explain or qualify as necessary.
   a. Investors demand higher expected rates of return on stocks with more variable rates of return.
   b. The capital asset pricing model predicts that a security with a beta of zero will provide an expected return of zero.
   c. An investor who puts $10,000 in Treasury bills and $20,000 in the market portfolio will have a portfolio beta of 2.0.
   d. Investors demand higher expected rates of return from stocks with returns that are highly exposed to macroeconomic changes.
   e. Investors demand higher expected rates of return from stocks with returns that are very sensitive to fluctuations in the stock market.

2. Consider the following two scenarios for the economy, and the returns in each scenario for the market portfolio, an aggressive stock A, and a defensive stock D.

	Rate of Return (%)		
Scenario	Market	Aggressive Stock A	Defensive Stock D
Bust	10	8	14
Boom	30	38	24

   a. Find the beta of each stock. In what way is stock D defensive?
   b. If each scenario is equally likely, find the expected rate of return on the market portfolio and on each stock.
   c. If the T-bill rate is 6 percent, what does the CAPM say about the fair expected rate of return on the two stocks?
   d. Which stock seems to be a better buy based on your answers to (a) through (c)?

3. Investors expect the market rate of return this year to be 14 percent. A stock with a beta of .8 has an expected rate of return of 12 percent. If the market return this year turns out to be 10 percent, what is your best guess as to the rate of return on the stock?

4. Figure 10.7 shows plots of monthly rates of return on three stocks versus the stock market index. The beta and standard deviation of each stock is given below its plot.
   a. Which stock is riskiest to a diversified investor?
   b. Which stock is riskiest to an undiversified investor who puts all her funds in one of these stocks?
   c. Consider a portfolio with equal investments in each stock. What would this portfolio's beta have been?

FIGURE 10.7
These plots show monthly rates of return for (*a*) Exxon, (*b*) Polaroid, and (*c*) Ford versus returns on the market portfolio. See Problem 4.

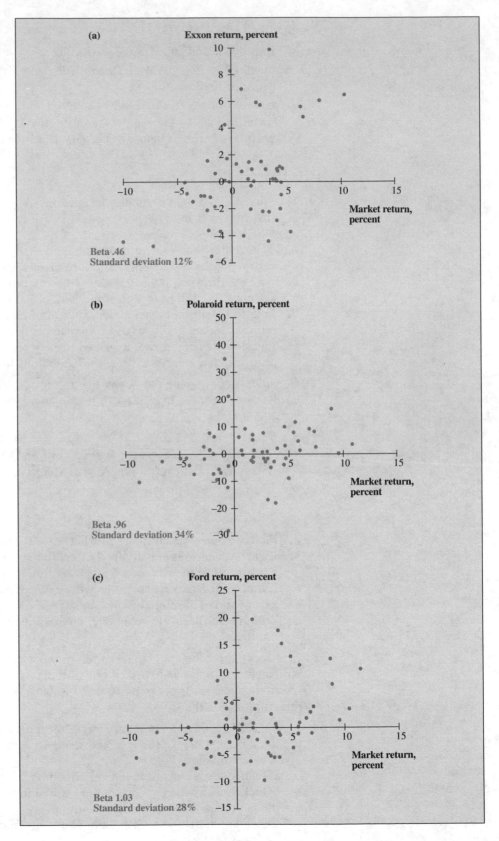

d. Consider a well-diversified portfolio made up of stocks with the same beta as Exxon. What are the beta and standard deviation of this portfolio's return? The standard deviation of the market portfolio's return is 20 percent.

e. What is the expected rate of return in each stock? Use the capital asset pricing model with a market risk premium of 8 percent. The risk-free rate of interest is 4 percent.

5. Following are several months' rates of return for Tumblehome Canoe Company. Prepare a plot like Figure 10.1. What is Tumblehome's beta?

Month	Market Return (%)	Tumblehome Return (%)
1	0	+1
2	0	−1
3	−1	−2.5
4	−1	−0.5
5	+1	+2
6	+1	+1
7	+2	+4
8	+2	+2
9	−2	−2
10	−2	−4

6. Figure 10.8 plots monthly rates of return from 1988 to 1992 for the Snake Oil mutual fund. Was this fund well-diversified? Explain.

FIGURE 10.8
Monthly rates of return for the Snake Oil mutual fund and the TSE Composite Index. See Problem 6.

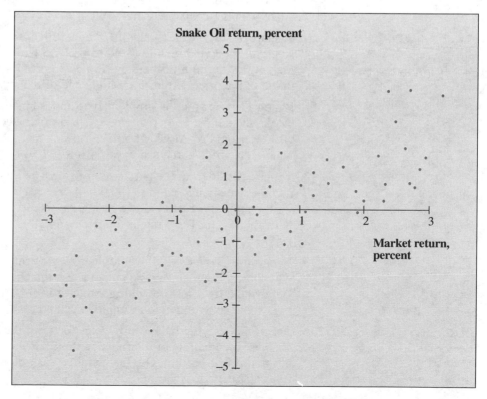

7. Draw the security market line when the Treasury bill rate is 10 percent and the market risk premium is 8 percent. What are the project costs of capital for new ventures with betas of .75 and 1.75? Which of the following capital investments have positive NPVs?

Project	Beta	Internal Rate of Return (%)
P	1.0	20
Q	0	10
R	2.0	25
S	0.4	16
T	1.6	25

8. You are a consultant to a firm evaluating an expansion of its current business. The cash-flow forecasts (in millions of dollars) for the project are:

Years	Cash Flow
0	−100
1–10	+ 15

Based on the behaviour of the firm's stock, you believe that the beta of the firm is 1.2. Assuming that the rate of return available on risk-free investments is 5 percent and that the expected rate of return on the market portfolio is 15 percent, what is the net present value of the project?

9. Reconsider the project in problem 8. What is the project IRR? What is the cost of capital for the project? Does the accept-reject decision using IRR agree with the decision using NPV?

10. A share of stock with a beta of .75 now sells for $50. Investors expect the stock to pay a year-end dividend of $3. The T-bill rate is 4 percent, and the market risk premium is perceived to be 8 percent. What is investors' expectation of the price of the stock at the end of the year?

11. Reconsider the stock in problem 10. Suppose investors actually believe the stock will sell for $54 at year-end. Is the stock a good or bad buy? What will investors do? At what point will the stock reach an "equilibrium" at which it again is perceived as fairly priced?

12. You are considering the purchase of real estate that will provide perpetual income that should average $50,000 per year. How much will you pay for the property if you believe its market risk is the same as the market portfolio's? The T-bill rate is 5 percent, and the expected market return is 12.5 percent.

13. According to the CAPM, would the expected rate of return on a security with a beta less than zero be more or less than the risk-free interest rate? Why would investors be willing to invest in such a security? *Hint:* Look back to the auto and gold example in Chapter 9.

14. The accompanying table shows betas for several companies. Calculate each stock's expected rate of return using the CAPM. Assume the risk-free rate of interest is 4 percent. Use the historical risk premium on the market portfolio of 7 percent.

Company	Beta
American Barrick Resouces	1.28
Canadian Pacific	1.20
Crestbrook Forest Industries	1.63
Jean Coutu Group	0.30
Thomson Corporation	0.72

15. Suppose Canadian Pacific is considering a new investment in the common stock of a publishing company. Which of the betas shown in the table in problem 14 is most relevant in determining the required rate of return for this venture? Explain why the expected return to Canadian Pacific stock is not the appropriate required return.

16. True or false? Explain or qualify as necessary.
    a. The expected rate of return on an investment with a beta of 2 is twice as high as the expected rate of return of the market portfolio.
    b. The contribution of a stock to the risk of a diversified portfolio depends on the market risk of the stock.
    c. If a stock's expected rate of return plots below the security market line, it is underpriced.
    d. A diversified portfolio with beta of 2 is twice as volatile as the market portfolio.
    e. An undiversified portfolio with beta of 2 is twice as volatile as the market portfolio.

17. Stock A had a beta of .5 and investors expect it to return 5 percent. Stock B has a beta of 1.5 and investors expect it to return 13 percent. Use the CAPM to find the market risk premium and the expected rate of return on the market.

18. A mutual fund manager claims that she expected her portfolio to earn a rate of return of 14 percent this year. She states that the beta of her portfolio is .8. If the rate of return available on risk-free assets is 5 percent and you expect the rate of return on the market portfolio to be 15 percent, should you invest in this mutual fund?

19. If the expected rate of return on the market portfolio is 14 percent and T-bills yield 6 percent, what must be the beta of a stock that investors expect to return 10 percent?

SOLUTION TO SELF-TEST PROBLEMS

10.1   See Figure 10.9 on page 260. Anchovy Queen's beta is 1.0.

10.2   A portfolio's beta is just a weighted average of the betas of the securities in the portfolio. In this case the weights are equal, since an equal amount is assumed invested in each of the stocks in Table 10.1. The average beta of these stocks is 1.03.

10.3   The standard deviation of a well-diversified portfolio's return is proportional to its beta. The standard deviation in this case is $.5 \times 20 = 10$ percent.

10.4
$$r = r_f + \beta(r_m - r_f)$$
$$= 6 + (1.5 \times 7) = 16.5\%$$

FIGURE 10.9
Each point shows the
performance of Anchovy
Queen stock when the
market is up or down by
1 percent. On average,
Anchovy Queen stock
follows the market; it has
a beta of 1.0.

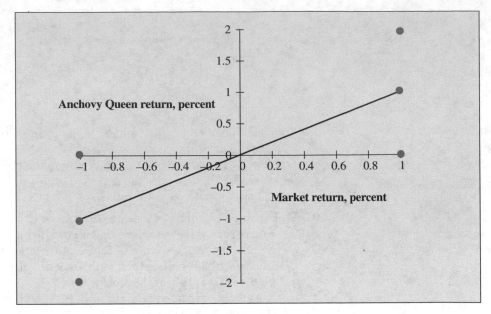

10.5   Put 25 percent of your money in the market portfolio and the rest in Treasury bills. The return on the market is

$$r_m = 6\% + 7\% = 13\%$$

The portfolio's beta is .25 and its expected return is

$$r_{portfolio} = (.75 \times 6) + (.25 \times 13) = 7.75\%$$

10.6 $$r_{portfolio} = (.4 \times 6) + (.6 \times 14.6) = 11.2\%$$

This portfolio's beta is .6, since $600,000, which is 60 percent of the investment, is in the market portfolio. Investors in a stock with a beta of .6 would not buy it unless it also offered a rate of return of 11.2 percent and would rush to buy if it offered more. The stock price would adjust until the stock's expected rate of return was 11.2 percent.

10.7   Present value = $50 million × 10-year annuity factor at 9.7%

= $311 million

If ß = 1.1, then the cost of capital rises to

$$r = 5.7\% + (1.2 \times 7\%) = 14.1\%$$

and the value of the 10-year annuity falls to $259 million.

10.8   Greyhound should use SHL Systemhouse's company cost of capital. Greyhound's company cost of capital tells us what expected rate of return investors demand from the bus transportation business. This is not the appropriate project cost of capital for Greyhound's venture into computer systems design and development. SHL Systemhouse designs and implements large-scale computer and communications systems.

In the last chapter you learned how to use the capital asset pricing model to estimate the expected return on a company's common stock. If the firm is financed wholly by common stock, then the stockholders own all the firm's assets and are entitled to all the cash flows. In this case, the expected return on the common stock and the company cost of capital are identical.

Most companies, however, are financed by a mixture of securities, including common stock, bonds, and often preferred stock or other securities. Each of these securities has different risks and therefore investors in them look for different rates of return. In these circumstances, the company cost of capital is no longer the same as the expected return on the common stock. It depends on the expected return from all the securities that the company has issued.

In this chapter we will show you how to calculate the company cost of capital when the firm is financed by a mixture of debt and equity. We will also show you how to use this figure to judge the appropriate discount rate for a new project. This chapter will also explain how financial managers translate the risks and returns on *securities* issued by the company into required rates of return for capital investment projects.

After studying this chapter you should be able to

● Calculate a firm's capital structure.
● Estimate the required rates of return on the securities issued by the firm.
● Calculate the weighted average cost of capital.
● Understand when the weighted average cost of capital is — or isn't — the appropriate discount rate for a new project.

11.1 THE COST OF CAPITAL

Jo Ann Cox, a recent graduate of a prestigious Canadian business school, poured a third cup of black coffee and tried again to remember what she once knew about project hurdle rates. Why hadn't she paid more attention in Finance 101? Why had she sold her finance text the day after passing the finance final?

Costas Thermopolis, her boss and CEO of Geothermal Corporation, had told her to prepare a financial evaluation of a proposed expansion of Geothermal's production. She was to report at 9:00 Monday morning. Thermopolis, whose background was geophysics, not finance, not only expected a numerical analysis; he expected her to explain it to him.[1]

Thermopolis had founded Geothermal in 1993 to produce electricity from geothermal energy trapped deep under Alberta. The company had pioneered this business and had been able to obtain perpetual production rights for a large tract on favourable terms from the Albertan government. When the 1997 oil shock drove up energy prices worldwide, Geothermal became an exceptionally profitable company. It was currently reporting a rate of return on book assets of 25 percent per year.

Now, in 1999, production rights were no longer cheap. The proposed expansion would cost $30 million and should generate a perpetual after-tax cash flow of $4.5 million annually. The projected rate of return was 4.5/30 = .15, or 15 per-

---

[1] This case is not prepared for class discussion, but to illustrate the proper analysis of a financial problem. It was prepared by Prof. John Major with research assistance from Charles DeGaulle.

cent, much less than the profitability of Geothermal's existing assets. However, once the new project was up and running, it would be no riskier than Geothermal's existing business.

Jo Ann realized that 15 percent was not necessarily a bad return — though of course 25 percent would have been better. Fifteen percent might still exceed Geothermal's cost of capital, that is, exceed the expected rate of return that outside investors would demand to invest money in the project. If the cost of capital was less than the 15 percent expected return, expansion would be a good deal and would generate net value for Geothermal and its stockholders.

Jo Ann remembered how to calculate the cost of capital for companies that used only common stock financing. Briefly she sketched the argument.

"I need the expected rate of return investors would require from Geothermal's real assets — the wells, pumps, generators, etc. That rate of return depends on the assets' risk. However, the assets aren't traded in the stock market, so I can't observe how risky they have been. I can only observe the risk of Geothermal's common stock.

"But if Geothermal issues only stock — no debt — then owning the stock means owning the assets, and the expected return demanded by investors in the stock must also be the cost of capital for the assets." She jotted down the following identities:

Value of business = value of stock

Risk of business = risk of stock

Rate of return on business = rate of return on stock

Investor's required return from business = investors' required return from stock

Unfortunately, Geothermal had borrowed a substantial amount of money; its stockholders did *not* have unencumbered ownership of Geothermal's assets. The expansion project was also going to be partly debt-financed. Jo Ann realized that she would have to look at Geothermal's **capital structure** — its mix of debt and equity financing — and consider the required rates of return of debtholders as well as equity investors.

capital structure: Firm's mix of long-term financing.

Geothermal had issued 22.65 million shares, now trading at $20 each. Thus shareholders valued Geothermal's equity at $20 × 22.65 million = $453 million. In addition, bonds totalling $194 million had been issued. The company's capital structure was therefore

Debt	$194	(30%)
Equity	453	(70%)
Total value	$647 million	(100%)

"Geothermal's worth more to investors than either its debt or its equity," Jo Ann mused. "But I ought to be able to find the overall value of Geothermal's business by adding up the debt and equity." She sketched a rough balance sheet:

Assets		Liabilities and Shareholders' Equity		
Assets = value of Geothermal's existing business	$647	Debt	$194	(30%)
		Equity	453	(70%)
Value	$647	Value	$647	(100%)

"Wow, I've got it!" Jo Ann exclaimed. "If I bought *all* the securities issued by Geothermal, debt as well as equity, I'd own the business unencumbered. That means. . . ." She jotted again:

$$\text{Value of business} = \frac{\text{value of portfolio of all the firm's debt}}{\text{and equity securities}}$$

$$\text{Risk of business} = \text{risk of portfolio}$$

$$\text{Rate of return on business} = \text{rate of return on portfolio}$$

$$\frac{\text{Investors' required return on business}}{\text{(company cost of capital)}} = \text{investors' required return on portfolio}$$

"All I have to do is calculate the expected rate of return on a portfolio of all the firm's securities. That's easy. The debt's yielding 8 percent, and Fred, that skinny banker, says that equity investors want 14 percent. The portfolio would contain 30 percent debt and 70 percent equity, so. . . ."

$$\text{Portfolio return} = (.3 \times 8\%) + (.7 \times 14\%) = 12.2\%$$

$$\text{Company cost of capital} = 12.2\%$$

It was all coming back to her now. The company cost of capital is just a weighted average of returns on debt and equity, with weights depending on relative market values of the two securities. The result, in this case 12.2 percent, is also the cost of capital for new investments with the same risk and financing.

"Looks like the expansion's a good deal. The 15 percent earned by Geothermal on the proposed expansion project is better than the 12.2 percent return required by Geothermal's investors. But I need a break."

11.2 THE COMPANY COST OF CAPITAL AND THE WEIGHTED-AVERAGE COST OF CAPITAL

Think again what the *company* cost of capital is, and what it is used for. We define it as the opportunity cost of capital for the firm's existing assets; we use it to value new assets that have the same risk as the old ones.

In this section we will start with the company cost of capital and then move on to its close relative, the weighted-average cost of capital, or WACC. WACC is a way of *estimating* the company cost of capital; it also incorporates an adjustment for the taxes a company saves when it borrows.

Calculating Company Cost of Capital as a Weighted Average

Calculating the company cost of capital is straightforward, though not always easy, when only common stock is outstanding. For example, a financial manager could estimate beta and calculate shareholders' required rate of return using the capital asset pricing model (CAPM). This would be the expected rate of return investors require on the company's existing assets and operations and also the expected return they will require on new investments that do not change the company's market risk.

But most companies issue debt as well as equity. That means that the company cost of capital is a *weighted average* of the returns demanded by debt and equity investors. It is the expected rate of return investors would demand on a portfolio of all the firm's outstanding securities.

Let's review Jo Ann Cox's calculations for Geothermal. The total value of that firm, which we denote as *V*, is the sum of the values of the outstanding debt *D* and the equity E. Thus firm value is $V = D + E = \$194$ million $+ \$453$ million $= \$647$ million. Debt accounts for 30 percent of the value and equity accounts for the remaining 70 percent. If you held all the shares and all the debt, your investment in Geothermal would be $V = \$647$ million. Between them, the debt and equity holders own *all* the firm's assets. So V is also the value of these assets — the value of Geothermal's existing business.

Suppose that Geothermal's equity investors require a 14 percent rate of return on their investment in the stock. What rate of return must a new project provide in order that all investors — both debtholders and stockholders — earn a fair rate of return? The debtholders require a rate of return of $r_{debt} = 8$ percent. So each year the firm will need to pay interest of $r_{debt} \times D = .08 \times \$194$ million $= \$15.52$ million. The shareholders, who have invested in a riskier security, require a return of $r_{equity} = 14$ percent on their investment of $\$453$ million. Thus in order to keep shareholders happy, the company needs additional income of $r_{equity} \times E = .14 \times \$453$ million $= \$63.42$ million. To satisfy both the debtholders and the shareholders, Geothermal needs to earn $\$15.52$ million $+ \$63.42$ million $= \$78.94$ million. This is equivalent to earning a return of $r_{assets} = 78.94/647 = .122$, or 12.2 percent.

Figure 11.1 illustrates the reasoning behind our calculations. The figure shows the amount of income needed to satisfy the debt and equity investors. Notice that debtholders account for 30 percent of Geothermal's capital structure but receive less than 30 percent of its income. On the other hand, they bear less than a 30 percent share of risk, since they have first cut at the company's income, and also first claim on its assets if the company gets in trouble. Shareholders expect a return of more than 70 percent of Geothermal's income because they bear correspondingly more risk.

FIGURE 11.1
Geothermal's debtholders account for 30 percent of the company's capital structure, but they get a smaller share of income because their return is guaranteed by the company. Geothermal's stockholders bear more risk and receive, on average, greater return. Of course if you buy all the debt and all the equity, you get all the income.

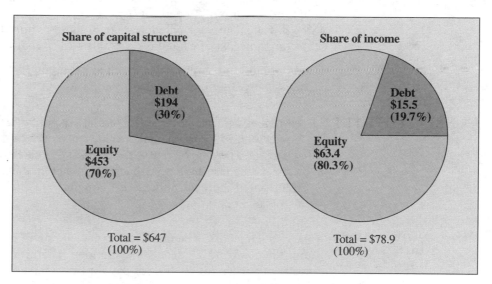

However, if you buy *all* Geothermal's debt and equity, you own its assets lock, stock, and barrel. You receive all the income and bear all the risks. The expected rate of return you'd require on this portfolio of securities is the same return you'd require from unencumbered ownership of the business. This rate of return — 12.2 percent in our example — is therefore the company cost of capital and the required rate of return from an equal-risk expansion of the business.

The bottom line is

Company cost of capital = weighted average of debt and equity returns

The underlying algebra is simple. Debtholders need income of ($r_{debt} \times D$) and the equity investors need income of ($r_{equity} \times E$). The total income that is needed is ($r_{debt} \times D$) + ($r_{equity} \times E$). The amount of their combined existing investment in the company is V. So to calculate the return that is needed on the assets, we simply divide the income by the investment:

$$r_{assets} = \frac{\text{total income}}{\text{value of investment}}$$

$$= \frac{(D \times r_{debt}) + (E \times r_{equity})}{V}$$

$$= \left(\frac{D}{V} \times r_{debt}\right) + \left(\frac{E}{V} \times r_{equity}\right)$$

For Geothermal,

$$r_{assets} = (.30 \times .08) + (.70 \times .14) = .122, \text{ or } 12.2\%$$

This figure is the expected return demanded by investors in the firm's assets.

Three Steps in Calculating Cost of Capital

There are three steps in calculating the weighted average:

Step 1. Calculate the market value of each security as a proportion of the firm's market value. For Geothermal, debt accounted for 30 percent of value ($D/V = .30$) and equity for 70 percent ($E/V = .70$).
Step 2. Determine the required rate of return on each security. For Geothermal, debtholders required a return of 8 percent ($r_{debt} = .08$) and the equity holders required a return of 14 percent ($r_{equity} = .14$).
Step 3. Calculate a weighted average of these required returns. For Geothermal, the company cost of capital is ($.3 \times .08$) + ($.7 \times .14$) = .122, or 12.2 percent.

Geothermal can use this cost of capital to value new projects that have the same risk as its existing business and that also support a 30 percent debt ratio.

SELF-TEST 11.1

Hot Rocks Corp., one of Geothermal's competitors, has issued long-term bonds with $50 million market value and a current required rate of return of 9 percent. The coupon rate of the bonds is 9.0 percent. It has 4 million shares outstanding trading for $10 each. At this price the shares offer an expected return of 17 percent. What is the company cost of capital for Hot Rocks's assets and operations?

Market versus Book Weights

The company cost of capital is the expected rate of return that investors demand from the company's assets and operations. Therefore, it must be based on what investors are actually willing to pay for the company's outstanding securities — that is, based on the securities' *market* values.

Market values usually differ from the values recorded by accountants in the company's books. The book value of debt is its value at maturity (the principal payment). The market value of debt is the present value of the interest (coupon) payments and principal. If market interest rates change, the book value of the debt does not change but the market value will. However, typically the market and book values of debt will be close. On the other hand, the difference between the book value of equity and the market value of equity can be large. The book value of equity (common shares plus retained earnings) reflects the investment shareholders have made in the company. The market value of equity reflects the future cash flows investors expect to receive. For example, Geothermal's market value of equity will include investors' assessment of Geothermal's excellent prospects. Investors are willing to pay more than the book value of equity for its shares.

Financial managers use book debt-to-value ratios for various other purposes, and sometimes they unthinkingly look to the books when calculating weights for the company cost of capital. That's a mistake, because the company cost of capital measures what investors want from the company, and it depends on how *they* value the company's securities. That value depends on future profits and cash flows, not on accounting history. Book values, while useful for many other purposes, only measure net cumulative historical outlays; they don't generally measure market values accurately.

SELF-TEST 11.2

Here is a book balance sheet for Anna Schwartz Associates. Figures are in millions.

Assets		Liabilities and Shareholders' Equity	
Assets (book value)	$75	Debt	$25
		Equity	50
	$75		$75

Unfortunately, the company has fallen on hard times. The 6 million shares are trading for only $4 apiece, and its debt securities are trading at a 20 percent discount from face (book) value.

Suppose shareholders now demand a 20 percent expected rate of return. The bonds are now yielding 14 percent. What is the company cost of capital?

Taxes and the Weighted-Average Cost of Capital

Our formula for the company cost of capital ignored taxes. Taxes are important because interest payments are deducted from income before tax is calculated. Therefore, the cost to the company of an interest payment is reduced by the amount of this tax saving.

The interest rate on Geothermal's debt is $r_{debt} = 8$ percent. However, with a corporate tax rate of $T_c = .35$, the government bears 35 percent of the cost of the interest payments. The government doesn't send the firm a cheque for this amount, but the income tax that the firm pays is reduced by 35 percent of its interest expense.

To see how this works, recall Geothermal pays 8 percent annual interest on its $194 million of outstanding debt. Thus the annual total interest payment is $.08 \times 194 = \$15.52$ million. Geothermal deducts this interest payment from its operating profits before calculating its income tax. Through this deduction, Geothermal reduces its taxes by the tax rate times the interest deduction: $.35 \times 15.52 = \$5.432$ million. Thus its after-tax interest expense is the pre-tax interest expense less the taxes saved from the interest deduction: $15.52 - 5.432 = \$10.088$ million. Geothermal's after-tax cost of debt is

$$\text{After-tax cost of debt} = \frac{\text{after-tax interest expense}}{\text{value of the debt}}$$

$$= \frac{10.088}{194} = 0.052 \text{ or } 5.2\%$$

Saying it another way, Geothermal's after-tax cost of debt is only $100 - 35 = 65$ percent of the 8 percent pretax cost:

$$\text{After-tax cost of debt} = \text{pretax cost} \times (1 - \text{tax rate})$$

$$= r_{\text{debt}} \times (1 - T_c)$$

$$= 8 \times (1 - .35) = 5.2\%$$

Payments to shareholders, such as dividends, are not tax-deductible by Geothermal. No tax saving arises from equity financing. Thus, Geothermal's after-tax cost of equity equals the before-tax cost, 14 percent.

We can now adjust our calculation of Geothermal's cost of capital to recognize the tax saving associated with interest payments:

$$\text{Company cost of capital, after-tax} = (.3 \times 5.2) + (.7 \times 14) = 11.4\%$$

weighted-average cost of capital (WACC): Expected rate of return on a portfolio of all the firm's securities.

This after-tax version of the company cost of capital is called the **weighted-average cost of capital**, or **WACC**. The general formula is

$$\text{Weighted-average cost of capital} = \left[\frac{D}{V} \times (1 - T_c) r_{\text{debt}} \right] + \left[\frac{E}{V} \times r_{\text{equity}} \right]$$

The WACC takes into consideration the tax deductibility of interest payments and is the rate of return the company must earn on its investments to satisfy the bondholders' and shareholders' required rates of return.

Geothermal's proposed expansion is actually better than Jo Ann Cox thought. The project's 15 percent rate of return is well in excess of 11.4 percent. The project is expected to earn $0.15 on each dollar invested but Geothermal must only pay $0.114 on each dollar of financing raised. You will recognize that this means the project has a positive NPV, which we calculate below.

We'll have more to say about taxes, debt interest, and project values. But first you may need a bit more practice in calculating WACC.

● Example 11.1 Weighted-Average Cost of Capital for Executive Fruit

Unlike Geothermal, Executive Fruit has issued three types of securities — debt, preferred stock, and common stock. The debtholders require a return of 6 percent, the preferred stockholders require an expected return of 12 percent, and the common stockholders require 18 percent. The debt is valued at $4 million ($D = 4$), the preferred stock at $2 million ($P = 2$), and the common stock at $6 million ($E = 6$). The corporate tax rate is 35 percent. What is Executive's weighted-average cost of capital?

Don't be put off by the third security, preferred stock. We simply work through the same three steps:

Step 1. Calculate the market value of each security as a proportion of the firm's market value. Firm value is $V = D + P + E = 4 + 2 + 6 = \$12$ million. So $D/V = 4/12 = .33$; $P/V = 2/12 = .17$; and $E/V = 6/12 = .5$.

Step 2. Determine the required rate of return on each security. We have already given you the answers: $r_{\text{debt}} = .06$, $r_{\text{preferred}} = .12$, and $r_{\text{equity}} = .18$.[2]

Step 3. Calculate a weighted average of the cost of the after-tax return on debt and the return on the preferred[3] and common stock:

---

[2] Financial managers often use "equity" to refer to *common* stock, even though a firm's equity strictly includes both common and preferred stock. We continue to use r_{equity} to refer specifically to the expected return on the common stock.

[3] Dividends on preferred stock are not tax-deductible.

$$\text{Weighted-average} \atop \text{cost of capital} = \left[\frac{D}{V} \times (1 - T_c)r_{\text{debt}}\right] + \left[\frac{P}{V} \times r_{\text{preferred}}\right] + \left[\frac{E}{V} \times r_{\text{equity}}\right]$$

$$= [.33 \times (1 - .35)\ .06] + (.17 \times .12) + (.5 \times .18)$$

$$= .123, \text{ or } 12.3\%$$

Wrapping Up Geothermal

We now turn one last time to Jo Ann Cox and Geothermal's proposed expansion. We want to make sure that she — and you — know how to *use* the weighted-average cost of capital.

Remember that the proposed expansion cost $30 million and should generate a perpetual cash flow of $4.5 million per year. A simple cash flow worksheet might look like this:[4]

Revenue	$10.00 million
Operating expenses	3.08
Pretax operating cash flow	6.92
Tax at 35%	2.42
After-tax cash flow	$ 4.50 million

Interest expense is not an operating expense and has not been deducted. These cash flows ignore the tax benefits of using debt.

Geothermal's managers and engineers forecast revenues, costs, and taxes as if the project was to be all-equity financed. The interest tax shields generated by the project's actual debt financing are not forgotten, however. They are accounted for by using the *after-tax* cost of debt in the weighted-average cost of capital.

Project net present value is calculated by discounting the cash flow (which is a perpetuity) at Geothermal's 11.4 percent weighted-average cost of capital:

$$\text{NPV} = -30 + \frac{4.5}{.114} = + \$9.5 \text{ million}$$

Expansion will thus add $9.5 million to the net wealth of Geothermal's owners.

Checking Our Logic

Any project offering a rate of return more than 11.4 percent will have positive NPV, assuming that the project has the same risk and financing as Geothermal's business. A project offering exactly 11.4 percent would be just break-even; it would generate just enough cash to satisfy both debtholders and stockholders.

Let's check that out. Suppose the proposed expansion had revenues of only $8.34 million and after-tax cash flows of $3.42 million:

Revenue	$8.34 million
Operating costs	3.08
Pretax operating cash flow	5.26
Tax at 35%	1.84
After-tax cash flow	$3.42 million

With an investment of $30 million, the internal rate of return is exactly 11.4 percent:

---

[4] For this example we ignore depreciation, a noncash but tax-deductible expense. (If the project were really perpetual, why depreciate?)

$$\text{Rate of return} = \frac{3.42}{30} = .114, \text{ or } 11.4\%$$

NPV is exactly zero:

$$\text{NPV} = -30 + \frac{3.42}{.114} = 0$$

When we calculated Geothermal's weighted-average cost of capital, we recognized that the company's debt ratio was 30 percent. When Geothermal's analysts use the weighted-average cost of capital to evaluate the new project, they are assuming that the $30 million additional investment would support the issue of additional debt equal to 30 percent of the investment, or $9 million. The remaining $21 million is provided by the shareholders.

The following table shows how the cash flows would be shared between the debtholders and shareholders. We start with the pretax operating cash flow of $5.26 million:

Cash flow before tax and interest	$5.26 million
Interest payment (.08 × $9 million)	.72
Pretax cash flow	4.54
Tax at 35%	1.59
Cash flow after tax	$2.95 million

Project cash flows before tax and interest are forecast to be $5.26 million. Out of this figure, Geothermal needs to pay interest of 8 percent of $9 million, which comes to $.72 million. This leaves a pretax cash flow of $4.54 million, on which the company must pay tax. Taxes equal .35 × 4.54 = $1.59 million. Shareholders are left with $2.95 million, just enough to give them the 14 percent return that they need on their $21 million investment. (Note that 2.95/21 = .14, or 14 percent.)

Therefore, everything checks out. If a project has zero NPV when the expected cash flows are discounted at the weighted-average cost of capital, then the project's cash flows are just sufficient to give debtholders and shareholders the return they require.

SELF-TEST 11.3
Calculate the weighted-average cost of capital for Anna Schwartz Associates. (See Self-Test 11.2.) The corporate tax rate is 35 percent.

MEASURING CAPITAL STRUCTURE

You now know the formula for calculating the weighted-average cost of capital. We will now look at some of the practical problems in applying that formula. Suppose that the financial manager of Big Oil has asked you to estimate the firm's weighted-average cost of capital. Your first step is to work out Big Oil's capital structure. But where do you get the data?

Financial managers usually start with the company's accounts, which show the *book* value of debt and equity, whereas the weighted-average cost of capital formula calls for their *market* values. A little work and a dash of judgment are needed to go from one to the other.

Table 11.1 shows the debt and equity issued by Big Oil. The firm has borrowed $200 million from banks and has issued a further $200 million of long-term bonds.

These bonds have a coupon rate of 8 percent and mature at the end of 12 years. Finally, there are 100 million shares of common stock outstanding, each with a par value of $1.00. But the accounts also recognize that Big Oil has in past years plowed back into the firm $300 million of retained earnings. The total book value of the equity shown in the accounts is $100 million + $300 million = $400 million.

TABLE 11.1

The *book* value of Big Oil's debt and equity (dollar figures in millions)

Bank debt	$200	25.0%
Long-term bonds (12-year maturity, 8% coupon)	200	25.0%
Total debt	$400	50.0%
Common equity (100 million shares)	$100	12.5%
Retained earnings	300	37.5%
Total equity	$400	50.0%
Total	$800	100.0%

The figures shown in Table 11.1 are taken from Big Oil's annual accounts and are therefore book values. Sometimes the differences between book values and market values are negligible. For example, consider the $200 million that Big Oil owes the bank. The interest rate on bank loans is usually a floating rate and thus linked to the general level of interest rates. Thus if interest rates rise, the rate charged on Big Oil's loan also rises to maintain the loan's value. As long as Big Oil is reasonably sure to repay the loan, the loan is worth close to $200 million. Most financial managers most of the time are willing to accept the book value of bank debt as a fair approximation of its market value.

What about Big Oil's long-term bonds? Since the bonds were originally issued, long-term interest rates have risen to 9 percent. If Big Oil's bonds are traded, you can simply look up their price. But many bonds are not regularly traded, and in such cases you need to infer their price by calculating the bond's value using the rate of interest offered by similar bonds. To be similar, the maturity dates must be close and the risk of default for the bonds must be comparable.

Suppose we find out that Big Oil's bonds are rated A by National Bond Rating Service. Other A rated long-term bonds are currently priced to yield about 9 percent. Using 9 percent as the current required rate of return on Big Oil's bonds, we can calculate the value today of each bond as follows.[5] There are 12 coupon payments of $.08 \times 200 = \$16$ million, and then repayment of principal 12 years out. Thus the final cash payment to the bondholders is $216 million. All the bond's cash flows are discounted back at the *current* interest rate of 9 percent:

$$PV = \frac{16}{1.09} + \frac{16}{(1.09)^2} + \frac{16}{(1.09)^3} + \ldots + \frac{216}{(1.09)^{12}} = \$185.7$$

Therefore, the bonds are worth only $185.7 million, 92.8 percent of their face value.

If you used the book value of Big Oil's long-term debt rather than its market value, you would be a little bit off in your calculation of the weighted-average cost of capital, but probably not seriously so. The bigger the difference between the bond's coupon rate and the current required rate of return to similar bonds, the greater will be the difference between book and market values.

---

[5] We assume that coupon payments are annual. Remember, most bonds in Canada actually pay interest twice a year.

The really big errors are likely to arise if you use the book value of equity rather than its market value. The $400 million book value of Big Oil's equity measures the total amount of cash that the firm has raised from shareholders in the past or has retained and invested on their behalf. But perhaps Big Oil has been able to find projects that were worth more than they originally cost or perhaps the value of the assets has increased with inflation. Perhaps investors see great future investment opportunities for the company. All these considerations determine what investors are willing to pay for Big Oil's common stock.

In September 1999 Big Oil stock was $12 a share. Thus the total *market value* of the stock was

Number of shares $\times$ share price = 100 million $\times$ $12 = $1200 million

In Table 11.2 we show the market value of Big Oil's debt and equity. You can see that debt accounts for 24.3 percent of company value ($D/V = .243$) and equity accounts for 75.7 percent ($E/V = .757$). These are the proportions to use when calculating the weighted-average cost of capital. Notice that if you looked only at the book values shown in the company accounts, you would mistakenly conclude that debt and equity each accounted for 50 percent of value.

TABLE 11.2

The *market* value of Big Oil's debt and equity (dollar figures in millions)

Bank debt	$ 200.0	12.6%
Long-term bonds (12-year maturity, 8% coupon)	185.7	11.7%
Total debt	$ 385.7	24.3%
Common equity (100 million shares at $12)	$1200.0	75.7%
Total	$1585.7	100.0%

11.4 CALCULATING REQUIRED RATES OF RETURN

To calculate Big Oil's weighted average cost of capital, you also need the rate of return that investors require from each security.

The Expected Return on Bonds

We know that Big Oil's bonds currently offer a yield to maturity of 9 percent. As long as the company does not go belly-up, that is the rate of return investors can expect to earn from holding Big Oil's bonds. If there is any chance that the firm may be unable to repay the debt, however, the yield to maturity of 9 percent represents the most favourable outcome and the *expected* return is lower than 9 percent.

For most large and healthy firms, the probability of bankruptcy is sufficiently low that financial managers are content to take the promised yield to maturity on the bonds as a measure of the expected return. But beware of assuming that the yield offered on the bonds of Fly-by-Night Corporation is the return that you can expect to receive.

The Expected Return on Common Stock

Estimates Based on the Capital Asset Pricing Model. In the last chapter we showed you how to use the capital asset pricing model to estimate the expected rate of return on common stock. The capital asset pricing model tells us that investors demand a higher rate of return from stocks with high betas. The formula is

$$\text{Expected return on stock} = \text{risk-free interest rate} + \left(\text{stock's beta} \times \text{expected market risk premium} \right)$$

Financial managers and economists measure the risk-free rate of interest by the yield on Treasury bills. To measure the expected market risk premium, they usually look back at capital market history, which suggests that investors have received an extra 7 to 9 percent a year from investing in common stocks rather than Treasury bills. Yet wise financial managers use this evidence with considerable humility, for who is to say whether investors in the past received more or less than they expected, or whether investors today require a higher or lower reward for risk than their parents did?

Let's suppose Big Oil's common stock beta is estimated at .85. The risk-free interest rate r_f is 6 percent and the expected market risk premium $(r_m - r_f)$ is 9 percent. Then the CAPM would put Big Oil's cost of equity at

$$\text{Cost of equity} = r_{\text{equity}} = r_f + \beta(r_m - r_f)$$

$$= 6 + .85(9) = 13.65\%$$

Of course no one can estimate expected rates of return to two decimal places, so we'll just round to 13.5 percent.

SELF-TEST 11.4

Jo Ann Cox decides to check whether Fred, the skinny banker, was correct in claiming that Geothermal's cost of equity is 14 percent. She estimates Geothermal's beta at 1.20. The risk-free interest rate in 1999 is 6 percent, and the long-run average market risk premium is 9 percent. What is the expected rate of return on Geothermal's common stock, assuming of course that the CAPM is true? Recalculate Geothermal's weighted-average cost of capital.

Dividend Discount Model Cost of Equity Estimates. Whenever you are given an estimate of the expected return on a common stock, always look for ways to check whether it is reasonable. One check on the estimates provided by the CAPM can be obtained from the dividend discount model (DDM). In Chapter 5 we showed you how to use the constant-growth DDM formula to estimate the return that investors expect from different common stocks. Remember the formula: if dividends are expected to grow indefinitely at a constant rate g, then the price of the stock is equal to

$$P_0 = \frac{\text{DIV}_1}{r_{\text{equity}} - g}$$

where P_0 is the current stock price, DIV_1 is the forecast dividend at the end of the year, and r_{equity} is the expected return from the stock. We can rearrange this formula to provide an estimate of r_{equity}:

$$r_{\text{equity}} = \frac{\text{DIV}_1}{P_0} + g$$

In other words, the expected return on equity is equal to the dividend yield (DIV_1/P_0) plus the expected growth rate in dividends (g).

This constant-growth dividend discount model is widely used in estimating expected rates of return on common stocks of public utilities. Utility stocks have a fairly stable growth pattern and are therefore tailor-made for the constant-growth formula. But remember that the constant-growth formula will get you into trouble if you apply it to firms with very high current rates of growth. Such growth can rarely be sustained indefinitely as the constant-growth DDM assumes. Using the formula in these circumstances will lead to an overestimate of the expected return.

**The Expected
Return on
Preferred Stock**

Preferred stock that pays a fixed annual dividend can be valued from the perpetuity formula:

$$\text{Price of preferred} = \frac{\text{dividend}}{r_{\text{preferred}}}$$

where $r_{\text{preferred}}$ is the appropriate discount rate for the preferred stock. Therefore, we can infer the required rate of return on preferred stock by rearranging the valuation formula to

$$r_{\text{preferred}} = \frac{\text{dividend}}{\text{price of preferred}}$$

For example, if a share of preferred stock sells for $20 and pays a dividend of $2 per share, the expected return on preferred stock is $r_{\text{preferred}} = \$2/\$20 = 10$ percent, which is simply the dividend yield.

11.5 CALCULATING THE WEIGHTED-AVERAGE COST OF CAPITAL

Now that you have worked out Big Oil's capital structure and estimated the expected return on its securities, you need only simple arithmetic to calculate the weighted-average cost of capital. Table 11.3 summarizes the necessary data. Now all you need to do is plug the data in Table 11.3 into the weighted-average cost of capital formula:

$$\begin{aligned}\text{Weighted-average} \atop \text{cost of capital} &= \left[\frac{D}{V} \times (1 - T_c)r_{\text{debt}}\right] + \left[\frac{E}{V} \times r_{\text{equity}}\right] \\ &= [.243 \times (1 - .35)\ .09] + (.757 \times .135) = .116, \text{ or } 11.6\% \end{aligned}$$

Suppose that Big Oil needed to evaluate a project with the same risk as its existing business that would also support a 24.3 percent debt ratio. The 11.6 percent weighted-average cost of capital is the appropriate discount rate for the cash flows.

TABLE 11.3
Data needed to calculate Big Oil's weighted-average cost of capital (dollar figures in millions)

Security Type	Capital Structure		Required Rate of Return
Debt	$D = \$385.7$	$D/V = .243$	$r_{\text{debt}} = .09$ or 9%
Common stock	$E = \$1200.0$	$E/V = .757$	$r_{\text{equity}} = .135$ or 13.5%
Total	$V = \$1585.7$		

Note: Corporate tax rate $= T_c = .35$

**Real Oil Company
WACCs**

Big Oil is entirely hypothetical — and not even very big compared to actual oil companies. Figure 11.2 shows estimated average costs of equity (r_{equity}) and WACCs for a sample of 10 to 12 large oil companies from 1965 to 1992. The latest estimates seem to be around 10 percent, less than our hypothetical figure for Big Oil.

The WACC estimates in Figure 11.2 decline steadily since the early 1980s. Some of that decline can be attributed to a decline in interest rates over the 1980s and early 1990s. We have included a plot of the risk-free rate (r_f) in Figure 11.2 as a reference point. However, the spread between the WACC estimates and these interest rates has also narrowed, suggesting that investors viewed the oil business as less risky in the early 1990s than a decade earlier.

Remember, the WACCs shown in Figure 11.2 are industry averages and therefore cover a wide range of activities. The large oil companies sampled are

FIGURE 11.2
The coloured line represents average weighted average costs of capital for a sample of large oil companies. Average costs of equity (for the same sample) and the risk-free rate of interest are also plotted for comparison.

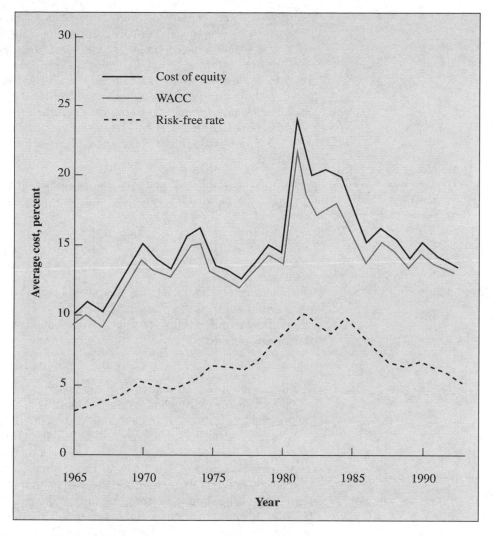

Source: The Brattle Group, Inc.

involved in some risky activities, such as exploration, and some relatively safe activities, such as franchising retail gas stations. The industry average may not be right for everything the industry does.

 INTERPRETING THE WEIGHTED-AVERAGE COST OF CAPITAL

When You Can and Can't Use WACC

We first discussed the company cost of capital in Chapter 10, but at that stage we did not know how to measure the company cost of capital when the firm has issued different types of securities or how to adjust for the tax-deductibility of interest payments. The weighted-average cost of capital formula solves those problems.

The weighted-average cost of capital is the rate of return that the firm must expect to earn on its average-risk investments in order to provide a fair expected return to all its security holders. We use it to value new assets that have the same risk as the old ones and that support the same ratio of debt. Strictly speaking, the weighted-average cost of capital is an appropriate discount rate only for a project that is a carbon copy of the firm's existing business. But often it is used as a company-wide benchmark discount rate; the benchmark is adjusted upward for unusually risky projects and downward for unusually safe ones.

There is a good musical analogy here. Most of us, lacking perfect pitch, need a well-defined reference point, like middle C, before we can sing on key. But anyone who can carry a tune gets *relative* pitches right. Businesspeople have good intuition about *relative* risks, at least in industries they are used to, but not about absolute risk or required rates of return. Therefore, they set a company- or industry-wide cost of capital as a benchmark. This is not the right hurdle rate for everything the company does, but judgmental adjustments can be made for more risky or less risky ventures.

Some Mistakes People Make Using the WACC

One danger with the weighted-average formula is that it tempts people to make logical errors. Think back to your estimate of the cost of capital for Big Oil:

$$\text{WACC} = \left[\frac{D}{V} \times (1 - T_c)r_{\text{debt}}\right] + \left[\frac{E}{V} \times r_{\text{equity}}\right]$$

$$= [.243 \times (1 - .35)\ .09] + (.757 \times .135) = .116, \text{ or } 11.6\%$$

Now you might be tempted to say to yourself, "Aha! Big Oil has a good credit rating. It could easily push up its debt ratio to 50 percent. If the interest rate is 9 percent and the required return on equity is 13.5 percent, the weighted-average cost of capital would be

$$\text{WACC} = [.50 \times (1 - .35)\ .09] + (.50 \times .135) = .097, \text{ or } 9.7\%$$

At a discount rate of 9.7 percent, we can justify a lot more investment."

That reasoning will get you into trouble. First, if Big Oil increased its borrowing, the lenders would almost certainly demand a higher rate of interest on the debt. Second, as the borrowing increased, the risk of the common stock would also increase and therefore the stockholders would demand a higher return. Thus there are actually two costs of debt finance. The explicit cost of debt is the rate of interest that bondholders demand. But there is also an implicit cost, because borrowing increases the required return to equity. When you jumped to the conclusion that Big Oil could lower its weighted-average cost of capital by borrowing more, you were recognizing only the explicit cost of debt and not the implicit cost.

How Changing Capital Structure Affects Expected Returns

We will illustrate how changes in capital structure affect expected returns by focusing on the simplest possible case, where the corporate tax rate T_c is zero.

Think back to our earlier example of Geothermal. Geothermal, you may remember, has the following market-value balance sheet:

Assets		Liabilities and Shareholders' Equity		
Assets = value of Geothermal's existing business	$647	Debt	$194	(30%)
		Equity	453	(70%)
Value	$647	Value	$647	(100%)

Geothermal's debtholders require a return of 8 percent and the shareholders require a return of 14 percent. Since we assume that Geothermal pays no corporate tax, its weighted-average cost of capital is simply the expected return on the firm's assets:

$$\text{WACC} = r_{\text{assets}} = (.3 \times .08) + (.7 \times .14) = .122, \text{ or } 12.2\%$$

This is the return you would expect if you held all Geothermal's securities and therefore owned all its assets.

Now think what will happen if Geothermal borrows an additional $97 million and uses the cash to buy back and retire $97 million of its common stock. The revised market-value balance sheet is:

Assets		Liabilities and Shareholders' Equity		
Assets = value of Geothermal's existing business	$647	Debt	$291	(45%)
		Equity	356	(55%)
Value	$647	Value	$647	(100%)

If there are no corporate taxes, the change in capital structure does not affect the total cash that Geothermal pays out to its security holders and it does not affect the risk of those cash flows. Therefore, if investors require a return of 12.2 percent on the total package of debt and equity before the financing, they must require the same 12.2 percent return on the package afterward. The weighted-average cost of capital is therefore unaffected by the change in capital structure.

Although the required return on the *package* of the debt and equity is unaffected, the change in capital structure does affect the required return on the individual securities. Since the company has more debt than before, the debt is riskier and debtholders are likely to demand a higher return. We will assume that the expected return on Geothermal's debt increases to 9 percent.

Geothermal's additional borrowing also puts common stockholders in a riskier position. The company has to pay out more interest before the stockholders get a penny of the company's cash flow. But just how much higher should stockholders' required return be? The answer is elegantly simple: the stockholders' required return rises by just enough to keep investors' overall required return (r_{assets}) constant. Remember, there is no reason for r_{assets} to change.

We then calculate r_{equity} as follows. Write down the basic equation for the return on Geothermal's assets and find the expected return on equity:

$$r_{assets} = \left(\frac{D}{V} \times r_{debt}\right) + \left(\frac{E}{V} \times r_{equity}\right)$$

$$.122 = (.45 \times .09) + (.55 \times r_{equity})$$

$$r_{equity} = .148, \text{ or } 14.8\%$$

Increasing the amount of debt increased debtholder risk and required return (r_{debt} rose from 8 to 9 percent). The higher level of debt also made the equity riskier and increased the return that shareholders required (r_{equity} rose from 14 to 14.8 percent). The company cost of capital remained at 12.2 percent:

$$r_{assets} = (.45 \times r_{debt}) + (.55 \times r_{equity})$$

$$= (.45 \times .09) + (.55 \times .148)$$

$$= .122, \text{ or } 12.2\%$$

SELF-TEST 11.5

Refer back to Table 11.5, and calculate Big Oil's weighted-average cost of capital assuming a corporate tax rate of zero ($T_c = 0$). What would Big Oil's cost of equity capital be if it moved its capital structure to 50 percent debt? Assume the cost of debt rises to 11 percent.

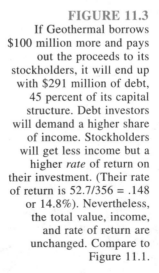

How Changing Capital Structure Affects Beta

asset beta: Market risk of the firm's projects.

We have looked at how changes in capital structure affect expected return. Let us now look at the effect on risk.

Both shareholders and debtholders receive a share of the cash flows and both bear part of the risk. For example, if the firm's assets turn out to be worthless, there will be no cash to pay either of them. But debtholders bear much less risk than shareholders. Debt betas of large blue-chip firms are close to zero — close enough that many financial analysts assume that $ß_{debt} = 0$.

If you owned a portfolio of all the firm's securities, you wouldn't share the firm's cash flows with anyone. You wouldn't share the risks with anyone either; you would bear them all. Thus the **asset beta**, that is, the beta of all the firm's assets, is equal to the beta of a portfolio of all the firm's debt and all its equity. This is just a weighted average of the debt and equity betas:

$$ß_{assets} = \left(\frac{D}{V} \times ß_{debt}\right) + \left(\frac{E}{V} \times ß_{equity}\right)$$

Think back to our Geothermal example. If the debt before the refinancing has a beta of .1 and the equity a beta of 1.2, then

$$ß_{assets} = (.3 \times .1) + (.7 \times 1.2) = .87$$

What happens after the refinancing? The risk of the total package is unaffected but both the debt and the equity are now riskier. Suppose that the debt beta increases to .15. We can work out the new equity beta:

$$ß_{assets} = \left(\frac{D}{V} \times ß_{debt}\right) + \left(\frac{E}{V} \times ß_{equity}\right)$$

$$.87 = (.45 \times .15) + (.55 \times ß_{equity})$$

$$ß_{equity} = 1.46$$

Look back to Figure 11.1, which shows how Geothermal's capital structure and expected income are shared between the debtholders and shareholders. Now suppose Geothermal buys back part of its equity. Figure 11.3 shows what happens after the change in capital structure. Both debt and equity are more risky, and therefore investors demand a higher expected return. But equity now accounts for a lower proportion of company value than before. As a result, the total risk of the

FIGURE 11.3
If Geothermal borrows $100 million more and pays out the proceeds to its stockholders, it will end up with $291 million of debt, 45 percent of its capital structure. Debt investors will demand a higher share of income. Stockholders will get less income but a higher *rate* of return on their investment. (Their rate of return is 52.7/356 = .148 or 14.8%). Nevertheless, the total value, income, and rate of return are unchanged. Compare to Figure 11.1.

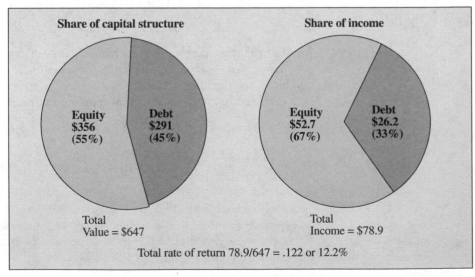

package of debt and equity is unchanged. The expected return on the package — that is, the company cost of capital — is also unchanged.

SELF-TEST 11.6

Turn one more time to Big Oil. Its common stock had a beta of $\beta_{equity} = .85$ at the existing capital structure shown in Table 11.4. What would Big Oil's β_{equity} be at a debt-value ratio of 50 percent? Assume the debt beta is .10 at the existing capital structure and .25 at 50 percent debt.

What Happens When the Corporate Tax Rate Is Not Zero

We have illustrated how changes in the debt ratio affect the expected return and risk of the equity when the corporate tax rate is zero. Unfortunately, taxes can complicate the picture.[6] For the moment, just remember

- It is the company cost of capital that is relevant to capital budgeting decisions, not the expected return on the common stock.
- The company cost of capital is a weighted average of the returns that investors expect from a package of all the debt and equity securities issued by the firm.
- If the firm increases its debt ratio, both the debt and the equity will become more risky (β_{debt} and β_{equity} rise). The debtholders and equity holders require a higher return to compensate for the increased risk (r_{debt} and r_{equity} rise).

11.7 THE WEIGHTED-AVERAGE COST OF CAPITAL AND CAPITAL BUDGETING

The company's weighted-average cost of capital is the correct discount rate for projects that have the same risks as the company's existing business. What do you do if the project you are considering has different risk than the company? If you use the company's weighted-average cost of capital to evaluate projects with different risks, you likely will reject projects that would increase the value of the firm and accept projects that reduce it. To avoid making costly mistakes, the discount rate appropriate for the project's risks must be assessed.

In Chapter 10 we introduced the concept of the project cost of capital, the minimum acceptable expected rate of return on a project, given its risks. When funds are invested in a project, the required rate of return on the investment depends on the *project's risk*, not on the source of funds. In Chapter 10 we discussed ways of finding a suitable estimate of a project's cost of capital. We now must extend the analysis to consider a project's weighted-average cost of capital.

We introduced the concept of the weighted-average cost of capital because firms typically are financed by a mixture of securities. The weighted-average cost of capital depends on the expected return from all the securities that the company has issued. In our analysis so far we have not answered an important question: Why is the firm financed this way? We have shown that in a world without taxes, the company's cost of capital is unaffected by how it is financed. With taxes, the analysis is more complex. We will deal with the details in Chapter 15. In the meantime, we can say that a firm selects its capital structure to maximize the firm's or project's value. Consequently, the determination of the cost of capital appropriate for a project has two components. First, the risks of the project's cash flows must be assessed. That is, the asset beta must be determined. Second, the best mixture of

---

[6] There's nothing wrong with our formulas and examples, provided that the tax deductibility of interest payments doesn't change the aggregate risk of the debt and equity investors. However, if the tax savings from deducting interest are treated as safe cash flows, the formulas get more complicated.

financing needs to be determined. The project's weighted-average cost of capital will reflect the project's overall risk and the best financing mix suitable for the project.

In Chapter 10 we discussed ways of estimating the project's cost of capital. We now know that the pure play approach for assessing the project's risk is complicated by the choice of capital structure. As a first step, you may want to use the pure play company's weighted-average cost of capital as a proxy for the project's weighted-average cost of capital. We want to caution you that such a simple approach may lead to poor investment decisions. You will want to be able to assess the appropriate capital structure for the project in question. We leave the details to Chapter 15.

 ## SUMMARY

1. The weighted-average cost of capital is an average of the required rates of return on all the securities issued by the firm.

2. Since interest payments can be used to reduce the firm's tax bill, the required return on debt is measured on an after-tax basis.

3. In calculating the weighted-average cost of capital, the required return on each security is weighted by its proportion of the firm's value. The proportions should be based on the market values of the securities, not their book values.

4. When you estimate the weighted-average cost of capital, the tricky part is to figure out the expected return on the firm's shares. Financial managers commonly use the capital asset pricing model to estimate expected return. But for steady-growth companies, it may also make sense to use the constant-growth discounted cash flow model. Remember, estimates of the expected return are less reliable for a single firm than for a sample of comparable-risk firms.

5. Do *not* assume that the expected return on each of the firm's securities will remain the same if the firm changes the proportions of debt and equity. For example, increasing the debt proportion will increase the risk of both debtholders and equity holders and cause them to demand a higher return.

6. The weighted-average cost of capital can be used to discount the after-tax cash flows on new projects that are carbon copies of the firm's existing business. That is, the firm's weighted-average cost of capital is the appropriate discount rate for new projects with risks identical to the firm's current risks.

7. For projects with risks different than the risk of the firm's existing business, the calculation of the weighted-cost of capital requires the determination of the project's overall (asset) risk and the best mixture of financing.

KEY TERMS

capital structure
weighted-average cost of capital (WACC)
asset beta

PROBLEMS

1. Advanced Spinoffs, Inc., issued 20-year debt last year at par value with a coupon rate of 9 percent, paid annually. Today, the debt is selling at $1050. If the firm's tax bracket is 35 percent, what is its after-tax cost of debt?

2. Passive Footwear has a WACC of 12 percent. Its debt sells at a yield to maturity of 9 percent, and its tax rate is 40 percent. Its cost of equity is 15 percent. What is the fraction of the firm financed with debt versus equity?

3. Reactive Industries has the following capital structure. Its corporate tax rate is 35 percent. What is its WACC?

Security	Market Value	Required Rate of Return
Debt	$20 million	8%
Preferred stock	$10 million	10%
Common stock	$50 million	15%

4. The common stock of Buildwell Conservation & Construction, Inc. has a beta of .80. The Treasury bill rate is 4 percent and the market risk premium is estimated at 8 percent. BCCI's capital structure is 30 percent debt paying a 5 percent interest rate, and 70 percent equity. What is BCCI's cost of equity capital? Its WACC? Buildwell pays no taxes.

5. BCCI (see problem 4) is evaluating a proposed project.
    a. In order to use BCCI's WACC calculated in problem 4, what must be true about the risk of the proposed project?
    b. If the project has an internal rate of return of 12 percent, should BCCI accept it?
    c. If the project will generate a cash flow of $100,000 a year for 7 years, what is the most BCCI should be willing to pay to initiate the project? What is the project's NPV and internal rate of return in this case?

6. Find the WACC of William Tell Computers. The total book value of the firm's equity is $10 million; book value per share is $20. The stock sells for a price of $30 per share, and the cost of equity is 15 percent. The firm's bonds have a par value of $5 million and sell at a price of 110 percent of par. The yield to maturity on the bonds is 9 percent, and the firm's tax rate is 40 percent.

7. On December 10, 1993, Freddie Mac preferred stock sold at a price of $27. The annual dividend on the preferred is $1.98 per share. What is the cost of preferred stock for Freddie Mac?

8. Examine the following book-value balance sheet. What is the capital structure of the firm based on market values? The preferred stock currently sells for $15 per share and the common stock for $20 per share. There are one million common shares outstanding.

BOOK VALUE BALANCE SHEET
(all values in millions)

Assets		Liabilities and Net Worth	
Cash and short-term securities	$1	Bonds, coupon = 8%, paid annually (maturity = 10 years, current yield to maturity = 9%)	$10.0
Accounts receivable	3	Preferred stock (par value $20 per share)	2.0
Inventories	7	Common stock	10
Plant and equipment	21	Retained earnings	10.0
Total	$32	Total	$32.0

9. Nodebt, Inc., is a firm with all-equity financing. Its equity beta is .80. The Treasury bill rate is 5 percent and the market risk premium is expected to be 10 percent. What is Nodebt's asset beta? What is Nodebt's weighted-average cost of capital? The firm is exempt from paying taxes.

10. Now suppose that Nodebt issues a little debt — so little debt, in fact, that investors perceive the bonds to be risk-free. The debt comprises 10 percent of the firm's capital structure, and the equity comprises 90 percent.
    a. What is the beta and required rate of return on the debt?
    b. What must be the new beta of and required rate of return on the firm's equity?
    c. Calculate the WACC of the firm under the new financing mix. Has WACC changed?
    d. Interpret your result. Calculate the weighted-average asset beta given the new financing mix. Has weighted-average beta changed?

11. The total market value of Muskoka Real Estate Company is $10 million, and the total value of its debt is $4 million. The treasurer estimates that the beta of the stock currently is 1.5 and that the expected risk premium on the market is 10 percent. The Treasury bill rate is 4 percent.
    a. What is the required rate of return on Muskoka stock?
    b. What is the beta of the company's existing portfolio of assets? The debt is perceived to be virtually risk-free.
    c. Estimate the company's cost of capital assuming a tax rate of 40 percent.
    d. Estimate the discount rate for an expansion of the company's present business.
    e. Suppose the company wants to diversify into the manufacture of rose-coloured glasses. The beta of optical manufacturers with no debt outstanding is 1.2. What is the required rate of return on Muskoka's new venture?

12. A firm with an asset beta of .9 engages in two lines of business. Aircraft production accounts for 70 percent of the value of the firm and sporting goods manufacturing accounts for the rest. If the asset beta of Consolidated Jets, which is exclusively engaged in aircraft production, is 1.0, what must be the beta of the sporting goods project?

SOLUTIONS TO SELF-TEST QUESTIONS

11.1 Hot Rocks's 4 million common shares are worth $40 million. Its market value balance sheet is:

Assets		Liabilities and Shareholders' Equity		
Assets	$90	Debt	$50	(56%)
		Equity	40	(44%)
Value	$90	Value	$90	

Company cost of capital = $(.56 \times .09) + (.44 \times .17) = .125$, or 12.5%

Note this question ignores taxes.

11.2 Schwartz's 6 million shares are now worth only $6 \times 4 = \$24$ million. The debt is selling for 80 percent of book, or $20 million. The market value balance sheet is:

Assets		Liabilities and Shareholders' Equity		
Assets	$44	Debt	$20	(45%)
		Equity	24	(55%)
Value	$44	Value	$44	

Company cost of capital = $(.45 \times .14) + (.55 \times .20) = .173$, or 17.3%

11.3   WACC = $.45 (1 - .35).14 + .55(.20) = .151$, or 15.1%

11.4   From the CAPM:

$$r_{equity} = r_f + \beta_{equity} (r_m - r_f)$$

$$= .06 + 1.20(.09) = .168, \text{ or } 16.8\%$$

$$WACC = .3(1 - .35) .08 + .7(.168) = .133, \text{ or } 13.3\%$$

11.5   If the tax rate is zero,

$$WACC = r_{assets} = (.243 \times .09) + (.757 \times .135) = .124, \text{ or } 12.4\%$$

The move to 50 percent debt doesn't change r_{assets}:

$$r_{assets} = .124 = (.50 \times .11) + .50r_{equity}$$

Solving for the new cost of equity,

$$r_{equity} = .138, \text{ or } 13.8\%$$

11.6   Big Oil's asset beta is

$$\beta_{assets} = (.243 \times .10) + (.757 \times .85) = .67$$

The move to 50 percent debt doesn't change the asset beta. If the debt beta increases to

$$\beta_{debt} - .25,$$

$$\beta_{assets} = .67 = (.50 \times .25) + .50\beta_{equity}$$

Solving for the equity beta, $\beta_{equity} = 1.09$.

PART FOUR

Financing

CHAPTER TWELVE

Corporate Financing and the Lessons of Market Efficiency

Up to this point we have concentrated almost exclusively on the firm's capital expenditure decision. Now we move to the other side of the balance sheet to look at how the firm can finance those capital expenditures. To put it crudely, you've learned how to spend money — now learn how to raise it.

In the next few chapters, therefore, we assume that the firm has already decided on which investment projects to accept and we focus on the best way to finance these projects. We begin in this chapter with some general lessons about the capital markets — the sources of financing.

Economists often talk about "efficient capital markets." By this they don't mean that the filing is up-to-date and desktops are tidy. They mean that information is widely and cheaply available to investors and that all relevant and ascertainable information is already reflected in security prices. New information is quickly reflected in stock prices. All stocks, bonds, and other securities are fairly priced in efficient markets and offer expected returns just sufficient to compensate for the securities' risks.

Why should a hard-nosed financial manager care about market efficiency? He or she just wants to raise financing at the lowest possible cost, right?

Right — but finding financing that's *truly* low-cost is not as easy as it looks. You've got to know where to look — and where not to look. Capital markets are full of traps and mirages for the unwary or naive. The wary and sophisticated financial manager, who understands the implications of capital market efficiency, is much less likely to make an expensive financing mistake.

Financial managers can't rely on issuing new shares at "cyclical highs" of the stock market. (Efficient markets have no predictable up and down cycles.)

Unscrupulous financial managers — there are a few — can't pump up their companies' stock prices just by choosing accounting policies that generate higher reported earnings. (Investors in efficient markets see through purely cosmetic accounting changes.)

Financing rules like "Borrow short-term when short-term rates are low, long-term otherwise" don't reduce financing costs in the long run. (In fact, financial managers facing absolutely efficient markets can't reduce the true, long-run costs of financing with any mechanical rule.)

Of course no human institution is perfect, and no financial market is perfectly efficient. But we always advise financial managers to start by assuming efficient capital markets. From that vantage point they can look out for the specific inefficiencies or imperfections (possibly due to taxes or government regulations) that can be used to create advantageous financing strategies.

After studying this chapter you should be able to

- Understand how competition among investors leads to efficient markets.
- Cite evidence that supports the hypothesis that security markets are efficient — as well as some that contradicts it.
- Understand the implications of market efficiency for a firm's financial decisions.

12.1 DIFFERENCES BETWEEN INVESTMENT AND FINANCING DECISIONS

In some ways financing decisions are more complicated than investment decisions. The number of different securities to choose from is large and continually expanding. You must also be aware of the major financial institutions that provide financing for business firms. Finally, you need to acquire a lot of new jargon. For example, in Chapters 13 and 14 you will learn about *swaps, eurodollars, red herrings, sinking funds*, and many other exotic beasts — and behind each lies an interesting story.

There are also ways in which financing decisions are easier than investment decisions. First, financing decisions do not have the same degree of finality as investment decisions. They are easier to reverse. For example, Stelco can issue a bond and buy it back later if second thoughts arise. It would be far more difficult for Stelco to dismantle or sell a blast furnace it decides is no longer needed.

Second, it's harder to make or lose money by smart or stupid financing strategies. It is difficult to make money — that is, to find cheap financing — because the investors who supply the financing demand fair terms. At the same time, it's harder to lose money because competition among investors prevents any one or group of them from demanding more than fair terms.

Competition in financial markets is more thorough and intense than in most product markets. In product markets, companies regularly find competitive advantages that allow positive-NPV investments. For example a company may have only a few competitors that specialize in the same line of business in the same geographical area. Or it may be able to capitalize on patents or technology, or on customer recognition and loyalty. All this opens up the opportunity to make superior profits and find projects with positive NPVs.

But there are few protected niches in *financial* markets. You can't patent the design of a new security. Moreover, in these markets you always face fast-moving competition, including all the other corporations seeking funds, to say nothing of the provincial, municipal, and federal governments, financial institutions, individuals, and foreign firms and governments that also come to Bay Street (Canada's financial centre), Wall Street (the United States' financial centre), London, or Tokyo for financing. The investors who supply financing are numerous, and they are smart — money attracts brains. Most likely, these investors can assess values of securities at least as well as you can.

A smart financing decision generates a positive NPV. For example, the firm might hope to sell a security for more than the present value of the cash flows it must pay the security holder. But if selling a security generates a positive NPV for you, it must generate a negative NPV for the buyer. What are the chances that your firm could consistently trick or persuade investors to purchase securities with negative NPVs to them? Pretty low. In general, firms should assume that the securities they issue sell for their true values.

But what do we mean by *true value*? It is a potentially slippery phrase. True value does not mean ultimate *future* value — we do not expect investors to be fortunetellers. It means a price that incorporates all the information currently available to investors. That is our definition of **efficient capital markets**. *If capital markets are efficient, all securities are fairly priced in light of the information available to investors.* If securities are fairly priced, then financing at prevailing market terms is always a zero-NPV transaction.

efficient capital markets: Financial markets in which security prices reflect all relevant information about asset values available.

Does that sound like a sweeping statement? It is. That is why we devote the rest of this chapter to the history, logic, and tests of market efficiency.

You may ask why we start our discussion of financing issues with this conceptual point, before you have even the most basic knowledge about securities, issue procedures, and financial institutions. We do it this way because financing decisions seem overwhelmingly complex if you don't learn to ask the right questions. You need to understand the efficient-market hypothesis, not because it is *universally* true but because it leads you to ask the right questions.

 WHAT IS AN EFFICIENT MARKET?

....
A Startling Discovery: Price Changes Are Random

random walk: Security prices change randomly, with no predictable trends or patterns.

As is so often the case with important ideas, the concept of efficient markets was a byproduct of a chance discovery. In 1953 the Royal Statistical Society met in London to discuss a rather unusual paper.[1] Its author, Maurice Kendall, was a distinguished statistician, and the subject was the behaviour of stock and commodity prices. Kendall had been looking for regular price cycles, but to his surprise he could not find them. Prices seemed to wander randomly, virtually equally likely to go up or go down on any particular day, *regardless of what had occurred on previous days*. In other words, prices seemed to follow a **random walk**.

If you are not sure what we mean by "random walk," consider the following example. You are given $100 to play a game. At the end of each week a coin is tossed. If it comes up heads, you win 3 percent of your investment; if it is tails, you lose 2.5 percent. Therefore, your capital at the end of the first week is either $103.00 or $97.50. At the end of the second week the coin is tossed again. Now the possible outcomes are as follows:

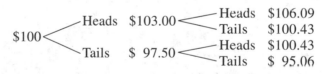

This process is a random walk because successive changes in the value of your stake are independent. That is, the odds of making money each week are 50 percent, regardless of the value at the start of the week or the pattern of heads or tails in the previous weeks.

If a stock's price follows a random walk, the odds of an increase or decrease during any day, month, or year do not depend at all on the stock's previous price moves. The historical path of prices gives no useful information about the future — just as a long series of recorded heads and tails gives no information about the next coin toss.

Some people find it difficult to believe that stock prices follow a random walk. If you are one of them, look at the two charts in Figure 12.1. One of these charts shows the outcome from playing our game for 5 years; the other shows the actual performance of the TSE 300 Price Index for a 5-year period. Can you tell which one is which?[2]

---

[1] See M. G. Kendall, "The Analysis of Economic Time-Series, Part I. Prices," *Journal of the Royal Statistical Society* 96 (1953):11–25.

[2] The top chart in Figure 12.1 shows the real TSE 300 Price Index for the years 1989 through 1993; the lower chart is the result of tossing a coin. Of course, 50 percent of you will have guessed right, but we bet it was just a guess and you weren't really that smart. A similar comparison between cumulated random numbers and actual price series was first suggested by H. V. Roberts, "Stock Market 'Patterns' and Financial Analysis: Methodological Suggestions," *Journal of Finance* 14 (March 1959):1–10.

FIGURE 12.1
One of these charts shows
the TSE 300 Composite
Index for a 5-year period.
The other shows the results
of playing our coin-toss
game for 5 years. Can you
tell which is which?

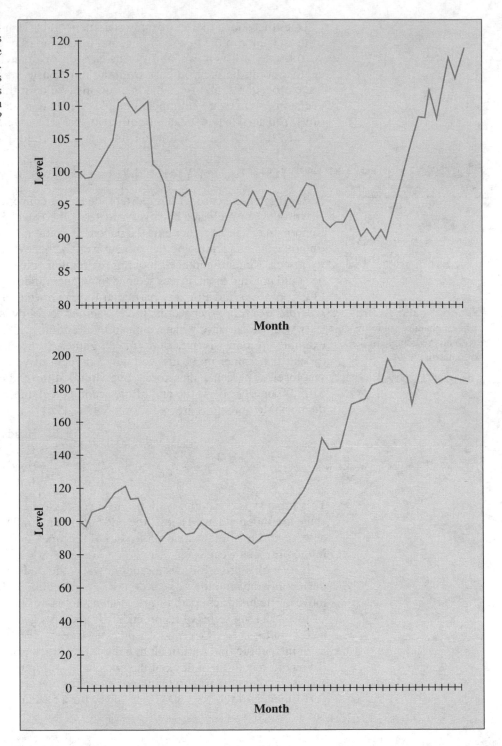

To most economists Maurice Kendall's suggestion that stock prices follow a random walk was at first startling and bizarre. However, as computers and data became more readily available, economists and statisticians rapidly amassed a large volume of supporting evidence. Let us look very briefly at the kinds of tests that they have used.

Suppose that you wished to assess whether there is any tendency for price changes to persist from one day to the next. You might begin by drawing a scatter diagram of price changes on successive days. Figure 12.2 is an example of such a diagram. Each point shows the change in the price of Canadian Pacific's stock on two successive days. The circled point in the southeast quadrant refers to a pair of days in which a 0.5 percent increase was followed by a 3.5 percent decrease. Points in the northeast quadrant refer to days in which a price increase was followed by another increase. The western quadrants show what happened after price declines.

FIGURE 12.2
Each point shows a pair of returns for Canadian Pacific stock on two successive days in 1991, 1992, and 1993. The circled point records a daily return of +.5 percent and then −3.5 percent on the next day. The scatter diagram shows no significant relationship between returns on successive days

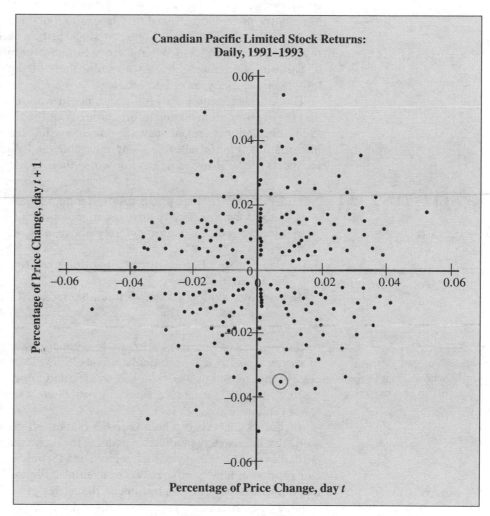

If there had been a systematic tendency for increases to be followed by decreases, there would be many points in the southeast quadrant and only a few in the northeast quadrant. On the other hand, if increases were usually followed by more increases, the northeast quadrant would be full and the southeast nearly empty.

If there was *no tendency* for returns to show any relationship to the previous day's return, then the points would be peppered randomly across the diagram — and this is exactly what the figure shows. One day's change in Canadian Pacific's stock price told investors nothing about the next day's.

We can test this random walk hypothesis more precisely by calculating the correlation coefficient between each day's price change and the next. If price movements persist, the correlation would be significantly positive; if price movements reverse, the coefficient would be negative; and if there were no relationship, it would be 0. In our example, the correlation was +.03 — there was a negligible tendency for price rises to be followed by further rises.

Figure 12.2 showed the behaviour of only one stock, but our finding is typical. Researchers have looked at many different stocks in many different countries and for many different periods; they have calculated the correlation coefficient between these price changes; they have looked for "runs" of consistently positive or negative price changes, and they have simulated mechanical trading rules that try to exploit "trends" or "cycles" in stock prices. With remarkable unanimity researchers have concluded that there is little useful information in the sequence of past stock price changes. As a result, many of the researchers have become famous. Few, if any, have become rich.

The fact that stock prices follow a random walk is consistent with the notion that they reflect all available information about the firm. If prices already reflect such information, then only new information will cause prices to change. But new information, by its nature, is unpredictable and equally likely to make the prospects of the firm seem better or worse than your current assessment.

SELF-TEST 12.1

True or false? If stock prices follow a random walk,
a. Successive stock price changes are not correlated.
b. Stock prices fluctuate randomly above and below a normal, long-run price.
c. The history of stock prices cannot be used to predict future returns to investors.
d. A historical plot of a stock's trading prices will show no apparent "peaks and valleys."

technical analysts: Analysts who attempt to find patterns in security price movements.

Some investors *try* to get rich by looking for patterns in stock prices. These investors are known as **technical analysts**. Some technical analysts are very successful investors, but we credit this to luck and good judgment, not to technical trading rules, because technical trading rules are useless when stock prices follow a random walk.

Technical analysts can help keep the market efficient, however. Their trading would extinguish any predictable patterns in stock prices. Suppose that there were a trend in some company's stock price. Then technical analysts could make superior profits, at least temporarily. For example, Figure 12.3 shows a hypothetical 2-month upswing for Establishment Industries (EI). The upswing started last month, when EI's stock price was $40, and it is expected to carry the stock price to $60 next month. What will happen when technicians perceive this bonanza? It will self-destruct. Since EI stock is a bargain at $50, investors will rush to buy. They will stop buying only when the stock offers a normal rate of return. Therefore, as soon as a price pattern becomes apparent to technical analysts, they immediately eliminate it by their trading.

weak-form efficiency: Situation in which market prices rapidly reflect all information contained in the history of past prices.

Three Forms of the Efficient-Market Theory

If stock prices follow a random walk, you can't make superior profits just by studying past stock prices. Any information in those stock prices is already reflected in today's price. So the market is at least efficient in this sense. Such a market is called **weak-form efficient**.

FIGURE 12.3
Cycles self-destruct as soon as they are recognized by investors. The stock price instantaneously jumps to the present value of the expected future price.

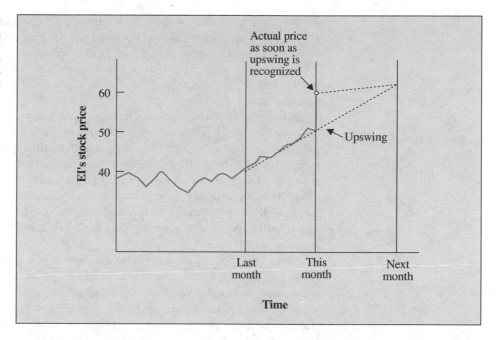

fundamental analysts: Analysts who attempt to find under- or overvalued securities by analyzing fundamental information, such as earnings, asset values, and business prospects.

semi-strong-form efficiency: Situation in which market prices reflect all publicly available information.

strong-form efficiency: Situation in which prices rapidly reflect all information that could in principle be used to determine true value.

But what about other kinds of information? Are they also immediately reflected in stock prices? After all, most investors don't just look at past stock prices. Instead they try to gauge a firm's business prospects by studying the financial and technical press, the company's financial accounts and the president's annual statement, the recommendations made by stockbrokers, and so on. These investors are **fundamental analysts**, in contrast to technical analysts, who examine past stock price movements.

Researchers have looked at stock price movements after announcements of earnings and dividends, forecasts of company earnings, disclosures of merger plans, and changes in accounting practices.[3] Most of this information was rapidly and accurately reflected in the price of the stock, so that investors were not able to earn superior profits by buying or selling immediately after the announcements.[4] A market in which it is impossible to make superior profits from such published information is said to be **semi-strong-form efficient**.

Finally, there's **strong-form efficiency**, in which prices reflect not just public information but *all* the information available about the company. This includes information that can be acquired by painstaking analysis of the company and the

[3] See, for example, R. Ball and P. Brown, "An Empirical Evaluation of Accounting Income Numbers," *Journal of Accounting Research*, 6 (Autumn 1968):159–178; R. R. Pettit, "Dividend Announcements, Security Performance, and Capital Market Efficiency," *Journal of Finance*, 27 (December 1972): 993–1007; G. Foster, "Stock Market Reaction to Estimates of Earnings Per Share by Company Officials," *Journal of Accounting Research*, 11: (Spring 1973):25–37; R. S. Kaplan and R. Roll, "Investor Evaluation of Accounting Information: Some Empirical Evidence," *Journal of Financial Economics*, 1 (December 1974):303–335; and G. Charest, "Returns to Dividend Splitting Stocks on the Toronto Stock Exchange," *Journal of Business Administration*, 12 (Fall 1980):1–18.

[4] The price reaction to news appears to be almost immediate. For example, within 5 to 10 minutes of earnings or dividend announcements appearing on the broad tape, most of the price adjustment has occurred and any remaining gain from acting on the news is less than the transaction costs. See J. M. Patell and M. A. Wolfson, "The Intraday Speed of Adjustment of Stock Prices to Earnings and Dividend Announcements," *Journal of Financial Economics*, 13 (June 1984):223–252; and Catherine Woodruff and A. J. Senchack, Jr., "Intraday Price–Volume Adjustments of NYSE Stocks to Unexpected Earnings," *Journal of Finance*, 43: 467–491.

economy by expert analysts. It also includes private or inside information available to some people by virtue of a special relationship with the company. Members of the board of directors, managers, and employees often have access to inside information before it is publicly announced. In such a market, prices would *always* be fair and *no* investor would be able to make consistently superior forecasts of stock prices.

Most tests of strong-form efficiency have analyzed the performance of professionally managed portfolios. Managers of such portfolios have every kind of published and unpublished information at their fingertips. If the market were not strong-form efficient, these managers ought to generate higher returns than ordinary investors. Yet no group of portfolio managers has been able to outperform the market consistently, after taking account of differences in risk. Some portfolios have done better than others, of course, but the differences are no greater than you would expect from chance.[5] This evidence supports the strong form of market efficiency.

When evidence of the only-average performance of professional investment managers first appeared, it was also greeted with skepticism — especially by the managers! But many investment managers are now convinced and indeed have given up the pursuit of superior performance. They simply "buy the index," which maximizes diversification and minimizes the costs of managing their portfolios. In the United States, over $250 billion of pension money (or about 10 percent of the total) is now "indexed."[6]

Indexing of professionally managed money makes sense if no manager can get useful information consistently ahead of the rest of the pack. When information does arrive, managers trade on it immediately, and stock prices respond right away. Such a market ends up strong-form efficient, even though the information moving stock prices is not readily available to the amateur investor.

Can no one outperform the market on a consistent basis? Some evidence suggests that if you have inside information, information about a company that has not yet been publicly announced, you may significantly outperform the market. If insider trading creates excess profits, then the market is not strong-form efficient. If it were, then the act of trading on inside information would lead to quick revision in asset prices, making it not possible for those with inside information to profit from their knowledge. It is questionable that many investors have access to inside information on a regular basis. Furthermore, as you can read in *Finance in Action: Insider Trading Laws*, it is illegal to trade on inside information.

SELF-TEST 12.2

Technical analysts, fundamental analysts, and professional portfolio managers all try to earn superior returns in the stock market. Explain how each group's efforts help keep the market efficient.

[5] The classic study was M. C. Jensen, "The Performance of Mutual Funds in the Period 1945–64," *Journal of Finance* 23 (May 1968):389–416. More recent studies include J. C. Bogle and J. M. Twardowski, "Institutional Investment Performance Compared: Banks, Investment Counselors, Insurance Companies, and Mutual Funds," *Financial Analysts Journal* 36 (January–February 1980):33–41; M. Grinblatt and S. Titman, "Mutual Fund Performance: An Analysis of Quarterly Portfolio Holdings," *Journal of Business* 62 (July 1989):393–416; and R. A. Ippolito, "Efficiency with Costly Information: A Study of Mutual Fund Performance, 1965–84," *Quarterly Journal of Economics* 104 (February 1989):1–23.
[6] An indexed portfolio is designed to replicate the investment performance of a particular stock market index. The portfolio is invested in each stock in proportion to the stock's weight in the index. Individual investors can index, too. See Example 10.2 in Chapter 10.

Finance in Action

Insider Trading Laws

* *

When a investor has information that no else knows, he or she may be able to act on the information before others figure out what is going on. Trading on private information can be a very successful way to make big returns in the stock market. However, if that information is inside information, received from someone who works for the company and not yet publicly announced, it is illegal to use. Investors guilty of trading on inside information face heavy financial penalties and possibly jail.

Consider the case of Mr. X, an assistant vice-president of Bell Canada, who made an $1100 profit from the sale of 10 put options he bought for $500, earning a healthy return of 222 percent in 5 days!!! How did he do it? Read on.

At 9 a.m., June 10, 1992, Mr. X was told that a proposed strategic alliance between his employer, Bell Canada, and SHL Systemhouse Inc., a computer company, had collapsed. A few minutes later, Mr. X placed an order with his broker to purchase 100 Systemhouse put option contracts. A put option gives an investor the right to sell a share at a predetermined price, within a certain time limit. Put options allow an investor to benefit from negative news that lowers the stock price and raises the value of the put.

At 9:41 a.m., trading in SHL options and stock was halted at the request of SHL. It is common practice for a company to ask the stock exchange to stop the trading of their stock shortly before they make a major announcement so no investors trade at an informational disadvantage.

At the time of the halt, SHL's stock was trading at $16 per share and the put options were selling at $0.50.

By the time the halt occurred, Mr. X's broker had purchased only 10 of the requested 100 put contracts. Each contract consisted of 100 puts, each put for one share. Each put was selling for $0.50. Each contract cost $50 ($0.50 per put × 100 puts = $50 per contract), for a total of $500 for the 10 contracts.

At 11:49 a.m., SHL issued a news release announcing the collapse of the deal with Bell Canada. Trading of SHL's stock resumed at 1:30 p.m. But now the price of SHL was only $11 3/8 ($11.375), a drop of $4.625 in just a few hours. In contrast, the price of the put had risen from $0.50 to $2.95.

Although trading on inside information can be profitable, it is illegal. According to Section 75.(1) of the Ontario Securities Act, no person in a "special relationship" with a company is permitted to purchase or sell securities of the company with the knowledge of a material fact or material change about the company that has not been generally disclosed. Furthermore, it is illegal to give information to others. The Act defines a person with a "special relationship" to include an employee, director, or officer of the company. In addition, a person with a special relationship includes someone who receives the inside information from someone who has a special relationship with the company. Thus, if you know that the

Insider Trading Laws *(continued)*

information came from an employee of the company, it is illegal for you to trade on the information.

Upon learning that it was illegal for him to purchase the put options, the assistant vice-president instructed his broker to not complete his order for the remaining 90 put contracts. He sold the put options the following week, netting an $1100 profit and immediately donated the profits to charity.

In the meantime, the department of the brokerage firm responsible for ensuring that the brokerage firm

obeys the law reported the purchase of the put options to the Ontario Securities Commission. The Ontario Securities Commission held a hearing and determined that the assistant vice-president had violated the Securities Act. His conduct "was unfair to other participants in the stock market and contrary to the public interest in that it undermines investor confidence in the integrity of the capital markets." He was fined $3300, three times the profit he made trading on the inside information.

Source: Lawrence Surtees, "OSC Hearing Set for Bell Canada Executive," *The Globe and Mail Report on Business,* June 11, 1994; *Ontario Securities Commission Bulletin,* (1994) 17 OSCB 2973.

What Market Efficiency Does and Does Not Imply

The efficient-market hypothesis is frequently misinterpreted. For example, some have suggested that stock prices cannot represent fair value because they go up and down. The truth is that they would not represent fair value unless they went up and down. It is because the future is so uncertain and people are so often surprised that prices fluctuate. (Of course, when we look back, nothing seems quite so surprising; it is easy to convince ourselves that we really knew all along how prices were going to change.)

Others are tempted to think that the inability of institutions to achieve superior portfolio performance shows that portfolio managers are incompetent. This is incorrect. Market efficiency exists only because competition is keen and managers are doing their job. If this were not the case, managers would "leave money on the table" by allowing other traders to find price bargains. The dearth of easy bargains shows that security prices are bid to correct levels.

SELF-TEST 12.3

Which of the following hypothetical "facts" would be violations of the efficient-market hypothesis? If inconsistent with market efficiency, which version of efficiency would be violated?
a. Stock returns tend to be more volatile in January than in other months.
b. Stocks that perform poorly in one week tend to outperform the rest of the market in the following week.
c. Roughly half of a group of professional portfolio managers "beat the market" in 1995.
d. Consistently superior returns are earned by buying a company's stock *the day after* announcement of good news, for example, after an increase in earnings.

No Theory Is Perfect

Few simple economic ideas are as well supported by the evidence as the efficient-market theory. But it would be wrong to pretend that there are no puzzles or apparent exceptions. For instance, company managers have made consistently superior profits when they deal in their own company's stock.[7] This does not square well with the strong form of the efficient-market theory. It implies that managers know more about their companies' prospects than even professional portfolio managers do.

It is not so surprising that insiders make superior profits, but there are other phenomena that take more explaining. For example, Figure 12.4 shows that investments in small firms have greatly outperformed investments in large firms, especially in the month of January.[8] This seems to violate even weak-form efficiency, since a mechanical trading rule ("Buy small stocks in December, sell in February") would apparently have generated superior returns.

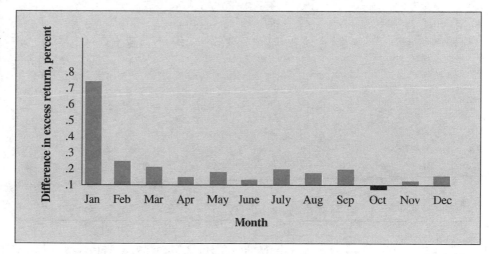

FIGURE 12.4
Average difference between daily excess returns of lowest-firm-size and highest-firm-size deciles by month between 1963 and 1979.

Source: Data from Donald B. Keim. (See fn. 8).

We believe that there is now widespread agreement that capital markets function well. So nowadays when economists come across instances where this apparently isn't true, they don't throw the efficient-market hypothesis onto the economic garbage heap. Instead they ask whether there is some missing ingredient that their theories ignore. Thus, despite the apparent superior performance of small-company stocks in January, few economists have to our knowledge been tempted to make a king-size investment in such stocks. Instead economists have assumed that investors aren't stupid and have looked at whether small-firm stocks suffer from some other defect, such as a lack of easy marketability, that is not allowed for in our theories or tests.

The Crash of 1987

On Monday, October 19, 1987, the Toronto Stock Exchange 300 Composite Index of stock prices fell 11 percent and the Standard and Poor's Composite Index of stock prices (the S&P 500) fell 20 percent in *1 day*. This crash fell in the midst of 2 weeks of incredible volatility, as you can see in Figure 12.5.

---

[7] See H. N. Seyhun, "Insiders' Profits, Costs of Trading, and Market Efficiency," *Journal of Financial Economics* 16 (June 1986):189–212.

[8] A readable summary of these size and seasonal effects is given by D. B. Keim, "The CAPM and Equity Return Regularities," *Financial Analysts Journal* 42 (May–June 1986):19–34. Research using Canadian data have found similar results. See Stephen Foerster and David Porter, "Calendar and Size-Based Anomalies in Canadian Stock Returns," *Canadian Capital Markets*, Michael Robinson and Brian Smith, eds. (The Toronto Stock Exchange and Western Business School, The University of Western Ontario), 1993:133–140.

FIGURE 12.5
Rate of return on the TSE 300 in 1987.

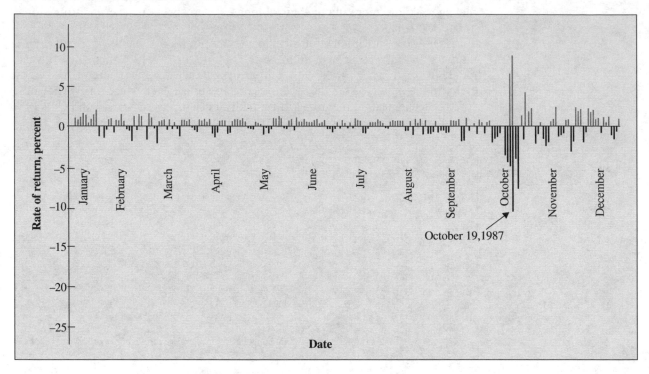

In the wake of Black Monday, investors asked why prices fell so sharply. There was no obvious *new* information to justify such a sharp decline. The idea that market prices accurately reflect all information available to investors, and thus are the best estimates of true values, seemed less compelling than before. It appears that prices were either irrationally high before Black Monday or irrationally low afterward. Could the theory of efficient markets be another casualty of the crash?

The crash reminds us of how exceptionally difficult it is to value common stocks from scratch. For example, suppose that in November 1994 you wanted to check whether common stocks were fairly valued. At least as a first stab, you might use the constant-growth formula that we introduced in Chapter 5. The annual dividend on the TSE 300 Composite Index was about $98.50.[9] If this dividend was expected to grow at a steady rate of 10 percent a year and investors required an annual return of 12.35 percent a year from common stocks,[10] the constant-growth formula gives a value for the index of

$$PV\ (Index) = \frac{DIV}{r - g} = \frac{98.50}{.1235 - .10} = 4191.5$$

which is close to the actual level of the index in November 1994. But how confident would you be about any of these figures? Suppose investors revised their assessment of the likely dividend growth rate to only 9.5 percent per year. This

[9] The level of the index was about 4190. If you had invested $4190, spread out across all the stocks in the index according to the stocks' weights, you would have received dividends of about $98.50 per year.
[10] The Treasury bill rate was about 5.35 percent at the time. If we assume investors expected a 7.0 percent risk premium from investing in the stock market — the same as the historical average risk premium — then the total expected market return was 5.35 + 7.0 = 12.35 percent.

would produce a downward revision of over 17.5 percent in your estimate of the correct level for the index, from 4191.5 to:

$$\text{PV (Index)} = \frac{\text{DIV}}{r - g} = \frac{98.50}{.1235 - .095} = 3456$$

In other words, a price drop like Black Monday's could have occurred in November 1994 if investors had suddenly become .5 percentage points (or about 5%) less optimistic about future dividend growth.

The extreme difficulty of valuing common stocks from scratch has two important consequences. First, investors almost always price a common stock relative to yesterday's price or relative to today's price of comparable securities. In other words, they generally take yesterday's price as correct, and then adjust it upward or downward according to today's information. If information arrives smoothly, then as time passes investors become more and more confident that today's market level is correct. However, when investors lose confidence in the benchmark of yesterday's price, there may be a period of confused trading and volatile prices before a new benchmark is established.

Second, the idea that stock price *always* equals true value is nearly impossible to test, precisely because it's so difficult to calculate value without referring to prices. Thus the crash didn't conclusively disprove the hypothesis. But many people now find it less plausible.

However, the crash does not undermine the evidence for market efficiency with respect to *relative* prices. Take, for example, CanWest Global Communications, the broadcasting company that owns Global Television, which sold for about $28 per share in November 1994. Could we *prove* that true value is $28? No, but we could be confident that CanWest's price should be substantially greater than Baton Broadcasting's (about $8.5 at the same time), since the two companies were in the same industry, but CanWest paid a higher dividend and had much higher forecast earnings per share. Moreover, if CanWest announced unexpectedly higher earnings, we could be quite confident that its share price would respond instantly and without bias. In other words, the subsequent price would be set correctly relative to the prior price.

Most of the corporate finance lessons of the efficient-markets hypothesis depend on these kinds of relative efficiency. Let us turn now to consider some of these lessons and at the same time introduce briefly some of the issues discussed in subsequent chapters.

LESSONS OF MARKET EFFICIENCY

Markets Have No Memory

The weak form of the efficient-market theory states that the sequence of past price changes contains no information about future changes. Economists express the same idea more concisely when they say that "stock prices follow a random walk" or "the market has no memory." Sometimes financial managers seem to act as if this were not the case. For example, they are often reluctant to issue stock after a fall in price. They are inclined to wait for a rebound. Similarly, managers favour equity rather than debt financing after an abnormal price rise. The idea is to "catch the market while it's high." But we know that the market has no memory and the cycles that financial managers seem to rely on do not exist. If such cycles did exist, that would be evidence that traders do not fully exploit the information available to them.

Sometimes a financial manager will have inside information indicating that the firm's stock is overpriced or underpriced. Suppose, for example, that there is some good news that the market does not know but managers do. The stock price will rise sharply when the news is revealed. Therefore, if the company sold shares at the current price, instead of waiting until the good news got out, it would be offering a bargain to new investors at the expense of present stockholders.

Naturally managers are reluctant to sell new shares when they have favourable inside information. But such inside information has nothing to do with the history of the stock price. Your firm's stock could be selling now at half its price of a year ago and yet you could have special information suggesting that it is *still* grossly overvalued. Or it may still be undervalued at twice last year's price.

There Are No Financial Illusions

In an efficient market there are no financial illusions. Investors are unromantically concerned with the firm's cash flows and the portion of those cash flows to which they are entitled.

There are occasions, however, on which managers seem to assume that investors suffer from financial illusions. For example, some firms devote enormous ingenuity to the task of manipulating earnings reported to stockholders. This is done by "creative accounting" — that is, by choosing accounting methods that stabilize and increase *reported* earnings without affecting the firm's cash flow. Presumably firms go to this trouble because management believes that stockholders take the earnings figures at face value. Some years ago, a leading accountant echoed this belief in the following complaint:

> *Let us assume that you sincerely want to report the profits in the way you feel fairly presents the true results of your company's business. This is an admirable and objective motive; but when you do this, you find that your competitor shows a relatively more favorable profit result than you do. This creates a demand for the competitor's stock, while yours lags behind. You put your analyst to work, and you find that if your competitor followed the same accounting practices you do, your results would be better than his. You show this analysis to your complaining stockholders. Naturally, they ask, "If this is true, and if your competitor's accounting practices are generally accepted, too, why not change your accounting practices and thus improve your profits?" At that point you try to explain why your accounting is much more factual and reliable than your competitor's. Your stockholders listen, but nothing you can say will convince them that they should give up a 20 percent, 50 percent, or 100 percent possible increase in the market value just because you like certain accounting practices better than others.[11]*

Was he right? Can the firm increase its market value by creative accounting? Or are the firm's shares traded in an efficient, well-functioning market, in which investors can see through such financial illusions?

A number of researchers have tried to resolve this question by looking at how the market reacts when companies change their accounting methods. In one classic study, Kaplan and Roll looked at what happens to stock prices when companies boost their reported profits by depreciating their assets more slowly.[12] This switch

[11] L. Spacek, "Business Success Requires an Understanding of Unsolved Problems of Accounting and Financial Reporting," address to the financial accounting class, Graduate School of Business Administration, Harvard University, September 25, 1959.

[12] R. S. Kaplan and R. Roll, "Investor Evaluation of Accounting Information: Some Empirical Evidence," *Journal of Business* 45 (April 1972):225–257.

is purely cosmetic. It reduces the reported depreciation charge but it does not affect the company's tax bill — the tax authorities allow firms to use accelerated depreciation for tax purposes and straight-line depreciation for reporting purposes.

Figure 12.6 shows the results of Kaplan and Roll's study. The preliminary announcement of increased earnings seems to prompt a slight abnormal rise in the stock price but this could simply be because investors were not informed at that stage of the accounting change. Within 3 months of the earnings announcement investors appear to have concluded that the accounting cosmetics were a sign of weakness rather than strength.

FIGURE 12.6
Kaplan and Roll's study shows that investors are not misled by accounting changes that are designed to inflate earnings. (Changes in price of the firms' stock are adjusted for general market movements.)

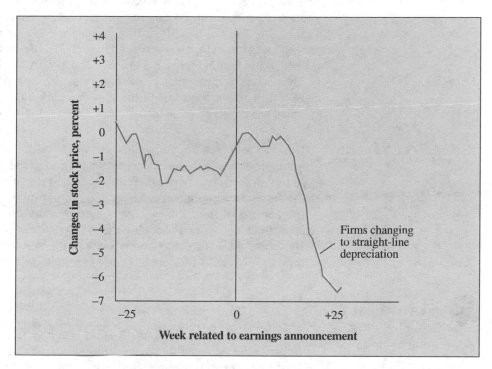

Source: R.S. Kaplan and R. Roll. "Investor Evaluation of Accounting Information: Some Empirical Evidence," *Journal of Business*, 45 (April 1972), fig. 1c, p. 239. © 1972 by the University of Chicago. All rights reserved.

SELF-TEST 12.4

Suppose that a company splits its stock two for one, meaning that it doubles the number of shares outstanding. Each shareholder is given a new share for each one previously held, so that the number of shares held doubles. The split is not associated with any change in the firm's investment policy.
a. Has the firm acquired any new assets as a result of the split?
b. Has anything happened to the value of the firm's real assets (its projects)?
c. What will happen to earnings per share?
d. What should happen to the firm's stock price?
e. What should happen to the dollar value of the shareholder's stock? Has investor wealth changed?

There Are No Free Lunches on Bay Street

In an efficient market you can trust market prices. To put it another way, there are no free lunches on Bay Street or in any other financial market. Here is an example.

Short-term interest rates are often different from long-term rates. For example, suppose that the interest rate on 1-year bonds is 4 percent and the rate on

2-year bonds is 6 percent. Does this mean that investors should sell all their 1-year bonds and rush to take advantage of the high interest rates on the 2-year bonds? Could firms reduce the cost of their borrowing by issuing 1-year rather than 2-year bonds?

If you believe that markets are efficient, you should be suspicious of any simple rule that says one type of bond is cheap and another expensive. So what's the explanation? One possibility is that investors expect short-term interest rates to rise over the coming year. For example, suppose that the 1-year interest rate is expected to rise to 8 percent. Then investors who buy a 1-year bond now and reinvest the proceeds in another 1-year bond at the end of the year can expect to earn a total return over the 2 years of just over 12 percent — almost identical to the total return that you would get from buying the 2-year bond.[13] Conversely, companies could not expect to borrow any more cheaply by issuing two 1-year bonds in succession than by issuing a 2-year bond.

Thus when you see that short-term rates are different from long-term rates, there is probably a good reason for it — the market may be telling you that interest rates are expected to change.[14]

SELF-TEST 12.5

By 1993 average dividend yields on stocks had fallen well below 3 percent. Some investors in the stock market were upset at the meager immediate cash return on their money and therefore switched into high-dividend stocks. For example, they might sell a diversified mutual fund and buy stocks of electric and gas utilities, many of which offered dividend yields of over 5 percent. Such a shift could double the dividends received per dollar invested. But were these investors really better off? Would you expect their total returns (dividends plus capital gains) to increase?

 **SUMMARY**

1. Sophisticated investors do not assume that superior returns come easy. Sophisticated financial managers do not assume that investors will willingly give them cheap financing. Both know that modern capital markets are highly competitive and efficient — and in particular that prices of stocks, bonds, and other securities react quickly and accurately when new information arrives.

2. Although capital markets are not always 100 percent efficient, smart financial managers generally start by assuming efficient capital markets. Financial traps and mirages are most easily seen from that vantage point. Of course financial managers sometimes find opportunities in the wake of inefficiencies and imperfections. In that case they abandon the efficient-markets vantage point and adapt financing strategy accordingly.

3. Competition between investors will tend to produce an efficient market. In such a market, prices will rapidly digest any new information, and it will be very difficult for investors to make consistently superior returns. We may indeed *hope* to beat the market, but in an efficient market all we can

---

[13] The total expected return on two 1-year bonds is $1.04 \times 1.08 - 1 = .1232$, or 12.32 percent. The total return on a 2-year bond is $1.06 \times 1.06 - 1 = .1236$, or 12.36 percent.

[14] Another explanation may be that the prices of long-term bonds fluctuate more than those of short-term bonds. A higher interest rate on long-term bonds is needed to compensate investors for this extra risk.

rationally *expect* is a return that is just sufficient on average to compensate for the time value of money and for the risks we bear.

4. The efficient-market hypothesis comes in three different flavours. The weak form states that prices efficiently reflect all the information contained in the past series of stock prices. In this case it is impossible to earn superior returns simply by looking for patterns in stock prices; in other words, price changes are a random walk. The semi-strong form states that prices reflect all published information. That means it is impossible to make consistently superior returns just by reading the newspaper, looking at the company's annual accounts, and so on. The strong form states that stock prices effectively impound all available information. This form tells us that useful private information is hard to find, because in pursuing it you are in competition with thousands — perhaps millions — of active, intelligent, and greedy investors. The best you can do in this case is to assume that securities are fairly priced.

5. The concept of an efficient market is astonishingly simple and remarkably well-supported by the facts. Less than 30 years ago any suggestion that security investment is a fair game was generally regarded as bizarre. Today it is not only widely accepted in business schools, but it also permeates investment practice and government policy toward the security markets. Futhermore, because security prices are set fairly, it is easier to add value to a firm by making smart investment decisions than by smart financing decisions.

6. An efficient market has no memory, financial illusions, or free lunches. Stock prices follow a random walk, in which the odds of a gain or loss tomorrow do not depend on past changes, so that managers cannot time security issues advantageously unless they have information the rest of the market does not. Moreover, because there are no financial illusions, managers cannot fool the market simply by manipulating accounting data.

KEY TERMS

efficient capital markets	**technical analysts**	**semi-strong-form efficiency**
random walk	**weak-form efficiency**	
	fundamental analysts	**strong-form efficiency**

SUGGESTED READINGS

An excellent and highly readable introduction to the efficient-market hypothesis is

B. G. Malkiel. *A Random Walk Down Wall Street.* New York: W. W. Norton, 1990.

PROBLEMS

1. Supply the missing words from the following list: *fundamental, semi-strong, strong, technical, weak.*

There are three forms of the efficient-market hypothesis. Tests of randomness in stock prices provide evidence for the _____ form of the hypothesis. Tests of stock price reaction to well-publicized news provide evidence for the _____ form and tests of the performance of professionally managed funds provide evidence for the _____ form. Market efficiency results from competition between investors. Many investors search for new information about the company's business that would help them to value the stock more accurately. This is known as _____ research. Such research helps to ensure that prices reflect all available information; in other words, it helps to keep the market efficient in the _____ form. Other investors study past stock prices for recurrent patterns that would allow them to make superior profits. This is known as _____ research. Such research helps to ensure that prices reflect all the information contained in past stock prices; in other words, it helps to keep the market efficient in the _____ form.

2. True or false?
   a. The efficient-market hypothesis asserts that investors have perfect forecasting ability.
   b. The semi-strong form of the efficient-market hypothesis states that prices reflect all publicly available information.
   c. In efficient markets the expected return on each stock is the same.
   d. Fundamental analysis by security analysts and investors helps keep markets efficient.
   e. If the efficient-market hypothesis is correct, managers will not be able to increase stock prices by "creative accounting," which boosts reported earnings.

3. How would you respond to the following comments?
   a. "Efficient market, my eye! I know of lots of investors who do crazy things."
   b. "Efficient market? Balderdash! I know at least a dozen people who have made a bundle in the stock market."
   c. "The trouble with the efficient-market theory is that it ignores investors' psychology."
   d. "The business cycle is at least somewhat predictable and stocks with positive betas respond to the state of the economy. Therefore, stock prices must be predictable."

4. Which of the following observations *appear* to violate market efficiency? Explain whether the inefficiency is weak, semi-strong, or strong.
   a. Managers make superior returns on their purchases of their company's stock.
   b. There is a positive relationship between the return on the market in one quarter and the change in aggregate corporate profits in the next quarter.
   c. Stocks of companies with unexpectedly high earnings appear to offer high returns for several months after the earnings announcement.[15]
   d. Very risky stocks on the average give higher returns than safe stocks.

5. Here are actual rates for the Standard and Poor's 500 Index for a 60-month period. Figures are in percent per month.

   +2.0, +1.0, −.3, +4.0, +.6, +8.4, +6.2, −.3, +1.3, −2.8, +8.3, +1.5, −3.5, 4.1, 7.1, −.04, −5.9, +4.1, +5.3, −3.3, −4.4, +6.6, −.5, +3.7, −4.0, −2.6, +2.2,

---

[15] This phenomenon has been documented in several studies. See, for example, G. Foster, C. Olsen, and T. Shevlin, "Earnings Releases, Anomalies, and the Behavior of Security Returns," *The Accounting Review* 59 (October 1984).

+3.9, +4.4, +.04, +1.3, −5.1, −6.0, −3.0, +2.3, −4.0, +4.5, −1.4, +3.3, +3.4, +2.1, +2.8, +4.5, +1.8, +5.0, +2.7, +2.8, +5.4, +.5, +.5, +.2, +4.0, +2.4, −.2, +3.6, −1.0, −4.4, +1.3, +1.9, +2.9

Now flip a coin 60 times and write down the returns that would be generated by the coin-toss game described at the start of Section 12.2. Calculate and plot the value of a $100 investment in the coin-toss game. Do the same calculation and plot for the actual market returns given above. See if your friends can tell which series is the real market.

6. "It's competition for information that makes securities markets efficient." Is this statement correct? Explain.

7. The top graph in Figure 12.1 shows the actual performance of the TSE 300 Index for a 5-year period. Two financial managers, Alpha and Beta, are contemplating this chart. Each manager's company needs to issue new shares of common stock sometime in the next year.

   Alpha: "My company's going to issue right away. The stock market cycle has obviously topped out, and the next move is almost surely down. Better to issue now and get a decent price for the shares."

   Beta: "You're too nervous — we're waiting. It's true that the market's been rising for the past year or so, but the figure clearly shows a basic upward trend. The market's on the way up to a new plateau."

   What would you say to Alpha and Beta?

8. "Long-term interest rates are at record highs. Most companies, therefore, find it cheaper to finance with common stock or relatively inexpensive short-term bank loans." Discuss.

9. In May 1987 Citicorp announced that it was bolstering its loan loss reserves by $3 billion in order to reflect its exposure to Third World borrowers. Consequently, second-quarter earnings were transformed from a $.5 billion profit to a $2.5 billion loss.

   In after-hours trading the price of Citicorp stock fell sharply from its closing level of $50, but the next day when the market had had a chance to digest the news, the price recovered to $53. Other bank stocks fared less well and *The Wall Street Journal* reported that Citicorp's decision "triggered a big sell-off of international banking stocks that roiled stock markets around the world."

   Response to the Citicorp action varied. The bank's chairman claimed that "it significantly strengthens the institution," and analysts and bankers suggested that it was a notable step toward realism. For example, one argued that it was the recognition of the problem that made the difference, while another observed that the action "is merely recognizing what the stock market has been saying for several months: that the value of the sovereign debt of the big U.S. money center banks is between 25% and 50% less than is carried in their books." The London *Financial Times* made the more cautionary comment that Citicorp had "simply rearranged its balance sheet, not strengthened its capital base" and the Lex column described the move as an "outsize piece of cosmetic self-indulgence rather than a great stride towards the reconstruction of Third World debt." A lead article in the same paper stated that "even if all this means that Citicorp shareholders are $3 billion poorer today, the group as a whole is better placed to absorb whatever shocks lie ahead."

There was also considerable discussion of the implications for other banks. As one analyst summed up, "There's no question that the market will put higher confidence in those institutions that can reserve more fully."

Discuss the general reaction to the Citicorp announcement. It is not often that a company announces a $2.5 billion loss in one quarter and its stock price rises. Do you think that the share price reaction was consistent with an efficient market?

10. Geothermal Corp. just announced good news: its earnings increased by 20 percent from last year's value. Most investors had anticipated an increase of 25 percent. Will Geothermal's stock price increase or decrease when the announcement is made?

11. If the yield curve is downward-sloping, meaning that long-term interest rates are lower than current short-term rates, what might investors believe about *future* short-term interest rates?

SOLUTIONS TO SELF-TEST QUESTIONS

12.1
a. True
b. False. There cannot be a long-run stock price. If there were, investors could make easy profits by investing in stocks when they are below the long-run price. This would be inconsistent with the notion that prices reflect all useful information about the firm.
c. True
d. False. Note the *apparent* peaks and valleys in Figure 12.1.

12.2 Each looks for information about over- or undervalued securities. Technical analysts look for patterns in past prices, and fundamental analysts focus on published information. Portfolio managers may use both technical and fundamental information and also have in-house analysts who try to uncover hidden or inside information. When any of them find useful information, indicating, say, an undervalued stock, they buy aggressively, trying to beat other investors to the bargain. This trading moves the stock price up until the bargain disappears. Then the favourable information is fully incorporated in the stock price.

Of course the process works in reverse if unfavourable information is discovered. In either case, trading by informed investors moves the price until the information is fully reflected in it. This is the efficient-market outcome.

12.3
a. No violation. Even if volatility is predictable, this offers no way for investors to make excessive profits. It could simply be that more information is released in January. More news would generate higher volatility, but that does not imply that prices are incorrect.
b. Violation of weak-form efficiency. If stocks tended to reverse their performance from one week to the next, it would be easy for investors to make easy money: simply buy stocks of firms that performed poorly last week. The knowledge of a stock's price history would provide a route to easy profits.
c. No violation. This outcome is normal in a strong-form efficient market where portfolio managers cannot beat the market on average. We expect roughly one-half of these managers to get lucky in any particular year.

d. Violation of semistrong efficiency. The good news ought to be fully incorporated in the stock price on the announcement day, leaving no superior profits for late buyers.

12.4

a. No. The split is purely a "paper transaction," in which more shares are printed and distributed to shareholders.

b. No. Operating profits continue as before the split.

c. Earnings per share will fall by half. With unchanged earnings and double the number of shares, all per-share values will fall by 50 percent.

d. The firm's stock price will fall by half. With unchanged total value and double the number of shares, price *per share* will fall by 50 percent.

e. The shareholder's wealth should be unaffected. Each owns double the number of shares, but the value of each share is only half of the original value.

These answers are actually only part of the story. Most stock split announcements are regarded as good news by investors, and stock prices generally increase. This is not because investors suffer from financial illusions, but because managers commit to splits only when they are confident that they can maintain or increase earnings. Thus the split is good news not because it multiplies the number of shares, but because it reveals management's confidence in the future.[16]

12.5 No and no. In an efficient market, investors are concerned with total return, including capital gains as well as dividends. Investors pursuing immediate dividend yield generally move into mature, low-growth companies and sacrifice the chance for substantial capital gains. Total return should depend on risk but not on the fraction of return received as dividends.

---

[16] See P. Asquith, P. Healy, and K. Palepu, "Earnings and Stock Splits," *The Accounting Review* 64 (July 1989), pp. 387-403.

An Overview of Corporate Financing

This chapter begins our analysis of long-term financing decisions. In later chapters this will involve a careful look at some classic finance problems, such as how much firms should borrow and what dividends they should pay their shareholders. But before getting down to specifics, we will provide a brief overview of types of long-term finance.

It is customary to classify sources of finance as debt or equity. When the firm borrows, it promises to repay the debt with interest. If it doesn't keep its promise, the debtholders may force the firm into bankruptcy. However, no such commitments are made to the equityholders. They are entitled to whatever is left over after the debtholders have been paid off. For this reason, equity is called a *residual claim* on the firm.

However, a simple division of sources of finance into debt and equity would miss the enormous variety of financing instruments that companies use today. For example, Table 13.1 shows the many long-term securities issued by Inco Limited, a leading producer of nickel and other metals. Yet Inco has not come close to exhausting the menu of possible securities.

This chapter introduces you to the principal families of securities and explains how they are used by corporations. We also draw attention to some of the interesting aspects of firms issuing these securities.

After studying this chapter you should be able to

- Describe the major genera and species of securities issued by firms to raise capital.
- Summarize recent trends in the use made by firms of different sources of finance.

TABLE 13.1

Large firms often use many different kinds of securities. Look at the variety of long-term securities issued by Inco:

Equity
    Common stock
    Preferred stock
Long-term debt
    Canadian dollar debentures
    U.S. dollar debentures
    Convertible U.S. dollar debentures
    U.S. dollar notes
    Sterling notes
    U.S. dollar revolving loans
    Floating-rate sterling term loan
    Silver loan

Source: Adapted from INCO Limited 1993 Annual Report.

COMMON STOCK

authorized share capital: Maximum number of shares that the company is permitted to issue, as specified in the firm's articles of incorporation.

All corporations in Canada issue common stock. Investors purchase shares of common stock and therefore are known as *shareholders* or *stockholders*. Table 13.2 shows how the investment by Inco's common shareholders is recorded in the company's books at the end of 1993.

The maximum number of shares that can be issued is known as the **authorized share capital** — for Inco, it is unlimited. This maximum is specified in the firm's

articles of incorporation: A legal document outlining the nature of the firm's business and the characteristics of its shares and the rights of its shareholders.

issued shares: Shares that have been issued by the company.

outstanding shares: Shares that have been issued by the company and are held by investors.

par value: Value of security shown on certificate.

articles of incorporation and can be changed only with the permission of the shareholders. Votes on proposed changes to the articles of incorporation occur at shareholders' meetings. As shares are sold to investors, they are said to be **issued**. Currently, Inco has issued 110,269,856 shares. Sometimes shares are said to be **outstanding** or issued and outstanding. The number of outstanding shares is the number actually owned by the shareholders. This will be less than the number issued if the firm has repurchased shares and is allowed to hold its own stock. These shares would be seen on the balance sheet as treasury stock. Treasury stock is not allowed in Canada. When Canadian companies repurchase their shares, the shares must be cancelled. Thus the number of issued shares always equals the number of shares outstanding.

When Inco issues new shares, the value of new shares is added to the common share account. This was not always the way firms recorded new share issues. In the past, a company would declare a **par value** for its shares, an arbitrarily set number. The price at which new shares were actually sold almost always exceeded par value. The difference was recorded as **additional paid-in capital**, *contributed surplus,* or *capital surplus*. A change to the Canadian Business Corporations Act ended this practice. Inco's capital surplus account is a remnant of the old system. To determine how much Inco has raised through new share issues, add together the common stock account and the capital surplus account. The practice of setting par value and using the additional paid-in capital account is still followed in the United States.

Besides buying new shares, stockholders also indirectly contribute new capital to the firm whenever profits that could be paid out as dividends are instead plowed back into the company. Table 13.2 shows that the cumulative amount of such **retained earnings** is $ 972,232,000.

TABLE 13.2

Book value of common stockholders' equity of Inco, December 31, 1993

Common shares	$ 640,844,000
Capital surplus	9,430,000
Retained earnings	972,232,000
Currency translation adjustment	(15,828,000)
Net common equity	$1,606,678,000

Note:
Shares

Authorized shares	unlimited
Issued shares	110,269,856

Source: Adapted from Inco Limited 1993 Annual Report.

additional paid-in capital: Difference between issue price and par value of stock. Also called capital surplus.

retained earnings: Earnings not paid out as dividends.

You will also see in Table 13.2 an account showing a minor adjustment for currency translation losses resulting from Inco's foreign operations. We'd rather not get into foreign exchange accounting here.

The sum of common shares and total retained earnings less currency translation losses is known as the *net common equity* of the firm. It equals the total amount contributed directly by shareholders when the firm issued new stock and indirectly when it plowed back part of its earnings.

Sometimes companies repurchase their shares for reasons we deal with in Chapter 16. The repurchased shares are cancelled and net common equity is reduced by the amount paid for the shares. The common shares account is reduced by the amount paid, up to the average issue price. Any amount in excess of the average issue price is subtracted from retained earnings. For example, suppose 1000 shares are repurchased for $25 per share and the average issue price was $20 per share. The total reduction in net common equity is $25 × 1000 or $25,000. The common stock account is reduced by $20 × 1000 or $20,000 and retained earnings are reduced by the remaining $5,000.

Book Value versus Market Value

We discussed the distinction between book and market value in Chapters 2 and 5, but it bears repeating. Book value is a backward-looking measure. It tells us how much capital the firm has raised from shareholders in the past. It does not measure the value that investors place on those shares today. The market value of the firm is forward-looking; it depends on the future dividends that shareholders expect to receive.

Inco's common equity has a book value of $1,606,678,000. With 110,269,856 shares outstanding, this translates to a book value of $1,606,678,000/110,269,856 = $14.57 per share. But in December 1993 Inco shares were priced at $35.50 each. So the total market value of the common stock was about 110 million shares × $35.50 per share = $3,905,000,000 about $2.3 billion higher than book.

Market value is usually greater than book value. This is partly because inflation has driven the value of many assets above what they originally cost. Also, firms raise capital to invest in projects with present values that exceed initial cost. So we would expect the market value of the firm to be higher than the amount of money put up by the shareholders.

However, sometimes projects do go awry and companies fall on hard times. In this case, market value can fall below book value.

SELF-TEST 13.1

No-name News can be established by investing $10 million in a printing press. The newspaper is expected to generate a cash flow of $2 million a year for 20 years. If the cost of capital is 10 percent, is the firm's market or book value greater? What if the cost of capital is 20 percent?

Stockholders' Rights

Stockholders have the ultimate control of the company's affairs. Occasionally companies need shareholder approval before they can take certain actions. For example, they need approval to increase the authorized capital or to merge with another company. On most other matters, shareholder control boils down to the right to vote on appointments to the board of directors. The board usually consists of the company's management and *nonexecutive directors*, who are not employed by the firm. In principle, the board is elected as an agent of the shareholders. It appoints and oversees the management of the firm and meets to vote on such matters as new share issues and to give guidance to management.

Most of the time the board will go along with the management, but in some situations it can be very independent. If the board must be particularly careful to make its own decision, a special committee of *independent directors*, those directors who are not part of management nor are large shareholders of the company, may be created. For example, when a takeover bid is made for a firm, in many provinces the board of directors must give their opinion on the attractiveness of the bid. Sometimes the opinion on the bid is made by a committee of independent directors, especially if a potential conflict of interest exists. For example, in 1993 Wine Acquisitions Inc. made an offer of $17 per share of T.G. Bright & Co. Ltd., a large, publicly owned Canadian wine producer. It is important to note that Mr. Leland Verner owned 61 percent of T.G. Bright and also was the head of Wine Acquisitions. In order that a fair opinion on the attractiveness of the takeover bid be given to the shareholders of Bright's, a committee of independent Bright's directors was formed. In their opinion, there were reasons both to accept or reject the offer.

Finance in Action

Labatt Brews Up a Storm of Protest with Poison Pill Plan

As discussed in Chapter 1, incorporation creates a separation between owner-ship and management. While managers are hired to look after the best interests of the shareholders, in large firms with widely distributed shares it may be difficult for small shareholders to make their wishes known. Imagine yourself, as owner of some Labatt's shares, trying to convince the other 12,300 shareholders about how the firm should be run. Management and the existing board of directors clearly have a huge advantage when it comes to explaining and defending their policies. However, recent events at Labatt indicate that management cannot afford to ignore shareholder sentiment. In question are some actions perceived as protecting the managers at the expense of shareholders.

In July 1994, John Labatt Ltd. announced that its board of directors had adopted a "shareholders' rights" plan. Commonly known as poison pills, such plans make it more difficult for investors to buy enough of a firm's stock to gain strong influence over a firm's policies and operations. Labatt justified the plan as one that would protect existing shareholders from having their shares bought before the firm had time to increase share values by selling off some broadcasting and sports business assets, and investing in the Mexican brewing and beverage industry.

Many Labatt shareholders disliked the poison pill. To some it was seen as a way for Labatt managers — who stood to be replaced if there was a takeover — to protect their high-paying jobs and independence by "protecting" shareholders from the gains that come when takeover bids push share prices up. (Despite investors' dislike, the jury is still out on whether poison pills hurt share value. Some evidence indicates that poison pills lead to higher ultimate prices for takeover bids, because the pills increase management's ability to bargain for higher bids.)

Lead by the institutional investors like mutual fund and pension fund managers who manage billion dollar pools of capital, Labatt shareholders defeated the poison pill plan at the firm's annual meeting that September. Such shareholder "revolts" used to be rare, but are becoming increasingly common. Militant shareholders have forced many companies to abandon or water down rules designed to make takeovers expensive or impossible. Companies where management has retreated or been defeated on the poison pill issue include Canadian forest products giant MacMillan Bloedel, Vancouver *Sun* and Montreal *Gazette* publisher Southam Inc., TransCanada PipeLines, and Lotus Development. A shareholder proposal to cancel Philip Morris' poison pill provisions received a surprising 40 percent of votes at that firm's annual meeting in April '94.).

If Labatt's managers were worried about their jobs, their worries may not be over. The firm has had difficulty in selling its non-brewing assets, the fall of Mexico's peso nearly halved the value of Labatt's recent $720 million investment in Mexico's Femsa Cerveza CA, and rumours of a takeover led by Onex Corp. were widely reported in April and May 1995.

If you want more information about takeover bids and defenses, look at Chapter 22 in this text.

Voting Procedures

majority voting: Voting system in which each director is voted on separately.

cumulative voting: Voting system in which all the votes one shareholder is allowed to cast can be cast for one candidate for the board of directors.

proxy contest: Takeover attempt in which outsiders compete with management for shareholders' votes.

restricted shares: Common shares that do not have voting rights equal to another class of common shares issued by the firm.

non-voting shares: Restricted shares that do not entitle shareholders the right to vote for the board of directors.

Classes of Stock

subordinate voting shares: Restricted shares that have fewer votes per share than another class of common shares.

multiple voting shares: Common shares with more than one vote per share. Multiple voting shares are always found in companies with subordinate voting shares.

In most companies stockholders elect directors by a system of **majority voting**. In this case each director is voted on separately and stockholders can cast one vote for each share they own. In some companies directors are elected by **cumulative voting**. The directors are then voted on jointly and the stockholders can, if they choose, cast all their votes for just one candidate.[1] Cumulative voting makes it easier for a minority group of the stockholders to elect a director to represent their interests. That is why minority groups devote so much effort to campaigning for cumulative voting.

On many issues a simple majority of the votes cast is enough to carry the day, but there are some decisions that require a "supermajority" of, say, 75 percent of those eligible to vote. For example, a supermajority vote is sometimes needed to approve a merger. This requirement makes it difficult for the firm to be taken over and therefore helps to protect the incumbent management. Supermajority voting requirements must be approved in a vote by shareholders and become part of the firm's articles of incorporation.

In some special situations, the vote must receive a "majority of the minority shareholders." Shareholders who own more than 10 percent of voting rights or who are directors or members of senior management are not allowed to vote on the issue. For example, under securities regulations in Ontario, if a firm wants to merge with another company owned by its current president, only the minority shareholders would be entitled to vote on the deal. The intention of the regulation is to give minority shareholders the opportunity to prevent large shareholders and management from doing deals that reduce the value of the minority shareholders' shares.

Shareholders can either vote in person or appoint a proxy to vote. The issues on which they are asked to vote are rarely contested, particularly in the case of large, publicly traded firms. Occasionally, however, there are **proxy contests** in which outsiders compete with the firm's existing management and directors for control of the corporation. But the odds are stacked against the outsiders, for the insiders can get the firm to pay all the costs of presenting their case and obtaining votes.

Many companies issue just one class of common stock. Sometimes, however, a firm may have two or more classes outstanding, which differ in their right to vote or receive dividends. Common shares without full voting rights are called **restricted shares**. If the restricted shares have no votes, they are called **non-voting**. For example, Andres Wines Class A non-voting shares trade on the Montreal, Toronto, and Vancouver Stock Exchanges. If the restricted shares have fewer votes per share than another class of common shares, they are called **subordinate voting**. St. Clair Paint and Wallpaper has two classes of common-like shares. Class A is subordinate voting and each share has 1 vote. Its Class B shares are **multiple voting**, each with 10 votes per share. A third type of restricted shares is known as **restricted voting**. Included in this group are stocks with a range of voting limitations. For example, UAP Class A restricted shares have 1 vote per share except during the election of the board of directors, in which case they have 10 votes per share but only are entitled to elect 20 percent of the board. UAP's Class B shares also have 1 vote per share but are entitled to elect 80 percent of the board. They too get 10 votes per share in the election. As of December 1993, 62 classes of non-

---

[1] For example, suppose there are five directors to be elected and you own 100 shares. You therefore have a total of $5 \times 100 = 500$ votes. Under majority voting you can cast a maximum of 100 votes for any one candidate. With a cumulative voting system you can cast all 500 votes for your favourite candidate.

restricted voting shares: Restricted shares that have special limitations on voting rights of shareholders. For example, only Canadian shareholders may be entitled to vote or each shareholder may have a maximum number of votes, regardless of the number of shares owned.

voting shares, 88 classes of subordinate voting shares, and 12 classes of restricted voting shares were trading on the Toronto Stock Exchange.

You may be wondering why firms create shares with different voting rights. Suppose that a firm needs fresh capital but its present stockholders do not want to give up control of the firm. The existing shares could be labeled class A voting , and then class B non-voting shares could be issued to outside investors. The class B shares would have no votes in the election of the board of directors, although they would probably sell for less as a result. In the 1980s it was not uncommon for firms to go public by offering restricted shares for sale. For example, when St. Clair Paint and Wallpaper sold shares to public investors, it offered non-voting shares only. The multiple voting shares were retained by its major shareholder, the Litwin family, and not traded on a public stock exchange.

In Canada, restricted shares have been accepted for trading on all stock exchanges for many years. However in the 1980s, in response to a flood of new non-voting and subordinate voting shares on the stock markets, new regulations were created to protect investors. To help investors identify restricted shares, the share name must mention voting restrictions. For example, Xerox Canada lists a class of shares called Xerox Canada Inc. Class B nv, where the "nv" refers to the fact that the shares are non-voting. If you see "sv," you know the shares are subordinate voting. You may also see the letters "mv" indicating the multiple voting shares counterpart to the subordinate voting class. The letters "rv" indicate that shares are restricted voting. Canadian securities regulators have also made it more difficult for a firm to convert an existing common shares class into two share classes with different voting rights. To make a conversion of such shares, a majority of the minority shareholders must approve. Finally, the stock exchanges will not list a new class of non-voting or subordinate voting shares unless the shares have the right to participate in takeover bids. This right is called a *coattail provision*.

A spectacular event in Canadian investment history illustrates how coattail provisions may be valuable. In 1986, a group of independent Canadian Tire Store dealers offered to purchase the Canadian Tire common (voting) shares for $160.24 each, while making no offer for the Class A non-voting stock, which traded at about $14.50. Their offer would have given them 49 percent of the common stock, which would have given them control of the firm, since they already had 17 percent of the voting stock. However, the Canadian Tire Class A non-voting stock had a coattail provision, which stated that in the event of a bid for all or substantially all of the voting common shares, the Class A shareholders would be entitled to tender their shares to the bidder. Were not the Class A shareholders also entitled to receive $160.24 per share? Was a bid for 49 percent a bid for "substantially all" of the common shares? The Class A non-voting shareholders went to court to stop the bid because they thought that 49 percent was "substantially all" of the voting shares and therefore the coattail provision should be triggered, allowing them to sell their shares for a big price. Ultimately the court decided in favour of the non-voting shareholders and the takeover bid was withdrawn.[2]

Unlike Canadian stock exchanges, the New York Stock Exchange has traditionally stood for "one share, one vote" and has banned companies that wanted to list two classes of stock with different voting rights. But the NYSE suspended its ban as a result of pressure from companies that wanted to deter hostile takeover bids. These companies felt that by concentrating voting power in a class

---

[2] For further information on the Canadian Tire case, see D. Toole, "A Subordinate Cause," *Moneywise, The Financial Post*, (August 1987):22–26.

of stock that can be held in friendly hands, they could protect themselves against "corporate raiders" and "takeover pirates." But perhaps pirates capture only the slower ships; many investors believe that the takeover specialists prey mostly on those management teams that are not doing a good job for their shareholders.

Dividends

Shareholders hope to receive a series of dividends on their investment. However, the company is not obliged to pay any dividend and the decision is up to the board of directors.

Because dividends are discretionary, they are not considered to be a business expense. Therefore, companies are not allowed to deduct dividend payments when they calculate their taxable income.

 ## 13.2 PREFERRED STOCK

preferred stock: Stock that takes priority over common stock in regard to dividends.

net worth: Book value of common stockholders' equity plus preferred stock.

Usually when investors talk about equity or stock, they are referring to common stock. You might have noticed in Table 13.1 that Inco also has issued **preferred stock**. As of December 31, 1993, Inco had issued 2,622,187 shares of 7.85 percent cumulative Series B preferred shares. When we add in the $59.6 million of preferred stock issued by Inco, book equity increases to $1606.7 million + $59.6 million = $1666.3 million. This figure is Inco's **net worth**. For Inco and most companies, preferred stock is much less important than common stock. However, it can be a useful method of financing in mergers and certain other special situations.

Like debt, preferred stock promises a series of fixed payments to the investor and with relatively rare exceptions preferred dividends are paid in full and on time. Nevertheless, preferred stock is legally an equity security. This is because payment of a preferred dividend is almost invariably within the discretion of the directors. The only obligation is that no dividends can be paid on the common stock until the preferred dividend has been paid. These days this obligation is usually cumulative. In other words, before the common stockholders get a cent, the firm must pay any preferred dividends that have been missed in the past. If the company goes out of business, the preferred stockholders get in the queue after the debtholders but before the common stockholders.

Preferred share dividends come in a wide variety. Some are *fixed rate* such as Inco's 7.85 percent preferred. To work out the dollar value of the dividend, you need to know the share's par value of $25. Thus, the annual dividend promised is $0.0785 \times \$25$ or $1.9625 per share. The dividends on some preferred shares are tied to other financial rates such as the Bank of Canada rate.

Like common stock, preferred stock does not have a final repayment date. However, roughly half the issues make some provision for periodic retirement and in many cases companies have the right to *redeem* or *call* preferred stock at a specified price. The Inco preferred stock are redeemable at the option of the company at $25 per share.

The contract that sets out the terms of the preferred stock also imposes restrictions on the company, including some limits on payments to common stockholders either as dividends or through repurchase of common stock. These restrictions may also stipulate that the company cannot make any payments to common stockholders unless it is able to maintain a minimum level of common equity and a minimum ratio of working capital to debt and preferred shares.

Preferred stock rarely confers full voting privileges. This is an advantage to firms that want to raise new money without sharing control of the firm with the new shareholders. However, if there is any matter that affects their place in the queue, preferred stockholders usually get to vote on it. Most issues also provide the holder with some voting power if the preferred dividend is skipped. For example, the preferred shareholders may receive the right to elect a member of the board if dividends have not been paid in eight successive quarters.

Companies cannot deduct preferred dividends when they calculate taxable income. Like common stock dividends, preferred dividends are paid from after-tax income. However, dividend income is generally not taxed when received by Canadian corporations, and is taxed at reduced rates when received by individuals. (This is discussed more fully in Chapter 16.) Thus preferred shares are a popular method of financing when the tax benefits in the hands of the investors are worth more than the tax burden imposed on the issuer.

The differential taxation of dividend income and interest income has created a tax-based incentive for firms paying little or no tax to issue preferred shares rather than debt. For example, suppose ABC Company pays no tax. Its bank has offered to make ABC a loan at 10 percent. After paying its tax on the interest at 36 percent, the bank will receive a net return of $(1 - .36) \times 10\% = 6.4\%$. Alternatively, the bank can earn an equally high return by buying ABC's preferred shares with a dividend yield of 6.4 percent, since the bank pays no tax on the preferred share dividends. Now consider ABC's perspective. Since ABC pays no tax, it cannot use the interest deduction from the bank loan to reduce its tax. ABC's before and after-tax costs of the bank loan are 10 percent. On the other hand, if it sells preferred shares with a 6.4 percent dividend yield, it has reduced its cost of funds from 10 percent to 6.4 percent. It is much cheaper for ABC to raise the needed money by selling preferred shares than by borrowing. In 1979, the Government of Canada recognized the potential erosion of its tax base and has made it more difficult for banks to buy preferred stock from other corporations. In 1987, the Canadian federal government attempted to further reduce the tax loophole by requiring issuers of preferred shares to pay a 40 percent tax on preferred dividends. The tax is refunded if the issuer is taxable. The effect of the tax has been to narrow but not close the loophole.[3]

In contrast to Canada, preferred shares are not as widely used in the United States. Again, the main reason is tax-driven. Individual U.S. investors do not have the dividend tax credit of Canadian investors and must pay the full personal tax on dividend income. U.S. corporations enjoy some tax relief on dividend income. If one corporation buys another's stock, only 30 percent of the dividends it receives is taxed. Also, regulated American public utilities, which can take tax payments into account when negotiating the rates they charge to customers, can effectively pass the tax disadvantage of preferred stock on to the consumer. As a result, a large fraction of the dollar value of American offerings of non-convertible preferred stock consists of issues by utilities.

floating-rate preferred: Preferred stock paying dividends that vary with short-term interest rates.

If you invest your firm's spare cash in a preferred stock, you will want to make sure that when it is time to sell the stock, it won't have plummeted in value. One problem with garden-variety preferred stock that pays a fixed dividend is that prices go up and down as interest rates change (because present values fall when rates rise). So one ingenious banker thought up a wrinkle: Why not link the dividend on the preferred stock to interest rates so that it goes up when interest rates rise and vice versa? The result is known as **floating-rate preferred**.

---

[3] See I. Fooladi, P.A. McGraw and G.S. Roberts, "Preferred Share Rule Freezes Out the Individual Investor," *CA Magazine* (April 11, 1988):38–41.

SELF-TEST 13.2

A company in a 35 percent tax bracket can buy a bond yielding 10 percent or a preferred stock of the same firm that is priced to yield 8 percent. Which will provide the higher after-tax yield?

 CORPORATE DEBT

When they borrow money, companies promise to make regular interest payments and to repay the principal (that is, the original amount borrowed). However, corporations have limited liability. By this we mean that the promise to repay the debt is not always kept. If the company gets into deep water, the stockholders have the right to default on the debt and to hand over the company's assets to the lenders. Clearly they will choose to do this only if the value of the assets is less than the amount of the debt. In practice, when companies go bankrupt, this handover of assets is far from straightforward. For example, when the furniture company Wickes went into bankruptcy, there were 250,000 creditors all jostling for a better place in the queue. Sorting out these problems is left to the bankruptcy court.

Because lenders are not regarded as owners of the firm, they don't normally have any voting power. Also, the company's payments of interest are regarded as a cost and are therefore deducted from taxable income. Thus interest is paid out of *before-tax* income, whereas dividends on common and preferred stock are paid out of *after-tax* income. This means that the government provides a tax subsidy on the use of debt, which it does not provide on stock.

Debt Comes in Many Forms

Some orderly scheme of classification is essential to cope with the almost endless variety of debt issues. We will walk you through the major distinguishing characteristics.

Interest Rate. The interest payment, or *coupon*, on most long-term loans is fixed at the time of issue. If a $1000 bond is issued with a coupon of 10 percent, the firm continues to pay $100 a year regardless of how interest rates change. As we pointed out in Chapter 4, you sometimes encounter zero-coupon bonds. In this case the firm does not make a regular interest payment. It just makes a single payment at maturity. Obviously, investors pay less for zero-coupon bonds.

Most loans from a bank and some long-term loans carry a *floating interest rate*. For example, your firm may be offered a loan at "1 percent over prime." The **prime rate** is the interest rate the bank charges on loans to its most favoured customers and is adjusted up and down with the general level of interest rates. When the prime rate changes, the interest on your floating-rate loan also changes.

Floating-rate loans are not always tied to the prime rate. Often they are tied to the rate at which international banks lend to one another. This is known as the *London Interbank Offered Rate*, or *LIBOR*.

prime rate: Interest rate at which banks lend to most favoured customers.

SELF-TEST 13.3

Would you expect the price of a 10-year floating-rate bond to be more or less sensitive to changes in interest rates than the price of a 10-year maturity fixed-rate bond?

long-term debt: Debt with more than 1 year remaining to maturity.

Maturity. Long-term debt is any debt repayable more than 1 year from the date of issue. Debt due in less than a year is termed *short-term* and is carried on the balance sheet as a current liability. Clearly it is artificial to call a 364-day debt short-term and a 366-day debt long-term (except on leap years).

There are corporate bonds of nearly every conceivable maturity. For example, Inco issued bonds in 1992 with a 30-year maturity. Canadian Pacific Limited has issued perpetuities — that is, bonds with no specific maturity. At the other extreme we find firms borrowing literally overnight.

sinking fund: Fund established to retire debt before maturity.

Repayment Provisions. Long-term loans are commonly repaid in a steady regular way, perhaps after an initial grace period. For bonds that are publicly traded, this is done by means of a **sinking fund**. Each year the firm puts aside a sum of cash into a sinking fund that is then used to buy back the bonds. When there is a sinking fund, investors are prepared to lend at a lower rate of interest. They know that they are more likely to be repaid if the company sets aside some cash each year than if the entire loan has to be repaid on one specified day.

callable bond: Bond that may be repurchased by firm before maturity at specified call price.

Most firms issuing debt to the public also reserve the right to *call* the debt — that is, issuers of **callable bonds** may buy back the bonds before the final maturity date. The price at which the firm can call the bonds is set at the time that the bonds are issued. Usually, lenders are given at least five years of call protection. During this period the firm cannot call the bonds.

This option to call the bond is attractive to the issuer. If interest rates decline and bond prices rise, the issuer may repay the bonds at the specified call price and borrow the money back at a lower rate of interest. The bond issuer enjoys a financial benefit and the bondholder loses. Since 1986, callable bonds issued in Canada have had a special call provision, known as the Canada Call, which prevents firms from calling the bonds for financial advantage. Thus firms call their bonds when they want to change their capital structure rather than to take advantage of lower interest rates.[4]

The sinking fund also contains an implicit call provision, because the firm may acquire bonds for the sinking fund for face value, even if the market price of the bond exceeds face value. The firm also may choose to buy the bonds back in the bond market, which means that it has an option to acquire the bonds for the *lower* of market price or face value.

These provisions come at the expense of bondholders, for they limit investors' capital gain potential. If interest rates fall and bond prices rise, holders of callable bonds may find their bonds called back by the firm for the call price. Similarly, the firm will retire bonds for the sinking funds by paying only the face value of the bond.

SELF-TEST 13.4

The company sometimes has the option to make additional contributions to the sinking fund and thus to retire more bonds. How will this affect the interest rate at which the firm can issue the bond to investors?

subordinated debt: Debt that may be repaid in bankruptcy only after senior debt is paid.

Seniority. Some debts are **subordinated**. In the event of default the subordinated lender gets in line behind the firm's general creditors. The subordinated lender holds a junior claim and is paid only after all senior creditors are satisfied.

When you lend money to a firm, you can assume that you hold a senior claim unless the debt agreement says otherwise. However, this does not always put you at the front of the line, for the firm may have set aside some of its assets specifically for the protection of other lenders. That brings us to our next classification.

---

[4] In the United States, callable bonds sometimes specify a period during which the firm is not allowed to call the bond if the purpose is simply to issue another bond at a lower interest rate. This has an effect similar to the Canada Call provision.

secured debt: Debt that has first claim on specified collateral in the event of default.

investment grade: Bonds rated B++ or above by the Canadian Bond Rating Service or BBB or above by the Dominion Bond Rating Service.

junk bond: Bond with a rating of B+ or below by the Canadian Bond Rating Service (BB or below by the Dominion Bond Rating Service).

Security. When you borrow to buy your home, the bank or trust company will take out a mortgage on the house. The mortgage acts as security for the loan. If you default on the loan payments, the bank can seize your home.

When companies borrow, they also may set aside certain assets as security for the loan. These assets are termed *collateral* and the debt is said to be **secured**. In the event of default, the secured lender has first claim on the collateral; unsecured lenders have a general claim on the rest of the firm's assets but only a junior claim on the collateral.

Default Risk. Seniority and security do not guarantee payment. A debt can be senior and secured but still as risky as a dizzy tightrope walker — it depends on the value and risk of the firm's assets.

Long-term bonds are described as **investment grade** if they qualify for one of the top four ratings from Canadian Bond Rating Service, Dominion Bond Rating Service, Moody's or Standard and Poor's rating services. Table 13.3 describes the rating criteria used by the Canadian Bond Rating Service. Bonds that are below investment grade are known as **junk bonds**.

TABLE 13.3
Key to CBRS's long-term bond ratings

Highest Quality A++

This category encompasses bonds of outstanding quality. They possess the highest degree of protection of principal and interest. Companies with debt rated A++ are generally large national and/or multinational corporations whose products or services are essential to the Canadian economy.

These companies are the acknowledged leaders in their respective industries and have clearly demonstrated their ability to best withstand adverse economic or trade conditions either national or international in scope.

Characteristically, these companies have had a long and creditable history of superior debt protection, in which the quality of their assets and earnings have been constantly maintained or improved, with strong evidence that this will continue.

Very Good Quality A+

Bonds rated A+ are similar in characteristics to those rated A++ and can also be considered superior in quality. These companies have demonstrated a long and satisfactory history of growth with above-average protection of principal and interest on their debt securities.

These bonds are generally rated lower in quality because the margin of assets or earnings protection may not be as large or as stable as those rated A++. In both these categories the nature and quality of the asset and earning coverages are more important than the numerical values of the ratios.

Good Quality A

Bonds rated A are considered to be good quality securities and to have favorable long-term investment characteristics. The main feature that distinguishes them from the higher rated securities is that these companies are more susceptible to adverse trade or economic conditions. Consequently, the protection is lower than for the categories of A++ and A+.

In all cases the A rated companies have maintained a history of adequate asset and earnings protection. There may be certain elements that may impair this protection sometime in the future. Confidence that the current overall financial position will be maintained or improved is slightly lower than for the securities rated above.

Medium Quality B++

Issues rated B++ are classified as medium or average grade credits and are considered to be investment grade. These companies are generally more susceptible than any of the higher rated companies to swings in economic or trade conditions that would cause a deterioration in protection should the company enter a period of poor operating conditions.

TABLE 13.3
(continued)

Medium Quality B++ *(continued)*

There may be factors present either from within or without the company that may adversely affect the long-term level of protection of the debt. These companies bear closer scrutiny but in all cases both interest and principal are adequately protected at the present time.

Lower Medium Quality B+

Bonds which are rated B+ are considered to be lower medium grade securities and have limited long-term protective investment characteristics. Assets and earnings coverage may be modest or unstable.

A significant deterioration in interest and principal protection may occur during periods of adverse economic or trade conditions. During periods of normal or improving economic conditions, assets and earnings protection are adequate. However, the company's ability to continually improve its financial position and level of debt protection is at present limited.

Poor Quality B

Securities rated B lack most qualities necessary for long-term fixed income investment. Companies in this category have a general history of volatile operating conditions, and the assurance has been in doubt that principal and interest protection will be maintained at an adequate level. Current coverages may be below industry standards and there is little assurance that debt protection will significantly improve.

Speculative Quality C

Securities in this category are clearly speculative. The companies are generally junior in many respects and there is little assurance that the adequate coverage of principal and interest can be maintained uninterruptedly over a period of time.

Default D

Bonds in this category are in default of some provisions in their trust deed and the companies may or may not be in the process of liquidation.

Rating Suspended

A company which has its rating currently suspended is experiencing severe financial or operating problems of which the outcome is uncertain. The company may or may not be in default but at present there is uncertainty as to the company's ability to pay off its debt.

Note: (High) and (Low) designations after a rating indicate an issuer's relative strength within a rating category.
Source: Canadian Bond Rating Service, "The CBRS Method of Rating Corporate and Government Securities," 1989 C.B.R.S. Inc., pp. 16–17.

Some junk issues are "fallen angels," securities that were investment grade when issued but that subsequently fell from grace. But in the late 1970s a *new-issue* junk bond market was created. Companies discovered a pool of investors willing to accept unusually high default risks in exchange for high promised yields. New issues of junk bonds in the United States leapt from about $1.5 billion in 1978 to $34.2 billion in 1986.[5] Junk bonds were often issued at short notice to finance mergers and acquisitions, such as Campeau Corporation's acquisition of Federated Stores in 1988.

Junk bonds combine the tax advantage of debt with the high risk and return characteristics of equity. In Chapter 15 we discuss the relative merits of debt and

[5] See E. I. Altman, "The Anatomy of the High-Yield Bond Market," *Financial Analysts Journal* 45 (July–August 1987):12–25.

equity financing. The relative tax advantage of debt over equity is much stronger in the United States than in Canada, because Canada offers tax relief to equity holders with a dividend tax credit. Thus, the new-issue junk bond market is not nearly so significant in Canada as it is in the United States. For example, although Campeau Corporation was a Canadian company, it issued its junk bonds in the United States when it acquired U.S.-based Federated Stores. The acquisition was so large that Campeau could not have quickly obtained equity or debt financing in Canada.

New issues of junk bonds took a hit in the mid-1980s when it emerged that a number of American savings and loan companies had speculated heavily in these bonds. The investment bank that had popularized junk bonds (Drexel Burnham Lambert) went into bankruptcy and the head of its junk bond operation (Michael Milken) went to prison. Since then, however, the U.S. junk bond market has rebounded and is a vital source of financing for corporations with low credit ratings. Canadian firms have also been tapping into the U.S. junk bond market. For example, Rogers Communications Inc. has borrowed $1.8 billion through the U.S. junk bond market since 1991. In addition, underwriters have been attempting to develop the junk bond market in Canada. These recent developments are discussed in the Finance in Action box below.

Finance in Action

Canadian Firms Crack U.S. Junk Market

NEW YORK — Ask Graham Savage, a senior vice-president at Rogers Communications Inc., what Canada's capital markets need, and you'll get a blunt answer.

"We need a Michael Milken in Canada," he says.

To most Canadians, Mr. Milken is the notorious financier who broke the law to reap astronomical profits from junk bonds. To financial executives throughout the United States and Canada, however, Mr. Milken's legacy is a thriving junk bond market that has given hundreds of corporations with low credit ratings an alternative source of long-term debt.

In the past decade, the U.S. junk bond market has exploded from a small pool of risky corporate bonds to a booming $200-billion (U.S.) market where household names such as Time Warner Inc. and RJR Nabisco Inc. regularly borrow money.

Until a few years ago, Canadian companies had a tough time breaking into the junk bond market. Conservative Canadian pension funds and institutional investors shied away from any bond rated below single-A-minus, while U.S. investors avoided little-known foreign companies.

But some aggressive U.S. investment banks have changed all that. Sensing an opportunity for new business, New York firms such as Merrill Lynch & Co. Inc., Salomon Brothers Inc. and Goldman Sachs & Co. have aggressively promoted the junk bond debt of Canadian companies to U.S. investors.

Junk bonds are securities that are sold by companies whose debt is rated below investment grade. They

Canadian Firms Crack U.S. Junk Market (*continued*)

are called junk or high-yield bonds because issuers must pay high interest rates to compensate investors for the speculative rating.

Mr. Milken served nearly two years in prison for securities fraud, and the junk market dived as some of his deals unravelled and legal troubles mounted. But since then, junk bonds have staged a strong comeback.

Since 1991, 20 Canadian companies have borrowed about $4.4-billion by selling junk bonds to U.S. investors. That's just for starters. Investment bankers estimate there are more than 50 Canadian companies with the necessary credit ratings and financial clout to sell junk bonds in the United States.

"The opportunity for Canadian issuers to raise high-yield bonds in the United States is unlimited. . . . You are going to see more and more Canadian companies going south of the border to borrow money," says Robert Gemmell, vice-chairman of Merrill Lynch Canada Inc.

The good news about the Canadian junk bond boom is that it offers businesses more flexible long-term debt. Most companies in Canada rated below single-A-minus can only borrow from banks, which seldom provide a loan for more than seven years. Junk bonds, however, can be issued for as long as 30 years and their financial terms, or covenants, are typically far less restrictive than those attached to bank loans.

The bad news, however, is that Canadians are selling junk bond debt outside Canada. For Canadian companies, this means most of their junk bond debt must be raised in U.S. dollars, forcing them to invest in complex and often inflexible swap instruments to minimize foreign currency swings.

"We are a Canadian company with Canadian revenues and we would like to be borrowing in Canada to mitigate our foreign exchange risk," says Mr. Savage of Rogers, which has borrowed $1.8-billion through the U.S. junk bond market since 1991.

Rogers, active in cable television and telecommunications, is one of the lucky companies. It has the profile and financial clout to attract U.S. investors to its junk bonds. By some estimates there are more than 100 Canadian companies that could sell junk bonds, but their borrowing needs fall below the $100-million minimum threshold in the United States.

Unless Canada can create its own junk bond market, its capital markets will tend to shrink as more local companies sell their debt outside the country. That means less revenue for Canadian securities firms, fewer local jobs and a domestic capital market that is less equipped to sell debt for Canadian companies.

"Obviously we simply can't stand still," says Reay Mackay, president of broker RBC Dominion Securities Inc. "We have to be a more viable competitor in this market place."

So far Canadian securites firms have been poor competitors. When Rogers asked a group of Canadian underwriters to test the domestic market for a junk bond issue last January, the firms couldn't find buyers for more than $50-million (Canadian) of the bonds. Adding insult to injury, prospective investors were demanding unusually tough financial restrictions on the bonds.

Frustrated, Rogers passed the deal to Merrill Lynch, which was able to sell $300-million of junk bonds to U.S. investors. Canadian investment firms were stunned, not only by the size of

Canadian Firms Crack U.S. Junk Market (*continued*)

Largest Junk Bond Issues by Canadian Companies

Offer Date	Issuer	S&P	Moody	$U.S. Million Principal Amount	Lead Managers
July, '91	Rogers Cantel Mobile	BB+	Ba3	$460	Merrill
Feb., '94	Doman Industries	BB–	Ba3	425	Bear Steams
Aug., '93	International Semi-Tech	B+	Ba2	300	Kidder Peabody
Jan., '94	Gulf Canada	B+	B2	300	Salomon Bros.
Nov., '93	Methanex	BB	Ba3	275	First Boston
April, '92	Rogers Comunications	BB–	Ba3	250	Merrill
July, '92	Rogers Cablesystems	BB+	Ba1	250	Merrill
Jan., '94	Rogers Cablesystems	BB+	Ba1	227	Merrill
Dec., '93	Stone Consolidated	B+	B1	225	Salomon
July, '92	Rogers Cantel Mobile	B	B2	200	Merrill
Aug., '92	Rogers Cablesystems	BB+	Ba1	200	Merrill
March, '93	Sherritt Gordon	BB–	Ba3	200	Goldman Sachs

Source: Merrill Lynch Canada

the Rogers issue, but by the fact that it was denominated in Canadian dollars. Rogers' bond sale was the first time a U.S. junk bond issue was sold in a foreign currency.

"It was a watershed deal. It showed you have a truly North American market for junk bonds in the U.S. that doesn't discriminate against world class Canadian companies," Mr. Gemmell says.

Well, maybe. While it's true that one other Canadian company, fertilizer and metals producer Sherritt Inc. of Fort Saskatchewan, Alta., was subsequently able to sell junk bonds to U.S. investors in Canadian dollars, it's doubtful that many other domestic companies will be so fortunate.

The Canadian dollar has swooned since Rogers and Sherritt sold their junk bonds, reducing returns of U.S. investors who bought the notes. With the political uncertainty in Quebec squeezing the dollar, it may be some time before U.S. investors are again willing to bet on Canadian-dollar junk issues.

If Canadian companies want to sell junk bonds in local currency, their best hope is a homegrown market. At the moment, however, prospects are bleak.

The biggest obstacle to a domestic junk bond market is the country's institutional investors. Canadian pension funds and insurance companies are highly conservative investors. For years they have regarded below-investment-grade debt securities as "fallen angels" that are to be avoided at all costs.

Their resistance to junk bonds frustrates Canadian companies and securities firms that are pushing institutional investors to broaden their investment horizons. The U.S. has dozens of mutual funds that have dedicated billions of dollars to junk bonds; Canada doesn't.

One Canadian institution, Manufacturers Life Insurance Co., is unusual in that it actively invests in junk bonds.

"Canadian institutions have a clear bias against high-yield securities," says Terry Garr, manager of Manulife's $650-million (U.S.) portfolio of junk bonds.

Canadian Firms Crack U.S. Junk Market *(continued)*

"There's an entrenched mindset at financial institutions that regards below-investment-grade bonds as accidents or mistakes."

Too bad Canadian institutions don't share Manulife's appetite for junk bonds. In the past three years, Mr. Garr's portfolio of mostly U.S. junk bonds has earned some of the company's biggest returns.

James Kiernan, president of Goldman Sachs Canada, says Canadian investors haven't investigated junk bonds because they are swamped with Canadian government bonds. "Canadian institutions have become somewhat lazy with the overwhelming amount of government debt they can choose from."

Meanwhile, Goldman Sachs has been lobbying Canadian institutions, sponsoring conferences and actively trading in below-investment-grade bonds to build a market for junk bonds.

So far the best Mr. Kiernan of Goldman Sachs can say about its progress is: "It's a slow process."

If Goldman Sachs fails, ultimately Canadian capital markets will lose. "If Canadian investors do not respond to the need for a high-yield market, more companies will be compelled to go outside Canada for their capital needs and Canadian capital markets will be left more and more to government bonds."

Source: Jacquie McNish, "Canadian Firms Crack U.S. Junk Market, *The Globe and Mail Report on Business*, July 11, 1994, pp. B1, B3.

Country and Currency. These days capital markets know few national boundaries and many large firms, especially those with significant overseas operations, borrow abroad. For example, a Canadian company may choose to finance a new plant in Spain by borrowing pesetas from a Spanish bank, or it may expand its Dutch operation by issuing a bond in Holland.

In addition to these national capital markets, there is also an international capital market centred mainly in London. There are some 500 banks in London from over 70 different countries and they include such giants as Citicorp, Union Bank of Switzerland, Deutsche Bank, Dai-ichi Kangyo Bank, Banque Nationale de Paris, and Barclays Bank. One reason they are there is to collect deposits in the major currencies. For example, suppose an Arab sheikh has just received payment in dollars for a large sale of oil to the United States. Rather than depositing the cheque in the United States, he may choose to open a dollar account with a bank in London. Dollars held in a bank outside the United States are known as eurodollars. Similarly, Canadian dollars held outside of Canada are called euroCanadian dollars, francs held outside France are known as eurofrancs, deutschemarks held outside Germany are known as eurodeutschemarks, and so on. The term **eurocurrency** is used to refer to money deposited in financial institutions outside of the currency's home country. Eurodollars (U.S. currency outside of the U.S.) dominates the eurocurrency market.

The London bank branch that is holding the sheikh's dollar deposit may temporarily lend those dollars to a company, in the same way that a bank in the United States may relend dollars that have been deposited with it. Thus a company can

eurocurrency: Money deposited in financial institutions outside the currency's home country. For example, euroCanadian dollars are Canadian dollars held outside of Canada.

eurobond: Bond that is marketed internationally, typically outside the country in whose currency the bond is denominated.

foreign bond: Bond that is marketed outside the country of the borrower and inside the country in whose currency it is denominated.

private placement: Sale of securities to a limited number of investors without a public offering.

protective covenant: Restriction on a firm to protect bondholders.

either borrow dollars from a bank in the United States or borrow eurodollars from a bank in London.[6]

If a firm wants to make an issue of long-term bonds, it can choose to do so in Canada. Alternatively, it can sell the bonds to investors in several countries. Such bonds are known as **eurobonds**. Eurobonds are usually sold to the London branches of the major international banks, which then resell them to investors throughout the world. What makes eurobonds unique is the fact that the bonds are issued in several countries but all are denominated in the same currency, often the currency of the issuer. Many large Canadian companies sell their Canadian dollar denominated bonds to international investors around the world.

In addition to eurobonds, a company may issue **foreign bonds**. A foreign bond is issued in a currency different from the currency of the issuer and is typically sold in the country in whose currency the bond is denominated. Inco, for example, has several foreign currency denominated bonds, including Swiss franc, deutschemark, U.S. dollar, and British sterling bonds.

Public versus Private Placements. Publicly issued bonds are sold to anyone who wishes to buy and, once they have been issued, they can be freely traded in the securities markets. In a **private placement**, the issue is sold directly to a small number of banks, insurance companies, or other investment institutions and individual investors who are deemed to be sophisticated. Privately placed bonds can only be traded among these qualified investors, excluding most individual investors.

Protective Covenants. When investors lend to a company, they are taking a risk; they might not get their money back. But they expect that the company will use their money well and not take unreasonable risks. To help ensure this, lenders usually impose a number of conditions, or **protective covenants**, on companies that borrow from them. An honest firm is willing to accept these conditions because it knows that they enable the firm to borrow at a reasonable rate of interest.

Companies that borrow in moderation are less likely to get into difficulties than those that are up to the gunwales in debt. So lenders usually restrict the amount of extra debt that the firm can issue. Lenders are also eager to prevent others from pushing ahead of them in the queue if trouble occurs. So they will not allow the company to create new debt that is senior to them or to put aside assets for other lenders.

Another possible hazard for lenders is that the company will pay a bumper dividend to the shareholders, leaving no cash for the debtholders. Therefore, lenders sometimes limit the size of the dividends that can be paid.

SELF-TEST 13.5

In 1988 RJR Nabisco, the American-based food and tobacco giant, had $5 billion of A-rated debt outstanding. In that year the company was taken over, and $19 billion of debt was issued and used to buy back equity. The debt ratio skyrocketed, and the debt was downgraded to BB. The holders of the previously issued debt were furious, and one filed a lawsuit claiming that RJR had violated an *implicit* obligation not to undertake major financing changes at the expense of existing bondholders. Why did these bondholders believe they had been harmed by the massive issue of new debt? What type of *explicit* restriction would you have wanted if you had been one of the original bondholders?

eurodollars deposits: Dollars held on deposit in a bank outside of Canada.

---

[6] Because the Federal Reserve requires banks in the United States to keep interest-free reserves, there is in effect a tax on dollar deposits in the United States. **Eurodollar deposits** are free of this tax and therefore banks can offer the borrower slightly lower interest rates on eurodollars.

A Debt by Any Other Name. The word debt sounds straightforward, but companies enter into a number of financial arrangements that look suspiciously like debt yet are treated differently in the accounts. Some of these obligations are easily identifiable. For example, accounts payable are simply obligations to pay for goods that have already been delivered and are therefore like a short-term debt.

Other arrangements are not so easy to spot. For example, instead of borrowing money to buy equipment, many companies **lease** or rent it on a long-term basis. In this case the firm promises to make a series of payments to the lessor (the owner of the equipment). This is just like the obligation to make payments on an outstanding loan. What if the firm can't make the payments? The lessor can then take back the equipment, which is precisely what would happen if the firm had *borrowed* money from the lessor, using the equipment as collateral for the loan.

lease: Long-term rental agreement.

An Example: The Terms of Inco's Bond Issue

Now that you are familiar with some of the jargon, you might like to look at an example of a bond issue. Table 13.4 (opposite) is a summary of the terms of a bond issue by Inco taken from *The Financial Post Yellow Cards*, produced by The Financial Post Data Group. We have added some explanatory notes.

Innovation in the Debt Market

We have discussed domestic bonds and eurobonds, fixed-rate and floating-rate loans, secured and unsecured loans, senior and junior loans, and much more. You might think that this gives you all the choice you need. Yet almost every day companies and their advisers dream up a new type of debt. Here are some examples of unusual bonds.

Indexed bonds make payments tied to some price index. For example, in high-inflation countries such as Brazil, payments on most debt are indexed to the rate of inflation. A few firms in Canada have tied payments to the price of a particular commodity. For instance, in 1986 Home Oil issued debentures with a two-part interest rate: a fixed component of 5 percent and a variable component based on the price of oil. The higher the price of oil, the higher the interest rate. Thus the bond was to give Home Oil protection against the vagaries of oil prices. If oil prices were depressed in 1992, for example, it is likely that the firm's income would be low. But in this case, the cost of debt would be low also.

Reverse floaters are floating-rate bonds that pay a higher rate of interest when other interest rates fall and a lower rate when other rates rise. Our favourite example of a reverse floater is a bond issued by the Norwegian Christiania Bank. This offered an interest rate of 12.8 percent *minus* the prime rate of interest. So if the prime rate rose, the interest payment on Christiania's bond fell (though it was not allowed to fall below zero). To complicate matters, the final payment on the bond was not fixed at 100 percent. Instead it was linked to the level of the Japanese stock market.

Pay in kind bonds (PIKs) make regular interest payments, but in the early years of the bonds' life, the issuer can choose to pay interest in the form of either cash or more bonds with the equivalent face value. This gives the firm a valuable option. If it falls on hard times and is strapped for cash, it can hand over more bonds to the investor rather than hard cash. Of course, the last thing that the investor wants is more bonds in a cash-starved firm.

These three examples illustrate the great variety of potential security designs. As long as you can convince investors of its attractions, you can issue a callable, subordinated, floating-rate bond denominated in deutschemarks. Rather than combining features of existing securities, you may be able to create an entirely new one. We can imagine a copper mining company issuing preferred shares on which the dividend fluctuates with the world copper price. We know of no such

TABLE 13.4

Inco's bond issue

Comment	Description of Bond
1. A "debenture" is an unsecured bond.	Inco Limited 9.875% Sinking Fund Debentures
2. The coupon rate is 9.875% of the $1,000 par value. The annual coupon is .09875 × $1000 = $98.75	
3. The bond was issued June 15, 1990 and is to be repaid on June 15, 2019.	Dated June 15, 1990; due June 15, 2019
4. Interest is payable at 6-month intervals on June and Dec. 15th.	Principal and half-yearly interest (June 15 and Dec. 15) payable in U.S. funds
5. Inco is authorized to issue (and has outstanding) U.S. $150 million of the bonds.	Authorized, issued and outstanding at Dec. 31, 1993 U.S. $150,000,000
6. A trustee is appointed to look after the bondholders' interests.	Trustee — Bank of New York

7. From 2000 onward, Inco has the right to redeem (i.e., call or buy back) the bond at specified prices. On the other hand, bondholders have the right to force Inco to repurchase the bonds at par only if the bond rating declines.

Redemption — Not redeemable prior to June 15, 1999, unless there is a rating decline whereby the holder can request Inco to purchase the debenture at par. Thereafter, redeemable in whole or in part, for other than sinking fund purposes, on 30 days' notice in the 12 months ending June 15 as follows:

2000	103.638	2005	101.819
2001	103.274	2006	101.455
2002	102.910	2007	101.091
2003	102.546	2008	100.728
2004	102.183	2009	100.364

and thereafter at par to maturity, plus accrued interest to the date fixed for redemption.

8. Every year for 17 years, beginning in 2000, Inco must satisfy the sinking fund by repurchasing bonds with face value of $7.5 million. Thus by 2019, when the bond matures, the outstanding principal will be $7.5 million at most.

Sinking Fund — Sufficient to retire on June 15 of the years 2000 to 2018, inclusive, U.S. $7,500,000 principal amount of the debentures. In addition, Inco has the noncumulative right to retire up to an additional U.S. $7,500,000 during the same period.

Offered — In June 1989, by a group headed by Morgan Stanley & Co. Inc., New York.

Source: The Financial Post Data Group.

security, but it is perfectly legal to issue it and — who knows? — it might generate considerable interest among investors.[7]

Variety is intrinsically good. People have different tastes, levels of wealth, rates of tax, and so on. Why not offer them a choice? Of course the problem is the expense of designing and marketing new securities. But if you can think of a new security that will appeal to investors, you may be able to issue it on especially favourable terms and thus increase the value of your company.

---

[7] However, our copper bond seems humdrum compared with some bonds that have been issued. For example, in 1990 the Swedish company Electrolux issued a bond whose final payment depends on whether there has been an earthquake in Japan.

13.4 CONVERTIBLE SECURITIES

warrant: Right to buy shares from a company at a stipulated price before a set date.

We have seen that companies sometimes have the option to repay an issue of bonds before maturity. There are also cases in which *investors* have an option. The most dramatic case is provided by a **warrant**, which is *nothing but* an option. A warrant gives its owner the right to purchase a set number of the company's shares at a set price before a set date. For example, on December 31, 1992 you could have bought a Quadra Logic Technologies warrant for $3.50. That warrant allowed you to purchase one share of Quadra Logic common stock at a price of $7 any time before December 1993. The Quadra Logic issue was originally issued in a package called a unit, which included one common Quadra Logic common share and one-half a common share warrant. Warrants are also often sold in units with bonds. The idea is to make the bond issue more attractive by including an "equity sweetener."

Suppose the price of Quadra Logic was $17 on December 31, 1993 when the warrant expired. In that case your original investment in the warrant would have paid off handsomely. You would have paid $3.50 for the warrant and then put up a further $7 to buy a share of common stock. So for a total outlay of $10.50, you would have acquired a share worth $17. Of course an investment in warrants also has its perils. In the event the price of Quadra Logic stock failed to rise above $7, the warrants expired worthless. As it happened, on December 31, 1993 the price of Quadra Logic stock was $10.50. If you had bought the warrant for $3.50, you would have broken even on a cash flow basis but made a loss in present value terms.

convertible bond: Bond that the holder may exchange for a specified amount of another security.

A **convertible bond** gives its owner the option to exchange the bond for a predetermined number of common shares. The convertible bondholder hopes that the company's share price will zoom up so that the bond can be converted at a big profit. But if the shares zoom down, there is no obligation to convert; the bondholder remains just that.

The convertible is rather like a package of a bond and a warrant. But there is an important difference: when the owners of a convertible wish to exercise their options to buy shares, they do not pay cash — they just exchange the bond for shares of the stock.

These examples do not exhaust the options encountered by the financial manager. We will see in Chapter 24 that *all* corporate securities contain an option. In fact once you read that chapter and learn how to analyze options, you will find that they are all around you.

13.5 DERIVATIVES

Most of the time we accept risk as part of life. A business is exposed to unpredictable changes in selling price, labour cost, tax rates, technology, and other hazards. There's nothing the manager can do about it.

That's not wholly true. To some extent the manager can protect the firm against particular risks, and in recent years a range of new tools has been developed to assist in this task. These tools are known as *derivative instruments* or, more simply, *derivatives*. Derivatives are side bets on stock prices, interest rates, exchange rates, commodity prices, and so on.

Here are four types of derivatives that have experienced rapid growth in the last decade.

Options

option: The right to buy or sell an asset in the future at a stipulated price.

An **option** gives the right (but not the obligation) to buy or sell an asset in the future at a price that is agreed today. We have already seen that firms sometimes issue options on their own or tacked onto other securities. But in addition there is a huge volume of business in options that are created by banks or traded on specialized options exchanges. Trading in options on common stocks took off in 1973 when the Chicago Board Options Exchange was established. Now you can deal in options to buy or sell a wide variety of common stocks, bonds, currencies, and commodities sold on options exchanges around the world.

Firms often use options to limit their risk. For example, suppose there is a chance that the firm will need to pay out 150,000 deutschemarks at the end of the year. At current exchange rates this amounts to $100,000. But imagine the deutschemark strengthens over the year; you could find yourself having to hand over a much larger number of dollars. One way to protect yourself against this risk is to take out a 1-year option to buy deutschemarks at the current exchange rate. In this case, you know that the most the deutschemarks will cost you is $100,000, plus the cost of the options.[8]

Futures

futures contract: Tradable contract to buy or sell an asset in the future at an agreed price.

A **futures contract** is an agreement to buy or sell an asset at a specified later date. The price is fixed when you place the order but you don't pay for the asset until the delivery date. Futures markets have existed for a long time in commodities such as copper, soybeans, and pork bellies. However, in the 1970s the futures exchanges began to trade contracts on financial assets, such as bonds, currencies, and stock market indexes. Within 15 years, the worldwide volume of transactions in these financial futures increased from zero to more than $30 *trillion* a year.

Suppose you are a farmer. The wheat crop is looking good, still you can't sleep. You are worried that when the time comes to sell the wheat, prices may have fallen through the floor. The solution to insomnia is to sell wheat futures. In this case, you agree to deliver so many bushels of wheat in the future at a price that is set today. Do not confuse this futures contract with an option, where the holder has a choice whether or not to make delivery; your futures contract is a firm promise to deliver wheat.

Forwards

forward contract: Non-tradeable contract to buy or sell an asset in the future at an agreed price.

Futures contracts are standardized products bought and sold on organized exchanges. A **forward contract** is a tailor-made futures contract that is not traded on an exchange. For example, your firm may know that it will receive 1 million yen in 6 months. If you don't want to take a chance on the future value of the yen, you can sell those yen forward at a price that is fixed today. Then, at the end of 6 months, you hand over the 1 million yen to the bank and receive in exchange the agreed number of dollars.[9]

Swaps

Think back to the oil-indexed debenture issued by Home Oil we mentioned above. In April, 1992, Home Oil decided that it would make more sense to have issued fixed rate debt.[10] Home Oil could have repaid its oil-indexed debentures by

---

[8] If the deutschemark strengthens, you exercise your options, pay the $100,000, and get 150,000 deutschemarks. If the deutschemark weakens, you throw the option away and buy your deutschemarks at the new cheap rate.

[9] Since 1983, banks have also been prepared to enter into forward contracts to borrow or lend money. If you buy one of these forward rate agreements (FRAs), you agree to borrow in the future at an interest rate that is fixed today; if you sell an FRA, you agree to lend in the future at an agreed rate.

[10] Home Oil's vice-president and chief financial officer explained the decision to fix (cap) the interest rate as follows, "The company believes that this rate provides an attractive cost of financing in today's markets....Crude oil prices were relatively low and people's expectations [about oil prices] for the long term were also relatively low." From Barry Critchely, "A New Twist in Home Oil's West Texas-indexed debt," *The Financial Post* (April 25–27, 1992):22.

swap: Agreement between two firms to exchange a series of future payments on different terms.

calling them and issued in its place a fixed-rate loan. But it was much simpler for Home Oil to arrange a **swap**, or, specifically, an *interest rate swap*. This worked as follows. A bank agreed to pay Home Oil each year the dollars that were needed to service its oil-indexed debt. In return Home Oil agreed to pay the bank the fixed rate of interest of 8.263 percent.

Companies also enter into *currency swaps*. For example, the bank may pay a firm the cost of servicing a Swiss franc loan, and in return the firm agrees to pay the bank the cost of servicing a similar U.S. dollar loan.[11] Inco, for example, engages in currency swaps to reduce its exposure to foreign currency. In 1993, it had total long-term debt with $1038 million face value, of which about 76 percent was denominated in U.S. dollars and the other 24 percent in non-U.S. dollar currencies. Through the use of currency swaps, Inco converts its non-U.S. dollar debt into U.S. dollar-denominated debt. In 1993, 92 percent of its long-term debt was effectively payable in U.S. dollars.

Swaps scarcely existed until the 1980s but they are now big business. By 1991 firms had entered into $4.5 trillion of swaps worldwide.

PATTERNS OF CORPORATE FINANCING

That completes our tour of corporate securities and derivatives. You may feel like the tourist who has just gone through 12 cathedrals in 5 days. But there will be plenty of time in later chapters for reflection and analysis. For now, let's look at how firms use these sources of finance.

Firms have two broad sources of cash. They can raise money from external sources by an issue of debt or equity. Or they can plow back part of their profits. When the firm retains cash rather than paying the money out as dividends, it is increasing shareholders' investment in the firm.

internally generated funds: Cash reinvested in the firm; depreciation plus earnings not paid out as dividends.

Figure 13.1 summarizes the sources of capital for Canadian corporations. The most striking aspect of this figure is the dominance of **internally generated funds**, defined as depreciation plus earnings that are not paid out as dividends.[12] Over the 16 years, 1977–1992, internally generated funds covered about 55 percent of firms' capital requirements. You might like to compare this proportion with the way that firms in other countries finance their operations. This is shown in Figure 13.2. Notice that the reliance on internally generated cash is the same the world over.

....
**Do Firms Rely
Too Heavily on
Internal Funds?**

Gordon Donaldson, in a survey of corporate debt policies, encountered several firms that acknowledged "that it was their long-term objective to hold to a rate of growth which was consistent with their capacity to generate funds internally." A number of other firms appeared to think less hard about expenditure proposals that could be financed internally.[13]

At first glance, this behaviour doesn't make sense. As we have already noted, retained profits are additional capital invested by shareholders and represent, in effect, a compulsory issue of shares. A firm that retains $1 million could have paid

---

[11] For example, in 1993 Toyota issued a huge $1.5 billion of eurobonds. The interest rate on these bonds was fixed at 5 5/8 percent. But Toyota also entered into an interest rate swap. This meant that a bank agreed to pay Toyota enough to cover the interest on the bond and in return Toyota agreed to pay the bank a sum that would go up and down as interest rates fluctuated. The net effect was that Toyota had borrowed at a floating rate.

[12] Remember that depreciation is a noncash expense.

[13] See G. Donaldson, *Corporate Debt Capacity*, Division of Research, Graduate School of Business Administration, Harvard University, Boston, 1961, Chapter 3, especially pp. 51–56.

FIGURE 13.1
Sources of funds as a percentage of total funds, Canadian non-financial enterprises.

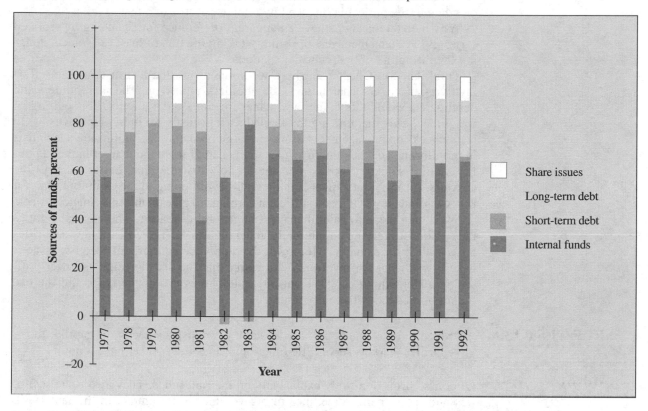

Source: Organization for Economic Cooperation and Development, "Non-Financial Enterprises Financial Statistics," 1993. © OECD, 1993, financial statistics. Reproduced by permission of the OECD.

FIGURE 13.2
Sources and uses of funds
1987–1991.

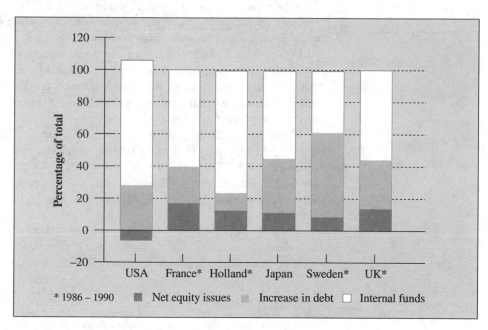

Source: OECD Financial Statistics and Flow of Funds

out the cash as dividends and then sold new common shares to raise the same amount of additional capital. The opportunity cost of capital ought not to depend on whether the project is financed by retained profits or a new stock issue.

Why then do managers have an apparent preference for financing by retained earnings? Perhaps managers are simply taking the line of least resistance, dodging the discipline of the securities markets.

Think back to Chapter 2 where we pointed out that a firm is a team effort involving managers, shareholders, debtholders, and so on. The shareholders and debtholders would like to monitor management to make sure that it is pulling its weight and truly maximizing market value. It is costly for individual investors to keep checks on management. However, large financial institutions are specialists in monitoring; so when the firm goes to the bank for a large loan or makes a public issue of stocks or bonds, managers know that they had better have all the answers. If they want a quiet life, they will avoid going to the capital market for new cash and they will retain sufficient earnings to give them some financial slack.

We do not mean to paint managers in general as loafers. There are also rational reasons for relying on internally generated funds. The costs of new securities are avoided, for example. Moreover, the announcement of a new equity issue is usually bad news for investors, who worry that the decision signals lower profits.[14] Raising equity capital from internal sources avoids the costs and the bad omens associated with equity issues.

SELF-TEST 13.6

"Since internal funds provide the bulk of industry's needs for capital, the securities markets serve little function." Does the speaker have a point?

External Sources of Capital

Of course firms don't rely exclusively on internal funds. They also issue securities and retire them, sometimes in big volume. For example, in the late 1980s Magna International dramatically increased its reliance on debt by issuing considerable amounts of bonds. In 1987 alone, the amount of its outstanding long-term debt increased more than 67 percent. After 1990, however, Magna gradually reduced its borrowing by repaid portions of outstanding issues with internally generated funds and proceeds from new share issues.

Figure 13.3 shows the ratio of the book value of Magna's total debt (current liabilities plus long-term debt) to the book value of assets. The ratio peaked in 1990 when Magna was 87 percent debt financed. By 1993, as debt was paid off and equity increased, the firm's total-debt-to-asset ratio was 46 percent, lower than any of the previous 10 years.

If you look back at Figure 13.1, you will see that Magna was not alone in its use of debt financing in the late 1980s. Total debt, short-term plus long-term, represented only 7.9 percent of funds raised in 1983 but increased over the decade. By 1988, total debt was 40 percent of total financing and in 1989 it was almost 42 percent of total financing. By 1992, total debt had fallen to 24.7 percent of total financing.

The net effect of these financing policies is shown in Figure 13.4, which shows that debt-to-asset ratios for Canadian non-financial corporations rose over the late 1980s, after declining over the early 1980s. Debt-to-asset ratios continued to

---

[14] Managers do have insiders' insights and naturally are tempted to issue stock when stock price looks good to them, that is, when they are less optimistic than outside investors. The outside investors realize all this and will buy a new issue only at a discount from the preannouncement price. Stock issues are discussed further in the next chapter.

FIGURE 13.3
Magna International total
debt to asset ratios
1983–1993.

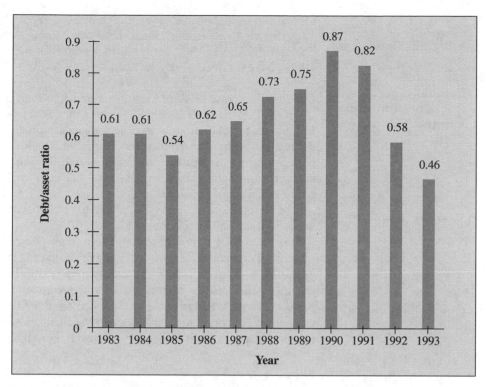

Source: Magna International Inc., 1993 Annual Report.

FIGURE 13.4
Total debt to assets, Canadian non-financial enterprises, 1977–1992.

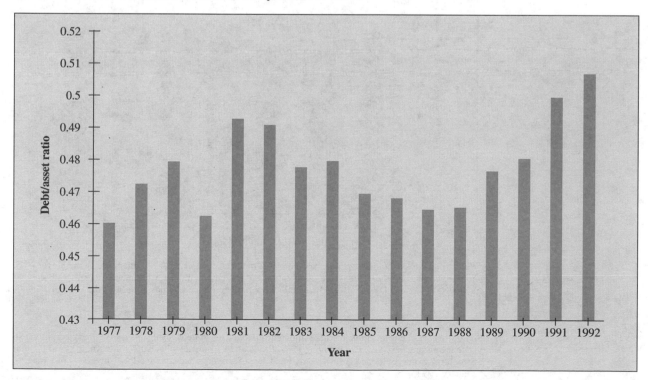

Source: Organization for Economic Cooperation and Development, "Non-Financial Enterprises Financial Statistics," 1993. © OECD, 1993, financial statistics. Reproduced by permission of the OECD.

increase in the 1990s, reaching a high of 50 percent in 1992. Comparing Figures 13.3 and 13.4 shows how remarkable was Magna's recovery from its very high debt levels. Unlike the average firm which was increasing its debt level in the 1990s, Magna successfully reduced its debt level.

Do Companies Borrow Too Much?

Canadian corporations are carrying more debt than they used to. Should we be worried? It is true that higher debt ratios mean that more companies are likely to fall into financial distress when a serious recession hits the economy. But all companies live with this risk to some degree, and it does not follow that less risk is better. Finding the optimal debt ratio is like finding the optimal speed limit: we can agree that accidents at 50 kilometres per hour are less dangerous, other things being equal, than accidents at 100 kilometres per hour, but we do not therefore set the national speed limit at 50. Speed has benefits as well as risks. So does debt, as we will see in Chapter 15.

It is interesting to compare the pattern of corporate financing in Canada to that of foreign companies. Figure 13.5 suggests that in Germany, Japan and Italy, for example, firms operate at significantly higher debt levels.[15] Much of this debt is owned by the banks, which take a very active and continuing interest in the company's activities. In Japan the lending bank and the borrower are often part of the same group of companies, called a *keiretsu*. This close connection between lender and borrower makes it easier for the firm to convince the borrower to contribute

FIGURE 13.5
Total debt to assets, for non-financial enterprises for various countries

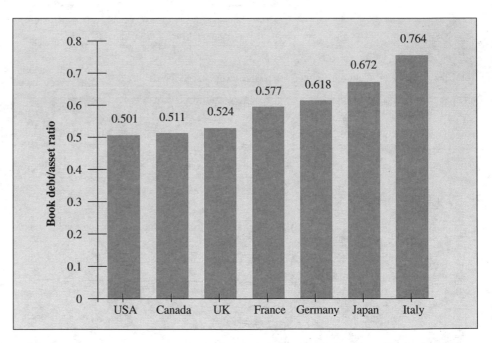

Note: Total book debt to asset ratios based on 1992 financial statements (1990 financial statements for UK).
Source: Organization for Economic Cooperation and Development, "Non-Financial Enterprises Financial Statistics," 1993. © OECD, 1993, financial statistics. Reproduced by permission of the OECD.

---

[15] A word of caution. Many of these apparent differences in debt levels may stem from variations in accounting practice. See, for example, R. G. Rajan and L. Zingales, "What Do We Know about Capital Structure? Some Evidence from International Data," unpublished manuscript, University of Chicago, January 1994.

additional capital and to help the firm sort out its problems if things go wrong. Some say that because firms in Japan and Germany have close links to their banks, they can operate safely at debt ratios that would sink a Canadian firm at the first onslaught of heavy weather.

It does seem that these international differences in sources of finance are diminishing. While the use of debt has increased somewhat in Canada, it has been falling in Japan, and some Japanese firms are breaking away from traditional bank relations and relying more on public debt markets.

13.7 SUMMARY

1. As owners of the corporation, the common stockholders elect the board of directors and vote on major issues. Companies may raise money from shareholders by issuing more shares. They also raise money indirectly by plowing back money that could otherwise have been paid out as dividends.

2. Preferred stock offers a fixed dividend but the company has the discretion not to pay it. It can't, however, then pay a dividend on the common stock. Despite its name, preferred stock is not a popular source of finance, but it is useful in special situations.

3. When companies issue debt, they promise to make a series of interest payments and to repay the principal. However, this liability is limited. Stockholders have the right to default on their obligation and to hand over the assets to the debtholders. Unlike dividends on common stock and preferred stock, the interest payments on debt are regarded as a cost and therefore they are paid out of before-tax income. Here are some of the various forms of debt:

   - *Fixed-rate* and *floating-rate* debt
   - *Long-term* and *short-term* debt
   - *Callable* and *sinking-fund* debt
   - *Senior* and *subordinated* debt
   - *Secured* and *unsecured* debt
   - *Investment grade* and *junk* debt
   - *Domestic* debt and *eurobonds*
   - *Publicly traded* debt and *private placements*

4. The fourth source of finance consists of options and optionlike securities. The simplest option is a warrant, which gives its holder the right to buy a share at a set price by a set date. Warrants are often sold in combination with other securities. Convertible bonds give their holder the right to convert the bond to shares. They therefore resemble a package of straight debt and a warrant.

5. One of the big growth areas in finance has been derivative instruments. These are not used to raise money. They are side bets that are used by companies to protect themselves against fluctuations in commodity prices, interest rates, and foreign exchange rates. We described four main types of derivatives: options, futures, forwards, and swaps.

6. Internally generated cash is the principal source of company funds. Some people worry about that; they think that if management does not go to the trouble of raising money, it may be profligate in spending it.

KEY TERMS

authorized share capital	multiple voting shares	eurodollars deposit
articles of incorporation	restricted voting shares	eurobond
issued shares	preferred stock	foreign bond
outstanding shares	net worth	private placement
par value	floating-rate preferred	protective covenant
additional paid-in capital	prime rate	lease
retained earnings	long-term debt	warrant
majority voting	sinking fund	convertible bond
cumulative voting	callable bond	option
proxy contest	subordinated debt	futures contract
restricted shares	secured debt	forward contract
non-voting shares	investment grade	swap
subordinate voting shares	junk bond	internally generated funds
	eurocurrency	

SUGGESTED READINGS

Donaldson describes a survey of corporate attitudes to different sources of finance in

> G. Donaldson. *Corporate Debt Capacity*, Division of Research, Graduate School of Business Administration, Boston: Harvard University, 1961.

Taggart and Marsh provide some evidence on why and when companies use different sources of finance.

> R. A. Taggart. "A Model of Corporate Financing Decisions," *Journal of Finance*, 32(December 1977):1467–1484.

> P. Marsh. "The Choice between Equity and Debt: An Empirical Study," *Journal of Finance*, 37(March 1982):12–144.

Taggart describes long-term trends in corporate financing in

> R. A. Taggart. "Secular Patterns in the Financing of Corporations," in B. M. Friedman, ed., *Corporate Capital Structures in the United States*, Chicago; University of Chicago Press, 1985.

Kester presents a detailed comparison and analysis of debt ratios for United States and Japanese companies.

> W. C. Kester. "Capital and Ownership Structure: A Comparison of United States and Japanese Manufacturing Corporations," *Financial Management* 15(Spring 1986):5–16.

PROBLEMS

1. The authorized share capital of the Alfred Cake Company is 100,000 shares and 80,000 are issued and outstanding. The equity is currently shown in the company's books as follows:

Common stock	$50,000
Retained earnings	30,000
Common equity	$80,000

a. How many more shares can be issued without the approval of share-holders?

b. If the company issues 10,000 shares at $2 a share, show the effect on the firm's accounts.

c. Calculate the market value and the book value of equity before and after the share issue.

d. Briefly explain the difference between the market value and the book value of equity.

2. Big Time Toys has 100,000 common shares issued and outstanding. The current market price is $30 per share. According to its recent financial statements, its equity is as follows:

Common stock	$750,000
Retained earnings	1,250,000
Common equity	$2,000,000

Big Time has decided to repurchase 20,000 shares. If the average issue price for its shares is $15, adjust the figures in its balance sheet to reflect the effect of the share repurchase.

3. In what ways is preferred stock like long-term debt? In what ways is it like common stock?

4. If there are 10 directors to be elected and a shareholder owns 80 shares, indicate the maximum number of votes that he or she can cast for a favourite candidate under
   a. majority voting
   b. cumulative voting

5. The shareholders of the Pickwick Paper Company need to elect five directors. There are 200,000 shares outstanding. How many shares do you need to own to ensure that you can elect at least one director if the company has
   a. majority voting
   b. cumulative voting
   Hint: How many votes in total will be cast? How many votes are required to ensure that at least one-fifth of votes are cast for your choice?

6. Fill in the blanks by choosing the appropriate term from the following list: *lease, long-term, floating-rate, eurobond, convertible, subordinated, call, sinking fund, prime rate, private placement, public issue, senior, short-term, eurodollar rate, warrant, debentures, term loan.*
   a. Debt maturing in more than 1 year is often called _____ debt.
   b. An issue of bonds that is sold simultaneously in several countries is called a(n) _____ .
   c. If a lender ranks behind the firm's general creditors in the event of default, the loan is said to be _____ .
   d. In many cases a firm is obliged to make regular contributions to a(n) _____ , which is then used to repurchase bonds.
   e. Most bonds give the firm the right to repurchase or _____ the bonds at specified prices.
   f. The rate that banks charge to their most creditworthy customers is generally termed the _____ .

g. The interest rate on bank loans is often tied to short-term interest rates. These loans are usually called _____ loans.

h. Where there is a(n) _____ , securities are sold directly to a small group of institutional investors. These securities cannot be resold to individual investors. In the case of a(n) _____ , debt can be freely bought and sold by individual investors.

i. A long-term rental agreement is called a(n) _____ .

j. A(n) _____ bond can be exchanged for shares of the issuing corporation.

k. A(n) _____ gives its owner the right to buy shares in the issuing company at a predetermined _____.

7. True or false? Explain.

a. Firms sell forward contracts primarily to raise money for new capital investment.

b. Firms trade in futures contracts to hedge their exposure to unexpected changes in interest rates, foreign exchange rates, or commodity prices.

c. A Canadian corporation pays tax on only 30 percent of the common or preferred dividends it receives from other Canadian corporations.

d. Because of the tax advantage, a large fraction of preferred shares is held by corporations.

8. Look back at Table 13.2.

a. Suppose that Inco issues 10 million shares at $30 a share. Rework Table 13.2 to show the company's equity after the issue.

b. Suppose that Inco *subsequently* repurchased 500,000 shares at $32 a share. Inco's average issue price is $25 a share. Rework Table 13.2 to show the effect of the further change.

9. Preferred stock of financially strong firms sometimes sells at lower yields than the bonds of those firms. For weaker firms, the preferred stock has a higher yield. What might explain this pattern?

10. *Income bonds* are unusual. Interest payments on such bonds may be skipped or deferred if the firm's income is insufficient to make the payment. In what way are these bonds like preferred stock? Why might a firm choose to issue an income bond instead of preferred stock?

11. Other things equal, will the following provisions increase or decrease the yield to maturity at which a firm can issue a bond?

a. A call provision

b. A restriction on further borrowing

c. A provision of specific collateral for the bond

d. An option to convert the bonds into shares

e. A sinking fund

12. Why might a bond agreement limit the amount of assets that the firm can lease?

SOLUTIONS TO SELF-TEST QUESTIONS

13.1   Book value is $10 million. At a discount rate of 10 percent, the market value of the firm ought to be $2 million × 20-year annuity factor at 10 percent = $17 million, which exceeds book value. At a discount rate of 20 percent, market value falls to $9.7 million, which is below book value.

13.2 The corporation's after-tax yield on the bonds is $10\% - (.35 \times 10\%) = 6.5\%$. The after-tax yield on the preferred is 8 percent, the same as the before-tax yield because the corporation pays no tax on dividend income from Canadian corporations. The preferred stock provides the higher after-tax rate despite its lower before-tax rate.

13.3 Because the coupon on floating-rate debt adjusts periodically to current market conditions, the bondholder is less vulnerable to changes in market yields. The coupon rate paid by the bond is not locked in for as long a period of time. Therefore, prices of floaters should be less sensitive to changes in market interest rates.

13.4 The option to increase sinking fund payments gives the firm the right (but not the obligation) to call back more bonds at par value when it is advantageous to do so, for example, when interest rates have fallen. The firm's advantage is the bondholder's disadvantage, and the bondholders will demand a higher rate of interest as compensation.

13.5 The extra debt makes it more likely that the firm will not be able to make good on its promised payments to its creditors. If the new debt is not junior to the already-issued debt, then the original bondholders suffer a loss when their bonds become more susceptible to default risk. A protective covenant limiting the amount of new debt that the firm can issue would have prevented this problem. Investors, having witnessed the problems of the RJR bondholders, generally demanded the covenant on future debt issues.

13.6 Capital markets provide liquidity for investors. Because individual stockholders can always lay their hands on cash by selling shares, they are prepared to invest in companies that retain earnings rather than pay them out as dividends. Well-functioning capital markets allow the firm to serve all its stockholders simply by maximizing value. Capital markets also provide managers with information. Without this information, it would be very difficult to determine opportunity costs of capital or to assess financial performance.

FOURTEEN

How Corporations Issue Securities

Bill Gates founded his software company, Microsoft, in 1975, when he was 19 years old. Eleven years later Microsoft shares were sold to the public for $21 a share and immediately zoomed to $35. Bill Gates's shares in Microsoft were worth $350 million.

In 1976 two college dropouts, Steve Jobs and Steve Wozniak, sold their most valuable possessions, a van and a couple of calculators, and used the cash to start manufacturing computers in a garage. In 1980, when Apple Computer went public, the shares were offered to investors at $22 and jumped to $36. The shares owned by the company's two founders were worth $414 million.

In 1988, Toronto-based Delrina Corporation was created by four ambitious young entrepreneurs. They started with the strategy to create a new category of software and avoid competing in the already crowded established markets. Their first niche was computerized business forms, PerForm, and it proved to be very successful. In 1990, when they took their company public, shares traded around $0.75. By year end 1994, the price had skyrocketed to $36 (on a pre-split basis).

Such stories illustrate that the most important asset of a new firm may be a good idea. But that is not all you need. To take an idea from the drawing board to a prototype and through to large-scale production requires ever greater amounts of capital.

To get a new company off the ground, entrepreneurs may rely on their own savings and personal bank loans. But this is unlikely to be sufficient to build a successful enterprise. *Venture capital* firms specialize in providing new equity capital to help firms over the awkward adolescent period before they are large enough to "go public." In the first part of this chapter we will explain how venture capital firms do this.

If the firm continues to be successful, there is likely to come a time when it needs to tap a wider source of capital. At this point it will make its first public issue of common stock. This is known as an *initial offering*, or *IPO*. In the second section of the chapter we will describe what is involved in an IPO.

A company's initial public offering is seldom its last. In Chapter 13 we saw that internally generated cash is not sufficient to satisfy the firm's needs. Established companies make up the deficit by issuing more equity or debt. The remainder of this chapter is taken up with looking at this process.

After studying this chapter you should be able to

● Understand how venture capital firms design successful deals.
● Understand how firms make initial public offerings and their costs.
● Know what is involved when established firms make a general cash offer, rights offer, or a private placement of securities.
● Explain the role of the underwriter in an issue of securities.

14.1 VENTURE CAPITAL

You have taken a big step. With a couple of friends, you have formed a corporation to open a number of fast-food outlets, offering innovative combinations of national dishes such as sushi with sauerkraut, curry Bolognese, and chow mein with Yorkshire pudding. Breaking into the fast-food business costs money, but, after pooling your savings and borrowing to the hilt from the bank, you have raised $100,000 and purchased 1 million shares in the new company. At this zero-stage investment, your company's assets are $100,000 plus the idea for your new product.

That $100,000 is enough to get the business off the ground, but if the idea takes off, you will need more capital to pay for large-scale production facilities. You therefore decide to look for an investor who is prepared to back an untried company in return for part of the profits. Equity capital in young businesses is known as **venture capital** and it is provided by specialist venture capital firms, wealthy individuals, and investment institutions such as pension funds.

> **venture capital:** Money invested to finance a new firm.

Most entrepreneurs are able to spin a plausible yarn about their company. But it is as hard to convince a venture capitalist to invest in your business as it is to get a first novel published. Your first step is to prepare a *business plan*. This describes your product, the potential market, the production method, and the resources — time, money, employees, plant, and equipment — needed for success. It helps if you can point to the fact that you are prepared to put your money where your mouth is. By staking all your savings in the company, you signal your faith in the business.

The venture capital company knows that the success of a new business depends on the effort its managers put in. Therefore, it will try to structure any deal so that you have a strong incentive to work hard. For example, if you agree to accept a modest salary (and look forward instead to increasing the value of your investment in the company's stock), the venture capital company knows you will be committed to working hard. However, if you insist on a watertight employment contract and a fat salary, you won't find it easy to raise venture capital.

You are unlikely to persuade a venture capitalist to give you as much money as you need all at once. Rather, the firm will probably give you enough to reach the next major checkpoint. Suppose you can convince the venture capital company to buy 1 million new shares for $.50 each. This will give it one-half ownership of the firm: it owns 1 million shares and the original partners own 1 million shares. Because the venture capitalist is paying $500,000 for a claim to half your firm, it is placing a $1 million value on the business. After this *first-stage* financing, your company's balance sheet looks like this:

FIRST-STAGE MARKET VALUE BALANCE SHEET
(figures in millions)

Assets		Liabilities and Shareholders' Equity	
Cash from new equity	$0.5	New equity from venture capital	$0.5
Other assets	0.5	Your original equity	0.5
Value	$1.0	Value	$1.0

SELF-TEST 14.1

Why might the venture capital company prefer to put up only part of the funds up-front? Would this affect the amount of effort put in by you, the entrepreneur? Is your willingness to accept only part of the venture capital that will eventually be needed a good signal of the likely success of the venture? You have written a letter to the venture capital company expressing your complete confidence in your firm's future. Is this another good signal?

Suppose that 2 years later your business has grown to the point at which it needs a further injection of equity. This *second-stage* financing might involve the issue of a further 1 million shares at $1 each. Some of these shares might be bought by the original backers and some by other venture capital firms. The balance sheet after the new financing would then be as follows:

SECOND-STAGE MARKET VALUE BALANCE SHEET
(figures in millions)

Assets		Liabilities and Shareholders' Equity	
Cash from new equity	$1.0	New equity from venture capital	$1.0
Other assets	2.0	Equity from first stage	1.0
		Your original equity	1.0
Value	$3.0	Value	$3.0

Notice the value of the initial 1 million shares owned by you and your friends has been marked up to $1 million. Does this begin to sound like a money machine? It was so only because you have made a success of the business and new investors are prepared to pay $1 to buy a share in the business. When you had started out, it wasn't clear that sushi and sauerkraut would catch on. If it hadn't caught on, the venture capital firm could have refused to put up more funds.

You are not yet in a position to cash in on your investment, but your gain is real. The second-stage investors have paid $1 million for a one-third share in the company. (There are now 3 million shares outstanding, and the second-stage investors hold 1 million shares.) Therefore, at least these impartial observers — who are willing to back up their opinions with a large investment — must have decided that the company was worth $3 million. Your one-third share is therefore also worth $1 million.

For every 10 first-stage venture capital investments, only two or three may survive as successful, self-sufficient businesses, and only one may pay off big.[1] From these statistics come two rules for success in venture capital investment. First, don't shy away from uncertainty; accept a low probability of success. But don't buy into a business unless you can see the *chance* of a big, public company in a profitable market. There's no sense taking a big risk unless the reward is big if you win. Second, cut your losses; identify losers early, and, if you can't fix the problem — by replacing management, for example — don't throw good money after bad.

 ## THE INITIAL PUBLIC OFFERING

Very few new businesses make it big, but venture capitalists keep sane by reminding themselves of the success stories — the investors who got in on the ground floor of firms like Newbridge Networks, Green Forest Lumber, and Lotus Development Corporation.[2]

---

[1] One study of venture capital investments between 1960 and 1975 found that about one in six were total failures. On the other hand, thanks to a few outstanding successes, the average return was about 19 percent a year. See B. Huntsman and J. P. Hoban, Jr., "Investment in New Enterprise: Some Empirical Observations on Risk, Return, and Market Structure," *Financial Management* 9 (Summer 1980):44–51.
[2] The founder of Lotus took a class from one of the authors of this textbook. Within 5 years the student had become a multimillionaire. Perhaps that will make you feel better about the cost of this book.

initial public offering (IPO): First offering of stock to the general public.

If a startup is successful, the firm may eventually decide to *go public*. This first sale of stock to the public is called an **initial public offering**, or **IPO**. An IPO is a *primary* offering when new shares are sold to raise additional cash for the company. It is a *secondary* offering when the company's founders and the venture capitalist cash in on some of their gains by selling shares. Sometimes IPOs are both primary and secondary offerings — new funds are raised and the company founders sell some of their shares. Hallmark Technologies Inc. is a company that engineers, designs, and manufactures sophisticated customized steel models employed in the production of precision plastic components used in automobile manufacturing. When Hallmark went public in December 1993, it offered 4.081 million common shares for sale. Of these, 1 million shares were a primary offering and the remaining 3.081 million shares were a secondary offering. Some of the biggest secondary offerings have involved governments selling off stock in nationalized enterprises. For example, the Japanese government raised $12.6 billion by selling its stock in Nippon Telegraph and Telephone and the British government took in $9 billion from its sale of British Gas. The Canadian government received over $700 million from its secondary offering of Air Canada shares in 1988 and 1989.

Arranging a Public Issue

underwriter: Firm that buys an issue of securities from a company and resells it to the public.

spread: Difference between public offer price and price paid by underwriter.

Once a firm decides to go public, the first task is to select the **underwriter** who will manage the new issue. Underwriters are investment dealers who act as financial midwives to a new issue. Usually they play a triple role — first providing the company with procedural and financial advice, then buying the stock, and finally reselling it to the public.

In the typical underwriting arrangement, called a *firm* commitment, the underwriters buy the securities from the firm and then resell them to the public. The underwriters receive payment in the form of a **spread** — that is, they are allowed to sell the shares at a slightly higher price than they paid for them. But the underwriters also accept the risk that they won't be able to sell the stock at the agreed offering price. If that happens, they will be stuck with unsold shares and must get the best price they can for them. In the more risky cases, the underwriter may not be willing to enter into a fixed commitment and handles the issue on a *best efforts* basis. In this case the underwriter agrees to sell as much of the issue as possible but does not guarantee the sale of the entire issue.

Before any stock can be sold to the public, the company must meet the requirements of the provinces' securities laws and regulations. In five provinces, (Quebec, Ontario, Manitoba, Alberta and British Columbia), this includes registering the stock with the appropriate securities commissions.[3] Although each province has its own securities laws, the laws are similar, partly because of the leadership role of the Ontario Securities Commission (OSC) and partly out of recognition that uniform laws make it easier for companies to sell their shares.

Registering the stock with the securities commission involves preparation of a detailed and sometimes cumbersome registration statement, which contains information about the proposed financing and the firm's history, existing business, and plans for the future. The securities commission does not evaluate the wisdom of an investment in the firm but it does check the registration statement for accuracy and completeness.

prospectus: Formal summary that provides information on an issue of securities.

The first part of the registration statement is distributed to the public in the form of a preliminary **prospectus**. Such a prospectus is generally known as a *red her-*

---

[3] In the U.S., the Securities and Exchange Commission (SEC) is responsible for securities regulation for the entire country.

ring because of the statement printed in red ink, denying that the firm is trying to sell securities before the securities commission has approved the registration statement. The preliminary prospectus contains financial statements as well as information about the proposed financing, the company's history, any existing business and plans for the future, but it does not contain some details such as the offering price of the issue.

One function of the prospectus is to warn investors about the risks involved in any investment in the firm. Some investors have joked that if they read prospectuses carefully, they would never dare buy any new issue. The appendix to this chapter is a possible prospectus for your fast-food business.

With the preliminary prospectus, the underwriter may attempt to "pre-sell" the issue or accept "indications of interest" from potential buyers.

After the securities commission has studied the preliminary prospectus, it notifies the company of any deficiencies and requests additions and changes. An amended prospectus is then filed, and so on, until the issue is approved. Once approved, the commission issues a receipt for the final prospectus and the issue can be legally sold.

With an approved final prospectus, the company and its underwriters now must finalize the issue price. To gauge how much the stock is worth, they work through a number of discounted cash-flow calculations like those described in Chapter 5. They look at the price-earnings ratios of the shares of the firm's principal competitors. They also use information gathered through their pre-selling efforts to gauge market interest in the issue.

The managers of the firm are eager to secure the highest possible price for their stock, but the underwriters are likely to be cautious because they will be left with any unsold stock if they overestimate investor demand. As a result, underwriters typically try to underprice the initial public offering. **Underpricing**, they argue, is needed to tempt investors to buy stock and to reduce the cost of marketing the issue to customers.

underpricing: Issuing securities whose offering price is set below true value of the security.

Underpricing represents a cost to the existing owners since the new investors are allowed to buy shares in the firm at a favourable price. The cost of underpricing may be very large. You can see this by looking at how the stock price moves up from the issue price in the days following the issue. For example, a study by Jog and Riding of 100 new issues on the Toronto Stock Exchange between 1971 and 1983 found average underpricing of 9.3 percent. For 116 new issues on the TSE between 1984 and 1987, Friedlan found average underpricing of 4.3 percent.[4] Similar evidence has been found for IPOs in the U.S., U.K., and other countries. Sometimes new issues are dramatically underpriced. For example, Boston Chicken stock was recently issued at $20 a share. On the first day after the issue the stock traded at $49. Investors who bought at the issue price received an immediate profit of 145 percent. On the other hand, not all IPOs are big winners. If you bought White Rose Crafts and Nursery Sales Limited common shares when it went public at $11 in March 1993, your shares would have been worth only $5 by August 1994, a 55 percent loss.[5]

---

[4] John Friedlan, "Understanding the IPO market," *CA Magazine*, March 1994:42–45.
[5] Research on the longer-term performance of IPOs, from 1 to 3 years from their initial offering, indicates that prices tend to fall. John Ritter in "The Long-Run Performance of Initial Public Offerings," *Journal of Finance* 46 (1991):3–27, found that on average over 1500 IPOs earned 15 percent lower return than comparable non-IPO stocks.

Finance in Action

The Drawbacks and Benefits of Going Public

The following is an excerpt from an article that describes the pros and cons of going public.

Stock market fever hit Canada's entrepreneurs last year, as dozens of owner-managers decided to raise capital through initial public offerings.

Looking at larger stock offerings of $5-million or more, 79 firms floated shares through IPOs in 1993 — more than in the previous five years combined. They raised a total of $3.7 billion — an average of $47 million each.

While the pace of IPOs has slackened a bit this year, experts still expect to see a healthy number of privately owned Canadian firms issue shares on the public markets in 1994....

[Paul Benson, national director of Ernst & Young's corporate finance practice,] recently published a booklet, The Public Decision, *that outlines the benefits and drawbacks of raising money on the stock markets.*

The advantages are well known. The money raised can be used to fuel the growth of a company and retained shares can be used to acquire other businesses (instead of paying cash). As well, publicly traded shares can be used as financial incentives for employees.

However, Mr. Benson also points out many disadvantages of going public, and in the process provides a balanced look at the phenomenon. The booklet would be extremely helpful to any company considering a public stock offering.

The top drawback: Once you go public, you lose your privacy and confidentiality. Suddenly, you must disclose highly sensitive information such as revenue and profit growth, company strategies and the compensation and incentives paid to top executives.

Because this information becomes publicly available, competitors along with investors will have access to it.

Mr. Benson said he recently advised a client not to go through a public offering. The firm, a Canadian manufacturer of telecommunications products, was experiencing annual revenue growth of 40 per cent, with strong profits.

While that level of financial performance would have made the company extremely attractive to investors, Mr. Benson noticed that barriers to entering the firm's business were extremely low.

"The capital requirements were small and qualified personnel were plentiful," he said. "If other companies saw how profitable the company was, they could have easily entered the same business."

Because the company was profitable, Mr. Benson advised it to get bank financing and use the money to expand into foreign markets. The company took the advice and established itself in Asia, Europe and the United States. Now, it would be much more difficult for competitors to enter the business and catch up.

"For that reason, they're taking another look at going public this year," Mr. Benson said. "They're now in a much better position to do it."

The Drawbacks and Benefits of Going Public (*continued*)

Other drawbacks to going public include:

- *Restrictions on management's decision-making abilities. While a privately held firm is free to act spontaneously, public companies must obtain the approval of the board of directors on major issues. Sometimes, they must even get a go-ahead from their shareholders.*

  Issues of this sort include the creation of employee compensation plans or the sale of significant assets.
- *Increased pressure for short-term performance. Investors judge a company's performance by the sales and profits that are racked up each quarter. That puts pressure on management to focus on the short term, instead of on long-range strategies.*

  Mr. Benson points out that many biotechnology companies, for example, are forced to seek regulatory approvals for clinical testing of their products before the research is fin- ished. *In some cases, they face delays and poor publicity when the results of the clinical tests are not as expected.*
- *Potential loss of control by the entrepreneur. If enough shares are issued, an outside investor or group of investors can wrest control of the company from the founders.*

Still, the benefits of IPOs are considerable. They can provide ample funds to finance research and development, expand to new markets or make a strategic acquisition.

And with investors ready to plow money into promising firms, many entrepreneurs will want to take a hard look at what the stock markets have to offer, Mr. Benson said.

"Investment dealers are interested in looking at any company that has a good story to tell, has strong growth prospects and may look attractive to public investors."

Source: Jerry Zeidenberg, "The Drawbacks and Benefits of Going Public," *The Globe and Mail Report on Business*, March 28, 1994.

Unfortunately, underpricing does not mean that anyone can become wealthy by buying stock in IPOs. If an issue is underpriced, everybody will want to buy it and the underwriters will not have enough stock to go around. You are therefore likely to get only a small share of these hot issues. If it is overpriced, other investors are unlikely to want it and the underwriter will be only too delighted to sell it to you. This phenomenon is known as the *winner's curse*.[6] It implies that, unless you can spot which issues are underpriced, you are likely to receive a small proportion of the cheap issues and a large proportion of the expensive ones. Since the dice are loaded against uninformed investors, they will play the game only if there is substantial underpricing on average.

● Example 14.1 Underpricing of IPOs and Investor Returns

Suppose that an investor will earn an immediate 10 percent return on underpriced IPOs and lose 5 percent on overpriced IPOs. But because of high

---

[6] The highest bidder in an auction is the participant who places the highest value on the auctioned object. Therefore, it is likely that the winning bidder has an overly optimistic assessment of true value. Winning the auction suggests that you have overpaid for the object — this is the winner's curse. In the case of IPOs, your ability to "win" an allotment of shares may signal that the stock is overpriced.

demand, you may get only half the shares you bid for when the issue is underpriced. Suppose you bid for $1000 of shares in two issues, one overpriced and the other underpriced. You are awarded the full $1000 of the overpriced issue, but only $500 worth of shares in the underpriced issue. The net gain on your two investments $(.10 \times \$500) - (.05 \times \$1000) = 0$. Your net profit is zero, despite the fact that, on average, IPOs are underpriced. You have suffered the winner's curse: you "win" a larger allotment of shares when they are overpriced.

SELF-TEST 14.2

What is the percentage profit earned by an investor who can identify the underpriced issues in Example 14.1? Who are such investors likely to be?

Underpricing is not the only cost to a new issue. There is also the underwriting spread. (Remember, underwriters make their profit by selling the issue at a higher price than they paid for it.) In addition, there are substantial administrative costs. For example, preparation of the registration statement and prospectus involves management, legal counsel, and accountants, as well as the underwriters and their advisers. These administrative costs can easily amount to several hundred thousand dollars.

Table 14.1 summarizes the costs of going public. The table includes the underwriting spread, administrative costs, and cost of underpricing. IPOs are especially costly for smaller firms. But even for the larger IPOs, total expenses average 16 percent of proceeds.

TABLE 14.1

Average expenses of 664 initial public offerings 1977–1982[a]

Value of Issue (millions of dollars)	Direct Costs (%)[b]	Average Initial Return (%)[b]	Total Costs (%)[c]
.1–1.9	19.5	26.9	31.7
2–3.9	17.4	20.7	24.9
4–5.9	14.8	12.6	20.9
6–9.9	12.3	9.0	17.9
10–120	9.3	10.3	16.3
All issues	14.0	14.8	21.2

Note: [a]The table includes only issues where there was a firm underwriting commitment.
[b]Direct costs and average initial return are expressed as a percentage of the issue price.
[c]Total costs are expressed as a percentage of the market price of the share.
Source: J. R. Ritter, "The Costs of Going Public," *Journal of Financial Economics*, 19(December 1987):269–283.

● **Example 14.2 Costs of an IPO**

When Microsoft went public in 1986, the sale was partly a primary issue (the company sold new shares to raise cash) and partly a secondary one (the company's original founders and backers cashed in some of their shares). The underwriters acquired a total of 2.8 million Microsoft shares for $19.69 each and sold them to the public at an offering price of $21. The underwriters' spread was therefore $21 – $19.69 = $1.31. The firm also paid $.5 million in legal fees and other costs. Within hours of public trading the stock price rose to $35.

Here are the costs of the Microsoft issue:

Direct Expenses	
Underwriting spread	2.8 million × $1.31 = $3.7 million
Other expenses	.5
Total direct expenses	$4.2 million

The firm and selling shareholders received 2.8 million × $19.69 – $.5 million = $54.6 million. Thus direct expenses absorbed 7.1 percent of the proceeds of the issue (that is, 4.2/(4.2 + 54.6) = .071).

In addition to these direct costs, we should also recognize the cost of underpricing. The market valued each share of Microsoft at $35, so the total market value of the shares was 2.8 million × $35 = $98 million. But the firm and selling shareholders received only $54.6 million. Thus a total of $98 – $54.6 = $43.4 million was absorbed by direct costs and the costs of underpricing. This was 44 percent of the market value of the shares.

SELF-TEST 14.3   Suppose that the underwriters acquired Microsoft shares for $25 each and sold them to the public at an offering price of $27. If all other features of the acquisition were unchanged (and the stock still sold for $35 a share), what would have been the direct costs of the issue and the costs of underpricing? What would have been the total costs as a proportion of the market value of the shares?

14.3 THE UNDERWRITERS

We have described underwriters as playing a triple role — providing advice, buying a new issue from the company, and reselling it to investors. Underwriters don't just help the company to make its initial public offering; they are called in whenever a company wishes to raise cash by selling securities to the public — commercial paper, debentures, preferred stock, and additional common stock and so on. We now need to step back and look more carefully at their activities.

If an issue is large, a group of underwriters, or *syndicate*, will usually get together to handle the sale. In this case one underwriter acts as syndicate manager and for this job keeps about 20 percent of the spread. A further 20 to 30 percent of the spread is used to pay those members of the group who buy the issue. The remaining 50 to 60 percent goes to the larger number of firms that provide the sales force for the issue.

The Investment Dealers Association (IDA) in Canada and the U.S. National Association of Security Dealers (NASD) require that the underwriting syndicate sell the issue at the stated offering price. However, if the issue obstinately remains unsold and the market price falls substantially below the offering price, the underwriters have no alternative but to break the syndicate. The members then dispose of their stock as best they can.

Most companies raise capital only occasionally, but underwriters are in the business all the time. Established underwriters are careful of their reputation and will not handle a new issue unless they believe the facts have been presented fairly to investors. Thus, in addition to handling the sale of an issue, the underwriters in effect give it their seal of approval. This implied endorsement may be worth quite a bit to a company that is coming to the market for the first time.

Underwriting is not always fun. On October 15, 1987, the British government finalized arrangements to sell its holding of British Petroleum (BP) shares at £3.30 a share. This huge issue involving more than $12 billion was the largest stock offering in history. It was underwritten by an international group of underwriters and simultaneously marketed in a number of countries. Four days after the underwriting arrangement was finalized, the October stock market crash occurred and stock prices nosedived. The underwriters appealed to the British government to cancel the issue but the government hardened its heart and pointed out that the underwriters knew the risks when they agreed to handle the sale.[7] By the closing date of the offer, the price of BP stock had fallen to £2.96, and the underwriters had lost more than $1 billion.

························
Who Are the Underwriters?

Since underwriters play such a crucial role in new issues, we should look at who they are. In Canada hundreds of investment banks, security dealers, and brokers are at least sporadically involved in underwriting. However, the market for the larger issues is dominated by the major investment dealers, which specialize in underwriting new issues, trading securities, providing financial research, and arranging mergers.[8] These firms enjoy great prestige, experience, and financial muscle. The big Canadian underwriters include RBC Dominion Securities, ScotiaMcLeod, Wood Gundy and Nesbitt Burns. Also prominent in Canada are several American underwriters, including Merrill Lynch and Goldman Sachs.

In Chapter 13 we pointed out that instead of issuing bonds in Canada, corporations issue eurobonds in London, which are then sold to investors outside of Canada. In addition, new equity issues by large multinational companies are increasingly marketed to investors throughout the world. Since these securities are sold in a number of countries, many of the major international banks are involved in underwriting the issues. For example, look at Table 14.2, which shows the names of the principal eurobond underwriters in the first 6 months of 1993. Notice that no Canadian firms are included in the list. However, Canadian underwriters are major players in the Canadian dollar denominated euro and foreign bond market. In Table 14.3 are the top 10 managing underwriters for the first six months of 1993. Canadian underwriters rank first, second and eighth.

TABLE 14.2

Managing underwriters, all public eurobond issues, January–June 1993 (figures in millions)

Goldman Sachs International	$21,751
Deutsche Bank	17,079
Morgan Stanley International	12,498
Merrill Lynch Capital Markets	12,124
CSFB/Credit Suisse	11,922
Salomon Brothers	11,245
Dresdner Bank	10,305
Union Bank of Switzerland	10,142
Industrial Bank of Japan	9,829
Nomura Securities	9,798
Daiwa Securities	8,664
J. P. Morgan	8,007
Lehman Brothers International	7,559
Paribas	7,218
S. G. Warburg Securities	6,602

Source: Euromoney, September 1993, p. 177.

Many companies develop a well-established relationship with a particular investment dealer, which underwrites the firm's security issues and provides other financial services. American utility holding companies are an exception,[9] for they are

---

[7] The government's only concession was to put a floor on the underwriters' losses by giving them the option to resell their stock to the government at £2.80 a share. The BP offering is described and analyzed in C. Muscarella and M. Vetsuypens, "The British Petroleum Stock Offering: An Application of Option Pricing," *Journal of Applied Corporate Finance* 1 (1989):74–80.

[8] The American equivalent to a Canadian investment dealer is an investment banker. But don't be confused — investment banks are not banks. They don't accept deposits nor do they make loans.

[9] A holding company is a firm whose only business is to hold the shares of other operating companies. Thus an electric utility holding company would own electric generating and distribution companies.

generally required to choose underwriters by competitive bids.[10] Utilities that are not organized as holding companies can do as they like. The competition is real. · Utilities almost always get two bids. For smaller issues, where fewer firms are needed to form a syndicate, four or five bids may be made.

TABLE 14.3

Managing underwriter, all Canadian dollar (C$) euro and global bonds, January–June 1993

	Total C$ (millions)	Nationality of Underwriter
Wood Gundy	2,950	Canadian
ScotiaMcLeod	2,862.5	Canadian
Goldman Sachs	1,850	American
Merrill Lynch	1,762.5	American
IBJ International	1,557.5	Japanese
Swiss Bank Corporation	1,375	Swiss
Banque Paribas	1,350	French
RBC Dominion	1,287.5	Canadian
Hambros	1,255	British
Salomon Brothers	1,000	American

Source: International Financing Review, June 19, 1993, p. 66.

 ## 14.4 LISTING THE NEW ISSUE

When a firm makes its initial public offering and transforms from being a privately held company to a publicly held company, it must decide where its newly issued shares will be traded. Obviously, the stocks will be bought and sold in the stock market, but which one? There are two types of stock markets: organized exchanges and over-the-counter markets.[11] The organized exchanges, such as the Toronto Stock Exchange, are physical entities where stocks are bought and sold through auctions. The price at which the stock is traded is determined through an auction that involves a number of dealers, acting as agents for investors or on behalf of their employer, who bid for the shares.

In contrast, the over-the-counter stock market is a loose network of securities traders who are involved in the buying and selling of stocks. A few of the traders are broker-dealers who are willing to buy or sell shares. The rest are brokers who trade with the dealers on behalf of investors wishing to buy or sell shares. The broker and dealer negotiate the price at which the shares are traded.

In Canada, there are five stock exchanges: (1) Toronto Stock Exchange; (2) Montreal Stock Exchange; (3) Vancouver Stock Exchange; (4) Alberta Stock Exchange and (5) Winnipeg Stock Exchange. You can see in Table 14.4 that the Toronto Stock Exchange leads all of the exchanges in terms of both trading value and trading volume. Both the Alberta and Winnipeg exchanges are regional exchanges, specializing in the stocks of local companies. Together, these small exchanges account for less than 1 percent of the total value of stocks traded in Canada.

Listing the stock on an organized exchange provides a readily available ("continuous") market for the stock. Orders for the stock are executed quickly and efficiently at prices set by competitive auction. In contrast, transactions in the Canadian over-the-counter market tend to take longer to execute and prices are

---

[10] When a holding company faces "unsettled market conditions," the securities regulator may relent and allow negotiation.

[11] See Chapter 5 for a brief discussion of how a stock exchange operates. For a detailed description of trading process used by the Toronto Stock Exchange see Sharpe, Alexander and Fowler, *Investments, 1st Canadian edition*, (Toronto: Prentice-Hall, 1993).

TABLE 14.4

Trading activity on
Canadian stock
exchanges

Stock Exchange	Trading Activity, November 1994	
	Value of Shares (millions of dollars)	Volume of Shares (millions of shares)
Toronto Stock Exchange	$13,128.0	1,120.3
Montreal Stock Exchange	2,444.3	197.8
Vancouver Stock Exchange	316.2	380.0
Alberta Stock Exchange	150.5	184.2

Source: TSE Review, Toronto Stock Exchange; *Monthly Review,* Montreal Exchange; *Review,* Vancouver Stock Exchange; *Monthly Review,* Alberta Stock Exchange.

determined through negotiation rather than auction. The competitiveness of the over-the-counter market has increased with the introduction of a computerized quotation system, the Canadian Dealing Network (CDN). The CDN provides up-to-date information on the current prices offered by dealers and statistics for the previous day. However, the market is still relatively small and primitive. In the U.S., the National Association of Security Dealers Automated Quotation (NASDAQ) system has made the U.S. over-the-counter market a major market for trading securities. It is a large and highly competitive market for trading stocks.

If organized exchanges provide easier and more efficient means of trading securities, why does the Canadian over-the-counter market exist? Firms must pay fees and meet minimum standards and reporting requirements to qualify for a stock exchange listing. The fees and listing requirements vary among exchanges. Table 14.5 contains a summary of the requirements for the Toronto Stock Exchange. The big and more prestigious the exchange, the more stringent are the listing requirements and the greater is the listing fee. For many small and some not so small companies, the cost of listing is not worth the added liquidity of the organized exchange.

TABLE 14.5

The Toronto Stock
Exchange's minimum
listing requirements for
industrial companies

Financial Requirements

(a) (i)   net tangible assets of $1,000,000;
    (ii) earnings of at least $100,000, before taxes and extraordinary items, in the fiscal year immediately preceding the filing of the listing application;
    (iii) pre-tax cash flow of $400,000, in the fiscal year immediately preceding the filing of the listing application; and
    (iv) adequate working capital and capitalization to carry on the business.

OR

(b) (i)   net tangible assets of $5,000,000;
    (ii) evidence, satisfactory to the Exchange, indicating a reasonable likelihood of future profitability; and
    (iii) adequate working capital and capitalization to carry on the business.

OR

(c) (i)   earnings of at least $200,000, before taxes and extraordinary items, in the fiscal year immediately preceding the filing of the listing application;
    (ii) pre-tax cash flow of $500,000 in the fiscal year immediately preceding the filing of the listing applications; and
    (iii) adequate working capital and capitalization to carry on the business.

Public Distribution

At least 1,000,000 freely-tradeable shares having an aggregate market value of $2,000,000 must be held by at least 300 public holders, each holding one board lot or more.

TABLE 14.5 *(continued)*	**Public Distribution** *(continued)*

Public Distribution *(continued)*

In circumstances where public distribution is achieved other than by way of a public offering, e.g., by way of a reverse takeover, share exchange offer of the other distribution, the Exchange may require evidence that a satisfactory market in the company's securities will develop. Prior trading on another market or sponsorship by a TSE member, which will assist in maintaining an orderly market, may satisfy this condition.

Management

The management of an applicant company shall be an important factor in the consideration of a listing application. In addition to the factors set out under "The Quality of Management of Listed Companies," the Exchange will consider the background and expertise of management in the context of the business of the company.

Sponsorship or Affiliation

While not mandatory, sponsorship of an applicant company by a member firm of the Exchange, or an affiliation with an established enterprise, can be a significant factor in the determination of the suitability of the company for listing, particularly where the company only narrowly meets the prescribed minimum listing requirements. Consideration will be given to the nature, as well as the existence, of the sponsorship or affiliation.

Other Factors

The Exchange may, in its discretion, take into account any factors it considers to be relevant in assessing the merits of a listing application and may refuse to grant an application notwithstanding that the prescribed minimum listing requirements are met.

Quality of Management of Listed Companies

The Toronto Stock Exchange seeks to provide the general public and its listed companies with a well-regulated, orderly, continuous auction market.

The Exchange reserves the right to exercise discretion in considering all factors related to the management of a company in order to determine the acceptability of that company for original listing and thereafter for continued listing. The Exchange's discretion will be exercised at all times in a manner which is reasonable and consistent with regulatory and statutory requirements.

1. Without in any way limiting the generality of the foregoing, the Exchange, in pursuit of its goal of public protection and to promote integrity and honesty in the capital markets shall require that any document submitted to the Exchange constitutes full, true and plain disclosure; and
2. may review the conduct of an officer, director, promoter, major shareholder or any other person or company or a combination of any of the above who in the Exchange's opinion holds sufficient of the company's securities to materially affect control, in order to satisfy itself that:
   a) the business of the company is and will be conducted with integrity and in the best interests of its security holders and the investing public; and
   b) the rules and regulations of the Exchange and all other regulatory bodies having jurisdiction are and will be complied with.

Source: Toronto Stock Exchange.

As the firm grows, it may decide to list its stock on an organized exchange or move from a smaller exchange to a larger one. A small, highly speculative company might begin trading as a publicly held company in the over-the-counter market or with a listing on the Vancouver Stock Exchange. As the company grows, it might also list on both the Montreal and Toronto Stock Exchanges. If a company assesses that U.S. investors will be interested in the stock, it might then add a listing on the NASDAQ. For example, Cinar Films Inc., best known for its animated films, went public in September 1993 and at that time listed its stock on both the

Montreal and Toronto Stock Exchanges. In March 1994, Cinar decided to list its stock on the NASDAQ as well to broaden its investor base. A large Canadian company might elect to list its stock on the "Big Board," the New York Stock Exchange, to increase its access to American and other investors. In April 1994, the Bank of Montreal announced its plans to list its common shares on the New York Stock Exchange. To do so, it must register its stock with the U.S. Securities and Exchange Commission. According to a spokeswoman at the Bank of Montreal, the initial fee for listing on the NYSE is $150,000, while the annual fee of $35,000 is required. Additional legal and accounting fees were estimated to bring the annual costs to $145,000.[12]

In summary, a stock exchange listing facilitates continuous trading in a stock and hence provides a continuous, competitively determined price for the shares. Knowing the pricing of existing shares, it is easier for a firm to price and sell more shares of its stock. In the next section, we examine the process of floating additional securities.

14.5 GENERAL CASH OFFERS BY PUBLIC COMPANIES

After the initial public offering a successful firm will continue to grow and from time to time it will need to raise more money by issuing stock or bonds. Any issue of securities needs to be formally approved by the firm's board of directors. If a stock issue requires an increase in the company's authorized capital, it also needs the consent of the stockholders. For additional issues of debentures and preferred shares, approval of existing security holders may be required.

rights issue: Issue of securities offered only to current stockholders.

Public companies can issue securities either by making a general cash offer to investors at large or by making a **rights issue**, which is limited to selling common shares to existing shareholders. In the latter case, the company offers the shareholders the opportunity, or *right*, to buy more shares at an "attractive" price. In this section we concentrate on the mechanics of general cash offers, which is used for virtually all debt issues and many equity issues. In the next section we describe rights issues.

General Cash Offers and the POP System

general cash offer: Sale of securities open to all investors by an already-public company.

When a public company makes a **general cash offer** of debt or equity, it goes through much the same procedure as when it first went public. In other words, it registers the issue with the securities commission and then sells it to an underwriter (or a syndicate of underwriters), which in turn offers the securities to the public. The procedure is fairly similar when a company issues a eurobond but, since the bond is not sold publicly in Canada, it is not registered with a Canadian securities commission.

The same procedures used in the initial public offering are used to distribute general cash offers. An underwriter or syndicate of underwriters is engaged to market the issue. The securities may be sold through a firm commitment arrangement or sold on a best-efforts basis.

In Canada, a variant of the firm commitment, known as a *bought deal*, has become quite popular. You will recall that with a firm commitment the underwriter contracts to pay the issuer a specified amount of money for the securities. Despite the commitment, certain events can trigger an escape clause for the underwriter that terminates the underwriter's responsibility to purchase the issue. For example, if the stock market crashes during the pre-selling period, the underwriter may

---

[12] Jacquie McNish, "B of M Eyes Fall NYSE Debut," *The Globe and Mail*, April 28, 1994.

terminate the contract. This escape clause is known as a "market out" clause. In a bought deal, the market out clause is removed and the underwriter has no escape from the contract and must pay the issuer of the securities for the specified amount. To reduce the risk of a significant change in market conditions, an underwriter of a bought deal quickly sells the issue to large investors. Consequently, critics of bought deals claim that small retail customers are denied access to many attractive new issues because they are already sold to big institutional investors. Others are concerned that underwriters take on excessive risks by giving up the market out clause. In a study comparing bought deal to the standard firm commitment deals, evidence was found that bought deals tend to be used to sell smaller sized issues, suggesting that underwriters reduce their risk by reducing their exposure to losses.[13]

The process of putting together a prospectus and getting it approved by the various securities commissions is costly and takes time, often more than 2 months. Recognizing that information about large, well-established companies that issue securities regularly is easily available to investors, the Ontario Securities Commission implemented a streamlined reporting and registration system called the *Prompt Offering Qualification System*, or **POP System**.[14] A qualifying company wishing to make a securities offering files a short-form version of a prospectus that is processed in about one week by the OSC. To ensure adequate disclosure about the company, the company is required to file financial information annually with the securities commission. Thus the POP system enables large, regularly reporting companies to make public offerings of common shares, preferred shares and investment grade non-convertible debt securities in a low cost, timely way.

Well-established companies are not restricted to the capital market in Canada; they can also raise money in the United States and offshore capital markets. The Canadian capital market cannot absorb large securities issues, so Canadian firms are often forced to use international capital markets, especially for large debt issues. We saw in Chapter 13 that can mean the company makes a foreign bond issue in another country's market and is subject to the laws and customs of that country. Alternatively, it can make an issue of eurobonds, which are offered internationally, but payable in domestic Canadian currency. Canadian firms now have a third option: issue securities in Canada and the United States under the Multi Jurisdictional Disclosure System (MJDS). Under MJDS, large Canadian and U.S. issuers can make public offerings of their securities in the other country using the disclosure documents required at home.

Magna International Inc. took advantage of MJDS in 1991 to issue equity in the United States and Canada. With MJDS, Magna avoided the normal U.S. SEC review of its prospectus because the prospectus had already been accepted by the OSC and other provincial regulators. Magna officials reported that the new system gave them faster and less expensive access to the U.S. market.[15]

POP System: A procedure that allows qualifying firms to file a short-form version of a prospectus with Ontario Securities Commission to speed up the issuing process.

[13] Lawrence Schwartz, "Bought Deals: The Devil that You Know," *Canadian Investment Review*, Vol. 7, no. 1 (Spring 1994):21–26.
[14] The U.S. system for streamlined securities offerings available is *shelf registration*. With shelf registration, the company files a single registration statement covering financing plans for up to 2 years in the future. The actual issues can then be sold to the public with scant additional paperwork, whenever the firm needs cash or thinks market conditions are advantageous for the firm.
[15] K. Michael Edwards, "Canadian Equity Markets: Taking Advantage of Change," *Canadian Business Review* (Spring 1992) pp.26–28.

The Bank of Montreal benefitted from MJDS when it decided to list its common stock on the New York Stock Exchange. In the past, Canadian banks have been reluctant to list their stock in the U.S. because the SEC rules required greater disclosure of corporate information than did Canadian securities regulators. Under MJDS, the Bank of Montreal must only satisfy Canadian disclosure requirement and avoids revealing additional information.[16]

....
Costs of the General Cash Offer

Whenever a firm makes a cash offer, it incurs substantial administrative costs. Also, the firm needs to compensate the underwriters by selling them securities below the price that they expect to receive from investors. Figure 14.1 shows the average underwriting spread and administrative costs for stock issues in the United States.[17] Costs are similar in Canada.

The figure clearly shows the economies of scale in issuing securities. Costs may absorb 15 percent of a $1 million issue but only 4 percent of a $500 million issue. This occurs because a large part of the issue cost is fixed.

FIGURE 14.1
Issue costs of general cash offers of common stock as a percentage of the proceeds.

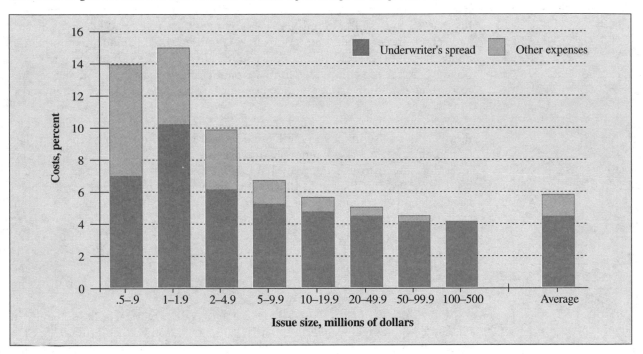

Source: Based on data from C.W. Smith, "Alternative Methods for Raising Capital: Rights versus Underwritten Offerings," *Journal of Financial Economics*, 5:273–307 (December 1977), table 1, p. 277.

SELF-TEST 14.4
•••••••••••••••

Use Figure 14.1 to compare the costs of 10 issues of $15 million of stock versus one issue of $150 million.

---

[16] Jacquie McNish, "B of M Eyes Fall NYSE Debut," *The Globe and Mail,* April 28, 1994.
[17] These figures do not capture all administrative costs. For example, they do not include management time spent on the issue.

Issue costs are lower for debt securities than for equity — the costs for a large debt issue are less than 1 percent — but show the same economies of scale. Debt issues are cheaper because administrative costs are somewhat less and because underwriters require compensation for the greater risk they take in buying and reselling stock.

Finance in Action

Issuing Securities

* *

The following article describes a recent $500.5-million stock issue by Canadian Pacific, including information about the specifics of the deal, the planned use of the funds to be raised, and general analysis of the financial situation of the company.

MONTREAL — Buoyed by its slowly improving operating results and a lively stock market, Canadian Pacific Ltd. is coming to market with a $500.5-million stock issue.

The Montreal-based conglomerate, which has businesses in the transportation, energy and real estate sectors, said it will sell 22 million common shares at $22.75 each to raise net proceeds of about $484-million.

"This issue increases our flexibility and puts our balance sheet on a sound footing at a time when the economy is recovering and our businesses' prospects are improving," said chief executive William Stinson.

CP is selling the shares to a group of underwriters led by RBC Dominion Securities Inc. and Nesbitt Thomson Inc. in a so-called bought deal. In other words, all the shares are sold in one chunk to a group of underwriters who then resell them to the public.

The other, less preferable way for a company to sell a new issue of stock is in instalments, usually three. CP used this method to sell its ailing Canadian Pacific Forest Products Ltd. subsidiary to a group of underwriters last year for about $700-million. It will

BIG SHARE ISSUES	
1993-95, $million	
International Semi-Tech*	$795
Horsham**	550
Canadian Pacific	501
Nova	500
CIBC	391
Air Canada	250
Cambridge Shopping Centres	250
Bombardier	210
TVX	201
Fletcher-Challenge	198

*Sold by instalment
**24-year debenture

receive three separate payments for the shares by 1995.

Zaheer Khan of Canadian Bond Rating Service Ltd. in Montreal said the fact that CP was able to arrange a bought deal for such a substantial amount of money suggests investors want stock in the company. "Not many other companies do a straight deal of this size," he said. "That proves there's a good market appetite for CP shares."

However, about 10 per cent of the 2,091,626 CP shares traded on the TSE yesterday changed hands at $22.62. The stock lost $1 on the day to close at the $22.75 issue price.

Issuing Securities *(continued)*
··

The most recent bought deal of this magnitude was a $500-million issue announced in January by Calgary-based oil and gas concern Nova Corp. to help it finance the expansion of its natural gas pipeline.

For its part, CP will use the money to pay for additions to major capital assets, property and equipment in its core businesses, and to reduce debt. As of Sept. 30, 1993, the long-term debt was $6.5-billion.

The company's debt-to-equity ratio is currently 50-50. CP spokesman Graeme McMurray said that because of the issue, the ratio "will certainly improve."

CP, which has been suffering crushing financial problems in recent years, mainly because of the performance of CP Forest, turned out a reasonable operating profit in 1993 and says its performance this year will be even better because of a stronger economy and its own efforts to reduce costs.

CP cut its losses for the year ended Dec. 31 to $190.6-million or 60 cents a share from $478.3-million or $1.50 in 1992.

Operating profit soared to $915.1-million from $163.2-million a year earlier, mainly through better results at CP Rail Systems, its freight railway subsidiary.

"Its recovery seems to be holding, certainly in the CP Rail," Mr. McMurray said.

The company had been under pressure to focus on a smaller number of core businesses. It also owns equity in waste-management company Laidlaw Inc. of Burlington, Ont., and long-distance telephone company Unitel Communications Inc. of Toronto.

CP will have 341 million shares outstanding after the issue, which, subject to regulatory approval, is expected to close by March 10.

The company said a short-form preliminary prospectus will be filed with securities commissions and relevant regulatory authorities in Canada by tomorrow.

The shares are only being sold in Canada.

Source: Ann Gibbon, "CP Issue To Raise $500.5-million," The Globe and Mail Report on Business, February 15, 1994, p. B15.

Market Reaction to Stock Issues

Because stock issues usually throw a sizable number of new shares onto the market, it is widely believed that they must temporarily depress the stock price. If the proposed issue is very large, this price pressure may, it is thought, be so severe as to make it almost impossible to raise money. If so, the firm faces severe capital rationing.

This belief in price pressure implies that a new issue depresses the stock price temporarily below its true value. However, that view doesn't appear to fit very well with the notion of market efficiency. If the stock price falls solely because of increased supply, then that stock would offer a higher return than comparable stocks and investors should be attracted to it as bees to honey.

Economists who have studied new issues of common stock have generally found that the announcement of the issue does result in a decline in the stock price. For industrial issues in the United States this decline amounts to about 3 percent.[18]

[18] See, for example, P. Asquith and D. W. Mullins, "Equity Issues and Offering Dilution," *Journal of Financial Economics* 15 (January–February 1986):61–90; R. W. Masulis and A. N. Korwar, "Seasoned Equity Offerings: An Empirical Investigation," *Journal of Financial Economics* 15 (January–February

While this may not sound overwhelming, such a price drop can amount to a huge issue cost. Suppose that a company with a market value of equity of $5 billion announces its intention to issue $500 million of additional equity and thereby causes the stock price to drop by 3 percent. The loss in value is .03 × $5 billion, or $150 million. That's 30 percent of the amount of money raised (.30 × $500 million = $150 million).

What's going on here? Is the price of the stock simply depressed by the prospect of the additional supply? Possibly, but here is an alternative explanation.

Suppose managers (who have better information about the firm than other investors) know that their stock is undervalued. If the company sells new stock at this low price, it will give the new shareholders a good deal at the expense of the old shareholders. In these circumstances managers might be prepared to forgo the new investment rather than sell shares at too low a price.

If managers know that the stock is *overvalued*, the position is reversed. If the company sells new shares at the high price, it will help its existing shareholders at the expense of the new ones. Managers might be prepared to issue stock even if the new cash were just put in the bank.

Of course investors are not stupid. They can predict that managers are more likely to issue stock when they think it is overvalued and therefore they mark the price of the stock down accordingly. Thus the decline in the price of the stock at the time of the issue may have nothing to do with the increased supply. Instead, the issue may simply be a signal that managers believe the stock is overpriced by the market.[19]

The Dilution Fallacy

Conventional wisdom is that firms should not issue more stock when the stock price is below book value, for that will result in *dilution*. The imagined dangers of this are dramatized by the sad tale of Quangle Hats. Quangle's profitability is as follows:

Book equity	$100,000
Number of shares	1000
Book value per share	$100,000/1000 = $100
Net earnings	$8000
Earnings per share	$8000/1000 = $8.00
Price-earnings ratio	10
Stock price	10 × $8.00 = $80.00
Total market value	$80,000

The total amount of money that has been put up by Quangle's shareholders is $100,000, or $100 per share. But that investment is earning only $8 per share — a book return of 8 percent. Investors evidently regard this as inadequate, for they are willing to pay only $80 per share for Quangle's stock.

Now suppose that Quangle raises $10,000 by issuing 125 additional shares at the market price of $80 per share, and suppose also that this $10,000 is invested

1986):91–118; W. H. Mikkelson and M. M. Partch, "Valuation Effects of Security Offerings and the Issuance Process," *Journal of Financial Economics* 15 (January–February 1986):31–60. There appears to be a smaller price decline for utility issues. Also Marsh observed a smaller decline for rights issues in the United Kingdom; see P. R. Marsh, "Equity Rights Issues and the Efficiency of the U.K. Stock Market," *Journal of Finance* 34 (September 1979):839–862.

[19] This explanation was developed in S. C. Myers and N. S. Majluf, "Corporate Financing and Investment Decisions When Firms Have Information that Investors Do Not Have," *Journal of Financial Economics* 13 (1984):187–222.

to earn a return of 8 percent. In that case, we would expect investors to continue to pay $10 each for $1 of Quangle's earnings. Now we have:

	Before the Issue	After the Issue
Book equity	$100,000	$110,000
Number of shares	1000	1125
Book value per share	$100,000/1000 = $100	$110,000/1125 = $97.78
Net earnings	$8000	8% of book equity = $8800
Earnings per share	$8000/1000 = $8.00	$8800/1125 = $7.822
Price-earnings ratio	10	10
Stock price	10 × $8.00 = $80.00	10 × $7.822 = $78.22
Total market value	$80,000	$88,000

Notice that by selling stock below book value, Quangle has *diluted* value per share from $100 to $97.78. Also, the stock price has fallen from $80 to $78.22.

But there are two things wrong with our example. First, we assumed that investors could be tricked into paying $80 for shares shortly destined to be worth $78.22. Actually, if Quangle wishes to raise $100,000, it will have to offer shares *worth* $100,000.

There is a second thing wrong with our example: we never questioned Quangle's decision to expand. It is raising $10,000 and getting only $8000 in additional market value. In other words, the market's verdict is that expansion has an NPV of –$2000. It is no wonder that the original shareholders suffer a loss of $2000.

What if the new investment earned a 10 percent return? In that case the issue of shares would cause the firm's market value to increase by $10,000 to $90,000 and the earnings per share and stock price would be unchanged.

The point is simple. There is no harm whatsoever in selling stock at prices below book value per share as long as investors know that you can earn an adequate rate of return on the new money. If the firm has good projects and needs equity capital to finance them, then dilution should not bar it from going to the market. Conversely, if investors don't believe you can earn an adequate return, then the stock price will fall regardless of whether you sell shares above or below book value.

SELF-TEST 14.5

Suppose that in a mistaken attempt to avoid dilution, the firm funds the project with a return on equity of 8 percent by issuing $100,000 of debt rather than equity. Show that book value per share is unchanged but that price per share must nevertheless fall. *Hint*: What must be the *market value* of the new debt issue? What is the *market value* of the project?

14.6 RIGHTS ISSUES

We have now looked at what happens when firms sell their securities to the public at large: now we must look at what happens when they restrict the offer to existing shareholders through a rights offering. In some countries rights issues are the most common or only method for issuing stock. In Canada they are less common. For example, in 1993, the Toronto Stock Exchange reported that over $9500 million of new equity was raised through general cash offerings, but only $7.6 million was raised through rights offerings.

Firms' articles of incorporation often state that shareholders have a pre-emptive right to subscribe to new offerings. Such a provision reinforces the fact that shareholders, as owners of the business, are entitled to anything of value that the company may distribute, including the potentially valuable opportunity to buy new issues of securities. The pre-emptive right is usually applied to common shares, convertible securities, and voting preferreds but not to issues of debt. Second, they do not apply to common stock that is issued as payment for a merger.

How Rights Issues Work

subscription price: Price to be paid per share in a rights offering.

In November 1994, Breakwater Resources issued over 239 million common shares through a rights issue. The preliminary stages of the issue were similar to those for any other public issue, including filing a prospectus with the securities commissions. The major difference lay in the selling procedures. Shareholders of record (that is, those listed on the company's books as share owners) on November 28, 1994, were sent "rights certificates" showing that they owned 1 right for each share they held. Each right entitled a shareholder to buy one additional share at a **subscription (or issue) price** of $0.10 at any time before December 19, 1994. To take advantage of the offer, the shareholder simply had to exercise the right by completing the subscription form on the rights certificate and forwarding it with payment to the firm's subscription agent.

Shareholders could either sell, exercise, or throw away these rights. The rights were listed for trading on the Toronto Stock Exchange. Those who didn't sell should have postponed any exercise decision until the expiry date. At that point, they should have taken advantage of the opportunity to buy the stock at $0.10 if, and only if, the stock price was higher than $0.10.

To guard against the danger that the price might end up below the subscription price, Breakwater arranged for the issue to be underwritten. Instead of actually buying the issue as in a cash offer, the underwriter, Canaccord Capital Corp., was paid a management fee or standby fee of $50,000.[20] In return, they stood ready to buy any unsubcribed or "residual" shares for the subscription price. In addition, Canaccord was able to deduct a take-up fee of $.0025 from the subscription price, to a maximum of $2,500 per subscriber. The underwriters were protected by a market-out clause, allowing them out of the standby arrangement in the event of significant adverse changes in market conditions.

As it turned out, Breakwater's shares closed out at $0.105 on the December 19, 1994 expiry date, making it profitable for investors to exercise the rights.

How does the rights issue affect the price of a stock? If you owned one share of Breakwater shortly before the rights issue, your share would have been worth about $0.155. The Breakwater offer gives you the opportunity to purchase one additional share for $0.10. If you buy the share immediately, your holding increases to 2 shares and, other things being equal, the value of the 2 shares is $0.155 + $.10 = $0.255. The price per share after the issue would no longer be $0.155, but $0.255/2 = $0.1275.

The only difference between the old $0.155 share and the new $0.1275 share is that the former carries the rights to subscribe to the new issue. Therefore, the old shares are generally called *cum-rights* or *rights-on* and the new shares are termed *ex-rights* shares. The $0.0275 difference in price between the two shares represents the price of one right. We can confirm that this is the correct price of the right by imagining a second investor who has no stock in Breakwater but who

[20] You can think of standby underwriting as providing shareholders with an option. In return for paying the standby fee, they can sell their stock to the underwriters at the issue price.

wishes to acquire some. One way to do this would be to buy a right at $0.0275 and then exercise it at a further cost of $0.10. The total cost of $0.1275 is the same outlay required to buy one of the new shares directly.

You might find it convenient to use the following formulas for calculating the ex-rights price of a share and the value of a right. If N is the number of rights required to buy one share, the theoretical ex-rights share price is

$$\text{Ex-rights price} = \frac{1}{N+1} (N \times \text{rights-on price} + \text{subscription price})$$

The rights-on price is the price of a share before the rights are issued.

The value of one right can be calculated with either the rights-on price or with the ex-rights price:

$$\text{Value of one right} = \frac{\text{rights-on price} - \text{subscription price}}{N+1}$$

or

$$\text{Value of one right} = \frac{\text{Ex-rights price} - \text{subscription price}}{N}$$

● Example 14.3 Rights Issue

Easy Writer Word Processing Company has 1 million shares outstanding, selling at $20 a share. To finance the development of a new software package, it plans a rights issue, allowing one new share to be purchased for each 10 shares currently held. The purchase price will be $10 a share. How many shares will be issued? How much money will be raised? What will be the stock price after the rights issue? What is the value of one right?

The firm will issue one new share for every 10 old ones, or 100,000 shares. So shares outstanding will rise to 1.1 million. The firm will raise $10 \times 100,000 = $1 million. Therefore, the total value of the firm will increase from $20 million to $21 million, and the stock price will fall to $21 million/1.1 million shares = $19.09 per share. To check the ex-rights price, we can use the formula:

$$\text{Ex-rights price} = \frac{1}{N+1} (N \times \text{rights-on price} + \text{subscription price})$$

$$= \frac{1}{10+1} (10 \times 20 + 10) = \$19.09$$

The value of one right is:

$$\text{Value of one right} = \frac{\text{rights-on price} - \text{subscription price}}{N+1}$$

$$= \frac{20 - 10}{10 + 1} = \$.91$$

As before, the difference between the rights-on price and the ex-rights price is equal to the value of one right: $20 - $19.09 = $.91.

Does the subscription price matter to the rights offering? No, as long as it is less than the stock price. The company can raise the same amount of money on a variety of terms. Suppose that Easy Writer set its subscription price at $5 per share, rather than $10. In this case, it would have to sell twice as many shares at half the price to raise the same total amount. To raise $1 million dollars, it must sell 200,000 shares: $1 million/$5 per share = 200,000 shares. How many rights will it take to purchase one new share? Divide the number of existing outstanding shares by the number of new shares to be sold:

$$\text{Number of rights needed to buy one new share} = \frac{\text{number of old shares}}{\text{number of new shares}}$$

$$= \frac{1,000,000}{200,000} = 5 \text{ rights}$$

Five rights plus $5 is needed to purchase one new share. The ex-rights share price is

$$\text{Ex-rights share price} = \frac{1}{5+1} (5 \times 20 + 5) = \$17.50$$

The value of one right is 20 – 17.50 = $2.50.

Do shareholders prefer one of these rights plans over the other? Consider a shareholder who owns 10 shares of Easy Writer. In Table 14.6, you can see that the value of the shareholder's holdings is the same under both rights plans. Although the ex-rights share price is lower when the subscription price is lower, the value of each right is higher. The net effect is shareholder's wealth is unchanged. After all, the subscription price cannot affect the real plant and equipment owned by the company or the proportion of these assets to which each shareholder is entitled.

TABLE 14.6		One New Share for 10 Rights and $10	One New Share for 5 Rights and $5
Subscription price in a rights offering does not affect shareholder's wealth	*Before Issue*		
	Number of shares held	10	10
	Price per share (rights-on)	$20	$20
	Value of holding	$200	$200
	After Issue		
	Number of new shares	1	2
	Cash spent on new shares	$10	$2 × 5 = $10
	Total value of holding	$210	$210
	Total number of shares	11	12
	Ex-rights share price	210/11 = $19.09	210/12 = $17.50
	Value of one right	20 – 19.09 = $0.91	20 – 17.50 = $2.50

The only thing a firm ought to worry about in setting the terms of the rights issue is the possibility of setting the subscription price too high. If it is set too high, the stock price might fall below it and shareholders will not take up their rights and the whole issue is torpedoed. You can avoid this danger by arranging a standby agreement with the underwriter. But standby agreements tend to be expensive. It may be cheaper just to set the issue price low enough to prevent the possibility of failure.

....

The Choice Between a Cash Offer and a Rights Issue

You now know about the two principal forms of public issue — the cash offer to all investors and the rights issue to existing shareholders. The former method is used for almost all debt issues and unseasoned stock issues. Rights issues are largely restricted to seasoned stock issues.

One essential difference between the two methods is that in a rights offering the issue price is largely irrelevant. Shareholders can sell their new stock or their rights in a free market. Therefore, they can expect to receive a fair price. In a cash offer, however, the issue price may be important. If the company sells stocks for less than the market would bear, the buyer has made a profit at the expense of the existing shareholders. The risk of this underpricing is greatest for initial public offerings. Unfortunately, a rights issue is not a feasible alternative for initial public offerings.

Although rights offerings have much lower flotation costs, cash offerings are more common. It does not seem sensible that rights offerings are used so infrequently. Perhaps there are hidden costs. However, until they are uncovered, we don't think you should rule out rights issues.

14.7 THE PRIVATE PLACEMENT

Whenever a company makes a public offering of shares or debt, it is required to obtain approval from the securities commissions for the jurisdictions in which it sells the securities. It can avoid this costly process by selling the issue privately. In Canada, this can be done if the securities are sold to "exempt-list purchasers." This group includes financial institutions such as banks, trust companies, insurance companies, and pension funds. Other exempt-list purchasers are senior officers of the firm making the offering or their close relatives, buyers of an issue sold to fewer than 25 investors who are acting as principals, and individual investors who purchase at least $150,000 worth of the issue. All of these exempt purchasers are considered to be "sophisticated investors," knowledgeable enough to not need the protection of the securities commission.

private placement: Sale of securities to a limited number of investors without a public offering.

Private placement allows firms to avoid the costly disclosure required for a public offer. However, one disadvantage of a private placement is that the investor must not resell the debt for a minimum of 6 months. Without restrictions on resale, the private placement system could be abused as a sneaky way to make a public offer at low cost: privately place the shares with exempt investors who then turn around and sell the issue publicly. The restriction on resale is less important to institutions such as life insurance companies, which invest huge sums of money in corporate debt for the long haul.

Until recently, the restrictions on resale of privately placed securities in the U.S. were considerably more stringent than in Canada. Consequently, U.S. investors required a higher rate of return to compensate for the lack of liquidity of a private placement. However, in 1990, the SEC relaxed its restrictions in Rule 144a, which allows large financial institutions (known as *qualified institutional buyers*) to trade privately placed securities among themselves, lowering the required rate of return. Canadian companies have taken advantage of lower cost to sell corporate debt in the U.S. private placement market.

As you would expect, it costs less to arrange a private placement than to make a public issue. That might not be so important for the very large issues where costs are less significant, but it is a particular advantage for companies making smaller issues.

Another advantage of the private placement is that the debt contract can be custom-tailored for firms with special problems or opportunities. Also, if the firm wishes later to change the terms of the debt, it is much simpler to do this with a private placement where only a few investors are involved.

Therefore, it is not surprising that private placements occupy a particular niche in the corporate debt market, namely, loans to small and medium-sized firms. These are the firms that face the highest costs in public issues, that require the most detailed investigation, and that may require specialized, flexible loan arrangements.

Of course these advantages are not free. Lenders in private placements have to be compensated for the risks they face and for the costs of research and negotiation. They also have to be compensated for holding an asset that is not easily resold. All these factors are rolled into the interest rate paid by the firm. It is difficult to generalize about the differences in interest rates between private placements and public issues, but a typical yield differential is on the order of half a percentage point.

14.8 SUMMARY

1. Infant companies raise venture capital to carry them through to the point at which they can make their first public issue of stock. More established publicly traded companies can issue additional securities in a general cash offer.

2. Financing choices should be designed to avoid conflicts of interest. This is especially important in the case of a young company that is raising venture capital. If both managers and investors have an important equity stake in the company, they are more likely to pull in the same direction. Remember that the company's financing decision may also *signal* management's confidence in the company's future.

3. Listing securities for trading on organized exchanges increases their liquidity and makes them more attractive to investors. However, listings are costly, both in terms of the listing fees and the increased disclosure required. Companies sometimes forgo a stock exchange listing because the benefits are outweighed by the costs. However if a company intends to grow by raising additional equity, chances are its objectives will be best achieved if the stock is listed on an organized exchange.

4. Larger is cheaper. There are always economies of scale in issuing securities. It is cheaper to go to the market once for $100 million than to make two trips for $50 million each. Consequently firms "bunch" security issues. That may mean relying on short-term financing until a large issue is justified. Or it may mean issuing more than is needed at the moment to avoid another issue later.

5. Firms often sell new issues of securities for less than their market value. This underpricing is a hidden cost to the existing shareholders. Fortunately, it is usually serious only for companies that are selling stock to the public for the first time.

6. New issues may depress the stock price. The extent of this price pressure varies, but for issues of common stocks by industrial firms the fall in the value of the existing stock may amount to a significant proportion of the money raised. The likely explanation for this pressure is the information the market reads into the company's decision to issue stock.

7. Prompt Offering Qualification System (POP System) streamlines the procedure for well-established Canadian companies wishing to make a public offering of common stock, preferred stocks, or investment grade non-convertible debt securities. The POP system reduces the time taken to arrange a new issue, it increases flexibility, and it may cut underwriting costs.

8. Through the Multi Jurisdictional Distribution System (MJDS), Canadian companies have easier access to the U.S. markets without having to meet the requirements of the U.S. Securities and Exchange Commission. This both reduces the paperwork involved and permits the company to avoid the tougher U.S. disclosure requirements.

9. Rights offerings provide a cheaper way for companies to issue equity to their existing shareholders. Shareholders receive one right per share held. To purchase a new share, a certain number of rights plus additional cash (the subscription price) is given to the issuer. Rights offers are less common in Canada than they used to be.

10. Private placements are well-suited for small, risky, or unusual firms. We do not mean that large, safe, and conventional firms should rule out private placements. Enormous amounts of capital are sometimes raised by this method. For example, AT&T once borrowed $500 million in a single private placement. But the special advantages of private placement stem from avoiding registration expenses and a more direct relationship with the lender. These are not worth as much to blue-chip borrowers.

KEY TERMS

venture capital	**spread**	**general cash offer**
initial public	**prospectus**	**POP System**
offering (IPO)	**underpricing**	**subscription price**
underwriter	**rights issue**	**private placement**

SUGGESTED READINGS

A useful general article on investment banking is

> C. W. Smith. "Investment Banking and the Capital Acquisition Process," *Journal of Financial Economics* 15(January–February 1986):3–29.

For an excellent case study of how one company went public see

> B. Uttal. "Inside the Deal That Made Bill Gates $350,000,000," *Fortune*, July 21, 1986.

There have been a number of studies of the market for initial public offerings of common stock. Good articles to start with are

> R. G. Ibbotson, J. L. Sindelar, and J. R. Ritter. "Initial Public Offerings," *Journal of Applied Corporate Finance* 1(Summer 1988):37–45.

> J. R. Ritter. "The 'Hot Issue' Market of 1980," *Journal of Business* 57(1984):215–240.

The effect of general cash offers on stock prices is examined in

> P. Asquith and D. W. Mullins. "Equity Issues and Offering Dilution," *Journal of Financial Economics* 15(January–February 1986):61–90.

> R. W. Masulis and A. N. Korwar. "Seasoned Equity Offerings: An Empirical Investigation," *Journal of Financial Economics* 15(January–February 1986):91–118.

> W. H. Mikkelson and M. M. Partch. "The Valuation Effects of Security Offerings and the Issuance Process," *Journal of Financial Economics* 15(January–February 1986):31–60.

A good analysis of the relative merits of negotiated underwriting and competitive bidding is given in

> S. Bhagat and P. A. Frost. "Issuing Costs to Existing Shareholders in Competitive and Negotiated Underwritten Public Utility Equity Offerings," *Journal of Financial Economics* 15(January–February 1986):213–232.

A collection that contains several articles on the issue of international securities is

A. M. George and I. H. Giddy, eds. *International Finance Handbook*, Vol. 1. New York: John Wiley & Sons, 1983.

PROBLEMS

1. a. Is a rights issue more likely to be used for an initial public offering or for subsequent issues of stock?
   b. Is a competitive general cash offer more likely to be used for a bond issue of an industrial company or a bond issue by a utility holding company?
   c. Is a private placement more likely to be used for issues of seasoned stock or seasoned bonds by an industrial company?
   d. Is the POP system more likely to be used for issues of unseasoned stocks or bonds by a large industrial company?

2. Each of the following terms is associated with one of the events beneath. Can you match them up?
   a. Red herring
   b. POP system
   c. Firm commitment
   d. Rights issue

   A. The company issues a preliminary prospectus.
   B. The underwriter agrees to buy the issue from the company at a fixed price.
   C. The company offers to sell stock to existing stockholders.
   D. The company files a short-form prospectus and is able to issue securities in 10 days, rather than the usual 4 weeks.

3. State for each of the following pairs of issues which you would expect to involve the lower proportionate underwriting and administrative costs, other things equal:
   a. A large issue/a small issue
   b. A bond issue/a common stock issue
   c. A large negotiated bond issue/a large competitive bond issue
   d. A small private placement of bonds/a small general cash offer of bonds

4. You need to choose between the following types of issues:

   A public issue of $10 million face value of 10-year debt. The interest rate on the debt would be 8.5 percent and the debt would be issued at face value. The underwriting spread would be 1.5 percent and other expenses would be $80,000.

   A private placement of $10 million face value of 10-year debt. The interest rate on the private placement would be 9 percent but the total issuing expenses would be only $30,000.

   a. What is the difference in the proceeds to the company net of expenses?
   b. Other things equal, which is the better deal?
   c. What other factors beyond the interest rate and issue costs would you wish to consider before deciding between the two offers?

5. Associated Breweries is planning to market unleaded beer. To finance the venture it proposes to make a rights issue with a subscription price of $10.

One new share can be purchased for each two shares held. The company currently has outstanding 100,000 shares priced at $40 a share. Assuming that the new money is invested to earn a fair return, give values for the

a. number of new shares
b. amount of new investment
c. total value of company after issue
d. total number of shares after issue
e. share price after the issue
f. the value of one right

6. "For small issues of common stock, the costs of flotation amount to about 15 percent of the proceeds. This means that the opportunity cost of external equity capital is about 15 percentage points higher than that of retained earnings." Does this follow?

7. When Microsoft went public, the company sold 2 million new shares (the primary issue). In addition, existing shareholders sold .8 million shares (the secondary issue) and kept 21.1 million shares. Suppose that the new shares had been issued to the underwriters at $33 each, rather than $19.69.

a. How many shares would the company have needed to issue to raise the same amount of money?
b. How much more would the existing shareholders have made from the sale?
c. What would have been the change in the value of the shares that they did not sell? *Hint:* Look at Example 14.2 for information on Microsoft's IPO. What was the market value of Microsoft's total outstanding stock? Would that value change if the company had raised the same amount of money from the underwriters? How many shares of stock would be outstanding if the shares had been issued for $33 each? What would the stock price be?

   Ignore in your calculations any legal and administrative expenses.

8. In 1994 Pandora, Inc., makes a rights issue at a subscription price of $5 a share. One new share can be purchased for every four shares held. Before the issue there were 10 million shares outstanding and the share price was $6.

a. What is the total amount of new money raised?
b. What is the expected stock price after the rights are issued?

9. Problem 8 contains details of a rights offering by Pandora. Suppose that the company had decided to issue the new stock at $4 instead of $5 a share. How many new shares would it have needed to raise the same sum of money? Recalculate the answers to problem 8. Show that Pandora's shareholders are just as well off if it issues the shares at $4 a share rather than the $5 assumed in problem 8.

10. The market value of the marketing research firm Fax Facts is $600 million. The firm issues an additional $100 million of stock, but as a result the stock price falls by 2 percent. What is the cost of the price drop to existing shareholders as a fraction of the funds raised?

11. Dilution Inc. has 100,000 shares outstanding, a book value of $30 per share, and stock price of $25. It issues another 40,000 shares at a price of $25 to raise to $1 million to invest in a new project. The NPV of the project is zero.

a. What will happen to book value per share?
b. What will happen to price per share?

12. Now suppose the NPV of the project in problem 11 is positive, and it is equal to $100,000.
    a. Does this fact affect either book value per share or dilution?
    b. What will happen to the market value of the firm?
    c. Assume the market value of the firm increases by $100,000 when the company announces its intention to pursue the positive-NPV project. If the new shareholders get equity worth only $1 million for the $1 million they pay for the stock, what must be the value of the stock held by the existing shareholders? What must be the price per share?
    d. How many shares of stock must the firm issue to raise the $1 million?
    e. Should the firm issue the shares?

13. Here are recent data on Pisa Construction Inc.:

Stock price	$40
Number of shares	10,000
Book value net worth	$500,000
Market value of firm	$400,000
Earnings per share	$4
Return on investment	8%

    Pisa has not performed well to date. However, it wishes to issue new shares to obtain $80,000 to finance expansion into a promising market. Pisa's financial advisers think a stock issue is a bad idea, because "sale of stock at a price below book value per share can only depress the stock price and decrease shareholders' wealth." To prove this point they construct the following example. "Suppose 2000 new shares are issued at $40 and the proceeds invested. Suppose return on investment doesn't change. Then after the issue,

Book net worth	$580,000
Total earnings	.08 × $580,000 = $46,400
Earnings per share	46,400/12,000 = $3.87

    Thus earnings per share declines, book value per share declines, and share price will decline proportionately to $38.70."
        Evaluate this argument with particular attention to the assumptions implicit in the numerical example.

14. Your broker calls and says that you can get 500 shares of an imminent IPO at the offering price. Should you buy? Are you worried about the fact that your broker called *you*?

15. Here is a difficult question. Pickwick Electronics is a new high-tech company financed entirely by 1 million ordinary shares, all of which are owned by George Pickwick. The firm needs to raise $1 million now for stage 1 and, assuming all goes well, a further $1 million at the end of 5 years for stage 2.
        First Cookham Venture Partners is considering two possible financing schemes:

    Buying 2 million shares now at their current valuation of $1.

    Buying 1 million shares at the current valuation and investing a further $1 million at the end of 5 years at whatever the shares are worth.

The outlook for Pickwick is uncertain, but as long as the company can secure the additional finance for stage 2, it will be worth either $2 million or $12 million after completing stage 2. (The company will be valueless if it cannot raise the funds for stage 2.) Show the possible payoffs for Mr. Pickwick and First Cookham and explain why one scheme might be preferred. Assume an interest rate of zero.

SOLUTIONS TO SELF-TEST QUESTIONS

14.1   Unless the firm can secure second-stage financing, it is unlikely to succeed. If the entrepreneur is going to reap any reward on his own investment, he needs to put in enough effort to get further financing. By accepting only part of the necessary venture capital, management increases its own risk and reduces that of the venture capitalist. This decision would be costly and foolish if management lacked confidence that the project would be successful enough to get past the first stage. A credible signal by management is one that only managers who are truly confident can afford to provide. However, words are cheap and there is little to be lost by *saying* that you are confident (except that, if you are proved wrong, you may find it difficult to raise money a second time).

14.2   If an investor can distinguish among overpriced and underpriced issues, she will bid only on the underpriced ones. In this case she will purchase only issues that provide a 10 percent gain. However, the ability to distinguish these issues requires considerable insight and research. The return to the informed IPO participant may be viewed as a return on the resources expended to become informed.

14.3   Direct expenses:

Underwriting spread = 2.8 million × ($27 – 25)	$ 5.6 million
Other expenses	.5
Total direct expenses	$ 6.1 million
Underpricing = 2.8 million × ($35 – 27)	$22.4
Total expenses	$28.5 million
Market value of issue = 2.8 million × $35	$98.0 million

Expenses as proportion of market value = 28.5/98 = .291 = 29.1%.

14.4   Ten issues of $15 million each will cost about 5.5 percent of proceeds, or .055 × $150 million = $8.3 million. One issue of $150 million will cost only 4 percent of $150 million, or $6 million.

14.5   Book-value balance sheet:

Assets		Liabilities and Net Worth	
Original project	$1,000,000	Stockholders' equity	$1,000,000
New project	100,000	New debt	100,000

Book value per share = $1,000,000/10,000 shares = $100 per share, which is the same as before the new project was initiated.

The new project is worth $8000/.10 = $80,000, so total market value of assets increases to $880,000. The new debt must be worth $100,000, the price that the bondholders are willing to pay for the debt. Therefore, the market value of stockholders' equity must fall to $880,000 - $100,000 = $780,000$. Notice that the market value of the stock falls by the (negative) NPV of the project. Therefore, price per share will fall even though no new shares are issued. The new market-value balance sheet becomes:

Assets		Liabilities and Net Worth	
Original project	$800,000	Stockholders' equity	$780,000
New project	80,000	New debt	100,000

Market value per share = $780,000/10,000$ shares = $78 per share, which is less than the share price before the project was initiated.

APPENDIX 14.1 HOTCH POT'S NEW ISSUE PROSPECTUS [21]

PROSPECTUS

800,000 Shares
Hotch Pot, Inc.
Common Stock ($.10 par value)

Of the 800,000 shares of Common Stock offered hereby, 500,000 shares are being sold by the Company and 300,000 shares are being sold by the Selling Stockholders. See "Principal and Selling Stockholders." The Company will not receive any of the proceeds from the sale of shares by the Selling Stockholders.

Before this offering there has been no public market for the Common Stock. **These securities involve a high degree of risk. See "Certain Factors."**

THESE SECURITIES HAVE NOT BEEN APPROVED OR DISAPPROVED BY THE SECURITIES COMMISSION NOR HAS THE COMMISSION PASSED ON THE ACCURACY OR ADEQUACY OF THIS PROSPECTUS. ANY REPRESENTATION TO THE CONTRARY IS A CRIMINAL OFFENSE.

	Price to Public	Underwriting Discount	Proceeds to Company[1]	Proceeds to Selling Shareholders[1]
Per share	$12.00	$1.30	$10.70	$10.70
Total	$9,600,000	$1,040,000	$5,350,000	$3,210,000

[1] Before deducting expenses payable by the Company estimated at $400,000, of which $250,000 will be paid by the Company and $150,445 by the Selling Stockholders.

The Common Stock is offered, subject to prior sale, when, as, and if delivered to and accepted by the Underwriters and subject to approval of certain legal matters by their counsel and by counsel for the Company and the Selling Shareholders. The Underwriters reserve the right to withdraw, cancel, or modify such offer and reject orders in whole or in part.

Silverman Pinch Inc.   **April 1, 1995**

No person has been authorized to give any information or to make any representations, other than as contained therein, in connection with the offer contained in this Prospectus, and, if given or made, such information or representations must not be relied upon. This Prospectus does not constitute an offer of any securities other than the registered securities to which it relates or an offer to any person in any jurisdiction where such an offer would be unlawful. The delivery of this Prospectus at any time does not imply that information herein is correct as of any time subsequent to its date.

IN CONNECTION WITH THIS OFFERING, THE UNDERWRITERS MAY OVER-ALLOT OR EFFECT TRANSACTIONS WHICH STABILIZE OR MAINTAIN THE MARKET PRICE OF THE COMMON STOCK OF THE COMPANY AT A LEVEL ABOVE THAT WHICH MIGHT OTHERWISE PREVAIL IN THE OPEN

---

[21] Most prospectuses have content similar to that of the Hotch Pot prospectus but go into considerably more detail. Also, we have omitted from the Hotch Pot prospectus the company's financial statements.

MARKET. SUCH STABILIZING, IF COMMENCED, MAY BE DISCONTINUED AT ANY TIME.

PROSPECTUS SUMMARY

The following summary information is qualified in its entirety by the detailed information and financial statements appearing elsewhere in this Prospectus.

The Company: Hotch Pot, Inc. operates a chain of 140 fast-food outlets in Canada offering unusual combinations of dishes.

The Offering: Common Stock offered by the Company 500,000 shares;
Common Stock offered by the Selling Stockholders 300,000 shares;
Common Stock to be outstanding after this offering 3,500,000 shares.

Use of Proceeds: For the construction of new restaurants and to provide working capital.

The Company

Hotch Pot, Inc. operates a chain of 140 fast-food outlets in Quebec, Ontario and Manitoba. These restaurants specialize in offering an unusual combination of foreign dishes.

The Company was organized in Ontario in 1987.

Use of Proceeds

The Company intends to use the net proceeds from the sale of 500,000 shares of Common Stock offered hereby, estimated at approximately $5 million, to open new outlets in the Maritime provinces and to provide additional working capital. It has no immediate plans to use any of the net proceeds of the offering for any other specific investment.

Dividend Policy

The company has not paid cash dividends on its Common Stock and does not anticipate that dividends will be paid on the Common Stock in the foreseeable future.

Certain Factors

Investment in the Common Stock involves a high degree of risk. The following factors should be carefully considered in evaluating the Company:

Substantial Capital Needs   The Company will require additional financing to continue its expansion policy. The Company believes that its relations with its lenders are good, but there can be no assurance that additional financing will be available in the future.

Competition   The Company is in competition with a number of restaurant chains supplying fast food. Many of these companies are substantially larger and better capitalized than the Company.

Capitalization

The following table sets forth the capitalization of the Company as of December 31, 1994, and as adjusted to reflect the sale of 500,000 shares of Common Stock by the Company.

	Actual	As Adjusted
	(in thousands)	
Long-term debt	$ —	$ —
Stockholders' equity:	30	50
Common stock – $.01 par value, 3,000,000 shares outstanding, 3,500,000 shares outstanding, as adjusted		
Paid-in capital	1,970	7,315
Retained earnings	3,200	3,200
Total stockholders' equity	5,200	10,550
Total capitalization	5,200	10,550

Selected Financial Data

[*The Prospectus typically includes a summary income statement and balance sheet.*]

Management's Analysis of Results of Operations and Financial Condition

Revenue growth for the year ended December 31, 1994, resulted from the opening of ten new restaurants in the Company's existing geographic area and from sales of a new range of desserts, notably crepes suzette with custard. Sales per customer increased by 20% and this contributed to the improvement in margins.

During the year the Company borrowed $600,000 from its banks at an interest rate of 2% above the prime rate.

Business

Hotch Pot, Inc. operates a chain of 140 fast-food outlets in Quebec, Ontario, and Manitoba. These restaurants specialize in offering an unusual combination of foreign dishes. 50% of company's revenues derived from sales of two dishes, sushi and sauerkraut and Curry bolognese. All dishes are prepared in three regional centres and then frozen and distributed to the individual restaurants.

Management

The following table sets forth information regarding the Company's directors, executive officers, and key employees:

Name	Age	Position
Emma Lucullus	28	President, Chief Executive Officer, & Director
Ed Lucullus	33	Treasurer & Director

Emma Lucullus   Emma Lucullus established the Company in 1987 and has been its Chief Executive Officer since that date.

Ed Lucullus   Ed Lucullus has been employed by the Company since 1987.

Executive Compensation

The following table sets forth the cash compensation paid for services rendered for the year 1994 by the Executive officers:

Name	Capacity	Cash Compensation
Emma Lucullus	President and Chief Executive Officer	$130,000
Ed Lucullus	Treasurer	$ 95,000

Certain Transactions

At various times between 1987 and 1994 First Cookham Venture Partners invested a total of $1.5 million in the Company.

Principal and Selling Stockholders

The following table sets forth certain information regarding the beneficial ownership of the Company's voting Common Stock as of the date of this prospectus by (i) each person known by the Company to be the beneficial owner of more than 5% of its voting Common Stock, and (ii) each director of the Company who beneficially owns voting Common Stock. Unless otherwise indicated, each owner has sole voting and dispositive power over his shares.

Name of Beneficial Owner	Shares Beneficially Owned prior to Offering		Shares Beneficially Owned after Offering		
	Number	Percent	Shares to be Sold	Number	Percent
Emma Lucullus	400,000	13.3	25,000	375,000	12.9
Ed Lucullus	400,000	13.3	25,000	375,000	12.9
First Cookham Venture Partners	1,700,000	66.7	250,000	1,450,000	50.0
Hermione Kraft	200,000	6.7	—	200,000	6.9

Description of Capital Stock

The Company's authorized capital stock consists of 10,000,000 shares of voting Common Stock.

As of the date of this Prospectus, there are 4 holders of record of the Common Stock.

Under the terms of one of the Company's loan agreements, the Company may not pay cash dividends on Common Stock except from net profits without the written consent of the lender.

Underwriting

Subject to the terms and conditions set forth in the Underwriting Agreement, the Underwriter, Silverman Pinch Inc., has agreed to purchase from the Company and the Selling Stockholders 800,000 shares of Common Stock.

There is no public market for the Common Stock. The price to the public for the Common Stock was determined by negotiation between the Company and the Underwriter and was based on, among other things, the Company's financial and operating history and condition, its prospects, and the prospects for its industry in general, the management of the Company, and the market prices of securities for companies in businesses similar to that of the Company.

Legal Matters

The validity of the shares of Common Stock offered by the Prospectus is being passed on for the Company by Major, Kohl, and Balladur and for the Underwriter by Keating de Klerk.

Legal Proceedings

Hotch Pot was served in January 1994 with a summons and complaint in an action commenced by a customer who alleges that consumption of the Company's products caused severe nausea and loss of feeling in both feet. The Company believes that the complaint is without foundation.

Experts

The consolidated financial statements of the Company have been so included in reliance on the reports of Hooper Firebrand, independent accountants, given on the authority of that firm as experts in auditing and accounting.

Financial Statements

[*Text and tables omitted.*]

A firm's basic resource is the stream of cash flows produced by its assets. When the firm is financed entirely by common stock, all those cash flows belong to the stockholders. When it issues both debt and equity, the firm splits the cash flows into two streams, a relatively safe stream that goes to the debtholders and a more risky one that goes to the stockholders.

The firm's mix of securities is known as its capital structure. Some high-tech firms, such as Delrina Corp. and Corel Corp., rely almost wholly on equity finance. Both Delrina's and Corel's ratio of book value of long-term debt to assets was zero in 1993. At the other extreme, debt accounts for a substantial part of the market value of oil and gas pipelines and utilities. TransCanada Pipelines book value of long-term debt to asset ratio was 53 percent. The long-term debt/asset ratio for Saskatchewan Power Corporation was almost 58 percent.

Capital structure is not immutable. Firms change their capital structure, sometimes almost overnight. For example, in late 1986 and early 1987 Goodyear bought back over 50 million shares at a cost of $2 1/2 billion. In their place it issued $2 1/2 billion of debt. Magna International did the reverse: it replaced debt with equity. In 1991, Magna was struggling to stay afloat with $1 billion of debt and only $250 million in equity. By 1994, after several equity issues, Magna had reduced its $1 billion debt load to almost zero and increased its equity to more than $1 billion.

In this chapter we discuss why some firms have more debt than others and why they sometimes change their capital structure. The choice of capital structure is fundamentally a marketing problem. The firm can issue dozens of distinct securities in countless combinations, but it attempts to find the particular combination that maximizes its overall market value.

Are these attempts worthwhile? We must consider the possibility that no combination has any greater appeal than any other. Perhaps the really important decisions concern the company's assets, and decisions about capital structure are mere details — matters to be attended to but not worried about.

In the first part of the chapter we will look at the circumstances in which capital structure *doesn't* matter. After that we will put back some of the things that *do* make a difference, such as taxes, bankruptcy, and the signals that your financing decisions may send to investors. At the end of the chapter we will be in a position to draw up a checklist for financial managers who need to decide on the firm's capital structure.

After studying this chapter you should be able to

- Analyze the effect of debt finance on the risk and required return of equityholders.
- Appreciate the advantages and disadvantages of debt finance.
- Cite the various costs of financial distress.
- Explain why the debt-equity mix varies across firms and across industries.

15.1   HOW BORROWING AFFECTS COMPANY VALUES IN A TAX-FREE ECONOMY

It is after the ball game and the pizza man is delivering a pizza to Yogi Berra. "Should I cut it into four slices as usual, Yogi?" asks the pizza man. "No," replies Yogi, "Cut it into eight; I'm hungry tonight."

capital structure: Firm's mix of financing.

If you understand why more slices won't sate Yogi's appetite, you will have no difficulty understanding why a company's choice of **capital structure** can't increase the underlying value of the cash flows generated by its real assets and operations. Think of a simple balance sheet:

$$\text{Value of assets} = \text{Value of liabilities plus shareholders' equity}$$

$$\frac{\text{Value of cash flows from}}{\text{real assets and operations}} = \frac{\text{Value of debt, common stock, and}}{\text{other securities issued to investors}}$$

The left-hand side determines the size of the pizza; the right-hand side determines how it is sliced. A company can slice its cash flow into as many parts as it likes, but the value of those parts will always sum back to the value of the unsliced cash flow. (Of course, we have to make sure that none of the cash-flow stream is lost in the slicing. We cannot say "The value of a pizza is independent of how it is sliced" if the seller is also a nibbler.)

The basic idea here (the value of a pizza does not depend on how it is sliced) has various applications. Yogi Berra got friendly chuckles for his misapplication. Franco Modigliani and Merton Miller received Nobel Prizes for applying it to corporate financing. Modigliani and Miller, always referred to as "MM," showed in 1958 that, in well-functioning capital markets, the market value of a company does not depend on its capital structure. In other words, financial managers cannot increase value by changing the mix of securities used to finance the company.

The following example retraces MM's original reasoning.

MM's Argument

Cleo, the president of River Cruises, is reviewing the firm's capital structure with Antony, the financial manager. Table 15.1 shows the current position. The company has no debt and all its operating income is paid as dividends to the shareholders. (We assume for now that there are no taxes.) The *expected* earnings and dividends per share are $1.25, but this figure is by no means certain — it could turn out to be more or less than $1.25. For example, earnings could fall to $.75 in a slump or they could jump to $1.50 in a boom.

TABLE 15.1

River Cruises is entirely equity-financed. Although it *expects* to have an income of $125,000 in perpetuity, this income is not certain. This table shows the return to the stockholder under different assumptions about operating income. We assume no taxes.

Data				
Number of shares	100,000			
Price per share	$10			
Market value of shares	$1 million			

Outcomes				
	State of the Economy			
	Slump	**Stagnant**	**Normal**	**Boom**
Operating income	$75,000	100,000	**125,000**	150,000
Earnings per share	$0.75	1.00	**1.25**	1.50
Return on shares	7.5%	10	**12.5**	15
			Expected outcome	

The price of each share is $10. The first expects to produce a level stream of earnings and dividends in perpetuity. With no growth forecast, stockholders' expected return is equal to the dividend yield — that is, the expected dividend per share divided by the price, $1.25/$10.00 = .125, or 12.5 percent.

Cleo has come to the conclusion that shareholders would be better off if the company had equal proportions of debt and equity. She therefore proposes to issue $500,000 of debt at an interest rate of 10 percent and to use the proceeds to repurchase 50,000 shares. This is called a **restructuring**. The assets and investment policy of the firm are not affected. Only the financing mix changes.

restructuring: Process of changing the firm's capital structure without changing its assets.

To support her proposal, Cleo has analyzed the situation under different assumptions about operating income. These calculations are shown in Table 15.2.

In order to see more clearly how debt finance would affect earnings per share, Cleo has also produced Figure 15.1. The solid line shows how earnings per share would vary with operating income under the firm's current all-equity financing. It is therefore simply a plot of the data in Table 15.1. The broken line shows how earnings per share would vary if the company moves to equal proportions of debt and equity. It is therefore a plot of the data in Table 15.2.

FIGURE 15.1
Borrowing increases River Cruises' earnings per share (EPS) when operating income is greater than $100,000, but reduces it when operating income is less than $100,000. Expected EPS rises from $1.25 to $1.50.

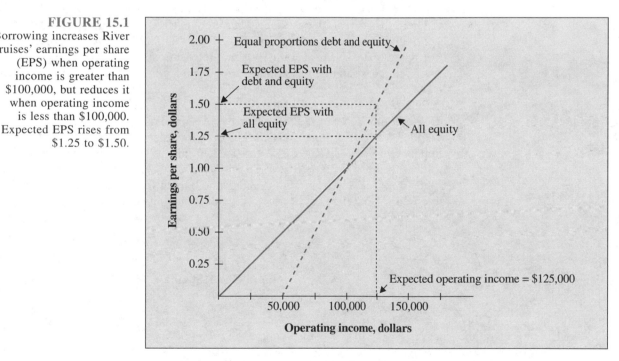

Cleo reasons as follows: "It is clear that debt could either increase or reduce the return to the equityholder. If income is greater than $100,000 (the value in a stagnant economy), the return to the equityholder is *increased* by the issue of debt. If income is less than $100,000, the return is *reduced* by debt. The return is unaffected when operating income is exactly $100,000. At this point, the return on the market value of the assets is 10 percent, which is exactly equal to the interest rate on the debt. Our capital structure decision therefore boils down to what we think about income prospects. Since we expect operating income to be above the $100,000 break-even point, I believe that we can best help our shareholders by going ahead with the debt issue."

TABLE 15.2

River Cruises is wondering whether to issue $500,000 of debt at an interest rate of 10 percent and repurchase 50,000 shares. This table shows the return to shareholders under different assumptions about operating income. Returns to shareholders are increased in normal and boom times, but fall more in slumps.

Data				
Number of shares	50,000			
Price per share	$10			
Market value of shares	$500,000			
Market value of debt	$500,000			

Outcomes				
	State of the Economy			
	Slump	**Stagnant**	**Normal**	**Boom**
Operating income	$75,000	100,000	**125,000**	150,000
Interest	$50,000	50,000	**50,000**	50,000
Equity earnings	$25,000	50,000	**75,000**	100,000
Earnings per share	$0.50	1.00	**1.50**	2.00
Return on shares	5%	10	**15**	20
			Expected outcome	

As financial manager, Antony should reply as follows: "I agree that borrowing will help the shareholder as long as our income is greater than $100,000. But your argument ignores the fact that River Cruises' shareholders have the alternative of borrowing on their own account. For example, suppose River Cruises does *not* borrow. In that case an investor could go to the bank, borrow $10, and then invest $20 in two shares. Such an investor would put up only $10 of her own money. Table 15.3 shows how the payoffs on this $10 investment vary with River Cruises' operating income. You can see that these payoffs are exactly the same as the investor would get by buying one share in the company after the restructuring. (Compare the last two lines of Tables 15.2 and 15.3.) It makes no difference whether shareholders borrow directly or whether River Cruises borrows on their behalf. Therefore, if River Cruises goes ahead and borrows, it will not allow investors to do anything that they could not do already, and so it cannot increase the value of the firm."

TABLE 15.3

Individual investors can replicate River Cruises' borrowing by borrowing on their own. In this example we assume that River Cruises has not restructured. However, the investor can put up $10 of her own money, borrow $10 more, and buy two shares at $20 apiece. This generates the same rates of return as in Table 15.2.

	State of the Economy			
	Slump	**Stagnant**	**Normal**	**Boom**
Earnings on two shares	$1.50	2.00	**2.50**	3.00
Less interest at 10%	$1.00	1.00	**1.00**	1.00
Net earnings on investment	$0.50	1.00	**1.50**	2.00
Return on $10 investment	5%	10	**15**	20
			Expected outcome	

"We can run the same argument in reverse and show that investors also won't be any *worse* off after the restructuring. Imagine an investor who owns two shares in the company before the restructuring. If River Cruises borrows money, there is some chance that the return on the shares will be lower than before. If that possibility is not to our investor's taste, he can buy one share in the restructured company and also invest $10 in the firm's debt. Table 15.4 shows how the payoff on this investment varies with River Cruises' operating income. You can see that these payoffs are exactly the same as the investor got before the restructuring. (Compare the last lines of Tables 15.1 and 15.4.) By lending half of his capital (by investing in River Cruises' debt), the investor exactly offsets the effect of the company borrowing. So, if River Cruises goes ahead and borrows, it won't *stop* investors from doing anything that they could previously do."

TABLE 15.4

Individual investors can also undo the effects of River Cruises' borrowings. Here the investor buys one share for $10 and lends out $10 more. Compare these rates of return to the original returns of River Cruises in Table 15.1

	State of the Economy			
	Slump	**Stagnant**	**Normal**	**Boom**
Earnings on one share	$0.50	1.00	**1.50**	2.00
Less interest at 10%	$1.00	1.00	**1.00**	1.00
Net earnings on investment	$1.50	2.00	**2.50**	3.00
Return on $10 investment	7.5%	10	**12.5**	15
			Expected outcome	

This recreates MM's argument. As long as investors can borrow or lend on their own account on the same terms as the firm, they are not going to thank companies for borrowing on their behalf. The value of the firm after the restructuring must be the same as before.

The argument that the value of the firm is unaffected by its capital structure is widely known as **MM's proposition I**. This proposition is also called the **MM debt irrelevance proposition**, because it shows that under ideal conditions the firm's debt policy shouldn't matter to shareholders.

MM's Proposition I (debt irrelevance proposition): The value of a firm is unaffected by its capital structure.

SELF-TEST 15.1

Suppose that River Cruises had issued $750,000 of debt, using the proceeds to buy back stock.
a. What would be the impact of a $25,000 change in operating income on earnings per share?
b. Show how a conservative investor could "undo" the change in River Cruises' capital structure by varying the investment strategy shown in Table 15.4. *Hint:* The investor will have to lend $3 for every dollar invested in River Cruises' stock.

How Borrowing Affects Risk and Return

operating risk, business risk: Risk in total income of the firm.

financial leverage: Increase in the variability of shareholder returns that comes from the use of debt.

Cleo's calculations in Table 15.2 showed that issuing debt would increase the shareholder's *expected* return. But what about risk? You can see that the company's operating income is the same after the restructuring. So the debt-equity ratio does not affect the **operating risk**, or equivalently, the **business risk** of the firm. But with less equity outstanding, a change in operating income has a greater impact on earnings per share. Suppose operating income drops from $150,000 to $125,000. Under all-equity financing, there are 100,000 shares; so earnings per share fall by $.25. With 50 percent debt, there are only 50,000 shares outstanding; so the same drop in operating income reduces earnings per share by $.50.

You can see now why the use of debt finance is known as **financial leverage**. It increases the spread of percentage stock returns. If the firm is financed entirely by equity, a decline of $25,000 in operating income reduces the return on the shares by 2.5 percent. If the firm issues debt, then the same decline of $25,000 in operating income reduces the return on the shares by 5 percent. (Compare Tables

financial risk: Risk to shareholders resulting from the use of debt.

15.1 and 15.2.) In other words, the effect of leverage is to double the magnitude of the swings in the price of River Cruises' shares. Whatever the beta of the firm's shares before the restructuring, it would be twice as high afterward. Thus debt finance does not affect the operating risk but it does add **financial risk**. With only half the equity to absorb the same amount of operating risk, risk per share must double.[1]

Before the proposed debt issue, the expected stream of earnings and dividends per share is $1.25. Investors require a return of 12.5 percent. So the share price (which for a perpetuity is equal to the expected dividends divided by the required return) is $1.25/.125 = $10. After the debt issue, expected earnings and dividends rise to $1.50 but investors now demand a return of 15 percent to compensate for the higher risk.[2] The share price is $1.50/.15 = $10 — exactly the same as before.

Thus leverage increases the expected return to shareholders but it also increases the risk. The two effects offset each other, leaving shareholder value unchanged.

Debt and the Cost of Capital

In Chapter 11 you learned that the expected return on the firm's bundle of assets is simply a weighted average of the expected return on the firm's securities. This is termed the *weighted-average cost of capital*, or *WACC*. WACC is the required rate of return for a project with the same risk as the firm's existing business. Firms use WACC as a discount rate for "average" projects and as a benchmark for thinking about the discount rate for safer or riskier projects.

The formula for the weighted-average cost of capital is

$$\text{WACC} = \frac{\text{expected return}}{\text{on firm's assets}} = \frac{\text{expected return}}{\text{on debt}} \times \frac{\text{proportion}}{\text{in debt}}$$

$$+ \frac{\text{expected return}}{\text{on equity}} \times \frac{\text{proportion}}{\text{in equity}}$$

$$\text{WACC} = r_{\text{assets}} = r_{\text{debt}} \left(\frac{D}{D+E} \right) + r_{\text{equity}} \left(\frac{E}{D+E} \right)$$

Note that we are ignoring taxes.[3] Also remember that D and E are the *market* values of the firm's debt and equity.

MM's proposition I states that the firm's choice of capital structure does not affect the firm's operating income or the value of its assets. So r_{assets}, the expected return on the package of debt and equity, is unaffected.

However, we have just seen that leverage does increase the risk of the equity and the return that shareholders demand. To see how the expected return on equity varies with leverage, we simply rearrange the weighted-average cost of capital formula as follows:

$$r_{\text{equity}} = r_{\text{assets}} + \frac{D}{E} (r_{\text{assets}} - r_{\text{debt}})$$

which in words says that

---

[1] Think back to Section 8.2, where we showed that fixed costs increase the variability in a firm's profits. These fixed costs are said to provide *operating leverage*. It is exactly the same with debt. Debt interest is a fixed cost and therefore debt magnifies the variability of profits after interest. These interest charges provide *financial leverage*.

[2] The interest rate is 10 percent. So before the debt issue, investors were content with a *risk premium* of 12.5 – 10 = 2.5 percent. We have seen that the debt issue doubles shareholder risk. So after the issue shareholders need a risk premium of 5 percent — that is, a return of 10 + 5 = 15 percent.

[3] When taxes are recognized, r_{debt} is multiplied by $(1 - T_c)$, where T_c is the marginal corporate tax rate. See Section 11.2 of Chapter 11.

$$\begin{pmatrix} \text{Expected} \\ \text{return} \\ \text{on equity} \end{pmatrix} = \begin{pmatrix} \text{Expected} \\ \text{return} \\ \text{on assets} \end{pmatrix} + \left[\begin{pmatrix} \text{Debt-} \\ \text{equity} \\ \text{ratio} \end{pmatrix} \times \left(\begin{pmatrix} \text{Expected} \\ \text{return on} \\ \text{assets} \end{pmatrix} - \begin{pmatrix} \text{Expected} \\ \text{return on} \\ \text{debt} \end{pmatrix} \right) \right]$$

MM's Proposition II: The required rate of return on equity increases as the firm's debt-equity ratio increases.

This is **MM's proposition II**. It states that the expected rate of return on the common stock of a levered firm increases in proportion to the debt-equity ratio (D/E), expressed in market values. Note that $r_{equity} = r_{assets}$ if the firm has no debt.

● **Example 15.1 River Cruises' Cost of Equity**

We can check out this formula for River Cruises. Before the decision to borrow

$$r_{equity} = r_{assets} = \frac{\text{expected operating income}}{\text{market value of all securities}}$$

$$= \frac{125,000}{1,000,000} = .125, \text{ or } 12.5\%$$

If the firm goes ahead with its plan to borrow, the expected return on assets, r_{assets}, is still 12.5 percent. So the expected return on equity is

$$r_{equity} = r_{assets} + \frac{D}{E}(r_{assets} - r_{debt})$$

$$= .125 + \frac{500,000}{500,000}(.125 - .10)$$

$$= .15, \text{ or } 15\%$$

We pointed out in Chapter 11 that you can think of a debt issue as having an explicit cost and an implicit cost. The explicit cost is the rate of interest charged on the firm's debt. When Cleo said that debt would benefit shareholders as long as the firm earned more than the interest rate on its assets, she was focusing on the explicit cost. But debt also increases shareholder risk and causes shareholders to demand a higher return on their investment. Once you recognize this implicit cost, debt is no cheaper than equity — the return that investors require on their assets is unaffected by the firm's borrowing decision.

SELF-TEST 15.2

When the firm issues debt, why does r_{assets}, the weighted-average cost of capital, remain fixed, while the expected return on equity, r_{equity}, changes? Why is it not the other way around?

You can now see how MM's theory underlies calculations of the weighted-average cost of capital. When in Chapter 11 we asserted that r_{assets} should not depend on the fractions of debt and equity financing, we were really relying on MM's proposition I; when we calculated r_{equity} for Geothermal, Inc., and Big Oil (in Section 11.5), we were really using MM's proposition II.

The general implications of MM's proposition II are shown in Figure 15.2. No matter how much the firm borrows, the expected return on the package of debt and equity, r_{assets}, is unchanged, but the expected rate of return on the separate parts of the package does change. How is this possible? Because the proportions of debt and equity in the package are also changing.

In Figure 15.2 we have drawn the rate of interest on the debt as constant no matter how much the firm borrows. That is not wholly realistic. It is true that most large companies could borrow a little more or less without noticeably affecting

FIGURE 15.2

MM's proposition II with risk-free debt. The expected return on equity rises linearly as the debt-equity ratio increases. The weighted average of the expected returns on debt and equity is constant, equal to the expected return on assets.

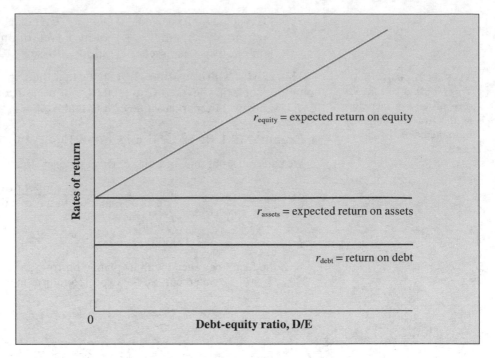

the interest rate that they pay. But at extreme debt levels lenders become concerned that they may not get their money back and demand higher rates of interest to reflect this. Figure 15.3 modifies Figure 15.2 to take account of this. You can see that as the firm borrows more, the risk of default increases and the firm has to pay higher rates of interest. Proposition II continues to predict that the expected return on the package of debt and equity does not change. However, the slope of the r_{equity} line now tapers off as D/E increases. Why? Essentially because holders of risky debt begin to bear part of the firm's operating risk. As the firm borrows more, more of that risk is transferred from stockholders to bondholders.

FIGURE 15.3

MM's proposition II. The expected return on equity r_{equity} increases linearly with the debt-equity ratio so long as debt is risk-free. But if leverage increases the risk of the debt, debt-holders demand a higher return on the debt. This causes the rate of increase in r_{equity} to slow down.

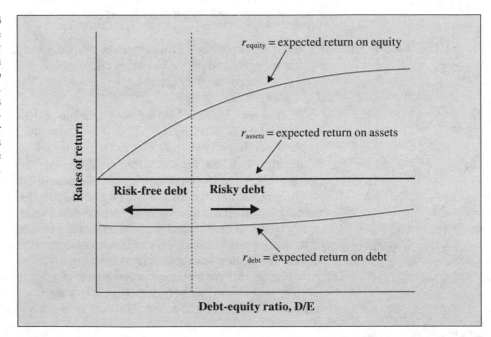

15.2 CORPORATE TAXES

The MM propositions suggest that debt policy should not matter in well-functioning capital markets. No matter how much the firm borrows, the value of the firm stays the same. So does the weighted-average cost of capital. Yet financial managers do worry about debt policy and for good reasons. Now we are ready to see why.

If debt policy were *completely* irrelevant, actual debt ratios would vary randomly from firm to firm and from industry to industry. Yet almost all airlines, utilities, banks, and real estate development companies rely heavily on debt. And so do many firms in capital-intensive industries like steel, aluminum, chemicals, petroleum, and mining. On the other hand, it is rare to find a drug company or advertising agency that is not predominantly equity-financed. Glamorous "growth" companies seldom use much debt despite rapid expansion and often heavy requirements for capital.

The explanation of these patterns lies partly in the things that we have so far left out of our discussion. We have ignored taxes, bankruptcy, potential conflicts of interest between the firm's security holders, and ways that the firm's financing decisions could affect its investment decisions. Now we will put all these things back in: taxes first, then the costs of bankruptcy and financial distress. This will lead us to conflicts of interest and to those possible interactions between financing and investment decisions. In the end we will see that debt policy *does* matter.

However, we will not throw away the MM theory. The MM propositions tell us when debt policy does *not* matter. As a result they also tell us where to look for reasons why firms *should* care about capital structure. Let's start looking.

Debt and Taxes at River Cruises

Debt financing has one important advantage. The interest that the company pays is a tax-deductible expense. Dividends and retained earnings are not.

To see the advantage of debt finance, let's look once again at River Cruises. Table 15.5 reworks Tables 15.1 and 15.2 and recognizes that profits are taxed at a rate of 35 percent. Panel A shows the position when the firm is financed entirely by equity. We assume that the shareholders continue to demand a 12.5 percent return if the firm is all-equity financed and therefore the company is valued at $81,250/.125 = $650,000.[4]

In panel B, we assume that River Cruises issues $325,000 of debt. Compare panels A and B of Table 15.5; you will notice that whatever happens to the economy, the combined income of the debt- and equityholders is higher by $11,375 when the firm is levered. This is because the interest payments are tax-deductible. Thus every dollar of interest reduces taxes by $.35. The total amount of tax savings is simply .35 × interest payments. In the case of River Cruises, the **interest tax shield** is .35 × 32,500 = $11,375 each year. Since the debtholders receive no more than the going rate of interest, all the benefit of this interest tax shield is captured by the shareholders.

interest tax shield: Tax savings resulting from deductibility of interest payments.

The interest tax shield is a valuable asset. Suppose that River Cruises plans to replace its bonds when they mature and to keep "rolling over" the debt indefinitely. It therefore looks forward to a permanent stream of tax savings of $11,375 per year. These savings depend only on the corporate tax rate and on the ability of River Cruises to earn enough to cover interest payments. So the risk of the tax shield is likely to be small. Therefore, if we wish to compute the present value of

---

[4] Notice in panel A that with corporate taxes, earnings, dividends, and company value are all reduced by 35 percent.

TABLE 15.5

Since debt interest is tax deductible, the combined income of River Cruises' debt- and equityholders is higher when the firm is leveraged, regardless of the state of the economy.

	State of the Economy			
	Slump	**Stagnant**	**Normal**	**Boom**
A. *Income with all-equity financing (dollars)*				
Operating income	75,000	100,000	**125,000**	150,000
Tax at 35%	26,250	35,000	**43,750**	52,500
After-tax income	48,750	65,000	**81,250**	97,500
			Expected outcome	

	State of the Economy			
	Slump	**Stagnant**	**Normal**	**Boom**
B. *Income assuming $325,000 of debt financing (dollars)*				
Operating income	75,000	100,000	**125,000**	150,000
Debt interest at 10%	32,500	32,500	**32,500**	32,500
Before-tax income	42,500	67,500	**92,500**	117,500
Tax at 35%	14,875	23,625	**32,375**	41,125
After-tax income	27,625	43,875	**60,125**	76,375
Combined debt and equity income (debt interest + after-tax income)	60,125	76,375	**92,625**	108,875
			Expected oucome	

all the future tax savings associated with permanent debt, we should discount the interest tax shields at a relatively low rate.

But what rate? The most common assumption is that the risk of the tax shields is the same as that of the interest payments generating them. Thus we discount at 10 percent, the expected rate of return demanded by investors who are holding the firm's debt. If the debt is permanent, then the firm can look forward to annual savings of $11,375 in perpetuity. Their present value is

$$\text{PV tax shield} = \frac{\$11,375}{.10} = \$113,750$$

This is what the tax savings are worth to River Cruises. With all-equity financing River Cruises is valued at $650,000. But if River Cruises issues $325,000 of permanent debt, the package of all the firm's securities increases by the value of the tax shield to $650,000 + $113,750 = $763,750.

Let us generalize. The interest payment each year equals the rate of interest times the amount borrowed, or $r_{debt} \times D$. The annual tax saving is the corporate tax rate T_c times the interest payment. Therefore,

$$\text{Annual tax shield} = \text{corporate tax rate} \times \text{interest payment}$$

$$= T_c \times (r_{debt} \times D)$$

If the tax shield is perpetual, we use the perpetuity formula to calculate its present value:

$$\text{PV tax shields} = \frac{\text{annual tax shield}}{r_{debt}} = \frac{T_c \times (r_{debt} \times D)}{r_{debt}} = T_c D$$

Of course the present value of the tax shield is less if the firm does not plan to borrow permanently or if it may not be able to use the tax shields in the future.

SELF-TEST 15.3

In 1992 Maritime Telephone and Telegraph (MT&T) paid out $58 million as debt interest. How much more tax would MT&T have paid if the firm was entirely equity-financed? What is the present value of MT&T's interest tax shield if (a) MT&T planned to keep its borrowing permanently at the 1992 level; (b) it intended to eliminate all debt after 1 year? Assume an interest rate of 8 percent and a corporate tax rate of 40 percent.

How Interest Tax Shields Contribute to the Value of Stockholders' Equity

MM's proposition I amounts to saying that "the value of the pizza does not depend on how it is sliced." The pizza is the firm's assets, and the slices are the debt and equity claims. If we hold the pizza constant, then a dollar more of debt means a dollar less of equity value.

But there is really a third slice — the government's. MM would still say that the value of the pizza — in this case the company value before taxes — is not changed by slicing. But anything the firm can do to reduce the size of the government's slice obviously leaves more for the others. One way to do this is to borrow money. This reduces the firm's tax bill and increases the cash payments to the investors. The value of their investment goes up by the present value of the tax savings.

In a no-tax world, MM's proposition I states that the value of the firm is unaffected by capital structure. But MM also modified proposition I to recognize corporate taxes:

$$\text{Value of levered firm} = \text{value if all-equity financed} + \text{present value of tax shield}$$

In the special case of permanent debt,

$$\text{Value of levered firm} = \text{value if all-equity financed} + T_c D$$

This "corrected" formula is illustrated in Figure 15.4. It implies that borrowing increases firm value and stockholders' wealth.

FIGURE 15.4
The coloured line shows how the availability of interest tax shields affects the market value of the firm. Additional borrowing decreases corporate income tax payments and increases the cash flows available to lenders and stockholders. Thus market value increases.

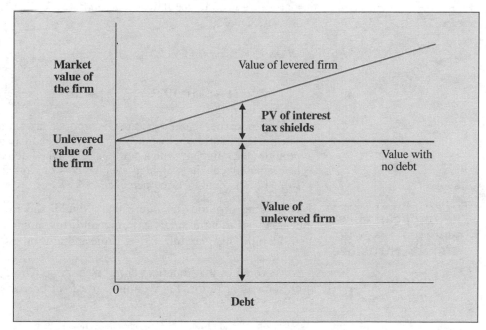

....
Corporate Taxes and the Weighted-Average Cost of Capital

We have shown that when there are corporate taxes, debt provides the company with a valuable tax shield. Few companies explicitly calculate the present value of interest tax shields associated with a particular borrowing policy. The tax shields are not forgotten, however, because they show up in the discount rate used to evaluate capital investments.

Since debt interest is tax-deductible, the government in effect pays 35 percent of the interest cost. So to keep its investors happy, the firm has to earn only the *after-tax* rate of interest on its debt and the full return required by shareholders. Once we recognize the tax benefit of debt, the weighted-average cost of capital formula becomes

$$\text{WACC} = r_{\text{assets}} = (1 - T_c)\, r_{\text{debt}} \left(\frac{D}{D + E}\right) + r_{\text{equity}} \left(\frac{E}{D + E}\right)$$

Notice that when we allow for the tax advantage of debt, the weighted-average cost of capital depends on the after-tax rate of interest, $(1 - T_c) \times r_{\text{debt}}$. Of course if the tax rate, T_c, is zero, we are back to our original formula, which ignored taxes.[5]

● Example 15.2 WACC and Debt Policy

We can use the weighted-average cost of capital formula to see how leverage affects River Cruises' cost of capital if the company pays corporate tax. When a company has no debt, the weighted-average cost of capital and the return required by shareholders are identical. In the case of River Cruises the WACC with all-equity financing is 12.5 percent.

Now let us calculate the weighted-average cost of capital if River Cruises issues \$325,000 of debt ($D = \$325,000$). Company value increases by the \$113,750 interest tax shield to \$763,750 ($D + E = \$763,750$) and therefore the value of equity must be $\$763,750 - \$325,000 = \$438,750$ ($E = \$438,750$). Panel B of Table 15.5 shows that when River Cruises borrows, the expected equity income and dividend is \$60,125. So the expected return to shareholders is $60,125/438,750 = 13.7$ percent ($r_{\text{equity}} = .137$). The interest rate is 10 percent ($r_{\text{debt}} = .10$) and the corporate tax rate is 35 percent ($T_c = .35$). This is all the information we need to see how leverage affects River Cruises' weighted-average cost of capital:

$$\text{WACC} = r_{\text{assets}} = (1 - T_c)\, r_{\text{debt}} \left(\frac{D}{D + E}\right) + r_{\text{equity}} \left(\frac{E}{D + E}\right)$$

$$= (1 - .35)\, .10 \left(\frac{325,000}{763,750}\right) + .137 \left(\frac{438,750}{763,750}\right) = .1064 \text{ or } 10.64\%$$

We saw earlier that if there are no corporate taxes, the weighted-average cost of capital is unaffected by borrowing. But when there are corporate taxes, debt provides the company with a new benefit — the interest tax shield. In this case leverage reduces the weighted-average cost of capital (in River Cruises' case from 12.5 percent to 10.64 percent).

....
The Implications of Corporate Taxes for Capital Structure

If borrowing provides an interest tax shield, the implied optimal debt policy appears to be embarrassingly extreme: all firms should borrow to the hilt to reduce their tax bill. This maximizes firm value and minimizes the weighted-average cost of capital.

MM were not that fanatical about it. No one would expect the gains to apply at extreme debt ratios. For example, if a firm borrows heavily, all its operating

---

[5] We developed the after-tax WACC formula in Section 11.2.

income may go to pay interest and therefore there are no corporate taxes to be paid. There is no point in such firms borrowing any more.

There may also be some tax *disadvantages* to borrowing, for bondholders have to pay personal income tax on any interest they receive. Stockholders, on the other hand, can get a tax break, because some of their returns come as dividends and capital gains. Dividends are taxed at a lower rate because of the dividend tax credit. Capital gains are not taxed until the stock is sold and may then be taxed at a lower rate.[6]

All this suggests that there may come a point at which the tax savings from debt level off and may even decline. But it doesn't explain why highly profitable companies with large tax bills often thrive with little or no debt. There are clearly factors besides tax to consider.

15.3 COSTS OF FINANCIAL DISTRESS

costs of financial distress: Costs arising from bankruptcy or distorted business decisions before bankruptcy.

Financial distress occurs when promises to creditors are broken or honoured with difficulty. Sometimes financial distress leads to bankruptcy. Sometimes it only means skating on thin ice.

As we will see, financial distress is costly. Investors know that levered firms may run into financial difficulty, and they worry about the **costs of financial distress**. That worry is reflected in the current market value of the levered firm's securities. Even if the firm is not now in financial distress, investors factor the potential for future distress into their assessment of current value. This means that the overall value of the firm is

$$\text{Overall market value} = \text{value if all-equity financed} + \text{PV tax shield} - \text{PV costs of financial distress}$$

The present value of the costs of financial distress depends both on the probability of distress and on the magnitude of the costs encountered if distress occurs.

Figure 15.5 shows how the trade-off between the tax benefits of debt and the costs of distress determines optimal capital structure. The present value of the tax shield initially increases as the firm borrows more but eventually levels off as the firm runs out of taxable profits. At moderate debt levels the probability of financial distress is trivial and therefore the tax advantages of debt dominate. But at some point the probability of financial distress increases rapidly with additional borrowing and the potential costs of distress begin to take a substantial bite out of firm value. The theoretical optimum is reached when the present value of tax savings due to additional borrowing is just offset by increases in the present value of costs of distress.

Let us now identify these costs of financial distress.

Bankruptcy Costs

In principle, bankruptcy is merely a legal mechanism for allowing creditors to take over the firm when the decline in the value of its assets triggers a default on outstanding debt. If the company cannot pay its debts, the company is turned over to the creditors, who become the new owners; the old stockholders are left with nothing. Bankruptcy is not the cause of the decline in the value of the firm. It is the result.

In practice, of course, anything involving courts and lawyers cannot be free. The fees involved in a bankruptcy proceeding are paid out of the remaining value

---

[6] Recall from Chapter 2, the capital gains are taxed at 3/4 of the full personal tax rate.

FIGURE 15.5
The trade-off theory of capital structure. The coloured line shows how the market value of the firm at first increases as the firm borrows, but finally decreases as the costs of financial distress become more and more important. The optimal capital structure balances the costs of financial distress against the value of the interest tax shields generated by borrowing.

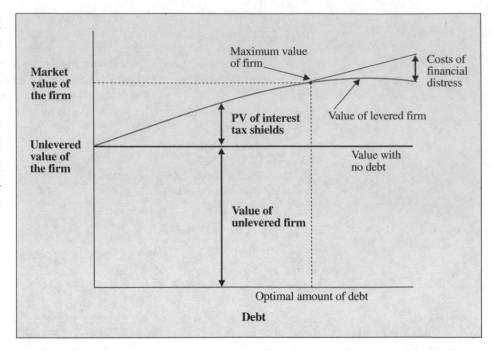

of the firm's assets. Creditors end up with only what is left after paying the lawyers and other court expenses. If there is a possibility of bankruptcy, the current market value of the firm is reduced by the present value of these potential costs.

It is easy to see how increased leverage affects the costs of financial distress. The more the firm owes, the higher the chance of default and therefore the greater the expected value of the associated legal costs. This reduces the current market value of the firm.

Creditors foresee the costs and realize that if default occurs, the lawyers' fees will come out of the value of the firm. For this they demand compensation in advance in the form of a higher promised interest rate. This reduces the possible payoffs to stockholders and reduces the current market value of their shares.

SELF-TEST 15.4

Suppose investors foresee $2 million of legal costs if the firm defaults on its bonds. How does this affect the value of the firm's bonds if bankruptcy occurs? How does it affect the value of the bonds *today*? Their promised yield to maturity?

Evidence on Bankruptcy Costs

Bankruptcy costs can add up fast. Manville, which declared bankruptcy in 1982 because of expected liability for asbestos-related health claims, spent $200 million on bankruptcy fees before it emerged from bankruptcy in 1988.[7] *Aviation Week and Space Technology* reported in 1984 that legal and professional fees of the Braniff International Corporation bankruptcy were $12 million; legal fees in the Continental Airlines bankruptcy were running $2 million a month.[8] Daunting as these numbers may seem, they are not a large fraction of these airlines' asset values. For example, in 1984 it cost about $95 million to buy *one* airplane, a Boeing 747.

---

[7] S. P. Sherman, "Bankruptcy's Spreading Blight," *Fortune*, June 3, 1991:123–132.
[8] *Aviation Week and Space Technology*, April 23, 1984, p. 35.

This is typical. Researchers have not found large legal and administrative costs of bankruptcies — that is, not large compared with the bankrupt companies' total values. J. B. Warner, who studied 11 railroad bankruptcies, found that legal and administrative costs averaged only 5.3 percent of the overall prebankruptcy market value of the railroads' debt and equity securities. The costs were only 1.4 percent of overall market value estimated 5 years before bankruptcy, when the railroads were in better health.[9]

A study by Edward Altman found direct bankruptcy costs were similar for retail companies but higher for bankrupt industrial companies.[10] Bankruptcy is also much more costly for small companies than for large ones — there are significant economies of scale in going bankrupt.

....
Direct versus Indirect Costs of Bankruptcy

Thus far we have discussed only the *direct* (that is, legal and administrative) costs of bankruptcy. There are also indirect costs, which are nearly impossible to measure. But we have circumstantial evidence indicating their importance.

The indirect costs reflect the difficulties of running a railroad — or any company — while it is going through bankruptcy. Management's efforts to prevent further deterioration in the firm's business are often undermined by the delays and legal tangles that go with bankruptcy. When Eastern Airlines entered bankruptcy in 1989, it was in severe financial trouble, but it still had some valuable, profit-making routes and readily saleable assets such as planes and terminal facilities. After nearly 2 years under the "protection" of a bankruptcy court, which allowed Eastern to continue loss-making operations, there was hardly anything of value left when it was finally forced to liquidate in 1991.

● **Example 15.3 Penn Central's Bankruptcy**

The Penn Central Railroad went under in June 1970. It was the largest and most dramatic corporate failure up to that time. Four years later, with bankruptcy proceedings nowhere near completion, *Business Week* published an article called "Why the Penn Central Is Falling Apart." Here are some excerpts.

> *As its creditors hound it — some of them want to shut it down to get back their money — the railroad must continue operations at a time when it can barely keep running without pouring in huge sums to rebuild its facilities. Those sums, however, will not be available until the railroad shows that it can be reorganized.*

Penn Central could have raised money by selling off some of its assets, but its creditors naturally opposed this:

> *Scores of other problems arise from lack of money. Agonizingly for everyone on the Penn Central, there is a tremendous source of capital that cannot be touched. For example, just about every abandoned mine branch in the Allegheny Mountains is chock full of old Penn Central cars destined for scrap. With today's scrap prices, they are a potential gold mine. But the creditors will not allow this asset to be turned into cash that will be reinvested in the estate, since that estate is eroding everyday.[11]*

---

[9] J. B. Warner, "Bankruptcy Costs: Some Evidence," *Journal of Finance* 26 (May 1977):337–348.
[10] See E. I. Altman, "A Further Empirical Investigation of the Bankruptcy Cost Question," *Journal of Finance* 39 (September 1984):1067–1089.
[11] Reprinted from the October 12, 1974, issue of *Business Week* by special permission, 1974 by McGraw-Hill, Inc., New York, NY 10020. All rights reserved.

Penn Central's problems show that some of the most important costs of bankruptcy are difficult to measure. The disruption of business activity is less visible but can be far more costly than the firm's legal bills.

We don't know how much such indirect costs add to the expenses of bankruptcy. We suspect it is a significant number, particularly in the case of large firms for which bankruptcy proceedings may be prolonged. Perhaps the best evidence is the reluctance of creditors to force a firm into bankruptcy. In principle, they would be better off to end the agony and seize the assets as soon as possible. But instead creditors often overlook defaults in the hope of nursing the firm over a difficult period. They do this in part to avoid the costs of bankruptcy. There is an old financial saying, "Borrow $1000 and you've got a banker. Borrow $10,000,000 and you've got a partner."

Finance in Action

Vultures Are Working Out!

Sometimes one firm's financial distress provides opportunities for another's financial gain. Certain investment funds specialize in buying bonds and bank loans of firms that have defaulted on the loans by failing to make the required payments. Guess what these funds are called?

A sophisticated group of investment managers operate what they call work-out funds or opportunity funds, which invest in the heavily-discounted securities of distressed companies. By buying the securities cheap and then waiting in hopes of a profitable offer for the securities or a turnaround in the firm's fortunes — or actively working to bring about a restructuring, sometimes against the strong objections of management — these funds seek high returns on their admittedly risky investments. Because they "feed" on weak or near-bankrupt companies, these funds are commonly known as vulture funds. Goldman, Sachs & Co., Lazard Freres, Oppenheimer, Morgens Waterfall & Co., and Amroc Investments are all operators of U.S. based vulture funds.

According to a story in *The Globe & Mail*, published April 29, 1994, U.S. vultures were "flocking north":

"Large U.S. bankruptcies that provide returns of 30–40% are almost gone, so such [vulture] investors are moving into Canada where they have invested an estimated $300 million in companies such as Bramalea Ltd., Domtar Inc., Olympia & York Developments Ltd., Repap Enterprises Ltd., Royal Trustco Ltd., and Stelco Ltd. O&Y became a big target because it was the first major company to fall back on the Canadian Companies Creditors Arrangement Act, similar to Chapter 11 bankruptcy in the U.S. Vultures are now particulary interested in Trizec Corp. Ltd., a $5 billion property development company that is the first of the cross-border companies in major trouble, and they are also watching Cadillac Fairview Inc."

Financial Distress without Bankruptcy

Not every firm that gets into trouble goes bankrupt. As long as the firm can scrape up enough cash to pay the interest on its debt, it may be able to postpone bankruptcy for many years. Eventually the firm may recover, pay off its debt, and escape bankruptcy altogether.

Skating on thin ice can be useful if it makes the skater concentrate. Likewise, some observers believe that managers of highly levered firms are more likely to work harder, run a leaner operation, and think more carefully before they spend money. This was one of the justifications for the increased use of leverage during the 1980s. For example, when Goodyear repurchased $2 billion of its stock and replaced it with debt, management was committing itself to paying out large sums of money as interest. That left it with little opportunity to fritter its cash away in corporate adventures or a comfortable life.

However, there are also drawbacks to extreme amounts of leverage. When a firm is in trouble, both bondholders and stockholders want it to recover, but in other respects their interests may be in conflict. In times of financial distress the security holders are like many political parties — united on generalities but threatened by squabbling on any specific issue.

Financial distress is costly when these conflicts get in the way of running the business. Stockholders are tempted to forsake the usual objective of maximizing the overall market value of the firm and to pursue narrower self-interest instead. They are tempted to play games at the expense of their creditors. These games add to the costs of financial distress.

We can illustrate some of the games with the case of Circular File Company. Here is Circular File's *book-value* balance sheet:

CIRCULAR FILE COMPANY BOOK-VALUE BALANCE SHEET

Net working capital	$ 20	Bonds outstanding	$ 50
Fixed assets	80	Common stock	50
Total assets	$100	Total liabilities	$100

Suppose that Circular's assets are barely generating income and the firm is tottering on the brink of bankruptcy. As a result, the market value of the assets is considerably less than the book value. Here is Circular's balance sheet in *market* values:

CIRCULAR FILE COMPANY MARKET-VALUE BALANCE SHEET

Net working capital	$20	Bonds outstanding	$25
Fixed assets	10	Common stock	5
Total assets	$30	Total liabilities	$30

This is a clear case of financial distress, since the face value of Circular's debt ($50) exceeds the firm's total market value. If the debt matured today, Circular owners would default, leaving the firm bankrupt. The debtholders would get $30, which is less than the $50 that they are owed, and the stockholders would get nothing.

But suppose that the debt actually matures 1 year hence and that there is enough cash for Circular to limp along for 1 year. The 1-year grace period explains why Circular shares still have value. The owners are betting on a stroke of luck that will rescue the firm, allowing it to pay off the debt with something left over. The bet is a long-shot — unless firm value increases from $30 to more than $50, the stock will be valueless. But the owners have a secret weapon: they control investment and operating strategy.

The First Game: Bet the Bank's Money. Suppose that Circular has $10 cash. The following investment opportunity comes up:

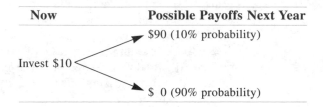

Now	Possible Payoffs Next Year
Invest $10	$90 (10% probability)
	$ 0 (90% probability)

This is a wild gamble and a lousy project. The expected payoff of the investment is only $9 [(.10 × $90) + (.90 × $0)]. That is less than the initial investment even *before* discounting. But you can see why the owner would be tempted to take it anyway. Why not go for broke? If the project pays off, there will be more than enough assets to pay off the debt and the surplus of $40 will go into the owners' pockets. If the project does not pay off, little is lost: Circular will probably go under anyway. Therefore, if the firm gambles on the project, it is essentially betting with the bondholder's money. But the equityholders get most of the loot if the project pays off.

One owner-manager of a small bankrupt company called KenDavis Industries put the point this way: "Everyone agrees there is no shareholder equity — so *we've* got *nothing* to lose. The *banks* have it all on the line now — not us." In another case, the managers of the failing firm took the incentive to gamble literally. They went to Las Vegas and bet the company's money, hoping to win enough to pay off the creditors. The effects of such distorted incentives to take on risk are usually not this blatant, but the results can be the same. For example, Sambo's Restaurants borrowed against unencumbered assets while in bankruptcy proceedings and used the funds to pay for a risky marketing initiative, changing the name and concept of its restaurants. When the gamble failed, unsecured creditors suffered most of the loss: they received only 11 cents of each dollar owed them.[12]

These kinds of warped strategies for capital budgeting clearly are costly for the bondholders and for the firm as a whole. Why do we say they create costs of financial distress? Because the temptation to follow such strategies is strongest when the odds of default are high. A healthy firm would never invest in Circular File's negative-NPV gamble, since it would be gambling with its own money, not the bondholders'. The healthy firm's creditors would not be vulnerable to this type of game.

The Second Game: Don't Bet Your Own Money. We have seen how stockholders, acting in their immediate, narrow self-interest, may take projects that reduce the overall market value of the firm. These are errors of commission. Conflicts of interest may also lead to errors of omission.

Assume now that a *good* opportunity for Circular File comes up: a relatively safe asset costing $10 with a present value of $15 and NPV = $5. Suppose Circular

---

[12] These cases are cited in Lynn M. LoPucki, "The Trouble with Chapter 11," *Wisconsin Law Review*, 1993, pp. 729–760.

issues $10 of new stock to go ahead with the investment and takes the project. The new balance sheet might then look like this:

CIRCULAR FILE COMPANY MARKET-VALUE BALANCE SHEET			
Net working capital	$20	Bonds outstanding	$33
Fixed assets	25	Common stock	12
Total assets	$45	Total liabilities	$45

The total value of the firm goes up by $15 ($10 of new capital plus the NPV of $5). So the probability of default has fallen and there are more assets to pay off the bondholder if default does occur. That should be reflected in the market value of the bonds. Before the injection of new capital, the bonds were worth $25; afterwards they might be worth (say) $33. Thus the new capital provides the bondholders with a capital gain of $8.

Because part of the value of the new project is captured by the bondholders, the equity value does not go up by $15 but by $15 – $8 = $7. The owner puts in $10 of fresh equity capital but gains only $7 in market value. Although going ahead is in the firm's interest, it is not in the owner's interest, and the project will be passed up.

Again, our example illustrates a general point. The value of any investment opportunity to the *firm's stockholders* is reduced because project benefits must be shared with the bondholders. Thus it may not be in the stockholders' self-interest to contribute fresh equity capital even if that means forgoing positive-NPV opportunities.

These problems theoretically affect all levered firms, but they are most serious when firms are staring bankruptcy in the face. If the probability of default is high, then stockholders will not put up new money that will be used to pay off the bondholders. They are more concerned with taking money out of the firm than with putting new money in.

SELF-TEST 15.5

> Go back to Circular File's original balance sheet. Now suppose that Circular issues $5 of new 1-year debt and uses the cash to buy back part of its stock. What happens to firm value? Who gains or loses? The new bondholders? The old bondholders? The stockholders?

What the Games Cost

The more the firm borrows, the greater the temptation to play such games. The increased odds of poor decisions in the future prompt investors to reduce today's assessment of the market value of the firm. Potential lenders, realizing that games may be played at their expense in the future, protect themselves by demanding better terms on the money they lend today. So the fall in value comes out of stockholders' pockets. This is the reason that it is ultimately in the stockholders' interest to avoid temptation. The easiest way to do this is to limit borrowing to levels at which the firm's debt is safe or close to it.

Here we have the economic rationale for all that fine print in the bond agreement. Debt contracts almost always limit the amount of additional borrowing. Often also they limit dividend payments to stockholders. But lawyers cannot anticipate all eventualities. For example, they can't ensure that the company accepts all positive-NPV projects.

We do not mean to leave the impression that managers and stockholders always succumb to temptation unless restrained. Usually they refrain voluntarily, not only from a sense of fair play, but also on pragmatic grounds: a firm or individual that makes a killing today at the expense of a creditor will be coldly received when the time comes to borrow again. Aggressive game playing is done only by out-and-out crooks and by firms in extreme financial distress. Firms limit borrowing precisely because they don't wish to land in distress and be exposed to the temptation to play.

....
Costs of Distress Vary with Type of Asset

Suppose your firm's only asset is a large downtown hotel, mortgaged to the hilt. A recession hits, occupancy rates fall, and the mortgage payments cannot be met. The lender takes over and sells the hotel to a new owner and operator. The stock is worthless and you use the firm's stock certificates for wallpaper.

What is the cost of bankruptcy? In this example, probably very little. The value of the hotel is, of course, much less than you hoped, but that is due to the lack of guests, not to bankruptcy. Bankruptcy does not damage the hotel itself. The direct bankruptcy costs are restricted to items such as legal and court fees, real estate commissions, and the time the lender spends sorting things out.

Suppose that we repeat the story of Heartbreak Hotel for Fledgling Electronics. Everything is the same, except for the underlying assets. Fledgling is a high-tech going concern and much of its value reflects investors' belief that its research team will come up with profitable ideas. Fledgling is a "people business"; its most important assets go down in the elevator and into the parking lot every night.

If Fledgling gets into trouble, the stockholders may be reluctant to put up money to cash in on those profitable ideas — why should they put up cash that will simply go to pay off the banks? Failure to invest is likely to be much more serious for Fledgling than for a company like Heartbreak Hotel.

If Fledgling finally defaults on its debt, the lender would find it much more difficult to cash in by selling off the assets. In fact, if trouble comes, many of those assets may drive into the sunset and never come back.

Some assets, like good commercial real estate, can pass through bankruptcy and reorganization largely unscathed; the values of other assets are likely to be considerably diminished. The losses are greater for intangible assets that are linked to the continuing prosperity of the firm. That may be why debt ratios are low in the pharmaceutical industry, where company values depend on continued success in research and development. It may also explain the low debt ratios in many service companies, whose main asset is their skilled labour. The moral of these examples is: *Do not think only about whether borrowing is likely to bring trouble. Think also of the value that may be lost if trouble comes.*

Finance in Action

Project Financing

Central to the selection of the debt/equity ratio is understanding its impact on the risks and costs of financial distress and bankruptcy. Firms can also manage the costs of financial distress and bankruptcy through the type of loan contract. A good example of this is *project financing*, a special type of debt that gives the lender the right to take over the entire project in the event of financial or operational difficulties. This reduces the opportunity

Project Financing *(continued)*

of the shareholders to play games with the lender's money.

In Canada, project financing typically is arranged through financial institutions such as chartered banks. To give you an idea of the issues involved in arranging project financing, we talked with Blair Roblin from the Canadian Imperial Bank of Commerce (CIBC). He has been involved in project finance as a Manager of the Project and Corporate Finance Division of CIBC and is currently Director of Mergers and Acquisitions.

Blair told us that the bank looks for projects that are economic units unto themselves. The project's cash flows and assets must be able to be isolated from the rest of the firm. Their operations must provide enough cash flow to cover operating expenses and service the debt — without looking for outside support. Furthermore, the risks of the project must be measurable and allocable to the parties to the deal. Project financing has been used to fund small hydro-electricity power plants, mines, and oil wells.

Small hydro-electricity projects are well-suited to project financing because they are very self-contained. Each involves building a power generating station on a river. The project's input is the river flow and electricity is the sole output. The risks of the project are well understood.

In a typical situation, an entrepreneur (the project sponsor) identifies a river with the potential to run a small hydro generating station. The sponsor then approaches the bank for a loan to build the generating station. Rather than making a traditional term loan, the bank often uses project financing — looking to the project itself for interest, principal repayment, and security — with little or no support

from the project sponsor. In essence, the bank is sharing with sponsors in the risks of project completion, operation, marketing, pricing, sales, and technology. In order to undertake these risks, the bank must have the right to take over the entire project in the event of financial or operational difficulties.

When arranging the project financing, the bank carefully analyzes all of the project's risks and does what it can to reduce these risks. This means shifting the risks to parties best suited to assess, monitor, and carry the risks. In our example, a key source of potential risk is the price of electricity, making the project's revenue uncertain. Variability in the project's revenues will make it difficult for the project to pay the interest and principal on the bank's loan. To reduce this variability, a long-term contract to sell all of the power is arranged with a hydro user or another hydro producer, such as Ontario Hydro. The small hydro station receives less revenue but has lower variability of its cash flow, which makes it better suited for project financing. The cost of the bank financing is lower than it would be if the firm had not lowered its risk.

In addition to these activities to allocate risks to other parties, the bank also ensures that it has the legal right to take over the project in the event that something goes wrong. Contracts are signed before the money is lent giving the bank the right to step in and run the project. Thus the project is isolated from the sponsor in both a financial sense and a legal contractual sense.

An important component to the bank's decision about lending money is the project's discounted cash flows. Blair told us that the bank measures the net present value of the project

> **Project Financing** *(continued)*
> ●●
>
> by forecasting the project's cash flows over a 50-year period, including inflation, and discounting the cash flows at the project's weighted average cost of capital. The discount rate used is built up from the current rate of return to existing hydro projects.
>
> Once the project has been funded, the work of the bank is far from over. The project financier must closely monitor the project during the construction phase to ensure that the project is on schedule and has not exceeded its budget. The bank does not receive any return on its loan until the hydro station is operational.
>
> We asked Blair what skills one needs to be a successful project financier. He stressed the need for analytical skills — the ability to model the project's cash flows and also to assess credit (lending) risks. Furthermore, negotiation skills are important because project financing involves many parties to the deal. Finally he told us, "You have to be nasty at times in order to protect the bank's interests. The bank does not make a lot of money. All of the contracts and arrangements must be locked up to ensure that the project is able to pay the interest on the bank loan."

 EXPLAINING FINANCING CHOICES

●●●●●●●●●●●●●●●●●●●●●
The Trade-off Theory

Financial managers often think of the firm's debt-equity decision as a trade-off between interest tax shields and the costs of financial distress. Of course, there is controversy about how valuable interest tax shields are and what kinds of financial trouble are most threatening, but these disagreements are only variations on a theme. Thus, Figure 15.5 illustrates the debt-equity trade-off.

trade-off theory: Theory that capital structure is based on a trade-off between tax savings and distress costs of debt.

This **trade-off theory** of capital structure recognizes that target debt ratios may vary from firm to firm. Companies with safe, tangible assets and plenty of taxable income to shield ought to have high target ratios. Unprofitable companies with risky, intangible assets ought to rely primarily on equity financing.

All in all, this trade-off theory of capital structure tells a comforting story. Unlike MM's theory, which seemed to say that with corporate taxes firms should take on as much debt as possible, it avoids extreme predictions and rationalizes moderate debt ratios. But what are the facts? Can the trade-off theory of capital structure explain how companies actually behave?

The answer is "yes and no." On the yes side, the trade-off theory successfully explains many industry differences in capital structure. For example, high-tech growth companies, whose assets are risky and mostly intangible, normally use relatively little debt. Utilities or retailers can and do borrow heavily because their assets are tangible and relatively safe.

On the no side, there are other things the trade-off theory cannot explain. It cannot explain why some of the most successful companies thrive with little debt. Consider, for example, the Canadian radio and television broadcaster CHUM Limited, which is basically all-equity financed. Granted, major valuable assets of CHUM's are intangible: its broadcasting licences. We know that intangible assets and conservative capital structures should go together. But CHUM also has a very large corporate income tax bill ($12.9 million in 1993 or 46 percent of earnings before interest and tax (EBIT)) and the highest possible credit rating. It could borrow enough to save millions of tax dollars without raising a whisker of concern about possible financial distress. In contrast, another Canadian broadcaster, Baton Broadcasting, has $166 million of short- and long-term debt (53 percent of book value of assets) and pays only $3.4 million in taxes (only 10.5 percent of EBIT).

CHUM and Baton illustrate an odd fact about real-life capital structures: the most profitable companies generally borrow the least. Here the trade-off theory fails, for it predicts exactly the reverse. Under the trade-off theory, high profits should mean more debt-servicing capacity and more taxable income to shield and therefore should give a *higher* debt ratio.

SELF-TEST 15.6

Rank these industries in order of predicted debt ratios under the trade-off theory of capital structure: (a) bioengineering; (b) auto manufacturing; (c) electric utilities.

A Pecking Order Theory

pecking order theory: Theory stating that firms prefer to issue debt rather than equity if internal finance is insufficient.

There is an alternative story that could explain why profitable companies borrow less. Financial managers worry about how investors may interpret an equity issue. Remember from Chapter 14 that the announcement of a stock issue drives down the stock price. It seems that investors believe managers are more likely to issue stock when they believe it is overpriced.

Issuing debt, on the other hand, seems to have a trifling effect on stock prices. Presumably this is because there is less scope for debt to be misvalued and therefore a debt issue is a less worrisome signal to investors.

These observations suggest a **pecking order theory** of capital structure. It goes like this:

1. Firms prefer internal finance, since these funds are raised without sending any adverse signals that may lower the stock price.
2. If external finance is required, firms issue debt first and issue equity only as a last resort. This pecking order arises because an issue of debt is less likely to be interpreted by investors as a bad omen.

In this story, there is no clear target debt-equity mix, because there are two kinds of equity, internal and external. The first is at the top of the pecking order and the second is at the bottom. The pecking order explains why the most profitable firms generally borrow less; it is not because they have low target debt ratios but because they don't need outside money. Less profitable firms issue debt because they do not have sufficient internal funds for their capital investment program and because debt is first in the pecking order for *external* finance.

15.5 SUMMARY

1. The firm's financing decision is a marketing problem. Think of the financial manager as taking all the firm's real assets and selling them to investors as a package of securities. Some financial managers choose the simplest package possible: all-equity financing. Others end up issuing dozens of debt and equity securities. The problem is to find the particular combination that maximizes the market value of the firm.

2. Modigliani and Miller's (MM's) famous proposition I states that no combination of securities is better than any other — the firm's overall market value (the value of all its securities) is independent of capital structure. MM agree that borrowing increases the expected rate of return on shareholders' investment. But it also increases the risk of the firm's shares. MM show that

the extra risk offsets the increase in expected return, leaving shareholders no better or worse off.

3. MM's proposition I is important because it exposes logical traps that unwary financial managers are sometimes lured into and it draws attention to the fact that debt has both an explicit cost (the interest rate) and an implicit cost (the increased risk of the equity). It also tells us *where* to look for reasons why capital structure could be important. We discussed two such reasons — tax and financial distress.

4. Debt interest is deductible when computing taxes. So borrowing provides an interest tax shield, which is equal to the marginal corporate tax rate T_c times the interest payment $r_{debt} \times D$. This tax is usually valued by discounting at the borrowing rate r_{debt}. In the special case of permanent debt

$$\text{PV tax shield} = T_c \frac{(r_{debt} \times D)}{r_{debt}} = T_c D$$

Of course this tax shield is valuable only for companies that are making profits and therefore paying taxes.

5. The costs of financial distress can be broken down as follows:

   ● Bankruptcy costs
      ● Direct costs include legal fees and administrative costs.
      ● Indirect costs reflect the difficulty of managing a company undergoing reorganization.
   ● Costs of financial distress short of bankruptcy
      ● Conflicts of interest between bondholders and stockholders of firms in financial distress may lead to poor operating performance and investment decisions.
      ● The fine print in debt contracts tries to prevent stockholders playing "games" that reduce the overall value of the firm but increase the costs of writing, monitoring, and enforcing the debt contract.

6. The capital structure choice is a trade-off between the tax advantages of borrowing and the costs of financial distress that maximizes firm value. Firms with safe, tangible assets and plenty of taxable income to shield ought to have high debt targets. Unprofitable companies with risky, intangible assets ought to rely primarily on equity financing.

7. There is an alternative pecking order theory of capital structure, which states that firms use internal finance when available and choose debt over equity when external finance is needed. This pecking order may reflect managers' desire to avoid the adverse signals that seem to be associated with the announcement of an equity issue.

8. There are no simple answers to the capital structure decision. For example, debt may be better than equity in some cases, worse in others. However, there are at least four things that firms need to think about:

   ● *Taxes:* If your firm is in a taxpaying position, an increase in leverage reduces the income tax paid by the company, though it may also increase the tax paid by investors. Of course you are not interested just in whether the company is currently paying taxes but whether it will do so throughout the life of the debt. Firms with high and stable income streams are more likely to remain in a taxpaying position.

- *Risk:* With or without bankruptcy, financial distress is costly. Other things equal, distress is more likely for firms with high business risk. That is why risky firms generally issue less debt.
- *Asset Type:* If distress does occur, the costs are likely to be greatest for firms whose value depends on intangible assets. These firms are more likely to forgo profitable investment opportunities and, if default occurs, their assets may erode rapidly. Hence such firms should borrow less than firms that hold tangible and saleable assets.
- *Financial Slack:* Since investors are likely to interpret an equity issue unfavourably, firms like to retain a certain amount of financial slack. Without such slack, a firm may be caught at the bottom of the pecking order and may be forced to choose between passing over a good investment opportunity or damaging the share price by an equity issue.

KEY TERMS

capital structure	**operating risk**	**costs of financial**
restructuring	**financial leverage**	**distress**
MM's proposition I	**financial risk**	**trade-off theory**
(debt irrelevance	**MM's proposition II**	**pecking order theory**
proposition)	**interest tax shield**	

SUGGESTED READINGS

The fall 1988 issue of the *Journal of Economic Perspectives* contains an anniversary collection of articles, including one by Modigliani and Miller, which review and assess the MM propositions. The summer 1989 issue of *Financial Management* contains three more articles under the heading "Reflections on the MM Propositions 30 Years Later."

The following articles analyze the conflicts of interest between bondholders and stockholders and their implications for financing policy:

M. C. Jensen and W. H. Meckling. "Theory of the Firm: Managerial Behavior, Agency Costs and Ownership Structure," *Journal of Financial Economics* 3(October 1976):305–360.

S. C. Myers. "Determinants of Corporate Borrowing," *Journal of Financial Economics* 5(1977):146–175.

Myers describes the pecking order theory in

S. C. Myers. "The Capital Structure Puzzle," *Journal of Finance* 39(July 1984):575–592.

PROBLEMS

1. Suppose that River Cruises, which currently is all-equity financed, issues $250,000 of debt and uses the proceeds to repurchase 25,000 shares. Assume the firm pays no taxes, and that debt finance has no impact on its market value.
   a. Rework Table 15.2 to show how earnings per share and share return now vary with operating income.
   b. If the beta of River Cruises' assets is .8 and its debt is risk-free, what would be the beta of the equity after the increased borrowing?

2. True or false? Explain briefly.
   a. Stockholders always benefit from an increase in company value.
   b. The reason that borrowing increases equity risk is because it increases the probability of bankruptcy.
   c. As long as the firm is *certain* that the return on assets will be higher than the interest rate, an issue of debt makes the shareholders better off.
   d. MM's proposition I implies that an issue of debt increases expected earnings per share and leads to an offsetting fall in the price-earnings ratio.

3. The common stock and debt of Northern Sludge are valued at $50 million and $30 million, respectively. Investors currently require a 16 percent return on the common stock and an 8 percent return on the debt.
   a. If Northern Sludge issues an additional $10 million of common stock and uses this money to retire debt, what happens to the expected return on the stock? Assume that the change in capital structure does not affect the risk of the debt and that there are no taxes.
   b. If the risk of the debt did change, would your answer underestimate or overestimate the expected return on the stock?

4. Reliable Gearing currently is all-equity financed. It has 5000 shares of equity outstanding, selling at $100 a share. The firm is considering a capital restructuring. The low-debt plan would entail a debt issue of $100,000 with the proceeds used to buy back stock. The high-debt plan would exchange $200,000 of debt for equity. The debt will pay an interest rate of 10 percent. The firm pays no taxes.
   a. What will be the debt-to-equity ratio after each possible restructuring?
   b. If earnings before interest and tax (EBIT) will be either $45,000 or $65,000, what will be earnings per share for each financing mix for both possible values of EBIT? If both scenarios are equally likely, what is expected EPS under each financing mix? Is the high-debt mix preferable?
   c. Suppose that EBIT is $50,000. What is EPS under each financing mix? Why are they the same in this particular case?

5. Schuldenfrei A.G. is financed entirely by common stock and has a beta of 1.0. The firm pays no taxes. The stock has a price-earnings multiple of 10 and is priced to offer a 10 percent expected return. The company decides to repurchase half the common stock and substitute an equal value of debt. If the debt yields a *risk-free* 5 percent, calculate
   a. the beta of the common stock after the refinancing.
   b. the required return and risk premium on the common stock before the refinancing.
   c. the required return and risk premium on the common stock after the refinancing.
   d. the required return on the debt.
   e. the required return on the company (i.e., stock and debt combined) after the refinancing.

   Assume that the operating profit of the firm is expected to remain constant. Give
   f. the percentage increase in earnings per share.
   g. the new price-earnings multiple. *Hint:* Has anything happened to the stock price?

6. Hubbard's Pet Foods is financed 80 percent by common stock and 20 percent by bonds. The expected return on the common stock is 12 percent and the rate of interest on the bonds is 6 percent. Assume that the bonds are default-free. Now assume that Hubbard's issues more debt and uses the proceeds to retire equity. The new financing mix is 60 percent equity and 40 percent debt. If the debt is still default-free, what happens to the expected rate of return on equity? What happens to the expected return on the package of common stock and bonds?

7. "MM totally ignore the fact that as you borrow more, you have to pay higher rates of interest." Explain carefully whether this is a valid objection.

8. Indicate what's wrong with the following arguments:
   a. As the firm borrows more and debt becomes risky, both stock- and bondholders demand higher rates of return. Thus by *reducing* the debt ratio we can reduce *both* the cost of debt and the cost of equity, making everybody better off.
   b. Moderate borrowing doesn't significantly affect the probability of financial distress or bankruptcy. Consequently, moderate borrowing won't increase the expected rate of return demanded by stockholders.
   c. A capital investment opportunity offering a 10 percent discounted cash flow rate of return is an attractive project if it can be 100 percent debt-financed at an 8 percent interest rate.
   d. The more debt the firm issues, the higher the interest rate it must pay. That is one important reason why firms should operate at conservative debt levels.

9. Smoke and Mirrors currently has EBIT of $25,000 and is all-equity financed. EBIT is expected to stay at this level indefinitely. The firm pays corporate taxes equal to 35 percent of taxable income. The discount rate for the firm's projects is 10 percent.
   a. What is the market value of the firm?
   b. Now assume the firm issues $100,000 of debt paying interest of 6 percent per year, using the proceeds to retire equity. The debt is expected to be permanent. What will happen to the total value of the firm (debt plus equity)?
   c. Recompute your answer to (b) under the following assumptions. The debt issue raises the possibility of bankruptcy. The firm has a 30 percent chance of going bankrupt after 3 years. If it does go bankrupt, it will incur bankruptcy costs of $200,000. The discount rate is 10 percent. Should the firm issue the debt?

10. Here are book- and market-value balance sheets of the United Frypan Company:

BOOK-VALUE BALANCE SHEET			
Net working capital	$ 20	Debt	$ 40
Long-term assets	80	Equity	60
	$100		$100

MARKET-VALUE BALANCE SHEET			
Net working capital	$ 20	Debt	$ 40
Long-term assets	140	Equity	120
	$160		$160

D/E = 25%

Assume that MM's theory holds with taxes. There is no growth and the $40 of debt is expected to be permanent. Assume a 35 percent corporate tax rate.

a. How much of the firm's value is accounted for by the debt-generated tax shield?

b. Now suppose that Parliament passes a law that eliminates the deductibility of interest for tax purposes after a grace period of 5 years. What will be the new value of the firm, other things equal? (Assume an 8 percent borrowing rate.)

11. Look back to Table 2.2 where we provided a summary 1994 income statement for Hudson's Bay Company. If the tax rate is 35 percent, what is HBC's interest tax shield? What is the present value of the annual tax shield if the company plans to increase its borrowing and interest payments by 5 percent a year indefinitely? Assume a discount rate of 8 percent.

12. The Salad Oil Storage Company (SOS) has financed a large part of its facilities with long-term debt. There is a significant risk of default, but the company is not on the ropes yet. Explain

a. why SOS stockholders could lose by investing in a positive-NPV project financed by an equity issue.

b. why SOS stockholders could gain by investing in a negative-NPV project financed by cash.

c. why SOS stockholders could gain from paying out a large cash dividend.

13. a. Who benefits from the fine print in bond contracts after the firm gets into financial trouble?

b. Who benefits from the fine print when the bonds are issued?

14. Let's go back to Circular File company. Its current *market-value* balance sheet is

Assets		Liabilities and Equity	
Net working capital	$20	Bonds outstanding	$25
Fixed assets	10	Common stock	5
Total assets	$30	Total liabilities and shareholders' equity	$30

Who would gain or lose from the following maneuvers?

a. Circular pays a $10 cash dividend.

b. Circular halts operations, sells its fixed assets for $6, and converts net working capital into $20 cash. It invests its $26 in Treasury bills.

c. Circular encounters an investment opportunity requiring a $10 initial investment with NPV = $0. It borrows $10 to finance the project by issuing more bonds with the same security, seniority, and so on, as the existing bonds.

d. Circular finances the investment opportunity in part (c) by issuing more common stock.

15. Ronald Masulis[13] has analyzed the stock price impact of *exchange offers* of debt for equity or vice versa. In an exchange offer, the firm offers to trade freshly issued securities for seasoned securities in the hands of investors.

---

[13] R. W. Masulis, "The Effects of Capital Structure Change on Security Prices: A Study of Exchange Offers," *Journal of Financial Economics* 8 (June 1980):139–177, and "The Impact of Capital Structure Change on Firm Value," *Journal of Finance* 38 (March 1983):107–126.

Thus a firm that wanted to move to a higher debt ratio could offer to trade new debt for outstanding shares. A firm that wanted to move to a more conservative capital structure could offer to trade new shares for outstanding debt securities. Masulis found that debt-for-equity exchanges were good news (stock price increased on announcement) and equity-for-debt exchanges were bad news.

a. Are these results consistent with the trade-off theory of capital structure?

b. Are the results consistent with the evidence that investors regard announcements of (i) stock issues as bad news, (ii) stock repurchases as good news, and (iii) debt issues as no news, or at most trifling disappointments?

SOLUTIONS TO SELF-TEST QUESTIONS

15.1

a. Data:

Number of shares	25,000
Price per share	$10
Market value of shares	$250,000
Market value of debt	$750,000

	State of the Economy			
	Slump	**Stagnant**	**Normal**	**Boom**
Operating income, dollars	75,000	100,000	**125,000**	150,000
Interest, dollars	75,000	75,000	**75,000**	75,000
Equity earnings, dollars	0	25,000	**50,000**	75,000
Earnings per share, dollars	0	1.00	**2.00**	3.00
Return on shares, percent	0	0	**20**	30

Every change of $25,000 in operating income leads to a change in the return to equityholders of 10 percent. This is double the swing in equity returns when debt was only $500,000.

b. The stockholder should lend out $3 for every $1 invested in River Cruises' stock. For example, he could buy one share for $10 and then lend $30. The payoffs are:

	State of the Economy			
	Slump	**Stagnant**	**Normal**	**Boom**
Earnings on one share	$0	1.00	**2.00**	3.00
Plus interest at 10%	$3.00	3.00	**3.00**	3.00
Net earnings	$3.00	4.00	**5.00**	6.00
Return on $40 investment	7.5%	10	**12.5**	15

15.2 The weighted-average cost of capital reflects the business risk of the firm's projects. That risk is unaffected by capital structure. As the financing mix changes, whatever equity is outstanding must absorb the fixed business risk of the firm. The less equity, the more risk per share. Therefore, as capital structure changes, r_{assets} is held fixed while r_{equity} adjusts.

15.3   Maritime Telegraph and Telephone's borrowing reduced taxable profits by $58 million. With a tax rate of 40 percent, tax was reduced by $.40 \times \$58 = \$23.2$ million. If the borrowing was permanent, MT&T would save this amount of tax each year. The present value of the tax saving would be $\$23.2/.08 = \$290$ million. If the tax shield lasted only for 1 year, the present value would be $\$23.2/1.08 = \$21.5$ million.

15.4   The bondholders will receive $2 million less than they would otherwise. This lowers the expected cash flow from the bond and reduces its present value. Therefore, the bonds will be priced lower and offer a higher *promised* yield to maturity. If the firm wants to issue the bonds at face value, it will need to offer a higher coupon rate and promised yield to maturity.

15.5   As long as the new bonds are issued at a fair price, the new bondholders don't lose and firm value is unaffected. The existing bondholders lose because Circular is more likely to default and the assets in the event of default will be shared with the new bondholders. The old bondholders' loss is the stockholders' gain.

15.6   The electric utility has the most stable cash flow. It also has the highest reliance on tangible assets that would not be impaired by a bankruptcy. It should have the highest debt ratio. The bioengineering firm has the least dependence on tangible assets and the most on assets that have value only if the firm continues as an ongoing concern. It probably also has the most unpredictable cash flows. It should have the lowest debt ratio.

Dividend Policy

In this chapter we explain how companies set their dividend payments and we discuss the controversial question of how dividend policy affects value.

Why should you care about these issues? Of course, if you are responsible for deciding on your company's dividend payment, you will want to know how it affects the value of your stock. But there is a more general reason. When we discussed the company's investment decision, we assumed that it was not affected by financing policy. In that case, a good project is a good project, no matter how it is ultimately financed. If dividend policy does not affect value, this still holds true. But suppose that it *does* affect value. Then the attractiveness of a project would depend on where the money was coming from. For example, if investors prefer companies with high payouts, then these firms might be reluctant to take on new projects that required them to reduce their dividend payout.

We start the chapter with a discussion of how dividends are paid. We then show that in an ideal world, the value of a firm would be independent of its dividend policy. This demonstration is in the same spirit as the Modigliani and Miller debt-irrelevance proposition of the previous chapter.

That leads us to look at the real-world complications that might favour one dividend policy over another. These complications include transaction costs, taxes, and the signals that investors might read into the firm's dividend announcement.

After studying this chapter you should be able to

- Describe how dividends are paid and how companies decide on dividend payments.
- Explain why dividend policy would not affect firm value in an ideal world.
- Explain why dividends may be used by management to signal the prospects of the firm.
- Show how differences in the tax treatment of dividends and capital gains might affect dividend policy.

 ## 16.1 HOW DIVIDENDS ARE PAID

Cash Dividends

cash dividend: Payment of cash by the firm to its shareholders.

On August 10, 1994, Spar Aerospace's board of directors met to discuss the company's dividends. The company announced a regular quarterly **cash dividend** of $.06 per share, making a total payment for the year of $.24. The term *regular* indicates that Spar expected to maintain the payment in the future. If it did not want to give that kind of assurance, it could have declared both a regular and an *extra* or *special dividend*. Investors realize that extra dividends are less likely to be repeated. For example, in April 1994 Imperial Oil declared a special dividend of $3.00 per share, well in excess of its usual regular dividend of $1.80 and not likely to be repeated in the near future.

Who receives the Spar dividend? That may seem an obvious question but, because shares trade constantly, the firm's records of who owns its shares can never be fully up-to-date. So Spar announced that it would send a dividend cheque to all shareholders recorded in its books on Monday, September 19. This is known as the *record date*.

The *payment date* for Spar's dividend was October 3. On that date the dividend cheques were mailed to investors. If Spar's records were not up-to-date, some of those cheques would be sent to the wrong investor. To handle this problem, stock exchanges fix a cutoff date, called the **ex-dividend date**, 4 business days prior to the record date. If you bought Spar stock on or after the ex-dividend date, which in this case was Tuesday, September 13, you were not entitled to the dividend. If Spar sent you that dividend by mistake, you had to send it on to the previous owner. If you owned the stock on Monday, September 12, you were entitled to the dividend. If Spar mistakenly sent that dividend to someone else, that person was obliged to pass it on to you.

Through September 12, Spar stock was said to be trading "with dividend" or "cum dividend." Beginning on September 13, the stock traded "ex dividend." The only difference between buying Spar before and after the ex-dividend date is that in the second case you miss out on the dividend. Other things equal, the stock is worth more when it is with dividend. Thus when the stock "goes ex," we would expect the stock price to drop by the amount of the dividend.

Figure 16.1 illustrates the sequence of the key dividend dates. This sequence is the same whenever companies pay a dividend (though of course the actual dates will differ).

ex-dividend date: Date that determines whether a stockholder is entitled to a dividend payment; anyone holding stock before this date is entitled to a dividend.

FIGURE 16.1
The key dates for Spar Aerospace's quarterly dividend.

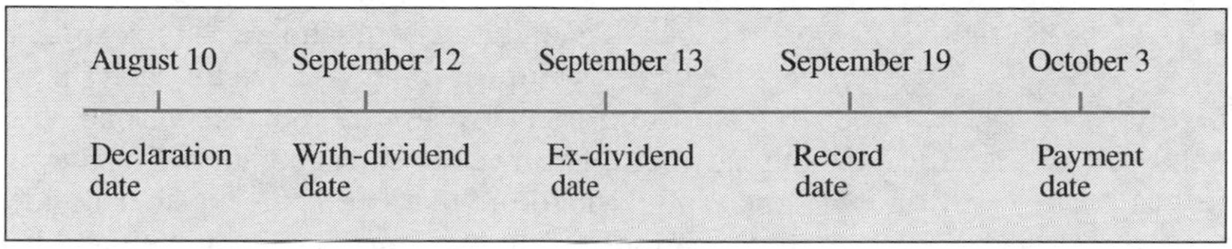

August 10	September 12	September 13	September 19	October 3
Declaration date	With-dividend date	Ex-dividend date	Record date	Payment date

SELF-TEST 16.1

Mick Milekin buys 100 shares of Junk Bombs, Inc., on Monday, June 1. The company has declared a dividend of $1 per share payable on June 30 to shareholders of record as of Friday, June 5. What is the ex-dividend date? Will Mick receive the dividend? When will the cheques go out in the mail?

Some shareholders may have desired the cash payment, but others preferred to reinvest the dividend in the company. To help these investors, firms offer dividend reinvestment plans. Imperial Oil, for example, has an automatic dividend reinvestment plan. If a shareholder belonged to this plan, his or her dividends were automatically used to buy additional shares.[1]

Some Legal Limitations on Dividends

Suppose that an unscrupulous board decided to sell all the firm's assets and distribute the money as dividends. That would not leave anything in the kitty to pay the company's debts. Therefore, bondholders often guard against this danger by placing limits on dividend payments.

Federal and provincial laws also help to protect the company's creditors against excessive dividend payments. For example, the Canada Business Corporations Act, which governs federally incorporated companies, prohibits payment of a dividend if there are "reasonable grounds for believing" that, after the

---

[1] Often the new shares in an automatic dividend investment plan are issued at a small discount from the market price; the firm offers this sweetener because it saves the underwriting costs of a regular share issue. Sometimes 10 percent or more of total dividends will be reinvested under such plans.

payment of the dividend, either, (a) the corporation would be "unable to pay its liabilities as they become due," or (b) "the realizable value of the corporation's assets would...be less than...its liabilities and stated capital...."[2] A company's stated capital is the total amount of stock issued. In effect, dividends must come out of the retained earnings and must not push the firm too close to insolvency.

If a firm decides to wholly or partially liquidate, it may repurchase its shares on the open market or pay a "liquidating dividend." However, this may reduce the realizable value of its assets below its liabilities plus stated capital. In that case, the firm must, by special resolution approved by the shareholders in a vote, reduce its stated capital.

These laws give most corporations a large degree of flexibility in deciding what to pay out. Nevertheless, they do help prevent unscrupulous managers from gutting the firm by paying out all its assets as dividends and then escaping their creditors.

Stock Dividends and Stock Splits

stock dividend: Distribution of additional shares to a firm's stockholders.

stock split: Issue of additional shares to firm's stockholders.

Spar's dividend was in the form of cash but companies often declare **stock dividends**. For example, the American firm Archer Daniels Midland has paid a yearly stock dividend of 5 percent for more than a decade. That means every year it sends each shareholder 5 additional shares for every 100 shares that are currently owned. In Canada, many firms have allowed shareholders the option of receiving cash or stock dividends.

A stock dividend is very much like a **stock split**. In both cases the shareholder is given a fixed number of new shares for each share held. For example, in a two-for-one split, each investor would receive one additional share for each share already held. The investor ends up with two shares rather than one. A two-for-one stock split is therefore like a 100 percent stock dividend. Both result in a doubling of the number of outstanding shares, but neither changes the total assets held by the firm. In both cases, therefore, we would expect the stock price to fall by half, leaving the total market value of the firm (price per share times shares outstanding) unchanged. Sometimes a company will undertake a reverse split or consolidation in which stocks are combined. For example, in August 1994 Bramalea shareholders approved a 1-for-20 share consolidation.

Why do firms pay stock dividends and split/consolidate their stock? One survey of managers indicated that 93.7 percent of splits are motivated by the desire to bring the stock price into an acceptable "trading range." They seem to believe that if the price is too high, investors won't be able to afford to buy a "round lot" of 100 shares. Of course that might be a problem for you or us, but it isn't a worry for insurance companies, pension funds or any other large institutional investors.[3]

● Example 16.1 Stock Dividends and Splits

Amoeba Products has issued 2 million shares currently selling at $15 each. Thus investors place a total market value on Amoeba of $30 million. The company now declares a 50 percent stock dividend. This means that each shareholder will receive one new share for every two shares that are currently held. So the total number of Amoeba shares will increase from 2 million to 3 million. The company's assets are not changed by this paper transaction and are still worth $30 million. The value of each share after the stock dividend is therefore $30/3 = $10.

---

[2] Canada Business Corporations Act, Section 40.
[3] J. Lakonishok and B. Lev, "Stock Splits and Stock Dividends: Why, Who, and When," *Journal of Finance* 42 (September 1987):913–932.

If Amoeba split its stock three for two, the effect would be the same.[4] In this case two shares would split into three. (Amoeba's motto is "divide and conquer.") So each shareholder has 50 percent more shares with the same total value. Share price must decline by a third.

There are other types of noncash dividends. For example, companies sometimes send shareholders a sample of their product. The British company Dundee Crematorium once offered its more substantial shareholders a discount cremation. Needless to say, you were not *required* to receive this dividend.

....

Share Repurchase

stock repurchase: Firm buys back stock from its shareholders.

When a firm wants to pay cash to its shareholders, it usually declares a cash dividend. But an alternative and increasingly popular method is for the firm to repurchase its own stock. In a **stock repurchase**, the company pays cash to repurchase shares from its stockholders and the shares are cancelled. These shares are usually kept in the company's treasury and then resold when the company needs money.

To see why share repurchase is similar to a dividend, look at panel A of Table 16.1, which shows the market value of Hewlard Pocket's assets and liabilities. Shareholders hold 100,000 shares worth in total $1 million, so price per share equals $1 million/100,000 = $10.

TABLE 16.1

Cash dividend versus share repurchase. Hewlard Pocket's market value balance sheet.

Assets		Liabilities and Shareholders' Equity	
A. Original balance sheet			
Cash	$ 150,000	Debt	$ 0
Other assets	850,000	Equity	1,000,000
Value of firm	$1,000,000	Value of Firm	$1,000,000

Shares outstanding = 100,000
Price per share = $1,000,000/100,000 = $10

B. After cash dividend			
Cash	$ 50,000	Debt	$ 0
Other assets	850,000	Equity	900,000
Value of firm	$ 900,000	Value of Firm	$ 900,000

Shares outstanding − 100,000
Price per share = $900,000/100,000 = $9

C. After stock repurchase			
Cash	$ 50,000	Debt	$ 0
Other assets	850,000	Equity	900,000
Value of firm	$ 900,000	Value of Firm	$ 900,000

Shares outstanding = ~~100,000~~ 90,000
Price per share = $~~900,000/100,000~~ = $9 00,000/90,000 = 10

Pocket is proposing to pay a dividend of $1 a share. With 100,000 shares outstanding, that amounts to a total payout of $100,000. Panel B shows the effect of this dividend payment. The cash account is reduced by $100,000 and the market value of the firm's assets falls to $900,000 Since there are still 100,000 shares outstanding, share price falls to $9. Suppose that before the dividend payment you owned 1000 shares of Pocket worth $10,000. After the payment you would have $1000 in cash and 1000 shares worth $9000.

---

[4] The distinction between stock dividends and stock splits is a technical one. A stock dividend is shown on the balance sheet as a transfer from the retained earnings account to the common equity account, whereas a split is shown as an increase in the number of shares outstanding. Neither affects the total book value of stockholders' equity.

Rather than paying out $100,000 as a dividend, Pocket could use the cash to buy back 10,000 shares at $10 each. Panel C shows what happens. The firm's assets fall to $900,000 just as in panel B, but only 90,000 shares remain outstanding, so price per share remains at $10. If you owned 1000 shares before the repurchase, you would own 1 percent of the company. If you then sold 100 of your shares to Pocket, you would still own 1 percent of the company. Your sale would put $1000 of cash in your pocket and you would keep 900 shares worth $9000. This is precisely the position that you would have been in if Pocket had paid a dividend of $1 per share.

It is not surprising that a cash dividend and a share repurchase are equivalent transactions. In both cases, the firm pays out some of its cash, which then goes into the shareholders' pockets. The assets that are left in the company are the same regardless of whether that cash was used to pay a dividend or to buy back shares. Later, however, we will see that how the company chooses to pay out cash may affect the tax that the investor is obliged to pay.

SELF-TEST 16.2

What would Table 16.1 look like if the dividend were $1.50 per share and the share repurchase were $150,000?

 ## HOW DO COMPANIES DECIDE ON DIVIDEND PAYMENTS?

What does the board of directors think about when it sets the dividend? To help answer this question, John Lintner conducted a classic series of interviews with corporate managers about their dividend policies.[5] His description of how dividends are determined can be summarized in four "stylized facts":

> **dividend payout ratio:** Percentage of earnings paid out as dividends.

1. Firms have long-run target **dividend payout ratios**. This ratio is the fraction of earnings paid out as dividends.
2. Managers focus more on dividend *changes* than on absolute levels. Thus paying a $2.00 dividend is an important financial decision if last year's dividend was $1.00, but it's no big deal if last year's dividend was $2.00.
3. Dividend changes follow shifts in long-run, sustainable levels of earnings rather than short-run changes in earnings. Managers are unlikely to change dividend payouts in response to temporary variation in earnings. Instead, they "smooth" dividends.
4. Managers are reluctant to make dividend changes that might have to be reversed. They are particularly worried about having to rescind a dividend increase.

A firm that always stuck to its target payout ratio would have to change its dividend whenever earnings changed. But the managers in Lintner's survey were loath to do this. They believed that shareholders prefer a steady progression in dividends. Therefore, even if circumstances appeared to warrant a large increase in their company's dividend, they would move only part way toward their target payment.

An extensive study by Fama and Babiak confirms Lintner's survey.[6] They found that if the company enjoys a good year, dividends may increase but to a lesser extent than earnings. Managers wait to see that the earnings increase is permanent before the dividend is fully adjusted.

---

[5] J. Lintner, "Distribution of Incomes of Corporations among Dividends, Retained Earnings, and Taxes," *American Economic Review* 46 (May 1956):97–113.
[6] E. F. Fama and H. Babiak, "Dividend Policy: An Empirical Analysis," *Journal of the American Statistical Association* 63 (December 1968):1132–1161. See p. 1134.

If managers are reluctant to make dividend changes that might have to be reversed, we should also expect them to take *future* prospects into account when setting the payment. And that is what we find. When companies pay unexpectedly low dividends, earnings on the average subsequently decline. When they pay unexpectedly high dividends, earnings subsequently increase.[7] That is why investors pay close attention to the dividend decision.

To see Lintner's model at work, consider Figure 16.2, which plots the dividends and earnings per share of Abitibi-Price Inc. While earnings per share fluctuate quite erratically, dividends per share do not. Between 1977 and 1988, both earnings per share and dividends per share grew but earnings varied much more from year to year. In 1989, Abitibi experienced a substantial drop in earnings and the decline continued over the next three years. Dividends fell in 1989 but remained constant between 1990 and 1992 as management seemed to cautiously wait for evidence that any further dividend decrease was needed. Finally, in 1993, Abitibi-Price cut its dividend. Over the 17 years, the average annual rate of growth of earnings per share was negative 11 percent (–11 percent) whereas the average annual rate of growth of dividends was 12 percent. Furthermore, the standard deviation of the annual earnings per share growth rate is 90 percent but the standard deviation of the annual dividend growth rate is only 50 percent, showing that dividends are much less variable than earnings per share.

FIGURE 16.2
Abitibi-Price earnings and dividends per share.

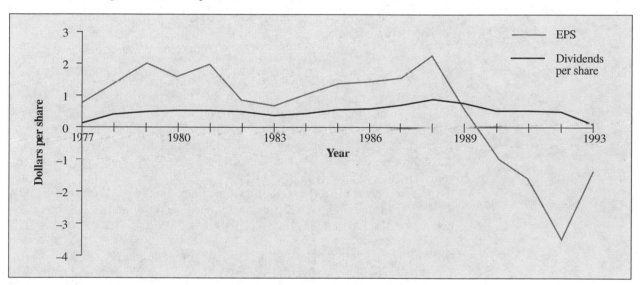

Source: Based on data from The Financial Post Datagroup, Historical Reports, "Abitibi-Price Inc."

 16.3 WHY DIVIDEND POLICY SHOULD NOT MATTER

The first step toward understanding dividend policy is to recognize that the phrase means different things to different people. Therefore, we must start by defining what we mean by it.

---

[7] See, for example, R. Watts, "The Information Content of Dividends," *Journal of Business* 46 (April 1973):191–211, for an analysis of the information effects in the United States.

A firm's decisions about dividends are often intertwined with other financing and investment decisions. Some firms pay low dividends because management is optimistic about the firm's future and wishes to retain earnings for expansion. In this case the dividend is a by-product of the firm's capital budgeting decision. Another firm might finance capital expenditures largely by borrowing. This frees up cash for dividends. In this case the firm's dividend is a by-product of the borrowing decision.

We wish to isolate dividend policy from other problems of financial management. The precise question we should ask is: "What is the effect of a change in cash dividends paid, *given the firm's capital budgeting and borrowing decisions*?" Of course the cash used to finance a dividend increase has to come from somewhere. If we fix the firm's investment outlays and borrowing, there is only one possible source — an issue of stock. Thus we define *dividend policy* as the trade-off between retaining earnings on the one hand and paying out cash and issuing shares on the other.

One nice feature of economics is that it can accommodate not just two, but three opposing points of view. And so it is with dividend policy. On one side there is a conservative group that believes high dividends increase firm value. On the other side there is a group that believes high dividends bring high taxes and therefore reduce firm value. And in the centre there is a middle-of-the-road party that believes dividend policy makes no difference.

Dividend Policy Is Irrelevant in Competitive Markets

The middle-of-the-road party was founded in 1961 by Miller and Modigliani (MM)[8] — the same two who showed that in idealized conditions capital structure also is irrelevant.

MM reasoned as follows. Suppose your firm has settled on its investment program. You have worked out how much of this program can be financed from borrowing, and you plan to finance the balance from retained earnings. Any surplus cash is to be paid out as dividends.

Now think what happens if you try to increase the dividend payment without changing the investment and borrowing policy. The extra money must come from somewhere. If the firm fixes its borrowing, the only way it can finance the extra dividend is to print some more shares and sell them. The new shareholders will part with their money only if you can offer them shares that are worth as much as they cost. But how is this possible when the firm's assets and earnings are unchanged? The answer is that some of the firm's future dividend payments that would previously have gone to the old shareholders must now be diverted to the new ones.

Since the old shareholders now have a reduced share in the firm's future dividends, they suffer a capital loss. This capital loss just offsets the extra cash dividend they receive.

Does it make any difference to the old shareholders that they receive an extra dividend payment plus an offsetting capital loss? It might if that was the only way they could get their hands on cash. But as long as capital markets are efficient, they can raise the cash by selling shares. Thus the old shareholders can cash in either by persuading the management to pay a higher dividend or by selling their shares. In either case there will be a transfer of ownership from old to new shareholders.

MM dividend-irrelevance proposition: Theory that under ideal conditions, the value of the firm is unaffected by dividend policy.

Because investors do not need dividends to get their hands on cash, MM argue that they will not pay higher prices for shares with higher payouts. Therefore, firms ought not to worry about dividend policy. This conclusion is known as the **MM dividend-irrelevance proposition.**

---

[8] M. H. Miller and F. Modigliani, "Dividend Policy, Growth and the Valuation of Shares," *Journal of Business* 34 (October 1961):411–433.

**Dividend
Irrelevance — An
Illustration**

We can illustrate the MM argument with the case of Rational Demiconductor, which at this moment has the following balance sheet:

RATIONAL DEMICONDUCTOR'S MARKET-VALUE BALANCE SHEET

Assets		Liabilities and Equity	
Cash ($2000 held for investment)	$ 2,000	Debt	$ 0
Fixed assets	9,000	Equity	12,000
NPV of investment opportunity ($2000 investment required)	1,000		
Total asset value	$12,000	Value of firm	$12,000

Rational Demiconductor has $2000 cash earmarked for a project requiring a $2000 investment. The project NPV is $1000, so after the project is paid for and undertaken, the total market value of the project will be $3000. Note that the balance sheet is constructed with market values; equity equals the market value of the firm's outstanding shares (price per share times number of shares outstanding). It is not necessarily equal to book equity.

Now suppose Rational Demiconductor uses its cash to pay a $2000 dividend to its stockholders. The benefit to them is obvious: $2000 of spendable cash. It is also obvious that there must be a cost. The cash is not free.

Where does the money for the dividend come from? Of course, the immediate source of funds is Rational Demiconductor's cash account. But this cash was earmarked for the investment project. Since we want to isolate the effects of dividend policy on shareholders' wealth, we assume that the company *continues* with the investment project. That means the $2000 cash must be raised by new financing. Since we assume borrowing to be fixed, Rational Demiconductor must end up financing the dividend with a $2000 stock issue. This is the sense in which dividend policy involves a trade-off between paying out cash and issuing new shares.

Now examine the balance sheet *after* the dividend is paid and the new stock is sold. Because Rational Demiconductor's investment and borrowing policies are unaffected by the dividend payment, its *overall* market value must be unchanged at $12,000. We know also that if the new stockholders pay a fair price for their shares, their stock must be worth $2000. That leaves us with only one missing number — the value of the shares held by the original stockholders. It is easy to see that this must be

$$\text{Value of original stockholders' shares} = \text{total value of company} \\ - \text{value of new shares}$$

$$= \$12{,}000 - \$2000 = \$10{,}000$$

The old shareholders have received a $2000 cash dividend and incurred a $2000 capital loss. Dividend policy doesn't matter.

RATIONAL DEMICONDUCTOR'S NEW MARKET-VALUE BALANCE SHEET

Assets		Liabilities and Equity	
Cash ($2000 from stock issue)	$ 2,000	New equity holders	$ 2,000
Fixed assets	9,000	Old equity holders	10,000
NPV of investment opportunity ($2000 investment required)	1,000		
Total asset value	$12,000	Value of firm	$12,000

By paying out $2000 with one hand and taking it back with the other, Rational Demiconductor is recycling cash. This benefits shareholders about as much as leaving the refrigerator door open cools the kitchen.

This example may seem artificial at first, for we do not observe firms scheduling a stock issue with every dividend payment. But there are many firms that pay dividends and also issue stock from time to time. They could avoid the stock issues by paying lower dividends and retaining more funds in the firm. Many other firms restrict dividends so that they *do not* have to issue shares. They could instead issue stock occasionally and increase the dividend.

Of course, our demonstration ignores taxes, issue costs, and a variety of other real-world complications. We will turn to those items shortly, but before we do, we note that the really crucial assumption in our proof is that the new shares are sold at a fair price. The shares sold to raise $2000 must actually be worth $2000.[9] In other words, we have assumed efficient capital markets.

Finance in Action

Shareholders Squeeze Cash from Chrysler

Does Mr. Kerkorian's demand for higher dividends contradict the dividend-irrelevance theory? No. His concern is with Chrysler's plans for the $6 billion of surplus cash. He wants the cash paid to shareholders and not spent by Chrysler. This is a battle over capital budgeting, not a question about dividend policy.

Kirk Kerkorian's takeover bid for Chrysler corporation received much publicity when it was announced in April 1995, but this was the second run that the billionaire had taken at the firm. In November 1994 Kerkorian, who then owned 9 percent of Chrysler's shares, sent a strongly worded letter to Chrysler's board of directors. This letter, which threatened legal action if not acted on by mid December, demanded that the firm distribute *billions* of dollars to its shareholders through a share buyback program and a large increase in dividend payments. Mr. Kerkorian's attention was, it seems, caught by the firm's cash holdings of well over $6 billion in U.S. funds.

Other recommendations in this letter focused on additional steps that Kerkorian believed would increase the value of Chrysler shares — implementation of a stock split, and relaxation of Chrysler's "poison pill" defense.

Kerkorian succeeded on three of the four counts, although spokespeople for Chrysler claimed that two of these initiatives were already in the works before his proposals were presented. Soon after receiving the letter Chrysler announced a major stock repurchase program to begin in 1995, boosted its quarterly dividend by 60 percent (from 25 to 40 cents per share), and weakened its poison pill provisions. The dividend increase will transfer over $200 million (U.S.) of cash to shareholders annually, and the share buyback will transfer one billion dollars U.S.

[9] Notice that the "old" shareholders get all the benefit of the positive-NPV project. The "new" shareholders require only a fair rate of return. They are making a zero-NPV investment.

....
Calculating Share Price

We have assumed that Rational Demiconductor's new shares can be sold at a fair price, but what is that price and how many new shares are issued?

Suppose that before this dividend payout the company had 1000 shares outstanding. Because the old stock was worth in total $12,000, this works out to $12,000/1000 = $12 per share. After the company has paid the dividend and completed the financing, the old stock is worth $10,000. That works out to $10,000/1000 = $10 per share. In other words, the price of the old stock falls by precisely the amount of the $2 per share dividend payment.

Now let us look at the new stock. Clearly, after the issue this must sell at the same price as the rest of the stock. In other words, it must be valued at $10. If the new stockholders get fair value, the company needs to issue $2000/$10 = 200 new shares in order to raise the $2000 that it needs.

● **Example 16.2 Dividend Irrelevance**

Panel A of Table 16.2 shows that Consolidated Pasta is expected to pay annual dividends of $10 a share in perpetuity. Shareholders expect a 10 percent rate of return from Consolidated stock and therefore the value of each share is

$$PV = \frac{10}{1.10} + \frac{10}{(1.10)^2} + \frac{10}{(1.10)^3} + \ldots = \frac{10}{.10} = \$100$$

Consolidated has issued 1 million shares. So the total forecast dividend payment in each year is 1 million × $10 = $10 million and the total value of Consolidated Pasta equity is 1 million × $100 = $100 million. The president, Al Dente, has read that the value of a share depends on the dividends it pays. That suggests an easy way to keep shareholders happy — increase next year's dividend to $20 per share. That way, he reasons, share price should rise by the present value of the increase in the first-year dividend to a new value of

$$PV = \frac{20}{1.10} + \frac{10}{(1.10)^2} + \frac{10}{(1.10)^3} + \ldots = \frac{10}{.10} + \frac{10}{1.10} = \$109.91$$

The president's heart is obviously in the right place. Unfortunately, his head isn't. Let's see why.

TABLE 16.2

Consolidated Pasta is currently expected to pay a dividend of $10 a share in perpetuity. However, the president is proposing to pay a one-time bumper dividend of $20 in Year 1. To replace the lost cash, the firm will need to issue more shares and the dividends that will need to be diverted to the new shareholders will exactly offset the effect of the higher dividend in Year 1.

A:	Old dividend plan	
	Dividend per share, Year 1	$10
	Dividend per share, Year 2 onwards	$10
	Price per share	$100
	Number of shares	1 million
	Total dividend, Year 1	$10 million
	Total dividend, Year 2 onwards	$10 million
	Total equity value	$100 million
B:	Revised dividend plan	
	Total dividend, Year 1	$20 million
	Total dividend, Year 2 onwards	$10 million
	Value of new shares issued in Year 1	$10 million
	Dividends paid on new shares, Year 2 onwards	$1 million
	Dividend paid on old shares, Year 2 onwards	$9 million
	Dividend per share, Year 1	$20
	Dividend per share, Year 2 onwards	$9
	Price per share	$100

Consolidated is proposing to pay out an extra $10 million in dividends. It can't do that *and* earn the same profits in the future, unless it also replaces the lost cash by an issue of shares. The new shareholders who provide this cash will require a return of 10 percent on their investment. So Consolidated will need to pay $1 million a year of dividends to the new shares ($1 million/$10 million = .10, or 10%). This is shown in panel B of Table 16.2.

As long as the company replaces the extra cash that it pays out, it will continue to earn the same profits and to pay out $10 million of dividends each year from Year 2. However, $1 million of this total will be needed to satisfy the new shareholders, leaving only $9 million (or $9 a share) for the original shareholders. Now recalculate the value of the original shares under the revised dividend plan:

$$PV = \frac{20}{1.10} + \frac{9}{(1.10)^2} + \frac{9}{(1.10)^3} + \dots = \frac{9}{.10} + \frac{11}{1.10} = \$100$$

The value of the shares is unchanged. The extra cash dividend in Year 1 is exactly offset by the reduction of dividends per share in later years. This reduction is necessary because some of the money paid out as dividends in later years is diverted to the new shareholders.

SELF-TEST 16.3

Suppose that Consolidated Pasta had issued $10 million in new bonds rather than new stock to pay the extra dividend. What would be the stock price? Assume that MM proposition I concerning debt irrelevance holds: specifically, ignore both the tax shields of debt as well as the potential costs of financial distress.

16.4   WHY DIVIDENDS MAY INCREASE FIRM VALUE

Many stockholders and businesspeople find it difficult to accept the suggestion that dividend policy is irrelevant. When faced with MM's argument, they often reply that dividends are cash in hand while capital gains are at best in the bush. It may be true, they say, that the recipient of an extra cash dividend forgoes an equal capital gain, but if the dividend is safe and the capital gain is risky, isn't the stockholder ahead?

It's correct that dividends are more predictable than capital gains. Managers can stabilize dividends but they cannot control stock price. From this it seems a small step to conclude that increased dividends make the firm less risky.[10] But the important point is, once again, that as long as investment policy and borrowing are held constant, a firm's *overall* cash flows are the same regardless of payout policy. The risks borne by *all* the firm's stockholders are likewise fixed by its investment and borrowing policies and unaffected by dividend policy.

A dividend increase financed by an issue of shares creates a transfer of ownership from "old" to "new" stockholders. The old stockholders — those who receive the increased dividend but do not buy their part of the stock issue — will find their stake in the firm reduced. They have indeed traded a safe receipt for an uncertain future gain. The reason their money is safe, however, is not because it

---

[10] In that case one might also argue that interest payments are even more predictable, so that a company's risk would be reduced by increasing the proportion of profits paid out as interest. How would you respond to that suggestion?

is special "dividend money" but because it is now in the bank. If the dividend had not been increased, the stockholders could have achieved an equally safe position just by selling part of their shares and putting the money in the bank.

If we really believed that old stockholders are better off by trading a risky asset for cash, then we would also have to argue that the new stockholders — those who trade cash for the newly issued shares — are worse off. But this doesn't make sense: the new stockholders are bearing risk, but they are getting paid for it. They are willing to buy because the new shares are priced to offer an expected return adequate to compensate for the risk.

MM's argument for the irrelevance of dividend policy does not assume a world of certainty; it assumes an efficient capital market. Market efficiency means that the transfers of ownership created by shifts in dividend policy are carried out on fair terms. And since the *overall* value of (old and new) stockholders' equity is unaffected, nobody gains or loses.

....
Market Imperfections

Most economists believe that MM's conclusions are correct, given their assumptions of perfect and efficient capital markets. However, nobody claims their model is an exact description of the so-called real world. Thus the impact of dividend policy finally boils down to arguments about imperfections and inefficiencies.

Those who believe that dividends are good argue that some investors have a natural preference for high-payout stocks. For example, some financial institutions are legally restricted from holding stocks lacking established dividend records. Trusts and endowment funds may prefer high-dividend stocks because dividends are regarded as spendable "income," whereas capital gains are "additions to principal," which may not be spent.[11]

In addition, many investors look to their stock portfolios for a steady source of cash to live on. In principle this cash can be generated from stocks paying no dividends at all; the investor can just sell off a small fraction of his or her holdings from time to time. For example an investor who holds 1000 shares of Canadian Pacific (CP) stock can sell 10 shares (1 percent of the total holdings) this year. This "homemade dividend" is equivalent to an increase of one percentage point in CP's annual dividend yield.

However, instead of CP's stockholders making regular sales, it is simpler and cheaper for the company to send them a dividend cheque. The costs of trading small numbers of shares can be extremely high. CP's regular dividends relieve many of its shareholders of these transaction costs and considerable inconvenience.

All this is undoubtedly true, but it does not follow that you can increase the value of *your* firm by increasing the dividend payout. Smart managers already have recognized that there is a clientele of investors who would be prepared to pay a premium for high-payout stocks. High-payout fans already have a wide variety of stocks to choose from.

You don't hear businesspeople argue that because there is a clientele of car buyers, their company should manufacture cars. So why should you believe that because there is a clientele of investors who like high payouts, your company can increase value by manufacturing a high payout? That clientele may have been satisfied long ago.

---

[11] Most colleges and universities are legally free to spend capital gains from their endowments, but this is rarely done.

SELF-TEST 16.4

Suppose an investor in Canadian Pacific does not need a regular income. What could she do to offset CP's "overly generous" payout policy? If there were no trading costs, would she have any reason to care about CP's dividend payout policy? What if there is a brokerage fee on the purchase of new shares? What if CP has a dividend reinvestment plan that allows the investor to buy shares at a 5 percent discount?

Dividends as Signals

Another line of argument for high payouts does not rely on market imperfections like trading costs. Think of a market in which investors receive very little reliable information about a firm's earnings. Such markets exist in some countries where a passion for secrecy and a tendency to construct many-layered corporate organizations produce earnings figures that are next to meaningless. Some people say that the situation is little better in Canada, thanks to creative accounting.

How might an investor in such a world separate marginally profitable firms from the real money makers? One clue is dividends. A firm that reports good earnings and pays a generous dividend is putting its money where its mouth is. Accounting numbers may lie, but dividends require the firm to come up with hard cash. We can understand why investors would favour firms with established dividend records. We can also see how investors would value the information content of dividends. Investors would refuse to believe a firm's reported earnings announcements unless they were backed up by an appropriate dividend policy.

Of course, firms can cheat in the short run by overstating earnings and scraping up cash to pay a generous dividend. But it is hard to cheat in the long run, for a firm that is not making money will not have the cash flow to pay out. Only the firms with sufficient cash flow will find that it pays to signal their good fortune by choosing a high dividend level. If a firm chooses a high dividend payout without the cash flow to back it up, that firm ultimately will face the high costs of a stock issue. Therefore, dividend increases may be taken as a valid signal of a company's good fortune.

For example, Healy and Palepu report that between 1970 and 1979 companies that made a dividend payment for the first time experienced relatively flat earnings growth until the year before the announcement.[12] In that year earnings grew by an average 43 percent. If managers thought that this was a temporary windfall, they might have been cautious about committing themselves to paying out cash. But it looks as if they had good reason to be confident about prospects, for over the next 4 years earnings grew by a further 164 percent.

Since dividends anticipate future earnings, it is no surprise to find that announcements of dividend cuts are usually taken as bad news (stock price typically falls) and that dividend increases are good news (stock price rises). For example, in a study by Aharony and Swary,[13] dividend increases were associated with a boost to the stock return of 1 percent, even after accounting for broad market movements. More significantly, firms announcing dividend decreases suffered a drop of 4 percent in stock market price.

It's important not to jump to the conclusion that these studies show that investors like higher dividends for their own sake. A dividend initiation or

[12] P. Healy and K. Palepu, "Earnings Information Conveyed by Dividend Initiations and Omissions," *Journal of Financial Economics* 21 (1988):149–175.
[13] J. Aharony and I. Swary, "Quarterly Dividend and Earnings Announcement and Stockholders' Return: An Empirical Analysis," *Journal of Finance* 35 (March 1980):1–12.

increase may be welcomed only as a sign of higher future earnings. Even investors who prefer low-dividend policies might find that a drop in the dividend is unwelcome news if they take it as a signal of the firm's prospects.[14]

---

[14] For example, in an article in *Fortune* Carol Loomis tells the story of General Public Utilities ("A Case for Dropping Dividends," *Fortune*, June 15, 1968, pp. 181ff.). In 1968 its management decided to reduce its cash dividend to avoid a stock issue. Despite the company's assurances, it encountered considerable opposition. Individual shareholders advised the president to see a psychiatrist, institutional holders threatened to sell their stock, the share price fell nearly 10 percent, and eventually management capitulated.

Finance in Action

Dividend Policy

Many firms strive to maintain constant dividend payout, regardless of changes in earnings. In the following excerpts from an article that appeared in The Globe and Mail Report on Business, *you will see evidence of the sticky dividend policy. Even the title of the article reveals the firms' reluctance to change dividend payouts: "Dividend growth lags profits." Notice the reference to dividend clienteles made by Nova's representative. Also, you will see evidence of firms attempting to communicate with their shareholders.*

...A sampling of recent corporate earnings shows there is plenty of room for improvement in dividend rates; banks, for example, are one of the most often-cited examples since they have been making bushels of money for several quarters and are expected to do equally well at year-end.

Yet, dividend yields remain in the 4.2- to 4.8-percent range — leading industry watchers to predict that most will bump up their dividends later this year or early next year, by as much as 10 per cent...

Another likely candidate for a dividend increase is cigarette and trust company conglomerate Imasco Ltd., whose profit was up 25 per cent in the third quarter. Although it raised its dividend in February to 39 cents from 37 cents, many observers say it's time for another boost.

"There is some speculation there will be another increase," agreed investor relations officer Peter McBride, adding that there may be some substance to the rumours — since chief executive Purdy Crawford hinted recently that analysts who predicted an increase "just may be right."

Other companies that have had healthy earnings increases include chemical giant Nova Corp., which almost doubled its third-quarter profit; Imperial Oil Ltd., whose earnings were up almost 70 per cent; and Noranda Inc., which has had a couple of profitable quarters after large losses last year.

None of these companies is contemplating a dividend increase any time soon, however.

Imperial Oil's dividend "hasn't changed since 1987," spokesman Jean Côté said. "For the last three years, the chairman has been asked by shareholders [about increasing it], and every time he has responded that we pay out $350 million annually in dividends — and for the past few years our earnings have been below that."

> ## Dividend Policy (*continued*)
> ●
>
> *Although "it appears very possible" that the company's earnings will be above that level this year, that doesn't mean investors should hold their breath waiting for a dividend rise, Mr. Côté said....*
>
> *Noranda representative Kevin Todd said the company's policy is "to maintain an even dividend during good and bad periods." He said Noranda ends up "in down times paying more than it should, and in good times paying less — but it all evens out in the long run."*
>
> *Nova's Bill Rowe said with a dividend yield of 1.86 per cent, the company is*
>
> *also "paying out more than we'd like to." A recent survey of shareholders on the subject of raising the dividend produced a "mixed response," he said — illustrating the kind of split in investment strategies that makes setting a dividend difficult.*
>
> *Institutional investors "wanted us to invest that money...because their focus is on capital appreciation," Mr. Rowe said. The ones who wanted an increase were primarily smaller investors, whose focus was "on a steady cash flow."*
>
> *Source:* Mathew Ingram, "Dividend Growth Lags Profits," *The Globe and Mail Report on Business*, November 15, 1994, p. B13.

SELF-TEST 16.5
● ● ● ● ● ● ● ● ● ● ● ● ● ●

In 1974 Consolidated Edison announced that it would omit its regular 45 cents per share cash quarterly dividend. It cited losses due to increased oil prices following the OPEC oil embargo. The stock price fell by about 30 percent in 1 day, from about $18 a share to $12 a share. Why would omission of a $.45 per share dividend result in a stock price drop of $6 a share?

 ## DIVIDENDS AND TAXES

How might paying dividends reduce firm value? If dividends are taxed more heavily than capital gains, then a company paying high-dividends causes its shareholders to pay higher taxes than an otherwise identical low-dividend paying company. Shareholders will pay less for the shares of the high-dividend paying company to compensate for the higher taxes. Firms should pay the lowest cash dividend they can get away with. Available cash should be retained and reinvested or used to repurchase shares.

Are dividends taxed more heavily than capital gains? For some shareholders it is true but some shareholders face higher capital gains tax. To examine the consequences for dividend policy, we first must look at the Canadian tax laws.

● ●

Taxation of Dividends and Capital Gains under Current Tax Law

Interest income is taxed as ordinary income when received either by an individual or a corporation. That is, interest income is taxed at the same rate as wage and salary income for individuals and at the same rate as income from operations for corporations.

Capital gains are taxed only when they are *realized* — that is when the asset is sold. Only 75 percent of the capital gains are taxable. This treatment applies to individuals as well as corporate investors.

Dividends are not taxed when received by a Canadian public corporation, such as one that is traded on a Canadian stock exchange. On the other hand, the *divi-*

dend tax credit (DTC) system applies to the taxation of Canadian dividends received by individual Canadian investors (that is, those who are not corporations). The dividend tax credit reduces the burden of the double taxation of shareholder income that occurs because the cash flows that produce dividend income are taxed at the corporate level as well as at the personal level.

To show how the dividend tax credit works, let's assume that you received $100 of dividend income in 1994 from Nova Scotia Power Inc. (NSP), a Canadian company. Let's say your marginal federal tax rate is 17 percent and you live in Ontario where the provincial tax rate is 58 percent of the federal rate. How much tax do you have to pay on the $100 of dividend income? First, "gross-up" the dividend income by 25 percent. The gross-up is designed to convert the dividend into its before tax equivalent. (Remember, that $100 dividend was paid out of after-corporate-tax income of NSP.) Then calculate your gross federal tax on your dividend income: $.17 \times \$125 = \$21.25$. To offset the federal dividend tax, you are allowed a dividend tax credit equal to 13.33 percent of the grossed-up dividend. Thus the dividend tax credit is worth $.1333 \times \$125 = \$16.67$. Your net federal tax is the gross federal tax less the dividend tax credit: $\$21.25 - \$16.67 = \$4.58$. The provincial tax is computed as 58 percent of the net federal tax: $.58 \times \$4.58 = \$2.66$. Thus the total combined federal and provincial tax is $\$4.58 + \$2.66 = \$7.24$. The dividend income tax rate is $\$7.24/\$100$ or 7.24 percent.

Table 16.3 describes the taxation of a $100 dividend, $100 capital gain, and $100 interest income for the three marginal federal tax rates — 17 percent, 26 percent, and 29 percent — when the province charges tax at 58 percent of the federal rate. Panel A shows the overall marginal tax rates for dividend income in those three cases: 7.24 percent, 25.01 percent, and 30.94 percent, respectively. In contrast, if the $100 had been retained in the firm and the investor sold the shares immediately to realize an incremental $100 capital gain that was subject to tax, the marginal personal tax rates on the capital gain would have been 20.15 percent, 30.81 percent and 34.37 percent, respectively, as seen in panel B of Table 16.3. For comparison, we show you the tax rate on $100 of interest income in panel C of Table 16.3. As you can see, the tax rate is highest for interest income: 26.86 percent, 41.08 percent, and 45.82 percent, respectively.

From a tax perspective, all investors would prefer dividends to immediately realized taxable capital gains. The tax advantage is much stronger, however, for the investors in the lower tax brackets — the high-income investor is almost indifferent between dividends and immediately realized capital gains.

However, many investors are in a position to defer some or all of their taxable capital gains because they need not sell their stock. Even those who desire regular annual income from their investments can defer much of their capital gains on "homemade dividends" because they don't have to sell off all of their investment at once. For example, suppose someone buys $10,000 of non-dividend-paying stock and sells 10 percent of that stock a year later as a homemade dividend when the stock price has increased by 12 percent to $11,200. The investor receives $1,120 for shares that cost $1,000 and thus realizes a $120 capital gain which is only 1.2 percent of the $10,000 investment. The remaining $1,000 of the homemade dividend is not taxed. Even though the investor has enjoyed a total capital gain of $11,200 — $10,000 or $1,200, no tax must be paid until the gain is realized by selling the shares. Thus the tax on the remaining capital gain, $1,200 - 120 = \$1,080$, is deferred. The deferral reduces the present value of any future capital gains tax. If the capital gains are deferred far enough into the future, the present value of the capital gains tax is negligible, and the effective tax rate on capital gains approaches zero.

TABLE 16.3

Personal taxation of
dividends, capital gains,
and interest income for
a provincial tax rate of
58 percent

	Marginal Personal Federal Tax Rate		
A. Dividend Income	17%	26%	29%
Dividend	$100	$100	$100
Taxable or grossed-up dividend (25% gross-up)	125	125	125
Gross federal tax	21.25	32.50	36.25
Dividend tax credit (13.33% of taxable dividend)	16.67	16.67	16.67
Net federal tax	4.58	15.83	19.58
Provincial tax (58% of federal tax)	2.66	9.18	11.36
Total personal tax on dividend	7.24	22.01	30.94
After-tax dividend	92.76	74.99	69.06
Dividend tax rate (dividend tax divided by dividend income)	7.24%	25.01%	30.94%
B. Capital Gains Income			
Capital gain	$100	$100	$100
Taxable capital gain (75% of capital gain)	75	75	75
Federal tax on capital gain	12.75	19.50	21.75
Provincial tax (58% of federal tax)	7.40	11.31	12.62
Total personal tax on capital gain	20.15	30.81	34.37
After-tax capital gain	79.85	69.17	65.63
Capital gains tax rate (capital gains tax divided by capital gain)	20.15%	30.81%	34.37%
C. Interest Income			
Interest income	$100	$100	$100
Federal tax on interest	17	26	29
Provincial tax (58% of federal tax)	9.86	15.08	16.82
Total personal tax on interest income	26.86	41.08	45.82
Interest income tax rate (interest income tax dividend by interest income)	26.86%	41.08%	45.82%

For all those investors who pay little or no tax on capital gains, by virtue of exemption or deferral, it would be more appropriate to compare the net tax on dividends in Table 16.3 to a zero capital gains tax rate. All such investors would prefer capital gains to dividends.

Let's call the group of investors that pays lower taxes on dividends "clientele D" and the other group that pays lower taxes on capital gains "clientele G." Clientele D includes Canadian investors in low tax brackets. Clientele G includes investors in high tax brackets, who do not trade their stocks. They prefer capital gains to dividends. Since Canadian corporations pay no tax on dividends they receive from other Canadian corporations, they are clientele D investors.

How Taxes Affect Share Values

We can now take a look at how taxes affect share value. Table 16.4 illustrates this. The stocks of firms A and B are equally risky and investors demand an expected after-tax rate of return of 10 percent on each. Investors expect A to be worth $114.45 per share next year. The share price of B is expected to be only $104.45, but a $10 dividend is also forecast, and so the total pretax payoff is the same, $114.45.

Both stocks offer the same pretax payoff. Yet clientele D investors should be willing to pay more for a share of stock B than of stock A and hence get a lower pretax rate of return from B. The reason is obvious: clientele D are taxed less heavily on dividends and B's return is mainly in the form of dividends. Table 16.4 shows that A and B are exactly equivalent investments to investors who are in the 26 percent marginal federal tax bracket, pay 58 percent provincial tax, and pay

TABLE 16.4

Effects of a shift in dividend policy when capital gains are taxed more heavily than dividends. The low payout stock (Firm A) must sell at a lower price in order to provide the same after-tax return because capital gains are taxed more heavily than dividends. The net tax rates on dividends and capital gains correspond to the 26 percent marginal tax rate and 58 percent provincial tax rate in Table 16.3.

	Firm A (no dividend)	Firm B (high dividend)
Next year's price	$114.45	$104.45
Dividend	$ 0.00	$ 10.00
Total *pretax* payoff	$114.45	$114.45
Today's stock price	$100	$100.73
Capital gain	$ 14.45	$ 3.72
Before-tax rate of return	$\frac{14.45}{100} \times 100 = 14.5\%$	$\frac{13.72}{100.73} \times 100 = 13.6\%$
Tax on dividend at 25.01%	$0.00	$.2501 \times 10 = \$2.50$
Tax on capital gain at 30.8%	$.3081 \times 14.45 = \$4.45$	$.3081 \times 3.72 = \$1.15$
Total after-tax income (dividends plus capital gains less taxes)	$(0 + 14.45) - 4.45 = \$10$	$(10 + 3.72) = (2.50 + 1.15) = \$10.07$
After-tax rate of return	$\frac{10}{100} \times 100 = 10\%$	$\frac{10.07}{100.73} = 10\%$

tax on capital gains annually. Each offers a 10 percent return after all taxes. The difference between the stock prices of A and B is exactly the present value of the extra taxes such investors face if they buy A.

Exactly the opposite is true for clientele G investors who are taxed more heavily on dividends than capital gains. They would pay more for stocks with low-dividend yields.

The question is which clientele predominates in the market: will high-dividend yield stocks sell for more or less than low-dividend yield stocks on the basis of taxes? An obvious way to answer the question is to look at the evidence and test whether high-yielding stocks offer different expected rates of return. Unfortunately, there are difficulties measuring these effects and so there are no definitive answers.[15]

Given the difficulties in measuring the relationship between expected yield and return, it is not surprising that different researchers have come up with different results. Furthermore, since tax laws change over time, we might expect that the relationship between dividends and expected return will also change. A significant change in the tax system occurred in 1972 when capital gains tax was introduced. Before 1972, capital gains were untaxed in Canada. Consequently, before 1972, the tax rate on dividend income was higher than on capital gains income for many investors and we would expect that high-dividend paying stocks would have to earn a higher pretax rate of return to compensate for the extra taxes. After 1972, when the difference between the tax on dividends and capital gains became smaller, we would expect that the pretax rate of return on high-dividend paying stocks would get smaller. Two Canadian studies have found these results: prior to

[15] To learn more about the issues involved in this research, see F. Black and M.S. Scholes, "The Effects of Dividend Yield and Dividend Policy on Common Stock Prices and Returns," *Journal of Financial Economics*, 1(May 1974):1–22, R.H. Litzenberger and K. Ramaswamy, "The Effects of Dividends on Common Stock Prices: Tax Effects or Information Effect," *Journal of Finance*, 37 (May 1982):429–443, and M.H. Miller, "Behavioral Rationality in Finance: The Case of Dividends," *Journal of Business*, 59 (October 1986):S451–S468.

1972, high-dividend paying stocks appeared to earn higher pretax rates of return, but after the introduction of the capital gains tax the differential reduced.[16]

The Canadian tax laws have not remained constant over time and the relationship between dividends and pre-tax rates of return has likely changed too. In the 1980s, new reforms increased the tax on capital gains. For example, a $100,000 lifetime capital gain exemption was ended in 1994. The net effect of these changes has been to reduce the difference in the taxes on capital gains and dividends. While there may have been a preponderance of clientele D investors in Canada prior to 1980's tax reform, the tax savings from moving between high and low dividend stocks are not as great as they used to be. With the current tax laws, there are still dividend and capital gains clienteles, but their borders are not so clear.

Dividend Clientele Effects

Despite all of our discussion of the effect of taxes on high-versus low-dividend paying stocks, it may still be true that dividend policy does not affect the value of a firm's shares. Changing the dividend policy of the firm attracts a new investor clientele but may not change the value of the firm. Why?

Suppose there is a predominance of clientele D investors who are taxed more heavily on capital gains than dividends. Then firms could increase their share prices if they increased their dividend payouts because this would make them more attractive to clientele D investors. The resulting increase in dividends would satisfy some of the overall demand of investors for high dividend stocks. Thus, they would require less of a pretax return premium per unit of dividend yield to compensate them for the higher tax on *any* low-dividend paying stocks. If enough firms were to convert to a high dividend yield, the premium would vanish and low dividend firms would have the same pretax return (and price) as high dividend firms of the same risk. Exactly the opposite would happen if there is a preponderance of clientele G investors — aggregate dividend yields would fall in response to the higher demand for capital gains as opposed to dividends.

Overall, we would expect to see firms shifting, in aggregate, to an optimal dividend policy at which there is no positive or negative premium required of high dividend stocks. The demand and supply of various dividend payouts would be equal. At this point, dividend policy would be irrelevant for each firm, even from a tax viewpoint. However, firms as a *whole* will have an optimal dividend policy.

According to the dividend clientele argument, when a firm changes its dividend policy, it will attract a different investor clientele. Suppose a company has a low dividend payout. If it switches to a high-payout policy, it will attract investors who prefer high-dividend paying stocks. Will the shares of the firm be worth more? No, as long as enough firms satisfy the demand for high-dividend paying stocks.

Share Repurchases as an Alternative to Cash Dividends

You already know that from the firm's perspective, a share repurchase is about the same as a cash dividend. However, the tax treatment for shareholders may not be. Stock repurchases by Canadian corporations generally get one of two tax treatments. If the shares are purchased on the open market, the selling shareholder receives a capital gains treatment, since it cannot be determined whether the buyer is a general member of the public or the corporation. If the shares are not repur-

---

[16] I.G. Morgan,("Dividends and Stock Price Behaviour in Canada," *Journal of Business Administration*, 12 (Fall 1980):91–106) found no difference in the before tax rates of return between high- and low-dividend paying stocks between 1972 and 1977. J. Rumsey,("An Efficient Technique for Testing Financial Modes with Time Varying Coefficients," Working Paper, York University (May 1989)), covered a longer period from 1972 to 1983 and found that high-dividend paying stocks had a higher pretax rate of return than low-dividend paying stocks, the differential in the rates of return had dropped substantially.

chased on the open market (for example, the shares are tendered directly to the corporation), the tax situation is more complex. In many cases, for example, when the shareholder is a Canadian dealing at "arms-length" with the corporation, the sale is also treated as a capital gain. In other cases, the share repurchase is treated as a combination of a "deemed dividend," a capital gain and a return of "paid-up capital" that is not taxed.

If a firm institutes a share repurchase program, typically it is allowed to buy back up to 5 percent of the outstanding shares. Such a program may be attractive to the firm's shareholders. Shareholders who pay higher tax on dividends than capital gains (clientele G) want to receive income from the firm and will be happy to sell some shares to the firm. They avoid paying the higher tax on the dividend income. Are you surprised that typically about one-third of TSE listed companies have stock repurchase programs? We must caution you: do not stop paying dividends altogether and only make regular share repurchases — like quarterly dividends. Firms that disguise dividends as repurchases — for example, proportional or regular repurchases — are liable to run into trouble with Revenue Canada. A firm that eliminates dividends and starts repurchasing stock on a regular basis may find that Revenue Canada would recognize the repurchase program for what it really is and would tax the payments accordingly. That is why financial managers have never announced that they are repurchasing shares to save stockholders taxes; they give some other reason.[17]

Nevertheless, one could argue that firms which pay dividends and as a result have to issue shares from time to time are making a serious mistake. Any such firm is essentially financing its dividends by issuing stock; it should cut its dividends at least to the point at which stock issues are unnecessary. This would not only save taxes for shareholders it would also avoid the transaction costs of stock issues.

16.6 SUMMARY

1. Dividends come in many forms. The most common is the regular cash dividend, but sometimes companies pay an extra cash dividend, and sometimes they pay a dividend in the form of stock. A firm is not free to pay whatever dividends it likes. It may have promised its bondholders it would not declare large dividends, and it is also prevented by federal and provincial laws from paying dividends if it is insolvent or if it has insufficient surplus.

2. When managers decide on the dividend, their primary concern seems to be to give shareholders a "fair" level of dividends. Most managers seem to have a notion of a target payout rate. But if firms simply applied this target payout rate to each year's earnings, dividends could fluctuate wildly. Managers therefore try to smooth dividends by moving only part way toward the target payout in each year. Also, they don't look just at past earnings: they try to look into the future when they set the payment. Investors are aware of this and they know that a dividend increase is often a sign of optimism on the part of management.

3. As an alternative to dividend payments, the company can repurchase its own stock. Although this has the same effect of distributing cash to shareholders, Revenue Canada taxes shareholders only on the capital gains that they may realize as a result of the repurchase.

---

[17] They might say, "Our stock is a good investment," or, "We want to have the shares available to finance acquisitions of other companies." What do you think of these rationales?

4. If we hold the company's investment policy and capital structure constant, then dividend policy is a trade-off between cash dividends and the issue or repurchase of common stock. If we lived in an ideally simple and perfect world, the choice would have no effect on market value. The dividend controversy centres on the effects of dividend policy in our flawed world. A common — though by no means universal — view in the investment community is that high payout enhances share price. While there are natural clienteles for high-payout stocks, we find it difficult to explain a *general* preference for dividends other than in terms of an irrational prejudice.

5. The most obvious and serious market imperfection has been the different tax treatment of dividends and capital gains. Dividend income offers tax advantages over realized capital gains income. However, investors who do not realize capital gains, defer their capital gains tax to the future, reducing the tax disadvantage of capital gains. For these investors, the tax on dividend income is higher. If dividend income is seriously tax-disadvantaged, we would expect investors to demand a higher before-tax return on high-payout stocks.

6. It is difficult to take a strong stand on dividend policy. Increases in the tax on capital gains have reduced the differences in taxes on dividends and capital gains; our sympathies lie with the middle-of-the-road view. Our recommendations to companies emphasize the following points. First, there is little doubt that sudden shifts in dividend policy can cause abrupt changes in stock price. The principal reason is the information that investors read into the company's actions. Given this, there is a clear case for smoothing dividends. If a sharp dividend change is necessary, then the company should provide as much forewarning and explanation as possible. Subject to this, we believe that, at the very least, a firm should adopt a target payout that is sufficiently low to minimize its reliance on external equity. Why pay out cash to stockholders if that requires issuing new shares to get the cash back? It's better to hold on to the cash in the first place.

KEY TERMS

cash dividend	stock split	MM dividend-
ex-dividend date	stock repurchase	irrelevance
stock dividend	dividend payout ratio	proposition

SUGGESTED READINGS

Lintner's classic analysis of how companies set their dividend payments is provided in

> J. Lintner. "Distribution of Incomes of Corporations among Dividends, Retained Earnings, and Taxes," *American Economic Review* 46(May 1956):97–113.

The pioneering article on dividend policy in the context of a perfect capital market is

> M. H. Miller and F. Modigliani. "Dividend Policy, Growth and the Valuation of Shares," *Journal of Business* 34(October 1961):411–433.

Merton Miller reviews research on the dividend controversy in

> M. H. Miller. "Behavioral Rationality in Finance: The Case of Dividends," *Journal of Business* 59 (October 1986):S451–S468.

PROBLEMS

1. In 1994 Trans Mountain Pipe Line paid a regular quarterly dividend of $.25 a share.

    a. Connect each of the following dates to the correct term:

        July 27, 1994   Record date
        August 30, 1993   Payment date
        August 31, 1994   Ex-dividend date
        September 6, 1994   Last with-dividend date
        September 30, 1994   Declaration date

    b. On one of these dates the stock price is likely to fall by about the value of the dividend. Why?
    c. The stock price in early September 1993 was $28. What was the prospective dividend yield?
    d. The earnings per share for 1994 were forecast at around $1.25. What was the percentage payout rate?
    e. Suppose that in 1994 the company paid a 10 percent stock dividend. What would be the expected fall in the stock price?

2. True or false? If false, correct the statement.

    a. A company may not generally pay a dividend out of legal capital.
    b. A company may not generally pay a dividend if it is insolvent.
    c. The *effective* tax rate on capital gains can be less than the stated tax rate on such gains.
    d. Corporations are not taxed on dividends received from other corporations.

3. The stock of Payout Corp. will go ex dividend tomorrow. The dividend will be $1.00 per share, and there are 20,000 shares of stock outstanding. The market-value balance sheet for Payout is shown below.

    a. What price is Payout stock selling for today?
    b. What price will it sell for tomorrow? Ignore taxes.

Assets		Liabilities and Equity	
Cash	$100,000	Equity	$1,000,000
Fixed assets	900,000		

4. Now suppose that Payout from question 3 announces its intention to repurchase $20,000 worth of stock instead of paying out the dividend.

    a. What effect will the repurchase have on an investor who currently holds 100 shares and sells 2 of those shares back to the company in the repurchase?
    b. Compare the effects of the repurchase to the effects of the cash dividend that you worked out in problem 3.

5. Now suppose that Payout again changes its mind and decides to issue a 2 percent stock dividend instead of either issuing the cash dividend or repurchasing 2 percent of the outstanding stock. How would this action affect a shareholder who owns 100 shares of stock? Compare with your answers to problems 3 and 4.

6. Suppose that you own 1000 shares of Nocash Corp. and the company is about to pay a 25 percent stock dividend. The stock currently sells at $50 per share.

    a. What will be the number of shares that you hold and the total value of your equity position after the dividend is paid?

    b. What will happen to the number of shares that you hold and the value of your equity position if the firm splits five for four instead of paying the stock dividend?

7. Respond to the following comment: "It's all very well saying that I can sell shares to cover cash needs, but that may mean selling at the bottom of the market. If the company pays a regular dividend, investors avoid that risk."

8. Good Values, Inc., is all-equity financed. The total market value of the firm currently is $100,000, and there are 2000 shares outstanding.

    a. The firm has declared a $1 per share dividend. The stock will go ex dividend tomorrow. At what price will the stock sell today? Ignore taxes.

    b. Now assume that the tax rate on dividend income is 25 percent (federal tax of 26 percent, provincial tax rate of 54 percent of the federal rate, 25 percent dividend gross-up, and 13.33 percent dividend tax credit) and the tax rate on capital gains is zero. At what price will the stock sell today?

9. Now suppose that instead of paying a dividend Good Values (from problem 8) plans to repurchase $10,000 worth of stock.

    a. What will be the stock price before and after the repurchase?

    b. Suppose an investor who holds 200 shares sells 20 of her shares back to the firm. If there are no taxes on dividends or capital gains, show that she should be indifferent between the repurchase and the dividend.

    c. Show that if dividends are taxed at 25 percent and capital gains are not taxed, the value of the firm is higher if it pursues the share repurchase instead of the dividend.

10. Investors require an after-tax rate of return of 10 percent on their stock investments. Assume that the tax rate on dividends is 25 percent while capital gains escape taxation. A firm will pay a $2 per share dividend 1 year from now, after which it is expected to sell at a price of $20.

    a. Find the current price of the stock.

    b. Find the expected before-tax rate of return for a 1-year holding period.

    c. Now suppose that the dividend will be $3 per share. If the expected after-tax rate of return is still 10 percent, and investors still expect the stock to sell at $20 in 1 year, at what price must the stock now sell?

    d. What is the before-tax rate of return? Why is it now higher than in part (b)?

11. Here are several "facts" about typical corporate dividend policies. Which of the "facts" are true and which false? Write out a corrected version of any false statements.

    a. Most companies set a target dividend payout ratio.

    b. They set each year's dividend equal to the target payout ratio times that year's earnings.

    c. Managers and investors seem more concerned with dividend changes than dividend levels.

    d. Managers often increase dividends temporarily when earnings are unexpectedly high for a year or two.

12. "Risky companies tend to have lower target payout ratios and more gradual adjustment rates." Explain what is meant by this statement. Why do you think it is so?

13. It is well documented that stock prices tend to rise when firms announce an increase in their dividend payouts. How then can it be said that dividend policy is irrelevant?

14. The expected pretax return on three stocks is divided between dividends and capital gains in the following way:

Stock	Expected Dividend	Expected Capital Gain
A	$ 0	$10
B	5	5
C	10	0

   a. If each stock is priced at $100, what are the expected net returns on each stock to (i) a pension fund that does not pay taxes, (ii) a corporation paying tax at 35 percent, and (iii) an individual paying federal tax at 29 percent and provincial tax at 54 percent of the federal rate. The dividend gross-up is 25 percent and the dividend tax credit is 13.33 percent of the grossed-up dividend.

   b. Suppose that stocks A, B, and C were priced to yield an 8 percent after-tax return to individual investors paying federal tax of 17 percent and provincial tax of 52 percent of the federal rate. Dividend gross-up is 25 percent and the dividend tax credit is 13.33 percent of the grossed-up dividend. What would A, B, and C each sell for?

15. Suppose all investments offered the same expected return *before* tax. Consider two equally risky shares, Hi and Lo. Hi shares pay a generous dividend and offer low expected capital gains. Lo shares pay low dividends and offer high expected capital gains. Which of the following investors would prefer the Lo shares? Which would prefer the Hi shares? Which wouldn't care? Explain.

   a. A pension fund.

   b. An individual in the highest tax bracket

   c. A corporation

   d. An individual in the lowest tax bracket

Assume that any stock purchased will be sold after 1 year.

16. Big Industries has the following market-value balance sheet. The stock currently sells for $20 a share, and there are 1000 shares outstanding. The firm will either pay a $1 per share dividend or repurchase $1000 worth of stock. Ignore taxes.

Assets		Liabilities and Equity	
Cash	$ 2,000	Debt	$10,000
Fixed assets	18,000	Equity	20,000

   a. What will be the price per share under each alternative (dividend versus repurchase)?

   b. If total earnings of the firm are $2000 a year, find earnings per share under each alternative.

   c. Find the price-earnings ratio under each alternative.

   d. Adherents of the "dividends-are-good" school sometimes point to the fact that stocks with high dividend payout ratios tend to sell at above-average price-earnings multiples. Is this evidence convincing? Discuss this argument with regard to your answers to parts (a)–(c).

17. For each of the following four groups of companies, state whether you would expect them to distribute a relatively high or low proportion of current earnings and whether you would expect them to have a relatively high or low price-earnings ratio.
    a. High-risk companies
    b. Companies that have recently experienced an unexpected decline in profits
    c. Companies that expect to experience a decline in profits
    d. "Growth" companies with valuable future investment opportunities

SOLUTIONS TO SELF-TEST QUESTIONS

16.1   The ex-dividend date is four business days prior to the date of record, or Monday, June 1. Therefore, Mick buys the stock ex dividend and will not receive the dividend. The cheques will be mailed on June 30.

16.2

Assets		Liabilities and Equity	
After cash dividend			
Cash	0	Debt	0
Other assets	850,000	Equity	850,000
Value of firm	$850,000	Value of firm	$850,000

Shares outstanding = 100,000
Price per share = $850,000/100,000 = $8.50

After stock purchase			
Cash	0	Debt	0
Other assets	850,000	Equity	850,000
Value of firm	$850,000	Value of firm	$850,000

Shares outstanding = 85,000
Price per share = $850,000/85,000 = $10

If a dividend is paid, the stock price falls by the amount of the dividend. If the company instead uses the cash for a share repurchase, the stock price remains unchanged, but with fewer shares left outstanding, the market value of the firm falls by the same amount as if the dividend had been paid. If a shareholder wants to receive the same amount of cash as if the firm had paid a dividend, he or she must sell shares, and the market value of the remaining stock will be the same as if the firm had paid a dividend.

16.3   Because we assume that the debt has no effect on the overall value of the firm, the total value of the firm remains at $100 million. Since the firm issues $10 million in new bonds and the total value of the firm is fixed, the total value of equity must fall by $10 million, which translates into the same $1 per share price drop as when equity was issued. If the firm starts out all-equity financed, the market-value balance sheet of the firm will be as follows (in millions):

Assets		Liabilities and Equity	
Assets	$100	Debt	$ 10
		Equity	90
Value of firm	$100	Value of firm	$100

Shares outstanding = 1 million
Price per share = $90 million/1 million = $90

16.4   An investor who prefers a zero-dividend policy can reinvest any dividends received. This will cause the value of the shares held to be unaffected by payouts. The price drop on the ex-dividend date is offset by the reinvestment of the dividends. However, if the investor had to pay brokerage fees on the newly purchased shares, she would be harmed by a high-payout policy since part of the proceeds of the dividends would go toward paying the broker. On the other hand, if the firm offers a dividend reinvestment plan (DRIP) with a 5 percent discount, she is better with a high-dividend policy. The DRIP is like a "negative trading cost." She can increase the value of her stock by 5 percent of the dividend just by participating in the DRIP.

16.5   The stock price dropped by more than the dividend because investors interpreted the news as a signal that in addition to omitting the current dividend Con Ed would have to reduce future dividends. The omitted dividend conveyed bad news about the future prospects of the firm.

PART SIX

FINANCIAL PLANNING

CHAPTER SEVENTEEN

Financial Statement Analysis

"Divide and conquer" is the only practical strategy for presenting a complex topic like financial management. That is why we have broken down the financial manager's job into separate areas: capital budgeting, dividend policy, equity financing, and debt policy. In the end the financial manager has to consider the combined effects of decisions in each of these areas on the firm as a whole. That is why we devote all of Part Six to financial planning. We begin in this chapter by looking at the analysis of financial statements.

Why do companies provide accounting information? Public companies have a variety of stakeholders, such as shareholders, bondholders, bankers, lenders, suppliers, employees, and management. These stakeholders all need to monitor how well their interests are being served. They rely on the company's periodic financial statements to provide the basic information on the profitability of the firm.

In this chapter we look at how you can use financial statements to analyze a firm's overall performance and assess its current financial standing. The tools you will learn can be applied in a wide variety of situations. For example, financial statement analysis may be useful in your assessment of a potential customer's financial health before you sell to them on credit. Financial statement analysis also may be used to understand the policies of a competitor, to help you decide the best policies for your company. Or you may need to check whether your own firm's financial performance meets standard criteria and, if not, the dimensions in which it can improve. Analyzing your company's financial performance and comparing it to your competitors may provide you with new insights about your performance.

As you can see, financial analysis is used for many reasons. In each case, the analyst must decide the questions that need to be answered and select the financial analysis tools best suited to shed light on the questions. For example, if you are a loans officer at a bank, you will want to know how likely it is that a loan applicant will pay the interest and principal owed on the loan. You will focus your analysis on the factors affecting the loan applicant's cash flow and assess its current debt level. On the other hand, if you are considering buying another company, you will want to use financial analysis to help understand how well run it is and assess its profitability.

We will look at how analysts summarize the large volume of accounting information by calculating some key financial ratios. We will then describe these ratios and look at some interesting relationships between them. Finally, we will show how the ratios are used and note the limitations of the accounting data on which most ratios are based.

After studying this chapter you should be able to

- Calculate and interpret measures of a firm's leverage, liquidity, profitability, asset management, and market valuation.
- Use the Du Pont formula to understand the determinants of the firm's return on its assets and equity.
- Evaluate the potential pitfalls of ratios based on accounting data.
- Interpret the company's earnings record.

17.1 FINANCIAL RATIOS

We have all heard stories of financial whizzes who can take a company's accounts apart in minutes and find its innermost secrets in financial ratios. The truth, however, is that financial ratios are no substitute for a crystal ball. They are just a convenient way to summarize large quantities of financial data and to compare firms' performance. Ratios help you to ask the right questions; they seldom answer them.

We will describe and calculate five types of financial ratios:

- Leverage ratios show how heavily the company is in debt.
- Liquidity ratios measure how easily the firm can lay its hands on cash.
- Efficiency or turnover ratios measure how productively the firm is using its assets.
- Profitability ratios are used to measure the firm's return on its investments.
- Market-value ratios show how the firm is valued by investors.

The company we will analyze is Green Forest Lumber Corporation (GFL), a Canadian distributor of lumber. Our objective is to assess GFL's recent overall financial performance and seek to identify weaknesses in the way the company is run. We will use the results to develop questions that the GFL's management may be able to use to improve its financial performance in the future. You'll find GFL's 1992 and 1993 income statement and balance sheet in Tables 17.1 and 17.2.

TABLE 17.1

INCOME STATEMENT FOR GREEN FOREST LUMBER CORPORATION
For the year ended March 31, 1993 and 1994
(All figures in millions)

	1994	1993
Sales revenue	376.7	302.6
Cost of goods sold	341.2	277.0
Gross profit	35.5	25.6
Selling and administrative expense	12.8	10.1
Depreciations and amortization	3.4	3.3
Amortization of goodwill	0.2	0.2
Earnings before interest and tax (EBIT)	19.1	12.0
Net interest expense	0.3	2.3
Other income	0.4	0.1
Income before tax	19.2	9.8
Taxes	7.5	4.1
Net income	11.7	5.7
Allocation of net income		
Addition to retained earnings	9.8	4.6
Dividends	1.9	1.0

Before diving headlong into the numbers, let's step back and look at Green Forest Lumber as a business. Without an understanding of the business, reading financial statements is like trying to put a puzzle together without knowing what it's a picture of — you may fit some pieces together but it's difficult to finish the job. A good place to start learning about the business is with the company's annual report. In the annual report you will find a company profile and management's analysis of the company's operations and performance along with all the financial statements and the accompanying notes. Don't forget to read the notes to the financial statements — they contain important information on how the accountants put the financial statements together.

According to its 1994 Annual Report, GFL is primarily a wholesaler of softwood lumber and oriented strand board (waferboard) to customers in residential construction and home improvement industries in Quebec, Ontario, and the eastern United States. GFL buys 85 percent of its lumber requirements from other sawmills and produces 15 percent at its own sawmill in Chapleau, Ontario. It has sales offices in Toronto and Bolton, Ontario, and distribution centres in Fort Erie, Windsor, Baltimore, Chicago and Charlotte, North Carolina.

income statement: Financial statement that shows the revenues, expenses, and net income of a firm over a period of time.

The **income statement** summarizes the firm's revenues and expenses over a period of time and the difference between the two, which is the firm's profit. For GFL, the income statement shows earnings made between April 1, 1993 and March 31, 1994. You can see that after deducting the cost of goods sold and other expenses, GFL had earnings before interest and taxes (EBIT) of $19 million. Of this sum, $0.14 million was used to pay debt interest (remember, interest is paid out of pretax income), and $7.5 million was set aside for taxes. GFL has no preferred stock so the balance of $11.7 million belonged to the common stockholders. However, GFL did not pay out all its earnings to the stockholders; dividends of $1.9 million were paid and $9.8 million was plowed back into the business.[1]

balance sheet: Financial statement that shows the value of the firm's assets and liabilities at a particular time.

Whereas the income statement summarizes activity during a period, the **balance sheet** presents a "snapshot" of the firm at a given moment. For example, the balance sheet in Table 17.2 shows a snapshot of GFL's assets and liabilities on March 31, 1994.

As we pointed out in Chapter 2, the accountant lists first the assets that are most likely to be turned into cash in the near future. They include cash itself, short-term securities, receivables (that is, bills unpaid by the firm's customers), and inventories of raw materials, work-in-process, and finished goods. These assets are all known as *current assets*. The second main group of assets consists of long-term assets such as building, land, machinery, and equipment. Note that the balance sheet does not show the market value of each asset. Instead the accountant records the amount that the asset originally cost and then, in the case of plant and equipment, deducts an annual charge for depreciation. GFL also has many valuable assets that are not shown on the balance sheet — a skilled labour force, for instance.

GFL's liabilities show the amount of the many claims on the firm's assets. These also are classified as current versus long-term. Current liabilities are bills that the company expects to pay in the near future. They include debts that are due to be repaid within the next year and payables (that is, amounts the company owes to its suppliers). In addition to these short-term debts, GFL has a lease that will not be repaid until 1995. This is shown as long-term debt.

After taking account of all the firm's liabilities, the remaining assets belong to the common stockholders. The shareholders' equity is simply the total value of the assets less the current and long-term liabilities and the preferred stock, if there is any. It is also equal to common stock plus retained earnings, that is, the net amount that the firm has raised from stockholders or reinvested on their behalf.

Table 17.2 also provides some other financial information about GFL, which is not part of the balance sheet. For example, it shows the market value of the common stock. It is often helpful to compare the *book value* of the equity shown on the company's balance sheet with the *market value* established in the capital markets.

---

[1] This is in addition to $3.58 million of cash flow earmarked for depreciation.

TABLE 17.2

BALANCE SHEET FOR GREEN FOREST LUMBER CORPORATION
As at March 31, 1994 and 1993
(All items in millions)

Assets	1994	1993	Liabilities and Shareholders' Equity	1994	1993
Current assets			Current liabilities		
Cash	2.3	0	Bank indebtedness	0	8.76
Accounts receivable	27.77	21.61	Accounts payable	31.34	29.15
Inventory	40.66	39.64	Income taxes payable	6.94	0.62
Other current assets	1.37	0.66	Current portion of long-term debt	0.07	0.06
Total current assets	72.10	61.91	Total current liabilities	38.35	38.59
Fixed assets			Long-term debt	0.05	0.12
Mortgage receivable	1.39	1.39	Shareholders' equity		
Capital assets	58.59	56.47	Capital stock	53.41	53.38
Less accumulated depreciation	23.27	20.68	Retained earnings	19.38	9.57
Net capital assets	35.32	35.79	Total shareholders' equity	72.79	62.95
Goodwill, deferred charges, and other assets	2.38	2.58			
Total assets	$111.19	$101.67	Total liabilities and shareholders' equity	$111.19	$101.67

Note: Columns may not add because of rounding.

Other financial information	As of March 31, 1994
Market value of equity	$98,136,430
Average number of shares	
Multiple voting shares	2,020,000
Subordinate voting shares	7,438,933
Total number of shares	9,458,933
Earnings per share	$ 1.24
Dividends per share	$ 0.20
Share price (subordinate voting shares)	$10.375

common-size balance sheet: Balance sheet that presents items as a percentage of total assets.

The balance sheet in Table 17.2 shows the dollar value of each asset or liability. Sometimes to facilitate comparison between firms, analysts calculate a **common-size balance sheet**. In this case all items are reexpressed as a percentage of total assets. Table 17.3 is GFL's common-size balance sheet. The table shows in 1994 65 percent of GFL assets were current assets and 35 percent were long-term assets. Inventory was the largest asset category, representing 37 percent of total assets. Accounts receivable were 25 percent of total assets. The main fixed asset category was capital assets, comprising 32 percent of total assets. You should not be surprised that GFL has more current assets than fixed assets. Think about GFL's main business: lumber wholesaler. GFL buys lumber from sawmills and resells it to retailers. Thus, it will have significant inventory of lumber. A wholesaler needs some fixed assets such as warehouses, trucks, and office equipment but the investment will not be large. Are you surprised that 78 percent of total assets of Acklands Limited, a distributor of automotive parts are current assets? Ackland's inventory alone is 49 percent of its total assets.

In contrast to wholesalers, manufacturers tend to have a majority of their total assets invested in fixed assets. Think of all the machinery and buildings needed to mine and refine ore into usable metals. You won't be surprised that Inco, a nickel and copper mining and manufacturing operation, has 66 percent of its assets in "property, plant, and equipment," a major fixed asset account. GFL has a man-

TABLE 17.3

COMMON-SIZE BALANCE SHEET FOR GREEN FOREST LUMBER CORPORATION
As at March 31, 1994 and 1993
(All items expressed as percentage of total assets)

Assets	1994	1993	Liabilities and Shareholders' Equity	1994	1993
Current assets			Current liabilities		
Cash	2%	0%	Bank indebtedness	0%	9%
Accounts receivable	25%	21%	Accounts payable	28%	29%
Inventory	37%	39%	Income taxes payable	6%	1%
Other current liabilities	1%	1%	Current portion of long-term debt	0%	0%
Total current assets	65%	61%	Total current liabilities	34%	38%
Fixed assets			Long-term debt	0%	0%
Mortgage receivable	1%	1%			
Capital assets	53%	56%	Shareholders' equity		
Less accumulated depreciation	21%	20%	Capital stock	48%	53%
Net capital assets	32%	35%	Retained earnings	17%	9%
Goodwill, deferred charges, and	2%	3%	Total shareholders' equity	65%	62%
other assets					
Total assets	100%	100%	Total liabilities and shareholders' equity	100%	100%

Note: Columns may not add because of rounding.

ufacturing business — it owns a sawmill and it also converts rough lumber into finished lumber ("remanufacturing"). It needs fixed assets for this too. The combined fixed assets for the wholesale business plus its manufacturing business results in fixed assets equal to 32 percent of its total assets.

On the liability and shareholders' equity side we see that GFL has significant accounts payable, a consequence of its purchases of lumber. GFL's long-term debt as a fraction of assets, only 0.1 percent in 1994, is very low. It appears that GFL has been able to finance its assets with almost no long-term debt and only 8.8 percent with bank financing. The main liability is accounts payable, financing 28.0 percent of total assets. The remaining financing is shareholders' equity.

....
Leverage Ratios

When a firm borrows money, it generally promises to make a series of fixed payments. Because the shareholders get only what is left over after the debtholders have been paid, debt is said to create *financial leverage*. Fluctuations in the firm's business have a greater impact on equity returns when firms are leveraged because the debtholders have first claim on the firm's revenues and assets. Since the interest and principal promised to debtholders is fixed by contract and paid before any payment can be made to shareholders, the more debt a firm has, the riskier is the shareholders' claim to cash flow from the firm. Therefore, financial leverage makes the rate of return on equity riskier. In extreme cases, if hard times come, firms with high leverage are liable to find that they cannot pay their debts.

Obviously, shareholders will be interested to know the extent of the company's financial leverage. The greater the leverage, the riskier are their shares. Creditors, too, assess the degree of financial leverage. The more leveraged a company is, the greater is the risk of financial distress and bankruptcy. This information may be useful when determining the interest rate to charge on a loan made to the company. A lender will want to include an extra interest charge to compensate for the risk of bankruptcy.

Debt Ratio. Financial leverage is usually measured by the ratio of long-term debt to total long-term capital. Since long-term lease agreements also commit the firm to a series of fixed payments, it makes sense to include the value of lease obligations with the long-term debt.[2] Thus for GFL:

$$\text{Long-term debt ratio} = \frac{\text{long-term debt} + \text{value of leases}}{\text{long-term debt} + \text{value of leases} + \text{equity}}$$

$$= \frac{.05}{.05 + 72.79} = 0.0007 \text{ or } 0.07\%$$

The long-term debt ratio is so low we may as well call it zero percent. Less than 1 cent of every dollar of long-term capital is in the form of long-term debt. In 1993, GFL's long-term debt ratio was 0.2 percent, or essentially zero.

Another way to express leverage is in terms of the company's debt-equity ratio:

$$\text{Debt-equity ratio} = \frac{\text{long-term debt} + \text{value of leases}}{\text{equity}}$$

$$= \frac{.05}{72.79} = 0.0007$$

For 1993, GFL's debt-equity ratio was .002.

Notice that both these measures make use of book (that is, accounting) values rather than market values.[3] The market value of the company finally determines whether debtholders get their money back, so you would expect analysts to look at the face amount of the debt as a proportion of the total *market value* of debt and equity. One reason that they don't do this is that market values are often not readily available. Does it matter much? Perhaps not; after all, the market value of the firm includes the value of intangible assets generated by research and development, advertising, staff training, and so on. These assets are not readily saleable and, if the company falls on hard times, the value of these assets may disappear altogether. For some purposes, it may be just as well to follow the accountant and to ignore these intangible assets entirely.

Both the long-term debt ratio and the long-term debt to equity ratio take account only of long-term debt obligations. Managers sometimes also define debt to include all liabilities. Total liabilities equal total assets minus shareholders' equity. The total debt ratio is:

$$\text{Total debt ratio} = \frac{\text{total liabilities}}{\text{total assets}}$$

GFL's total liabilities are $111.19 − $72.79 = $38.4 million. The total debt ratio is:

$$\text{Total debt ratio} = \frac{38.4}{111.19} = .35$$

Therefore, GFL is financed 35 percent with debt, both long-term and short-term, and 65 percent with equity. We could also say that its ratio of total debt to equity is 35/65 = .54. In 1993, GFL's total debt ratio was 38 percent and its total debt to equity ratio was 38/62 = .61

---

[2] A lease is a long-term rental agreement and therefore commits the firm to make regular rental payments. As we emphasized in Chapter 13, leases are quite similar to debt obligations.

[3] In the case of leased assets accountants try to estimate the present value of the lease commitments. In the case of long-term debt they simply show the face value. This can sometimes be very different from present values. For example, the present value of low-coupon debt may be only a fraction of its face value.

Are you impressed that the debt ratio can be calculated so many ways? Don't be fooled! Each of the ratios gives the same basic message: GFL has very little debt relative to its assets. Why do we bother to show you so many different ways to measure the debt ratio? You may encounter these ratios at one time or another and need to know how to calculate them. Even more important, we want you to be a cautious user of debt ratios. Whenever you see a debt ratio, the first question you must ask is, "How is this debt ratio calculated?" If you don't, you may find yourself making serious errors in the analysis of the firm's leverage.

Times Interest Earned Ratio. Another measure of the financial leverage is the extent to which interest is covered by earnings. A healthy firm will generate earnings far in excess of interest payments. Therefore, analysts often calculate the ratio of earnings before interest and taxes (EBIT) to interest payments. For GFL:[4]

$$\text{Times interest earned} = \frac{\text{EBIT}}{\text{interest payments}} = \frac{19.1}{0.3} = 63.7$$

GFL's earnings would need to fall by a factor of 63.7 before they were exceeded by its interest obligations. This high times interest earned is a reflection of GFL's very low level of debt. Compare it to GFL's 1993 times interest earned of 12/2.3 = 5.2. GFL's bank indebtedness plus long-term debt was about $9 million in 1993 but only $100,000 in 1994.

The regular interest payment is a hurdle that companies must keep jumping if they are to avoid default. The *times interest earned ratio* measures how much clear air there is between hurdle and hurdler. However, always bear in mind that such summary measures tell only part of the story. For example, it might make sense to include in the measure other fixed charges such as regular repayments of existing debt, preferred share sinking fund payments and dividends or long-term lease obligations. The *fixed charge coverage ratio* shows how many times greater is EBIT relative to the fixed payments that the company is obliged to make.

Some fixed payments must be made from earnings remaining after taxes have been paid. Such non-tax-deductible payments include principal repayment, preferred share dividends, and preferred share sinking fund payments. These payments must be converted to a before-tax basis to show the before-tax amount of earnings needed to cover them. For example, GFL must repay $71,000 of long-term debt ("current portion of long-term debt"). Its tax rate is approximately 40 percent. Thus on a before-tax basis, the required principal repayment is

$$\text{before-tax cost of principal repayment} = \frac{\text{principal repayment}}{(1 - \text{corporate tax rate})}$$

$$= \frac{71,000}{1 - .4} = \$118,333.$$

In other words, in order that GFL cover its $71,000 principal repayment, it must earn $118,333 in before-tax earnings. The same adjustment is made to all other non-tax-deductible payments. GFL has no preferred shares and hence no fixed payments associated with preferred shares. GFL has operating lease payments of $603,000 in 1994. GFL's fixed charge coverage ratio is:

---

[4] The numerator of times interest earned can be defined in several ways. Sometimes it is just net earnings plus interest — that is, earnings before interest *but after tax*. This definition seems inappropriate to us, because the point of times interest earned is to assess the risk that the firm won't have enough money to pay interest. If EBIT falls below interest obligations, taxable income will be negative, and the firm won't pay any income taxes. Interest is paid before the firm pays income taxes.

$$\text{Fixed charge coverage} =$$

$$\frac{\text{EBIT + lease payments}}{\text{Interest + lease payments + before tax cost of repayments of long-term debt}}$$

$$= \frac{19.1 + .6}{.3 + .118} = 47.1$$

Again, this ratio indicates a high comfort level of clear air between earnings and fixed charges. In 1993, GFL's fixed charge coverage was 5.9.

Cash Flow Coverage Ratio. We have pointed out that depreciation and amortization are deducted when calculating the firm's earnings even though no cash goes out the door. Thus, rather than asking whether *earnings* are sufficient to cover interest payments, it might be more interesting to calculate the extent to which interest is covered by the *cash flow* from the firm's operations. This is measured by the cash flow coverage ratio. As with the fixed charge coverage ratio, any fixed charges that must be paid out of after-tax earnings must be converted into their before-tax equivalent. For GFL:

$$\text{Cash flow coverage ratio} = \frac{\text{EBIT + depreciation + amortization}}{\text{interest payments + before-tax cost of long-term debt repayment}}$$

$$= \frac{19.1 + 3.4 + .2}{.3 + .118} = 54.3$$

In 1993, GFL's cash flow coverage ratio was 7.4.

Again, we have given you a variety of ratios that measure essentially the same thing. This time, we were interested in the extent to which the firm has the ability to pay its fixed obligations. All of the ratios lead to the same conclusion: Currently, GFL has no trouble meeting its fixed payments.

Will you want to use all of these ratios at the same time? Clearly the answer is no because they give you the same sort of information. Pick the one you believe will give the best information. The cash flow coverage ratio is the most complete and may be the most informative. However, if you have times interest earned ratios for four competitors of the company you are analyzing, you will want to calculate times interest earned.

SELF-TEST 17.1
· · · · · · · · · · · ·

A firm buys back $10 million par value of outstanding debt and issues $10 million of new debt with a lower rate of interest. What happens to its long-term debt ratio? What happens to its times interest earned and cash flow coverage ratios? Assume a 40 percent tax rate.

· · · · · · · · · · · · · · · · · · · ·
Liquidity Ratios

liquidity: Ability of an asset to be converted to cash quickly at low cost.

If you are extending credit or lending to a company for a short period, you are interested in more than the company's leverage. You want to know whether it will be able to lay its hands on the cash to repay you. That is why credit analysts and bankers look at several measures of **liquidity.** Liquid assets are those that can be converted into cash quickly and easily.

Think, for example, what you would do if you had to meet a large unexpected bill. You might have some assets that are easily sold, but it would not be so easy to convert old sweaters into cash. Companies also own assets with different degrees of liquidity. For example, accounts receivable and inventories of finished goods are generally quite liquid. As inventories are sold and customers pay their bills, cash flows into the firm. At the other extreme, real estate may be quite *illiquid*. It can be hard to find a buyer, negotiate a fair price, and close a deal at short notice.

Another reason that managers focus on liquid assets is that the accounting figures are more reliable. The book value of a catalytic cracker may be a poor guide to its true value, but at least you know what cash in the bank is worth.

Liquidity ratios also have some *less* desirable characteristics. Because short-term assets and liabilities are easily changed, measures of liquidity can rapidly become outdated. You might not know what the catalytic cracker is worth, but you can be fairly sure that it won't disappear overnight. Also, companies often choose a slack period for the end of their financial year. For example, retailers may end their financial year in January after the Christmas boom. At these times the companies are likely to have more cash and less short-term debt than during busier seasons.

Net Working Capital to Total Assets Ratio. We have seen that current assets are those which the company expects to turn into cash in the near future; current liabilities are liabilities that it expects to meet in the near future. The difference between the current assets and current liabilities is known as *net working capital*. It roughly measures the company's potential reservoir of cash. Managers often express net working capital as a proportion of total assets. For GFL:

$$\frac{\text{Net working capital}}{\text{Total assets}} = \frac{72.10 - 38.35}{111.19} = 0.3$$

GFL's net working capital is 30 percent of its total assets.

Current Ratio. Another measure that serves a similar purpose is the current ratio:

$$\text{Current ratio} = \frac{\text{current assets}}{\text{current liabilities}} = \frac{72.10}{38.35} = 1.88$$

So GFL has $1.88 in current assets for every $1 in current liabilities. In 1993, GFL's net working capital to total assets was .23 and its current ratio was 1.6. Comparing 1993's ratio to 1994's ratio shows that GFL has become more liquid.

Rapid decreases in the current ratio sometimes signify trouble. For example, a firm that drags out its payables to delay paying its bills will suffer an increase in current liabilities and a decrease in the current ratio.

Changes in the current ratio can mislead, however. For example, suppose that a company borrows a large sum from the bank and invests it in marketable securities. Current liabilities rise and so do current assets. Therefore, if nothing else changes, net working capital is unaffected but the current ratio changes. For this reason, it might be preferable to net short-term investments against short-term debt when calculating the current ratio.

Quick (or Acid-Test) Ratio. Some assets are closer to cash than others. If trouble comes, inventory may not sell at anything above fire-sale prices. (Trouble typically comes because the firm can't sell its finished-product inventory for more than production cost.) Thus managers often exclude inventories and other relatively less liquid components of current assets (such as prepaid expenses, which are typically part of the "other current assets" account) when comparing current assets to current liabilities. They instead focus only on cash, marketable securities, and bills that customers have not yet paid. This results in the quick ratio:

$$\text{Quick ratio} = \frac{\text{cash + marketable securities + receivables}}{\text{current liabilities}}$$

$$= \frac{2.30 + 27.77}{38.35} = 0.79$$

In 1993, GFL's quick ratio was .56, lower than 1994. GFL has improved its comfort level with regard to meeting its current liabilities.

SELF-TEST 17.2

> a. A firm has $1.2 million in current assets and $1.0 million in current liabilities. If it uses $.5 million of cash to pay off some of its accounts payable, what will happen to the current ratio? What happens to net working capital?
> b. A firm uses cash on hand to pay for additional inventories. What will happen to the current ratio? To the quick ratio?

Cash Ratio. A company's most liquid assets are its holdings of cash and marketable securities. That is why financial analysts also look at the cash ratio:

$$\text{Cash ratio} = \frac{\text{cash + marketable securities}}{\text{current liabilities}} = \frac{2.30}{38.35} = 0.06$$

GFL has $.06 of cash and securities for every dollar of current liabilities. In 1993, GFL had no cash or marketable securities so its cash ratio was zero. Is GFL in dire financial trouble because its 1994 cash ratio is almost zero? We want to take this opportunity to remind you that financial analysis is much more than just calculating ratios. Ratios must be interpreted in the context of the firm. A cash ratio of zero may mean that the firm is in financial trouble. However, lack of cash may not matter if the firm can borrow on short notice. Who cares whether the firm has actually borrowed from the bank or whether it has a guaranteed line of credit that enables it to borrow whenever it chooses? None of the standard liquidity measures takes the firm's "reserve borrowing power" into account. Given GFL's very low level of debt, it is likely that it has a lot of reserve borrowing power. We will want to look at its profitability but we can make a preliminary assessment that GFL's lack of cash is a deliberate decision of management and not an indication of financial trouble.

Interval Measure. Instead of looking at a firm's liquid assets relative to its current liabilities, it may be useful to measure whether liquid assets are large relative to the firm's regular cash outgoings. We ask how long the firm could keep up with its bills using only its cash and other liquid assets. This is the so-called interval measure, which is computed by dividing liquid assets by daily expenditures:

$$\text{Interval measure} = \frac{\text{cash + marketable securities + receivables}}{\text{average daily expenditures from operations}}$$

For GFL the cost of goods sold amounted to $341.2 million over the year and there were selling and administrative expenses of $12.8 million. Therefore,

$$\text{Interval measure} = \frac{2.3 + 27.77}{(341.2 + 12.8)/365} = 31 \text{ days}$$

GFL has sufficient liquid assets to finance operations for 31 days even if it receives no further cash. In contrast, in 1993, GFL's interval measure was 25.2 days. GFL has improved its ability to finance its operations from its liquid assets.

....
Efficiency Ratios

Financial analysts employ another set of ratios to judge how efficiently the firm is using its assets.

Asset Turnover Ratio. The sales-to-assets ratio, also known as asset turnover, shows how hard the firm's assets are being put to use. It measures the revenue generated per dollar of assets. For GFL, each dollar of assets resulted in $3.54 in sales:

$$\text{Asset turnover} = \frac{\text{sales}}{\text{average total assets}} = \frac{376.7}{(111.19 + 101.67)/2} = 3.54$$

A high ratio compared to other firms in the industry could indicate that the firm is working close to capacity. It may prove difficult to generate further business without an increase in invested capital. Asset turnover in 1993 was 3.52, not much different than in 1994.

Notice that since the assets are likely to change over the year, we use the average of the assets at the beginning and the end of the year. Averages are usually used whenever a flow figure (in this case, *annual sales*) is compared with a snapshot figure (*total assets*).

Instead of looking at the ratio of sales to *total* assets, managers sometimes look at how hard particular types of assets are being put to use. For example, they might look at the value of sales per dollar invested in fixed assets. Or they might look at the ratio of sales to net working capital.

Thus for GFL, each dollar of fixed assets supported $10.60 of revenue:

$$\text{Fixed asset turnover} = \frac{\text{sales}}{\text{average fixed assets}} = \frac{376.7}{(35.32 + 35.79)/2} = 10.6$$

and each dollar of net working capital (NWC) was associated with $13.19 of sales:

$$\text{NWC turnover} = \frac{\text{sales}}{\text{average net working capital}} = \frac{376.7}{(33.75 + 23.32)/2} = 13.2$$

Fixed asset turnover in 1993 was 302.6/[(35.8 + 26.4)/2]= 9.7 and net working capital turnover was 302.6/[(23.3 + 11.1)/2] = 17.6. GFL has increased its fixed asset turnover relative to 1993 but has reduced its net working capital turnover. Before we start to worry about the decline in net working capital turnover, several other efficiency ratios must be examined.

Inventory Turnover Ratio. Managers may also monitor the rate at which the company is turning over its inventories. In GFL's case:[5]

$$\text{Inventory turnover} = \frac{\text{cost of goods sold}}{\text{average inventory}} = \frac{342.2}{(40.66 + 39.64)/2} = 8.5$$

A high inventory turnover ratio compared to other firms in the industry is often regarded as a sign of efficiency. But don't jump to conclusions — it may sometimes indicate that the firm is living from hand to mouth.

In 1993, GFL's inventory turnover was 277.0/[(39.6 + 27.2)/2] = 8.3, slightly lower than in 1994.

Another useful measure of how rapidly inventory turns over is the number of days' sales in inventory. First convert cost of goods sold to a daily basis by

---

[5] The denominator in the inventory turnover ratio is the level of inventories, which is valued at cost. Therefore, we use the cost of goods sold (that is, the value of the goods drawn out of inventory) in the numerator rather than sales.

dividing by 365. Then express inventories as a multiple of daily sales. The result is the number of days it would take to sell off the firm's current level of inventory:

$$\text{Days' sales in inventories} = \frac{\text{average inventory}}{\text{cost of goods sold}/365}$$

$$= \frac{(40.66 + 39.64)/2}{341.2/365} = 43 \text{ days}$$

Notice that days' sales in inventories is the reciprocal of inventory turnover multiplied by 365. The fewer the number of days' sales in inventory, the faster the inventory is moving. On average, GFL has 43 days' worth of sales in inventory. In 1993, days' sales in inventory was 44 days, again only marginally longer than 1994.

Average Collection Period Ratio. The average collection period measures the speed with which customers pay their bills. It expresses accounts receivable in terms of daily sales:

$$\text{Average collection period} = \frac{\text{average receivables}}{\text{average daily sales}}$$

$$= \frac{(27.77 + 21.61)/2}{376.7/365} = 23.9 \text{ days}$$

Therefore, GFL's accounts receivable corresponds to about 24 days' worth of sales. This can be interpreted as the average delay before GFL's customers pay their bills. A comparatively low ratio is often believed to indicate an efficient collection department. Sometimes, however, it is the result of an unduly restrictive credit policy. In such cases, the firm may offer credit only to customers that can be relied on to pay promptly.[6]

In 1993, GFL's average collection period was 20.0 days. Compared to 1993, 1994 collections are taking about 3 days longer. Whether this indicates a decline in the efficiency of the collection department or more generous credit sales we cannot say. A logical next step for a manager responsible for accounts receivable would be to determine if 3 days variation in the average collection period is normal by looking at the collection pattern for several earlier years. In addition, a closer look at the activities of the credit department may be warranted. Once again, the usefulness of the ratio analysis is not the number uncovered but the questions it leads to.

SELF-TEST 17.3

The average collection period measures the number of days it takes GFL to collect its bills. But GFL also delays *paying* its own bills. Use the information in Tables 17.1 and 17.2 to calculate the average number of days that it takes the company to pay its bills.

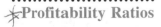

Profitability Ratios

Other measures of the efficiency and success of the firm are provided by several profitability measures. These focus on the firm's earnings. Profitability measures provide an overall indication of the firm's performance. You should not be surprised to learn that profitability ratios are calculated in a variety of ways. One group of ratios, referred to as profit margins, measures some form of profits or

---

[6] If possible, it would make more sense to divide average receivables by average daily *credit* sales. Otherwise a low ratio might simply indicate that only a small proportion of sales was made on credit.

earnings as a fraction of sales. Profit margins indicate how much money was made per dollar of sales. The second group of profitability measures, called return ratios, look at the ratio of profits to assets. Return ratios show how much profit was earned on the assets invested.

What profits are used in a profitability ratio? Several definitions of profits are commonly used. Gross profit, or revenues minus cost of goods sold, reflects the firm's mark-up over its cost of goods sold as well as the ability of its management to minimize the cost of producing the revenues. Operating profits, or earnings before interest and tax, measures what the firm has earned after it has paid for the cost of goods sold and its operating expenses. If you subtract taxes as well, you have operating profits after tax. Operating profits after tax is a good overall measure of the firm's operating performance. It tells how much the firm has earned, after all costs of producing the product, including taxes. Net income is operating profits minus interest payments and taxes and shows how much shareholders have earned.

For each definition of profits there is a corresponding profit margin.

Gross Profit Margin. The gross profit margin is a very basic measure of the firm's success at its business. After taking into account the cost of goods involved in producing the goods, how much did the firm make as a percentage of sales? For GFL in 1994, its gross profit margin was

$$\text{Gross profit margin} = \frac{\text{Gross profit}}{\text{Sales}} = \frac{35.5}{376.7} = 0.094 \text{ or } 9.4\%$$

In 1993, GFL's gross profit margin was 8.5 percent. Comparing the two ratios, we see that GFL is earning more per dollar of sales. This could be due to better operating efficiencies, which reduce the cost of goods sold, and/or due to higher mark-up over the cost of goods.

Operating Profit Margin or Basic Earnings Power. If you want to know the proportion of revenues left after all costs of producing the sales, including overhead and other operating expenses and taxes, you look at the operating profit margin or basic earnings power. Thus[7]

$$\text{Operating profit margin} = \frac{\text{EBIT} - \text{taxes}}{\text{Sales}}$$

$$= \frac{19.1 - 7.5}{376.7} = 0.031 \text{ or } 3.1\%$$

For every dollar of sales GFL made in 1994, it earned 3.1 cents in operating profits. GFL's operating profit margin in 1993 was 2.6 percent. Again, we see evidence of improvements in GFL's profitability from 1993 to 1994.

Net Profit Margin. If you want to know the proportion of revenue that finds its way into profits for shareholders, you look at the net profit margin. Thus

$$\text{Net profit margin} = \frac{\text{Net income}}{\text{Sales}} = \frac{11.7}{376.7} = 0.031 \text{ or } 3.1\%$$

In 1993, GFL's net profit margin was 1.9 percent. Since net income is a measure of shareholders' earnings, another way to interpret the net profit margin is the

---

[7] Sometimes operating profit margin is defined as EBIT/Sales. We prefer to subtract taxes as well, as taxes are a cost of doing business.

percentage of sales that is available to pay to shareholders. Out of every dollar of sales, shareholders earned 3.1 cents in 1994.

The net profit margin is a commonly used summary measure of the firm's profitability. However, we prefer the operating profit margin as an overall measure of a firm's profitability. The net profit margin measures profits as net income rather than EBIT in the numerator. (Remember that net income equals EBIT − tax − interest expense.) We think that net income is an inappropriate measure of overall profits: one should not deduct interest on debt in calculating overall profits because we would not wish to conclude that a firm is less profitable simply because it relies more heavily on debt finance.

SELF-TEST 17.4

Compare Green Forest Lumber's 1994 operating profit margin and net profit margin. Explain why the two margins are essentially the same.

Holding everything else constant, a firm would naturally prefer a high profit margin. But all else cannot be held constant. A high-price and, hence, high-margin strategy typically will result in lower sales. So while Holt Renfrew might have higher margins than Zeller's, it will not necessarily enjoy higher profits. A low-margin but high-volume strategy can be quite successful. We return to this issue later. (See Table 17.5.)

Return on Assets (ROA). In addition to the profit margins, managers often measure the performance of a firm by the ratio of profits to total assets. We prefer to measure profits as earnings before interest but after taxes, EBIT − taxes. Again, some use net income rather than EBIT − tax to compute ROA. Because net income measures profits net of interest expense, this practice makes the apparent profitability of the firm a function of its capital structure. It is better to use income before interest because we are measuring the return on *all* the firm's assets, not just the equity investment:[8]

$$\text{Return on assets} = \frac{\text{EBIT} - \text{tax}}{\text{average total assets}}$$

$$= \frac{19.1 - 7.5}{(111.19 + 101.67)/2} = .109 = 10.9\%$$

In 1993, GFL had a return on assets of 9.2%.

The assets in a company's books are valued on the basis of their original cost (less any depreciation). A high return on assets does not always mean that you

---

[8] This definition of ROA also can be misleading if it is used to compare firms with different capital structures. The reason is that firms that pay more interest pay less taxes. Thus this ratio reflects differences in financial leverage as well as in operating performance. If you want a measure of operating performance alone, we suggest adjusting taxes by adding back interest tax shields (interest payments × marginal tax rate). This gives the taxes the firm would pay if all-equity financed. Thus, using the 1994 tax rate of 40 percent for GFL,

$$\text{Return on total assets} = \frac{\text{EBIT} - (\text{tax} + \text{interest tax shields})}{\text{average total assets}}$$

$$= \frac{19.1 - (7.5 + .4 \times .03)}{(112.19 + 101.67)/2} = .109 \text{ or } 10.9\%$$

We could use this measure to compare the operating performance of two firms even if they had radically different debt ratios. With GFL's very low debt level and hence very low interest payments, it has a very small interest tax shield. Consequently, the return on assets is essentially unchanged. A firm with more significant interest payments would see its ROA lowered by this adjustment.

could buy the same assets today and get a high return. Nor does a low return on assets imply that the assets could be better employed elsewhere. But it does suggest that you should ask some searching questions.

Return on Equity (ROE). Another measure of profitability focuses on the return on shareholders' equity:

$$\text{Return on equity} = \frac{\text{earnings available for common stock}}{\text{average equity}}$$

$$= \frac{11.7}{(72.79 + 62.95)/2} = .172 \text{ or } 17.2\%$$

In 1993, GFL earned a 9.1 percent return on equity.

Payout Ratio. The payout ratio measures the proportion of earnings that is paid out as dividends. Thus

$$\text{Payout ratio} = \frac{\text{dividend per share}}{\text{earnings per share}} = \frac{1.9}{11.7} = .162 \text{ or } 16.2\%$$

GFL paid out 16 percent of its earnings to common shareholders in 1994. In 1993, GFL's payout ratio was 14 percent.

We saw in Section 16.2 that managers don't like to cut dividends because of a shortfall in earnings. Therefore, if a company's earnings are particularly variable, management is likely to play safe by setting a low average payout ratio.

When earnings fall unexpectedly, the payout ratio is likely to rise temporarily. Likewise, if earnings are expected to rise next year, management may feel that it can pay somewhat more generous dividends than it would otherwise have done.

Earnings not paid out as dividends are retained, or plowed back into the business. The proportion of earnings reinvested in the firm is called the *plowback ratio.*

$$\text{Plowback ratio} = 1 - \text{payout ratio}$$

$$= \frac{\text{earnings} - \text{dividend}}{\text{earnings}} = \frac{\text{retained earnings}}{\text{earnings}}$$

If you multiply this figure by the return on equity, you can see how rapidly shareholders' equity is growing as a result of retained earnings. Thus for GFL, retained earnings increase the book value of equity by 14.4 percent:

$$\text{Growth in equity from plowback} = \frac{\text{retained earnings}}{\text{equity}}$$

$$= \frac{\text{retained earnings}}{\text{earnings}} \times \frac{\text{earnings}}{\text{equity}}$$

$$= \text{plowback ratio} \times \text{ROE}$$

$$= .84 \times .172 = .144 \text{ or } 14.4\%$$

If GFL can continue to earn 17.2 percent on its book equity and plow back 84 percent of earnings, both earnings and equity will grow at 14.4 percent a year.[9]

Is this a reasonable prospect? We saw in Chapter 5 that such high growth rates are unlikely to persist. While GFL might continue to grow rapidly for a while, as

---

[9] Analysts sometimes refer to this figure as the *sustainable rate of growth*. We discuss the sustainable rate of growth at greater length in Section 5.5.

the firm and its industry matures, such rapid growth will inevitably slow. At best, in the long term, a company can hope to grow with rate of growth of the economy. Even that may be difficult.

....
Market-Value Ratios

There is no law prohibiting the financial manager from introducing data that are not in the company accounts. For example, if you were analyzing a steel company, you might want to look at the cost per tonne of steel produced or the sales per employee. Frequently managers also find it helpful to look at ratios that combine accounting and stock market data. Here are four of these market-based ratios.

Price-Earnings Ratio. The price-earnings, or P/E, ratio is a common measure of the esteem in which the company is held by investors. In the case of GFL, the stock market price on March 31, 1994 was $10 3/8 or $10.375 and earnings per share are $1.24.[10] Therefore,

$$\text{P/E ratio} = \frac{\text{stock price}}{\text{earnings per share}} = \frac{10.375}{1.24} = 8.4$$

What does it mean when a company's stock sells at a high or low P/E? To answer this question, you might find it helpful to look back to the dividend discount model that we introduced in Chapter 5. If a company's dividends are expected to grow at a steady rate, then the current stock price (P_0) is

$$P_0 = \frac{\text{DIV}_1}{r - g}$$

In this formula DIV_1 measures the expected dividend next year, r is the expected return that investors require from similar investments, and g is the expected rate of dividend growth. In order to find the P/E ratio, simply divide through by expected earnings per share:

$$\frac{P_0}{\text{EPS}_1} = \frac{\text{DIV}_1}{\text{EPS}_1} \times \frac{1}{r - g}$$

Thus a high P/E ratio may indicate that (1) investors expect high dividend growth (g); or (2) the stock has low risk and therefore investors are content with a low prospective return (r); or (3) the company is expected to achieve average dividend growth despite paying out a high proportion of earnings ($\text{DIV}_1/\text{EPS}_1$).

Dividend Yield. The stock's dividend yield is simply the expected dividend as a proportion of the stock price. Thus for GFL:

$$\text{Dividend yield} = \frac{\text{dividend per share}}{\text{stock price}} = \frac{.20}{10.375} = .019 \text{ or } 1.9\%$$

Again it is helpful to consider a company with a steady expected growth in dividends. In this case

$$\text{Dividend yield} = \frac{\text{DIV}_1}{P_1} = r - g$$

Thus a high dividend yield may indicate that investors expect low dividend growth or that they require a high rate of return.

---

[10] We follow common practice when we use 1994 earnings per share and the price at the end of the fiscal year, March 31, 1994. Since stockholders always look forward, not back, it would be better to use earnings that were forecast for the 1995 fiscal year. See Section 5.4.

Market-to-Book Ratio. The market-to-book ratio is the ratio of stock price to book value per share:

$$\text{Market-to-book ratio} = \frac{\text{stock price}}{\text{book value per share}} = \frac{10.375}{7.70} = 1.35$$

Book value per share is just stockholders' book equity divided by the number of shares outstanding. Book equity equals common stock plus retained earnings — the net amount that the firm has received from stockholders plus what it has reinvested on their behalf. For GFL, book value of equity is 72.79/9.45 or $7.70 per share. Thus GFL's market-to-book ratio of 1.35 means that the market value of the stock is 1.35 times the sum of paid-in capital and retained earnings.

SELF-TEST 17.5

Show that ROE equals the market-to-book ratio divided by the price-earnings ratio. Are firms with a high ROE necessarily good stock market investments?

Table 17.4 is a summary of the financial ratios we have discussed.

TABLE 17.4
Summary of financial ratios

I. Leverage ratios

$$\text{Long-term debt ratio} = \frac{\text{Long-term debt} + \text{present value of lease commitments}}{\text{Long-term debt} + \text{value of leases} + \text{equity}}$$

$$\text{Debt-equity ratio} = \frac{\text{Long-term debt} + \text{value of lease commitments}}{\text{Equity}}$$

$$\text{Total debt ratio} = \frac{\text{Total liabilities}}{\text{Total assets}}$$

$$\text{Times interest earned} = \frac{\text{EBIT}}{\text{Interest payments}}$$

$$\text{Cash flow coverage} = \frac{\text{EBIT} + \text{depreciation} + \text{lease payments}}{\text{Interest payments} + \text{lease payments} + \text{before-tax principal payments} + \text{before-tax preferred share payment}}$$

II. Liquidity ratios

$$\text{NWC to assets} = \frac{\text{Net working capital}}{\text{Total assets}}$$

$$\text{Current ratio} = \frac{\text{Current assets}}{\text{Current liabilities}}$$

$$\text{Quick ratio} = \frac{\text{Cash} + \text{marketable securities} + \text{accounts receivable}}{\text{Current liabilities}}$$

$$\text{Cash ratio} = \frac{\text{Cash} + \text{marketable securities}}{\text{Current liabilities}}$$

$$\text{Interval measure} = \frac{\text{Cash} + \text{marketable securities} + \text{receivables}}{\text{Average daily expenditures from operations}}$$

III. Efficiency ratios

$$\text{Total asset turnover} = \frac{\text{Sales}}{\text{Average total assets}}$$

$$\text{NWC turnover} = \frac{\text{Sales}}{\text{Average net working capital}}$$

TABLE 17.4
(continued)

III. Efficiency ratios *(continued)*

$$\text{Inventory turnover} = \frac{\text{Cost of goods sold}}{\text{Average inventory}}$$

$$\text{Days' sales in inventories} = \frac{\text{Average inventory}}{\text{Cost of goods sold}/365}$$

$$\text{Average collection period} = \frac{\text{Average receivables}}{\text{Average daily sales}}$$

IV. Profitability ratios

$$\text{Gross profit margin} = \frac{\text{Gross profit}}{\text{Sales}}$$

$$\text{Operating profit margin} = \frac{\text{EBIT} - \text{tax}}{\text{Sales}}$$

$$\text{Net profit margin} = \frac{\text{Net income}}{\text{Sales}}$$

$$\text{Return on assets} = \frac{\text{EBIT} - \text{tax}}{\text{Average total assets}}$$

$$\text{Return on equity} = \frac{\text{Earnings available for common stock}}{\text{Average equity}}$$

V. Market-value ratios

$$\text{P/E ratio} = \frac{\text{Stock price}}{\text{Earnings per share}}$$

$$\text{Dividend yield} = \frac{\text{Dividend per share}}{\text{Stock price}}$$

$$\text{Market-to-book ratio} = \frac{\text{Stock price}}{\text{Book value per share}}$$

THE DU PONT SYSTEM

Du Pont System: Group of relationships that breaks down ROE and ROA into component ratios.

Some profitability or efficiency ratios can be linked in useful ways. These relationships are often referred to as the **Du Pont system**, in recognition of the chemical company that popularized them.

The first relationship links the return on assets (ROA) with the firm's turnover ratio and its profit margin:

$$\text{ROA} = \frac{\text{EBIT} - \text{taxes}}{\text{assets}} = \frac{\text{Sales}}{\text{Assets}} \times \frac{\text{EBIT} - \text{taxes}}{\text{Sales}}$$

$$= \underset{\uparrow}{\text{Asset turnover}} \times \underset{\uparrow}{\text{Operating profit margin}}$$

Managers use the decomposition of ROA into asset turnover and operating profit margin as a guide to understanding the firm's financial performance. The asset turnover indicates how efficiently the firm is utilizing the assets in place. A low asset turnover relative to past performance or to competitors suggests that the firm should either increase its sales or consider reducing its investment in assets. The operating profit margin indicates how much profit is generated per dollar of sales. A low operating margin, relative to past margins or competitors' margins, suggests that the firm might not be controlling its costs effectively. Armed with the insights from the ratio analysis, a manager must explore further the reasons for the observed ratios and implement changes in the firm's operations to improve performance.

All firms would like to earn a higher return on assets, but their ability to do so is limited by competition. If the expected return on assets is fixed by competition, firms face a trade-off between the turnover ratio and the profit margin. Thus we find that fast-food chains, which have high turnover, also tend to operate on low profit margins. Hotels have relatively low turnover ratios but tend to compensate for this with higher margins. The example in Table 17.5 illustrates the trade-off. Both the fast-food chain and the hotel have the same return on assets. However, their profit margins and turnover ratios are entirely different.

TABLE 17.5

Fast-food chains and hotels may have a similar return on assets but different asset turnover ratios and profit margins.

	Turnover Ratio × Profit Margin = Return on Assets		
Fast-food chains	2.0	5%	10%
Hotels	0.5	20	10

Firms often seek to improve their profit margins by acquiring a supplier. The idea is to capture the supplier's profit as well as their own. Unfortunately, unless they have some special skill in running the new business, they are likely to find that any gain in profit margin is offset by a decline in the sales-to-assets ratio.

A few numbers may help to illustrate this point. Table 17.6 shows the sales, profits, and assets of Admiral Motors and its components supplier Diana Corporation. Both earn a 10 percent return on assets, though Admiral has a lower profit margin (20 percent versus Diana's 25 percent). Since all of Diana's output goes to Admiral, Admiral's management reasons that it would be better to merge the two companies. That way, the merged company could capture the profit margin on both the auto components and the assembled car.

TABLE 17.6

Merging with suppliers or customers will generally increase the profit margin but this will be offset by a reduction in the turnover ratio.

	Millions of Dollars					
	Sales	**Profits**	**Assets**	**Asset Turnover**	**Profit Margin**	**ROA**
Admiral Motors	$20	$4	$40	.50	20%	10%
Diana Corp.	8	2	20	.40	25%	10%
Diana Motors	$20	$6	60	.33	30%	10%

The bottom line of Table 17.6 shows the effect of the merger. The merged firm does indeed earn the combined profits. Total sales remain at $20 million, however, because all of the components produced by Diana are used within the company. With higher profits and unchanged sales, the profit margin increases. Unfortunately, the asset turnover ratio is *reduced* by the merger since the merged firm operates with higher assets. This exactly offsets the benefit of the higher profit margin. The return on assets is unchanged.

It is also useful to break down financial ratios to show how the return on equity (ROE) depends on the return on assets and leverage:

$$\text{ROE} = \frac{\text{earnings available for common stock}}{\text{equity}} = \frac{\text{EBIT} - \text{taxes} - \text{interest}}{\text{equity}}$$

$$= \frac{\text{assets}}{\text{equity}} \times \frac{\text{sales}}{\text{assets}} \times \frac{\text{EBIT} - \text{taxes}}{\text{sales}} \times \frac{\text{EBIT} - \text{taxes} - \text{interest}}{\text{EBIT} - \text{taxes}}$$

$$\uparrow \qquad\qquad \uparrow \qquad\qquad \uparrow \qquad\qquad\qquad \uparrow$$

$$= \begin{array}{c}1 + \text{total debt} \\ - \text{equity ratio}\end{array} \times \begin{array}{c}\text{asset} \\ \text{turnover}\end{array} \times \begin{array}{c}\text{profit} \\ \text{margin}\end{array} \times \quad \text{``debt burden''}$$

Notice that the product of the two middle terms is the return on assets. This depends on the firm's production and marketing skills and is unaffected by the firm's financing mix.[11] However, the first and fourth terms do depend on the debt-equity mix. The first term, assets/equity, can be expressed as (equity + liabilities)/equity, which equals 1 + total debt – equity ratio. The last term, which we call the "debt burden," measures the proportion by which interest expense reduces profits.

Suppose that the firm is financed entirely by equity. In this case both the first and fourth terms are equal to 1.0 and the return on equity is identical to the return on assets. If the firm is highly leveraged, the first term is greater than 1.0 (assets are greater than equity) and the fourth term is less than 1.0 (part of the profits are absorbed by interest). Thus leverage can either increase or reduce return on equity. In fact we showed in Section 15.1 that leverage increases ROE when the firm earns a return higher than the interest rate on its debt.

SELF-TEST 17.6

a. Sappy Syrup has a profit margin below the industry average, but its ROA equals the industry average. How is this possible?

b. Sappy Syrup's ROA equals the industry average, but its ROE exceeds the industry average. How is this possible?

 ## USING FINANCIAL STATEMENTS

Many years ago a British bank chairman observed that not only did the bank's accounts show its true position but the actual situation was a little better still.[12] Since that time accounting standards have been much more carefully defined but companies still have considerable discretion in calculating profits and deciding what to show on the balance sheet. Thus when you calculate financial ratios, you need to look below the surface and understand some of the potential pitfalls of accounting data.

For example, the entry for other long-term assets shown in GFL's balance sheet includes a figure of $2.4 million for "goodwill, deferred charges and other assets." Goodwill is the difference between the amount that GFL paid when it acquired a company and the book value of its assets. GFL writes off 5 percent of this goodwill from each year's profits. We don't want to debate whether goodwill is really an asset, but we should warn you about the dangers of comparing ratios of firms whose balance sheets include a substantial goodwill element with those that do not.

---

[11] There is a minor complication here if the amount of taxes paid depends on the financing mix. We suggested in our discussion of ROA above that it would be better to add back any interest tax shields when calculating the firm's profit margin.

[12] Speech by the chairman of the London and County Bank at the Annual Meeting, February 1901. Reported in *The Economist*, 1901, p. 204, and cited in C. A. E. Goodhart, *The Business of Banking 1891–1914* (London: Weidenfeld and Nicholson, 1972), p. 15.

Another pitfall arises because many of the company's liabilities are not shown in the balance sheet at all. For example, long-term leases are shown in the balance sheet as a liability but short-term lease agreements are not included even though the threshold for long- versus short-term is necessarily arbitrary. There may be little difference between a lease that barely counts as long-term and another that barely escapes the net.

off-balance sheet items: Assets and liabilities that are not shown on the balance sheet but nonetheless have genuine financial consequences for the firm, such as short-term leases and swaps.

Assets and liabilities that do not appear on the balance sheet are called **off-balance sheet items**. Fire insurance is an asset but it is not shown on the balance sheet. Certain types of financial arrangements such as swaps are not required to be revealed. Some firms disclose swaps and other financial transactions in the notes accompanying their financial statements but are not required by law to do so. Accounting regulations evolve more slowly than does financial innovation. Currently, Canadian accounting standards are under review and we expect to see new rules for reporting firms' involvement in off-balance sheet activities.

The list of difficulties with the use of financial ratios is very long. For example, Canadian accounting standards are not the same as elsewhere in the world, making it challenging to compare companies from different countries. Another potential problem is the impact of inflation on the financial statements. Revenues will tend to rise with inflation but costs of goods sold may not, depending on the inventory accounting rules used. Thus ratios may be corrupted by inflation.

If accounting standards give managers considerable discretion in reporting their financial situation and do not cover all of a firm's assets and liabilities, is it pointless to analyze financial statements? We believe that valuable information can be uncovered through financial statement analysis. However, we also believe that a manager must not rely exclusively on the financial statements. Read the notes accompanying the financial statements to learn more about the specifics of the firm's financial activities. Furthermore, financial statements are historical documents, reporting the financial situation of the firm during the past year. Remember, past financial performance is not guaranteed to continue in the future. A loan officer at a Canadian chartered bank put it well saying, "Using only financial statements to evaluate a firm's financial situation is like driving down the expressway looking only at the rearview mirror."[13] Gather information from other sources including news reports, industry studies, and interviews with the company. High quality financial analysis combines the information collected with a good understanding of accounting rules, economic reasoning, and common sense.

Choosing a Benchmark

We have shown you how to calculate the principal financial ratios for GFL. We suggest, however, that you should be selective in your choice of ratios. Many of them measure essentially the same thing and there is nothing to be gained by calculating all of them. Knowing which ratios will be most meaningful will depend on the nature of the business and on your reasons for doing financial analysis. For example, if you are analyzing a company in a high technology industry, you might be very interested to compare the ratio of research and development expenditures (R&D) to sales among competitors. On the other hand, R&D is of little importance to a lumber wholesaler. However, inventory management is central to the efficient operation of a wholesaler. If you were a potential supplier to a company, your financial analysis will focus on how quickly the company pays its bills and on its solvency. You may be less interested in its operating efficiency.

---

[13] We want to thank an anonymous reviewer of the book for this apt description of poor financial analysis.

Once you have selected and calculated the important ratios, you still need some way of judging whether they are high or low. A good starting point is to compare them with the equivalent figures for the same company in earlier years. The analysis of several years' worth of ratios is referred to as trend analysis. We have summarized the 1994 and 1993 ratios in the first two columns of Table 17.7.

Comparing 1993 and 1994 financial ratios reveals that GFL has enjoyed an improvement in its financial performance. Both ROE and ROA are higher in 1994 than 1993. Most of its efficiency ratios have improved. An exception is the decline in net working capital turnover and an increase in the average collection period.

TABLE 17.7

Financial ratios for Green Forest Lumber and Goodfellow Inc.

	Green Forest Lumber Corporation		Goodfellow Inc.
	March 31, 1994	**March 31, 1993**	**August 31, 1993**
Leverage ratios			
Long-term debt ratio	.0007	.002	.25
Total debt ratio	.35	.38	.51
Times interest earned	63.7	5.2	2.3
Fixed charge coverage	47.1	5.9	1.32
Cash coverage	54.3	7.4	1.76
Liquidity ratios			
NWC to assets	.30	.23	.30
Current ratio	1.88	1.6	1.73
Quick ratio	.79	.56	.89
Cash ratio	.06	0.00	.01
Interval measure	31 days	25 days	48 days
Efficiency ratios			
Asset turnover	3.54	3.52	3.0
Fixed asset turnover	10.6	9.7	9.8
NWC turnover	13.2	17.6	9.5
Inventory turnover	8.5	8.3	8.6
Average collection period	24 days	20 days	42 days
Profitability ratios			
Gross profit margin (%)	9.4	8.5	na*
Operating profit margin (%)	3.1	2.6	1.9
Net profit margin (%)	3.1	2.6	0.8
Return on assets (%)	10.9	9.2	5.8
Return on equity (%)	17.2	9.1	5.7
Market value ratios			
Price-earnings ratio	8.4	11.3	11.8
Dividend yield (%)	1.9	2.4	1.0
Market-to-book ratio	1.35	1.20	0.7

*na = not available

When making comparisons of this kind remember our earlier warning about the need to dig behind the figures. For example, should we be concerned about the decline in the net working capital turnover? To answer the question, we must look at the components of net working capital. We see that part of the decline is due to an increase in the average collection period. An increase in the average collection period may indicate that customers of GFL are having difficulty paying for the lumber purchased. However, a four-day increase in the average collection period is not too serious but should be monitored. The other factor contributing to the decline in the net working capital turnover is the increase in GFL's cash position. In 1993, GFL had no cash. We may take some comfort knowing that GFL's operations have generated more cash in 1994. GFL may have been operating in 1993 with too little cash. If the decline in net working capital turnover had arisen because GFL had a decrease in inventory turnover, we would have more cause for concern. Unsold inventory is much less liquid than excess cash in the bank. In summary, although net working capital turnover has declined, there is little evidence to indicate a deterioration in GFL's management of its working capital.

It is also helpful to compare GFL's financial position with that of other firms. However, you would not expect companies in different industries to have similar financial ratios. For example, a lumber wholesaler is unlikely to have the same profit margin as a shoe manufacturer or the same leverage as a finance company. It makes sense, therefore, to limit the comparison to other firms in the same industry.

The third column of Table 17.7 shows the financial ratios for Goodfellow Inc., one of Green Forest Lumber's competitors. Both Goodfellow and GFL have similar liquidity ratios. Both have adequate levels of working capital but neither has lots of cash. However, GFL has significantly less debt than Goodfellow, which you see in the differences in their leverage ratios. In a pinch, GFL will likely be able to borrow more money faster than Goodfellow can. The efficiency ratios of the two companies are similar, although GFL ratios are somewhat larger. This indicates that GFL operates more efficiently than Goodfellow. In fact, the average collection period of GFL is nearly half that of Goodfellow. This might warrant further investigation. Does Goodfellow sell to a different type of customer than GFL? Overall, GFL is a more profitable company. They make more money on each dollar of sales and on each dollar of assets.

Financial statistics and ratios for industries are published by Statistics Canada, Dun and Bradstreet, Robert Morris Associates (U.S. data), and others. Table 17.8 shows the principal ratios for several major industry groups. These ratios were calculated with the financial statistics reported quarterly by Statistics Canada. This should give you a feel for some of the differences between industries.

We don't recommend that you use industry averages as your benchmark for analyzing a company's financial performance. The problem with averages is that you do not know exactly which companies are included. The firms may differ in size or may be involved in several different industries. Consequently, the average ratios may not be well-matched to your company. Furthermore, you may not know how the ratios have been calculated. We recommend that you select one or two companies similar to the company you are analyzing. You might augment these individual companies' ratios with industry average data but don't rely exclusively on the industry averages.

17.4 THE EARNINGS RECORD

Figure 17.1 on page 464 summarizes GFL's earnings record over the past seven years. But GFL is affected by the state of the economy as a whole and by the prosperity of its particular industry. Thus to interpret this record you need to take into account what was happening to other companies.

Figure 17.1 also shows Goodfellow's earnings performance. Notice that GFL's earnings record closely mirrors that of its competitor until 1993 when GFL had a significant improvement in earnings. This tells us that if we want to understand GFL's recent growth in profits, we probably need to look at events affecting the

TABLE 17.8
Financial ratios for selected industry groups, fourth quarter 1993

	Total Non-financial Industries	Food (including Retail)	Iron, Steel and Related Products	Petroleum and Natural Gas	Electronic Equipment and Computer Services
Leverage ratios					
Short-term + long-term debt ratio[a]	.57	.55	.52	.49	.44
Total debt ratio[b]	.64	.65	.54	.53	.65
Liquidity ratios					
Net working capital to total assets	.06	.08	.19	.01	.15
Current ratio	1.23	1.24	1.92	1.1	1.42
Quick ratio	.75	.66	1.06	.80	1.07
Efficiency ratios					
Average collection period (days)	43.1	21.7	61.8	47.0	91.9
Total asset turnover	1.05	2.38	.90	.68	1.19
Profitability ratios					
Net profit margin (%)	3.26	1.75	3.53	7.36	1.63
Return on assets (%)	3.42	4.2	3.2	5.02	1.94
Return on equity (%)	3.79	5.4	6.0	7.78	2.43
Payout ratio	1.73	.87	.51	.51	2.03

Notes:
[a] Separate data on long-term debt was not available.
[b] Deferred taxes are included with shareholders' equity and not with total liabilities.
Source: Statistics Canada, *Quarterly Financial Statistics for Enterprises,* Fourth Quarter, 1993. Reproduced by authority of the Minister of Industry, 1995.
Readers wishing further information on data provided through the cooperation of Statistics Canada may obtain copies of related publications by mail from: Publications Sales, Statistics Canada, Ottawa, Ontario, K1A 0T6, by calling 1-613-951-7277 or toll-free 1-800-267-6677. Readers may also facsimile their order by dialing 1-613-951-1584.

Finance in Action

Controversial Financial Statements

Analyzing financial statements is a skill that requires a solid understanding of accounting and finance as well as the company's business. Even so, sometimes one person's assessment of the financial health of a company is strikingly different from someone else's assessment. Take the case of the financial statements of Cott Corp., a Canadian soft-drink manufacturer, which drew the attention of stock analysts and accountants between 1992 and 1994. Some accountants and stock analysts saw in Cott's financial state-

ments a profitable, growing, highly successful company that warranted its high share price. Other accountants and stock analysts saw artificially inflated profits and earnings per share due to improper accounting techniques. For these analysts, Cott's $50 stock price was not warranted, based on their assessment of the financial statements. A number of these analysts recommended that investors "sell short" the stock of Cott Corp. because they believed that the stock was overvalued and must fall. To sell short, an investor

Controversial Financial Statements *(continued)*

borrows shares, immediately sells them, and replaces the shares in the future. The hope of a short-seller is that the price of the shares falls so that the replacement shares are bought for less than the borrowed shares were sold.

Those who questioned Cott's financial statements were concerned with the way Cott accounted for certain costs they incurred doing business. For example, Cott capitalized its development costs — money spent designing the packaging of products, for example — and its contract costs — money spent to secure shelf space at grocery stores for Cott pop. Critics argue that these costs should be expensed, as they are with other major pop manufacturers. When costs are capitalized, only part of the cost is charged against income in the year in which the costs are incurred. The rest of the costs are charged in subsequent years. Of course, Cott had to pay for the development and contract activities when the services were provided. Its cash flow is reduced by the full amount of money paid for the activities. By not expensing the full cost of these activities, Cott was able to report higher profits. In a report on Cott's accounting practices, Al Rosen (accounting professor, York University and practicing forensic accountant) wrote, "Every day that Cott operates, it consumes much more cash than it generates from sales. Eventually, companies with such problems go bankrupt, because they run out of GAAP [generally accepted accounting principles] diversions.... Unless Cott raises more equity...or entices some naive long-term creditor to lend it money, or *shrinks* in sales volume, the company will be bankrupt in 18 to 36 months."

Another question must be asked: "Do the accounting practices matter to the market's assessment of the value of Cott?" Studies have shown that the market sees through the accounting techniques and cares only about the expected cash flow to shareholders. Indeed as the stock price fell in the summer of 1994, it was reported that "...even ignoring its accounting methods, Cott faced a troubled future, what with the pressures of a new economy: a hostile market for raising more equity capital, enormous cash flow demands [to fund the assets needed for sales growth], shrinking profit margins (thanks in part to pop price wars)...." Did Cott's stock price fall because people finally woke up and realized that its aggressive accounting was hiding the true situation of the company or did economic conditions change, reducing the expected cash flows to shareholders?

The evidence seems to suggest that changing market conditions had a significant role to play. By late October, 1994, virtually all analysts who had recommended investors buy the stock had changed their recommendations to "moderately attractive" or even "high risk, avoid." The reasons cited for the change included declining profit margins partly because of stiff competitive pricing from soft-drink giants Coca-Cola Co. and Pepsi-Cola Co. In addition, the cost of aluminum and plastic, the key packaging materials, were expected to rise up to 15 percent. Packaging costs account for 55 percent of total costs.

By the end of 1994, Cott's stock price was around $12 per share, a far cry from its year high of $42.37. The short-sellers had made the right call.

Source: Adapted from Jennifer Wells, "Cott Short," *The Globe and Mail Report on Business Magazine,* September 1994, pp. 36–50; and Marina Strauss, "Cott Loses Its Sparkle of Wall Street Brokers," *The Globe and Mail,* October 22, 1994, p. B2.

FIGURE 17.1
Earnings per share of Green
Forest Lumber and
Goodfellow, 1988–1994.

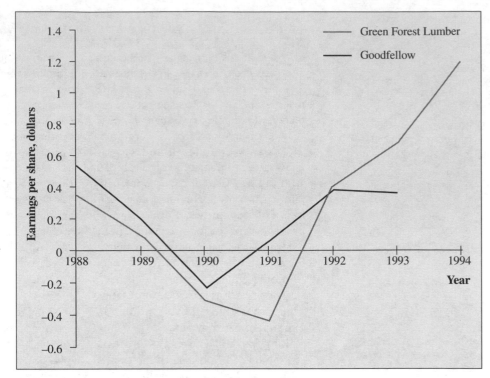

FIGURE 17.1
Earnings per share of Green Forest Lumber and Goodfellow, 1988–1994.

whole industry. For example, you can see the impact that the 1989–1991 recession had on both GFL's and Goodfellow's earnings.

Does GFL's growth in earnings bode well for the future? Not necessarily. Statisticians who have studied the time path of firms' reported earnings conclude that earnings behave much as stock prices — that is, they follow a random walk.[14] There is almost no relationship between a company's earnings growth in one period and that in the next. Therefore, you should never extrapolate growth mechanically. A firm with above-average earnings growth is equally likely to follow up with either below-average or above-average future growth. There is little point in fitting a trend line to past earnings, and such a trend line tells you little about likely future earnings.

Of course there are many sources of information that may help you forecast earnings. For example, when a firm enjoys a high P/E ratio despite disappointing earnings, this suggests that investors expect an earnings rebound. Or suppose a firm announces a significant technological jump ahead of its competitors; you don't need a Ph.D. to figure out the likely impact on earnings.

 **SUMMARY**

1. If you are analyzing a company's financial statements, there is a danger of being overwhelmed by the sheer volume of data. Managers use a few salient ratios to summarize the firm's leverage, liquidity, efficiency, profitability, and market valuation.

---

[14] See, for example, R. Ball and R. Watts, "Some Time Series Properties of Accounting Income," *Journal of Finance* 27 (June 1972):663–682.

2. Leverage ratios measure the indebtedness of the firm. Liquidity ratios measure how easily the firm can obtain cash. Efficiency ratios measure the firm's return on its investments. Market-value ratios measure how the firm is valued by investors. Be selective in your choice of ratios. Different ratios often tell you similar things.

3. The Du Pont system provides a useful way to link ratios to explain the firm's return on assets and equity.

4. Financial ratio analysis will rarely be useful if practiced mechanically. It requires a good dose of good judgement. Financial ratios seldom provide answers but they do help you ask the right questions. There is no international standard for financial ratios. A little thought and common sense are worth far more than blind application of formulas.

5. You need a benchmark for assessing a company's financial position. It is usual to compare financial ratios with the company's ratios in earlier years and with the ratios of other firms in the same business.

KEY TERMS

income statement	**liquidity**	**off-balance sheet**
balance sheet	**Du Pont system**	**items**
common-size balance sheet		

SUGGESTED READINGS

There are some good general texts on financial statement analysis. See, for example,

G. Foster. *Financial Statement Analysis*, 2d ed. Englewood Cliffs, N.J.: Prentice-Hall, 1986.

B. Lev. *Financial Statement Analysis: A New Approach*, Englewood Cliffs, N.J.: Prentice-Hall, 1978.

PROBLEMS

1. Here are the 1994 financial statements of Nynex Corporation:

INCOME STATEMENT
(figures in millions of dollars)

Net sales	13,194
Cost of goods sold	4,060
Other expenses	4,049
Depreciation	2,518
Earnings before interest and taxes (EBIT)	2,566
Interest expenses	685
Income before tax	1,882
Taxes	570
Net income	1,311
Dividends	856

BALANCE SHEET
(figures in millions of dollars)

	End of Year	Start of Year
Assets		
Cash and marketable securities	89	158
Receivables	2,382	2,490
Inventories	187	238
Other current assets	867	932
Total current assets	3,524	3,818
Net property, plant, and equipment	19,973	19,915
Other long-term assets	4,216	3,770
Total assets	27,714	27,503
Liabilities and Shareholders' Equity		
Payables	2,564	3,040
Short-term debt	1,419	1,573
Other current liabilities	811	787
Total current liabilities	4,795	5,400
Long-term debt and leases	7,018	6,883
Other long-term liabilites	6,178	6,149
Shareholders' equity	9,724	9,120
Total liabilities and shareholders' equity	27,714	27,503

Calculate the following financial ratios:
a. Long-term debt ratio
b. Total debt ratio
c. Times interest earned
d. Cash flow coverage ratio
e. Current ratio
f. Quick ratio
g. Net profit margin
h. Inventory turnover
i. Days in inventory
j. Average collection period
k. Return on equity
l. Return on assets
m. Payout ratio

2. Suppose that Nynex shut down operations. For how many days could it pay its bills?

3. What was Nynex's gross investment in plant and other equipment in 1994?

4. If the market value of Nynex stock was $17.2 billion at the end of 1994, what was the price-to-book ratio? If there were 205 million shares outstanding, what were earnings per share? The P/E ratio?

5. There are no universally accepted definitions of financial ratios, but some of the following ratios make no sense at all. Substitute the correct definitions.

a. $\text{Debt-equity ratio} = \dfrac{\text{long-term debt} + \text{values of leases}}{\text{long-term debt} + \text{value of leases} + \text{equity}}$

b. $\text{Return on equity} = \dfrac{\text{EBIT} - \text{tax}}{\text{average equity}}$

c. $\text{Profit margin} = \dfrac{\text{EBIT} - \text{tax}}{\text{sales}}$

d. $\text{Inventory turnover} = \dfrac{\text{sales}}{\text{average inventory}}$

e. $\text{Current ratio} = \dfrac{\text{current liabilities}}{\text{current assets}}$

f. $\text{Interval measure} = \dfrac{\text{current assets} - \text{inventories}}{\text{average daily expenditure from operations}}$

g. $\text{Average collection period} = \dfrac{\text{sales}}{\text{average receivables}/365}$

h. $\text{Quick ratio} = \dfrac{\text{cash} + \text{marketable securities} + \text{receivables}}{\text{current liabilities}}$

i. $\text{Payout ratio} = \dfrac{\text{dividend}}{\text{stock price}}$

6. As you can see, someone has spilled ink over some of the entries in the balance sheet and income statement of Transylvania Railroad. Can you use the following information to work out the missing entries:

Long-term debt ratio	.4
Times interest earned	8.0
Current ratio	1.4
Quick ratio	1.0
Cash ratio	.2
Return on assets	18%
Return on equity	41%
Inventory turnover	5.0
Average collection period	71.2 days

INCOME STATEMENT
(figures in millions of dollars)

Net sales	• • •
Cost of goods sold	• • •
Selling, general, and administrative expenses	10
Depreciation	20
Earnings before interest and taxes (EBIT)	• • •
Interest expense	• • •
Income before tax	• • •
Tax	• • •
Net income	• • •

BALANCE SHEET
(figures in millions of dollars)

	This Year	Last Year
Assets		
Cash and marketable securities	• • •	20
Receivables	• • •	34
Inventories	• • •	26
Total current assets	• • •	80
Net property, plant, and equipment	• • •	25
Total assets	• • •	105

BALANCE SHEET *(continued)*
(figures in millions of dollars)

	This Year	Last Year
Liabilities and Shareholders' Equity		
Accounts payable	25	20
Notes payable	30	35
Total current liabilities	•••	55
Long-term debt	•••	20
Shareholders' equity	•••	30
Total liabilities and shareholders' equity	115	105

7. Suppose that at year-end 1994 Green Forest Lumber had unused lines of credit that would have allowed it to borrow a further $10 million. Suppose also that it used this line of credit to raise short-term loans of $10 million and invested the proceeds in marketable securities. Would the company have appeared to be (a) more or less liquid, (b) more or less highly leveraged? Calculate the appropriate ratios.

8. How would the following actions affect a firm's current ratio?
   a. Inventory is sold.
   b. The firm takes out a bank loan to pay its accounts due.
   c. A customer pays its accounts receivable.
   d. The firm uses cash to purchase additional inventories.

9. A firm uses $1 million in cash to purchase inventories. What will happen to its current ratio? Its quick ratio?

10. Chik's Chickens has average accounts receivable of $6333. Sales for the year were $9800. What is its days in receivables?

11. Salad Daze maintains an inventory of produce worth $400. Its total bill for produce over the course of the year was $73,000. How old on average is the lettuce it serves its customers?

12. If a firm's inventory level of $10,000 represents 30 days' sales, what is the annual cost of goods sold? What is the inventory turnover ratio?

13. Lever Age pays an 8 percent coupon on outstanding debt with face value $10 million. The firm's EBIT was $1 million.
   a. What is times interest earned?
   b. If depreciation is $200,000, what is cash flow coverage?
   c. If the firm must retire $300,000 of debt for the sinking fund each year, what is its "fixed-payment cash-coverage ratio" (the ratio of cash flow to interest plus other fixed debt payments)?

14. Use the income statement and balance sheets in problem 1 to
   a. calculate the ROE for Nynex
   b. demonstrate that the product of Nynex's debt burden ratio, turnover ratio, operating profit margin, and leverage ratio equals its ROE

15. Keller Cosmetics maintains a profit margin of 5 percent and asset turnover ratio of 3.
   a. What is its ROA?
   b. If its debt-equity ratio is 1.0, its interest payments and taxes are each $8,000, and EBIT is $20,000, what is its ROE?

16. Torrid Romance Publishers has total receivables of $3000, which represents 20 days' sales. Average total assets are $75,000. The firm's operating profit margin is 5 percent. Find the firm's ROA and asset turnover ratio.

17. A firm has a long-term debt-equity ratio of .4. Shareholders' equity is $1 million. Current assets are $200,000 and the current ratio is 2.0. The only current liabilities are notes payable. What is the total debt ratio?

18. In each of the following cases, explain briefly which of the two companies is likely to be characterized by the higher ratio:
    a. Debt-equity ratio: a shipping company or a computer software company
    b. Payout ratio: United Foods Inc. or Computer Graphics Inc.
    c. Ratio of sales to assets: an integrated pulp and paper manufacturer or a paper mill
    d. Average collection period: Regional Electric Power Company or Z-Mart Discount Outlets
    e. Price-earnings multiple: Basic Sludge Company or Fledgling Electronics

SOLUTIONS TO SELF-TEST QUESTIONS

17.1 Nothing will happen to the long-term debt ratio computed using book values, since the face values of the old and new debt are equal. However, times interest earned and cash flow coverage will increase since the firm will reduce its interest expense.

17.2
a. The current ratio starts at 1.2/1.0 = 1.2. The transaction will reduce current assets (specifically cash) to $.7 million and current liabilities (accounts payable) to $.5 million. The current ratio increases to .7/.5 = 1.4. Net working capital is unaffected: current assets and current liabilities fall by equal amounts.
b. The current ratio is unaffected, since the firm merely exchanges one current asset (cash) for another (inventories). However, the quick ratio will fall since inventories are not included among the most liquid assets.

17.3 Average daily expenses are (2041 + 761 + 2)/365 = $7.68 million. Average accounts payable are (135 + 166)/2 = 150.5 million. The average payment delay is therefore 150.5/7.68 = 19.6 days.

17.4 In 1994, Green Forest Lumber had almost no debt and therefore paid almost no interest. Thus operating profits after tax, EBIT – taxes, equals net income, EBIT – interest – taxes. Shareholders of Green Forest Lumber receive all of the operating profits.

17.5

$$\text{Market-to-book} = \frac{\text{price}}{\text{book value per share}}$$

$$\frac{\text{Market-to-book}}{\text{Price/earnings per share}} = \frac{\text{price/book value per share}}{\text{price/earnings per share}}$$

$$= \frac{\text{earnings per share}}{\text{book value per share}} = \text{ROE}$$

Firms with high ROE are not necessarily good investments. A high ROE will be associated with a high stock price. Even though the firm earns a good return on its investments, investors in the *firm's stock* might not earn attractive returns on their investments since they buy into the firm at prices that already reflect the attractive ROE. (In fact, we've just shown that the market-to-book ratio is proportional to ROE.) There is a difference between a "good firm" and a "good stock."

17.6

a.   The firm must compensate for its below-average profit margin with an above-average turnover ratio. Remember that ROA is the *product* of margin × turnover.
b.   If ROA equals the industry average but ROE exceeds the industry average, the firm must have above-average leverage. As long as ROA exceeds the borrowing rate, leverage will increase ROE.

CHAPTER EIGHTEEN

Financial Planning

It's been said that a camel looks like a horse designed by committee. If a firm made all its financial decisions piecemeal, it would end up with a financial camel. Therefore, smart financial managers consider the overall effect of future investment and financing decisions. This process is called *financial planning*, and the end result is called a *financial plan*.

Investment and financing decisions are interconnected, thus they cannot be made independently. Financial planning forces managers to think systematically about the relationships among their goals for growth, investment, and financing. Planning should reveal any inconsistencies in these goals.

Planning also helps managers avoid some surprises and think about how they should react to those surprises that cannot be avoided. In Chapter 8 we stressed that good financial managers insist on understanding what makes projects work and what could go wrong with them. The same approach is, or should be, taken when investment and financing decisions are considered as a whole.

Finally, financial planning helps establish concrete goals to motivate managers and provide standards for measuring performance.

We start the chapter by summarizing what financial planning involves and we describe the contents of a typical financial plan. We then discuss the use of financial models in the planning process. Finally, we examine the relationship between a firm's growth and its need for new financing.

After studying this chapter you should be able to
- Describe the contents and uses of a financial plan.
- Construct a simple financial planning model.
- Estimate the effect of growth on the need for external financing.

 WHAT IS FINANCIAL PLANNING?

Financial planning is a process consisting of:

1. Analyzing the investment and financing choices open to the firm.
2. Projecting the future consequences of current decisions.
3. Deciding which alternatives to undertake.
4. Measuring subsequent performance against the goals set forth in the financial plan.

Notice that financial planning is not designed to minimize risk. Instead it is a process of deciding which risks to take and which are unnecessary or not worth taking.

Firms must plan for both the short-term and the long-term. Short-term planning rarely looks ahead further than the next 12 months. It is largely the process of making sure the firm has enough cash to pay its bills and that short-term borrowing and lending are arranged to the best advantage. We discuss short-term planning in the next chapter.

Here we are more concerned with long-term planning, where a typical **planning horizon** is 5 years (although some firms look out 10 years or more). For example, it can take at least 10 years for an electric utility to design, obtain approval for, build, and test a major generating plant.

planning horizon: Time horizon corresponding to a financial plan.

Many of the firm's capital expenditures are proposed by plant managers. But the final budget must also reflect strategic plans made by senior management. These strategic plans attempt to identify the businesses in which the firm has a genuine competitive advantage and that should be expanded. They also seek to identify businesses to sell or liquidate as well as businesses that should be allowed to run down.

Strategic planning involves capital budgeting on a grand scale. In this process, financial planners try to look at the investment by each line of business and avoid getting bogged down in details. Of course, some individual projects are large enough to have significant individual impact. When Ford committed $6 billion to the development of its self-proclaimed world car, the Mondeo, you can bet that this project was explicitly analyzed as part of Ford's long-range financial plan. Normally, however, financial planners do not work on a project-by-project basis. Smaller projects are always aggregated into a unit that is treated as a single project.

At the beginning of the planning process the corporate staff might ask each division to submit three alternative business plans covering the next 5 years:

1. A *best case* or aggressive growth plan calling for heavy capital investment and new products, rapid growth of existing markets, or entry into new markets.
2. A *normal growth* plan in which the division grows with its markets but not significantly at the expense of its competitors.
3. A plan of *retrenchment* if the firm's markets contract. This is planning for lean economic times.

Of course, the planners might also want to look at the opportunities and costs of moving into a wholly new area where the company may be able to exploit some of its existing strengths. Often they may recommend entering a market for "strategic" reasons — that is, not because the *immediate* investment has a positive net present value, but because it establishes the firm in a new market and creates *options* for possibly valuable follow-up investments.

As an example,consider the decision by CanWest Global Communications, a Canadian broadcaster, to acquire a 50 percent interest in La Red Television Network of Santiago, Chile, a struggling television network. CanWest chairman, I.H. Aspler stated, "We view this investment as an important experiment which, if successful, could lead to CanWest International developing a portfolio of broadcasting properties in selected Hispanic markets".[1]

Because the firm's future is likely to depend on the options that it acquires today, we would expect planners to take a particular interest in these options.

In the simplest plans, capital expenditures might be forecast to grow in proportion to sales. In even moderately sophisticated models, however, the need for additional investments will recognize the firm's ability to use its fixed assets at varying levels of intensity by adjusting overtime or by adding additional shifts. Similarly, the plan will alert the firm to needs for additional investments in working capital. For example, if sales are forecast to increase, the firm should plan to increase inventory levels and should expect an increase in accounts receivable.

Most plans also contain a summary of planned financing. This part of the plan should logically include a discussion of dividend policy, because the more the firm pays out, the more capital it will need to find from sources other than retained earnings.

---

[1] *The Globe and Mail Report on Business*, May 31, 1994, B1–B2.

Growing firms will need to pay for investments in plant, equipment, and working capital. A commitment to pay interest on debt and a desire to pay dividends also require cash. If cash flows from operations are not sufficient for these outflows, the firm will have to raise additional funds. Therefore, the completed financial plan will outline a strategy for raising any necessary additional funds. The plan might specify bank borrowing, debt issues, equity issues, or other means to raise capital.

Some firms need to worry much more than others about raising money. A firm with limited investment opportunities, ample operating cash flow, and a moderate dividend payout accumulates considerable "financial slack" in the form of liquid assets and unused borrowing power. Life is relatively easy for the managers of such firms, and their financing plans are routine. Whether that easy life is in the interests of their stockholders is another matter.

Other firms have to raise capital by selling securities. Naturally, they give careful attention to planning the kinds of securities to be sold and the timing of the offerings. Such firms may also find their financing plans complicated by covenants on their existing debt. For example, electric utility bonds often prohibit the firm from issuing more bonds if interest coverage drops below a certain level. Typically, the minimum level is two times earnings.

Financial Planning Is Not Just Forecasting

Forecasting concentrates on the most likely future outcome. But financial planners are not concerned solely with forecasting. They need to worry about unlikely events as well as likely ones. If you think ahead about what could go wrong, then you are less likely to ignore the danger signals and you can react faster to trouble.

Companies have developed a number of ways of asking "what-if" questions about both their projects and the overall firm. We examined some of these techniques in Chapter 8. Often planners work through the consequences of the plan under the most likely set of circumstances and then use *sensitivity analysis* to vary the assumptions one at a time. For example, they might look at what would happen if a policy of aggressive growth coincided with a recession. Companies using *scenario analysis* might look at the consequence of each business plan under different plausible scenarios in which several assumptions are varied at once. For example, one scenario might envisage high interest rates leading to a slowdown in world economic growth and lower commodity prices. A second scenario might involve a buoyant domestic economy, high inflation, and a weak currency.

Three Requirements for Effective Planning

Planning involves forecasting, but it is more than just forecasting. It also requires you to choose among competing financial and investment policies and to think ahead about how you might react to surprises.

Forecasting. The firm will never have perfectly accurate forecasts. If it did, there would be less need for planning. Still, managers must strive for the best forecasts possible.

Forecasting should not be reduced to a mechanical exercise. Naive extrapolation or fitting trends to past data is of limited value. Planning is needed because the future is not likely to resemble the past.

Do not forecast in a vacuum. By this we mean that your forecasts should recognize that your competitors are developing their own plans. For example, your ability to implement an aggressive growth plan and increase market share depends on what the competition is likely to do. So, planning should not be conducted in a vacuum. *When you are presented with a set of corporate forecasts, do not accept them at face value. Probe behind the forecasts and try to identify the economic model on which they are based.*

Finance in Action

Finance — More Important Than Marketing?

When CEOs of 2600 entrepreneurial American firms were sent open-ended questions asking what management skills were most important to their ability to succeed, their responses identified financial management as the most important skill. The survey, which was done by the San Diego-based Center for Creative Leadership, so intrigued Canada's Bank of Montreal that the Bank collaborated with the Center on follow-up surveys in the U.S. and Canada.

Geoff Cannon, Vice-President and Executive Director of the Bank of Montreal's Institute for Small Business, explained the meaning of the term "financial management" as follows: "The American CEOs define financial management as the ability to find and maintain adequate capital for survival and growth of the business."

The follow-up study, which included mailing surveys to over 3700 entrepreneurial Canadian firms, led the B of M's Institute to publish, in early 1995, a report entitled *Entrepreneurial Success Factors: Linking Leadership and Growth.*

This second study, while indicating that financial management skills were considered important by the American and the Canadian respondents, suggested that the views of the relative importance of the financial skills dif- fer north and south of the border. American respondents, when ranking the importance of management skills and when reporting the frequency with which the skills are used, rated financial management ahead of nine skills including sales, marketing, and organizing! The only skills the Americans ranked as being *both* more important and more frequently used than financial management were "vision" and "ethics." Responses from Canadian managers did not put vision-creating and ethics-related skills consistently ahead of financial management, but substituted listening, leadership, delegating, industry knowledge, and customer/vendor relationship skills.

Asked about the study, Cannon remarked on the apparent differences between the Canadian and American perceptions. "More detailed analysis of the Canadian responses suggests that financial management skills become more strongly linked with success when entrepreneurial Canadian firms enter the high growth stage of development." Further work is underway to explore how factors like firm size — Canadian firms in the sample were, on average, smaller than those in the American sample — may colour the findings.

Source: Interview with Geoff Cannon, May 1995.

Planners draw on information from many sources. Therefore, inconsistency may be a problem. For example, forecast sales may be the sum of separate forecasts made by many product managers, each of whom may make different assumptions about inflation, growth of the national economy, availability of raw materials, and so on. In such cases, it makes sense to ask individuals for forecasts based on a common set of macroeconomic assumptions.

Choosing the Optimal Financial Plan. In the end, the financial manager has to choose which is best. We would like to tell you exactly how to make this choice. Unfortunately, we can't. There is no model or procedure that encompasses all the complexity and intangibles encountered in financial planning.

You sometimes hear managers state corporate goals in terms of accounting numbers. They might say, "Our objective is to achieve annual sales growth of 20 percent," or "We want a 25 percent return on book equity and a profit margin of 10 percent." On the surface such objectives don't make sense. Shareholders want to be richer, not to have the satisfaction of a 10 percent profit margin. Also, a goal that is stated in terms of accounting ratios is nonoperational unless it is translated back into what that means for business decisions. For example, a higher profit margin can result from higher prices, lower costs, a move into new, high-margin products, or taking over the firm's suppliers.[2] Setting profit margin as a goal gives no guidance as to which of these strategies is to be preferred.

So why do managers define objectives in this way? In part such goals may be a mutual exhortation to work harder, like singing the company song before work. But we suspect that managers are often using a code to communicate real concerns. For example, the goal to increase sales rapidly may reflect management's belief that increased market share is needed to achieve scale economies. Or a target profit margin may be a way of saying that in pursuing sales growth the firm has allowed costs to get out of control.

The danger is that everyone may forget the code and the accounting targets may be seen as goals in themselves.

Watching the Plan Unfold. Financial plans are out of date as soon as they are complete. Often they are out of date even earlier. For example, suppose that profits in the first year turn out to be 10 percent below forecast. What do you do with your plan? Scrap it and start again? Stick to your guns and hope profits will bounce back? Revise down your profit forecasts for later years by 10 percent? A good financial plan should be easy to adapt as events unfold and surprises occur.

Long-term plans can also be used as a benchmark to judge subsequent performance as events unfold. But performance appraisals have little value unless you also take into account the business background against which they were achieved. You are likely to be much less concerned if profits decline in a recession than if they decline when the economy is buoyant and your competitors' sales are booming. If you know how a downturn is likely to throw you off plan, then you have a standard to judge your performance during such a downturn and a better idea of what to do about it.

18.2 FINANCIAL PLANNING MODELS

Financial planners often use a financial planning model to help them explore the consequences of alternative financial strategies. These models range from simple models, such as the one presented later in this chapter, to models that incorporate hundreds of equations.

Financial planning models support the financial planning process by making it easier and cheaper to construct forecast financial statements. The models auto-

---

[2] If you take over a supplier, total sales are not affected (to the extent that the supplier is selling to you), but you capture both the supplier's and your own profit margin. See Chapter 17, Table 17.7, for an example.

mate an important part of planning that would otherwise be boring, time-consuming, and labour-intensive.

Programming these financial planning models used to consume large amounts of computer time and high-priced talent. These days standard spreadsheet programs such as Lotus 1-2-3 and Microsoft Excel are regularly used to solve complex financial planning problems.

Components of a Financial Planning Model

A completed financial plan for a large company is a substantial document. A smaller corporation's plan would have the same elements but less detail and documentation. For the smallest, youngest businesses, the financial plan may be entirely in the financial manager's head. The basic elements of the plans will be similar, however, for firms of any size.

Financial plans all include three components: inputs, the planning model, and outputs. The relationship among these components is represented in Figure 18.1. Let's look at these components in turn.

FIGURE 18.1
The components of a financial plan.

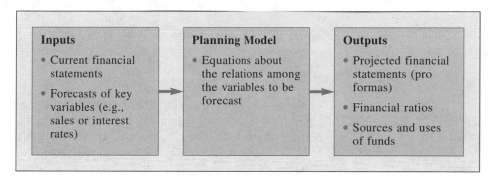

Inputs	Planning Model	Outputs
• Current financial statements	• Equations about the relations among the variables to be forecast	• Projected financial statements (pro formas)
• Forecasts of key variables (e.g., sales or interest rates)		• Financial ratios
		• Sources and uses of funds

Inputs. The inputs to the financial plan consist of the firm's current financial statements and its forecasts about the future. Usually, the principal forecast is the likely growth in sales, since many of the other variables such as labour requirements and inventory levels are tied to sales. These forecasts are only in part the responsibility of the financial manager. Obviously, the marketing department will play a key role in forecasting sales. In addition, because sales will depend on the state of the overall economy, large firms will seek forecasting help from firms that specialize in preparing macroeconomic and industry forecasts.

The Planning Model. The financial planning model calculates the implications of the manager's forecasts for profits, new investment, and financing. This involves an estimate of how a change in sales is likely to affect costs, working capital, fixed assets, and financing requirements. For example, the financial model may specify that the total cost of goods produced may increase by 80 cents for every $1 increase in total sales, that accounts receivable will be a fixed proportion of sales, and that the firm will need to increase fixed assets by 8 percent for every 10 percent increase in sales.

Outputs. The output of the financial model consists of financial statements like income statements, balance sheets, and statements describing sources and uses of cash. These statements are called **pro formas**, which means that they are forecasts based on the inputs and the assumptions built into the plan. Usually the output of financial models also includes many of the financial ratios we discussed in the last chapter. These ratios indicate whether the firm will be financially fit and healthy at the end of the planning period.

pro formas: Projected or forecast financial statements.

We can illustrate the basic components of a planning model with a very simple example. In the next section we will start to add some complexity.

Suppose that Executive Cheese has prepared the simple balance sheet and income statement shown in Table 18.1. The firm's financial planners forecast that total sales next year will increase by 10 percent from this year's level. They expect that costs will be a fixed proportion of sales, so they too will increase by 10 percent. Almost all the forecasts for Executive Cheese are proportional to the forecast of sales. Such models are therefore called **percentage of sales models**. The result is the pro forma, or forecast, income statement in Table 18.2, which shows that next year's income will be $200 × 1.10 = $220.

percentage of sales model: Planning model in which sales forecasts are the driving variables and other variables are proportional to sales.

TABLE 18.1

Financial statements of Executive Cheese Company for past year

INCOME STATEMENT			
Sales	$1,200		
Costs	1,000		
Net income	$ 200		

BALANCE SHEET, YEAR END			
Assets	$2,000	Debt	$ 800
		Equity	1,200
Total	$2,000	Total	$2,000

Executive Cheese has no spare capacity, and in order to sustain this higher level of output, it must increase plant and equipment by 10 percent, or $200. Therefore, the left-hand side of the balance sheet, which lists total assets, must increase to $2200. What about the right-hand side? The firm must decide how it intends to finance its new assets. Suppose that it decides to maintain a fixed debt-equity ratio. Then both debt and equity would grow by 10 percent, as shown in the pro forma balance sheet in Table 18.2. Notice that this implies that the firm must issue $80 in additional debt. On the other hand, no equity needs to be issued. The 10 percent increase in equity can be accomplished by retaining $120 of earnings.

TABLE 18.2

Pro forma financial statements of Executive Cheese

INCOME STATEMENT			
Sales	$1,320		
Costs	1,100		
Net income	$ 220		

BALANCE SHEET			
Assets	$2,200	Debt	$ 880
		Equity	1,320
Total	$2,200	Total	$2,200

This raises a question, however. If income is forecast at $220, why does equity increase by only $120? The answer is that the firm must be planning to pay a dividend of $220 − $120 = $100. Notice that this dividend payment is not chosen independently but is a *consequence* of the other decisions. Given the company's need for funds and its decision to maintain the debt-equity ratio, dividend policy is completely determined. Any other dividend payment would be inconsistent with the two conditions that (1) the right-hand side of the balance sheet increase by $200, and (2) both debt and equity increase by 10 percent. For this reason we call dividends the **balancing item**, or *plug*. The balancing item is the variable that adjusts to make the sources of funds equal to the uses.

balancing item: Variable that adjusts to maintain the consistency of a financial plan. Also called *plug*.

There is no requirement that dividends be the balancing item. Instead of maintaining a fixed debt-equity ratio, the firm could commit to some other dividend payment, for example, $180, and raise the extra money it needs by an issue of debt. In this case the amount of debt becomes the balancing item. With the dividend set at $180, retained earnings would be only $40, so the firm would have to issue $160 in new debt to help pay for the additional $200 of assets. Table 18.3 is the new balance sheet.

TABLE 18.3

Pro forma balance sheet with dividends fixed at $180 and debt used as the balancing item

Assets	$2,200	Debt	$ 960
		Equity	1,240
Total	$2,200	Total	$2,200

Is the second plan better than the first? It's hard to give a simple answer. The choice of dividend payment depends partly on how investors will interpret the decision. If last year's dividend was only $50, investors might regard a dividend payment of $100 as a sign of a confident management; if last year's dividend was $150, investors might not be so content with a payment of $100. The alternative of paying $180 in dividends and making up the shortfall by issuing more debt leaves the company with a debt-equity ratio of 77 percent. That is unlikely to make your bankers edgy, but you may worry about how long you can continue to finance expansion predominantly by borrowing.

SELF-TEST 18.1

Suppose that the firm is prevented by bond covenants from issuing more debt. It is committed to increasing assets by 10 percent to support the forecast increase in sales, and it strongly believes that a dividend payment of $180 is in the best interests of the firm. What must be the balancing item? What is the implication for the firm's financing activities in the next year?

An Improved Model

Now that you have grasped the idea behind financial planning models, we can move on to a more sophisticated example.

Table 18.4 shows current (year-end 1994) financial statements for Executive Fruit Company. Judging by these figures, the company is ordinary in almost all respects. Its earnings before interest and taxes were 10 percent of sales revenue. Net income was $96,000 after payment of taxes and 10 percent interest on $400,000 of long-term debt. The company paid out two-thirds of its net income as dividends.

Next to each item on the financial statements in Table 18.4 we have entered a comment about the relationship between that variable and sales. In most cases, the comment gives the value of each item as a percentage of sales. This may be useful for forecasting purposes. For example, it would be reasonable to assume that cost of goods sold will remain at 90 percent of sales even if sales grow by 10 percent next year. Similarly, it is reasonable to assume that net working capital will remain at 10 percent of sales.

On the other hand, the fact that long-term debt currently is 20 percent of sales does not mean that we should assume that this ratio will continue to hold next period. Any of many financing plans with varying combinations of debt issues, equity issues, and dividend payouts may be considered without affecting the firm's operations.

Now suppose that you are asked to prepare pro forma financial statements for Executive Fruit for 1995. You are told to assume that (1) sales and operating costs are expected to be up 10 percent over 1994. You interpret "business as usual" to

TABLE 18.4

Financial statements for Executive Fruit Co., 1994 (all figures in thousands)

INCOME STATEMENT		
		Comment
Revenue	$2,000	
Cost of goods sold	1,800	90% of sales
EBIT	200	Difference = 10% of sales
Interest	40	10% of debt at start of year
Earnings before taxes	160	EBIT – interest
Provincial and federal tax	64	40% of (EBIT – interest)
Net income	$ 96	EBIT – interest – taxes
Dividends	$ 64	Payout ratio = 2/3
Retained earnings	$ 32	Net income – dividends

BALANCE SHEET		
Assets		
Net working capital	$ 200	10% of sales
Fixed assets	800	40% of sales
Net assets	$1,000	50% of sales
Liabilities & Shareholders' Equity		
Long-term debt	$ 400	
Shareholders' equity	600	
Total liabilities & shareholders' equity	$1,000	Equals total assets

mean that (2) interest rates will remain at their current level, (3) the firm will stick to its traditional dividend policy of paying out two-thirds of earnings, and (4) fixed assets and net working capital will need to increase by 10 percent to support the larger sales volume.

In Table 18.5 we present the resulting first-stage pro forma calculations for Executive Fruit. These calculations show what would happen if the size of the firm

TABLE 18.5

First-stage pro forma statements for Executive Fruit Co., 1995 (all figures in thousands)

INCOME STATEMENT		
		Comment
Revenue	$2,200	10% higher
Cost of goods sold	1,980	10% higher
EBIT	220	10% higher
Interest	40	Unchanged
Earnings before taxes	180	EBIT – interest
Provincial and federal tax	72	40% of (EBIT – interest)
Net income	$ 108	EBIT – interest – taxes
Dividends	$ 72	2/3 of net income
Retained earnings	$ 36	Net income – dividends

BALANCE SHEET		
Assets		
Net working capital	$ 220	10% higher
Fixed assets	880	10% higher
Total assets	$1,100	10% higher
Liabilities & Shareholders' Equity		
Long-term debt	$ 400	Temporarily held fixed
Shareholders' equity	636	Increased by retained earnings
Total liabilities & shareholders' equity	$1,036	Sum of debt plus equity
Required external financing	$ 64	Balancing item or plug (= $1,100 – $1,036)

increases along with sales, but at this preliminary stage, the plan does not specify a particular mix of new security issues.

Without any security issues, the balance sheet will not balance: assets will increase to $1,100,000 while debt plus shareholders' equity will amount to only $1,036,000. Somehow the firm will need to raise an extra $64,000 to help pay for the increase in assets. In this first pass, external financing is the balance item. Given the firm's growth forecasts and its dividend policy, the financial plan calculates how much money the firm needs to raise.

In the second-stage pro forma, the firm must decide on the financing mix that best meets its needs. It must choose some combination of new debt or new equity that supports the contemplated acquisition of additional assets. For example, it could issue $64,000 of equity or debt, or it could choose to maintain its long-term debt-equity ratio at two-thirds by issuing both debt and equity.

Table 18.6 shows the second-stage pro forma balance sheet if the required funds are raised by issuing $64,000 of debt. Therefore, in Table 18.6, debt is treated as the balancing item. Notice that while the plan requires the firm to specify a financing plan *consistent* with its growth projections, it does not provide guidance as to the *best* financing mix.

TABLE 18.6

Second-stage pro forma balance sheet for Executive Fruit Co., 1995 (All figures in thousands)

			Comment
Assets			
Net working capital	$	220	10% higher
Fixed assets		880	10% higher
Total assets		$1,100	10% higher
Liabilities & Shareholders' Equity			
Long-term debt	$	464	10% higher (New borrowing = $64; this is the balancing item)
Shareholders' equity	$	636	Increased by retained earnings
Total liabilities & shareholders' equity		$1,100	Again equals total assets

Table 18.7 sets out the firm's sources and uses of funds. It shows that the firm requires an extra investment of $20,000 in working capital and $80,000 in fixed assets. Therefore, it needs $100,000 from retained earnings and new security issues. Retained earnings are $36,000, so $64,000 must be raised from the capital markets. Under the financing plan presented in Table 18.6, the firm borrows the entire $64,000.

TABLE 18.7

Pro forma statement of sources and uses of funds for Executive Fruit in 1995 (all figures in thousands)

Sources		**Uses**	
Retained earnings	$ 36	Investment in working capital	$ 20
Net borrowing	64	Investment in fixed assets	80
Total sources	$100	Total uses	$100

SELF-TEST 18.2

a. Suppose that Executive Fruit is committed to its expansion plans and to its dividend policy. It also wishes to maintain its debt-equity ratio at 2/3. What are the implications for external financing?

b. If the company is prepared to freeze dividends at the 1994 level, how much external financing would be needed?

We have spared you the trouble of actually calculating the figures necessary for Tables 18.5 to 18.7. The calculations do not take more than a few minutes for this simple example, *provided* you set up the calcuiations correctly and make no arithmetic mistakes. If that time requirement seems trivial, remember that in reality you probably would be asked for four similar sets of statements covering each year from 1994 to 1998. Probably you would be asked for alternative projections under different assumptions (for example, 5 percent instead of 10 percent growth rate of revenue) or different financial strategies (for example, freezing dividends at their 1994 level of $64,000). This would be far more time-consuming. Moreover, actual plans will have many more line items than this simple one. Building a model and letting the computer toil in your place have obvious attractions.

18.3 PLANNERS BEWARE

Pitfalls in Model Design

The Executive Fruit model is too simple for practical application. You probably have already noticed several ways to improve it. For example, we ignored depreciation of fixed assets. Depreciation is important because it provides a tax shield. If Executive Fruit deducts depreciation before calculating its tax bill, it could plow back more money into new investments and would need to borrow less. We also ignored the fact that there would probably be some interest to pay in 1995 on the new borrowing, which would cut into the cash for new investment.

You would certainly want to make these obvious improvements. But beware: there is always the temptation to make a model bigger and more detailed. You may end up with an exhaustive model that is too cumbersome for routine use.

Exhaustive detail gets in the way of the intended use of corporate planning models, which is to project the financial consequences of a variety of strategies and assumptions. The fascination of detail, if you give in to it, distracts attention from crucial decisions like stock issues and dividend policy and allocation of capital by business area.

Shortcomings of Percentage of Sales Models

Percentage of sales models are useful first approximations for financial planning. However, in reality, many variables will not be proportional to sales. For example, we will see in Chapter 20 that important components of working capital such as inventories and cash balances will generally rise less than proportionally with sales.

In addition, fixed assets such as plant and equipment are typically not added in small increments as sales increase. Instead, they are added in large or "lumpy" increments. Factories normally operate at less than full capacity. As sales initially increase, the factory utilization rate will increase, so the additional sales can be supported without a major addition to fixed assets. Ultimately, however, if sales continue to increase, the firm will need to add new capacity. Therefore, when the financial plan is prepared, the contemplated addition to fixed assets should not simply track sales growth; it will depend also on the current level of excess capacity. If there is considerable excess capacity, even rapid sales growth may not require big additions to fixed assets. On the other hand, if the firm is already operating near capacity, even small sales growth may call for large investments in plant and equipment.

There Is No Finance in Financial Planning Models

Why do we say that there is no finance in corporate financial models? The first reason is that most such models incorporate an accountant's view of the world. They are designed to forecast accounting statements. Consequently, the models do not emphasize the tools of financial analysis: incremental cash flow, present value, market risk, and so on.[3]

---

[3] Of course there is no reason that the manager can't use the output to calculate the present value of the firm (given some assumptions about growth beyond the planning period), and this is sometimes done.

Second, corporate financial models produce no signposts pointing toward optimal financial decisions. They do not even tell which alternatives are worth examining. All this is left to their users.

For example, the Executive Fruit model tells the firm only how much capital it needs to raise if it decides to pay out two-thirds of its earnings as a dividend. It does not disclose whether this dividend payment makes sense or whether the firm should issue long-term debt, short-term debt, or some other security. While the plan enforces consistency in assumptions, it is silent on the best of the many feasible strategies.

SELF-TEST 18.3

Which of the following questions will a financial plan help to answer?
a. Is the firm's assumption for asset growth consistent with its plans for debt and equity issues and dividend policy?
b. Will accounts receivable increase in direct proportion to sales?
c. Will the contemplated debt-equity mix maximize the value of the firm?

EXTERNAL FINANCING AND GROWTH

We started this chapter by noting that financial plans force managers to be consistent in their goals for growth, investments, and financing. Before leaving the topic of long-term planning, therefore, we should look at the relationship between a firm's growth objectives and its requirements for external financing.

Recall that Executive Fruit started with $1,000,000 of fixed assets and working capital. It forecast sales growth of 10 percent. This higher sales volume required a 10 percent addition to its assets. Thus

$$\text{New investment} = \text{growth rate} \times \text{initial assets}$$

$$\$100,000 = .10 \times \$1,000,000$$

Part of the funds to pay for the new assets is provided by retained earnings. The remainder must come from external financing. Therefore,

$$\text{Required external financing} = \text{new investment} - \text{retained earnings}$$

$$= (\text{growth rate} \times \text{assets}) - \text{retained earnings}$$

This simple equation highlights that the amount of external financing depends on the firm's projected growth. The faster the firm grows, the more it needs to invest and therefore the more it needs to raise new capital.

In the case of Executive Fruit,

$$\text{Required external financing} = (.10 \times \$1,000,000) - \$36,000$$

$$= \$100,000 - \$36,000$$

$$= \$64,000$$

The sloping line in Figure 18.2 illustrates how required external financing increases with the growth rate. At low growth rates, the firm generates more funds than necessary for expansion. In this sense, its requirement for further external funds is negative. It may choose to use its surplus to pay off some of its debt or buy back its stock. In fact, the intercept in Figure 18.2, at zero growth, is the negative of retained earnings. When growth is zero, no funds are needed for expansion, so all the retained earnings are surplus.

FIGURE 18.2
External financing and
growth.

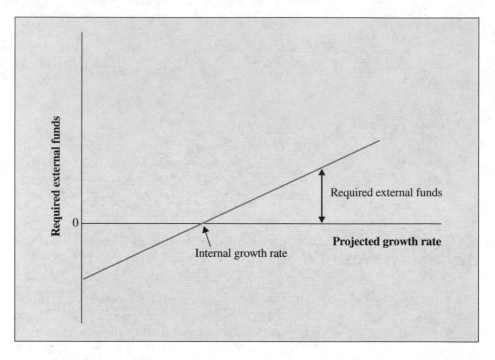

As the firm's projected growth rate increases, more funds are needed to pay for the necessary investments. Therefore, the plot in Figure 18.2 is upward-sloping. For high rates of growth the firm must issue new securities to pay for new investments. Where the sloping line crosses the horizontal axis, external financing is zero: the firm is growing as fast as possible without resorting to new security issues. This is called the **internal growth rate**. The growth rate is internal in the sense that it can be maintained without resort to additional external sources of capital.

internal growth rate:
Maximum rate of growth without external financing.

Notice that if we set external financing to zero, we can solve for the internal growth rate as

$$\text{Internal growth rate} = \frac{\text{retained earnings}}{\text{assets}}$$

Thus the firm's rate of growth without additional external sources of capital will equal the ratio of retained earnings to assets. This means that a firm with a high volume of retained earnings relative to its assets can generate a higher growth rate without needing to raise more capital.

We can gain more insight into what determines the internal growth rate by multiplying the top and bottom of the expression for internal growth by *net income* and *equity* as follows:

$$\text{Internal growth rate} = \frac{\text{retained earnings}}{\text{net income}} \times \frac{\text{net income}}{\text{equity}} \times \frac{\text{equity}}{\text{assets}}$$

$$= \text{plowback ratio} \times \text{return on equity} \times \frac{\text{equity}}{\text{assets}}$$

A firm can achieve a higher growth rate without raising external capital if (1) it plows back a high proportion of its earnings, (2) it has a high return on equity (ROE), and (3) it has a low debt-to-asset ratio.

Instead of focusing on the maximum growth rate that can be supported without *any* external financing, firms also may be interested in the growth rate that can be sustained without additional *equity* issues. Of course, if the firm is able to issue enough debt, virtually any growth rate can be financed. It makes more sense to assume that the firm has settled on an optimal capital structure that it will maintain even as equity is augmented by retained earnings. The firm issues only enough debt to keep its debt-equity ratio constant. The **sustainable growth rate** is the highest growth rate the firm can maintain without increasing its financial leverage. It turns out that the sustainable growth rate depends only on the plowback ratio and return on equity:[4]

> **sustainable growth rate:**
> Steady rate at which a firm can grow without changing leverage; plowback ratio × return on equity.

$$\text{Sustainable growth rate} = \text{plowback ratio} \times \text{return on equity}$$

You may remember this formula from Chapter 5, where we first used it when we looked at the valuation of the firm and the dividend discount model.

● Example 18.1 Internal and Sustainable Growth for Executive Fruit

Executive Fruit has chosen a plowback ratio of 1/3, its return on equity[5] is ROE = 96/600 = .16, and its ratio of equity to assets is 600/1000 = .60. If it is unwilling to raise new capital, its maximum growth rate is

$$\text{Internal growth rate} = \text{plowback} \times \text{ROE} \times \frac{\text{equity}}{\text{assets}}$$

$$= \frac{1}{3} \times .16 \times 60$$

$$= .032, \text{ or } 3.2\%$$

This is much less than the 10 percent growth it projects, which explains its need for external financing.

If Executive is prepared to maintain its current ratio of equity to total assets, it can issue an additional 40 cents of debt for every 60 cents of retained earnings. In this case, the maximum growth rate would be

---

[4] Here is a proof.

$$\text{Required equity issues} = \text{growth rate} \times \text{assets} - \text{retained earnings} - \text{new debt issues}$$

We find the sustainable growth rate by setting required new equity issues to zero and solving for growth:

$$\text{Sustainable growth rate} = \frac{\text{retained earnings} + \text{new debt issues}}{\text{assets}}$$

$$= \frac{\text{retained earnings} + \text{new debt issues}}{\text{debt} + \text{equity}}$$

However, because both debt and equity are growing at the same rate, new debt issues must equal retained earnings multiplied by the ratio of debt to equity, *D/E*. Therefore, we can write the sustainable growth as

$$\text{Sustainable growth rate} = \frac{\text{retained earnings} \times (1 + D/E)}{\text{debt} + \text{equity}}$$

$$= \frac{\text{retained earnings} \times (1 + D/E)}{\text{equity} \times (1 + D/E)} = \frac{\text{retained earnings}}{\text{equity}}$$

$$= \frac{\text{retained earnings}}{\text{net income}} \times \frac{\text{net income}}{\text{equity}} = \text{plowback} \times \text{ROE}$$

[5] Note that, when calculating sustainable growth rates, ROE is measured by earnings as a proportion of equity at the start of the year rather than as a proportion of the average of outstanding equity at the start and end of the year.

$$\text{Sustainable growth rate} = \text{plowback} \times \text{ROE}$$

$$= \frac{1}{3} \times .16$$

$$= .0533, \text{ or } 5.33\%$$

Executive's planned growth rate of 10 percent requires not only new borrowing but an increase in the debt-equity ratio. In the long run the company will need to either issue new equity or cut back its rate of growth.[6]

SELF-TEST 18.4

Suppose Executive Fruit reduces the dividend payout rate to 25 percent. Calculate its growth rate assuming (a) that no new debt or equity will be issued and (b) that the firm maintains its equity-to-asset ratio at .60.

 **SUMMARY**

1. Most firms take financial planning seriously and devote considerable resources to it. The tangible product of the planning process is a financial plan describing the firm's financial strategy and projecting its future consequences by means of pro forma balance sheets, income statements, and statements of sources and uses of funds. The plan establishes financial goals and is a benchmark for evaluating subsequent performance. Usually it also describes why that strategy was chosen and how the plan's financial goals are to be achieved.

2. The plan is the end result. The process that produces the plan is valuable in its own right. Planning forces the financial manager to consider the combined effects of all the firm's investment and financing decisions. This is important because these decisions interact and should not be made independently.

3. Planning, if it is done right, forces the financial manager to think about events that could upset the firm's progress and to devise strategies to be held in reserve for counterattack when unfortunate surprises occur. Planning is more than forecasting, because forecasting deals with the most likely outcome. Planners also have to think about events that may occur even though they are unlikely.

4. In long-range, or strategic, planning, the planning horizon is usually 5 years or more. This kind of planning deals with aggregate decisions; for example, the planner would worry about whether the farm equipment division should go for heavy capital investment and rapid growth, but not whether the division should choose machine tool A versus tool B. In fact, planners must be constantly on guard against the fascination of detail, because giving in to it means slighting crucial issues like investment strategy, debt policy, and the choice of a target dividend payout ratio.

5. There is no theory or model that leads straight to *the* optimal financial strategy. Consequently, financial planning proceeds by trial and error. Many different strategies may be projected under a range of assumptions about the future before one strategy is finally chosen. The dozens of separate projec-

---

[6] As the firm issues more debt, its return on equity also changes. But Executive would need to have a very high debt-equity ratio before it could support a growth rate of 10 percent a year and maintain a constant debt ratio.

tions that may be made during this trial-and-error process generate a heavy load of arithmetic and paperwork. Firms have responded by developing corporate planning models to forecast the financial consequences of specified strategies and assumptions about the future. These models are efficient and widely used. But remember that there is not much finance in them. Their primary purpose is to produce accounting statements. The models do not search for the best financial strategy, but only trade out the consequences of a strategy specified by the model user.

KEY TERMS

planning horizon	**percentage of sales model**	**internal growth rate**
pro formas	**balancing item**	**sustainable growth rate**

SUGGESTED READINGS

Corporate planning has an extensive literature of its own. Good books and articles include

G. Donaldson. "Financial Goals and Strategic Consequences," *Harvard Business Review* 63:(May–June 1985):57–66.

G. Donaldson. *Strategy for Financial Mobility*. Boston: Harvard Business School Press, 1986.

A. C. Hax and N. S. Majluf. *Strategic Management: An Integrative Perspective*. Englewood Cliffs, N.J.: Prentice-Hall, 1984.

P. Lorange and R. F. Vancil. *Strategic Planning Systems*. Englewood Cliffs, N.J.: Prentice-Hall, 1977.

Our description of what planning is and is not was influenced by

P. Drucker. "Long-Range Planning: Challenge to Management Science," *Management Science* 5(April 1959):238–249.

The links among capital budgeting, strategy, and financial planning are discussed in

S. C. Myers. "Finance Theory and Financial Strategy," *Interfaces* 14:(January–February 1984):126–137.

PROBLEMS

1. True or false? Explain.
   a. Financial planning should attempt to minimize risk.
   b. The primary aim of financial planning is to obtain better forecasts of future cash flows and earnings.
   c. Financial planning is necessary because financing and investment decisions interact and should not be made independently.
   d. Firms' planning horizons rarely exceed 3 years.
   e. Individual capital investment projects are not considered in a financial plan unless they are very large.
   f. Financial planning requires accurate and consistent forecasting.
   g. Financial planning models should include as much detail as possible.

2. What are the dangers and disadvantages of using a financial model? Discuss.

3. Corporate financial plans are often used as a basis for judging subsequent performance. What can be learned from such comparisons? What problems might arise and how might you cope with such problems?

4. Why do we say that "there is no finance in financial planning models"?

5. Here are the abbreviated financial statements for Planners Corporation:

INCOME STATEMENT, 1995

Sales	$2,000
Costs	1,500
Net income	$ 500

BALANCE SHEET, YEAR END

	1994	1995		1994	1995
Assets	$2500	$3000	Debt	$ 833	$1000
			Equity	1667	2000
Total	$2500	$3000	Total	$2500	$3000

If sales increase by 20 percent, and the company uses a strict percentage of sales planning model (meaning that all items on the income and balance sheet also increase by 20 percent), what must be the balancing item? What will be its value?

6. If the dividend payout ratio in problem 5 is 50 percent, calculate the required total external financing for growth rates of 15 percent, 20 percent, and 25 percent.

7. What is the maximum possible growth rate for Planners Corporation (see problem 5) if the payout ratio remains at 50 percent and
   a. no external debt or equity is to be issued
   b. the firm maintains a fixed debt ratio but issues no equity

8. How would Executive Fruit's financial model change if the dividend payout ratio were cut to 1/3? Use the revised model to generate a new financial plan for 1995 assuming that debt is the balancing item. Show how the financial statements given in Table 18.6 would change. What would be required external financing?

9. Executive Fruit's financial manager believes that sales in 1995 could rise by as much as 20 percent or by as little as 5 percent.
   a. Recalculate the first-stage pro forma financial statements (Table 18.5) under these two assumptions. How does the rate of growth in revenues affect the firm's need for external funds?
   b. Assume any required external funds will be raised by issuing long-term debt and that any surplus funds will be used to retire such debt. Prepare the completed (second-stage) pro forma balance sheet.

10. Eagle Sport Supply has the following financial statements. Assume that Eagle's assets are proportional to its sales.

INCOME STATEMENT

Sales	$950
Costs	250
EBIT	700
Taxes	200
Net income	$500

	BALANCE SHEET, YEAR END				
	1994	1995		1994	1995
Assets	$2700	$3000	Debt	$ 900	$1000
			Equity	1800	2000
Total	$2700	$3000	Total	$2700	$3000

a. Find Eagle's required external funds if it maintains a dividend payout ratio of 60 percent and plans a growth rate of 15 percent.

b. If Eagle chooses not to issue new shares of stock, what variable must be the balancing item? What will its value be?

c. Now suppose that the firm plans instead to increase long-term debt only to $1100 and does not wish to issue any new shares of stock. Why must the dividend payment now be the balancing item? What will its value be?

11. a. What is the internal growth rate of Eagle Sports (see problem 10) if the dividend payout ratio is fixed at 60 percent?

b. What is the sustainable growth rate if the equity-to-asset ratio is fixed at 2/3?

12. The following tables contain financial statements for Dynastatics Corporation. Although the company has not been growing, it now plans to expand and will increase net fixed assets (that is, assets net of depreciation) by $200 per year for the next 5 years and forecasts that the ratio of revenues to total assets will remain at 1.50. Annual depreciation is 10 percent of fixed assets at the start of the year. Fixed costs are expected to remain at $56 and variable costs at 80 percent of revenue. The company's policy is to pay out two-thirds of net income as dividends and to maintain a book debt ratio of 25 percent of total capital.

a. Produce a set of financial statements for 1995. Assume that net working capital will equal 50 percent of fixed assets.

b. If the balancing item is debt, and no equity is to be issued, prepare a completed pro forma balance sheet for 1995. What is the projected debt ratio for 1995?

BALANCE SHEET, YEAR-END
(figures in thousands of dollars)

Revenue		$1800
Fixed costs		56
Variable costs (80% of revenue)		1440
Depreciation		80
Interest (8% of beginning-of-the-year debt)		24
Taxable income		200
Taxes (at 40%)		80
Net income		120
Dividends	$80	
Retained earnings	$40	

BALANCE SHEET, YEAR-END
(figures in thousands of dollars)

	1993	1994
Assets		
Net working capital	$ 400	$ 400
Fixed assets	800	800
Total assets	$1,200	$1,200

BALANCE SHEET, YEAR-END *(continued)*
(figures in thousands of dollars)

	1993	1994
Liabilities and Shareholders' Equity		
Debt	$ 300	$ 300
Equity	900	900
Total liabilities and shareholders' equity	$1,200	$1,200

13. Go Go Industries is growing at 30 percent per year. It is all-equity financed and has total assets of $1 million. Its return on equity is 20 percent. Its plowback ratio is 40 percent.
    a. What is the internal growth rate?
    b. What is the firm's need for external financing this year?
    c. By how much would the firm increase its internal growth rate if it reduced its payout ratio to zero?
    d. By how much would such a move reduce the need for external financing? What do you conclude about the relationship between dividend policy and requirements for external financing?

14. A firm's profit margin is 10 percent and its asset turnover ratio is .5. It has no debt, net income of $10 per share, and pays dividends of $4 per share. What is the sustainable growth rate?

15. An all-equity-financed firm plans to grow at an annual rate of at least 10 percent. Its return on equity is 15 percent. What is the maximum possible dividend payout rate the firm can maintain without resorting to additional equity issues?

16. Suppose the firm in the previous question has a debt-equity ratio of 1/3. What is the maximum dividend payout ratio it can maintain without resorting to any external financing?

17. A firm has an asset turnover ratio of 2.0. Its plowback ratio is 50 percent, and it is all-equity financed. What must its profit margin be if it wishes to finance 8 percent growth using only internally generated funds?

18. If the profit margin of the firm in the previous problem is 6 percent, what is the maximum payout ratio that will allow it to grow at 8 percent without resorting to external financing?

19. If the profit margin of the firm in problem 17 is 6 percent, what is the maximum possible growth rate that can be sustained without external financing?

20. A firm has decided that its optimal capital structure is 100 percent equity financed. It perceives its optimal dividend policy to be a 40 percent payout ratio. Asset turnover is sales/assets = .8, the profit margin is 10 percent, and the firm has a target growth rate of 5 percent.
    a. Is the firm's target growth rate consistent with its other goals?
    b. If not, by how much does it need to increase asset turnover to achieve its goals?
    c. How much could it increase the profit margin instead?

SOLUTIONS TO SELF-TEST QUESTIONS

18.1   The firm cannot issue debt, and its dividend payment is effectively fixed, which limits retained earnings to $40. Therefore, the balancing item must be new equity issues. The firm must raise $200 – $40 = $160 through equity sales in order to finance its plans for $200 in asset acquisitions.

18.2

a.   The *total amount* of external financing is unchanged, since the dividend payout is unchanged. The $100,000 increase in total assets will now be financed by a mixture of debt and equity. If the debt-equity ratio is to remain at 2/3, the firm will need to increase equity by $60,000 and debt by $40,000. Since retained earnings already increase shareholders' equity by $36,000, the firm needs to issue an additional $24,000 of new equity and $40,000 of debt.

b.   If dividends are frozen at the 1994 level of $64,000 instead of increasing to $72,000 as envisioned in Table 18.5, then the required external funds fall by $8000 to $56,000.

18.3

a.   This question is answered by the planning model. Given assumptions for asset growth, the model will show the need for external financing, and this value can be compared to the firm's plans for such financing.

b.   Such a relationship may be *assumed* and built into the model. However, the model does not help to determine whether it is a reasonable assumption.

c.   Financial models do not shed light on the best capital structure. They can tell us only whether contemplated financing decisions are consistent with asset growth.

18.4

a.   If the payout ratio were reduced to 25 percent, the maximum growth rate assuming no external financing would be .75 × 16 percent × .6 = 7.2 percent.

b.   If the firm also can issue enough debt to maintain its equity-to-asset ratio unchanged, the sustainable growth rate will be .75 × 16 percent = 12 percent.

CHAPTER NINETEEN

Working Capital Management and Short-Term Planning

Much of this book is devoted to long-term financial decisions such as capital budgeting and the choice of capital structure. These decisions are called *long-term* for two reasons. First, they usually involve long-lived assets or liabilities. Second, they are not easily reversed and thus may commit the firm to a particular course of action for several years.

Short-term financial decisions generally involve short-lived assets and liabilities, and usually they are easily reversed. Compare, for example, a 60-day bank loan for $50 million with a $50 million issue of 20-year bonds. The bank loan is clearly a short-term decision. The firm can repay it 2 months later and be right back where it started. A firm might conceivably issue a 20-year bond in January and retire it in March, but it would be extremely inconvenient and expensive to do so. In practice, such a bond issue is a long-term decision, not only because of the bond's 20-year maturity, but because the decision to issue it cannot be reversed on short notice.

A financial manager responsible for short-term financial decisions does not have to look far into the future. The decision to take the 60-day bank loan could properly be based on cash-flow forecasts for the next few months only. The bond issue decision will normally reflect forecast cash requirements 5, 10, or more years into the future.

Short-term financial decisions do not involve many of the difficult conceptual issues encountered elsewhere in this book. In a sense, short-term decisions are easier than long-term decisions — but they are not less important. A firm can identify extremely valuable capital investment opportunities, find the precise optimal debt ratio, follow the perfect dividend policy, and yet founder because no one bothers to raise the cash to pay this year's bills. Hence the need for short-term planning.

In this chapter, we will review the major classes of short-term assets and liabilities, show how long-term financing decisions affect the firm's short-term financial planning problem, and describe how financial managers trace changes in cash and working capital. We will also describe how managers forecast month-by-month cash requirements or surpluses and how they develop short-term investment and financing strategies.

After studying this chapter you should be able to

- Understand *why* the firm needs to invest in net working capital.
- Show how long-term financing policy affects short-term financing requirements.
- Trace a firm's sources and uses of cash and evaluate its need for short-term borrowing.
- Develop a short-term financing plan that meets the firm's need for cash.

 19.1 WORKING CAPITAL

The Components of Working Capital

Short-term, or *current*, assets and liabilities are collectively known as *working capital*. Table 19.1 gives a breakdown of current assets and liabilities for non-financial enterprises in Canada at the end of 1993. Note that total current assets were $302 billion and total current liabilities were $246 billion.

Current Assets. One important current asset is *accounts receivable*. When one company sells goods to another company, it does not usually expect to be paid immediately. These unpaid bills, or *trade credit*, make up the bulk of accounts receivable. Companies also sell some goods on credit to the final consumer. This *consumer credit* makes up the remainder of accounts receivable. We will discuss the management of receivables in Chapter 21.

Another important current asset is *inventory*. Inventories may consist of raw materials, work in process, or finished goods awaiting sale and shipment. Table 19.1 shows that firms in Canada have about the same amount invested in inventories as in accounts receivable.

TABLE 19.1
Current assets and liabilities, Canadian non-financial industries (Fourth quarter, 1993, figures in millions)

Current Assets		Current Liabilities	
Cash	$ 36,392	Accounts payable and accrued liabilities	$141,185
Accounts receivable	122,604	Other current liabilities	109,465
Inventories	122,060		
Other current assets	28,177		
Total	$309,233	Total	$250,650

Notes: Net working capital (current assets – current liabilities) equals $309,233 – $250,650 = $58,583 million. Limited information was available on most of the current liability accounts.
Source: Statistics Canada, *Quarterly Financial Statistics for Enterprises*, Fourth Quarter, 1993 p. 54. Reproduced by authority of the Minister of Industry, 1995.

The remaining current asset accounts are cash and other current assets. The cash consists partly of currency, but most of the cash is in the form of bank deposits. These may be *demand deposits* (money in chequing accounts that the firm can pay out immediately) and *time deposits* (money in savings accounts that can be paid out only with a delay). Included in other current assets are marketable securities. The principal marketable security is *commercial paper* (short-term unsecured debt sold by other firms). Other securities include *Treasury bills*, which are short-term debts sold by the federal government, and provincial and local government securities.

In managing their cash companies face much the same problem you do. There are always advantages to holding large amounts of ready cash — they reduce the risk of running out of cash and having to borrow more on short notice. On the other hand, there is a cost to holding idle cash balances rather than putting the money to work earning interest. In Chapter 20 we will tell you how the financial manager collects and pays out cash and decides on an optimal cash balance.

Current Liabilities. We have seen that a company's principal current asset consists of unpaid bills. One firm's credit must be another's debit. Therefore, it is not surprising that a company's principal current liability consists of *accounts payable* — that is, outstanding payments due to other companies.

The other major current liability consists of short-term borrowing. We will have more to say about this later in the chapter.

net working capital:
Current assets minus current liabilities. Often called working capital.

Working Capital and the Cash Conversion Cycle

The difference between current assets and current liabilities is known as **net working capital**, but financial managers often refer to the difference simply (but imprecisely) as *working capital*. Usually current assets exceed current liabilities — that is, firms have positive net working capital. For Canadian non-financial companies, current assets are on average about 1 1/4 times current liabilities.

To see why firms need net working capital, imagine a small company, Simple Souvenirs, that makes small novelty items for sale at gift shops. It buys raw materials such as leather, beads, and rhinestones for cash, processes them into finished goods like wallets or costume jewelry, and then sells these goods on credit. Figure 19.1 shows the whole cycle of operations.

FIGURE 19.1
Simple cycle of operations.

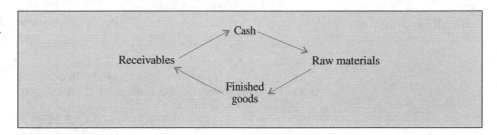

If you prepare the firm's balance sheet at the beginning of the process, you see cash (a current asset). If you delay a little, you find the cash replaced first by inventories of raw materials and then by inventories of finished goods (also current assets). When the goods are sold, the inventories give way to accounts receivable (another current asset) and finally, when the customers pay their bills, the firm takes out its profit and replenishes the cash balance.

The components of working capital constantly change with the cycle of operations, but the amount of working capital is fixed. That is one reason why net working capital is a useful summary measure of current assets or liabilities.

The longer the production process, the more cash the firm must keep tied up in inventories. Similarly, the longer it takes customers to pay their bills, the higher the value of accounts receivable. On the other hand, if Simple Souvenirs can delay paying for its own materials, it may reduce the amount of cash it needs. In other words, accounts payable *reduce* net working capital.

Figure 19.2 depicts four key dates in the production cycle that influence the firm's investment in working capital. The firm starts the cycle by purchasing raw materials, but it does not pay for them immediately. This delay is the *accounts payable period*. The firm processes the raw material and then sells the finished goods. The delay between the initial investment in inventories and the sale date is the *inventory period*. Some time after the firm has sold the goods its customers pay their bills. The delay between the date of sale and the date at which the firm is paid is the *accounts receivable period*.

Figure 19.2 shows that the *total* delay between initial purchase of raw materials and ultimate payments from customers is the sum of the inventory and accounts receivable periods: first the raw materials must be purchased, processed, and sold, and then the bills must be collected. However, the *net* time that the company is

FIGURE 19.2
Cash conversion cycle.

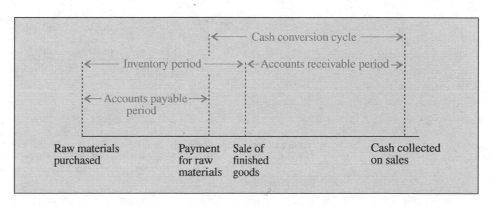

cash conversion cycle:
Period between firm's
payment for materials and
collection on its sales.

out of cash is reduced by the time it takes to pay its bills. The length of time between the firm's payment for its raw materials and the collection of payment from the customer is known as the firm's **cash conversion cycle**. To summarize,

$$\text{Cash conversion cycle} = (\text{inventory period} + \text{receivables period}) \\ - \text{accounts payable period}$$

The longer the cash conversion cycle, the more the firm must invest in working capital.

In Chapter 17 we showed you how the firm's financial statements can be used to estimate the inventory period, also called days' sales in inventory:

$$\text{Inventory period} = \frac{\text{average inventory}}{\text{annual cost of goods sold}/365}$$

The denominator in this equation is the firm's daily output. The ratio of inventory to daily output measures the average number of days from the purchase of the inventories to the final sale.

We can estimate the accounts receivable period and the accounts payable period in a similar way:[1]

$$\text{Accounts receivable period} = \frac{\text{average accounts receivable}}{\text{annual sales}/365}$$

$$\text{Accounts payable period} = \frac{\text{average accounts payable}}{\text{annual cost of goods sold}/365}$$

● Example 19.1 Cash Conversion Cycle

Table 19.2 provides the information necessary to compute the cash conversion cycle for non-financial firms in Canada in 1993. We can use the table to answer four questions. How long on average does it take firms to produce and sell their product? How long does it take to collect bills? How long does it take to pay bills? And what is the cash conversion cycle?

The delays in collecting cash are given by the inventory and receivables period. The delay in paying bills is given by the payables period. The net delay in collecting payments is the cash conversion cycle. We calculate these periods as follows:

$$\text{Inventory period} = \frac{\text{average inventories}}{\text{annual cost of goods sold}/365}$$

$$= \frac{(120,075 + 122,060)/2}{965,775/365} = 45.8 \text{ days}$$

$$\text{Receivables period} = \frac{\text{average accounts receivable}}{\text{annual sales}/365}$$

$$= \frac{(118,977 + 122,604)/2}{1,005,834/365} = 43.8 \text{ days}$$

---

[1] Because inventories are valued at cost, we divide inventory levels by cost of goods sold rather than sales revenue to obtain the inventory period. This way, both numerator and denominator are measured by cost. The same reasoning applies to the accounts payable period. On the other hand, because accounts receivable are valued at product price, we divide average receivables by annual sales revenue to find the receivables period.

$$\text{Payables period} = \frac{\text{average accounts payable}}{\text{annual cost of goods sold}/365}$$

$$= \frac{(137,039 + 141,185\ )/2}{965,775/365} = 52.6 \text{ days}$$

The cash conversion cycle is

$$\text{(Inventory period + receivables period) – accounts payable period}$$
$$= (45.8 + 43.8) - 52.5 = 37.1 \text{ days}$$

It is taking Canadian non-financial companies an average of five weeks from the time that they lay out money on inventories to collect payment from their customers.

TABLE 19.2

These data can be used to calculate the cash conversion cycle for Canadian non-financial enterprises in 1993 (figures in millions)

Income Statement Data		Balance Sheet Data		
			Beginning of 1993	End of 1993
Sales	$1,005,834	Inventory	$120,975	$122,060
Cost of goods sold	965,775	Accounts receivable	118,977	122,604
		Accounts payable	137,039	142,185

Source: Statistics Canada, *Quarterly Financial Statistics for Enterprises,* Fourth Quarter, 1993 p. 54. Reproduced by authority of the Minister of Industry, 1995.

SELF-TEST 19.1

a. Suppose Canadian firms are able to reduce inventory levels to a year-average value of $110 billion and average accounts receivable to $112 billion. By how many days will this reduce the cash conversion cycle?

b. Suppose that with the original level of inventories, accounts receivable, and accounts payable, Canadian companies can increase production and sales by 10 percent. What will be the effect on the cash conversion cycle?

Managing Working Capital

Of course the cash conversion cycle is not cast in stone. To a large extent it is within management's control. Working capital can be *managed.* For example, accounts receivable are affected by the terms of credit the firm offers to its customers. You can cut the amount of money tied up in receivables by getting tough with customers who are slow in paying their bills. (You may find, however, that in the future they take their business elsewhere.) Similarly, the firm can reduce its investment in inventories of raw materials. (Here the risk is that it may one day run out of inventories and production will grind to a halt.)

These considerations show that investment in working capital has both costs and benefits. For example, the cost of the firm's investment in receivables is the interest that could have been earned if customers had paid their bills earlier. The firm also forgoes interest income when it holds idle cash balances rather than putting the money to work in marketable securities. The cost of holding inventory includes not only the opportunity cost of capital but also storage and insurance costs and the risk of spoilage or obsolescence. All of these **carrying costs** encourage firms to hold current assets to a minimum.

carrying costs: Costs of maintaining current assets, including opportunity cost of capital.

While carrying costs discourage large investments in current assets, too low a level of current assets makes it more likely that the firm will face **shortage costs**. For example, if the firm runs out of inventory of raw materials, it may have to shut down production. Similarly, a producer holding a small finished goods inventory is more likely to be caught short, unable to fill orders promptly. There are also disadvantages to holding small "inventories" of cash. If the firm runs out of cash, it

shortage costs: Costs incurred from shortages in current assets.

may have to sell securities and incur unnecessary trading costs. The firm may also maintain too low a level of accounts receivable. If the firm tries to minimize accounts receivable by restricting credit sales, it may lose customers.

The job of the financial manager is to strike a balance between the costs and benefits of current assets, that is, to find the level of current assets that minimizes the sum of carrying costs and shortage costs. We will have more to say about these trade-offs in the next two chapters.

SELF-TEST 19.2

How will the following affect the size of the firm's optimal investment in current assets?
a. The interest rate rises from 6 percent to 8 percent.
b. A just-in-time inventory system is introduced that reduces the risk of inventory shortages.
c. Customers pressure the firm for a more lenient credit sales policy.

19.2 LINKS BETWEEN LONG-TERM AND SHORT-TERM FINANCING

Businesses require capital — that is, money invested in plant, machinery, inventories, accounts receivable, and all the other assets it takes to run a company efficiently. Typically, these assets are not purchased all at once but are obtained gradually over time as the firm grows. The total cost of these assets is called the firm's *total capital requirement.*

For most firms, the total capital requirement grows irregularly, like the wavy line in Figure 19.3. This line shows a clear upward trend as the firm's business grows. But there is also seasonal variation around the trend: in our illustration the

FIGURE 19.3
The firm's total capital requirement grows over time. It also exhibits seasonal variation around the trend.

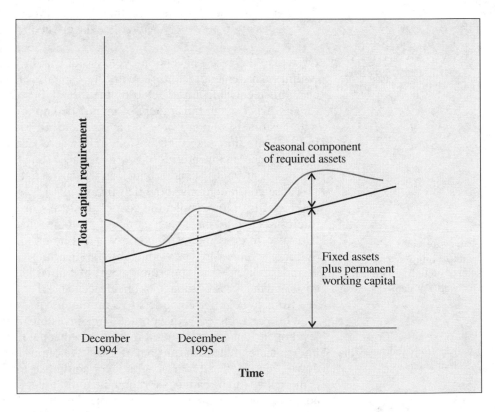

capital requirements line peaks late in each year. Finally, there would be unpredictable week-to-week and month-to-month fluctuations, but we have not attempted to show these in Figure 19.3.

The total capital requirement can be met through either long- or short-term financing. When long-term financing does not cover the total capital requirement, the firm must raise short-term capital to make up the difference. When long-term financing *more* than covers the total capital requirement, the firm has surplus cash available for short-term investment. Thus the amount of long-term financing raised, given the total capital requirement, determines whether the firm is a short-term borrower or lender.

The three panels in Figure 19.4 illustrate this. Each depicts a different long-term financing strategy. The "relaxed strategy" in panel (a) always implies a short-term cash surplus. This surplus will be invested in marketable securities. The "restrictive" policy illustrated in panel (c) implies a permanent need for short-term borrowing. Finally, panel (b) illustrates the most common strategy: the firm is a short-term lender during the part of the year when total capital requirements are relatively low and a borrower during the rest of the year when capital requirements are relatively high.

What is the *best* level of long-term financing relative to the total capital requirement? It is hard to say. We can make several practical observations, however.

1. *Matching maturities.* Most financial managers attempt to "match maturities" of assets and liabilities. That is, they finance long-lived assets like plant and machinery with long-term borrowing and equity. Short-term assets like inventory and accounts receivable are financed with short-term bank loans or by issuing short-term debt like commercial paper.

2. *Permanent working-capital requirements.* Most firms have a permanent investment in net working capital (current assets less current liabilities). By this we mean that they plan to have at all times a positive amount of working capital. This is financed from long-term sources. This is an extension of the maturity-matching principle. Since the working capital is permanent, it is funded with long-term sources of financing.

3. *The comforts of surplus cash.* Many financial managers would feel more comfortable under the relaxed strategy illustrated in Figure 19.4a than the restrictive strategy in panel (c). A firm with a surplus of long-term financing never has to worry about borrowing to pay next month's bills. But is the financial manager paid to be comfortable? Firms usually put surplus cash to work in Treasury bills or other marketable securities. This is at *best* a zero-NPV investment for a tax-paying firm.[2] Thus we think that firms with a *permanent* cash surplus ought to go on a diet, retiring long-term securities to reduce long-term financing to a level at or below the firm's total capital requirement. That is, if the firm is described by panel (a), it ought to move down to panel (b), or perhaps even lower.

---

[2] Why do we say *at best* zero NPV? Not because we worry that the Treasury bills may be overpriced. Instead, we worry that when the firm holds Treasury bills, the interest income is subject to double taxation, first at the corporate level, and then again at the personal level when the income is passed through to investors as dividends. The extra layer of taxation can make corporate holdings of Treasury bills a negative-NPV investment even if the bills would provide a fair rate of interest to an individual investor.

FIGURE 19.4
Alternative approaches to
long-term versus short-term
financing. (*a*) Relaxed
strategy. The firm is always
a short-term lender.
(*b*) Middle of the road.
(*c*) Restricted policy. The
firm always is a short-
term borrower.

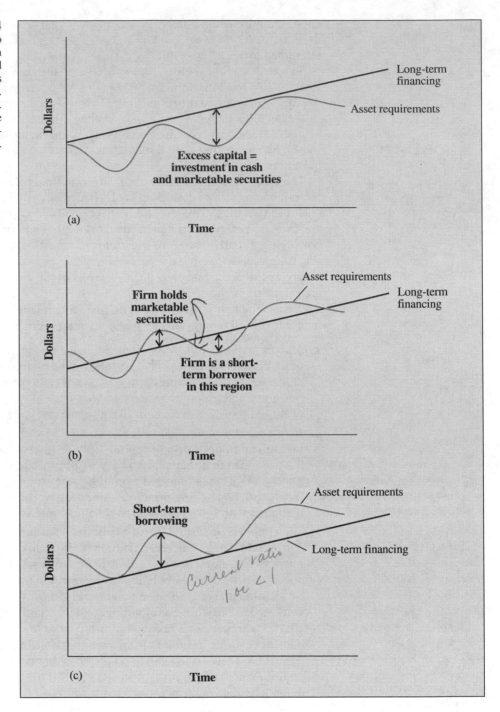

TRACING CHANGES IN CASH AND WORKING CAPITAL

Table 19.3 compares 1994 and 1995 year-end balance sheets for Dynamic
Mattress Company. Table 19.4 shows the firm's income statement for 1995. Note
that Dynamic's cash balance increased by $1 million during 1995. What caused
this increase? Did the extra cash come from Dynamic Mattress Company's additional long-term borrowing? From reinvested earnings? From cash released by

TABLE 19.3

Year-end balance sheets for Dynamic Mattress Company (figures in millions)

Assets	1994	1995	Liabilities and shareholders' equity	1994	1995
Current assets			Current liabilities		
Cash	$ 4	$ 5	Bank loans	$ 5	$ 0
Marketable securities	0	5	Accounts payable	20	27
Inventory	26	25	Total current liabilities	$25	$ 27
Accounts receivable	25	30			
Total current assets	$55	$ 65	Long-term debt	5	12
			Net worth (equity and retained earnings)	65	76
Fixed assets					
Gross investment	$56	$ 70	Total liabilities and owners' equity	$95	$115
Less depreciation	16	20			
Net fixed assets	$40	$ 50			
Total assets	$95	$115			

reducing inventory? Or perhaps it came from extra credit extended by Dynamic's suppliers. (Note the increase in accounts payable.)

Financial analysts often summarize sources and uses of cash in a statement like the one shown in Table 19.5. The statement shows that Dynamic *generated* cash from the following source:

1. It issued $7 million of long-term debt.

2. It reduced inventory, releasing $1 million.

3. It increased its accounts payable, in effect borrowing an additional $7 million from its suppliers.

4. By far the largest source of cash was Dynamic's operations, which generated $16 million. Note that the $12 million net income reported in Table 19.4 understates cash flow because depreciation is deducted in calculating income. Depreciation is *not* a cash outlay. Thus it must be added back in order to obtain operating cash flow.

Dynamic *used* cash for the following purposes:

1. It paid a $1 million dividend. (*Note:* The $11 million increase in Dynamic's equity is due to retained earnings: $12 million of equity income, less the $1 million dividend.)

2. It repaid a $5 million short-term bank loan.

3. It invested $14 million. This shows up as the increase in gross fixed assets in Table 19.3.

TABLE 19.4

Income statement for 1995 for Dynamic Mattress Company (figures in millions)

Sales	$350
Operating costs	321
Depreciation	4
EBIT	25
Interest	1
Pretax income	24
Tax at 50 percent	12
Net income	$ 12

Note: Dividend = $1 million; Retained earnings = $11 million

TABLE 19.5

Sources and uses of
cash for Dynamic
Mattress Company
(figures in millions)

Sources	
Issued long-term debt	$ 7
Reduced inventories	1
Increased accounts payable	7
Cash from operations:	
Net income	12
Depreciation	4
Total sources	$31
Uses	
Repaid short-term bank loan	$ 5
Invested in fixed assets	14
Purchased marketable securities	5
Increased accounts receivable	5
Dividend	1
Total uses	$30
Increase in cash balance	$ 1

4. It purchased $5 million of marketable securities.

5. It allowed accounts receivable to expand by $5 million. In effect, it lent this additional amount to its customers.

SELF-TEST 19.3

How will the following affect *cash* and *net working capital*?
a. The firm takes out a short-term bank loan and uses the funds to pay off some of its accounts payable.
b. The firm uses cash on hand to buy raw materials.
c. The firm repurchases outstanding stock.
d. The firm sells long-term bonds and puts the proceeds in its bank account.

 ## CASH BUDGETING

The financial manager's task is to forecast *future* sources and uses of cash. These forecasts serve two purposes. First, they alert the financial manager to future cash needs. Second, the cash-flow forecasts provide a standard, or budget, against which subsequent performance can be judged.

There are several ways to produce a quarterly cash budget. Many large firms have developed elaborate "corporate models"; others use a spreadsheet program to plan their cash needs. The procedures of smaller firms may be less formal. But no matter what method is chosen, there are common issues that all firms must face when they forecast. We will illustrate these issues by continuing the example of Dynamic Mattress.

Cash Inflows

Most of Dynamic's cash inflow comes from the sale of mattresses. We therefore start with a sales forecast by quarter for 1996:[3]

Quarter:	First	Second	Third	Fourth
Sales, millions of dollars	87.5	78.5	116	131

---

[3] For simplicity, we present a quarterly forecast. However, most firms would forecast by month instead of by quarter. Sometimes weekly or even daily forecasts are made.

But unless customers pay cash on delivery, sales become accounts receivable before they become cash. Cash flow comes from *collections* on accounts receivable.

Most firms keep track of the average time it takes customers to pay their bills. From this they can forecast what proportion of a quarter's sales is likely to be converted into cash in that quarter and what proportion is likely to be carried over to the next quarter as accounts receivable. This proportion depends on the lags with which customers pay their bills. For example, if customers wait 1 month to pay their bills, then on average one-third of the bills will not be paid until the following quarter. If the payment delay is 2 months, then two-thirds of sales will be collected in the following quarter.

Suppose that 80 percent of sales are collected in the immediate quarter and the remaining 20 percent in the next. Table 19.6 shows forecast collections under this assumption.

TABLE 19.6
Dynamic Mattress's collections on accounts receivable, 1996 (figures in millions)

		Quarter			
		First	**Second**	**Third**	**Fourth**
1.	Receivables at start of period	$30.0	$32.5	$ 30.7	$ 38.2
2.	Sales	87.5	78.5	116.0	131.0
3.	Collections				
	Sales in current period (80%)	70.0	62.8	92.8	104.8
	Sales in last period (20%)	15.0[a]	17.5	15.7	23.2
	Total collections	$85.0	$80.3	$108.5	$128.0
4.	Receivables at end of period				
	(4 = 1 + 2 − 3)	$32.5	$30.7	$ 38.2	$ 41.2

[a] Sales in the fourth quarter of the previous year were $75 million.

In the first quarter, for example, collections from current sales are 80 percent of $87.5 million, or $70 million. But the firm also collects 20 percent of the previous quarter's sales, or .20 × $75 million = $15 million. Therefore, total collections are $70 million + $15 million = $85 million.

Dynamic started the first quarter with $30 million of accounts receivable. The quarter's sales of $87.5 million were *added* to accounts receivable, but $85 million of collections was *subtracted*. Therefore, as Table 19.6 shows, Dynamic ended the quarter with accounts receivable of $30 million + $87.5 million − $85 million = $32.5 million. The general formula is

Ending accounts receivable = beginning accounts receivable + sales − collections

The top section of Table 19.7 shows forecast sources of cash for Dynamic Mattress. Collection of receivables is the main source but it is not the only one. Perhaps the firm plans to dispose of some land or expects a tax refund or payment of an insurance claim. All such items are included as "other" sources. It is also possible that you may raise additional capital by borrowing or selling stock, but we don't want to prejudge that question. Therefore, for the moment we just assume that Dynamic will not raise further long-term finance.

Cash Outflows

There always seem to be many more uses for cash than there are sources. For simplicity, in Table 19.7 we condense the uses into four categories:

1. *Payments of accounts payable.* Dynamic has to pay its bills for raw materials, parts, electricity, and so on. The cash-flow forecast assumes all these bills are paid on time, although Dynamic could probably delay payment to some extent. Delayed payment is sometimes called *stretching your*

TABLE 19.7

Dynamic Mattress's cash budget for 1996 (figures in millions)

	Quarter			
	First	**Second**	**Third**	**Fourth**
Sources of cash				
Collections on accounts receivable	$ 85.0	$80.3	$108.5	$128
Other	1.5	0	12.5	0
Total sources of cash	$ 86.5	$80.3	$121.0	$128
Uses of cash				
Payments of accounts payable	$ 65.0	$60.0	$ 55.0	$ 50
Labour and administrative expenses	30.0	30.0	30.0	30
Capital expenditures	32.5	1.3	5.5	8
Taxes, interest, and dividends	4.0	4.0	4.5	5
Total uses of cash	$131.5	$95.3	$ 95.0	$ 93
Net cash inflow equals sources minus uses	–$ 45.0	–$15.0	+$ 26.0	+$ 35

payables. Stretching is one source of short-term financing, but for most firms it is an expensive source, because by stretching they lose discounts given to firms that pay promptly. (This is discussed in more detail in Chapter 20.)

2. *Labour, administrative, and other expenses.* This category includes all other regular business expenses.

3. *Capital expenditures.* Note that Dynamic Mattress plans a major outlay of cash in the first quarter to pay for a long-lived asset.

4. *Taxes, interest, and dividend payments.* This includes interest on presently outstanding long-term debt and dividend payments to stockholders.

The Cash Balance

The forecast net inflow of cash (sources minus uses) is shown on the bottom row of Table 19.7. Note the large negative figure for the first quarter: a $45 million forecast *outflow.* There is a smaller forecast outflow in the second quarter, and then substantial cash inflows in the second half of the year.

Table 19.8 calculates how much financing Dynamic will have to raise if its cash-flow forecasts are right. It starts the year with $5 million in cash. There is a $45 million cash outflow in the first quarter, and so Dynamic will have to obtain at least $45 million – $5 million = $40 million of additional financing. This would leave the firm with a forecast cash balance of exactly zero at the start of the second quarter.

Most financial managers regard a planned cash balance of zero as driving too close to the edge of the cliff. They establish a *minimum operating cash balance* to absorb unexpected cash inflows and outflows. We will assume that Dynamic's minimum operating cash balance is $5 million. That means it will have to raise

TABLE 19.8

Short-term financing requirements for Dynamic Mattress (figures in millions)

Cash at start of period	$ 5	–$40	–$55	–$29
+ Net cash inflow (from Table 19.7)	– 45	– 15	+ 26	+ 35
= Cash at end of period[a]	– 40	– 55	– 29	+ 6
Minimum operating cash balance	5	5	5	5
Cumulative short-term financing required (minimum cash balance minus cash at end of period)[b]	$45	$60	$34	–$ 1

[a] Of course firms cannot literally hold a negative amount of cash. This line shows the amount of cash the firm will have to raise to pay its bills.
[b] A negative sign indicates a cash *surplus.*

$45 million instead of $40 million in the first quarter, and $15 million more in the second quarter. Thus its *cumulative* financing requirement is $60 million in the second quarter. Fortunately, this is the peak; the cumulative requirement declines in the third quarter when its $26 million net cash inflow reduces its cumulative financing requirement to $34 million. (Notice that the change in cumulative short-term financing in Table 19.8 equals the net cash inflow in that quarter from Table 19.7). In the final quarter Dynamic is out of the woods. Its $35 million net cash inflow is enough to eliminate short-term financing and actually increase cash balances above the $5 million minimum acceptable balance.

Before moving on, we offer two general observations about this example:

1. The large cash outflows in the first two quarters do not necessarily spell trouble for Dynamic Mattress. In part they reflect the capital investment made in the first quarter: Dynamic is spending $32.5 million, but it should be acquiring an asset worth that much or more. The cash outflows also reflect low sales in the first half of the year; sales recover in the second half.[4] If this is a predictable seasonal pattern, the firm should have no trouble borrowing to help it get through the slow months.

2. Table 19.7 is only a best guess about future cash flows. It is a good idea to think about the *uncertainty* in your estimates. For example, you could undertake a sensitivity analysis, in which you inspect how Dynamic's cash requirements would be affected by a shortfall in sales or by a delay in collections.

Our next step will be to develop a short-term financing plan that covers the forecast requirements in the most economical way possible.

SELF-TEST 19.4

Calculate Dynamic Mattress's quarterly collectibles if customers pay for only 60 percent of purchases in the current quarter and pay the remaining 40 percent in the following quarter.

A SHORT-TERM FINANCING PLAN

Options for Short-Term Financing

Suppose that Dynamic can borrow up to $40 million from the bank at an interest cost of 8 percent per year or 2 percent per quarter. Dynamic can also raise capital by putting off paying its bills. In effect, this is taking a loan from its suppliers. Accounts payable are called *trade credit* and amount to another form of short-term borrowing. The financial manager believes that Dynamic can defer the following amounts in each quarter:

Quarter:	First	Second	Third	Fourth
Amount deferrable, millions of dollars	52	48	44	40

That is, $52 million can be saved in the first quarter by *not* paying bills in that quarter. (Note that Table 19.7 was prepared assuming these bills *are* paid in the first quarter.) If deferred, these payments *must* be made in the second quarter. Similarly, $48 million of the second quarter's bills can be deferred to the third quarter and so on.

---

[4] Maybe people buy more mattresses late in the year when the nights are longer.

Stretching payables is often costly, however, even if no ill will is incurred.[5] This is because many suppliers offer discounts for prompt payment, so that Dynamic loses the discount if it pays late. In this example we assume the lost discount is 5 percent of the amount deferred. In other words, if a $52 million payment is delayed in the first quarter, the firm must pay 5 percent more, or $54.6 million in the next quarter. This is like borrowing at an interest rate of over 20 percent ($1.05^4 - 1 = .216$, or 21.6%).

With these two options, the short-term financing strategy is obvious: use the lower cost bank loan first. Stretch payables only if you can't borrow enough from the bank.

Table 19.9 shows the resulting plan. The first panel (cash requirements) sets out the cash that needs to be raised in each quarter. The second panel (cash raised) describes the various sources of financing the firm plans to use. The third and fourth panels describe how the firm will use net cash inflows when they turn positive.

TABLE 19.9

Dynamic Mattress's financing plan (figures in millions)

	Quarter			
	First	**Second**	**Third**	**Fourth**
Cash Requirements				
1. Cash required for operations[a]	$45	$15	–$26	–$35
2. Interest on line of credit[b]	0	0.8	0.8	0.6
3. Interest on stretched payables[c]	0	0	0.8	0
4. Total cash required	$45	$15.8	–$24.4	–$34.4
Cash Raised				
5. Line of credit	$40	$ 0	$ 0	$ 0
6. Stretched payables	0	15.8	0	0
7. Securities sold	5	0	0	0
8. Total cash raised	$45	$15.8	$ 0	$ 0
Repayments				
9. Of stretched payables	0	0	$15.8	$ 0
10. Of line of credit	0	0	8.6	$31.4
Increase in cash balances				
11. Addition to cash balances	$ 0	$ 0	$ 0	$ 3
Line of Credit				
12. Beginning of quarter	$ 0	$40	$40	$31.4
13. End of quarter	40	40	31.4	0

[a] From Table 19.7, bottom line. A negative cash requirement implies positive cash flow from operations.
[b] The interest rate on the line of credit is 2 percent per quarter applied to the line of credit outstanding in the previous quarter. Thus the interest due in the second quarter is .02 × $40 million = $0.8 million.
[c] The "interest" cost of the stretched payables is 5 percent of the amount of payment deferred. For example, in the third quarter, 5 percent of $15.8 million stretched in the second quarter is about $.8 million.

In the first quarter the plan calls for borrowing the full amount available from the bank ($40 million). In addition, the firm sells the $5 million of marketable securities it held at the end of 1995. Thus under this plan it raises the necessary $45 million in the first quarter.

In the second quarter, an additional $15 million must be raised to cover the net cash outflow predicted in Table 19.7. In addition, $.8 million must be raised to

---

[5] In fact, ill will can be incurred. Firms that stretch payments risk being labelled as credit risks. Since stretching is so expensive, suppliers reason that only customers that cannot obtain credit at reasonable rates elsewhere will resort to it. They naturally may be reluctant to act as the lender of last resort.

pay interest on the bank loan. Therefore, the plan calls for Dynamic to maintain its bank borrowing and to stretch $15.8 million in payables. Notice that in the first two quarters, when net cash flow from operations is negative, the firm maintains its cash balance at the minimum acceptable level. Additions to cash balances are zero. Similarly, repayments of outstanding debt are zero. In fact outstanding debt rises in each of these quarters.

In the third and fourth quarters, the firm generates a cash-flow surplus, so the plan calls for Dynamic to pay off its debt. First it pays off stretched payables, as it is required to do, and then it uses any remaining cash flow surplus to pay down its bank loan. In the third quarter, all of the net cash inflow is used to reduce outstanding short-term borrowing. In the fourth quarter, the firm pays off its remaining short-term borrowing and uses the extra $3 million to increase its cash balances.

SELF-TEST 19.5

> Revise Dynamic Mattress's short-term financial plan assuming it can borrow up to $45 million through its line of credit. Assume that the firm will still sell its $5 million of short-term securities in the first quarter.

Evaluating the Plan

Does the plan shown in Table 19.9 solve Dynamic's short-term financing problem? No — the plan is feasible, but Dynamic can probably do better. The most glaring weakness of this plan is its reliance on stretching payables, an extremely expensive financing device. Remember that it costs Dynamic 5 percent *per quarter* to delay paying bills — 20 percent per year at simple interest. This first plan should merely stimulate the financial manager to search for cheaper sources of short-term borrowing.

The financial manager would ask several other questions as well. For example:

1. Does Dynamic need a larger reserve of cash or marketable securities to guard against, say, its customers stretching their payable (thus slowing down collections on accounts receivable)?
2. Does the plan yield satisfactory current and quick ratios?[6] Its bankers may be worried if these ratios deteriorate.
3. Are there hidden costs to stretching payables? Will suppliers begin to doubt Dynamic's creditworthiness?
4. Does the plan for 1996 leave Dynamic in good financial shape for 1997? (Here the answer is yes, since Dynamic will have paid off all short-term borrowing by the end of the year.)
5. Should Dynamic try to arrange long-term financing for the major capital expenditure in the first quarter? This seems sensible, following the rule of thumb that long-term assets deserve long-term financing. It would also dramatically reduce the need for short-term borrowing. A counterargument is that Dynamic is financing the capital investment *only temporarily* by short-term borrowing. By year-end, the investment is paid for by cash from operations. Thus Dynamic's initial decision not to seek immediate long-term financing may reflect a preference for ultimately financing the investment with retained earnings.
6. Perhaps the firm's operating and investment plans can be adjusted to make the short-term financing problem easier. Is there any easy way of deferring

---

[6] These ratios are discussed in Chapter 17.

the first quarter's large cash outflow? For example, suppose that the large capital investment in the first quarter is for new mattress-stuffing machines to be delivered and installed in the first half of the year. The new machines are not scheduled to be ready for full-scale use until August. Perhaps the machine manufacturer could be persuaded to accept 60 percent of the purchase price on delivery and 40 percent when the machines are installed and operating satisfactorily.

Short-term financing plans are developed by trial and error. You lay out one plan, think about it, then try again with different assumptions on financing and investment alternatives. You continue until you can think of no further improvements.

A Note on Short-Term Financial Planning Models

Working out a consistent short-term plan requires burdensome calculations. Fortunately, much of the arithmetic can be delegated to a computer. Many large firms have built short-term financial planning models to do this. Smaller companies like Dynamic Mattress do not face so much detail and find it easier to work with a spreadsheet program on a personal computer. In either case the financial manager specifies forecast cash requirements or surpluses, interest rates, credit limits, and so forth, and the model grinds out a plan like those shown in Table 19.9. The computer can also be used to produce balance sheets, income statements, and other special reports the financial manager may require.

 ## SOURCES OF SHORT-TERM FINANCING

We suggested that Dynamic's manager might want to investigate alternative sources of short-term borrowing. Here are some of the possibilities.

Bank Loans

line of credit: Agreement by a bank that a company may borrow at any time up to an established limit.

The simplest and most common source of short-term finance is an unsecured loan from a bank. For example, Dynamic might have a standing arrangement with its bank allowing it to borrow up to $40 million. The firm can borrow and repay whenever it wants so long as it does not exceed the credit limit. This kind of arrangement is called a **line of credit.**

A close relative of the line of credit is the *revolving credit arrangement*. The major differences are that revolving credit arrangements usually last for a few years and formally commit the bank to providing loans up to some limit for the term of the agreement. In contrast, lines of credit are typically reviewed annually and can be cancelled if the firm's creditworthiness deteriorates. The borrowing firm must pay a commitment fee to establish a revolving credit arrangement, in part to compensate the bank for its legal obligation to honour the agreement.

Lines of credit usually require the firm to maintain some amount of money on balance at the bank. This is called a *compensating balance*. For example, Dynamic might have to maintain a balance of 20 percent of the amount of the loan. In other words, if the firm wants to raise $100, it must actually borrow $125, because $25 (20 percent of $125) must be left on deposit in the bank.

If the compensating balance does not pay interest (or pays a below-market rate of interest), the actual interest rate on the line of credit is higher than the stated rate. This is because the borrower must pay interest on the full amount borrowed but has access to only part of the funds. For example, if the stated rate on Dynamic's loan is 8 percent and it borrows $125, it will have to pay interest of $125 \times .08 = 10 per year. However, it gets use of only $100, so the effective interest rate is $10/$100 = 10$ percent. In general, the effective rate is

$$\text{Effective interest rate on compensating balance} = \frac{\text{actual interest paid}}{\text{borrowed funds available}}$$

$$= \frac{\text{stated interest rate}}{\text{fraction of funds available}}$$

For Dynamic Mattress,

$$\text{Effective interest rate} = \frac{\$10}{\$100} = \frac{8\%}{.80} = 10\%$$

Commercial Paper

commercial paper: Short-term unsecured notes issued by firms.

Large, safe, and well-known companies can bypass the banking system by issuing their own short-term unsecured notes. These notes are known as **commercial paper**. Only a nationally known company can find a market for its commercial paper, and even then, only if there is little uncertainty about its financial position. Companies generally back their issue of commercial paper by arranging a special backup line of credit with a bank. This guarantees that they can find the money to repay the paper. The risk of default is therefore small.

By cutting out the intermediary (the bank), major companies are able to borrow at rates that may be 1 percent to 1 1/2 percent below the prime rate charged by banks. Even after allowing for an investment dealer's sales commission and the cost of compensating balances on any backup line of credit, there is still a substantial saving. Although the amount of commercial paper outstanding is less than bank loans, this form of financing has grown rapidly in recent years. Banks have felt the competition from commercial paper and have been prepared to reduce their rates to blue-chip customers.

Banker's acceptances are another form of unsecured short-term financing a firm may issue. A banker's acceptance begins life as a draft (which is essentially a post-dated cheque) for the bank to pay a given sum at a future date. The bank then guarantees the draft by writing "accepted" on it, although there is a clear agreement that the writer of the draft (the borrower) will deposit enough funds with the bank in time to cover the future payment. Once accepted, the draft becomes the bank's *and* the borrower's IOU. The bank then sells the instrument to an investor who has funds to invest for the short-term. Buyers of banker's acceptances include pension funds, insurance companies, money market funds, and banks.

banker's acceptance: Short-term unsecured notes issued by a firm and guaranteed by a bank.

Secured Loans

Many short-term loans are unsecured, but sometimes the company may offer its inventory or receivables as security. Since the bank is lending on a short-term basis, the security generally consists of liquid assets such as receivables, inventories, or securities. For example, a firm may decide to borrow short-term money secured by its accounts receivable. When its customers have paid their bills, it can use the cash to repay the loan. An alternative procedure is to *sell* the receivables to a financial institution known as a *factor* and let it collect the money. In other words, some companies solve their financing problem by borrowing on the strength of their current assets; others solve it by selling their current assets.

Accounts Receivable Financing. Firms can either assign receivables or factor them. When receivables are assigned, and the firm fails to repay its loan, the bank can collect the receivables from the firm's customers and use the cash to pay off the debt. However, the firm is still responsible for the loan even if the receivables ultimately cannot be collected. The risk of default on the receivables is therefore borne by the firm. Under factoring, in contrast, the firm actually sells its receivables at a discount to a factoring firm. Once sold, the factor bears all responsibility for collecting on the accounts. Therefore, the factor may play three roles:

it administers collection of receivables, takes responsibility for bad debts, and provides finance.

To illustrate factoring, suppose that the firm sells its accounts receivables to a factor at a 2 percent discount. This means that the factor pays 98 cents for each dollar of accounts receivable. If the average collection period is 1 month, then in a month the factor should be able to collect $1 for every 98 cents it paid today. Therefore, the implicit interest rate is 2/98 = 2.04 percent per month, which corresponds to an effective annual interest rate of $(1.0204)^{12} - 1 = .274$, or 27.4 percent.

While factoring would appear from this example to be an expensive source of financing for the firm, part of the apparently steep interest rate represents payment for the assumption of default risk as well as for the cost of running the credit operation.

Inventory Financing. Banks also lend on the security of inventory, but they are choosy about the inventory they will accept. They want to make sure that they can identify and sell it if you default. Automobiles and other standardized nonperishable commodities are good security for a loan; work in progress and ripe strawberries are poor collateral.

Banks need to monitor companies to be sure they don't sell their assets and run off with the money. Consider, for example, the story of the great salad oil swindle. Fifty-one banks and companies made loans of nearly $200 million to the Allied Crude Vegetable Oil Refining Corporation in the belief that these loans were secured on valuable salad oil. Unfortunately, they did not notice that Allied's tanks contained false compartments that were mainly filled with seawater. When the fraud was discovered, the president of Allied went to jail and the 51 lenders stayed out in the cold looking for their $200 million.

To protect themselves against this sort of risk, lenders often insist on *field warehousing*. An independent warehouse company hired by the bank supervises the inventory pledged as collateral for the loan. As the firm sells its product and uses the revenue to pay back the loan, the bank directs the warehouse company to release the inventory back to the firm. If the firm defaults on the loan, the bank keeps the inventory and sells it to recover the debt.

 **SUMMARY**

1. Short-term financial planning is concerned with the management of the firm's short-term, or *current*, assets and liabilities. The most important current assets are cash, marketable securities, inventory, and accounts receivable. The most important current liabilities are bank loans and accounts payable. The difference between current assets and current liabilities is called *net working capital.*

2. Net working capital arises from lags between the time the firm obtains the raw materials for its product and the time it finally collects its bills from customers. The cash conversion cycle is the length of time between the firm's payment for materials and the date that it gets paid by its customers. The cash conversion cycle is partly within management's control. For example, it can choose to have a higher or lower level of inventories. Management needs to trade off the benefits and costs of investing in current assets.

3. The nature of the firm's short-term financial planning problem is determined by the amount of long-term capital it raises. A firm that issues large amounts

of long-term debt or common stock, or that retains a large part of its earnings, may find that it has permanent excess cash. Other firms raise relatively little long-term capital and end up as permanent short-term debtors. Most firms attempt to find a golden mean by financing all fixed assets and part of current assets with equity and long-term debt. Such firms may invest cash surpluses during part of the year and borrow during the rest of the year.

4. The starting point for short-term financial planning is an understanding of sources and uses of cash. Firms forecast their net cash requirement by forecasting collections on accounts receivable, adding other cash inflows, and subtracting all forecast cash outlays. If the forecast cash balance is insufficient to cover day-to-day operations and to provide a buffer against contingencies, you will need to find additional finance. For example, you may borrow from a bank on an unsecured line of credit, you may borrow by offering receivables or inventory as security, or you may issue your own short-term notes known as commercial paper.

5. The search for the best short-term financial plan inevitably proceeds by trial and error. The financial manager must explore the consequences of different assumptions about cash requirements, interest rates, limits on financing from particular sources, and so on. Firms are increasingly using computerized financial models to help in this process.

KEY TERMS

net working capital	**shortage costs**	**commercial paper**
cash conversion cycle	**line of credit**	**bankers' acceptances**
carrying costs		

SUGGESTED READINGS

Here are some general textbooks on working-capital management:

G. W. Gallinger and P. B. Healey. *Liquidity Analysis and Management.* Reading, Mass.: Addison-Wesley, 1987.

K. V. Smith. *Readings on the Management of Working Capital*, 2d ed, New York: West, 1980.

J. H. Van der Weide and S. F. Maier. *Managing Corporate Liquidity: An Introduction to Working Capital Management.* New York: John Wiley & Sons, 1985.

J. D. Wilson and J. F. Duston. *Financial Information Systems Manual.* Boston: Warren, Gorham and Lamont, 1986.

PROBLEMS

1. Indicate how each of the following six different transactions that Dynamic Mattress might make would affect (i) cash and (ii) net working capital:
   a. Paying out a $2 million cash dividend.
   b. A customer paying a $2500 bill resulting from a previous sale.
   c. Paying $5000 previously owed to one of its suppliers.
   d. Borrowing $1 million long-term and investing the proceeds in inventory.
   e. Borrowing $1 million short-term and investing the proceeds in inventory.
   f. Selling $5 million of marketable securities for cash.

2. Here is a forecast of sales by National Bromide for the first 4 months of 1995 (figures in thousands of dollars):

Month:	1	2	3	4
Cash sales	15	24	18	14
Sales on credit	100	120	90	70

On the average, 50 percent of credit sales are paid for in the current month, 30 percent in the next month, and the remainder in the month after that. What are expected cash collections in months 3 and 4?

3. Fill in the blanks in the following statements:
   a. A firm has a cash surplus when its _____ exceeds its _____. The surplus is normally invested in _____.
   b. In developing the short-term financial plan, the financial manager starts with a(n) _____ budget for the next year. This budget shows the _____ generated or absorbed by the firm's operations and also the minimum _____ needed to support these operations. The financial manager may also wish to invest in _____ as a reserve for unexpected cash requirements.

4. State how each of the following events would affect the firm's balance sheet. State whether each change is a source or use of cash and whether it is a source or use of funds.
   a. An automobile manufacturer increases production in response to a forecast increase in demand. Unfortunately, the demand does not increase.
   b. Competition forces the firm to give customers more time to pay for their purchases.
   c. The firm sells a parcel of land for $100,000. The land was purchased 5 years earlier for $200,000.
   d. The firm repurchases its own common stock.
   e. The firm doubles its quarterly dividend.
   f. The firm issues $1 million of long-term debt and uses the proceeds to repay a short-term bank loan.

5. The accompanying tables show Dynamic Mattress's year-end 1993 balance sheet and its income statement for 1994. Use these tables (and Table 19.3) to work out a statement of sources and uses of cash for 1994.

YEAR-END BALANCE SHEET FOR 1993
(figures in millions of dollars)

Current assets		Current liabilities	
Cash	4	Bank loans	4
Marketable securities	2	Accounts payable	15
Inventory	20	Total current liabilities	19
Accounts receivable	22		
Total current assets	48	Long-term debt	5
		Net worth (equity and retained	
Fixed assets		earnings)	60
Gross investment	50		
Less depreciation	14	Total liabilities and net worth	84
Net fixed assets	36		
Total assets	84		

INCOME STATEMENT FOR 1994
(figures in millions of dollars)

Sales	300
Operating costs	285
	15
Depreciation	2
EBIT	13
Interest	1
Pretax income	12
Tax at 50 percent	6
Net income	6

Note: Dividend = $1 million and retained earnings = $5 million.

6. Suppose that Dynamic Sofa (a subsidiary of Dynamic Mattress) has a line of credit with a stated interest rate of 10 percent and a compensating balance of 25 percent. The compensating balance earns no interest.
   a. If the firm needs $10,000, how much will it need to borrow?
   b. Suppose that Dynamic's bank offers to forget about the compensating balance requirement if the firm pays interest at a rate of 12 percent. Should the firm accept this offer? Why or why not?
   c. Redo part (b) if the compensating balance pays interest of 4 percent. *Warning:* You cannot use the formula in the chapter for the effective interest rate when the compensating balance pays interest. Think about how to measure the effective interest rate on this loan.

7. What effect will the following have on the cash conversion cycle?
   a. Customers are given a larger discount for cash transactions.
   b. The inventory turnover ratio falls from 8 to 6.
   c. New technology streamlines the production process.
   d. The firm adopts a policy of reducing outstanding accounts payable.
   e. The firm starts producing more goods in response to customers' advance orders instead of for inventory.
   f. A temporary glut in the commodity market induces the firm to stock up on raw materials while prices are low.

8. Calculate the accounts receivable period, accounts payable period, inventory period, and cash conversion cycle for the following firm:

   Income statement data:

Sales	5000
Cost of goods sold	4200

   Balance sheet data:

	Beginning of Year	End of Year
Inventory	500	600
Accounts receivable	100	120
Accounts payable	250	290

9. If a firm pays its bills with a 30-day delay, what fraction of its purchases will be paid for in the current quarter? In the following quarter? What if its payment delay is 60 days?

10. Paymore Products places orders for goods equal to 75 percent of its sales forecast in the next quarter. What will be the orders in each quarter of the year if the sales forecasts for the next five quarters are:

	Quarter in Coming Year				Following Year
	First	**Second**	**Third**	**Fourth**	**First quarter**
Sales forecast	$372	$360	$336	$384	$384

11. Calculate Paymore's cash payments to its suppliers under the assumption that the firm pays for its goods with a 1-month delay. Therefore, on average, two-thirds of purchases are paid for in the quarter that they are purchased and one-third are paid in the following quarter. Assume that sales in the last quarter of the previous year were $336.

12. Now suppose that Paymore's customers pay *their* bills with a 2-month delay. What is the forecast for Paymore's collectibles in each quarter of the coming year?

13. Assuming that Paymore's labour and administrative expenses are $65 per quarter and that interest on long-term debt is $40 per quarter, work out the net cash inflow for Paymore for the coming year using a table like Table 19.7.

14. Suppose that Paymore's cash balance at the start of the first quarter is $40 and its minimum acceptable cash balance is $30. Work out the short-term financing requirements for the firm in the coming year using a table like Table 19.8. The firm pays no dividends.

15. Now assume that Paymore can borrow up to $100 from a line of credit at an interest rate of 2 percent per quarter. Prepare a short-term financing plan. Use Table 19.9 to guide your answer.

16. The following data are from the budget of Ritewell Publishers. Half the company's sales are transacted on a cash basis. The other half are paid for with a one-month delay. The company pays all of its credit purchases with a 1-month delay. Credit purchases in January were $30 and total sales in January were $180.

	February	**March**	**April**
Total sales	200	220	180
Cash purchases	70	80	60
Credit purchases	40	30	40
Labour and administrative expenses	30	30	30
Interest on long-term debt	10	10	10
Capital purchases	100	0	0

Complete the following cash budget:

	February	**March**	**April**
Sources of cash			
Collections on current sales			
Collections on accounts receivable			
Total sources of cash			

	February	**March**	**April**
Uses of cash			
Payments of accounts payable			
Cash purchases			
Labour and administrative expenses			
Capital expenditures			
Taxes, interest, and dividends			
Total uses of cash			
Net cash inflow			
Cash at start of period	100		
+ Net cash inflow			
= Cash at end of period			
+ Minimum operating cash balance	100	100	100
= Cumulative short-term financing required			

SOLUTIONS TO SELF-TEST QUESTIONS

19.1

a. The new values for the accounts receivable period and inventory period are

$$\text{Days in inventory} = \frac{110,000}{965,775/365} = 41.6$$

This is a reduction of 4.2 days from the original value of 45.8 days.

$$\text{Days in receivables} = \frac{112,000}{1,005,834/365} = 40.6$$

This is a reduction of 3.2 days from the original value of 43.8 days.
The cash conversion cycle falls by a total of 4.2 + 3.2 = 5.4 days.
b. The inventory period, accounts receivable period, and accounts payable period will all fall by a factor of 1.10. (The numerators are unchanged, but the denominators are higher by 10 percent.) Therefore, the conversion cycle will fall from 37.1 days to 37.1/1.10 = 33.7 days.

19.2

a. An increase in the interest rate will increase the cost of carrying current assets. The effect is to reduce the optimal level of such assets.
b. The just-in-time system lowers the expected level of shortage costs and reduces the amount of goods the firm ought to be willing to keep in inventory.
c. If the firm decides that more lenient credit terms are necessary to avoid lost sales, it must then expect customers to pay their bills more slowly. Accounts receivable will increase.

19.3

a. This transaction merely substitutes one current liability (short-term debt) for another (accounts payable). Neither cash nor net working capital is affected.
b. This transaction will increase inventory at the expense of cash. Cash falls but net working capital is unaffected.
c. The firm will use cash to buy back the stock. Both cash and net working capital will fall.
d. The proceeds from the sale will increase both cash and net working capital.

19.4

	Quarter			
	First	**Second**	**Third**	**Fourth**
Sales	$87.5	$78.5	$116.0	$131.0
Collections				
Sales in current period (60%)	52.5	47.1	69.6	78.6
Sales in last period (40%)	30.0[a]	35.0	31.4	46.4
Total collections	$82.5	$82.1	$101.0	$125.0

[a] Sales in the fourth quarter of the previous year were $75 million.

19.5   The major change in the plan is the substitution of the extra $5 million of borrowing via the line of credit in the second quarter and the corresponding reduction in the stretched payables. This substitution is advantageous because the line of credit is a cheaper source of funds. Notice that the cash balance at the end of the year is higher under this plan than in the original plan.

	Quarter			
	First	**Second**	**Third**	**Fourth**
Cash Requirements				
1. Cash required for operations	$45	$15	−$26	−$35
2. Interest on line of credit	0	0.8	0.9	0.6
3. Interest on stretched payables	0	0	0.5	0
4. Total cash required	$45	$15.8	−$24.6	$34.4
Cash raised				
5. Line of credit	$40	$ 5	$ 0	$ 0
6. Stretched payables	0	10.8	0	0
7. Securities sold	5	0	0	0
8. Total cash raised	$45	$15.8	$ 0	$ 0
Repayments				
9. Of stretched payables	$ 0	$ 0	$10.8	$ 0
10. Of line of credit	0	0	13.8	31.2
Increases in cash balances				
11. Addition to cash balances	$ 0	$ 0	$ 0	$ 3.2
Line of credit				
12. Beginning of quarter	$ 0	$40	$45	$31.2
13. End of quarter	40	$45	31.2	0

CHAPTER TWENTY

Cash and Inventory Management

During 1994 citizens and corporations in Canada held approximately $54 billion in cash. This included about $24 billion of currency and $30 billion of demand deposits (chequing accounts) with banks. Cash pays no interest. Why, then, do sensible people hold it? Why, for example, don't you take all your cash and invest it in interest-bearing securities? The answer is that cash gives you more *liquidity* than securities. By this we mean that you can use it to buy things. It is hard enough getting cab drivers to give you change for a $20 bill, but try asking them to split a Treasury bill.

Of course, rational investors will not hold an asset like cash unless it provides the same benefit on the margin as other assets such as Treasury bills. The benefit from holding Treasury bills is the interest that you receive; the benefit from holding cash is that it gives you a convenient store of liquidity. When you have only a small proportion of your assets in cash, a little extra can be extremely useful; when you have a substantial holding, any additional liquidity is not worth much. Therefore, as a financial manager you want to hold cash balances up to the point where the value of any additional liquidity is equal to the value of the interest forgone.

Cash is simply a raw material that companies need to carry on production. As we will explain later, the financial manager's decision to stock up on cash is in many ways similar to the production manager's decision to stock up on inventories of raw materials. We will therefore look at the general problem of managing inventories and then show how this helps us to understand how much cash you should hold.

But first you need to learn about the mechanics of cash collection and disbursement. This may seem a rather humdrum topic but you will find that it involves some interesting and important decisions.

After studying this chapter you should be able to

- Measure float and explain why it arises and how it can be controlled.
- Calculate the value of changes in float.
- Understand the costs and benefits of holding inventories.
- Cite the costs and benefits of holding cash.
- Understand how models of inventory management can be useful for cash management.

CASH COLLECTION, DISBURSEMENT, AND FLOAT

Companies don't keep their cash in a little tin box; they keep it in a bank deposit. To understand how they can make best use of that deposit, you need to understand what happens when companies withdraw money from their account or pay money into it.

Float

Suppose that the Canadian Carbon Company has $1 million in a demand deposit (chequing account) with its bank. It now pays one of its suppliers by writing and mailing a cheque for $200,000. The company's records are immediately adjusted to show a cash balance of $800,000. Thus the company is said to have a *ledger balance* of $800,000.

payment float: Cheques written by a company that have not yet cleared.

But the company's bank won't learn anything about this cheque until it has been received by the supplier, deposited at the supplier's bank, and finally presented to Canadian Carbon's bank for payment. During this time Canadian Carbon's bank continued to show in *its* ledger that the company has a balance of $1 million.

While the cheque is clearing, the company obtains the benefit of an extra $200,000 in the bank. This sum is often called disbursement, or **payment float.**

Company's ledger balance + Payment float
$800,000 + $200,000

equals

Bank's ledger balance
$1,000,000

Float sounds like a marvellous invention; every time you spend money, it takes the bank a few days to catch on. Unfortunately it can also work in reverse. Suppose that in addition to paying its supplier, Canadian Carbon *receives* a cheque for $120,000 from a customer. It first processes the cheque and then deposits it in the bank. At this point both the company and the bank increase the ledger balance by $120,000:

Company's ledger balance + Payment float
$920,000 + $200,000

equals

Bank's ledger balance
$1,120,000

availability float: Cheques already deposited that have not yet been cleared.

But this money isn't available to the company immediately. The bank doesn't actually have the money in hand until it has sent the cheque to the customer's bank and received payment. Since the bank has to wait, it makes Canadian Carbon wait too — usually 1 or 2 business days. In the meantime, the bank will show that Canadian Carbon still has an available balance of only $1 million. The extra $120,000 has been deposited but is not yet available. It is therefore known as **availability float**.

Company's ledger balance + Payment float
$920,000 + $200,000

equals

Bank's ledger balance
$1,120,000

equals

Available balance + Availability float
$1,000,000 + $120,000

net float: Difference between payment and availability float.

Notice that the company gains as a result of the payment float and loses as a result of availability float. The **net float** available to the firm is the difference between payment and availability float.

Net float = payment float − availability float

In our example, the net float is $80,000. The company's available balance is $80,000 greater than the balance shown in its ledger.

SELF-TEST 20.1

Your bank account currently shows a balance of $940. You now deposit $100 into the account and write a cheque for $40.
a. What is the ledger balance in your account?
b. What is the availability float?
c. What is payment float?
d. What is the bank's ledger balance?
e. Show that your ledger balance plus payment float equals the bank's ledger balance, which in turn equals the available balance plus availability float.

Valuing Float

Float results from the delay between your writing a cheque and the reduction in your bank balance. The amount of float will therefore depend on the size of the cheque and the delay in collection. For example, suppose that your firm writes cheques worth $6000 per day. It may take 3 days to mail these cheques to your suppliers, who then take a day to process the cheques and deposit them with their bank. Once the cheque is deposited in the bank, it is very quickly cleared, typically within 1 day and almost always within 2 days.[1] The total delay is 6 days and the payment float is 6 × $6000 = $36,000. On average, the available balance at the bank will be $36,000 more than is shown in your firm's ledger.

As financial manager your concern is with the available balance, not with the company's ledger balance. If you know that it is going to be a week before some of your cheques are presented for payment, you may be able to get by on a smaller cash balance. The smaller you can keep your cash balance, the more funds you can hold in interest-earning accounts or securities. This game is often called *playing the float*.

You can increase your available cash balance by increasing your net float. This means that you want to ensure that cheques paid in by customers are cleared rapidly and those paid to suppliers are cleared slowly. Perhaps this may sound like rather small change, but think what it can mean to a company like Canadian Pacific. CP's daily sales average over $24 million. If it could speed up collections by 1 day, and the interest rate is .02 percent per day (about 7.3 percent per year), it would increase earnings by .0002 × $24 million = $4,800 *per day*.

What would be the present value to CP if it could *permanently* reduce its collection period by 1 day? That extra interest income would then be a perpetuity, and the present value of the income would be $4,800/.0002 = $24 million, exactly equal to the reduction in float.

Why should this be? Think about the company's cash-flow stream. It receives $24 million a day. At any time, suppose that 4 days' worth of payments are deposited and "in the pipeline." When it speeds up the collection period by a day, the pipeline will shrink to 3 days' worth of payments. At that point, CP receives an extra $24 million cash flow: it receives the "usual" payment of $24 million, and it also receives the $24 million for which it ordinarily would have had to wait an extra day. From that day forward, it continues to receive $24 million a day, exactly as before. So the net effect of reducing the payment pipeline from 4 days to 3 is that CP gets an extra up-front payment equal to 1 day of float, or $24

---

[1] The Canadian financial system is recognized as having one of the world's mot efficient payment systems. At the centre of the payment system is the Canadian Payments Association (CPA), which operates a national clearing and settlement system for cheques and electronic forms of payments made through automated banking machines, point-of-sale terminals, magnetic tape, and other sources. For more information, see Bruce McDougall, "Hidden highways: Canada's payments clearing and settlement system," *Canadian Banker* (January/February 1994) 27–30.

million. We conclude that the present value of a permanent reduction in float is simply the amount by which float is reduced.

However, you should be careful not to become overenthusiastic at managing the float. Writing cheques on your account for the sole purpose of creating float and earning interest is called *cheque kiting* and is illegal. In 1985 the brokerage firm E.F. Hutton pleaded guilty to 2000 separate counts of mail and wire fraud. Hutton admitted that it had created nearly $1 billion of float by shuffling funds between its branches and through various accounts at different banks.

SELF-TEST 20.2

Suppose CP's stock price is about $20 per share, and there are 340 million shares of CP outstanding. Now suppose that technological improvements in the cheque-clearing process reduce availability float from 4 days to 2 days. What would happen to the stock price? How much should CP be willing to pay for a new computer system that would reduce availability float by 2 days?

20.2 MANAGING FLOAT

There are several kinds of delay that create float, and so people in the cash management business refer to several kinds of float. Figure 20.1 shows the three sources of float:

- The time that it takes to mail a cheque.
- The time that it takes the company to process the cheque after it has been received.
- The time that it takes the bank to clear the cheque and adjust the firm's account.

The total collection time is the sum of these three sources of delay.

Of course the delays that help the payer hurt the recipient. Recipients try to speed up collections. Payers try to slow down disbursements.

You probably have come across attempts by companies to reduce float in your own financial transactions. For example, some stores now encourage you to pay bills with your bank debit card[2] instead of a credit card. The payment is automatically debited from your bank account on the day of the transaction, which eliminates the considerable float you otherwise would enjoy until you were billed by your credit card company and paid your bill. Similarly, many companies now arrange *preauthorized payments* with their customers. For example, if you have a mortgage payment on a house, the lender can arrange to have your bank account debited by the amount of the payment each month. The funds are automatically transferred to the lender. You save the work of paying the bill by hand, and the lender saves the few days of float during which your cheque would have been processed through the banking system.

concentration banking: System whereby customers make payments to a regional collection centre that transfers funds to a principal account.

Speeding Up Collections

One way to speed up collections is by a method known as **concentration banking**. In this case customers in a particular area make payments to a local branch office rather than to company headquarters. The local branch office then deposits the cheques into a local branch bank account. Surplus funds are periodically trans-

---

[2] The debit card system is also known as "electronic funds transfer at point of sale" or "EFT/POS." In its first year of operation in Canada, this direct payment system has transferred $2.5 billion for 13 million cardholders.

FIGURE 20.1
Delays create float. Each
heavy arrow represents a
source of delay. Recipients
try to reduce delay to get
available cash sooner.
Payers prefer delay so they
can use their cash longer.
Note: The delays causing
availability float and
presentation float are equal
on average, but can differ
from case to case.

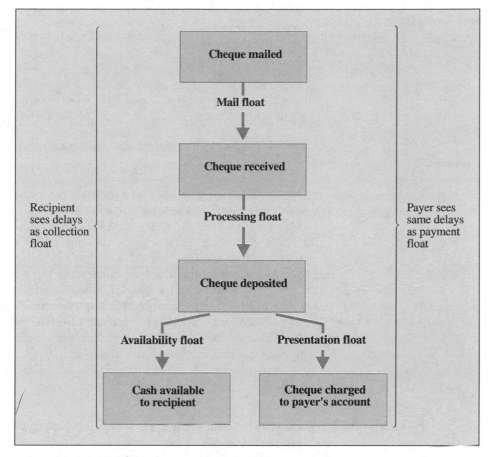

ferred to a concentration account at the company's principal branch, which is
known as the *concentration branch*. Sometimes the company's branch office does
not even have its own bank account, and instead makes a deposit at a local bank
branch directly into the head office account. In other cases the company's branch
office deals with a different bank from head office, in which case the funds are
transferred to the bank of the head office by a *depository transfer cheque or DTC*.
This is a preprinted cheque used to transfer funds between specified accounts. The
funds become available within 2 days. The main advantage of concentration banking is the reduction in mailing time that arises because the branch office is nearer
to the customer.

Often concentration banking is combined with a **lock-box system**. It works as
follows. The company rents a locked post office box in each principal region. All
customers within a region are instructed to send their payments to the post office
box. The local branch, as agent for the company, empties the box at regular intervals (as often as several times per day) and deposits the cheques in your company's principal account.

How many collection points do you need if you use a lock-box system or concentration banking? The answer depends on where your customers are and on the
speed of Canada Post. For example, suppose that you are thinking of opening a
lock box. The local bank shows you a map of mail delivery times. From that and
knowledge of your customers' locations, you come up with the following data:

lock-box system: System
whereby customers send
payments to a post office
box and a local bank col-
lects and processes
cheques.

Average number of daily payments to lock box	= 150
Average size of payment	= $1200
Rate of interest *per day*	= .02 percent
Saving in mailing time	= 1.2 days
Saving in clearing time	= .8 day

On this basis, the lock box would reduce collection float by

150 items per day × $1200 per item × (1.2 + .8) days saved = $360,000

Invested at .02 percent per day, that gives a daily return of

.0002 × $360,000 = $72.00

The bank's charge for operating the lock-box system depends on the number of cheques processed. Suppose that the bank charges $.26 per cheque. That works out to 150 × $.26 = $39.00 per day. You are ahead by $72.00 – $39.00 = $33.00 per day, plus whatever your firm saves from not having to process the cheques itself.

Our example assumes that the company has only two choices. It can do nothing or it can operate the lock box. But maybe there is some other lock-box location, or some mixture of locations, that would be still more effective. Of course, you can always find this out by working through all possible combinations, but many banks have computer programs that find the best locations for lock boxes.[3]

Canadian firms can also arrange for lock boxes to receive payments from American customers. Sometimes the lock boxes are with U.S. subsidiaries. In other cases, the lock boxes are located in cities near the border and transferred by courier to a nearby Canadian city for processing.

SELF-TEST 20.3

How will the following conditions affect the price that a firm should be willing to pay for a lock-box service?
a. The average size of its payments increases.
b. The number of payments per day increases (with no change in average size of payments).
c. The interest rate increases.
d. The average mail time saved by the lock-box system increases.
e. The processing time saved by the lock-box system increases.

Controlling Disbursements

Speeding up collections is not the only way to increase the net float. You can also do this by slowing down disbursements. One tempting strategy is to increase mail time. For example, Canadian Carbon could pay its Toronto suppliers with cheques mailed from Medicine Hat, Alberta, and its Vancouver suppliers with cheques mailed from Summerside, P.E.I.

But on second thought you will realize that these kinds of post office tricks are unlikely to help you. Suppose you have promised to pay a Toronto supplier on March 29. Does it matter whether you mail the cheque from Medicine Hat on the 26th or from Toronto on the 28th? Such mailing games would buy you time only if your creditor cares more about the date you mailed the cheque than the day it arrives. This is unlikely: with the notable exception of tax returns sent to Revenue Canada, mailing dates are irrelevant. Of course you could use a remote mailing

---
[3] These usually involve linear programming. Linear programming is an efficient method of hunting through the possible solutions to find the optimal one.

address as an excuse to pay late, but that's a trick easily seen through. If you have to pay late, you may as well mail late.

Another strategy might be to pay the Toronto supplier with a cheque drawn on your account at the Medicine Hat branch of your bank.[4] However, this too is not likely to be much of an advantage due to the way in which cheques are cleared in Canada. All banks *must* join an organization called the Canadian Payments Association and near banks such as trust companies and credit unions can join if they wish. The system has ten clearing centres located in major Canadian cities to facilitate the exchange of cheques and magnetic tapes. Items presented before 15:00 Eastern Time are settled on the same day. With same-day settlement there is little float created by the clearing system.

Finance in Action

Electronic Cash Management

Cash management activities of businesses are changing with the advent of new electronic products. The following article discusses some of the traditional and emerging electronic cash management services offered by Canadian financial institutions.

Banks in Canada have been using electronic commerce to serve customer needs for many years. Banks offer on-line balance and transaction reporting systems that help cash managers in their day-to-day activities. Latest information on cheques cleared, deposits made from remote locations, and balances in all accounts can all be accessed from the comfort of the cash manager's office. Funds can be moved between accounts, and payments can be sent via wire transfers around the world.

Electronic funds transfer (EFT) has been a common delivery vehicle for employee payroll deposits for decades. Companies processing their own payroll can transmit payment files to their bank for deposit to employees' accounts in virtually all Canadian financial institutions. Companies using payroll services [offered by a bank] can update their employee records electronically.

Emerging Trends
Many firms are looking to expand the use of electronic commerce with their banks. Buoyed by the successes in using electronic data exchange (EDI) for purchase orders, several Canadian companies have started to pay their suppliers using EDI. Organizations like The University of Manitoba, IBM, and Eaton's are all far beyond the pilot stage. They send their banks electronic files that include payment instructions and all the supporting information that would traditionally be printed on a cheque stub, or accompanying statement. The bank debits their account for the full amount of the payments in the file, and forwards the payments and remittance data to the suppliers'

---

[4] This technique, known as remote disbursement, works well in the United States where the cheque clearing process is slow and banks have been prohibited from having widespread branches.

Electronic Cash Management (continued)

banks on the same day as the payers originated the instructions.

This use of EDI for payment processing allows these pioneers to keep absolute control of payment timing, improve relationships with their suppliers, and reduce total processing costs.

Federal and provincial governments are actively encouraging the use of EDI for companies sending tax remittances. Seven major financial institutions have signed agreements with Revenue Canada to forward employer payroll deductions to Revenue Canada. Processing of other company taxes, including GST, is in testing stages.

Companies involved in downsizing/rightsizing or consolidation of divisional accounting groups can look to their bankers for even more innovative products. Complete outsourcing of payment disbursement is available.

A single electronic file sent to a bank can contain payments to be made by EFT (payment with minimal supporting data), EDI (payment accompanied by all supporting data), or by cheque, printed by the bank. This significantly reduces the manual effort and associated cost, without compromising control over the payment decision or timing of the payment. Companies using this service retain all decisions, but outsource the processing of their payments, and reap the benefits of cost reduction.

Future Products

Banks are actively pursuing new service offerings that use technology to serve customers. Telephone banking, imaging, network services, are all being integrated to meet the needs of a changing market.

Source: Reprinted from an article appearing in *CMA* magazine by Tom Provencher, June 1994 issue, with permission of The Society of Management Accountants of Canada.

20.3 INVENTORIES AND CASH BALANCES

So far we have focused on managing the *flow* of cash efficiently. We have seen how efficient float management can improve a firm's income and its net worth. Now we turn to the management of the *stock* of cash that a firm chooses to keep on hand and ask, How much cash does it make sense for a firm to hold?

At the beginning of this chapter we stated that cash management involves a trade-off. If the cash were invested in securities, it would earn interest. On the other hand, you can't use securities to pay the firm's bills. If you had to sell those securities every time you needed to pay a bill, you would incur heavy transactions costs. The art of cash management is to balance these costs and benefits.

If that seems more easily said than done, you may be comforted to know that production managers must make a similar trade-off. Ask yourself why they carry inventories of raw materials, work in progress, and finished goods. They are not obliged to carry these inventories; for example, they could simply buy materials day by day, as needed. But then they would pay higher prices for ordering in small lots, and they would risk production delays if the materials were not delivered on time. That is why they order more than the firm's immediate needs. Similarly, the firm holds inventories of finished goods to avoid the risk of running out of product and losing a sale because it cannot fill an order.

But there are costs to holding inventories: the money that is tied up in inventories does not earn interest; storage and insurance must be paid for; and often there is spoilage and deterioration. Production managers must try to strike a sensible balance between the costs of holding too little inventory and those of holding too much.

In this sense, cash is just another raw material you need for production. There are costs to keeping an excessive inventory of cash (the lost interest) and costs to keeping too small an inventory (the cost of repeated sales of securities).

Managing Inventories

Let us take a look at what economists have had to say about managing inventories and then see whether some of these ideas may help us to manage cash balances. Here is a simple inventory problem.

Dole's Bookstore experiences a steady demand for *Fundamentals of Corporate Finance* from customers who find that it makes a serviceable bookend. Suppose that the bookstore sells 100 copies of the book a year and that it orders Q books at a time from the publisher. Then it will need to place $100/Q$ orders per year:

$$\text{Number of orders per year} = \frac{\text{sales}}{Q} = \frac{100}{Q}$$

Just before each delivery, the bookstore has effectively no inventory of *Fundamentals of Corporate Finance*. Just after each delivery it has an inventory of Q books. Therefore, its average inventory is midway between 0 books and Q books:

$$\text{Average inventory} = \frac{Q}{2} \text{ books}$$

For example, if the store increases its regular order by 1 book, the average inventory increases by 1/2 book.

There are two costs associated with this inventory. First, there is the *carrying cost*. This includes the opportunity cost of the capital that is tied up in inventory, the cost of shelf space, insurance, and losses due to deterioration. Let us suppose that these costs work out to a dollar per book per year. Then the annual cost of storage is

$$\text{Total carrying cost} = \text{carrying cost per book} \times \text{average inventory of books}$$

$$= \$1 \text{ per book} \times \frac{Q}{2}$$

$$= \frac{Q}{2}$$

Notice that carrying costs increase in direct proportion to the level of average inventories.

The second type of cost is the *order cost*. Imagine that each order placed with the publisher involves a fixed clerical and handling expense of $2. Because there are $100/Q$ orders per year, total order costs are $\$2 \times (100/Q)$. In general, if the firm orders Q books at a time,

$$\text{Total order costs} = \text{orders per year} \times \text{cost per order}$$

$$= \frac{\text{Sales}}{Q} \times \text{cost per order}$$

Notice that orders per year, and therefore total order costs, are lower when the order size, Q, is greater.

Table 20.1 illustrates what happens to order costs as you increase the size of each order. You can see that the bookstore gets a large reduction in costs when it

TABLE 20.1
How order cost varies
with order size

Order Size, Number of Books	Number of Orders per Year	Total Order Costs
1	100	$200
2	50	100
3	33	66
4	25	50
10	10	20
100	1	2

orders two books at a time rather than one, but thereafter the savings from increases in order size steadily diminish.

Here, then is the kernel of the inventory problem. As the bookstore increases its order size, the number of orders falls but the average inventory rises. Costs that are related to the number of orders decline; those that are related to inventory size increase.

The optimal order size strikes a balance between these two costs. A graphical solution to the problem is presented in Figure 20.2. The downward-sloping curve is a graph of annual order costs. The upward-sloping straight line is a graph of carrying costs. The U-shaped curve is the sum of these two costs. Total costs are minimized in this example when the order size $Q = 20$ books. Five times a year the bookstore should place an order for 20 books, and it should work off this inventory over the following 10 weeks. Its inventory of *Fundamentals of Corporate Finance* will therefore follow the sawtoothed pattern in Figure 20.3.

FIGURE 20.2
Determination of optimal
order size.

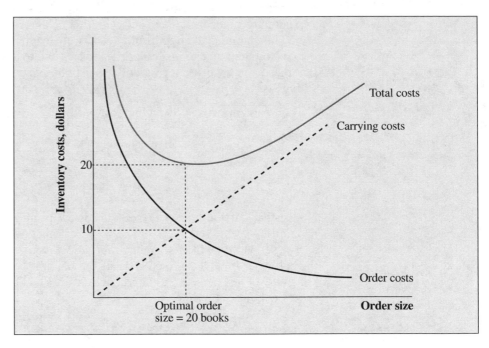

In fact, it is relatively easy to find the precise formula for the optimal order size. Note that it is worth increasing order size as long as the decrease in total order costs outweighs the increase in carrying costs. The optimal order size is the point at which these two effects exactly offset each other. This order size is called the **economic order quantity.**

economic order quantity: Order size that minimizes total inventory costs.

FIGURE 20.3
Dole's Bookstore minimizes
inventory costs by placing 5
orders per year for 20
books per order. That is,
it places orders at about
10-week intervals.

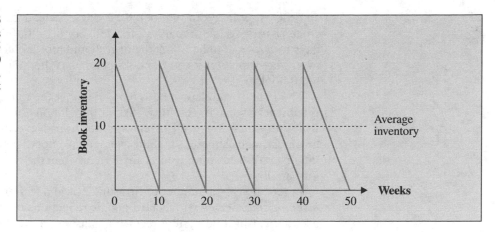

We've seen that adding 1 more book to each order increases the average inventory by 1/2 book and therefore the carrying cost by $1/2 \times \$1.00 = \$.50$. Thus the extra, or *marginal*, carrying cost is a constant $.50:

$$\text{Marginal carrying cost} = \frac{\text{carrying cost per book}}{2} = \$.50$$

We've also seen that order costs fall as the order size increases. In fact the *marginal*, or incremental, reduction in order costs falls with the square of the order size:

$$\text{Marginal reduction in order cost} = \frac{\text{sales} \times \text{cost per order}}{Q^2}$$

$$= \frac{\$200}{Q^2}$$

The general formula for optimum order size is found by setting the marginal reduction in order cost equal to the marginal increase in carrying costs and solving for Q. At this point the firm just balances the reduction in order costs with the increase in storage costs. The optimal value of Q, denoted Q^*, is the economic order quantity.

$$\text{Marginal reduction in order cost} = \text{marginal carrying cost}$$

$$\frac{\text{Sales} \times \text{cost per order}}{Q^2} = \frac{\text{carrying cost per book}}{2}$$

$$Q^2 = \frac{2 \times \text{sales} \times \text{cost per order}}{\text{carrying cost}}$$

$$Q^* = \text{economic order quantity} = \sqrt{\frac{2 \times \text{sales} \times \text{cost per order}}{\text{carrying cost}}}$$

In our example,

$$\text{economic order quantity} = \sqrt{\frac{2 \times 100 \times 2}{1}} = \sqrt{400} = 20$$

There are several possible improvements that you might want to make to this simple model. For example, rather than allowing inventories to decline to zero, the firm would want to allow for the time it takes to reorder new goods. If it takes 5 days to fill an order, and the store waits until it runs out of stock before placing an order, it will be out of stock for 5 days. Instead, the *reorder point* should be some positive value that allows for delivery lags. In this case, because it takes 5 days for an order to be filled, the firm should reorder when its stock of books falls to a 5-day supply. If it sells 2 books per day, it should reorder when its stock falls to 10 books.

The firm might also want to recognize that the rate at which it sells its goods is subject to some uncertainty. It should maintain a minimum *safety stock* below which it would not want inventories to drop. Nevertheless, the main thrust of inventory management is that the average inventory level should be kept low when interest rates and storage costs are high or when the costs of restocking the inventory are low.

In recent years a number of firms have used a technique known as *just-in-time inventory management* to make dramatic reductions in inventory levels. Firms that use the just-in-time system receive a nearly continuous flow of deliveries, with no more than 2 or 3 hours' worth of parts inventory on hand. Just-in-time systems require close cooperation between the firm and its suppliers.

SELF-TEST 20.4

Dole's Bookstore has experienced an increase in demand for *Fundamentals of Corporate Finance*. It now expects to sell 200 books a year. Unfortunately, inventory carrying costs have increased to $2 per book per year, whereas order costs have remained steady at $2 per order.
a. How many orders should the store place per year?
b. What is its average inventory?

Managing Inventories of Cash: The Baumol Model

William Baumol was the first to notice that this simple inventory model can tell us something about the management of cash balances.[5] Suppose that you keep a reservoir of cash that is steadily drawn down to pay bills. When it runs out you replenish the cash balance by selling short-term securities. In these circumstances your inventory of cash also follows a sawtoothed pattern like the pattern for inventories we saw in Figure 20.3.

In other words, your cash management problem is just like the problem of optimum order size faced by Dole's Bookstore. You simply need to redefine variables. Instead of books per order, Q becomes the value of short-term securities sold each time the cash balance is replenished. Cost per order becomes the cost per sale of securities. The carrying cost of cash is just the interest rate. Total cash disbursement takes the place of books sold. Thus the optimum amount of securities to be sold is

$$Q^* = \sqrt{\frac{2 \times \text{annual cash disbursements} \times \text{cost per sale of securities}}{\text{interest rate}}}$$

● **EXAMPLE 20.1 The Baumol Model**

Suppose that you can invest spare cash in Government of Canada Treasury bills at an interest rate of 8 percent, but every sale of bills costs you $20. Your firm pays out cash at a rate of $105,000 per month, or $1,260,000 per year. Therefore, the optimum amount of Treasury bills that you should sell at one time is

$$Q^* = \sqrt{\frac{2 \times 1,260,000 \times 20}{.08}} = \$25,100$$

---

[5] W. J. Baumol, "The Transactions Demand for Cash: An Inventory Theoretic Approach," *Quarterly Journal of Economics* 66 (November 1952):545–556.

Thus your firm would sell approximately $25,000 of Treasury bills four times a month — about once a week. Its average cash balance will be $25,000/2, or $12,500.

In Baumol's model a higher interest rate implies smaller sales of bills. In other words, when interest rates are high, you should hold more of your funds in interest-bearing securities and make small sales of these securities when you need the cash. On the other hand, if you use up cash at a high rate or if there are high costs to selling securities, you want to hold large average cash balances. Think about that for a moment. *You can hold too little cash.* Many financial managers point with pride to the tight control that they exercise over cash and to the extra interest that they have earned. These benefits are highly visible. The costs are less visible but they can be very large. When you allow for the time that the manager spends in monitoring the cash balance, it may make sense to forgo some of that extra interest.

SELF-TEST 20.5

Suppose now that the interest rate is only 4 percent. How will this affect the optimal initial cash balance derived in Example 20.1? What will be the *average* cash balance? Annual trading costs? Explain why the optimal cash position now involves fewer trades.

The Miller-Orr Model

Baumol's model works well as long as the firm is steadily using up its cash account. But that is not what usually happens. In some weeks the firm may collect a large unpaid bill and therefore receive a net *inflow* of cash. In other weeks it may pay its suppliers and so incur a net *outflow* of cash.

Economists and management scientists have developed a variety of more elaborate and realistic models that allow for the possibility of both cash inflows and outflows. Let us look briefly at a model developed by Miller and Orr.[6] It represents a nice compromise between simplicity and realism.

Miller and Orr consider how the firm should manage its cash balance if it cannot predict day-to-day cash inflows and outflows. Their answer is shown in Figure 20.4. You can see that the cash balance meanders unpredictably until it reaches an upper limit. At this point the firm *buys* enough securities to return the cash balance to a more normal level. Once again the cash balance is allowed to meander until this time it hits a lower limit. When it does, the firm *sells* enough securities to restore the balance to a normal level. Thus the rule is to allow the cash holding

FIGURE 20.4
In Miller and Orr's model the cash balance is allowed to meander until it hits an upper or lower limit. At this point the firm buys or sells securities to restore the balance to the return point, which is the lower limit plus one-third of the spread between the upper and lower limits.

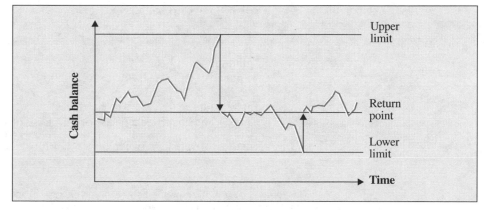

[6] M. H. Miller and D. Orr, "A Model of the Demand for Money by Firms," *Quarterly Journal of Economics* 80 (August 1966):413–435.

to wander freely until it hits an upper or lower limit. When this happens, the firm buys or sells securities to regain the desired balance.

How far should the firm allow its cash balance to wander? Miller and Orr show that the answer depends on three factors. If the day-to-day variability in cash flows is large or if the cost of buying and selling securities is high, then the firm should set the upper and lower limits far apart. Conversely, if the rate of interest is high, it should set the limits close together. The formula for the distance between the barriers is[7]

$$\begin{array}{c}\text{\textit{Spread} between} \\ \text{upper and lower} \\ \text{cash balance limits}\end{array} = 3\left(\frac{3}{4} \times \frac{\text{transaction cost} \times \text{variance of cash flows}}{\text{interest rate}}\right)^{1/3}$$

Have you noticed one odd feature about Figure 20.4? The firm does not return to a point halfway between the lower and upper limits. The firm always returns to a point one-third of the distance from the lower to the upper limit. In other words, the return point is

$$\text{Return point} = \text{lower limit} + \frac{\text{spread}}{3}$$

Always starting at this return point means the firm hits the lower limit more often than the upper limit. This does not minimize the number of transactions — that would require always starting exactly in the middle of the spread. However, always starting in the middle would mean a larger average cash balance and larger interest costs. The Miller-Orr return point minimizes the sum of transaction costs and interest costs.

The Miller-Orr model is easy to use. The first step is to set the lower limit for the cash balance. This may be zero, some minimum safety margin above zero, or a balance necessary to keep the bank happy. The second step is to estimate the variability of cash flows. For example, you might record net cash inflows or outflows for each of the last 100 days and compute the variance of those 100 sample observations.[8] More sophisticated measurement techniques could be applied if there were, say, seasonal fluctuations in the volatility of cash flows. The third step is to observe the interest rate and the transaction cost of each purchase or sale of securities. The final step is to compute the upper limit and the return point. Here is a numerical example.

● EXAMPLE 20.2 Miller-Orr Model

A. Assumptions:

1. Minimum cash balance = $10,000
2. Variance of daily cash flows = 6,250,000 (equivalent to a standard deviation of $2,500 per day)
3. Interest rate = .025 percent per day
4. Transaction cost for each sale of purchase of securities = $20

B. Calculation of spread between upper and lower cash balance limits:

---

[7] This formula assumes the expected daily change in the cash balance is zero. Thus it assumes that there are no systematic upward or downward trends in the cash balance. If the Miller-Orr model is applicable, you need know only the variance of the daily cash flows, that is, the variance of the daily *changes* in the cash balance.

[8] We showed you how to calculate variance in Chapter 9.

$$\text{Spread} = 3 \left(\frac{3}{4} \times \frac{\text{transaction cost} \times \text{variance of cash flows}}{\text{interest rate}} \right)^{1/3}$$

$$= 3 \left(\frac{3}{4} \times \frac{20 \times 6,250,000}{.00025} \right)^{1/3}$$

$$= \$21,634 \text{ or about } \$21,600$$

C. Calculate upper limit and return point:

$$\text{Upper limit} = \text{lower limit} + 21,600 = \$31,600$$

$$\text{Return point} = \text{lower limit} + \frac{\text{spread}}{3}$$

$$= 10,000 + \frac{21,600}{3} = \$17,200$$

D. Decision rule: If cash balance rises to $31,600, invest $31,600 – 17,200 = $14,400 in marketable securities; if cash balance falls to $10,000, sell $7200 of marketable securities and replenish cash.

The Miller-Orr model's practical usefulness is limited by the assumptions it rests on. For example, few managers would agree that cash inflows and outflows are entirely unpredictable, as Miller and Orr assume. The manager of Toys "R" Us knows that there will be substantial cash inflows around Christmas. Financial managers know when dividends will be paid and when income taxes will be due. In Chapter 19 we described how firms forecast cash inflows and outflows and how they arrange short-term investment and financing decisions to supply cash when needed and put cash to work earning interest when it is not needed.

This kind of short-term financial plan is usually designed to produce a cash balance that is stable at some lower limit. But there are always fluctuations that financial managers cannot plan for, certainly not on a day-to-day basis. You can think of the Miller-Orr policies as responding to the cash inflows and outflows that cannot be predicted, or that are not *worth* predicting. Trying to predict *all* cash flows would chew up enormous amounts of management time.

You should therefore think of these models as helping us to *understand* the problem of cash management. But they are not generally used for day-to-day management and would probably not yield substantial savings compared with policies based on a manager's judgment, providing of course that the manager understands the trade-offs we have discussed.

SELF-TEST 20.6

How would you expect a firm's cash balance to respond to the following changes?
a. Interest rates increase.
b. The volatility of daily cash flow decreases.
c. The transaction cost of buying or selling marketable securities goes up.

Raising Cash by Borrowing

Thus far we have assumed that surplus cash is invested in securities such as Treasury bills and that cash is replenished when necessary by selling these securities. The alternative may be to replenish cash by borrowing — for example, by drawing on a bank line of credit.

While borrowing avoids the cost of selling securities, it raises another problem. The interest rate that you pay to the bank is likely to be higher than the rate that you receive on securities. As financial manager, you therefore face another trade-off. To earn the maximum interest on your funds, you want to hold low cash balances in the bank, but this means that you are more likely to have to borrow to cover an unexpected cash outflow. For example, suppose you can either hold cash that pays no interest or invest in securities that pay interest at 10 percent. The cost of keeping cash balances is the interest forgone by not investing the money in securities:

$$\text{Cost of cash balances} = 10 \text{ percent}$$

If you need more cash at short notice, it may be difficult or costly to sell securities, but you can borrow from the bank at 12 percent. In this case, there is a simple rule for maximizing expected return. You should adjust the cash balances until the probability that you will need to borrow from the bank equals[9]

$$\frac{\text{Cost of cash balances}}{\text{Cost of borrowing}} = \frac{10}{12} = .83$$

When we look at the problem this way, the best cash balance depends on the cost of borrowing and the extent of uncertainty about future cash flow. If the cost of borrowing is high relative to the interest rate on securities, you should make sure that there is only a low probability that you will be obliged to borrow. If you are very uncertain about the future cash flow, you may need to keep a large cash balance in order to be confident that you will not have to borrow. If you are fairly sure about cash flow, you can keep a lower cash balance.

SELF-TEST 20.7

Suppose that you can hold cash that pays no interest or invest in securities paying interest of 8 percent. Since the securities are not easily sold on short notice, you must make up any cash deficiency by drawing on a bank line of credit that charges interest at 10 percent. Should you invest more or less in securities if
a. You are unusually uncertain about future cash flows?
b. The interest rate on bank loans rises to 11 percent?
c. You revise downward your forecast of future cash needs?

Cash Management in the Largest Corporations

For very large firms, the transaction costs of buying and selling securities become trivial compared with the opportunity cost of holding idle cash balances. Suppose that the interest rate is 4 percent per year, or roughly $4/365 = .011$ percent per day. Then the daily interest earned by \$1 million is $.00011 \times \$1,000,000 = \$110$. Even at a cost of \$50 per transaction, which is generous, it pays to buy Treasury bills today and sell them tomorrow rather than to leave \$1 million idle overnight.

A corporation with \$1 billion of annual sales has an average daily cash flow of \$1,000,000,000/365, about \$2.7 million. Firms of this size end up buying or selling securities once a day, every day, unless by chance they have only a small positive cash balance at the end of the day.

Why do such firms hold any significant amounts of cash? For two reasons. First, cash may be left in non-interest-bearing accounts to compensate banks for the services they provide. Second, large corporations may have literally hundreds of accounts with dozens of different banks. It is often less expensive to leave idle cash in some of these accounts than to monitor each account daily and make daily transfers between them.

[9] See, for example, J. H. W. Goslings, "One-Period Optimal Cash Balances," unpublished paper presented to the European Finance Association, Scheveningen, Holland, 1981.

One major reason for the proliferation of bank accounts is decentralized management. You cannot give a subsidiary operating freedom to manage its own affairs without giving it the right to spend and receive cash.

Good cash management nevertheless implies some degree of centralization. You cannot maintain your desired inventory of cash if all the subsidiaries in the group are responsible for their own private pools of cash. And you certainly want to avoid situations in which one subsidiary is investing in spare cash at 8 percent while another is borrowing at 10 percent. It is not surprising, therefore, that even in highly decentralized companies there is generally central control over cash balances and bank relations.

Investing Idle Cash: The Money Market

money market: Market for short-term financial assets.

We have seen that when firms have excess funds, they can invest the surplus in interest-bearing securities. Treasury bills are only one of many securities that might be appropriate for such short-term investments. More generally, firms may invest in a variety of securities in the **money market**, the market for short-term financial assets.

Only fixed-income securities with maturities less than 3 years are considered to be part of the money market. In fact, however, most instruments in the money market have considerably shorter maturity. Limiting maturity has two advantages for the cash manager. First, short-term securities entail little interest-rate risk. Recall from Chapter 4 that price risk due to interest-rate fluctuations increases with maturity. Very-short-term securities, therefore, have almost no interest-rate risk. Second, it is far easier to gauge financial stability over very short horizons. One need not worry as much about deterioration in financial strength over a 90-day horizon as over the 30-year life of a bond. These considerations imply that high-quality money-market securities are a safe "parking spot" to keep idle balances until they are converted back to cash.

Most money-market securities are also highly marketable or *liquid*, meaning that it is easy and cheap to sell the asset for cash. This property, too, is an attractive feature of securities used as temporary investments until cash is needed. Treasury bills are the most liquid asset. Treasury bills are issued by the federal and some provincial governments with original maturities ranging from 90 days to 1 year.

Some of the other important instruments of the money market are

Commercial paper. This is the short-term, usually unsecured debt of large and well-known companies. While maturities can range up to one year, commercial paper usually is issued with maturities of less than 2 months. Both Dominion Bond Rating Service and Canada Bond Rating Service rate commercial paper in terms of the default risk of the issuer.

Certificates of deposit. CDs are time deposits at banks, usually in denominations greater than $100,000. Unlike demand deposits (chequing accounts), time deposits cannot be withdrawn from the bank on demand: the bank pays interest and principal only at the maturity of the deposit. However, short-term CDs (with maturities less then 3 months) are actively traded, so a firm can easily sell the security if it needs cash.

Buy Backs. Also known as *repos, repurchase agreements* are in effect collateralized loans. A government bond dealer sells Treasury bills to an investor, with an agreement to repurchase them at a later date at a higher price. The increase in price serves as implicit interest, so the investor in effect is lending money to the dealer, first giving money to the dealer and later getting it back with interest. The bills serve as collateral for the loan: if the dealer fails, and cannot buy back the bill, the investor can keep it. Repurchase agreements are usually very short term, with terms of only a few days.

SUMMARY

1. The cash shown in the company ledger is not the same as the available balance in your bank account. The difference is the net float. When you write a cheque, it takes time before your bank balance is adjusted downward. During this time the available balance will be larger than the ledger balance. When you deposit a cheque, there is again a delay before it gets credited to your bank account. In this case the available balance will be smaller than the ledger balance. If you can predict how long it will take cheques to clear, you may be able to play the float and get by on a smaller cash balance.

2. You can also manage the float by speeding up collections and slowing down payments. One way to speed collections is by concentration banking. Customers make payments to a regional office, which then pays the cheques into a local branch account. Surplus funds are transferred from the local account to a concentration account. A related technique is lock-box banking. In this case customers send their payments to a local post office box. A local branch empties the box at regular intervals and clears the cheques. Concentration banking and lock-box banking reduce mailing time and the time required to clear cheques.

3. Cash provides liquidity, but it doesn't pay interest. Securities pay interest, but you can't use them to buy things. As financial manager you want to hold cash up to the point where the incremental or marginal value of liquidity is equal to the interest that you could earn on securities.

4. Cash is simply a raw material that you need to do business. It is expensive keeping capital tied up in large inventories of any raw material when it could be earning interest. So why do you hold inventories at all? Why not order materials as and when you need them? The answer is that it is also expensive to keep placing many small orders. You need to strike a balance between holding too large an inventory of cash (and losing interest on the money) and making too many small adjustments to your inventory (and incurring additional administrative costs). If interest rates are high, you want to hold relatively small inventories of cash. If your cash needs are variable and your administrative costs are high, you want to hold relatively large inventories.

5. If the securities are not easily sold, you have the alternative of borrowing to cover a cash deficiency. Again, you face a trade-off. Since banks charge a high interest rate on borrowing, you want to keep sufficiently large liquid funds that you don't need to keep borrowing. On the other hand, by having large liquid balances, you are also not earning the maximum return on your cash.

6. Firms can invest idle cash in the money market, the market for short-term financial assets. These assets tend to be short-term, low risk, and highly liquid, making them ideal instruments in which to invest funds for short periods of time before cash is needed.

KEY TERMS

payment float	concentration banking	economic order quantity
availability float	lock-box system	money market
net float		

SUGGESTED READINGS

The *Journal of Cash Management*, published by the National Corporate Cash Management Association, is a good reference for recent developments. Useful specialized texts include

J. G. Kallberg, K. L. Parkinson, and J. R. Ochs, eds. *Essentials of Cash Management*. Newtown, Conn.: National Corporate Cash Management Association, 1989.

N. C. Hill and W. L. Sartoris. *Short-Term Financial Management*. New York: Macmillan, 1988.

J. Van der Weide and S. F. Maier. *Managing Corporate Liquidity: An Introduction to Working Capital Management*. New York: John Wiley & Sons, 1985.

PROBLEMS

1. On January 25, Coot Company has $250,000 deposited with a local bank. On January 27, the company writes and mails cheques of $20,000 and $60,000 to suppliers. At the end of the month, Coot's financial manager deposits a $45,000 cheque received from a customer in the morning mail and picks up the end-of-month account summary from the bank. The manager notes that only the $20,000 payment of the 27th has cleared the bank. What are the company's ledger balance and payment float? What is the company's net float?

2. A company has the following cash balances:

   Company's ledger balance = $600,000
   Bank's ledger balance = $625,000
   Available balance = $550,000

   a. Calculate the payment float and availability float.
   b. Why does the company gain from the payment float?

3. General Products writes cheques that average $20,000 daily. These cheques take an average of 6 days to clear. It receives payments that average $22,000 daily. It takes 3 days before these cheques are available to the firm.
   a. Calculate payment float, availability float, and net float.
   b. What would be General Products's annual savings if it could reduce availability float to 2 days? The interest rate is 6 percent per year. What would be the present value of these savings?

4. Anne Teak, the financial manager of a furniture manufacturer, is considering operating a lock-box system. She forecasts that 300 payments a day will be made to lock boxes with an average payment size of $1500. The bank's charge for operating the lock boxes is $.40 a cheque. The interest rate is .015 percent per day.
   a. If the lock box saves 2 days in collection float, is it worthwhile to adopt the system?
   b. What minimum reduction in the time to collect and process each cheque is needed to justify use of the lock-box system?

5. Sherman's Sherbet currently takes about 6 days to collect and deposit cheques from customers. A lock-box system could reduce this time to 4 days. Collections average $10,000 daily. The interest rate is .02 percent per day.

    a. By how much will the lock-box system reduce collection float?

    b. What is the daily interest savings of the system?

    c. Suppose the lock-box service is offered for a fixed monthly fee instead of payment per cheque. What is the maximum monthly fee that Sherman's should be willing to pay for this service? (Assume a 30-day month.)

6. The financial manager of JAC Cosmetics is considering opening a lock box in Hamilton. Cheques cleared through the lock box will amount to $300,000 per month. The lock box will make cash available to the company 3 days earlier.

    a. Suppose that the bank offers to run the lock box at no charge as long as your company keeps a minimum $20,000 'compensating balance' in your chequing account. Is the lock box worthwhile?

    b. Suppose that the bank offers to run the lock box for a fee of $.10 per cheque cleared instead of a compensating balance. What must the average cheque size be for the fee alternative to be less costly? Assume an interest rate of 6 percent per year.

    c. Why did you need to know the interest rate to answer (b) but not to answer (a)?

7. Complete the following passage by choosing the appropriate term from the following list: *lock-box banking, payment float, concentration banking, availability float, net float, depository transfer cheque.*

The firm's available balance is equal to its ledger balance plus the _____ and minus the _____. The difference between the available balance and the ledger balance is often called the _____. Firms can increase their cash resources by speeding up collections. One way to do this is to arrange for payments to be made to regional offices that pay the cheques into local branches. This is known as _____. Surplus funds are then transferred from the local branch to the company's main accounts. Transfer may be made through a _____. Another technique is to arrange for a local branch to collect the cheques directly from a post office box. This is known as _____.

8. Assume that Dole's Bookstore uses up cash at a steady rate of $20,000 a year. The interest rate is 2 percent and each sale of securities costs $2.

    a. How many times a year should the store sell securities?

    b. What is its average cash balance?

9. In the Miller-Orr cash balance model the firm should allow the cash balance to move within limits.

    a. What three factors determine how far apart these limits are?

    b. How far should the firm adjust its cash balance when it reaches the upper or lower limit?

    c. Why does it not restore the cash balance to the halfway point?

10. Refer to Example 20.2. Calculate the optimal strategy under the following alternative assumptions:

Minimum cash balance = $20,000
Standard deviation of daily cash flows = $5000
Interest rate = .03 percent per day
Transaction cost of each purchase or sale of securities = $25

11. Suppose that the rate of interest increases from 4 to 8 percent per year. Would firms' cash balances go up or down relative to sales? Explain.

12. Knob, Inc., is a nationwide distributor of furniture hardware. The company now uses a central billing system for credit sales of $182.5 million annually. Montreal Dominion, Knob's principal bank, offers to establish a new concentration banking system for a flat fee of $100,000 per year. The bank estimates that mailing and collection time can be reduced by 3 days.

   a. By how much will Knob's availability float be reduced under the new system?

   b. How much extra interest income will the new system generate if the extra funds are used to reduce borrowing under Knob's line of credit with Montreal Dominion? Assume the borrowing rate is 12 percent.

   c. Finally, should Knob accept Montreal Dominion's offer if collection costs under the old system are $40,000 per year?

13. A few years ago, Merrill Lynch increased its float by mailing cheques drawn on West Coast banks to customers in the East and cheques drawn on East Coast banks to customers in the West. A subsequent class action suit against Merrill Lynch revealed that in 28 months from September 1976 Merrill Lynch disbursed $1.25 billion in 365,000 cheques to New York State customers alone. The plaintiff's lawyer calculated that by using a remote bank Merrill Lynch had increased its average float by 1 1/2 days.[10]

   a. How much did Merrill Lynch disburse per day to New York State customers?

   b. What was the total gain to Merrill Lynch over the 28 months, assuming an interest rate of 8 percent?

   c. What was the present value of the increase in float if the benefits were expected to be permanent?

   d. Suppose that the use of remote banks had involved Merrill Lynch in extra expenses. What was the maximum extra cost per cheque that Merrill Lynch would have been prepared to pay?

14. Suppose that your weekly cash expenses are $80. Every time you withdraw money from the automatic teller at your bank, you are charged 15 cents. Your bank account pays interest of 3 percent annually.

   a. How often should you withdraw funds from the bank?

   b. What is the optimal-sized withdrawal?

   c. What is your average amount of cash on hand?

15. A large consulting firm orders photocopying paper by the carton. The firm pays a $30 delivery charge on each order. The total cost of storing the paper, including forgone interest, storage space, and deterioration, comes to about $1.50 per carton per month. The firm uses about 1000 cartons of paper per year.

   a. Fill in the following table:

	Order Size			
	100	**200**	**250**	**500**
Orders per year	_____	_____	_____	_____
Total order cost	_____	_____	_____	_____
Average inventory	_____	_____	_____	_____
Total carrying costs	_____	_____	_____	_____
Total inventory costs	_____	_____	_____	_____

---

[10] See I. Ross, "The Race Is to the Slow Payer," *Fortune*, April 1983, pp. 75–80.

    b. Calculate the economic order quantity. Is your answer consistent with your findings in part (a)?

16. Genuine Gems orders a full month's worth of precious stones at the beginning of every month. Over the course of the month, it sells off its stock, at which point it restocks inventory for the following month. It sells 200 gems per month, and the monthly carrying cost is $1 per gem. The fixed order cost is $20 per order. Should the firm adjust its inventory policy? If so, should it order smaller stocks more frequently or larger stocks less frequently?

17. Patty's Pancakes orders pancake mix once a week. The mix is used up by the end of the week, at which point more is reordered. Each time Patty orders pancake mix, she spends about a half hour of her time, which she estimates is worth $20. Patty sells 200 pounds of pancakes each week. The carrying cost of each pound of the mix is 5 cents per week. Should Patty restock more or less frequently? What is the cost-minimizing order size? How many times per month should Patty restock?

18. A just-in-time inventory system reduces the cost of ordering additional inventory by a factor of 100. What is the change in the optimal order size predicted by the economic order quantity model?

19. According to the economic order quantity inventory model and the Baumol model of cash management, what will happen to cash balances and inventory levels if the firm's production and sales both double? What is the implication of your answer for percentage of sales models?

SOLUTIONS TO SELF-TEST QUESTIONS

20.1
a. The ledger balance is $940 + $100 − $40 = $1000.
b. Availability float is $100, since you do not yet have access to the funds you have deposited.
c. Payment float is $40, since the cheque that you wrote has not yet cleared.
d. The bank's ledger balance is $940 + $100 = $1040. The bank is aware of the cheque you deposited but is not aware of the cheque you wrote.
e. Ledger balance plus payment float = $1000 + $40 = $1040, which equals the bank's ledger balance. Available balance + availability float = $940 + $100 = $1040, also equal to the bank's ledger balance.

20.2 The current market value of CP is $6800 million. The 2-day reduction in float is worth $48 million. This increases the value of CP to $6848 million. The new stock price will be $20.14 per share. CP should be willing to pay up to $48 million for the system, since the present value of the savings is $48 million.

20.3 The benefit of the lock-box system, and the price the firm should be willing to pay for the system, is higher when:
a. Payment size is higher (since interest is earned on more funds).
b. Payments per day are higher (since interest is earned on more funds).
c. The interest rate is higher (since the cost of float is lower).
d. Mail time saved is higher (since more float is saved).
e. Processing time saved is higher (since more float is saved).

20.4 The economic order quantity is

$$Q^* = \sqrt{\frac{2 \times \text{cost per order} \times \text{annual sales}}{\text{carrying cost}}}$$

$$= \sqrt{\frac{2 \times 2 \times 200}{2}} = \sqrt{400} = 20$$

a. The effects of the higher sales and higher carrying costs offset: the optimal order size is unchanged. However, orders per year double to 400/20 = 20, since twice the number of books are sold each year while the order size is still 20.
b. Average inventory is one-half of the order size, or 10 books.

20.5 At an interest rate of 4 percent, the optimal initial cash balance is

$$\sqrt{\frac{(2 \times 1,260,000 \times 20)}{.04}} = \$35,496.$$

The average cash balance will be one-half this amount, or $17,748. The firm will need to order goods 1,260,000/35,496 = 35.5 times per year. Therefore, annual trading costs will be 35.5 × $20 = $710 per year. Since the carrying cost of cash, the interest rate, has fallen, more is carried in inventory. With higher average inventories, fewer sales are needed each year.

20.6
a. Higher interest rates will lead to lower cash balances.
b. Higher volatility will lead to higher cash balances.
c. Higher transaction costs will lead to higher cash balances.

20.7
a. Higher uncertainty about cash balances will lead to a higher cash balance and therefore less investment in securities.
b. A higher interest rate on loans makes the cost of running out of cash higher. The firm will hold more cash and less in securities.
c. Lower cash needs will lead the firm to invest more in securities.

CHAPTER TWENTY-ONE

Credit Management and Bankruptcy

When companies sell their products, they sometimes demand cash on delivery, but in most cases they allow a delay in payment. If you turn back to the balance sheet in Table 19.1, you can see that accounts receivable constitute on the average more than one-third of a firm's current assets. These receivables include both trade credit to other firms and consumer credit to retail customers. The former is by far the larger and will therefore be the main focus of this chapter. Credit management involves the following steps, which we will discuss in turn.

First, you must establish the *terms of sale* on which you propose to sell your goods. How long are you going to give customers to pay their bills? Are you prepared to offer a cash discount for prompt payment?

Second, you must decide what evidence you need that the customer owes you money. Do you just ask the buyer to sign a receipt, or do you insist on a more formal IOU?

Third, you must consider which customers are likely to pay their bills. This is called *credit analysis*. Do you judge this from the customer's past payment record or past financial statements? Do you also rely on bank references?

Fourth, you must decide on *credit policy*. How much credit are you prepared to extend to each customer? Do you play safe by turning down any doubtful prospects? Or do you accept the risk of a few bad debts as part of the cost of building up a large regular clientele?

Fifth, after you have granted credit, you have the problem of collecting the money when it becomes due. This is called *collection policy*. How do you keep track of payments and pursue slow payers? If all goes well, this is the end of the matter. But sometimes you will find that the customer is bankrupt and cannot pay. In this case you need to understand how bankruptcy works.

After studying the chapter you should be able to

- Measure the implicit interest rate on credit.
- Understand when it makes sense to ask the customer for a formal IOU.
- Explain how firms can assess the probability that a customer will pay.
- Decide whether it makes sense to grant credit to that customer.
- Summarize the bankruptcy procedures when firms cannot pay their creditors.

21.1 TERMS OF SALE

Not all business transactions involve credit. For example, if you are supplying goods to a wide variety of irregular customers, you may require cash on delivery (COD). And if you are producing goods to the customer's specification or incurring heavy delivery costs, then it may be sensible to ask for cash before delivery (CBD). Thus you must establish the **terms of sale**.

terms of sale: Credit and discount terms offered on a sale.

Some contracts provide for *progress payments* as work is carried out. For example, a large consulting contract might call for 30 percent payment after completion of field research, 30 percent more on submission of a draft report, and the remaining 40 percent when the project is finally completed.

When we look at transactions that do involve credit, we encounter a wide variety of arrangements (and a wide variety of jargon). Each industry seems to have its own typical payment terms. These terms have a rough logic. For example, the seller will naturally demand earlier payment if its customers are financially less secure, if their accounts are small, or if the goods are perishable or quickly resold.

When you buy goods on credit, the supplier will state a final payment date. To encourage you to pay *before* the final date, it is common to offer a cash discount for prompt settlement. For example, a manufacturer may require payment within 30 days but offer a 5 percent discount to customers who pay within 10 days. These terms would be referred to as 5/10, net 30:

5	/	10	net 30
↑		↑	↑
percent discount for early payment		number of days that discount is available	number of days before payment is due

Similarly, if a firm sells goods on terms of 2/30, net 60, customers receive a 2 percent discount for payment within 30 days or else must pay in full within 60 days. If the terms are simply net 30, then customers must pay within 30 days of the invoice date, and no discounts are offered for early payment.

For many items that are bought regularly, it is inconvenient to require separate payment for each delivery. A common solution is to pretend that all sales during the month in fact occur at the end of the month (EOM). Thus goods may be sold on terms of 8/10, EOM, net 60. This allows the customer a cash discount of 8 percent if the bill is paid within 10 days of the end of the month; otherwise the full payment is due within 60 days of the invoice date.

When purchases are subject to seasonal fluctuations, manufacturers often encourage customers to take early delivery by allowing them to delay payment until the usual order season. This practice is known as *season dating*. For example, summer products might have terms of 2/10, net 30, but the invoice might be dated May 1 even if the sale takes place in February. The discount is then available until May 10, and the bill is not due until May 30.

Firms that buy on credit are in effect borrowing money from their suppliers. Of course, a free loan is always worth having. But if you pass up a cash discount, then the loan may prove to be very expensive. For example, a customer who buys on terms of 3/10, net 30 may decide to forgo the cash discount and pay on the thirtieth day. The customer obtains an extra 20 days' credit by deferring payment from 10 to 30 days after the sale but pays about 3 percent more for the goods. This is equivalent to borrowing money at a rate of 74.3 percent a year. To see why, consider an order of $100. If the firm pays within 10 days, it gets a 3 percent discount and pays only $97. If it waits the full 30 days, it pays $100. The extra 20 days of credit increase the payment by the fraction $3/97 = .0309$, or 3.09 percent. Therefore, the implicit interest charged to extend the trade credit is 3.09 percent *per 20 days*. There are $365/20 = 18.25$ twenty-day periods in a year, so the effective annual rate of interest on the loan is $(1.0309)^{18.25} - 1 = .743$, or 74.3 percent.

Of course any firm that delays payment beyond day 30 gains a cheaper loan but damages its reputation for creditworthiness.

● EXAMPLE 21.1 Trade Credit Rates

What would happen to the implied interest rate on the trade credit if the discount for early payment were reduced to 2/10, net 30?

The discount for prompt payment is only $2, so the per-period discount falls to $2/98 = .0204$, or 2.04 percent. This is equivalent to an annual interest rate of

Effective annual rate = $(1.0204)^{18.25} - 1 = .446$, or 44.6%

You might wonder why the effective interest rate on trade credit is typically so high. Part of the rate should be viewed as compensation for the costs the firm anticipates in collecting from slow payers. After all, at such steep effective rates, most purchasers will choose to pay early and receive the discount. Therefore, you might interpret the choice to stretch payables as a sign of financial difficulties. It follows that the interest rate you charge to these firms should be high.

SELF-TEST 21.1

What would be the effective annual interest rate in Example 21.1 if the terms of the loan were 2/10, net 60? Why is the rate lower?

21.2   CREDIT AGREEMENTS

open account: Agreement whereby sales are made with no formal debt contract.

The terms of sale define the amount of any credit but not the nature of the contract. Repetitive sales are almost always made on **open account** and involve only an implicit contract. There is simply a record in the seller's books and a receipt signed by the buyer.

Sometimes you might want a more formal agreement that the customer owes you money. Where the order is very large and there is no complicating cash discount, the customer may be asked to sign a *promissory note*. This is just a straightforward IOU, worded along the following lines:

Antigonish, Nova Scotia
April 1, 1995

Sixty days after date I promise to pay to the order of the XYZ Company one thousand dollars ($1000) for value received.

Signature

Such an arrangement is not common but it does eliminate the possibility of any subsequent disputes about the existence of the debt; the customer knows that he or she may be sued immediately for failure to pay on the due date.

If you want a clear commitment from the buyer, it is more useful to have it *before* you deliver the goods. In this case the common procedure is to arrange a *commercial draft*. This is simply jargon for an order to pay.[1] It works as follows. The seller prepares a draft ordering payment by the customer and sends this draft to the customer's bank. If payment is required immediately, the draft is termed a *sight draft*; otherwise it is known as a *time draft*. Depending on whether it is a sight or a time draft, the customer either tells the bank to pay up or acknowledges the debt by adding the word *accepted* and a signature. Once accepted, a time draft is like a postdated cheque and is called a *trade acceptance*. This trade acceptance is then forwarded to the seller, who holds it until the payment becomes due.

If the customer's credit is for any reason suspect, the seller may ask the customer to arrange for his or her bank to accept the time draft. In this case, the bank guarantees the customer's debt and the draft is called a *banker's acceptance*.

---

[1] For example, a cheque is an example of a draft. Whenever you write a cheque, you are ordering the bank to make a payment.

Banker's acceptances are often used in overseas trade. They are actively traded in the money market, the market for short-term high-quality debt.

If you sell goods to a customer who proves unable to pay, you cannot get your goods back. You simply become a general creditor of the company, in common with other unfortunates. You can avoid this situation by making a *conditional sale*, so that ownership of the goods remains with the seller until full payment is made. The conditional sale is common in Europe. In Canada it is usually used only for goods that are bought on installment. In this case, if the customer fails to make the agreed number of payments, then the equipment can be immediately repossessed by the seller.

21.3   CREDIT ANALYSIS

credit analysis: Procedure to determine the likelihood a customer will pay its bills.

There are a number of ways to find out whether customers are likely to pay their debts, that is, to carry out **credit analysis**. The most obvious indication is whether they have paid promptly in the past. Prompt payment is usually a good omen, but beware of the customer who establishes a high credit limit on the basis of small payments and then disappears, leaving you with a large unpaid bill.

If you are dealing with a new customer, you will probably check with a credit agency. Dun and Bradstreet is by far the largest of these agencies; its regular *Reference Book* provides credit ratings on nearly 3 million firms. In addition to its rating service, Dun and Bradstreet provides on request a full credit report on a potential customer.[2]

Credit agencies usually report the experience that other firms have had with your customer, but you can also get this information by contacting the firm directly or through a credit bureau.

Your bank can also make a credit check. It will contact the customer's bank and ask for information on the customer's average bank balance, access to bank credit, and general reputation.

In addition to checking with your customer's bank, it might make sense to check what everybody else in the financial community thinks about your customer's credit standing. Does that sound expensive? Not if your customer is a public company. You just look at the Canada Bond Rating Service or Dominion Bond Rating Service's rating for the customer's bonds.[3] You can also compare prices of these bonds to the prices of other firms' bonds. (Of course the comparisons should be between bonds of similar maturity, coupon, and so on.) Finally, you can look at how the customer's stock price has been behaving recently. A sharp fall in price doesn't mean that the company is in trouble, but it does suggest that prospects are less bright than formerly.

Financial Ratio Analysis

We have suggested a number of ways to check whether your customer is a good risk. You can ask your collection manager, a specialized credit agency, a credit bureau, a banker, or the financial community at large. But if you don't like relying on the judgment of others, you can do your own homework. Ideally this would involve a detailed analysis of the company's business prospects and financing, but this is usually too expensive. Therefore, credit analysts concentrate on the company's financial statements, using rough rules of thumb to judge whether the firm is a good credit risk. The rules of thumb are based on *financial ratios*. Chapter 17 described how these ratios are calculated and interpreted.

---

[2] These reports are now available on line.
[3] We described bond ratings in Chapter 4, Section 4.1.

Numerical Credit Scoring

Analyzing credit risk is like detective work. You have a lot of clues — some important, some fitting into a neat pattern, others contradictory. You must weigh these clues to come up with an overall judgment.

When the firm has a small, regular clientele, the credit manager can easily handle the process informally and make a judgment about what are often termed the *five Cs of credit*:

1. The customer's *character*
2. The customer's *capacity* to pay
3. The customer's *capital*
4. The *collateral* provided by the customer
5. The *condition* of the customer's business

When the company is dealing directly with consumers or with a large number of small trade accounts, some streamlining is essential. In these cases it may make sense to use a scoring system to prescreen credit applications.

If you apply for a credit card or bank loan, you will be asked various questions about your job, home, and financial position. One medium-sized bank required each loan applicant to answer a standard questionnaire, of which a condensed variation is shown in Table 21.1 on page 548.[4] It found that in total only 1.2 percent of these loans subsequently defaulted. Some categories of borrower, however, proved to be much worse credit risks than others. We have added the actual default rates for each category in the right-hand margin of Table 21.1. For example, you can see that 7.0 percent of the borrowers who had no telephone subsequently defaulted. Similarly, below-average credit risks included borrowers who lived in rented rooms, had no bank account, needed the loan to pay medical bills, and so on.

Given this experience, it might make sense for the bank to calculate an overall risk index for each applicant.[5] For example, it could construct a rough-and-ready index simply by adding up all the probabilities in Table 21.1. In this case, the higher the score, the worse the credit rating. The wretch who gave the most unfavourable response to each question would have a risk index of

$$7.0 + 7.3 + 2.6 + \ldots = 51.8$$

As if he (or she) didn't have enough troubles!

SELF-TEST 21.2

How much better would the score be if the person bought a phone? What feature in Table 21.1 is potentially the most important determinant of credit rating?

The questionnaire in Table 21.1 is of course dated — not many loan applicants have a monthly income below $200! We wish we could give a real, current example, but they are all top secret: a bank with a superior method for identifying good and bad borrowers has a significant advantage over the competition.

Many users of credit scoring systems employ ad hoc formulas. For example, just adding up the separate probabilities, as in our bank example, ignores the interactions between the different factors. It may be much more alarming when a family of eight rents a single room than when a single applicant does.

---

[4] See P. F. Smith, "Measuring Risk on Consumer Installment Credit," *Management Science* 11 (November 1964): 327–340.
[5] There are some measures you *cannot* use in calculating this risk index or in any other credit evaluation — the applicant's sex or race, for example.

TABLE 21.1

A condensed version of a questionnaire used by a bank for personal loan applicants. We have added in parentheses the percentage of borrowers in each category who subsequently defaulted.

1. Do you have:		7. What is your marital status:	
1 or more telephones?	(.7)	Single?	(1.6)
No telephone?	(7.0)	Married?	(1.0)
2. Do you:		Divorced?	(2.9)
Own your home?	(.7)	8. What is your postal zone?	(.1 to 11.4)
Rent a house?	(2.2)	9. For how long do you require the loan:	
Rent an apartment?	(3.3)	12 months or less?	(1.6)
Rent a room?	(7.3)	More than 12 months?	(1.0)
3. Do you:		10. What is your occupation?	(.4 to 3.5)
Have 1 or more bank accounts?	(.8)	11. What is your monthly income:	
No bank account?	(2.6)	$200 or less?	(2.3)
4. Is the purpose of the loan:		$200 to $1000?	(1.1)
To buy an automobile?	(.8)	More than $1000?	(.7)
To buy household goods?	(.6)	12. What is your age:	
To pay medical expenses?	(2.5)	25 or under?	(1.5)
Other?	(1.3)	26 to 30?	(1.8)
5. How long did you spend in your last residence:		More than 30?	(1.0)
6 months or less?	(3.1)	13. How many are there in your family:	
7 to 60 months?	(1.4)	One?	(1.6)
More than 60 months?	(1.8)	Two to seven?	(1.1)
6. How long did you spend in your last job?		Eight or more?	(2.6)
6 months?	(3.2)		
7 to 60 months?	(1.5)		
More than 60 months?	(.9)		

Source: Reprinted by permission from P. F. Smith, "Measuring Risk on Consumer Installment Credit," *Management Science*, II:327–340 (November 1964), Copyright 1964 The Institute of Management Science.

Firms use several statistical techniques to separate the creditworthy sheep from the impecunious goats. One common method employs multiple discriminant analysis to produce a measure of solvency called a *Z score*. For example, a study by Edward Altman suggested the following relationship between a firm's financial ratios and its creditworthiness (*Z*):[6]

$$Z = 3.3 \frac{\text{EBIT}}{\text{total assets}} + 1.0 \frac{\text{sales}}{\text{total assets}} + .6 \frac{\text{market value of equity}}{\text{book debt}}$$

$$+ 1.4 \frac{\text{retained earnings}}{\text{total assets}} + 1.2 \frac{\text{working capital}}{\text{total assets}}$$

This equation did a good job at distinguishing the bankrupt and nonbankrupt firms. Of the former, 94 percent had Z scores *less* than 2.7 before they went bankrupt. In contrast, 97 percent of the nonbankrupt firms had Z scores *above* this level.[7]

When to Stop Looking for Clues

We told you earlier where to start looking for clues about a customer's creditworthiness, but we never said anything about when to *stop*. A detailed credit analysis costs money, so you need to keep the following principles in mind:

[6] EBIT is earnings before interest and taxes. E. I. Altman, "Financial Ratios, Discriminant Analysis and the Prediction of Corporate Bankruptcy," *Journal of Finance* 23 (September 1968), 589–609.
[7] This equation was fitted with hindsight. The equation did slightly less well when used to predict bankruptcies after 1965.

1. *Don't undertake a full credit analysis unless the order is big enough to justify it.* If the maximum profit on an order is $100, it is foolish to spend $200 to check whether the customer is a good prospect. Rely on a less detailed credit check for the smaller orders and save your energy and your money for the big orders.

2. *Undertake a full credit analysis for the doubtful orders only.* If a preliminary check suggests that a customer is almost certainly a good prospect, then the extra gain from a more searching inquiry is unlikely to justify the costs. That is why many firms use a numerical credit scoring system to identify borderline applicants, who are then the subject of a full-blown detailed credit check. Other applicants are either accepted or rejected without further question.

21.4 THE CREDIT DECISION

credit policy: Standards set to determine the amount and nature of credit to extend to customers.

You have taken the first three steps toward an effective credit operation. In other words, you have fixed your terms of sale; you have decided whether to sell on open account or to ask your customers to sign an IOU; and you have established a procedure for estimating the probability that each customer will pay up. Your next step is to decide on **credit policy.**

If there is no possibility of repeat orders, the credit decision is relatively simple. Figure 21.1 summarizes your choice. On the one hand, you can refuse credit and pass up the sale. In this case you make neither profit nor loss. The alternative is to offer credit. Suppose that the probability that the customer will pay up is p. If the customer does pay, you receive additional revenues (REV) and you deliver goods that you incurred costs to produce; your net gain is the present value of REV – COST. Unfortunately, you can't be certain that the customer will pay; there is a probability $(1 - p)$ of default. Default means you receive nothing but still incur the additional costs of the delivered goods. The *expected profit* from the two sources of action is therefore as follows:

Refuse credit: 0

Grant credit: $p \times \text{PV}(\text{REV} - \text{COST}) - (1 - p) \times \text{PV}(\text{COST})$

You should grant credit if the expected profit from doing so is greater than the expected profit from refusing.

FIGURE 21.1
If you refuse credit, you make neither profit nor loss. If you offer credit, there is a probability p that the customer will pay and you will make REV – COST; there is a probability $(1 - p)$ that the customer will default and you will lose COST.

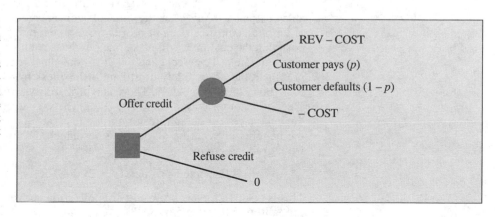

● **EXAMPLE 21.2 The Credit Decision**

Consider the case of the Cast Iron Company. On each nondelinquent sale Cast Iron receives revenues with a present value of $1200 and incurs costs with a present value of $1000. Therefore, the company's expected profit if it offers credit is

$$p \times PV(REV - COST) - (1 - p) \times PV(COST) = p \times 200 - (1 - p) \times 1000$$

If the probability of collection is 5/6, Cast Iron can expect to break even:

$$\text{Expected profit} = 5/6 \times 200 - (1 - 5/6) \times 1000 = 0$$

Thus Cast Iron's policy should be to grant credit whenever the chances of collection are better than 5 out of 6.

SELF-TEST 21.3

What is the break-even probability of collection if the present value of the revenues from the sale are $1100 rather than $1200? Why does the probability increase? Use your answer to decide whether firms that sell high-profit-margin or low-margin goods should be more willing to issue credit.

Credit Decisions with Repeat Orders

What effect does the possibility of repeat orders have on your credit decision? One of the reasons for offering credit today is that you may get yourself a good, regular customer.

Cast Iron has been asked to extend credit to a new customer. You can find little information on the firm and you believe that the probability of payment is no better than .8. If you grant credit, the expected profit on this order is

$$\text{Expected profit on initial order} = p \times PV(REV - COST) - (1 - p) \times PV(COST)$$

$$= (.8 \times 200) - (.2 \times 1000) = -\$40$$

You decide to refuse credit.

This is the correct decision *if* there is no chance of a repeat order. But now consider future periods. If the customer does pay up, there will be a reorder next year. Having paid once, the customer will seem less of a risk. For this reason, any repeat order is very profitable.

● **EXAMPLE 21.3 Credit Decisions with Repeat Orders**

To illustrate, let's look at an extreme case. Suppose that if a customer pays up on the first sale, you can be *sure* you will have a regular and completely reliable customer. In this case, the value of such a customer is not the profit on one order but an entire stream of profits from repeat purchases. For example, suppose that the customer will make one purchase each year from Cast Iron. If the discount rate is 10 percent and the profit on each order is $200 a year, then the present value of an indefinite stream of business from a good customer is not $200 but $200/.10 = $2000. There is a probability p that Cast Iron will secure a good customer with a value of $2000. There is a probability of $(1 - p)$ that the customer will default, resulting in a loss of $1000. So, once we recognize the benefits of securing a good and permanent customer, the expected profit from granting credit is

$$\text{Expected profit} = (p \times 2000) - (1 - p) \times (1000)$$

This is positive for any probability of collection above .33. Thus the break-even probability falls from 5/6 to 1/3.

SELF-TEST 21.4

> How will the break-even probability vary with the discount rate? Try a rate of 20 percent. What is the intuition behind your answer?

Some General Principles

Real-life situations are generally far more complex than our simple examples. Customers are not all good or all bad. Many pay late consistently; you get your money, but it costs more to collect and you lose a few months' interest. And estimating the probability that a customer will pay up is far from an exact science.

Like almost all financial decisions, credit allocation involves a strong dose of judgment. Our examples are intended as reminders of the issues involved rather than as cookbook formulas. Here are the basic things to remember.

1. *Maximize profit.* As credit manager your job is not to minimize the number of bad accounts; it is to maximize profits. You must recognize, therefore, that you are concerned with a trade off. The best that can happen is that the customer pays promptly; the worst is default. In the one case the firm receives the full additional revenues from the sale less the additional costs; in the other it receives nothing and loses the costs. You must weigh the chances of these alternative outcomes. If the margin of profit is high, you are justified in a liberal credit policy; if it is low, you cannot afford many bad debts.

2. *Concentrate on the dangerous accounts.* You should not expend the same effort on analyzing all credit decisions. If an application is small or clear-cut, your decision should be largely routine; if it is large or doubtful, you may do better to move straight to a detailed credit appraisal. Most credit managers don't make credit decisions on an order-by-order basis. Instead they set a credit limit for each customer. The sales representative is required to refer the order for approval only if the customer exceeds this limit.

3. *Look beyond the immediate order.* Sometimes it may be worth accepting a relatively poor risk as long as there is a likelihood that the customer will grow into a regular and reliable buyer. (This is why credit card companies are eager to sign up college students even though few students can point to an established credit history.) New businesses must be prepared to incur more bad debts than established businesses because they have not yet formed relationships with low-risk customers. This is part of the cost of building up a good customer list.

21.5 COLLECTION POLICY

It would be nice if all customers paid their bills by the due date. But they don't, and, since you may also "stretch" your payables, you can't altogether blame them.

Slow payers impose two costs on the firm. First, they require the firm to spend more resources in collecting payments. They also force the firm to invest more in working capital. Recall from Chapter 17 that accounts receivable are proportional to the average collection period (also known as days' sales in receivables):

$$\text{Accounts receivable} = \text{daily sales} \times \text{average collection period}$$

collection policy: Procedures to collect and monitor receivables.

When your customers stretch payables, you end up with a longer collection period and a greater investment in accounts receivable. Thus you must establish a **collection policy.**

The credit manager keeps a record of payment experiences with each customer. In addition, the manager monitors overdue payments by drawing up a schedule

aging schedule: Classification of accounts receivable by time outstanding.

of the aging of receivables. The **aging schedule** classifies accounts receivable by the length of time they are outstanding. This may look roughly like Table 21.2. The table shows that customer A, for example, is fully current: there are no bills outstanding for more than a month. Customer Z, however, might present problems, as there are $15,000 in bills that have been outstanding for more than 3 months.

TABLE 21.2

An aging schedule of receivables

Customer's Name	Less than 1 Month	1–2 Months	2–3 Months	More than 3 Months	Total Owed
A	$ 10,000	$ 0	$ 0	$ 0	$ 10,000
B	8,000	3,000	0	0	11,000
.	.	.	.	.	.
.	.	.	.	.	.
.	.	.	.	.	.
Z	5,000	4,000	6,000	15,000	30,000
Total	$200,000	$40,000	$15,000	$43,000	$298,000

When a customer is in arrears, the usual procedure is to send a *statement of account* and to follow this at intervals with increasingly insistent letters, telephone calls, or fax messages. If none of these has any effect, most companies turn the debt over to a collection agency or an attorney. The fee for such services is usually between 15 and 40 percent of the amount collected.

SELF-TEST 21.5

Suppose a customer who buys goods on terms 1/10, net 45 always forgoes the cash discount and pays on the 45th day after sale. If the firm typically buys $10,000 of goods a month, spread evenly over the month, what will the aging schedule look like?

There is always a potential conflict of interest between the collection department and the sales department. Sales representatives commonly complain that they no sooner win new customers than the collection department frightens them off with threatening letters. The collection manager, on the other hand, bemoans the fact that the sales force is concerned only with winning orders and does not care whether the goods are subsequently paid for.

On the other hand, there are also instances of cooperation between sales managers and the financial managers who worry about collections. For example, the specialty chemicals division of a major pharmaceutical company actually made a business loan to an important customer that had been suddenly cut off by its bank. The pharmaceutical company bet that it knew its customer better than the customer's bank did — and the pharmaceutical company was right. The customer arranged alternative bank financing, paid back the pharmaceutical company, and became an even more loyal customer. It was a nice example of financial management supporting sales.

21.6 BANKRUPTCY

bankruptcy: The reorganization or liquidation of a firm that cannot pay its debts.

Each year about 40,000 individuals and 10,000 businesses file for **bankruptcy** in Canada. So it is a rare firm that never has a customer who becomes bankrupt. In this section we outline the procedures involved.

Our focus here is on business bankruptcies. These account for only about 20 percent of the total number of bankruptcies, but because they are larger than individ-

Finance in Action

Near Death Experiences

....

It's tempting to believe that it's safe to skip the credit checking if you are deal-ing with large, well-known companies. But there is no such safety, and even gov-ernments can be bad credit risks, as suppliers to Orange County, California recently learned when the County filed for bankruptcy. When it comes to decid-ing what firms to give credit to, neither a great product, nor tremendous prod-uct recognition, nor even profitable and growing sales is necessarily enough to save a firm from glimpsing the great beyond. And perhaps defaulting on any credit you have unwisely given to them.

Companies that have come extremely close to bankruptcy include Grey-hound Lines, Federal Express, the West Edmonton Mall, Magna International, and Chrysler Corporation.

Companies that have demon-strated that there can be life after death include Henry Birks and Sons, People's Jewellers, The Penn Central Railroad, and Algoma Steel.

Despite their fame, Nutri/system, Mother's Pizza, Multitech Warehouse Direct, and Beaver Canoe all went to the brink. Still, the strongest warning to all who would ignore the need for careful financial management and plan-ning comes from one firm now emerg-ing from bankruptcy — Hayes Micro-computer Systems. Hayes spent twelve years as the world's best-known and largest producer of modems for per-sonal computers. However, being a profitable firm with great name recog-nition and with rapidly growing rev-enue was not enough to save Hayes from filing for protection from its creditors in November 1994. Modem orders had surged rapidly during the previous year, and when Hayes attempted to meet the huge growth by subcontracting for additional man-ufacturing facilities, it had problems getting production on stream. As inventories of parts and work in progress soared while shipments of finished goods were delayed, Hayes succumbed to severe cash flow prob-lems and filed for bankruptcy protec-tion under the American "Chapter 11" legislation.

ual bankruptcies, they involve about half of all claims by value. There are also more complications when a business declares bankruptcy than when an individual does so.

....
Bankruptcy Procedures

A corporation that cannot pay its debts will often try to come to an informal agree-ment with its creditors. This is known as a **workout**. A workout may take several forms. For example, the firm may negotiate an *extension*, that is, an agreement with its creditors to delay payments. Or the firm may negotiate a *composition*, in which the firm makes partial payments to its creditors in exchange for being relieved of its debts. The company may also try to *restructure* its debt by exchang-ing outstanding debt for new securities, often including equity.

workout: Informal ar-rangement between debtor and creditor establishing steps debtor may take to avoid declaring bank-ruptcy.

The advantage of a negotiated agreement is that the costs and delays of formal bankruptcy are avoided. However, the larger the firm, and the more complicated its capital structure, the less likely it is that a negotiated settlement can be reached. (For example, when Confederation Life collapsed it owed money to

170,000 life insurance policyholders and had issued debt in British pounds, Japanese yen, and Luxembourg francs.)

If the firm cannot get an agreement, then it may end up having to deal with a bankruptcy judge. Bankruptcy law in Canada is usually governed by the *Bankruptcy Act*. In addition, some companies are governed by the *Winding-up Act* and the *Companies Creditors' Arrangement Act*. These laws provide mechanisms through which creditors can try to collect on what they are owed by having a firm **liquidated** and the proceeds distributed. Secured creditors get the proceeds from the assets they have title to while unsecured creditors share in what is left over.

liquidation: Sale of bankrupt firm's assets.

There is a pecking order of unsecured creditors. First come claims for expenses that arise after bankruptcy is filed, such as attorney's fees. Next come claims for wages and employee benefits earned in the period immediately prior to the filing. Taxes are next in line, together with debts to some government agencies such as the Workers' Compensation Board. Finally come general unsecured claims such as bond debentures or unsecured trade debt.

In addition to providing for the liquidation of the firm, the laws governing bankruptcy also provide for an alternative to liquidation. The process of avoiding liquidation starts with the sometimes lengthy negotiation outside of court that we mentioned above and, if claimants cannot settle, continues with formal negotiations under the supervision of the court. A recent example is the case of Cadillac Fairview, the real estate company that owns such well-known landmarks as Portage Place in Winnipeg, Pacific Centre in Vancouver, and Eaton Centre and Toronto-Dominion Centre in Toronto. In February of 1994 the company announced that it would attempt to restructure about $5.8 billion in debt. In March the company failed to make payments on some of its mortgage debt. The company continued to negotiate with its creditors but when one of them, Goldman Sachs & Co., took legal action against the firm in December, Cadillac Fairview responded by seeking court *protection* from its creditors. This protection came in the form of a *stay* granted to the firm under the Companies Creditors' Arrangement Act. The stay prevents creditors from taking action to collect on its debt until the firm files a *proposal* or a *proposal for arrangement*. Furthermore, the court also requires time for the proposal to be considered and voted upon by the creditors.

In some cases, this procedure results in a newly structured firm emerging from financial distress. In others, however, things just don't work out and protection from creditors does not last forever. For example, less than a week after the court granted bankruptcy protection to Cadillac Fairview, a judge lifted the stay under which Pennington's had been trying to restructure for several months. Once the stay was lifted, creditors were able to proceed with liquidation.

reorganization: Restructuring of financial claims on failing firm to allow it to keep operating.

An informal **reorganization** plan offered outside of court or the formal proposal filed with a court are basically statements of who gets what; each class of creditors gives up its claim in exchange for new securities. (Sometimes creditors receive cash as well.) The problem is to design a new capital structure for the firm that will (1) satisfy the creditors and (2) allow the firm to solve the business problems that got the firm into trouble in the first place. Sometimes only a plan of baroque complexity can satisfy these two requirements. When the Penn Central Corporation was finally reorganized in 1978 (7 years after it became the largest railroad bankruptcy ever), more than a dozen new securities were created and parceled out among 15 classes of creditors.

....
The Choice between Liquidation and Reorganization

Here is an idealized view of the bankruptcy decision. Whenever a payment is due to creditors, management checks the value of the firm. If the firm is worth more than the debt, the firm pays the creditors (if necessary, raising the cash by an issue of shares). If not, the equity is worthless, and the firm defaults on its debt and petitions for bankruptcy. If in the court's judgment the assets of the bankrupt firm can be put to better use elsewhere, the firm is liquidated and the proceeds are used to pay off the creditors. Otherwise, the creditors simply become the new owners and the firm continues to operate.

In practice, matters are rarely so simple. For example, we observe that firms often petition for bankruptcy even when the equity has a positive value. And firms are often reorganized even when the assets could be used more efficiently elsewhere. We next discuss some reasons.

First, although the reorganized firm is legally a new entity, it is entitled to any tax-loss carry-forwards belonging to the old firm. If the firm is liquidated rather than reorganized, any tax-loss carry-forwards disappear. Thus there is an incentive to continue in operation.

Second, if the firm's assets are sold off, it is easy to determine what is available to pay the creditors. However, when the company is reorganized, it needs to conserve cash as far as possible. Therefore, claimants are generally paid in a mixture of cash and securities. This makes it less easy to judge whether they receive their entitlement. For example, each bondholder may be offered $300 in cash and $700 in a new bond that pays no interest for the first 2 years and a low rate of interest thereafter. A bond of this kind in a company that is struggling to survive may not be worth much in the eyes of the creditors. But the bankruptcy court may disagree and decide that with the new securities the bondholders have received as much as they would have if the firm was liquidated.

Senior creditors who know they are likely to get a raw deal in a reorganization are likely to press for a liquidation. Shareholders and junior creditors prefer a reorganization. They hope that the court will not interpret the pecking order too strictly and that they will receive some crumbs.

Third, although shareholder and junior creditors are at the bottom of the pecking order, they have a secret weapon: they can play for time. Bankruptcies often take several years before a plan is presented to the court and agreed to by each class of creditor. (The bankruptcy proceedings of the Missouri Pacific Railroad took a total of 22 years.) When they use delaying tactics, the junior claimants are betting on a turn of fortune that will rescue their investment. On the other hand, the senior creditors know that time is working against them, so they may be prepared to accept a smaller payoff as part of the price for getting a plan accepted. Also, prolonged bankruptcy cases are costly (Pennington's creditors claimed that the firm was spending $100,000 a week on consulting, legal, and other fees). Senior claimants may see their money seeping into lawyers' pockets and therefore decide to settle quickly.

Finally, profitable companies may file for court protection to avoid "burdensome" suits. For example, in 1982 Manville Corporation was threatened by 16,000 damage suits alleging injury from asbestos. Manville filed for bankruptcy protection, and the bankruptcy judge agreed to put the damage suits on hold until the company was reorganized. This took 6 years. Of course legislators worry that these actions are contrary to the original intent of the bankruptcy acts.

 **SUMMARY**

1. The first step in credit management is to set normal terms of sale. This means that you must decide the length of the payment period and the size of any cash discounts. In most industries these conditions are standardized.

2. Your second step is to decide the form of the contract with your customer. Most domestic sales are made on open account. In this case the only evidence that the customer owes you money is the entry in your ledger and a receipt signed by the customer. Sometimes, you may require a more formal commitment before you deliver the goods. For example, the supplier may arrange for the customer to provide a trade acceptance.

3. The third task is to assess each customer's creditworthiness. There are various sources of information: your own experience with the customer, the experience of other creditors, the assessment of a credit agency, a check with the customer's bank, the market value of the customer's securities, and an analysis of the customer's financial statements. Firms that handle a large volume of credit information often use a formal system for combining the various sources into an overall credit score.

4. When you have made an assessment of the customer's credit standing, you can establish sensible credit limits. The job of the credit manager is not to minimize the number of bad debts; it is to maximize profits. This means that you need to weigh the odds that the customer will pay, providing you with a profit, or that the customer will default, resulting in a loss. Remember not to be too shortsighted when reckoning the expected profit. It is often worth accepting the marginal applicant if there is a chance that the applicant may become a regular and reliable customer.

5. The next problem is to collect. This requires tact and judgment. You want to be firm with the truly delinquent customer, but you don't want to offend the good one by writing demanding letters just because a cheque has been delayed in the mail. You will find it easier to spot troublesome accounts if you keep a careful record of the aging of receivables.

6. Firms that cannot meet their obligations may end up dealing with bankruptcy laws, in which case the business may be liquidated or reorganized. Liquidation means that the firm's assets are sold and the proceeds used to pay creditors. Reorganization means that the firm is maintained as an ongoing concern, and creditors are compensated with securities in the reorganized firm. Ideally, reorganization should be chosen over liquidation when the firm as a going concern is worth more than its liquidation value. However, the conflicting interests of the different parties can result in violations of this principle.

KEY TERMS

terms of sale	**collection policy**	**workout**
open account	**aging schedule**	**liquidation**
credit analysis	**bankruptcy**	**reorganization**
credit policy		

SUGGESTED READINGS

A standard text on the practice and institutional background of credit management is

R. H. Cole. *Consumer and Commercial Credit Management*, 8th ed. Homewood, Ill.: Richard D. Irwin, 1987.

A general overview of bankruptcy is provided in

E. A. Altman. *Corporate Financial Distress: A Complete Guide to Predicting, Avoiding and Dealing with Bankruptcy.* New York: John Wiley & Sons, 1983.

PROBLEMS

1. Company X sells on a 1/20, net 60, basis. Customer Y buys goods with an invoice of $1000.
   a. How much can Y deduct from the bill if he or she pays on Day 20?
   b. How many extra days of credit can Company Y receive if it passes up the cash discount?
   c. What is the effective annual rate of interest if Y pays on the due date rather than Day 20?

2. Indicate which firm of each pair you would expect to grant shorter or longer credit periods:
   a. One firm sells hardware; the other sells bread.
   b. One firm has an inventory turnover ratio of 10; the other has turnover of 15.
   c. The bonds of one firm are rated A+ by Canada Bond Rating Service; the other's bonds are rated B+.

3. The lag between purchase date and the date at which payment is due is known as the *terms lag*. The lag between the due date and the date on which the buyer actually pays is termed the *due lag*, and the lag between the purchase and actual payment dates is the *pay lag*. Thus

   $$\text{Pay lag} = \text{terms lag} + \text{due lag}$$

   State how you would expect the following events to affect each type of lag:
   a. The company imposes a service charge on late payers.
   b. A recession causes customers to be short of cash.
   c. The company changes its terms from net 10 to net 20.

4. A firm currently offers terms of sale of 3/20, net 40. What effect will the following actions have on the implicit interest rate charged to customers that pass up the cash discount? State whether the implicit interest rate will increase or decrease.
   a. The terms are changed to 4/20, net 40.
   b. The terms are changed to 3/30, net 40.
   c. The terms are changed to 3/20, net 30.

5. A firm currently makes only cash sales. It estimates that allowing trade credit on terms of net 30 would increase monthly sales from 200 to 220 units per month. The price per unit is $101 and the cost (in present value terms) is $80. The interest rate is 1 percent per month.
   a. Should the firm change its credit policy?
   b. Would your answer to (a) change if 5 percent of all customers will fail to pay their bills under the new credit policy?
   c. What if 5 percent of only the new customers fail to pay their bills? The current customers take advantage of the 30 days of free credit but remain safe credit risks.

6. Complete the following passage by selecting the appropriate terms from the following list (some terms may be used more than once): *acceptance,*

open, commercial, trade, the Canada, his or her own, note, draft, account, promissory, bank, banker's, the customer's, shipping, documents.

Most goods are sold on _____ . In this case the only evidence of the debt is a record in the seller's books and a signed receipt. When the order is very large, the customer may be asked to sign a(n) _____ , which is just a simple IOU. An alternative is for the seller to arrange a(n) _____ ordering payment by the customer. In order to obtain the _____ , the customer must acknowledge this order and sign the document. This signed acknowledgment is known as a(n) _____ . Sometimes the seller may also ask _____ bank to sign the document. In this case it is known as a(n) _____ .

7. Locust Software sells computer training packages to its business customers at a price of $101. The cost of production (in present value terms) is $95. Locust sells its packages on terms of net 30 and estimates that about 7 percent of all orders will be uncollectible. An order comes in for 20 units. The interest rate is 1 percent per month.
   a. Should the firm extend credit if this is a one-time order? The sale will not be made unless credit is extended.
   b. What is the break-even probability of collection?
   c. Now suppose that if a customer pays this month's bill, it will place an identical order each month indefinitely and can be safely assumed to pose no risk of default. Should credit be extended?
   d. What is the break-even probability of collection in the repeat-sales case?

8. The Branding Iron Company sells its irons for $50 apiece wholesale. Production cost is $40 per iron. There is a 25 percent chance that a prospective customer will go bankrupt within the next half year. The customer orders 1000 irons and asks for 6 months' credit. Should you accept the order? Assume a 10 percent per year discount rate, no chance of a repeat order, and that the customer will pay either in full or not at all.

9. Look back at Example 21.2. Cast Iron's costs have increased from $1000 to $1050. Assuming there is no possibility of repeat orders, and that the probability of successful collection from the customer is $p = .9$, answer the following:
   a. Should Cast Iron grant or refuse credit?
   b. What is the break-even probability of collection?

10. This is a bit harder. Use the data in Example 21.2. Now suppose, however, that 10 percent of Cast Iron's customers are slow payers, and that slow payers have a probability of 30 percent of defaulting on their bills. If it costs $5 to determine whether a customer has been a prompt or slow payer in the past, should Cast Iron undertake such a check? *Hint:* What is the expected savings from the credit check? It will depend on both the probability of uncovering a slow payer and the savings from denying these payers credit.

11. Look back at problem 10, but now suppose that if a customer defaults on a payment, you can eventually collect about half the amount owed to you. Will you be more or less tempted to pay for a credit check once you account for the possibility of partial recovery of debts?

12. True or false?
   a. It makes sense to monitor the credit manager's performance by looking at the proportion of bad debts.

b. When a company becomes bankrupt, it is usually in the interests of the equityholders to seek a liquidation rather than a reorganization.

c. A reorganization plan must be presented for approval by each class of creditor.

d. Revenue Canada has first claim on the company's assets in the event of bankruptcy.

e. In a reorganization, creditors may be paid off with a mixture of cash and securities.

f. When a company is liquidated, one of the most valuable assets to be sold is often the tax-loss carry-forward.

13. As treasurer of the Universal Bed Corporation, Aristotle Procrustes is worried about his bad debt ratio, which is currently running at 6 percent. He believes that imposing a more stringent credit policy might reduce sales by 5 percent and reduce the bad debt ratio to 4 percent. If the cost of goods sold is 80 percent of the selling price, should Mr. Procrustes adopt the more stringent policy?

14. Jim Khana, the credit manager of Velcro Saddles, is reappraising the company's credit policy. Velcro sells on terms of net 30. Cost of goods sold is 85 percent of sales and fixed costs are a further 5 percent of sales. Velcro classifies customers on a scale of 1 to 4. During the past 5 years, the collection experience was as follows:

Classification	Defaults as Percentage of Sales	Average Collection Period in Days for Nondefaulting Accounts
1	0	45
2	2	42
3	10	50
4	20	80

The average interest rate was 15 percent. What conclusions (if any) can you draw about Velcro's credit policy? Should the firm deny credit to any of its customers? What other factors should be taken into account before changing this policy?

15. Financial ratios were described in Chapter 17. If you were the credit manager, to which financial ratios would you pay most attention? Which do you think would be the least informative?

16. Explain why equity can sometimes have a positive value even when companies petition for bankruptcy.

17. Reliant Umbrellas has been approached by Plumpton Variety Stores of Manitoba. Plumpton has expressed interest in an initial purchase of 5000 umbrellas at $10 each on Reliant's standard terms of 2/30, net 60. Plumpton estimates that if the umbrellas prove popular with customers, its purchases could be in the region of 30,000 umbrellas a year. After deducting variable costs, this would provide an addition of $47,000 to Reliant's profits.

Reliant has been eager for some time to break into the lucrative Manitoba market, but its credit manager has some doubts about Plumpton. In the past 5 years, Plumpton had embarked on an aggressive program of store openings. In 1991, however, it went into reverse. The recession combined with aggressive price competition caused a cash shortage. Plumpton laid off employees, closed one store, and deferred store openings. The company's Canada Bond Rating Service rating is only fair and a check with Plumpton's other suppliers reveals that although Plumpton has traditionally taken cash discounts, it has recently been paying 30 days slow. A check through Reliant's bank indicates that Plumpton has unused credit lines of $350,000 but has entered into discussions with the banks for a renewal of a $1,500,000 term loan due at the end of the year. The accompanying tables summarize Plumpton's latest financial statements.

a. As credit manager of Reliant, what is your attitude to extending credit to Plumpton? Specifically, what must be the probability of payment to justify sales?

b. How might you use financial ratio analysis to help make your decision? Ratios for the nonfinancial industries are given in Table 17.8.

BALANCE SHEET
(figures in millions)

	1994	1993		1994	1993
Cash	$ 1.0	$ 1.2	Payables	$ 2.3	$ 2.5
Receivables	1.5	1.6	Short-term loans	3.9	1.9
Inventory	10.9	11.6	Long-term debt	1.8	2.6
Fixed assets	5.1	4.3	Equity	10.5	11.7
Total assets	$18.5	$18.7	Total liabilities and equity	$18.5	$18.7

INCOME STATEMENT
(figures in millions)

	1994	1993
Sales	$55.0	$59.0
Cost of goods sold	32.6	35.9
Selling, general, and administrative expenses	20.8	20.2
Interest	.5	.3
Tax	.5	1.3
Net income	.6	1.3

18. Galenic, Inc. is a wholesaler for a range of pharmaceutical products. Before deducting any losses from bad debts, Galenic operates on a profit margin of 5 percent. For a long time the firm has employed a numerical credit scoring system based on a small number of key ratios. This has resulted in a bad debt ratio of 1 percent.

Galenic has recently commissioned a detailed statistical study of the payment record of its customers over the past 8 years and, after considerable experimentation, has identified five variables that could form the basis of a new credit scoring system. On the evidence of the past 8 years, Galenic calculates that for every 10,000 accounts it would have experienced the following default rates:

Credit Score under Proposed System	Number of Accounts		
	Defaulting	**Paying**	**Total**
Better than 80	60	9,100	9,160
Worse than 80	40	800	840
Total	100	9,900	10,000

By refusing credit to firms with a poor credit score (worse than 80) Galenic calculates that it would reduce its bad debt ratio to 60/9160, or just under .7 percent. While this may not seem like a big deal, Galenic's credit manager reasons that this is equivalent to a decrease of one-third in the bad debt ratio and would result in a significant improvement in the profit margin.

a. What is Galenic's current profit margin, allowing for bad debts?

b. Assuming that the firm's estimates of default rates are right, how would the new credit scoring system affect profits?

c. Why might you suspect that Galenic's estimates of default rates will not be realized in practice? What are the likely consequences of overestimating the accuracy of such a credit scoring scheme?

d. Suppose that one of the variables in the proposed new scoring system is whether the customer has an existing account with Galenic (new customers are more likely to default). How would this affect your assessment of the proposal? *Hint:* Think about repeat sales.

SOLUTIONS TO SELF-TEST QUESTIONS

21.1   Passing up the discount results in 50 extra days of credit, at the cost of a 2 percent discount. The implied interest rate is 2/98 = 2.041% per 50 days. As an effective annual rate, this corresponds to $(1.02041)^{365/50} - 1 = .159$, or 15.9 percent. The annualized rate is lower than in Example 21.1 because more days of additional credit can be obtained by forfeiting the 2 percent discount.

21.2   The credit score would improve by 6.3, the difference between the score for no telephone (7.0) and one or more telephones (.7). The feature with the potentially greatest impact on credit score is the postal zone.

21.3   The present value of costs is still $1000. Present value of revenues are now $1100. The break-even probability is defined by

$$p \times 100 - (1 - p) \times 1000 = 0$$

which implies that $p = .909$. The break-even probability is higher because the profit margin is now lower. The firm cannot afford as high a bad debt ratio as before since it is not making as much on its successful sales. We conclude that high-margin goods will be offered with more liberal credit terms.

21.4   The higher the discount rate the less important are future sales. Because the value of repeat sales is lower, the break-even probability on the initial sale is higher. For instance, we saw that the break-even probability was 1/3 when the discount rate was 10 percent. When the discount rate is 20 percent, the value of a perpetual flow of repeat sales falls to $200/.20 = $1000, and the break-even probability increases to 1/2:

$$1/2 \times \$1000 - 1/2 \times \$1000 = 0$$

21.5   The customer pays bills 45 days after the invoice date. Because goods are purchased daily, at any time there will be bills outstanding with "ages" ranging from 1 to 45 days. At any time, the customer will have 30 days' worth of purchases, or $10,000, outstanding for a period of up to 1 month, and 15 days' worth of purchases, or $5000, outstanding for between 1 month and 45 days. The aging schedule will appear as follows:

Age of Account	Amount
< month	$10,000
1–2 months	$ 5,000

PART EIGHT

Special Topics

CHAPTER TWENTY-TWO

Mergers, Acquisitions, and Corporate Control

The pace of merger activity by Canadian companies is sometimes remarkable. The money involved is sometimes even more remarkable. (Table 22.1 lists some of the more impressive recent takeovers.) During periods of intense merger activity, financial managers spend significant amounts of time searching for firms to acquire or worrying that some other firm will acquire them.

When one company buys another, it is making an investment, and the basic principles of capital investment decisions apply. You should go ahead with the purchase if it makes a net contribution to shareholders' wealth. But mergers are often awkward transactions to evaluate. First, you have to be careful to define benefits and costs properly. Second, buying a company is more complicated than buying a new machine; special tax, legal, and accounting issues must often be addressed.

Many mergers are arranged amicably, but in other cases one firm will make a hostile takeover bid for the other. We describe the principal techniques of modern merger warfare, and since the threat of hostile takeovers has stimulated corporate restructurings and leveraged buy-outs (LBOs), we describe them too, and attempt to explain why these deals have generated rewards for investors. We close with a look at who gains and loses from mergers and we discuss whether mergers are beneficial on balance.

After studying this chapter you should be able to

- Describe ways the companies change their ownership or management.
- Explain why it may make sense for companies to merge.
- Estimate the gains and costs of mergers to the acquiring firm.
- Describe takeover defenses.
- Summarize the evidence on whether mergers increase efficiency and on how the gains from mergers are distributed between shareholders of the acquired and acquiring firms.

THE MARKET FOR CORPORATE CONTROL

The shareholders are the owners of the firm. But most shareholders do not feel like the boss, and with good reason. Try buying a share of Molson Co. stock and marching into the boardroom for a chat with your employee, the chief executive officer.

There is substantial separation between the *ownership* and *management* of large corporations. Shareholders do not directly appoint or supervise the firm's managers. They elect the board of directors, who act as their agents in choosing and monitoring the managers of the firm. Shareholders have a direct say in very few matters. Control of the firm is in the hands of the managers, subject to the general oversight of the board of directors.

What ensures that the board has engaged the most talented managers? What happens if managers are inadequate? What if the board of directors is derelict in monitoring the performance of managers? Or what if the firm's managers are fine, but resources of the firm could be used more efficiently by merging with another firm? Can we count on managers to pursue arrangements that would put them out of jobs?

These are all questions about the *market for corporate control*, the mechanisms by which firms are matched up with management teams and owners who can make the most of the firm's resources. You should not take a firm's current ownership and management for granted. If it is possible for the value of the firm to be enhanced by changing management or by reorganizing under new owners, there will be incentives for someone to make the changes.

There are four general ways in which the management of a firm can change. These are (1) a successful proxy fight in which a group of stockholders votes in a new group of directors, who then pick a new management team; (2) the purchase of one firm by another in a merger or acquisition; (3) a leveraged buy-out of the firm by a private group of investors; and (4) a divestiture, in which a firm either sells part of its operations to another company or spins it off as an independent firm. We will review briefly each of these methods.

Proxy Contests

Shareholders elect the board of directors to serve as their agents by keeping a watch on management and replacing unsatisfactory managers. If the board is lax, shareholders are free to elect a different board. Therefore, in theory the corporation should be run in the best interests of shareholders.

In practice things are not so clear-cut. Ownership in large corporations is widely dispersed among diversified investors. Usually even the largest single shareholder holds only a small fraction of the shares. Most shareholders have little notion who is on the board or what the members stand for. Management, on the other hand, deals directly with the board and has a personal relationship with its members. In most corporations, management sits on the committee that nominates candidates for the board. It is not surprising that some boards seem less than aggressive in forcing managers to run a lean operation or to act primarily in the interests of shareholders.

When a group of investors believes that the board and its management team should be replaced, they can engage in a **proxy contest**. A proxy is the right that one shareholder can give to another to vote his or her shares. In a proxy contest, the dissident shareholders attempt to obtain enough proxies to elect their own slate to the board of directors. Once the new board is in control, management can be replaced. A proxy fight is therefore a direct contest for control of the corporation.

proxy contest: Takeover attempt in which outsiders compete with management for shareholders' votes. Also called *proxy fight*.

However, the great majority of proxy contests fail. Dissidents who engage in such fights must use their own money, while management can use the corporation's funds and lines of communication with shareholders to defend itself. Such fights can cost millions of dollars[1].

Institutional shareholders such as large pension funds recently have become aggressive in pressing for managerial accountability. These funds have been able to gain concessions from firms without initiating proxy contests. For example, firms have agreed to split the jobs of chief executive officer and chairman of the board of directors. This ensures that an outsider is responsible for keeping watch over the company.

Acquisitions

Proxy contests are rare, and successful ones are rarer still. Poorly performing managers face a greater risk from acquisition. If the management of one firm observes another firm underperforming, it can try to acquire the business and replace the poor managers with its own team. If the new team is better, investors will revise

---

[1] P. Dodd and J. Warner have written a detailed description and analysis of proxy fights. See "On Corporate Governance: A Study of Proxy Contests," *Journal of Financial Economics* 2 (April 1985), pp. 401–438.

their expectations of performance and the stock price of the acquired firm will increase. Thus, in practice, corporate takeovers are the arenas where contests for corporate control are usually fought.

There are three ways for one firm to acquire another. Although we usually refer to all combinations of two firms as a *merger*, this is too broad in a legal sense. The one possibility that is legally referred to as a **merger**[2] occurs when the acquiring company assumes all the assets and all the liabilities of the other. Such a merger must have the approval of at least 50 percent of the stockholders of each firm[3]. The acquired firm ceases to exist, and its former shareholders receive cash and/or securities in the acquiring firm. In many mergers there is a clear acquiring company, whose management then runs the enlarged firm. However, a merger is often a combination of two equals with both managements having a major say in the running of the new company. The merger between Time and Warner Communications was an example of a merger of equals.

A second alternative is for the acquiring firm to buy the target firm's stock in exchange for cash, shares, or other securities. The acquired firm may continue to exist as a separate entity, but it is now owned by the acquirer. The approval and cooperation of the target firm's managers are generally sought, but even if they resist, the acquirer can attempt to purchase a majority of the outstanding shares. By offering to buy shares directly from shareholders, the acquiring firm can bypass the target firm's management altogether. The offer to purchase stock is called a tender offer. If the **tender offer** is successful, the buyer obtains control and can, if it chooses, toss out incumbent management.

The third approach is to buy the target firm's assets. In this case ownership of the assets needs to be transferred, and payment is made to the selling firm rather than directly to its stockholders. Usually, the target firm sells only some of its assets. For example, in 1995 Thomson Corp. put 25 small U.S. newspapers that it owns up for sale. Thompson, one of Canada's biggest companies, will continue to operate its other newspapers and businesses. Occasionally, the target firm sells *all* its assets. It continues to exist as an independent entity, but it becomes an empty shell — a corporation engaged in no business activity.

Table 22.1 lists some recent important mergers and acquisitions.

merger: Combination of two firms into one, with the acquirer assuming assets and liabilities of the target firm.

tender offer: Takeover attempt in which outsiders directly offer to buy the stock of the firm's shareholders.

leveraged buy-out (LBO): Acquisition of the firm by a private group using substantial borrowed funds.

Leveraged Buy-outs

management buy-out (MBO): Acquisition of the firm by its own management in a leveraged buy-out.

Sometimes a group of investors buys the firm by means of a **leveraged buy-out**, or **LBO**. In an LBO the group takes the firm private and its shares no longer trade in the securities markets. Usually a considerable proportion of its financing is obtained by borrowing funds, hence the term *leveraged* buy-out. Often the investor group is led by the management of the firm, in which case the takeover is called a **management buy-out**, or **MBO**. In this case, the firm's managers actually buy the firm from the shareholders and continue to run it. They become owner-managers. We will discuss LBOs and MBOs later in the chapter.

Divestitures and Spin-offs

Firms not only acquire businesses; they also sell them. *Divestitures* are part of the market for corporate control. In recent years the number of divestitures has been about half the number of mergers.

Instead of selling a business to another firm, companies may spin off a subsidiary by separating it from the parent firm and distributing stock in the newly independent company to the shareholders of the parent company. For example, the British chemical company ICI spun off its pharmaceutical business into a new $2

---

[2] In Canada this is more precisely referred to as a *statutory amalgamation*.
[3] Corporate charters sometimes specify a higher percentage.

TABLE 22.1

Some large mergers and
acquisitions

Selling Company	Acquiring Company	Payment (billions)
MCA/Matsushita (Japan)	Seagrams	5.7
Allied Stores (U.S.)	Campeau Corp.	4.8
Federated Stores (U.S.)	Campeau Corp.	8.8
Maclean Hunter	Rogers Communications Inc.	3.1
Lac Minerals	American Barrick	2.2
Bow Valley Resources	Talisman	1.8

billion company, Zeneca. Each shareholder in ICI was given stock in Zeneca. Of course, the value of their shares in ICI declined when it no longer had its valuable pharmaceutical business.

Probably the most frequent motive for spin-offs is improved efficiency. Companies sometimes refer to a business as being a "poor fit." By spinning off a poor fit, the management of the parent company can concentrate on its main activity. If each business must stand on its own feet, there is no risk that funds will be siphoned off from one in order to support unprofitable investments in the other. Moreover, if the two parts of the business are independent, it is easy to see the value of each and to reward managers accordingly.

22.2 SENSIBLE MOTIVES FOR MERGERS

Mergers are often categorized as *horizontal, vertical, or conglomerate*. A horizontal merger is one that takes place between two firms in the same line of business; the merged firms are former competitors. Most of the mergers around the turn of the century were of this type. Recent examples include the purchase of Lac Minerals by American Barrick to form one of the largest gold producers in the world.

During the 1920s, vertical mergers were predominant. Today they are much rarer but occasionally observed. A vertical merger is one in which the buyer expands backward toward the source of raw material or forward in the direction of the ultimate consumer. For example, in 1995 Seagrams announced that it had purchased Atlas Comercial of Bogota, the Colombian company that had been distributing several of its brands for over twenty years.

A conglomerate merger involves companies in unrelated lines of business. For example, Imasco Ltd. owns Imperial Tobacco, a cigarette manufacturer; Canada Trust, a financial services company; Hardee's, a U.S. fast food operation; Shoppers Drug Mart, a retailer; Genstar, a real estate operation; and UCS, a magazine store chain. Conglomerate mergers were common in the 1960s and 1970s. However, the number of conglomerate mergers declined in the 1980s. In fact, much of the action in the 1980s came from breaking up the conglomerates that had been formed 10 to 20 years earlier.

SELF-TEST 22.1

Are the following hypothetical mergers horizontal, vertical, or conglomerate?
a. Hudson's Bay Company acquires Wal Mart.
b. Imperial Oil Limited acquires Loblaws.
c. Loblaws acquires Cott Beverages.
d. Cott Beverages acquires Consumers' Gas.

We have already seen that one motive for a merger is to replace the existing management team. If this motive is important, one would expect that poorly performing firms would tend to be targets for acquisition; this seems to be the case.[4] However, firms also acquire other firms for reasons that have nothing to do with inadequate management. Many mergers and acquisitions are motivated by possible gains in efficiency from combining operations. These mergers create *synergies*. By this we mean that the two firms are worth more together than apart.

It would be nice if we could say that certain types of mergers are usually successful and other types fail. Unfortunately, we know of no such simple generalizations. Many mergers that appear to make sense nevertheless fail because managers cannot handle the complex task of integrating two firms with different production processes, accounting methods, and corporate cultures. Moreover, the value of most businesses depends on *human assets* — managers, skilled workers, scientists, and engineers. If these people are not happy in their new roles in the acquiring firm, the best of them will leave. Beware of paying too much for assets that go down in the elevator and out to the parking lot at the close of each business day.

With this caveat in mind, we will now consider possible sources of synergy.

Economies of Scale

Just as most of us believe that we would be happier if only we were a little richer, so managers always seem to believe their firm would be more competitive if only it were just a little bigger. They hope for *economies of scale*, that is, the opportunity to spread fixed costs across a larger volume of output.

These economies of scale are the natural goal of horizontal mergers. But they have been claimed in conglomerate mergers, too. The architects of these mergers have pointed to the economies that come from sharing central services such as accounting, financial control, and top-level management.

Economies of Vertical Integration

Large industrial companies commonly like to gain as much control and coordination as possible over the production process by expanding back toward the output of the raw material and forward to the ultimate consumer. One way to achieve this is to merge with a supplier or a customer.

Do not assume that more vertical integration is necessarily better than less. Carried to extremes, it is absurdly inefficient. For example, LOT, the Polish state airline, found itself raising pigs to make sure that its employees had fresh meat on their tables. (Of course, in a centrally managed economy it may prove necessary to grow your own meat, since you can't be sure you'll be able to buy it.)

Combining Complementary Resources

Many small firms are acquired by large firms that can provide the missing ingredients necessary for the firm's success. The small firm may have a unique product but lack the engineering and sales organization necessary to produce and market it on a large scale. The firm could develop engineering and sales talent from scratch, but it may be quicker and cheaper to merge with a firm that already had ample talent. The two firms have *complementary resources* — each has what the other needs — and so it may make sense for them to merge. Also, the merger may open up opportunities that neither firm would pursue otherwise.

Mergers as a Use for Surplus Funds

Suppose that your firm is in a mature industry. It is generating a substantial amount of cash, but it has few profitable investment opportunities. Ideally such a firm should distribute the surplus cash to shareholders by increasing its dividend

[4] For example, Palepu found that investors in firms that were subsequently acquired earned relatively low rates of return for several years before the merger. See K. Palepu, "Predicting Takeover Targets: A Methodological and Empirical Analysis," *Journal of Accounting and Economics 8* (March 1986):3–36.

payment or by repurchasing its shares. Unfortunately, energetic managers are often reluctant to adopt a policy of shrinking their firm in this way.

If the firm is not willing to purchase its own shares, it can instead purchase someone else's. Thus firms with a surplus of cash and a shortage of good investment opportunities often turn to mergers *financed by cash* as a way of deploying their capital.

Firms that have excess cash and do not pay it out or redeploy it by acquisition often find themselves targets for takeover by other firms that propose to redeploy the cash for them. During the oil price slump of the early 1980s, many cash-rich oil companies found themselves threatened by takeover. This was not because their cash was a unique asset. The acquirers wanted to capture the companies' cash flow to make sure it was not frittered away on negative-NPV oil exploration projects. We return to this *free-cash-flow* motive for takeovers later in this chapter.

22.3 DUBIOUS REASONS FOR MERGERS

The benefits that we have described so far all make economic sense. Other arguments sometimes given for mergers are more dubious. Here are two.

Diversification

We have suggested that the managers of a cash-rich company may prefer to see that cash used for acquisitions. That is why we often see cash-rich firms in stagnant industries merging their way into fresh woods and pastures new.

What about diversification as an end in itself? It is obvious that diversification reduces risk. Isn't that a gain from merging?

The trouble with this argument is that diversification is easier and cheaper for the stockholder than for the corporation. Why should firm A buy firm B to diversify when the shareholders of firm A can buy shares in firm B to diversify their own portfolios? It is far easier and cheaper for individual investors to diversify than it is for firms to combine operations.

The Bootstrap Game

During the 1960s some conglomerate companies made acquisitions that offered no evident economic gains. Nevertheless, the conglomerates' aggressive strategy produced several years of rising earnings per share. To see how this can happen, let us look at the acquisition of Muck and Slurry by the well-known conglomerate World Enterprises.

The position before the merger is set out in the first two columns of Table 22.2. Notice that because Muck and Slurry has relatively poor growth prospects, its stock sells at a lower price-earnings ratio than World Enterprises (line 3). The merger, we assume, produces no economic benefits, and so the firms should be worth exactly the same together as apart. The value of World Enterprises after the merger is therefore equal to the sum of the separate values of the two firms (line 6).

Since World Enterprises stock is selling for double the price of Muck and Slurry stock (line 2), World Enterprises can acquire the 100,000 Muck and Slurry shares for 50,000 of its own shares. Thus World will have 150,000 shares outstanding after the merger.

World's total earnings double as a result of the acquisition (line 5), but the number of shares increases by only 50 percent. Its earnings per share rise from $2.00 to $2.67. We call this a *bootstrap effect* because there is no real gain created by the merger and no increase in the two firms' combined value. Since World's stock

TABLE 22.2

Impact of merger on market value and earnings per share of World Enterprises

		World Enterprises (before Merger)	Muck and Slurry	World Enterprises (after acquiring Muck and Slurry)
1.	Earnings per share	$2.00	$2.00	$2.67
2.	Price per share	$40.00	$20.00	$40.00
3.	Price-earnings ratio	20	10	15
4.	Number of shares	100,000	100,000	150,000
5.	Total earnings	$200,000	$200,000	$400,000
6.	Total market value	$4,000,000	$2,000,000	$6,000,000
7.	Current earnings per dollar invested in stock (line 1 divided by line 2)	$.05	$.10	$.067

Note: When World Enterprises purchases Muck and Slurry, there are no gains. Therefore, total earnings and total market value should be unaffected by the merger. But earnings *per share* increase. World Enterprises issues only 50,000 of its shares (priced at $40.00) to acquire the 100,000 Muck and Slurry shares (priced at $20.00).

price is unchanged by the acquisition of Muck and Slurry, the price-earnings ratio falls (line 3).

Before the merger, $1 invested in World Enterprises bought 5 cents of current earnings and rapid growth prospects. On the other hand, $1 invested in Muck and Slurry bought 10 cents of current earnings but slower growth prospects. If the *total* market value is not altered by the merger, then $1 invested in the merged firm gives World shareholders 6.7 cents of immediate earnings but slower growth. Muck and Slurry shareholders get lower immediate earnings but faster growth. Neither side gains or loses provided that everybody understands the deal.

But financial manipulators sometimes try to ensure that the market does *not* understand the deal. Suppose that investors are fooled by the exuberance of the president of World Enterprises and mistake the 33 percent postmerger increase in earnings per share for *sustainable* growth. If they do, the price of World Enterprises stock rises and the shareholders of both companies receive something for nothing.

You should now see how to play the bootstrap game. Suppose that you manage a company enjoying a high price-earnings ratio. The reason why it is high is that investors anticipate rapid growth in future earnings. You achieve this growth not by capital investment, product improvement, or increased operating efficiency, but by purchasing slow-growing firms with low price-earnings ratios. The long-run result will be slower growth and a depressed price-earnings ratio, but in the short run earnings per share can increase dramatically. If this fools investors, you may be able to achieve the higher earnings per share without suffering a decline in your price-earnings ratio. But in order to keep *fooling* investors, you must continue to expand by merger *at the same compound rate*. Obviously you cannot do this forever; one day expansion must slow down or stop. Then earnings growth will cease, and your house of cards will fall.

SELF-TEST 22.2

Suppose that Muck and Slurry has even worse growth prospects than in our example and its price-earnings ratio is only 5. Recalculate the effects of the merger in this case. You should find that earnings per share increase by a greater amount, since World Enterprises can now buy the same *current* earnings for fewer shares.

22.4 ESTIMATING THE ECONOMIC GAINS AND COSTS

Estimating the Gains

Suppose that you are the financial manager of firm A and you wish to analyze the possible purchase of firm B. The first thing to think about is whether there is an *economic gain* from the merger. There is an economic gain *only if the two firms are worth more together than apart*. For example, if you think that the combined firm would be worth PV_{AB} and that the separate firms are worth PV_A and PV_B, then

$$\text{Gain} = PV_{AB} - (PV_A + PV_B)$$

If the gain is positive, there is an economic justification for merger. But you also have to think about the *cost* of acquiring firm B. Take the easy case in which payment is made in cash. Then the cost of acquiring B is equal to the cash payment minus B's value as a separate entity. Thus

$$\text{Cost} = \text{cash} - PV_B$$

The cost equals the portion of the economic gain captured by the shareholders of firm B. The net present value to A of a merger with B is measured by the difference between the gain and the cost. Therefore, you should go ahead with the merger if its net present value, defined as

$$\text{NPV} = \text{gain} - \text{cost} = PV_{AB} - (PV_A + PV_B) - (\text{cash} - PV_B)$$

is positive.

We like to write the merger criterion in this way because it focuses attention on two distinct questions. When you estimate the benefit, you concentrate on whether there are any gains to be made from the merger. When you estimate cost, you are concerned with the *division* of these gains between the two companies.

An example may help make this clear. Firm A has a value of $100 million, and B has a value of $50 million. Merging the two would allow cost savings with a present value of $25 million. This is the gain from the merger. Thus

$$PV_A = \$100 \quad PV_B = \$50 \quad \text{Gain} = +25 \quad PV_{AB} = \$175 \text{ million}$$

Figure 22.1 shows how the value of the new merged firm is increased by the $25 million value of the cost savings.

Suppose that B is bought for $65 million in cash. The cost of the merger is

$$\text{Cost} = \text{cash} - PV_B = 65 - 50 = \$15 \text{ million}$$

Note that the stockholders of firm B — the people on the other side of the transaction — are ahead by $15 million. *Their gain is your cost*. They have captured

FIGURE 22.1
Firms A and B are worth $25 million more together than apart. This is the gain from merger.

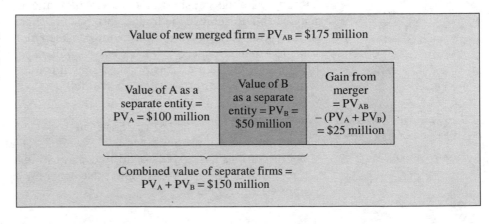

$15 million of the $25 million merger gain. Thus when we write down the NPV of the merger from A's viewpoint, we are really calculating that part of the gain that A's stockholders get to keep. The NPV to A's stockholders equals the overall gain to the merger less that part of the gain captured by B's stockholders:

$$NPV = 25 - 15 = +\$10 \text{ million}$$

Just as a check, let's confirm that A's stockholders really come out $10 million ahead. They start with a firm worth $PV_A = \$100$ million. They pay out $65 million in cash to B's stockholders and end up with a firm worth $175 million. Thus their net gain is

$$PV = \text{wealth with merger} - \text{wealth without merger}$$

$$= (PV_{AB} - \text{cash}) - PV_A$$

$$= (\$175 - \$65) - \$100 = +\$10 \text{ million}$$

Figure 22.2 shows that the value of firm A is increased by the net present value of the merger.

When investors learn of the merger between A and B, the value of B's stock will rise from $50 million to $65 million, a 30 percent increase. The market value of A's stock will increase by $10 million, or only a 10 percent increase.

FIGURE 22.2
The NPV of the merger to firm A is equal to the gain from the merger less that portion of the gain that is paid to B's shareholders.

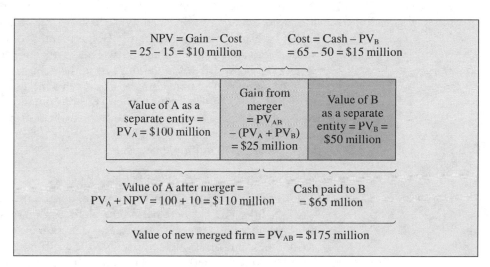

<table>
<tr><td colspan="2">NPV = Gain − Cost
= 25 − 15 = \$10 million</td><td colspan="2">Cost = Cash − PV_B
= 65 − 50 = \$15 million</td></tr>
<tr><td>Value of A as a separate entity = PV_A = \$100 million</td><td>Gain from merger
= PV_{AB}
− (PV_A + PV_B)
= \$25 million</td><td colspan="2">Value of B as a separate entity = PV_B = \$50 million</td></tr>
<tr><td colspan="2">Value of A after merger =
PV_A + NPV = 100 + 10 = \$110 million</td><td colspan="2">Cash paid to B
= \$65 mllion</td></tr>
<tr><td colspan="4">Value of new merged firm = PV_{AB} = \$175 million</td></tr>
</table>

SELF-TEST 22.3

Killer Shark Inc. makes a surprise cash offer of $22 a share for Goldfish Industries. Before the offer, Goldfish was selling for $18 a share. Goldfish has 1 million shares outstanding. What must Killer Shark believe about the present value of the improvement it can bring to Goldfish's operations?

Right and Wrong Ways to Estimate Merger Gains

Some companies begin their merger analyses with a forecast of the target firm's future cash flows. Any revenue increases or cost reductions attributable to the merger are included in the forecasts, which are then discounted back to the present and compared with the purchase price:

Estimated net gain = DCF valuation of target including merger benefits − cash required for acquisition

This is a dangerous procedure. Even the brightest and best-trained analyst can make large errors in valuing a business. The estimated net gain may come up positive not because the merger makes sense, but simply because the analyst's cash-flow forecasts are too optimistic. On the other hand, a good merger may not be pursued if the analyst fails to recognize the target's potential as a stand-alone business.

A better procedure *starts* with the target's current and stand-alone market value and concentrates instead on the *changes* in cash flow that would result from the merger. Always ask why the two firms should be worth more together than apart. Remember, *you add value only if you can generate additional economic benefits* — some competitive edge that other firms can't match and that the target firm's managers can't achieve on their own.

It makes sense to keep an eye on the value that investors place on the gains from merging. If A's stock price falls when the deal is announced, investors are sending a message that the merger benefits are doubtful or that A is paying too much for them.

Estimating the Costs

To recapitulate, you should go ahead with a merger if the gain exceeds the cost. The gain is the difference between the value of the merged firm and the value of the separate entities. We have looked at where these gains may come from and how to estimate them. It is now time to focus on the costs.

The cost of a merger is the premium the acquirer pays for the target firm over its value as a separate entity. It is a straightforward problem to estimate cost as long as the merger is financed by cash. However, it is important to bear in mind that if investors *expect* A to acquire B, the market value of B may be a poor measure of its value as a separate entity. This is because the price of B may already reflect the possibility of a premium from the acquiring firm.

Estimating cost is more complicated when a merger is financed by an exchange of shares. Let's return to our earlier example. Suppose that firm A has 1 million shares outstanding, each worth $100. Instead of offering $65 million in cash for firm B, A decides to offer 650,000 shares. Since A's share price is $100 and B on its own is worth $50 million, the cost *appears* to be $15 million, the same as before:

$$\text{Apparent cost} = 650{,}000 \times \$100 - \$50{,}000{,}000 = \$15{,}000{,}000$$

However, the apparent cost may not equal the true cost. Are A's shares really worth $100 each? They are before the merger is announced but not afterward. We assumed that the merger is expected to generate cost savings worth $25 million, so that the value of the merged firm is $175 million. After the merger the firm will have $1{,}000{,}000 + 650{,}000 = 1{,}650{,}000$ shares outstanding. Therefore, the share price will be

$$\text{New share price} = \frac{\$175{,}000{,}000}{1{,}650{,}000} = \$106.06$$

The true cost is

$$\text{Cost} = (650{,}000 \times \$106.06) - \$50{,}000{,}000 = \$18{,}939{,}000$$

This is the value of the shares in the new firm that are given to B's shareholders.

We can now calculate the net present value of the merger when it is financed by shares:

$$\text{Gain} = \$25{,}000{,}000$$

$$\text{Cost} = \$18{,}939{,}000$$

$$\text{NPV} = \text{gain} - \text{cost} = 25{,}000{,}000 - 18{,}939{,}000 = \$6{,}061{,}000$$

There is a key distinction between cash and stock as financing instruments. If cash is offered, the cost of the merger is unaffected by the size of the merger gains. If stock is offered, the cost depends on the gains because the gains show up in the postmerger share price.

Stock financing also mitigates the effect of overvaluation or undervaluation of either firm. Suppose, for example, that A overestimates B's value as a separate entity, perhaps because it has overlooked some hidden liability. Thus A makes too generous an offer. Other things equal, A's stockholders are better off if it is a stock offer rather than a cash offer. With a stock offer, the inevitable bad news about B's value will fall partly on the shoulders of B's stockholders.

SELF-TEST 22.4

Suppose that A offers B's shareholders a choice of $15 million in cash or 600,000 shares. Which is the more attractive offer? Resketch Figure 22.2 showing the value of the share offer to B, the cost of the merger, and its NPV.

22.5 MERGER TACTICS

Many mergers are agreed upon by both parties, but in other cases the acquirer will go over the heads of the target firm's management and make a *tender offer* directly to its stockholders. The management of the target firm may advise shareholders to accept the tender, or it may attempt to fight the bid in the hope that the acquirer will either raise its offer or throw in the towel.

The rules of merger warfare are largely set by federal and provincial laws[5] and the courts act as referee to see that contests are conducted fairly. We will look at one classic contest, which illustrates many of the tactics and weapons employed.

The Fight for Cities Service[6]

The battle for Cities began in May 1982 when T. Boone Pickens, the chairman of Mesa Petroleum, began buying Cities shares as preparation for a takeover bid. Foreseeing the bid, Cities made an issue of equity that diluted Mesa's holding and followed this up with a retaliatory offer for Mesa.[7] Over the following month Mesa's bid was revised once and Cities's bid was revised twice before both companies agreed to drop their bids for the other. Cities repurchased Mesa's holding — at an $80 million profit to Mesa — and in exchange Mesa agreed not to attempt a hostile takeover of Cities for 5 years.

The principal reason for the cessation of hostilities between Mesa and Cities was the announcement that Cities has found a more congenial partner in Gulf Oil. Also, Gulf was prepared to pay substantially more than Mesa for Cities's stock. Unfortunately, this proposal fell afoul of the U.S. Federal Trade Commission (FTC), the American equivalent of Canada's Bureau of Competition, which is responsible for ensuring that mergers do not reduce competition. The FTC issued a temporary restraining order and shortly thereafter Gulf withdrew its offer.

In response, Cities charged Gulf with not attempting to resolve the FTC's objections, and it filed a $3 billion lawsuit against Gulf. At the same time it began to look for another **white knight** to take it over in a friendly acquisition. The only interested suitor was Occidental Petroleum. Occidental's initial offer for Cities

white knight: Friendly potential acquirer sought by a target company threatened by an unwelcome suitor.

---

[5] The principal federal law governing takeovers is the *Competition Act* passed into law in 1986. Under this act, companies planning a merger must report to the *Bureau of Competition Policy*, which reviews the proposed transaction.

[6] The Cities Service takeover is described in R. S. Ruback, "The Cities Service Takeover: A Case Study," *Journal of Finance* 38 (May 1983):319–330.

[7] This practice of defending yourself against merger by making a counterbid for the predator's stock is sometimes known as the *Pacman defence*.

was revised twice and finally accepted. The battle for Cities Service had lasted 3 months and involved a total of nine bids from four separate companies.

In several instances the bidders employed both carrot and stick; for example, Occidental followed up its initial friendly offer for Cities with a hostile tender offer before finally reaching a friendly agreement.

The generous Gulf offer would have provided Cities's shareholders with a profit of almost 80 percent, but the collapse of that offer and the shortage of other suitors caused Cities's stock price to lose all its earlier gains. From then on Cities was in a relatively weak bargaining position, and the Occidental offer resulted in a profit of only 12 percent for Cities's stockholders. The merger scarcely affected Occidental's stock price, which suggests that investors believed the merger to be a zero-NPV investment for Occidental. Gulf's stockholders fared worst. Its high-priced offer led to a 14 percent fall in the price of Gulf stock. Even though this offer was subsequently withdrawn, the prospect of a costly lawsuit left Gulf's stock price depressed.

As with many real-life stories, there is an epilogue. One year after losing its battle for Cities, Gulf itself became a takeover target, when Mesa Petroleum proposed to buy Gulf stock in order to break the company up and sell it in pieces. At this point Chevron came to the rescue and acquired Gulf for $13.2 billion, more than double its value of 6 months earlier. Chevron's bid gave Mesa a profit of $760 million on the Gulf shares that it had bought. Asked for his views, Pickens commented, "Shucks, I guess we lost another one."

Takeover Defenses

shark repellent: Amendments to a company charter made to forestall takeover attempts.

poison pill: Measure taken by a target firm to avoid acquisition; for example, the right for existing shareholders to buy additional shares at an attractive price if a bidder acquires a large holding.

The Cities Service case illustrates some of the stratagems of modern merger warfare. Firms that are worried about being taken over usually prepare their defenses in advance. A common first step is to persuade the shareholders to agree to **shark-repellent** changes in the corporate charter to dissuade potential acquirers from attempting a takeover. For example, the charter may be amended to require that any merger must be approved by a *supermajority* of 80 percent of the shares rather than the normal 50 percent.

A firm may also deter potential bidders by devising **poison pills**, which make the company unappetizing. Often the poison pill will give existing shareholders the right to buy the company's shares at half price as soon as a bidder acquires more than 15 percent of the shares. The bidder is not entitled to the discount. Thus the bidder resembles Tantalus — as soon as it has acquired 15 percent of the shares, control is lifted further away from its reach. By 1995 more than 40 Canadian companies had poison pills in place. However, the use of poison pills is limited by both regulators and the company's own shareholders. For instance, in 1994 the Ontario Securities Commission (OSC) prevented Lac Minerals from putting a poison pill in place because it did not feel that a poison pill would lead to higher bids for the firm. In the same year the shareholders of Labatt's were the first in Canadian history to defeat a management proposal to introduce a poison pill.

Who Gets the Gains?

Is it better to own shares in the acquiring firm or the target? In our example, the stockholders of the target firm (Cities Service) made a profit of 12 percent. Investors in Occidental broke even and Gulf's shareholders lost money.

In general, shareholders of the target firm do best. Figure 22.3 summarizes the results of Eckbo's study of about 1700 buying firms and 400 selling firms in Canadian mergers that took place between 1964 to 1983.[8] The study tracked

---

[8] B.E. Eckbo, "Mergers and the Market for Corporate Control: the Canadian Evidence," *Canadian Journal of Economics* 19 (May 1986):236–260.

returns to shareholders over a 24-month period centred on the dates when the acquisitions were first announced in the press.[9] You can see that selling stockholders received a healthy gain. (Note also how much of this gain occurs before press day. Investors anticipate the announcement of the acquisition and the good news it brings.) On the other hand, stockholders in the acquiring companies also gained but not as much as the acquired firm.

FIGURE 22.3
Eckbo's study shows that both selling firms and buying firms in Canada experience gains from take-overs, although the gains to selling firms are larger.

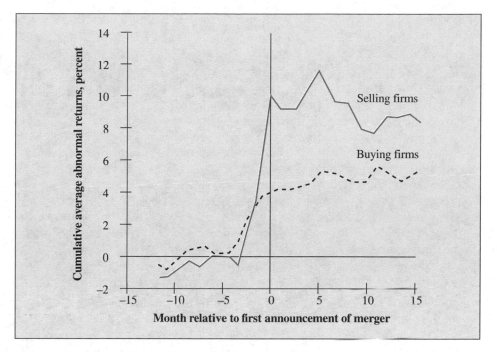

Source: B.E. Eckbo, "Mergers and the Market For Corporate Control: the Canadian Evidence," *Canadian Journal of Economics* 19:236–260 (May 1986).

The fact that there are gains for both buying and selling firms in Canada contrasts with the results of studies of takeovers in the United States. For instance, Figure 22.4 summarizes the results of a study by Asquith of 200 mergers during the period 1962 to 1976. The study tracked abnormal returns to shareholders over 120 periods centred on the date that the acquisition was first announced. You can see that selling stockholders received a healthy gain. On the other hand, the acquiring companies' stockholders gained much less. On average, it appears that investors expect acquiring companies to just about break even.[10]

SELF-TEST 22.5

If the original stock price of a firm is $100, and the firm becomes a takeover target, by how much can we expect the stock price to rise? Use Figure 22.3 to guide your answer.

---

[9] These returns are adjusted to account for general movements in the stock market. They can be interpreted as returns in excess of what one would otherwise expect given the performance of the overall market. The excess returns are therefore attributed to the announcement of a takeover attempt.
[10] The small initial gain to the shareholders of acquiring firms is not statistically significant, although most researchers have observed a similar small positive return.

FIGURE 22.4
Asquith's study confirms
that selling firms receive
substantial premiums.
Stockholders of buying
firms roughly break even.
Note: The cumulative
returns are adjusted to
remove price fluctuations
attributable to movements
of the overall stock market.

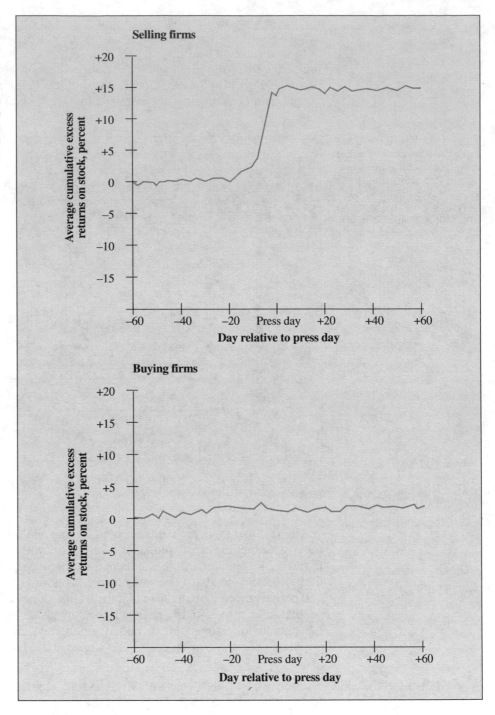

Source: P. Asquith, "Merger Bids, Uncertainty, and Stockholder Returns," *Journal of Financial Economics* 11:51–83 (April 1983), figures 1 and 2, pp. 62–63. Published with permission of the *Journal of Financial Economics*, Elsevier Science BV.

How do we explain the conflicting evidence? Why do sellers earn higher returns? There are two possible explanations. First, buyers in the United States are typically much larger than sellers, whereas in Eckbo's study of Canada they were about the same size. When the buyer is much bigger it might be that even significant net benefits would not show up clearly in the buyers' share price. Suppose, for example that company A buys another company B, which is only one-tenth A's size. Suppose the dollar value of the net gain to the merger is split equally between A and B. Each company's shareholders received the same dollar profit but B's receive ten times A's in *percentage* return.

A second reason is competition among potential bidders. Once the first bidder puts the target company "in play," one or more additional suitors often jump in, sometimes as white knights at the invitation of the target firm's management. Every time one suitor tops another's bid, more of the merger gain slides toward the target. At the same time the target firm's management may mount various legal and financial counterattacks, ensuring that capitulation, if and when it comes, is at the highest attainable price. So it might be that competition among bidders in the United States is more intense than it is in Canada.

Of course, bidders and targets are not the only possible winners. Unsuccessful bidders often win, too, by selling off their holdings in target companies at substantial profits. Such shares may be sold on the open market or sold back to the target company.[11] Sometimes they are sold to the successful suitor. We saw how Mesa Petroleum earned $80 million by selling its Cities Service shares back to Cities Service and $760 million by selling its Gulf stock to Chevron, the winning bidder.

Other winners include investment bankers, lawyers, accountants, and in some cases arbitrageurs, or "arbs," who speculate on the likely success of takeover bids.

"Speculate" has a negative ring, but it can be a useful social service. A tender offer may present shareholders with a difficult decision. Should they accept, should they wait to see if someone else produces a better offer, or should they sell their stock in the market? This quandary presents an opportunity for the arbitrageurs. In other words, they buy from the target's shareholders and take on the risk that the deal will not go through.[12]

Of course, as Ivan Boesky demonstrated, arbitrageurs can make even more money if they can learn about the offer *before* it is publicly announced. Because arbitrageurs may accumulate large amounts of stock, they can have an important effect on whether a deal goes through, and the bidding company or its investment bankers may be tempted to take the arbitrageurs into their confidence. At this point, a legitimate and useful activity becomes illegal and harmful.

22.6 LEVERAGED BUY-OUTS

Leveraged buy-outs, or *LBO*s, differ from ordinary acquisitions in two ways. First, a large fraction of the purchase price is debt-financed. Some, perhaps all, of this debt is junk, that is, below investment grade. Second, the shares of the LBO no longer trade on the open market. The remaining equity in the LBO is privately held by a small group of (usually institutional) investors. When this group is led by the company's management, the acquisition is called a *management buy-out* (*MBO*). Many LBOs are in fact MBOs.

In the 1970s and 1980s many management buy-outs were arranged for unwanted divisions of large, diversified companies. Smaller divisions outside the companies' main lines of business often lacked top management's interest and

---

[11] When a company sells the shares back to the target, the transaction is known as *greenmail*.
[12] Strictly speaking, an arbitrageur is an investor who makes a riskless profit. Arbitrageurs in merger battles often take very large risks indeed. Their activities are sometimes known as "risk arbitrage."

commitment, and divisional management chafed under corporate bureaucracy. Many such divisions flowered when spun off as MBOs. Their managers, pushed by the need to generate cash for debt service and encouraged by a substantial personal stake in the business, found ways to cut costs and compete more effectively.

During the 1980s MBO/LBO activity shifted to buy-outs of entire businesses, including large, mature public corporations. The largest, most dramatic, and best-documented LBO of them all was the $25 billion takeover of RJR Nabisco in 1988 by Kohlberg Kravis Roberts (KKR). The players, tactics, and controversies of LBOs are writ large in this case.

RJR Nabisco[13]

On October 28, 1988, the board of directors of RJR Nabisco revealed that Ross Johnson, the company's chief executive officer, had formed a group of investors prepared to buy all the firm's stock for $75 per share in cash and take the company private. Johnson's group was backed up and advised by Shearson Lehman Hutton, the investment bank subsidiary of American Express.

RJR's share price immediately moved to about $75, handing shareholders a 36 percent gain over the previous day's price of $56. At the same time RJR's bonds fell, since it was clear that existing bondholders would soon have a lot more company.

Johnson's offer lifted RJR onto the auction block. Once the company was in play, its board of directors was obliged to consider other offers, which were not long coming. Four days later, a group of investors led by LBO specialists Kohlberg Kravis Roberts bid $90 per share, $79 in cash plus preferred stock valued at $11.

The bidding finally closed on November 30, some 32 days after the initial offer was revealed. In the end it was Johnson's group against KKR. KKR offered $109 per share, after adding $1 per share (roughly $230 million) at the last hour. The KKR bid was $81 in cash, convertible subordinated debentures valued at about $10, and preferred shares valued at about $18. Johnson's group bid $112 in cash and securities.

But the RJR board chose KKR. True, Johnson's group had offered $3 per share more, but its security valuations were viewed as "softer" and perhaps overstated. Also, KKR's planned asset sales were less drastic; perhaps their plans for managing the business inspired more confidence. Finally, the Johnson group's proposal contained a management compensation package that seemed extremely generous and had generated an avalanche of bad press.

But where did the merger benefits come from? What could justify offering $109 per share, about $25 billion in all, for a company that only 33 days previously had been selling for $56 per share?

KKR and other bidders were betting on two things. First, they expected to generate billions of additional dollars from interest tax shields, reduced capital expenditures, and sales of assets not strictly necessary to RJR's core businesses. Asset sales alone were projected to generate $5 billion. Second, they expected to make those core businesses significantly more profitable, mainly by cutting back on expenses and bureaucracy. Apparently there was plenty to cut, including the RJR "Air Force," which at one point operated 10 corporate jets.

In the year after KKR took over, new management was installed. This group sold assets and cut back operating expenses and capital spending. There were also layoffs. As expected, high interest charges meant a net loss of $976 million for

---

[13] The story of the RJR Nabisco buy-out is reconstructed by B. Burrough and J. Helyar in *Barbarians at the Gate: The Fall of RJR Nabisco* (New York: Harper & Row, 1990).

1989, but pretax operating income actually increased, despite extensive asset sales, including the sale of RJR's European food operations.

While management was cutting costs and selling assets, prices in the junk market were rapidly declining, implying much higher future interest charges for RJR and stricter terms on any refinancing. In mid-1990 KKR made an additional equity investment, and later that year the company announced an offer of cash and new shares in exchange for $753 million of junk bonds. By 1993 the burden of debt had been reduced from $26 billion to $14 billion. For RJR, the world's largest LBO, it seemed that high debt was a temporary, not permanent, virtue.

Barbarians at the Gate?

The buy-out of RJR crystallized views on LBOs, the junk bond market, and the takeover business. For many it exemplified all that was wrong with finance in the 1980s, especially the willingness of "raiders" to carve up established companies, leaving them with enormous debt burdens, basically in order to get rich quick.

There was plenty of confusion, stupidity, and greed in the LBO business. Not all the people involved were nice. On the other hand, LBOs generated enormous increases in market value, and most of the gains went to selling stockholders, not raiders. For example, the biggest winners in the RJR Nabisco LBO were the company's stockholders.

We should therefore consider briefly where these gains may have come from before we try to pass judgment on LBOs. There are several possibilities.

The Junk Bond Markets. LBOs and debt-financed takeovers may have been driven by artificially cheap funding from the junk bond markets. With hindsight it seems that investors in junk bonds underestimated the risks of default in junk bonds. Default rates climbed painfully in 1989 and 1990. At the same time the junk bond market became much less liquid after the demise of Drexel Burnham Lambert, the chief market maker. Yields climbed dramatically, and new issues dried up. Suddenly junk-financed LBOs seemed to disappear from the scene.[14]

If junk bond investors in 1985 had appreciated the risk of what actually happened in 1990, junk finance would have been dearer. That would have slowed down LBOs and other highly leveraged transactions.

Leverage and Taxes. As we explained in Chapter 18, borrowing money saves taxes. But taxes were not the main driving force behind LBOs. The value of interest tax shields was just not big enough to explain the observed gains in market value.

Of course, if interest tax shields were the main motive for LBOs' high debt, then LBO managers would not be so concerned to pay off debt. We saw that this was one of the first tasks facing RJR Nabisco's new management.

Other Stakeholders. It is possible that the gain to the selling stockholders is just someone else's loss and that no value is generated overall. Therefore, we should look at the total gain to *all* investors in an LBO, not just the selling stockholders.

Bondholders are the obvious losers. The debt they thought was well-secured may turn into junk when the borrower goes through an LBO. We noted how market prices of RJR Nabisco debt fell sharply when Ross Johnson's first LBO offer was announced. But again, the value losses suffered by bondholders in LBOs are not nearly large enough to explain stockholder gains.

[14] There was a sharp revival of junk bond sales in 1992 and 1993 but many of these issues simply replaced existing bonds. It remains to be seen whether junk bonds will make a lasting recovery.

Leverage and Incentives. Managers and employees of LBOs work harder and often smarter. They have to generate cash to service the extra debt. Moreover, managers' personal fortunes are riding on the LBO's success. They become owners rather than employees.

It is hard to measure the payoff from better incentives, but there is some preliminary evidence of improved operating efficiency in LBOs. Kaplan, who studied 48 management buyouts between 1980 and 1986, found average increases in operating income of 24 percent over the following 3 years. Ratios of operating income and net cash flow to assets and sales increased dramatically. He observed cutbacks in capital expenditures but not in employment. Kaplan suggests that these operating changes "are due to improved incentives rather than layoffs or managerial exploitation of shareholders through inside information."[15]

Free Cash Flow. The free-cash-flow theory of takeovers is basically that mature firms with a surplus of cash will tend to waste it. This contrasts with standard finance theory, which says that firms with more cash than positive-NPV investment opportunities should give the cash back to investors through higher dividends or share repurchases. But we see firms like RJR Nabisco spending on corporate luxuries and questionable capital investments. One benefit of LBOs is to put such companies on a diet and force them to pay out cash to service debt.

The free-cash-flow theory predicts that mature, "cash cow" companies will be the most likely targets of LBOs. We can find many examples that fit the theory, including RJR Nabisco. The theory says that the gains in market value generated by LBOs are just the present value of the future cash flows that would otherwise have been frittered away.[16]

We do not endorse the free-cash-flow theory as the sole explanation for LBOs. We have mentioned several other plausible rationales, and we suspect that most LBOs are driven by a mixture of motives. Nor do we say that all LBOs are beneficial. On the contrary, there are many mistakes and even soundly motivated LBOs can be dangerous, as the bankruptcies of Campeau, Revco, National Gypsum, and many other highly leveraged companies prove. However, we do take issue with those who portray LBOs *simply* as Wall Street barbarians breaking up the traditional strengths of corporations. In many cases LBOs have generated true gains.

In the next section we sum up the long-run impact of mergers and acquisitions, including LBOs, in the economy. We warn you, however, that there are no neat answers. Our assessment has to be mixed and tentative.

 # 22.7 MERGERS AND THE ECONOMY

Merger Waves

Mergers take place in waves. The first episode of intense merger activity in North America occurred at the turn of the century and the second in the 1920s. There was a further boom from 1967 to 1969 and then again in the 1980s. Each episode coincided with a period of buoyant stock prices, though in each case there were substantial differences in the types of companies that merged and how they went about it.

---

[15] S. Kaplan, "The Effects of Management Buyouts on Operating Performance and Value," *Journal of Financial Economics* 24 (October 1989):217–254.

[16] The free-cash-flow theory's chief proponent is Michael Jensen. See M. C. Jensen, "The Eclipse of the Public Corporation," *Harvard Business Review* 67 (September-October 1989):61–74, and "The Agency Costs of Free Cash Flow, Corporate Finance and Takeovers," *American Economic Review* 76 (May 1986):323–329.

We don't really understand why merger activity is so volatile. If mergers are prompted by economic motives, at least one of these motives must be "here today, gone tomorrow," and it must somehow be associated with high stock prices. But none of the economic motives that we review in this chapter have anything to do with the general level of the stock market. None of the motives burst on the scene in 1967, departed in 1970, and reappeared for most of the 1980s.

Some mergers may result from mistakes in valuation on the part of the stock market. In other words, the buyer may believe that investors have underestimated the value of the seller or may hope that they *will* overestimate the value of the combined firm. Why don't we see just as many firms hunting for bargain acquisitions when the stock market is low? It is possible that "suckers are born every minute," but it's difficult to believe that they can be harvested only in bull markets.

During the 1980s merger boom, only the very largest companies were immune from attack from a rival management team. For example, in 1985 Pantry Pride, a small supermarket chain recently emerged from bankruptcy, made a bid for the cosmetics company Revlon. Revlon's assets were more than five times those of Pantry Pride. What made the bid possible (and eventually successful) was the ability of Pantry Pride to finance the takeover by borrowing $2.1 billion. The growth of leveraged buy-outs during the 1980s depended on the development of a junk bond market that allowed bidders to place low-grade bonds rapidly and in high volume.

By the end of the decade the merger environment had changed. Many of the obvious targets had disappeared, and the battle for RJR Nabisco highlighted the increasing cost of victory. Institutions were reluctant to increase their holdings of junk bonds. Moreover, the market for these bonds had depended to a remarkable extent on one individual, Michael Milken, of the investment bank Drexel Burnham Lambert. By the late 1980s Milken and his employer were in trouble. Milken was indicted by a grand jury on 98 counts and was subsequently sentenced to jail and ordered to pay $600 million. Drexel filed for bankruptcy, but by that time the junk bond market was moribund and the finance for highly leveraged buy-outs had largely dried up.[17] Finally, in reaction to the perceived excess of the merger boom, public opinion and the courts began to lean against takeovers.

....
Do Mergers Generate Net Benefits?

There are undoubtedly good acquisitions and bad acquisitions, but economists find it hard to agree on whether acquisitions are beneficial *on balance*. We do know that mergers generate substantial gains to stockholders of acquired firms.

Since buyers seem at least to break even and sellers make substantial gains, it seems that there are positive gains to mergers. But not everybody is convinced. Some believe that investors analyzing mergers pay too much attention to short-term earnings gains and don't notice that these gains are at the expense of long-term prospects.

Since we can't observe how companies would have fared in the absence of a merger, it is difficult to measure the effects on profitability. Studies of recent merger activity suggest that mergers do seem to improve real productivity. For example, Healy, Palepu, and Ruback examined 50 large mergers between 1979 and 1983 and found an average increase in the companies' pretax returns of 2.4

---

[17] For a history of the role of Milken in the development of the junk bond market, see C. Bruck, *The Predator's Ball: The Junk Bond Raiders and the Man Who Staked Them*, (New York: Simon and Schuster, 1988).

percentage points.[18] They argue that this gain came from generating a higher level of sales from the same assets. There was no evidence that the companies were mortgaging their long-term futures by cutting back on long-term investments; expenditures on capital equipment and research and development tracked the industry average.

If you are concerned with public policy toward mergers, you do not want to look only at their impact on the shareholders of the companies concerned. For instance, we have already seen that in the case of RJR Nabisco some part of the shareholders' gain was at the expense of the bondholders and the U.S. taxpayer (through the enlarged interest tax shield). The acquirer's shareholders may also gain at the expense of the target firm's employees, who in some cases are laid off or are forced to take pay cuts after takeovers.

Many people worry that the merger wave of the 1980s led to excessive debt levels and left many companies ill-equipped to survive a recession. Also, many savings and loan companies and some large insurance firms invested heavily in junk bonds. Defaults on these bonds threatened, and in some cases extinguished, their solvency.

Perhaps the most important effect of acquisition is felt by the managers of companies that are *not* taken over. For example, one effect of LBOs was that the managers of even the largest corporations could not feel safe from challenge. Perhaps the threat of takeover spurs all corporations to try harder. Unfortunately, we don't know whether on balance the threat of merger makes for more active days or sleepless nights.

We do know that merger activity is very costly. For example in the RJR Nabisco buy-out, the total fees paid to the investment banks, lawyers, and accountants amounted to over $1 billion.

Even if the gains to the community exceed these costs, one wonders whether the same benefits could not be achieved more cheaply another way. For example, are leveraged buy-outs necessary to make managers work harder? Perhaps the problem lies in the way that many corporations reward and penalize their managers. Perhaps many of the gains from takeover could be captured by linking management compensation more closely to performance.

SUMMARY

1. If the board of directors fails to replace an inefficient management, there are four general ways that the change may be brought about: (a) shareholders may engage in a proxy fight to replace the board, (b) the firm may be acquired by another, (c) the firm may be purchased by a private group of investors in a leveraged buy-out, or (d) it may sell off part of its operations to another company.

2. A merger may be undertaken in order to replace an inefficient management. But there may also be synergies from combining the operations of two firms. These may stem from economies of scale, economies of vertical integration, the combination of complementary resources, or redeployment of surplus funds. We don't know how common these benefits are, but they do make

---

[18] See P. Healey, K. Palepu, and R. Ruback, "Does Corporate Performance Improve after Mergers?" *Journal of Financial Economics* 31 (April 1992):135–175. The study examined the pretax returns of the merged companies relative to industry averages.

economic sense. Sometimes mergers are undertaken to diversify risks or artificially increase growth of earnings per share. These motives are dubious.

3. A merger generates an economic gain if the two firms are worth more together than apart. You should go ahead with the merger if the gain exceeds the cost. The cost is the premium that the buyer pays for the selling firm over its value as a separate entity. When payment is in the form of shares, the value of this payment naturally depends on what those shares are worth after the merger is complete.

4. There are three ways for one firm to acquire another. It can merge all the assets and liabilities of the target into those of its own company; it can buy the stock of the target; or it can buy the individual assets of the target. Mergers are often amicably negotiated between the management and directors of the two companies; but if the seller is reluctant, the would-be buyer can decide to make a tender offer for the stock. We sketched some of the offensive and defensive tactics used in takeover battles. We also observed that when the target firm loses, its shareholders typically win: target firms' shareholders earn large abnormal returns. The bidding firm's shareholders roughly break even. The typical merger generates positive net benefit to investors and somewhat smaller benefits to the buying firm. The lower gains to bidders may result from the fact that bidders are much larger than targets with the results that gains are hard to measure. It may also be due to competition among bidders and active defense by target managements that pushes most of the gains toward selling shareholders.

5. In a leveraged buy-out (LBO) or management buy-out (MBO), all public shares are repurchased and the company "goes private." LBOs tend to involve mature businesses with ample cash flow and modest growth opportunities. LBOs and other debt-financed takeovers are driven by a mixture of motives, including (a) the value of interest tax shields; (b) transfers of value from bondholders, who may see the value of their bonds fall as the firm piles up more debt; and (c) the opportunity to create better incentives for managers and employees, who have a personal stake in the company. In addition, many LBOs were designed to force firms with surplus cash to distribute it to shareholders rather than plowing it back. Investors feared such companies would channel free cash flow into negative-NPV investments.

6. Mergers seem to generate economic gains, but they are also costly. Investment bankers, lawyers, and arbitrageurs thrived during the 1980s merger and LBO boom. Many companies were left with heavy debt burdens and will have to sell assets or improve performance to stay solvent. By the end of 1990, the new-issue junk bond market had dried up, and the corporate jousting field was strangely quiet. But 1994 brought another increase in merger activity with this round heavily involving foreign companies. In that year Canadian companies spent $7 billion on foreign takeovers and foreigners in turn spent $5.8 billion on the purchase of Canadian companies. As we write this chapter in early 1995 we may be on the verge of a new merger wave.

KEY TERMS

proxy contest	**leveraged buy-out (LBO)**	**shark repellent**
merger	**management buy-out (MBO)**	**poison pill**
tender offer	**white knight**	

SUGGESTED READINGS

The extensive empirical work on mergers is reviewed in

M. C. Jensen and R. S. Ruback. "The Market for Corporate Control: The Scientific Evidence," *Journal of Financial Economics* 11(April 1983): 5–50.

Two useful recent books on takeovers are

J. F. Weston, K. S. Chung, and S. E. Hoag. *Mergers, Restructuring, and Corporate Control*, Englewood Cliffs, N.J.: Prentice-Hall, 1990.

R.S. Khemani, D.M. Shapiro, and W.T. Stanbury, *Mergers, Corporate Concentration and Power in Canada*, The Institute for Research on Public Policy, Halifax, 1988.

PROBLEMS

1. Immense Appetite, Inc., believes that it can acquire Sleepy Industries and improve efficiency to the extent that the market value of Sleepy will increase by $5 million. Sleepy currently sells for $20 a share, and there are 1 million shares outstanding.
   a. Sleepy's management is willing to accept a cash offer of $25 a share. Can the merger be accomplished on a friendly basis?
   b. What will happen if Sleepy's management holds out for an offer of $28 a share?

2. Velcro Saddles is contemplating the acquisition of Pogo Ski Sticks, Inc. The values of the two companies as separate entities are $20 million and $10 million, respectively. Velcro Saddles estimates that by combining the two companies, it will reduce marketing and administrative costs by $500,000 per year in perpetuity. Velcro Saddles is willing to pay $14 million cash for Pogo. The opportunity cost of capital is 10 percent.
   a. What is the gain from merger?
   b. What is the cost of the cash offer?
   c. What is the NPV of the acquisition under the cash offer?

3. Suppose that instead of making a cash offer as in problem 2, Velcro Saddles considers offering Pogo shareholders a 50 percent holding in Velcro Saddles.
   a. What is the value of the stock in the merged company held by the original Pogo shareholders?
   b. What is the cost of the stock alternative?
   c. What is its NPV under the stock offer?

4. Which of the following motives for mergers make economic sense?
   a. Merging to achieve economies of scale.
   b. Merging to reduce risk by diversification.
   c. Merging to redeploy cash generated by a firm with ample profits but limited growth opportunities.
   d. Merging to increase earnings per share.

5. True or false?
   a. Sellers almost always gain in mergers.
   b. Buyers almost always gain in mergers.
   c. Firms that do unusually well tend to be acquisition targets.
   d. Merger activity in North America varies dramatically from year to year.

e. On the average, mergers produce substantial economic gains.

f. Tender offers require the approval of the selling firm's management.

g. The cost of a merger is always independent of the economic gain produced by the merger.

6. Connect each term to its correct definition or description:

LBO	Attempt to gain control of a firm by winning the votes of its stockholders.
Poison pill	Changes in corporate charter designed to deter unwelcome takeover.
Tender offer	Friendly potential acquirer sought by a threatened target firm.
Shark repellent	Shareholders are issued rights to buy shares if bidder acquires large stake in the firm.
Proxy contest	Offer to buy shares directly from stockholders.
White knight	Company or business bought out by private investors, largely debt-financed.

7. True or false?

a. One of the first tasks of an LBO's financial manager is to pay down debt.

b. Shareholders of bidding companies earn higher abnormal returns when the merger is financed with stock than in cash-financed deals.

c. Targets for LBOs in the 1980s tended to be profitable companies in mature industries with limited investment opportunities.

8. The Muck and Slurry merger has fallen through (see Section 22.3). But World Enterprises is determined to report earnings per share of $2.67. It therefore acquires the Wheelrim and Axle Company. You are given the following facts:

	World Enterprises	Wheelrim and Axle	Merged Firm
Earnings per share	$2.00	$2.50	$2.67
Price per share	$40.00	$25.00	_____
Price-earnings ratio	20	10	_____
Number of shares	100,000	200,000	_____
Total earnings	$200,000	$500,000	_____
Total market value	$4,000,000	$5,000,000	_____

Once again there are no gains from merging. In exchange for Wheelrim and Axle shares, World Enterprises issues just enough of its own shares to ensure its $2.67 earnings per share objective.

a. Complete the above table for the merged firm.

b. How many shares of World Enterprises are exchanged for each share of Wheelrim and Axle?

c. What is the cost of the merger to World Enterprises?

d. What is the change in the total market value of those World Enterprises shares that were outstanding before the merger?

9. As treasurer of Leisure Products, Inc., you are investigating the possible acquisition of Plastitoys. You have the following basic data:

	Leisure Products	Plastitoys
Earnings per share	$5.00	$1.50
Dividend per share	$3.00	$.80
Number of shares	1,000,000	600,000
Stock price	$90.00	$20.00

You estimate that investors currently expect a steady growth of about 6 percent in Plastitoys's earnings and dividends. You believe that Leisure Products could increase the growth rate to 8 percent per year, without any additional capital investment required.

a. What is the gain from the acquisition?

b. What is the cost of the acquisition if Leisure Products pays $25 in cash for each share of Plastitoys?

c. What is the cost of the acquisition if Leisure Products offers one share of Leisure Products for every three shares of Plastitoys?

d. How would the cost of the cash offer and the share offer alter if the expected growth rate of Plastitoys were not increased by the merger?

SOLUTIONS TO SELF-TEST QUESTIONS

22.1

a. Horizontal merger. The Hudson's Bay Company is in the same industry as Wal Mart.

b. Conglomerate merger. Imperial Oil and Loblaws are in different industries.

c. Vertical merger. Loblaws is expanding backwards to acquire one of its suppliers, Cott Beverages.

d. Conglomerate merger. Cott Beverages and Consumers Gas are in different industries.

22.2   Given current earnings of $2.00 a share, and a price-earnings ratio of only 5, Muck and Slurry would sell for only half as much, $10 a share, and have a market value of $1,000,000. It can be acquired for only half as many shares of World Enterprises, 25,000 shares. Therefore, the merged firm will have 125,000 shares outstanding and earnings of $400,000, resulting in earnings per share of $3.20, higher than the $2.67 value in the third column of Table 22.2.

22.3   The cost of the merger is $4 million: the $4 per share premium offered to Goldfish shareholders times 1 million shares. If the merger has positive NPV to Killer Shark, the gain must be greater than $4 million.

22.4   In the case of the share offer there will be 1,600,000 shares after the merger. Each will be worth 175/1.6 = $109.38. Therefore the total offer is worth 600,000 × $109.38 = $65,625,000. This is *marginally* higher than the cash alternative.

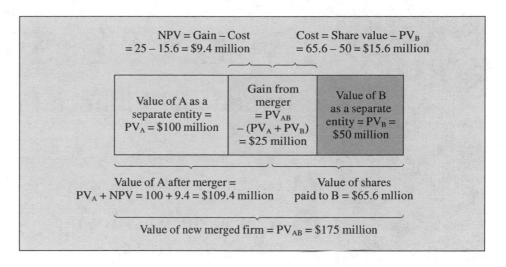

22.5 Figure 22.3 shows that shareholders of target firms enjoy excess returns of about 10 percent. This would translate to a price jump of $10 on a stock originally selling at $100 a share.

CHAPTER TWENTY-THREE

International Financial Management

Thus far we have talked principally about doing business at home. But many companies have substantial overseas interests. Of course the objectives of international financial management are still the same. You want to buy assets that are worth *more* than they cost, and you want to pay for them by issuing liabilities that are worth *less* than the money raised. But when you try to apply these criteria to an international business, you come up against some new wrinkles.

One of the most important differences in international financial management is that you need to deal with more than one currency. Therefore we open this chapter with a look at foreign exchange markets.

The financial manager must also remember that interest rates differ from country to country. For example, early in 1995 the interest rate on long-term government bonds was about 4.5 percent in Japan, about 7.5 percent in Germany and the U.S., 8.5 percent in the United Kingdom, and 9.2 percent in Canada. We will discuss the reasons for these differences in interest rates, along with some of the implications for financing overseas operations.

Exchange rate fluctuations can knock companies off course and transform black ink into red. We will therefore discuss how firms can protect themselves against exchange risks.

We will also discuss how international companies decide on capital investments. How do they choose the discount rate? You'll find that the basic principles of capital budgeting are the same as for domestic projects, but there are a few pitfalls to watch for.

After studying this chapter you should be able to

- Understand the difference between spot and forward exchange rates.
- Understand the basic relationships between spot exchange rates, forward exchange rates, interest rates, and inflation rates.
- Formulate simple strategies to protect the firm against exchange rate risk.
- Perform an NPV analysis for projects with cash flows in foreign currencies.

FOREIGN EXCHANGE MARKETS

A Canadian company that imports goods from Switzerland may need to exchange its dollars for Swiss francs in order to pay for its purchases. A Canadian company exporting to Switzerland may *receive* Swiss francs, which it sells in exchange for dollars. Both firms must make use of the foreign exchange market, where currency is traded.

The foreign exchange market has no central marketplace. All business is conducted by electronic means, telephone, or telex. The principal dealers are the large chartered banks, and any corporation that wants to buy or sell currency usually does so through a bank.

Turnover in the foreign exchange markets is huge. In London about $300 billion of currency changes hands each day (that is, about $75 *trillion* a year). New York and Tokyo between them account for a further $300 billion of turnover a day. Compare this to trading volume on the New York Stock Exchange, by far the largest stock exchange in the world, where the volume is about $7 billion on a typical day.

exchange rate: Amount of one currency needed to purchase one unit of another.

Exchange rates in Canada are the amount of one country's currency needed to purchase one unit of another currency. Table 23.1 shows exchange rates for a sample of major currencies.[1] The column, labeled "Cdn $ per unit," tells you how many Canadian dollars it takes to buy one unit of foreign exchange. For example, it takes 1.0945 Canadian dollars to buy one Swiss franc (Sfr). This is sometimes written as $1.0945/Sfr (that is, $1.0945 = Sfr1). If 1.0945 Canadian dollars buys 1 Swiss franc, then 1 Canadian dollar must buy 1/1.0945 =.9137 Swiss francs or, more concisely, Sfr.9137/$. The second column labelled "U.S. $ per unit" provides the same information but for trade into U.S. dollars.

TABLE 23.1
Spot and forward exchange rates Feb. 2, 1995

FOREIGN EXCHANGE

Mid-market rates in Toronto at noon, Feb. 2, 1995. Prepared by the Bank of Montreal Treasury Group.

		$1 U.S. in Cdn$ =	$1 Cdn. in U.S.$ =	Country	Currency	Cdn. $ per unit	U.S. $ per unit
U.S./Canada spot		1.4064	0.7110	Fiji	Dollar	0.9929	0.7060
1 month forward		1.4084	0.7100	Finland	Markka	0.2988	0.2125
2 months forward		1.4107	0.7089	France	Franc	0.2671	0.1899
3 months forward		1.4127	0.7079	Greece	Drachma	0.00594	0.00422
6 months forward		1.4176	0.7054	Hong Kong	Dollar	0.1819	0.1293
12 months forward		1.4241	0.7022	Hungary	Forint	0.01264	0.00899
3 years forward		1.4599	0.6650	Iceland	Krona	0.02093	0.01488
5 years forward		1.5089	0.6627	India	Rupee	0.04486	0.03190
7 years forward		1.5664	0.6384	Indonesia	Rupiah	0.000637	0.000453
10 years forward		1.6489	0.6065	Ireland	Punt	2.2102	1.5715
Canadian dollar	High	1.3976	0.7155	Israel	N Shekel	0.4674	0.3323
in 1995:	Low	1.4267	0.7009	Italy	Lira	0.000876	0.000623
	Average	1.4125	0.7080	Jamaica	Dollar	0.04395	0.03125
				Jordan	Dinar	2.0091	1.4286

Country	Currency	Cdn. $ per unit	U.S. $ per unit
Britain	Pound	2.2263	1.5830
1 month forward		2.2288	1.5825
2 months forward		2.2317	1.5820
3 months forward		2.2339	1.5813
6 months forward		2.2396	1.5799
12 months forward		2.2456	1.5769
Germany	Mark	0.9260	0.6584
1 month forward		0.9282	0.6590
3 months forward		0.9331	0.6605
6 months forward		0.9400	0.6631
12 months forward		0.9519	0.6684
Japan	Yen	0.014140	0.010054
1 month forward		0.014203	0.010084
3 months forward		0.014348	0.010156
6 months forward		0.014565	0.010274
12 months forward		0.014998	0.010532
Algeria	Dinar	0.0332	0.0236
Antigua, Grenada and St. Lucia	E.C. Dollar	0.5219	0.3711
Argentina	Peso	1.40640	1.00000
Australia	Dollar	1.0661	0.7580
Austria	Schilling	0.13169	0.09363
Bahamas	Dollar	1.4064	1.0000
Barbados	Dollar	0.7067	0.5025
Belgium	Franc	0.04490	0.03193
Bermuda	Dollar	1.4064	1.0000
Brazil	Real	1.670309	1.187648
Bulgaria	Lev	0.0211	0.0150
Chile	Peso	0.003452	0.002454
China	Renminbi	0.1667	0.1185
Cyprus	Pound	2.9955	2.1299
Czech Rep	Koruna	0.0509	0.0362
Denmark	Krone	0.2348	0.1670
Egypt	Pound	0.4136	0.2941

Country	Currency	Cdn. $ per unit	U.S. $ per unit
Lebanon	Pound	0.000856	0.00609
Luxembourg	Franc	0.04490	0.03193
Malaysia	Ringgit	0.5507	0.3916
Mexico	N Peso	0.2619	0.1862
Netherlands	Guilder	0.8267	0.5878
New Zealand	Dollar	0.9015	0.6410
Norway	Krone	0.2115	0.1504
Pakistan	Rupee	0.04571	0.03250
Philippines	Peso	0.05694	0.04049
Poland	Zloty	0.5768663	0.4101723
Portugal	Escudo	0.00896	0.00637
Romani	Leu	0.0008	0.0006
Russia	Ruble	0.000345	0.000245
Saudi Arabia	Riyal	0.3750	0.2667
Singapore	Dollar	0.9686	0.6887
Slovakia	Koruna	0.0463	0.0329
South Africa	Rand	0.3966	0.2820
South Korea	Won	0.001788	0.001271
Spain	Peseta	0.01066	0.00758
Sudan	Dinar	0.0366	0.0260
Sweden	Krona	0.1891	0.1345
Switzerland	Franc	1.0945	0.7782
Taiwan	Dollar	0.0539	0.0383
Thailand	Baht	0.0563	0.0401
Trinidad, Tobago	Dollar	0.2478	0.1762
Turkey	Lira	0.0000346	0.0000246
Venezuela	Boilvar	0.00829	0.00590
Zambia	Kwacha	0.002099	0.001493
European Currency Unit		1.7469	1.2421
Special Drawing Right		2.0666	1.4694

The U.S. dollar closed at $1.4057 in terms of Canadian funds, down $0.0020 from Wednesday. The pound sterling closed at $2.2238, down $0.0032.

In New York, the Canadian dollar closed up $0.0010 at $0.7114 in terms of U.S. funds. The pound sterling was unchanged at $1.5820.

Source: The Globe and Mail February 3, 1995.

[1] The rates in Table 23.1 are taken from the daily table of exchange rates that is published in *The Globe and Mail*.

● **EXAMPLE 23.1 A Yen For Trade**

How many yen will it cost a Japanese importer to purchase $1000 worth of grain from a Manitoba farmer? How many dollars will it take for that farmer to buy a Japanese VCR priced in Japan at 30,000 yen (¥)?

The spot exchange rate is $.01414 per ¥ or equivalently ¥70.72 per $. The $1000 of grain will require the Japanese importer to come up with $1000 × 70.72 = ¥70,720. The VCR will require the Canadian farmer to come up with 30,000/70.72 = $424.21.

The number of dollars needed to buy one unit of foreign currency is called the *direct* exchange rate. For example, column 1 shows that the direct exchange rate for the British pound is $2.2263/£. The number of units of foreign currency that you can buy for one dollar is known as the *indirect* or *European* exchange rate. The indirect rate for Japanese yen is ¥70.72/$. Usually, when a bank quotes an exchange rate, it will state the indirect rate. But, to make life confusing, the pound sterling (and the Irish punt) is usually quoted as a direct rate — that is, a bank quotes the number of dollars per pound.

spot exchange rate: Exchange rate for an immediate transaction.

Foreign exchange dealers quote spot and forward exchange rates. The **spot exchange rate** is the price of currency for immediate delivery.[2] Except where otherwise noted, the quotes in Table 23.1 show spot exchange rates. For example, if you need yen immediately, you will pay the spot exchange rate of ¥70.72/$. If you need British pounds immediately, you will pay the spot rate of $2.2263/£.

Suppose that you have agreed to purchase a consignment of Japanese VCRs for ¥100 million and you need to make the payment when you take delivery of the VCRs at the end of 12 months. You could wait until the 12 months have passed and then buy 100 million yen at the spot exchange rate. If the spot rate is unchanged at ¥70.72/$, then the VCRs will cost you 100 million/70.72 = $1,414,027. But you are taking a risk by waiting, for the yen may become more expensive. For example, if the yen appreciated to ¥60/$, then you would have to pay out 100 million/60 = $1,666,667 million.

forward exchange rate: Exchange rate for a forward transaction.

You can avoid this risk and fix the dollar cost of VCRs by "buying the yen forward," that is, by arranging now to buy yen in the future. The **forward exchange rate** is the price of currency for delivery at some time in the future. Table 23.1 also shows forward exchange rates for a number of currencies. For example, the 12-month forward rate for the yen is quoted at .014998 dollar per yen (or 66.675 yen per dollar). If you buy 100 million yen forward, you don't pay anything today; you simply fix today the price that you will pay for your yen in the future. At the end of the 12 months you receive your 100 million yen and hand over 100 million × .014998 = $1,499,800 in payment.

Notice that if you buy Japanese yen forward, you get fewer yen for your dollar than if you buy spot. In this case, the yen is said to trade at a forward *premium* relative to the dollar. Expressed as a percentage, the forward premium is

$$\frac{(70.72 - 66.675)}{66.675} \times 100 = 6.07\%$$

You could also say that the dollar was selling at a 6.07 percent *forward discount*.

A forward purchase or sale is a made-to-order transaction between you and the bank. It can be for any currency, any amount, and any delivery day. You could buy,

---

[2] The term *immediate delivery* is a relative one; usually it takes 2 days before you receive your foreign currency.

say, 99,999 Vietnamese dong or Haitian gourdes for a year and a day forward as long as you can find a bank ready to deal. Most forward transactions are for 6 months or less, but banks are prepared to buy or sell the major currencies for up to 10 years forward.

There is also an organized market for currency for future delivery known as the currency *futures* market. Futures contracts are highly standardized — they exist only for the main currencies, they are for specified amounts, and choice of deliv-

Finance in Action

Currency Turmoil Hits Importers

OTTAWA — Toronto currency adviser John Newland has seen the damage that wild currency fluctuations can cause Canadian importers. And he says they quickly learn how to protect themselves. Take the case of one of his clients, an importer of Austrian clothes. The Austrian shilling, which generally moves with the German mark, has soared in the past few months along with several other foreign currencies like the Japanese yen and the British pound.

"He has just been clobbered," said Mr. Newland, who works for Refco Futures (Canada) Ltd., the Canadian arm of a Chicago-based currency trader. "He's having a hell of a time because he had not protected himself on some of his dollars, and this year he wants to make damn sure he locks in because he does not want to take the chance again."

Here's the problem — the importer agreed to buy goods last spring in Austrian shillings. Then, he turned around and made a deal with domestic retailers in Canadian dollars, building in a reasonable profit. But no money actually changed hands until this winter, wiping out his margin when the Canadian dollar dropped in value.

It is the classic importer squeeze and it is only one example of the mil-lions of dollars lost in the chain of events triggered by the recent sharp fall in the dollar. With the Canadian and U.S. dollars at post-war lows against the yen, and well down against the mark and other European currencies, importers are scrambling.

Some importers are compensating by raising prices, eating part or all of their margin to maintain sales or sourcing goods in markets where their dollars stretch further — namely in North America. Or they go to currency experts like Mr. Newland for a little peace of mind, buying a forward contract in the currency of their choice and locking in at today's exchange rates — a technique known as currency hedging.

Soren Larsen, Canadian vice-president of German printing press maker MAN Roland, said his company has been able to avoid frequent price increases, but it has not been easy.

"We have a policy of hedging our prices out into the future," Mr. Larsen said from Chicago. "But you nonetheless have to increase your prices when you deplete your inventory, so to speak, of foreign currency at a certain rate because you have to buy new foreign currency to pay your bills."

Source: *The Globe and Mail*, April 24, 1995, p. B1.

ery dates is limited. The advantage of this standardization is that there is a very low-cost market in currency futures. Huge numbers of contracts are bought and sold daily on the futures exchanges.

SELF-TEST 23.1

A skiing vacation in Switzerland costs Sfr1500.
a. How many dollars does that represent? Use the exchange rates in Table 23.1.
b. Suppose that the dollar depreciates by 10 percent relative to the Swiss franc, so that each dollar buys 10 percent fewer Swiss francs than before. What will be the new values of the direct and indirect exchange rates?
c. If the Swiss vacation continues to cost the same number of Swiss francs, what will happen to the cost in dollars?
d. If the tour company that is offering the vacation keeps the price fixed in dollars, what will happen to the number of Swiss francs that it will receive?

 23.2 SOME BASIC RELATIONSHIPS

The president of VCR Importers has also been looking at the financial pages and has dashed off the following memo to you:

I have been looking at The Globe and Mail *and I am not happy with some of the policies that we have been following.*

First, we have been buying yen forward to cover the cost of our imports. You say that this ensures us against the risk that the dollar may depreciate over the next 12 months, but it is incredibly expensive insurance. Each dollar buys only 66.675 yen when we buy forward, compared with the current spot rate of 70.72 yen to the dollar. We could save a fortune by buying yen as and when we need them rather than buying them forward.

Another possibility has occurred to me. If we are worried that the dollar may depreciate, why don't we buy yen today at the low spot rate of ¥70.72/$ and then put them on deposit until we have to pay for the VCRs?

I am also worried that we are missing out on some cheap financing. It is true that the interest rate on our bank loans is much lower than it used to be but Japanese interest rates are even lower. Why don't we repay our dollar loans and borrow yen instead? That would slash our interest payments.

Before you respond to the president's memo, you need some understanding of how exchange rates are determined and why one country may have a lower interest rate than another. These are complex issues but as a first cut we suggest that you think of spot and forward exchange rates, interest rates, and inflation rates as being linked together as in Figure 23.1. Let's explain.

Exchange Rates and Inflation

Consider first the relationship between changes in the exchange rate and inflation rates (the two boxes on the right of Figure 23.1). Suppose you notice that gold can be bought in Toronto for $525 an ounce and sold in Tokyo for ¥40,000. You think you may be onto a good thing. You buy gold for $525 and put it on the first plane to Tokyo, where you sell it for ¥40,000. Then you exchange your ¥40,000 for 40,000/70.72 = $566. You have made a gross profit of $41 an ounce. Of course you have to pay transportation and insurance costs out of this, but there should still be something left over for you.

FIGURE 23.1
Some simple theories
linking spot and forward
exchange rates, interest
rates, and inflation rates.

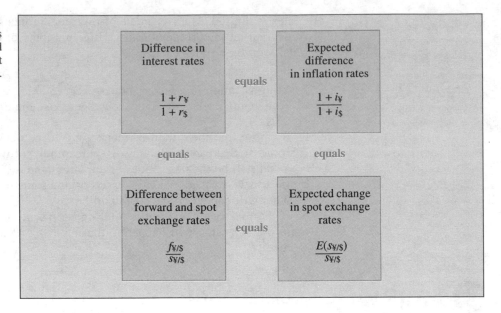

At these prices you would have a sure-fire profit. Sure-fire profits don't exist — not for long. As others notice the disparity between the price of gold in Tokyo and the price in Toronto, the price will be forced down in Tokyo and up in Toronto until the profit opportunity disappears. This ensures that the dollar price of gold is about the same in the two countries.[3]

Gold is a standard and easily transportable commodity, but to some degree you might expect that the same forces would be acting to equalize the domestic and foreign prices of other goods. Those goods that can be bought more cheaply abroad will be imported, and that will force down the price of the domestic product. Similarly, those goods that can be bought more cheaply in Canada will be exported, and that will force down the price of the foreign product.

law of one price: Theory that prices of goods in all countries should be equal when translated to a common currency.

This conclusion is often called the **law of one price**. Just as the price of goods in The Bay must be roughly the same as the price of goods in Eaton's, so the price of goods in Japan when converted into dollars must be roughly the same as the price in Canada:

$$\text{Dollar price of goods in Canada} = \frac{\text{yen price of goods in Japan}}{\text{number of yen per dollar}}$$

$$\$525 = \frac{\text{yen price of gold in Japan}}{70.72}$$

$$\text{Price of gold in Japan} = 525 \times 70.72 = ¥39,603$$

No one who has compared prices in foreign stores with prices at home really believes that the law of one price holds exactly. Look at the first column of Table 23.2, which shows the price of a Big Mac in different countries in 1993. Using the exchange rates at that time (second column), we can convert the local price to U.S. dollars (third column). You can see that the price varies considerably across

---

[3] Activity of this kind is known as *arbitrage*. The arbitrageur makes a riskless profit by noticing discrepancies in prices.

TABLE 23.2
Price of a Big Mac in
different countries

	Price in Local Currency	Exchange Rate (currency/dollar)	Local Price Converted to Dollars
Australia	A$2.45	1.39	1.76
Belgium	BFr109	32.5	3.36
Canada	C$2.76	1.26	2.19
Denmark	DKr25.75	6.06	4.25
France	FFr18.50	5.34	3.46
Germany	DM4.60	1.58	2.91
Holland	F15.45	1.77	3.07
Hong Kong	HK$9.00	7.73	1.16
Ireland	Ir£1.48	0.65	2.29
Italy	L4500	1523	2.95
Japan	¥391	113	3.45
Korea	W2300	796	2.89
Spain	Pts325	114	2.85
Sweden	SKr25.50	7.43	3.43
Switzerland	Sf5.70	1.45	3.94
United Kingdom	£1.79	.64	2.79
United States	US$2.28	—	2.28

Source: "Big MacCurrencies," *The Economist,* April 17, 1993, p. 101. © *The Economist,* April 1993.

countries. For example, Big Macs were almost twice as expensive in Denmark as in Canada and about half the price in Hong Kong.[4]

This suggests a possible way to make a quick buck. Why don't you buy a hamburger-to-go in Canada for $2.19 and take it for resale to Denmark where the price in dollars is $4.25? The answer, of course, is that the gain would not cover the costs. The law of one price works very well for commodities like gold where transportation costs are relatively small; it works far less well for Big Macs and very badly indeed for haircuts and appendectomies, which cannot be transported at all.

● EXAMPLE 23.2 The Cost of a Hangover

Table 23.3 provides another example where the law of one price does not give the whole story. The cost of a hangover appears to differ substantially in different cities. What would the exchange rate need to be to equalize the cost of a

TABLE 23.3
The cost of a hangover
in different cities

City	1 Litre of Scotch, Dollars	36 Alka-Seltzer, Dollars	Exchange Rate[a]
Copenhagen	48.22	4.63	6.11
Singapore	42.33	5.33	1.63
Frankfurt	21.49	11.46	1.59
Hong Kong	23.95	5.24	11.80
London	23.81	4.61	0.66
Paris	20.32	6.85	5.37
New York	22.84	3.85	
Toronto	19.42	3.57	1.27
Moscow	12.95	4.70	250.00

[a]Exchange rate is the number of units of foreign currency to one dollar in November 1992.
Source: Financial Times, December 16, 1992.

---

[4] Of course, it could also be that Big Macs come with a bigger smile in Denmark. If the quality of the hamburgers or the service differs, we are not comparing like with like.

litre of scotch in Toronto and Copenhagen? What would it need to be to equalize the cost of Alka Seltzer in Toronto and Frankfurt?

Scotch costs $19.42 in Toronto[5] and $48.22 × 6.11 = DKr294.62 in Copenhagen. The cost of scotch would be the same in the two countries if $19.42 could be exchanged for exactly DKr294.62. That implies that $1 would need to be equal in value to 294.62/19.42 = DKr15.17. This compares with the *actual* exchange rate of $1 = DKr6.11.

Similarly, Alka-Seltzer costs $3.57 in Toronto and $11.46 × 1.59 = DM18.22 in Frankfurt. The cost would be the same in the two countries if $3.57 were equivalent to DM18.22 — that is, if $1 were equivalent to DM5.10. The actual exchange rate was $1 = DM1.59.

purchasing power parity (PPP): Theory that the cost of living in different countries is equal, and exchange rates adjust to offset inflation differentials across countries.

A weaker version of the law of one price is known as **purchasing power parity**, or **PPP**. PPP states that although some goods may cost different amounts in different countries, the *general* cost of living should be the same in any two countries.

Purchasing power parity implies that if prices increase faster in one country than another, there must be an offsetting change in the exchange rate. For example, by 1992 prices in Peru were about 336,000 times their level in 1986. To put it another way, you could say that the purchasing power of the new sol (the Peruvian currency) declined by about 99.9999 percent relative to other currencies. With Peruvian prices 336,000 times their previous values, Peruvian exporters would have found it impossible to sell their goods if exchange rates had not adjusted. But, of course, exchange rates did adjust. In fact, on average, one new sol bought 99.999 percent fewer dollars than before. Thus a 99.999 percent relative decline in purchasing power was offset by a 99.999 percent decline in the value of the Peruvian currency.

Peru is an extreme case, but in Figure 23.2 we have plotted the relative change in purchasing power for a sample of countries against the change in the exchange

FIGURE 23.2
Countries with high inflation rates tend to see their currencies depreciate.

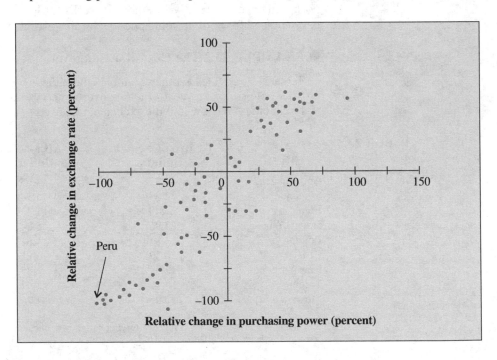

---

[5] The prices are all in U.S. dollars. Although the *Financial Times* is a British publication they follow the widely used convention of basing comparisons of this sort on U.S. dollars.

rate. Peru is tucked in the bottom left-hand corner. You can see that although the relationship is far from exact, large differences in inflation rates are generally accompanied by an offsetting change in the exchange rate. In fact, if you had to make a long-term forecast of the exchange rate, it is very difficult to do much better than to assume that it will offset the effect of any differences in the inflation rates.

If purchasing power parity holds, then your forecast of the difference in inflation rates is also your best forecast of the change in the spot rate of exchange. Thus the expected difference between inflation rates in Japan and Canada is given by the right-hand boxes in Figure 23.1:

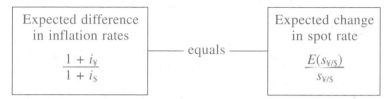

For example, if inflation is expected to be 2 percent in Canada and 1 percent in Japan, then purchasing power parity implies that the expected spot rate for the yen is ¥70.03/$:

Current spot rate × expected difference in inflation rates = expected spot rate

$$70.72 \times \frac{1.01}{1.02} = 70.03$$

SELF-TEST 23.2

Suppose that gold currently costs $532 an ounce in Canada and £260 an ounce in Great Britain.
a. What must be the pound/dollar exchange rate?
b. Suppose that gold prices rise by 2 percent in Canada and by 5 percent in Great Britain. What will be the price of gold in the two currencies at the end of the year? What must be the exchange rate at the end of the year?
c. Show that at the end of the year each dollar buys about 3 percent more pounds as predicted by PPP.

Inflation and Interest Rates

Now for the relationship between the top two boxes in Figure 23.1 — between the interest rates in different countries and expected inflation rates.

Interest rates in Canada are about 8 percent, whereas in Brazil they are nearly 3000 percent. So why don't you (and a few million other investors) rush into Brazilian bonds, where the return seems to be much greater?

The answer lies in the distinction that we made in Chapter 4 between nominal and real rates of interest. Bonds promise you a fixed nominal rate of interest but they don't promise what that money will buy. If you invest 100 Brazilian cruzeiros for a year at an interest rate of 3000 percent, you will have 3000 percent more cruzeiros at the end of the year than you did at the start. But you won't be 3000 better off. With an inflation rate in Brazil approaching 3000 percent, you will be able to buy only (say) 3 percent more goods than you can today. The nominal rate of interest is 3000 percent but the real rate is close to zero. Investors in Brazil *need* that high nominal interest rate to compensate them for Brazil's high rate of inflation.

The nominal rate of interest is much lower in Canada, but then so is the inflation rate. The real rate of interest is likely to be similar in the two countries.

There is a general law at work here. Just as water always flows downhill, so capital always flows where returns are greatest. But it is the *real* returns that concern investors, not the *nominal* returns. Two countries may have different nominal interest rates but the same expected real interest rate.

Do you remember from Chapter 4 Irving Fisher's theory that changes in the expected inflation rate are reflected in the nominal interest rate? We have just described here the **international Fisher effect** — international variations in the expected inflation rate are reflected in the nominal interest rates:

international Fisher effect: Theory that real interest rates in all countries should be equal, with differences in nominal rates reflecting differences in expected inflation.

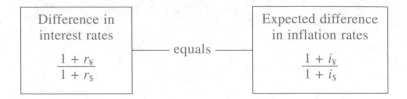

In other words, capital market equilibrium requires that *real* interest rates be the same in any two countries. For example, the nominal interest rate in Japan is 5 percent and the expected inflation rate is about 1 percent. Thus

$$r_\yen(\text{real}) = \frac{1 + r_\yen}{E(1 + i_\yen)} - 1 = \frac{1.05}{1.01} - 1 = .039 \text{ or } 3.9\%$$

In the United States, where the nominal interest rate is 7.5 percent and inflation is 3 percent, the real interest rate is almost the same at about :

$$r_\$(\text{real}) = \frac{1 + r_\$}{E(1 + i_\$)} - 1 = \frac{1.075}{1.03} - 1 = .044, \text{ or } 4.4\%$$

In Canada, however, the nominal interest rate is 9 percent. Inflation in recent years has been even less than in the U.S. Suppose that we thought expected inflation was the same in Canada as in the U.S., about 3 percent. This means that the real interest rate is much higher at about 6 percent:

$$r_\$(\text{real}) = \frac{1 + r_\$}{E(1 + i_\$)} - 1 = \frac{1.09}{1.03} - 1 = .058, \text{ or } 5.8\%$$

This illustrates how hard it is to see if the theory in fact works. This is because we cannot directly observe *expected* inflation. Is Canada's real rate higher than that of Japan and the U.S. or are investors expecting a much higher inflation rate, despite the recent record? In general, however, the relationship between inflation and nominal rates works pretty well. In Figure 23.3 we have plotted the average interest rate in each of 16 countries against the inflation that subsequently occurred. You can see that the countries with the highest interest rates generally had the highest inflation rates. There were much smaller differences between the real rates of interest than between nominal rates.

SELF-TEST 23.3

Canadian investors can invest $1000 at an interest rate of 8 percent. Alternatively, they can convert those funds to 1080 German deutschemarks and invest at 6.5 percent in Germany. If expected inflation in Canada is 2 percent and if real rates in the two countries are the same, what must be investors' forecast of the inflation rate in Germany?

FIGURE 23.3
Countries with the highest interest rates generally have the highest subsequent inflation rates. In this diagram, each point represents a different country.

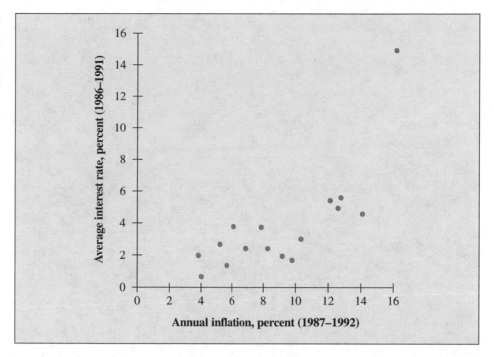

Interest Rates and Exchange Rates

You are an investor with $1 million to invest for 1 year. The 1-year interest rate in Japan is 1.8 percent and in Canada it is 8 percent. Is it better to make a yen loan or a dollar loan?

The answer seems obvious: Isn't it better to earn an interest rate of 8 percent than 1.8 percent? But appearances may be deceptive. If you lend in Japan, you first need to convert your $1 million into yen. When the loan is repaid at the end of the year, you need to convert your yen back into dollars. Of course you don't know what the exchange rate will be at the end of the year but you can fix the future value of your yen by selling them forward. If the forward rate of exchange is sufficiently attractive, it may compensate you for the lower rate of interest in Japan.

Let's use the data from Table 23.1 to check which loan is the better deal:

- *Dollar loan*: The rate of interest on a 1-year dollar loan is 8 percent. Therefore, at the end of the year you get $1,000,000 \times 1.08 = \$1,080,000$.
- *Yen loan*: The current rate of exchange (from Table 23.1) is ¥70.72/$. Therefore, for $1 million, you can buy $1,000,000 \times 70.72 = ¥70,720,000$. The rate of interest on a 1-year yen loan is 1.8 percent. So at the end of the year, you get $¥70,720,000 \times 1.018 = ¥71,992,960$. Of course, you don't know what the exchange rate will be at the end of the year. But that doesn't matter. You can nail down the price at which you can sell your yen. The 1-year forward rate is ¥66.675/$. Therefore, by selling the ¥71,992,960 forward, you make sure that you will get $71,992,960/66.675 = \$1,079,750$.

Thus the two investments offer almost exactly the same rate of return. They have to — they are both risk-free. If the domestic interest rate were different from the "covered" foreign rate, you would have a money machine: you could borrow in the market with the lower rate and lend in the market with the higher rate.

When you make a yen loan, you lose because you get a lower interest rate. But you gain because you sell the yen forward at a higher price than you have to pay for them today. The interest rate differential is

$$\frac{1 + r_¥}{1 + r_\$} = \frac{1.018}{1.08} = .9425$$

and the differential between the forward and spot exchange rate is nearly identical:

$$\frac{f_{¥/\$}}{s_{¥/\$}} = \frac{66.68}{70.72} = .9428$$

interest rate parity: Theory that forward premium equals interest rate differential.

Interest rate parity theory says that the interest rate differential must equal the differential between the forward and spot exchange rates. Thus

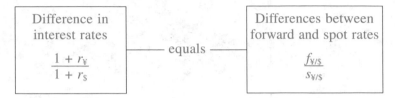

- ● **EXAMPLE 23.3 What Happens if Interest Rate Parity Theory Does Not Hold?**

Suppose that the forward rate on the yen is not ¥66.675/$ but is ¥70.72/$, the same as today's spot rate. Here is what you do. Borrow ¥1 million at an interest rate of 1.8 percent and change these yen into dollars at the spot exchange rate of ¥70.72/$. That gives you $14,140, which you invest for a year at 8 percent. At the end of the year you will have $14,140 \times 1.08 = \$15,271$. Of course, this is not money to spend because you need to repay your yen loan. The amount that you need to repay is $1,000,000 \times 1.018 = ¥1,018,000$. If you buy the yen forward, you can fix in advance the number of dollars that you will need to lay out. With a forward rate of ¥70.72/$, you need to set aside $1,018,000/70.72 = \$14,395$. Thus, after paying off your yen loan, you walk away with a risk-free profit of $15,271 - 14,395 = \$876$. It is a pity that in practice interest rate parity almost always holds and the opportunities for such easy profits are rare.

SELF-TEST 23.4

Look at the exchange rates in Table 23.1. Does the United States dollar sell at a forward premium or discount on the dollar (twelve month)? Does this suggest that the interest rate in the U.S. is higher or lower than in Canada? Use the interest rate parity relationship to estimate the interest rate in the United States.

The Forward Rate and the Expected Spot Rate

If you buy yen forward, you get fewer yen for your dollar than if you buy them spot. So the yen is selling at a forward premium. Now let us think how the forward premium is related to expected changes in spot rates of exchange.

The 1-year yen forward rate is ¥66.675/$. Would you buy yen forward at this rate if you expected the spot rate for yen at the end of the year to bc higher than this? Probably not. You would be tempted to wait and get more yen for your dollar in the spot market. If other traders felt the same way, nobody would buy yen forward and the forward exchange rate would fall. Similarly, if traders expected the spot rate for yen at the end of the year to be *lower* than ¥66.675/$, they might be reluctant to *sell* forward and the forward exchange rate would rise.[6]

---

[6] The expectations theory ignores risk. If a forward purchase reduces your risk sufficiently, you *might* be prepared to buy forward even if you expected to pay more as a result. Similarly, if a forward sale reduces risk, you *might* be prepared to sell forward even if you expected to receive less as a result.

This is the reasoning behind the *expectations theory* of exchange rates, which predicts that the forward rate equals the expected future spot exchange rate: $f_{\yen/\$} = E(s_{\yen/\$})$. Equivalently, we can say that the *percentage* difference between the forward rate and today's spot rate is equal to the expected *percentage* change in the spot rate:

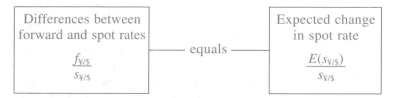

This is the final leg of our quadrilateral in Figure 23.1.

The expectations theory of forward rates does not imply that managers are perfect forecasters. Sometimes the *actual* future spot rate will turn out to be above the previous forward rate. Sometimes it will fall below. But if the theory is correct, we should find that *on the average* the forward rate is equal to the future spot rate. The theory passes this simple test reasonably well. This is important news for the financial manager; it means that a company that always covers its foreign exchange commitments by buying or selling currency in the forward market does not have to pay a premium to avoid exchange rate risk: *on average*, the forward price at which it agrees to exchange currency will equal the eventual spot exchange rate, no better but no worse.

We should also warn you that the forward rate does not tell you very much about the future spot rate. This does not mean that the forward rate is a poor measure of managers' expectations; it just means that exchange rates are very tough to predict.

Some Implications

Our four simple relationships ignore many of the complexities of interest rates and exchange rates. But they capture the more important features and emphasize that international capital markets and currency markets function well and offer no free lunches. For example, in the late 1980s, several Australian banks observed that interest rates in Switzerland were about 8 percentage points lower than those in Australia and advised their clients to borrow Swiss francs. Was this advice correct? According to the international Fisher effect, the lower Swiss interest rate indicated that investors were expecting a lower inflation rate in Switzerland than in Australia and this in turn would result in an appreciation of the Swiss franc relative to the Australian dollar. Thus it was likely that the advantage of the low Swiss interest rate would be offset by the fact that it would cost the borrowers more Australian dollars to repay the loan. As it turned out, the Swiss franc appreciated very rapidly, the Australian banks found that they had a number of very irate clients and agreed to compensate them for the losses they had incurred. *Moral*: Don't assume automatically that it is cheaper to borrow in a currency with a low nominal rate of interest.

Here is another case where our simple relationships can stop you falling into a trap. Managers sometimes talk as if you make money simply by buying currencies that go up in value and selling those that go down. But if investors anticipate the change in the exchange rate, then it will be reflected in the interest rate differential; therefore, what you gain on the currency you will lose in terms of interest income. You make money from currency speculation only if you can predict whether the exchange rate will change by more or less than the interest rate differential. In other words, you must be able to predict whether the exchange rate will change by more or less than the forward premium.

SELF-TEST 23.5

In 1986 the U.S. tobacco company Philip Morris borrowed 100,000 New Zealand dollars at an interest rate of 17.25 percent when the exchange rate between the New Zealand and U.S. dollar was NZ$1.91/$. The exchange rate was NZ$1.69/$ in 1987 and NZ$1.52/$ in 1988. When Philip Morris came to repay its loan in 1989 the exchange rate was about NZ$1.67/$. Calculate in U.S. dollars the amount that Philip Morris borrowed and the amounts that it paid in interest and principal (assume annual interest payments). What was the effective *U.S. dollar* interest rate on the loan? If you don't have a financial calculator, you will need a little trial and error to find the internal rate of return.

● EXAMPLE 23.4 Measuring Currency Gains

The financial manager of Universal Waffle is proud of his acumen. Instead of keeping his cash in Canadian dollars, he has invested in deutschemark deposits. At the end of 1980 the exchange rate was DM1.55/$. By the end of 1994 a dollar bought only DM1.12. Thus the manager calculates that he has made a currency gain of about 38 percent, or 2.3 percent a year. Has he really gained from investing in foreign currency? Let's check.

The compound rate of interest on dollar deposits between 1980 and 1994 was about 9 percent. The compound rate of interest on deutschemark deposits was about 7 percent. If Universal Waffle had kept its funds in dollar deposits, each $100 would have grown to $100 \times 1.09^{14} = \$334$. Compare this figure with the amount that Universal made by investing the same sum in Germany. At the end of 1980, $100 could be exchanged for $100 \times 1.55 = DM155$. Invested at an interest rate of 7 percent, this sum would have grown to $155 \times 1.07^{14} = DM399.67$. Exchanged back at the 1994 exchange rate, it would have produced $399.67/1.12 = \$357$. The currency gain was almost all wiped out by the lower rate of interest on deutschemark deposits.

The interest rate differential (which is equal to the forward premium) is a measure of the market's expectations of the change in the value of the currency. The difference between the German and Canadian interest rates during this period suggests that the market was expecting the deutschemark to appreciate by about 2 percent a year.[7] As it happened, Universal Waffle invested in a currency that performed slightly better than investors expected.

23.3 HEDGING EXCHANGE RATE RISK

Firms with international operations are subject to exchange rate risk. As exchange rates fluctuate, the dollar value of the firm's revenues or expenses also fluctuates. It helps to distinguish two types of exchange rate risk: contractual and noncontractual. By *contractual* risk, we mean that the firm is committed either to pay or to receive a known amount of foreign currency. For example, our VCR importer was committed to pay ¥100 million at the end of 12 months. If the value of the yen appreciates rapidly over this period, those VCRs will cost more dollars than the firm expected.

---

[7] If the interest rate is 9 percent on dollar deposits and 7 percent on deutschemark deposits, our simple relationship implies that the expected change in the value of the deutschemark was $(1 + r_\$)/(1 + r_{DM}) - 1 = 1.09/1.07 - 1 = .018$ or 1.8 percent.

Noncontractual risk arises because exchange rate fluctuations can affect the competitive position of the firm. For example, during 1991 and 1992 the value of the deutschemark appreciated relative to that of other major currencies. As a result, Porsche and other German luxury car manufacturers found it increasingly difficult to compete in North America. Canadian dealers that had a franchise to sell German luxury cars also took a bath. Thus the German car producers and their dealers in Canada were exposed to exchange rate changes even though they may have had no fixed obligations to pay or receive dollars.

Exchange rate changes can get companies into *big* trouble and therefore most companies aim to limit at least their contractual exposure to currency fluctuations. Let us look at an example of how this can be done.

In 1989 a British company, Enterprise Oil, bought some oil properties from Texas Eastern for $440 million.[8] Since the payment was delayed a couple of months, Enterprise's plans for financing the purchase could have been thrown out of kilter if the dollar had strengthened during this period.

Enterprise therefore decided to avoid, or *hedge*, this risk. It did so by borrowing pounds, which it converted into dollars at the current spot rate and invested for 2 months. In that way Enterprise guaranteed that it would have just enough dollars available to pay for the purchase. Of course it was possible that the dollar would *depreciate* over the 2 months, in which case Enterprise would have regretted that it did not wait and buy the dollars spot. Unfortunately, you cannot have your cake and eat it too. By fixing its dollar cost, Enterprise forfeited the chance of pleasant as well as unpleasant surprises.

Was there any other way that Enterprise could hedge against exchange loss? Of course. It could buy $440 million 2 months forward. No cash would change hands immediately but Enterprise would fix the price at which it buys its dollars at the end of 2 months. It would therefore eliminate all exchange risk on the deal. Interest rate parity theory tells us that the difference between buying spot and buying forward is equal to the difference between the rate of interest that you pay at home and the interest that you earn overseas. In other words, the two methods of eliminating risk should be equivalent.

Let us check this. In March 1989 the 2-month interest rate in the United States was about 9.7 percent and the interest rate in the United Kingdom was 13.0 percent. The spot exchange rate was $1.743 to the pound and the 2-month forward rate was $1.730/£. Table 23.4 shows that the cash flows from the two methods of hedging the dollar payment for Texas Eastern were almost identical.[9]

What is the cost of such a hedge? You sometimes hear managers say that it is equal to the difference between the forward rate and *today's* spot rate. This is wrong. If Enterprise did not hedge, it would pay the spot rate for dollars at the time that the payment for Texas Eastern was due. Therefore, the cost of hedging is the difference between the forward rate and the *expected* spot rate when payment is received.

Hedge or speculate? We generally vote for hedging. First, it makes life simpler for the firm and allows it to concentrate on its own business. Second, it does not cost much. (In fact the cost is zero if the forward rate equals the expected spot rate, as our simple relations imply.) Third, the foreign exchange market seems reasonably efficient, at least for the major currencies. Speculation should be a

---

[8] See "Enterprise Oil's Mega Forex Option," *Corporate Finance* 53 (April 1989), p. 13.
[9] We are not sure of Enterprise's borrowing rate but the company is rumoured to have hedged at an effective forward rate of $1.73/£.

TABLE 23.4
Enterprise Oil could
hedge its future dollar
payment either by
borrowing sterling and
lending dollars or by
buying dollars forward

	Cash Flow, Millions	
	£	$
Method 1: Borrow sterling, convert proceeds to dollars, and invest dollars until needed		
Now:		
Borrow £248.6m at 13%	+248.6	
Convert to $ at $1.743/£	−248.6	+433.3
Invest $433.3m for 2 months at 9.7%		−433.3
Net cash flow now	0	0
Month 2:		
Repay £ loan with interest	−253.7	
Receive payment on $ loan		+440
Pay for oil properties		−440
Net cash flow, Month 2	−253.7	0
Method 2: Buy dollars forward		
Now:		
Buy $440m forward at $1.73/£	0	0
Month 2:		
Pay for $	−254.3	+440
Payment for oil properties		−440
Net cash flow, Month 2	−254.3	0

zero-sum game unless financial managers have superior information to the pros who make the market.

SELF-TEST 23.6

You should now be in a position to reply to that memo you received from the president of VCR Importers (see page 595). What is the cost to the company of ensuring against exchange rate changes by buying yen forward? Is the president correct to compare the forward rate with the current spot rate? What is the disadvantage of buying yen now and leaving them on deposit? Is it better to do this than to buy yen forward? And what do you think of the president's suggestion of borrowing yen at a "low" interest rate of 1.8 percent?

23.4 INTERNATIONAL CAPITAL BUDGETING

Net Present Value Analysis

Consider Outland Steel Corporation, a Canadian firm that manufactures and sells steel both at home and abroad. Its export business has risen to the point at which it is proposing to establish a subsidiary in Holland to hold inventories of steel. Outland's decision to invest overseas should be based on the same criteria as its decision to invest in Canada — that is, the company must forecast the incremental cash flows, discount them at a rate that reflects the opportunity cost of capital, and accept projects with a positive NPV. Let's examine two ways that Outland could calculate the NPV of its Dutch venture:

Method 1: Value cash flows in dollars. Outland could follow the practice of many multinational companies and do all its capital budgeting calculations in dollars. In this case it must first estimate the guilder cash flows from its Dutch operation and convert these into dollars at the projected exchange rate. These dollar cash flows can then be discounted at the *dollar* cost of capital to give the investment's net present value in dollars.

Method 2: Value cash flows in guilders. In order to avoid making forecasts of the exchange rate, Outland could simply calculate the project's net present value entirely in terms of guilders, using a *guilder* cost of capital. Outland could then convert this figure into dollars at the current exchange rate.

Each method has three steps, but the orders of steps 2 and 3 are different:

	Method 1	**Method 2**
Step 1	Estimate future cash flow in guilders	Estimate future cash flow in guilders
Step 2	Convert to dollars (at forecast exchange rates)	Calculate present value (use guilder discount rate)
Step 3	Calculate present value (use dollar discount rate)	Convert to dollars (use spot rate)

Does it matter which of our two methods Outland uses to appraise its investment? It does if Outland employs its own forecasts of the exchange rate and inflation rate. However, as long as Outland assumes our simple relationships between interest rates, exchange rates, and inflation, the two methods will give the same answer.

Suppose that Outland's managers do not go along with what market prices are telling them. For example, perhaps they believe that the guilder is likely to appreciate relative to the dollar. Should they plug their own currency forecasts into their net present value calculations? We think not. It would be stupid to undertake what might be an unprofitable investment just because management is optimistic about the currency. Outland would do better to pass up the investment in a Dutch steel business and buy guilders.

What about the reverse? Should Outland be deterred from going ahead with a foreign investment that has a negative NPV only because management is unusually pessimistic about the foreign currency? Again, the answer is "No"; it would do much better to go ahead with the project and protect the firm against the currency depreciation by selling guilders forward. In that way, the company would get the best of both worlds.[10]

● EXAMPLE 23.5 Outland Steel's Foreign Project

Suppose Outland's Dutch facility is expected to generate the following cash flows in guilders:

Year	1	2	3	4	5
Cash flow in thousands of guilders	400	416	433	450	468

How much is this cash flow worth today if Outland requires a 15 percent *dollar* return from its investment?

Outland's financial manager looks in the newspaper and finds that the current exchange rate is 2 guilders (fl) per dollar, fl2/$, and that the risk-free

---

[10] There is a general point here that is not confined to international investment. Whenever you face an investment that appears to have a positive NPV, decide what it is that you are betting on and then see if there is a more direct way to place the bet. For example, if a copper mine looks profitable only because you are unusually optimistic about the price of copper, then maybe you would do better to buy copper rather than open a copper mine.

interest rate is 4 percent in Canada ($r_\$ = .04$) and 5 percent in Holland ($r_{fl} = .05$). Right away it is clear that if real interest rates are expected to be the same in the two countries, then the consensus forecast for the Dutch inflation rate, i_{fl}, must be approximately one percentage point higher than the inflation rate in Canada, $i_\$$. For example, if the expected rate of inflation in Canada is 3 percent, then the expected inflation rate in Holland is about 4 percent.[11] The financial manager therefore checks that the guilder cash-flow forecasts are consistent with this inflation rate.

The manager also realizes that since the expected inflation rate is higher in Holland than in Canada, the guilder is likely to depreciate against the dollar. According to purchasing power parity (PPP),

$$\begin{array}{c}\text{Expected spot exchange rate} \\ \text{at end of year}\end{array} = \begin{array}{c}\text{spot exchange rate} \\ \text{at start of year}\end{array} \times \begin{array}{c}\text{inflation rate} \\ \text{differential}\end{array}$$

For example, the spot exchange rate is currently 2.00 guilders to the dollar. Therefore,

$$\begin{array}{c}\text{Expected spot exchange} \\ \text{rate at end of year}\end{array} = 2.00 \times \frac{1.04}{1.03} = 2.02 \text{ guilders per dollar}$$

The forecast exchange rates for each year of the project are calculated in a similar way as follows:

Year	Forecast Exchange Rate	
0	Spot exchange rate	= fl2.00/$
1	$2.00 \times (1.04/1.03)$	= fl2.02/$
2	$2.00 \times (1.04/1.03)^2$	= fl2.04/$
3	$2.00 \times (1.04/1.03)^3$	= fl2.06/$
4	$2.00 \times (1.04/1.03)^4$	= fl2.08/$
5	$2.00 \times (1.04/1.03)^5$	= fl2.10/$

The financial manager can use these projected exchange rates to convert the forecast guilder cash flows into dollars:

Year	1	2	3	4	5
Dollar value of guilder cash flow	$\frac{400}{2.02}$	$\frac{416}{2.04}$	$\frac{433}{2.06}$	$\frac{450}{2.08}$	$\frac{468}{2.10}$
	= \$198	= \$204	= \$210	= \$216	= \$223

Now the manager uses method 1 and discounts these *dollar* cash flows at the 15 percent *dollar* cost of capital:

$$\text{PV} = \frac{198}{1.15} + \frac{204}{1.15^2} + \frac{210}{1.15^3} + \frac{216}{1.15^4} + \frac{223}{1.15^5} = 699, \text{ or } \$699,000$$

---

[11] We approximate. The formula is

$$\frac{1 + r_{fl}}{1 + r_\$} = \frac{1 + i_{fl}}{1 + i_\$}$$

If $r_{fl} = .05$, $r_\$ = .04$, and $i_\$ = .03$, then

$$\frac{1 + i_{fl}}{1 + .03} = \frac{1 + .05}{1 + .04}$$

$$i_{fl} = \frac{1.03 \times 1.05}{1.04} - 1 = .0399, \text{ or } 3.99\%$$

Notice that the manager discounted at 15 percent, not the risk-free domestic interest rate of 4 percent. The cash flow is risky, so a risk-adjusted rate is appropriate.

Just as a check, the financial manager tries method 2. Since the guilder interest rate is higher than the dollar rate, the risk-adjusted discount rate must be correspondingly higher:[12]

	1 + Risk-Adjusted Discount Rate	=	1 + Nominal Interest Rate	×	1 + Risk Premium
In dollars	1.15	=	1.04	×	1.106
In guilders	1.16	=	1.05	×	1.106

To use method 2 the manager discounts the *guilder* cash flows by the *guilder* discount rate:

$$PV = \frac{400}{1.16} + \frac{416}{1.16^2} + \frac{433}{1.16^3} + \frac{450}{1.16^4} + \frac{468}{1.16^5} = 1403, \text{ or fl1,403,000}$$

Now convert to dollars at the spot rate, fl2.00/$:

$$NPV = \frac{1403}{2.0} = 701, \text{ or } \$701,000$$

The answers are the same, save for rounding error.

SELF-TEST 23.7

Suppose that the nominal risk-free interest rate in Canada is 6 percent rather than 4 percent. The exchange rate is still fl2.00/$ and the real interest rate in Canada is expected to be 1 percent, the same as before.
a. Does this new situation affect your estimate of expected inflation in Holland? Should it affect the NPV of the project using method 2?
b. Given your answer to (a) can the NPV of the project using method 1 be affected? Check whether you are right by using method 1 to recalculate NPV.
c. Interpret your answer. If the real rate in Holland is unchanged, what must have caused the rise in the nominal interest rate in Canada?

The Cost of Capital for Foreign Investment

We did not say how Outland Steel arrived at a 15 percent dollar discount rate for its investment in a Dutch steel facility. That depends on the risk of overseas investment and the reward that investors require for taking this risk. These are issues on which few economists can agree, but we will tell you where we stand.[13]

Remember that the risk of an investment cannot be considered in isolation; it depends on the securities that the investor holds in his or her portfolio. For example, suppose Outland's shareholders invest mainly in companies that do business in Canada. They would find that the value of Outland's Dutch venture was

---

[12] We *multiply* (1 + risk-free rate) by (1 + risk premium) in these calculations. In the CAPM we *added* the risk premium to the risk-free rate. Why the difference? Think of it this way. If the inflation rate in Canada is 3 percent, then the *real* cost of capital on a risky investment is 1.15/1.03 − 1 = .117, or 11.7 percent. If the real cost of capital is .117 and the Dutch inflation rate is 4 percent, then the nominal cost of capital in Holland must be 1.04 × 1.117 − 1 = .16, or 16 percent.

[13] Why don't economists agree? One fundamental reason is that economists have never been able to agree on what makes one country different from another. Is it just that they have different currencies? Or is it that their citizens have different tastes? Or is it that they are subject to different regulations and taxes? The answer affects the relationship between security prices in different countries.

relatively unaffected by fluctuations in the value of Canadian shares. So an investment in the Dutch steel industry would appear to be a relatively low-risk project to Outland's shareholders. That would not be true of a Dutch company, whose shareholders are already exposed to the fortunes of the Dutch market. To them an investment in the Dutch steel industry might seem a relatively high-risk project. In this case Outland's shareholders would be satisfied with a lower return on the project than the shareholders of a similar Dutch company would demand.

Avoiding Fudge Factors

We certainly don't pretend that we can put a precise figure on the cost of capital for foreign investment. But you can see that we disagree with the frequent practice of *automatically* increasing the domestic cost of capital when foreign investment is considered. We suspect that managers mark up the required return for foreign investment because it is more costly to manage an operation in a foreign country and to cover the risk of expropriation, foreign exchange restrictions, or unfavourable tax changes. A fudge factor is added to the discount factor to cover these costs.

We think managers should leave the discount rate alone and reduce expected cash flows instead. For example, suppose that Outland is expected to earn fl500,000 in the first year *if no penalties are placed on the operations of foreign firms*. Suppose also that there is a 20 percent chance that Outland's operation may be expropriated without compensation.[14] The *expected* cash flow is not fl500,000 but $.8 \times 500 = fl400,000$.

The end result may be the same if you pretend that the expected cash flow is fl500,000 but add a fudge factor to the discount rate. Nevertheless, adjusting cash flows brings management's assumptions about "political risks" out in the open for scrutiny and sensitivity analysis.

23.5 POLITICAL RISK

Managers of multinational companies do worry about political risk and with reason. For example, when the revolutionary government came to power in Libya, it seized foreign oil investments.

Think about what the political risk of a foreign investment really is. It is the threat that a foreign government will change the rules of the game — that is, break a promise or understanding — *after* the investment is made. Some managers think of political risks as inescapable. But the most successful multinational companies structure their business to reduce political risks.

Foreign governments are not likely to expropriate a local business if it cannot operate without the support of its parent. For example, the foreign subsidiaries of Canadian manufacturers of flight simulators or pharmaceutical companies would have relatively little value if they were cut off from the know-how of their parents. Such operations are much less likely to be expropriated than, say, a mining operation that can be run as a stand-alone venture.

We are not recommending that you turn your silver mine into a pharmaceutical company, but you may be able to plan overseas manufacturing operations to improve your bargaining position with foreign governments. For example, Ford has integrated its overseas operations so that the manufacture of components, subassemblies, and complete automobiles is spread across plants in a number of coun-

---

[14] Our example is fanciful. Most measures of political risk place Holland as one of the most stable environments for investment.

tries. None of these plants would have much value on its own, and Ford can switch production between plants if the political climate in one country deteriorates.

Multinational corporations have also devised financing arrangements to help keep foreign governments honest. For example, suppose your firm is contemplating investing $500 million to reopen the San Tom silver mine in Costaguana, with modern machinery, smelting equipment, and shipping facilities.[15] The Costaguanan government agrees to invest in roads and other infrastructure and to take 20 percent of the silver produced by the mine in lieu of taxes. The agreement is to run for 25 years.

The project's NPV on these assumptions is quite attractive. But what happens if a new government comes to power 5 years from now and imposes a 50 percent tax on "any precious metals exported from the Republic of Costaguana"? Or changes the government's share of output from 20 to 50 percent? Or simply takes over the mine "with fair compensation to be determined in due course by the Minister of Natural Resources of the Republic of Costaguana"?

No contract can absolutely restrain a sovereign power. But you can arrange project financing to make these acts as painful as possible for the foreign government. For example, you might set up the mine as a subsidiary corporation, which then borrows a large fraction of the required investment from a consortium of major international banks. If your firm guarantees the loan, make sure the guarantee stands only if the Costaguanan government honours its contract. The government will be reluctant to break the contract if that causes a default on the loans and undercuts the country's credit standing with the international banking system. If possible, you should finance part of the project with a loan from the World Bank (or one of its affiliates). Few governments will take on the World Bank.

These arrangements do work. In the late 1960s Kennecott Copper financed a major expansion of a copper mine in Chile using arrangements like those we have just described. In 1970 a new government was elected, headed by Salvador Allende, who vowed to take over all foreign holdings in Chile giving "ni un centavo" in exchange. Kennecott's mine was spared.

Political risk is not confined to the risk of expropriation. Multinational companies are always exposed to the criticism that they siphon funds out of countries in which they do business, so that governments are tempted to limit their freedom to repatriate profits. This is most likely to happen when there is considerable uncertainty about the rate of exchange, which is usually when companies would most like to get their money out.

Here again a little forethought can help. For example, there are often tougher restrictions on the payment of dividends to the parent than on the payment of interest on debt. So it may be better for the parent to put up part of the funds in the form of a loan.[16]

SUMMARY

1. To produce order out of chaos, the international financial manager needs some model of the relationship between exchange rates, interest rates, and inflation rates. Four very simple theories prove useful:

---

[15] The early history of the San Tom mine is described in Joseph Conrad's *Nostromo*.
[16] Royalty payments and management fees are also less politically sensitive than dividends, particularly if they are levied equally on all foreign operations. A company can also, within limits, alter the price of goods that are bought or sold within the group, and it can require more or less prompt payment for such sales.

- In its strict form, purchasing power parity states that $1 must have the same purchasing power in every country. You only need to take a vacation abroad to know that this doesn't square well with the facts. Nevertheless, *on average* changes in exchange rates match differences in inflation rates and, if you need a long-term forecast of the exchange rate, it is difficult to do much better than to assume that the exchange rate will offset the effect of any differences in the inflation rates.

- In an open world capital market *real* rates of interest would have to be the same. Thus differences in *nominal* interest rates result from differences in expected inflation rates. This suggests that firms should not simply borrow where interest rates are lowest. Those countries are also likely to have the lowest inflation rates and the strongest currencies.

- Interest rate parity theory states that the interest differential between two countries must be equal to the difference between the forward and spot exchange rates. In the international markets, arbitrage ensures that parity almost always holds.

- The expectations theory of foreign exchange rates tells us that the forward rate equals the expected spot rate (though it is very far from being a perfect forecaster of the spot rate).

2. Our simple theories about forward rates have two practical implications for the problem of hedging overseas operations. First, the expectations theory suggests that hedging exchange risk is on average costless. Second, there are two ways to hedge against exchange risk — one is to buy or sell currency forward, the other is to lend or borrow abroad. Interest rate parity tells us that the cost of the two methods should be the same.

3. A strong view about future exchange rates may lead a manager to make foolish international capital budgeting decisions. There are two methods for evaluating overseas projects. In one case you need to translate the forecast cash flows into dollars and discount them at the dollar discount rate. In the other case you discount the foreign currency cash flows at the foreign discount rate. Both methods give the same answer as long as you assume that prices, interest rates, and exchange rates are linked by the simple theories described above. One problem is the difficulty of estimating the return that your shareholders require from foreign investments; adding a premium for the "extra risks" of overseas investment is not a good solution.

4. Finally, multinational companies must assess political risk and structure their overseas business and financing to reduce the chance that a foreign government will discriminate against them.

KEY TERMS

exchange rates	**law of one price**	**international Fisher**
spot exchange rate	**purchasing power**	**effect**
forward exchange rate	**parity (PPP)**	**interest rate parity**

SUGGESTED READINGS

There are a number of useful textbooks in international finance. One good text is

M.D. Levi, *International Finance: the Markets and Financial Management of Multinational Business*, 2nd ed., McGraw-Hill, New York, 1990.

Euromoney and *Euromoney Corporate Finance* are two journals concerned with international finance. It is worth leafing through them for current events and developments.

International investment decisions and associated exchange risks are discussed in

A. C. Shapiro. "International Capital Budgeting," *Midland Corporate Finance Journal* 1 (Spring 1983):26–45.

B. Cornell and A. C. Shapiro. "Managing Foreign Exchange Risks," *Midland Corporate Finance Journal* 1 (Fall 1983):16–31.

E. Flood and D. Lessard. "On the Measurement of Operating Exposure to Exchange Rates: A Conceptual Approach," *Financial Management* 15 (Spring 1986):25–36.

PROBLEMS

1. Look at Table 23.1.
   a. How many British pounds do you get for your dollar?
   b. What is the 12-month forward rate for the British pound?
   c. Is the pound at a forward discount or premium on the dollar?
   d. Calculate the annual percentage discount or premium on the pound.
   e. If the 12-month interest rate on dollars is 8 percent, what do you think is the 12-month interest rate on pounds?
   f. According to the expectations theory, what is the expected spot rate for the pound in 12 months' time?
   g. According to purchasing power parity, what then is the expected difference in the rate of price inflation in Canada and Britain?

2. Define each of the following theories in a sentence or simple equation:
   a. Interest rate parity theory.
   b. Expectations theory of forward rates.
   c. Law of one price.
   d. International Fisher effect (relationship between interest rates in different countries).

3. The following table shows interest rates and exchange rates for the Canadian dollar and Greek drachma. The spot exchange rate is 168 drachmas per dollar. Complete the missing entries:

	1 Month	1 Year
Dollar interest rate (annually compounded)	7.6%	8.7%
Drachma interest rate (annually compounded)	27.9%	_____
Forward drachmas per dollar	_____	200.00

Hint: When calculating the 1-month forward rate, remember to translate the annual interest rate into a monthly interest rate.

4. An importer in Canada is due to take delivery of silk scarves from Italy in 6 months. The price is fixed in lire. Which of the following transactions could eliminate the importer's exchange risk?
   a. Buy lire forward.
   b. Sell lire forward.
   c. Sell lire in the currency futures market.

   d. Borrow lire, buy dollars at the spot exchange rate.

   e. Sell lire at the spot exchange rate, lend dollars.

5. Sanyo produces audio and video consumer goods and exports a major fraction of its output to North America under its own name and the Fisher brand name. It prices its products in yen, meaning that it seeks to maintain a fixed price in terms of yen. Suppose the yen moves from ¥70.72/$ to ¥65/$. What currency risk does Sanyo face? How can it reduce its exposure?

6. A firm in Canada is due to receive payment of DM1 million in 8 years' time. It would like to protect itself against a decline in the value of the deutschemark but finds it difficult to arrange a forward sale for such a long period. Is there any other way that it can protect itself?

7. **a.** Which of the following items do you need if you do all your capital budgeting calculations in your own currency?

   Forecasts of future exchange rates
   Forecasts of the foreign inflation rate
   Forecasts of the domestic inflation rate
   Foreign interest rates
   Domestic interest rates

   b. Which of the preceding items do you need if you do all your capital budgeting calculations in the foreign currency?

8. Table 23.1 shows the 12-month forward rate on the deutschemark.

   a. Is the dollar at a forward discount or a premium on the mark?

   b. What is the annual *percentage* discount or premium?

   c. If you have no other information about the two currencies, what is your best guess about the spot rate on the mark 12 months hence?

   d. Suppose that you expect to receive DM100,000 in 12 months. How many dollars is this likely to be worth?

9. A Canadian investor buys 100 shares of London Enterprises at a price of £50 when the exchange rate is $1.60/£. A year later the shares are selling at £52. No dividends have been paid.

   a. What is the rate of return to a Canadian investor if the exchange rate is still $1.60/£?

   b. What if the exchange rate is $1.70/£?

   c. What if the exchange rate is $1.50/£?

10. Look at Table 23.1. If the 3-month interest rate on dollars is 8 percent a year, what do you think is the 3-month sterling (U.K.) interest rate? Explain what would happen if the rate were substantially above your figure. *Hint*: In your calculations remember to convert the annually compounded interest rate into a rate for 3 months.

11. Look at Table 23.1. How many French francs can you buy for $1? How many deutschemarks can you buy? What rate do you think a German bank would quote for buying or selling French francs? Explain what would happen if it quoted a rate that was substantially above your figure.

12. Ms. Rosetta Stone, the treasurer of International Reprints, Inc., has noticed that the interest rate in Switzerland is below the rates in most other countries. She is therefore suggesting that the company should make an issue of Swiss franc bonds. What considerations should she first take into account?

13. Suppose that the inflation rate in the United States is 4 percent and in Canada it is 5 percent. What would you expect is happening to the exchange rate between the United States and Canadian dollars?

14. A Canadian firm is evaluating an investment in Portugal. The project costs 500 million Portuguese escudos and it is expected to produce an income of 250 million escudos a year in *real* terms for each of the next 3 years. The expected inflation rate in Portugal is 8 percent a year and the firm estimates that an appropriate discount rate for the project would be about 8 percent above the risk-free rate of interest. Calculate the net present value of the project in dollars using each of the two methods described in this chapter. Exchange rates are given in Table 23.1. The interest rate was about 10 percent in Portugal and 8 percent in Canada.

15. Suppose that you do use your own views about inflation and exchange rates when valuing an overseas investment proposal. Specifically, suppose that you believe that inflation will be 2 percent in Holland and 4 percent in Canada but that the exchange rate will remain unchanged. Recalculate the NPV of the Outland project using both of our methods. Each NPV implies a different financing strategy. What are they?

16. You have bid for a possible export order that would provide a cash inflow of DM1 million in 12 months. The spot exchange rate is DM1.708/$ and the 12-month forward rate is DM1.735/$. There are two sources of uncertainty: (1) the deutschemark could appreciate or depreciate, and (2) you may or may not receive the export order. Illustrate in each case the profits or losses that you would make if you sell DM1 million forward by filling in the following table. Assume that the exchange rate in 6 months will be either DM1.90/$ or DM1.60/$.

	Profit/Loss	
Spot Rate	**Receive Order**	**Lose Order**
DM1.90/$	_____	_____
DM1.60/$	_____	_____

17. General Gadget Corp. (GGC) is a Canadian-based multinational firm that makes electrical coconut scrapers. These gadgets are made only in Canada using local inputs. The scrapers are sold mainly to Asian and West Indian countries where coconuts are grown.
    a. If GGC sells scrapers in Trinidad, what is the currency risk faced by the firm?
    b. In what currency should GGC borrow funds to pay for its investment in order to mitigate its foreign exchange exposure?
    c. Suppose that GGC begins manufacturing its products in Trinidad using local (Trinidadian) inputs and labour. How does this affect its exchange rate risk?

18. If investors recognize the impacts of inflation and exchange rate changes on a firm's cash flows, changes in exchange rates should be reflected in stock prices. How would the stock price of each of the following Swiss companies be affected by an unanticipated appreciation in the Swiss franc of 10 percent, only 2 percent of which could be justified by comparing Swiss inflation to that in the rest of the world:

a. *SwissAir:* More than two-thirds of its employees are Swiss. Most revenues come from international fares set in U.S. dollars.
b. *Nestlé:* Fewer than 5 percent of its employees are Swiss. Most revenues are derived from sales of consumer goods in a wide range of countries with competition from local producers.
c. *Union Bank of Switzerland:* Most employees are Swiss. All non-Swiss franc monetary positions are fully hedged.

SOLUTIONS TO SELF-TEST QUESTIONS

23.1
a. $1500 \times 1.0945 = \$1641.75$ (or equivalently $1500/ .9137 = \$1641.75$).
b. Indirect: $\$1 = .9 \times .9137 = 0.8223$ francs. Direct: 1 franc $= 1.0945/.9 = \$1216$.
c. $1500/0.8223 = \$1824.15$. The dollar price increases.
d. $1641.75 \times .8223 = 1350.01$ francs.

23.2
a. £260 = \$532. Therefore £1 = 532/260 = \$2.05
b. In Canada, price = $\$532 \times 1.02 = \$542.64$. In Great Britain, price = £260 × 1.05 = £273. The new exchange rate = \$542.64/£273 = \$1.9876/£.
c. Initially \$1 buys $1/2.05 = £.488$. At the end of the year, \$1 buys $1/1.9876 = £.503$, which is about 3 percent higher than the original value of £.488.

23.3 The real interest rate in Canada is $1.08/1.02 - 1 = .0588$, or 5.88%. If the real rate is the same in Germany, then expected inflation must be (1 + nominal rate)/(1 + real rate) − 1 = 1.065/1.0588 − 1 = .0059, or 0.59%.

23.4 The U.S. dollar is at a forward premium (that is, you get fewer U.S. dollars for \$1 Canadian in the forward market). This implies that interest rates in Canada are higher than in the United States. Interest rate parity states

$$\frac{1 + r_{US\$}}{1 + r_{Cdn\$}} = \frac{f_{US\$/Cdn\$}}{s_{US\$/Cdn\$}}$$

$$r_{US\$} = 1.08 \times .7022/.7110 - 1 = .067, \text{ or } 6.7\%.$$

23.5 Cash flows in dollars were

$$1986: \frac{+100,000}{1.91} = +\$52,356$$

$$1987: \frac{-17,250}{1.69} = -\$10,207$$

$$1988: \frac{-17,250}{1.52} = -\$11,349$$

$$1989: \frac{-117,250}{1.67} = -\$70,210$$

The internal rate of return on these flows is about 24 percent, that is,

$$+52,356 - \frac{10,207}{1.24} - \frac{11,349}{1.24^2} - \frac{70,210}{1.24^3} = 0$$

23.6 The points you should make are

a.   When judging the cost of forward cover, the relevant comparison is between the forward rate and the *expected* spot rate. Since the forward rate is *on average* close to the subsequent spot rate, the cost of insurance is low.

b.   The firm could buy spot yen today but would then receive the low yen rate of interest for 1 year rather than the higher dollar rate. Interest rate parity states that the two methods of hedging (buying yen forward or buying spot and investing in yen deposits) have similar cost.

c.   The yen interest rate is likely to be low because investors expect the yen to appreciate against the dollar. The firm can expect the benefit of borrowing at the low interest rate to be offset by the extra cost of buying yen to pay the interest and principal. Also, borrowing yen would add currency risk and it would be odd to do this at the same time as buying yen and putting them on deposit.

23.7

a.   If the Canadian real interest rate is 1 percent and the nominal rate is 6 percent, expected inflation is $1.06/1.01 - 1 = .05$, or 5.0%. If the real interest rate is the same in Holland and Canada, the guilder discount rate is unchanged and method 2 gives the same NPV as before.

b.   With 5 percent expected inflation in Canada forecast exchange rates are as follows:

Year	Forecast Exchange Rate
0	Spot exchange rate = fl2.00/$
1	$2.00 \times (1.04/1.05)$ = fl1.98/$
2	$2.00 \times (1.04/1.05)^2$ = fl1.96/$
3	$2.00 \times (1.04/1.05)^3$ = fl1.94/$
4	$2.00 \times (1.04/1.05)^4$ = fl1.92/$
5	$2.00 \times (1.04/1.05)^5$ = fl1.91/$

The financial manager can use these projected exchange rates to convert the forecast guilder cash flows into dollars:

Year:	1	2	3	4	5
Dollar value of guilder cash flow	$\dfrac{400}{1.98}$	$\dfrac{416}{1.96}$	$\dfrac{433}{1.94}$	$\dfrac{450}{1.92}$	$\dfrac{468}{1.91}$
	= $202	= $212	= $223	= $234	= $245

The dollar cost of capital is now

$(1 + \text{risk premium}) \times (1 + \text{nominal interest rate}) - 1 = 1.106 \times 1.06 - 1 = .1724$

Discounting the dollar cash flows at the dollar cost of capital gives

$$\text{PV} = \frac{202}{1.172} + \frac{212}{1.172^2} + \frac{223}{1.172^3} + \frac{234}{1.172^4} + \frac{245}{1.172^5} = 700$$

c.   If the real interest rate is unchanged, the higher nominal interest rate reflects a higher expected inflation rate in Canada and therefore suggests that the dollar will depreciate against the guilder. Since the guilder cash flows are unchanged, the project will produce more dollars but these dollars must be discounted at a higher rate. Value is unaffected.

CHAPTER TWENTY-FOUR

Options

Figure 24.1(a) shows your payoff if you buy BCE stock at $45. You gain dollar-for-dollar if the stock price goes up and lose dollar-for-dollar if it falls. That's trite — it doesn't take a genius to draw a 45-degree line.

Look now at panel (b), which shows the payoffs from an investment strategy that retains the upside potential of BCE stock but gives complete downside protection. In this case your payoff stays at $45 even if BCE stock falls to $20, $10, or zero. Panel (b)'s payoffs are clearly better than panel (a)'s. If a financial alchemist could turn panel (a) into (b), you'd be willing to pay for the service.

Panel (c) is still better. Here your payoff increases regardless of whether BCE goes up or down. A financial alchemist who was able to deliver panel (c) could demand an even greater fee.

FIGURE 24.1
Payoffs to four investment strategies for BCE stock. (*a*) You buy one share for $45. (*b*) No downside. Your payoff stays at $45, even if stock price falls below $45. (*c*) Here your payoff increases if stock rises or if it falls. (*d*) A strategy for masochists? Your payoff falls if stock price rises or if it falls.

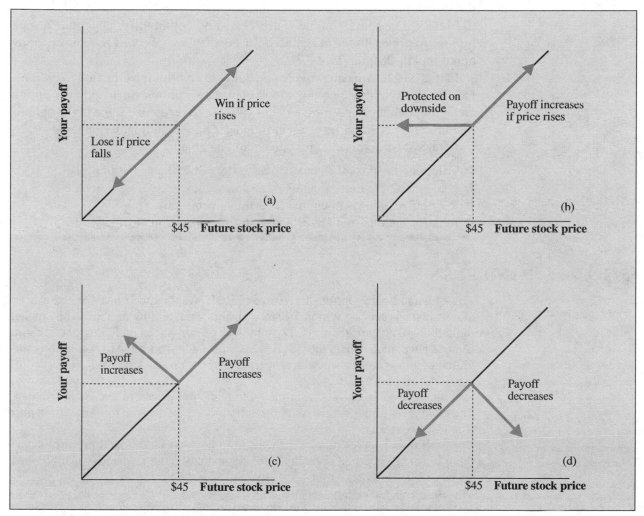

Of course alchemy has its dark side. Panel (d) shows an investment strategy for masochists. If you *like* to lose, or if somebody pays you enough to take the strategy on, these payoffs fall dollar-for-dollar regardless of which way BCE moves.

Now, as you have probably suspected, all this financial alchemy is for real. You really can do all the transmutations shown in Figure 24.1. You do them with options. And we will show you how.

But why should the financial manager of an industrial company read further? There are several reasons. First, most capital budgeting projects have options embedded in them, for example, that allow the company to expand at a future date or to bail out. These options allow the company to profit if things go well but give downside protection when they don't. Those managers who build flexibility into investment projects are also practicing financial alchemy.

Second, many of the securities that firms issue include an option. For example, companies often issue convertible bonds. The holder has the option to exchange the bond for common stock. Most corporate bonds also contain a call provision, meaning that the issuer has the option to buy back the bond from the investor.

Finally, managers routinely use currency, commodity, and interest-rate options to protect the firm against a variety of risks. (We will have more to say about this in Chapter 25.)

In one chapter we can provide you with only a brief introduction to options. Our first goal in this chapter is to explain how options work and how option value is determined. Then we will tell you how to recognize some of the options that crop up in capital investment proposals and in company financing.

After studying this chapter you should be able to

- Calculate the payoff to buyers and sellers of call and put options.
- Understand the determinants of option values.
- Recognize options in capital investment proposals.
- Identify options that are provided in financial securities.

24.1 CALLS AND PUTS

The Chicago Board Options Exchange (CBOE) was founded in 1973 and was an almost instant success. Within 5 years investors were trading options to buy or sell more than 10 million shares daily. A number of exchanges including a number in Canada have since copied the CBOE's example and, in addition to options on individual common stocks, you can now trade options on stock indexes, bonds, commodities, and foreign exchange.

Table 24.1 is an extract from the table of option prices in a daily newspaper. The table gives prices for two types of option — *calls* (the first four rows) and *puts* (the last two rows).

call option: Right to buy an asset at a specified exercise price on or before the exercise date.

A **call option** gives its owner the right to buy stock at a fixed *exercise price*[1] on or before a specified *exercise date*.[2] For example, the first entry in Table 24.1

---

[1] The exercise price is sometimes known as the *strike price*.
[2] In some cases, the option can be exercised only on one particular day, and it is then conventionally known as a *European* call; in other cases, it can be exercised on or before that day, and it is then known as an *American* call.

TABLE 24.1
BCE Option Prices

Stock	Option	Exercise Date	Exercise Price	Option Price
BCE	Call	February	$45.00	$0.20
	Call	March	$45.00	$0.50
	Call	May	$45.00	$1.30
	Call	August	$47.50	$0.90
	Put	February	$45.00	$1.05
	Put	August	$42.50	$1.00

shows that you would need to pay $0.20 for an option to buy BCE stock (a call option) at $45 (the exercise price) any time until February (the exercise date).

The diagram in Figure 24.2a shows the possible values of this option just before it expires in February. If the price of BCE stock in February turns out to be less than $45, you would not want to exercise your option to buy the share for $45. (Who would want to pay $45 for BCE stock if it could be bought in the market for less?) In that case your call option will prove to be valueless and you will have lost the $0.20 that you paid for it.

On the other hand, if BCE's share price turns out to be *greater* than $45 in February, it will pay you to exercise your option to buy the share. In this case, just before the option expires, it will be worth the market price of the share minus the $45 that you must pay to buy the share. For example, if BCE's stock price in February is $50, the option at that point is worth $5 since the option would give you the right to buy for $45 a stock worth $50.

FIGURE 24.2
Payoffs to buyers of call and put options on BCE stock (exercise price = $45).

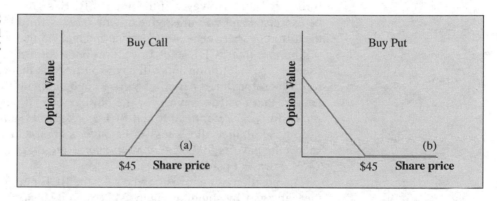

In summary, the value of the call option at expiration is as follows:

Stock Price at Expiration	Value of Call Option at Expiration
Greater than exercise price	Stock price – exercise price
Less than exercise price	Zero

put option: Right to sell an asset at a specified exercise price on or before the exercise date.

Now look at the next-to-last row in Table 24.1. It shows that for $1.05 you can buy a **put option** on BCE stock with the same $45 exercise price. Whereas the call gives you the right to *buy* the share for $45, the put gives you the right to *sell* it for $45. Therefore, the circumstances in which the put option will be valuable are just opposite to those in which the call will be valuable. You can see this from the diagram in Figure 24.2(b). If BCE share price turns out to be *greater* than $45 in February when the option expires, you will not want to exercise your option to sell the share for $45. Your put option will be worthless and you will have lost the $1.05 that you paid for it.

However, if BCE's share price turns out to be *less* than $45, it will pay to buy the share at the low price and then exercise your option to sell it for $45. For example, suppose BCE stock price in February is $30. Then you could buy the share for $30 and resell it for $45. In this case, the put would be worth $45 – $30 = $15.

In general, the value of a put option at expiration is as follows:

Stock Price at Expiration	Value of Put Option at Expiration
Greater than exercise price	Zero
Less than exercise price	Exercise price – stock price

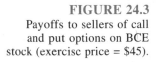

Selling Calls and Puts

The traded options that you see quoted in the financial pages are not sold by the companies themselves but by other investors. If one investor buys an option on BCE stock, some other investor must be on the other side of the bargain. We will look now at the position of the investor who sells an option.[3]

We have already seen that the February-maturity BCE calls are trading at $0.20. Thus if you *sell* the February call option on BCE stock, the buyer pays you $0.20. However, in return you promise to sell BCE shares at a price of $45 if the call buyer decides to exercise his option. The option seller's obligation to *sell* BCE is just the other side of the coin to the option holder's right to buy the stock. If the share price is below the exercise price of $45 when the option expires in February, holders of the call will not exercise their option and you, the seller, will have no further liability. However, if the price of BCE is greater than $45, the option will be exercised and you must give up your shares for $45 each. You therefore lose the difference between the share price and the $45 that you receive from the buyer.

Suppose that BCE's stock price turns out to be $60. In this case the buyer will exercise the call option and will pay $45 for stock that can be resold for $60. The buyer therefore has a payoff of $15 — not bad on an investment of only $.20. Of course, that positive payoff for the *buyer* means a negative payoff for you the *seller*, for you are obliged to sell BCE stock worth $60 for only $45.

In general, the seller's loss is the buyer's gain, and vice versa. Figure 24.3(a) shows the payoffs to the call option seller. Note that Figure 24.3(a) is just Figure 24.2(a) drawn upside down.

The position of an investor who sells the BCE put option can be shown in just the same way by standing Figure 24.2(b) on its head. The put *buyer* has the right

FIGURE 24.3
Payoffs to sellers of call and put options on BCE stock (exercise price = $45).

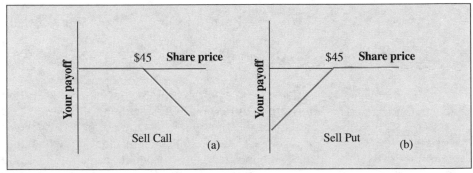

---

[3] The option seller is known as the *writer*.

to sell a share for $45; so the seller of the put has agreed to pay $45 for the share if the put buyer should demand it. Clearly the seller will be safe as long as the share price remains above $45 but will lose money if the share price falls below this figure. The worst thing that can happen to the put seller is for the stock to be worthless. The seller would then be obliged to pay $45 for a worthless stock. The payoff to the seller would be –$45.

Table 24.2 summarizes the rights and obligation of buyers and sellers of calls and puts.

TABLE 24.2

Rights and obligations of various options positions

	Buyer	**Seller**
Call option	Right to buy asset	Obligation to sell asset
Put option	Right to sell asset	Obligation to buy asset

SELF-TEST 24.1

Fill in the following table that shows the payoff to investors in BCE options when the options expire in February. All options have exercise prices of $45.

	Stock Price at Option Expiration		
	$30	**$45**	**$50**
Buyer of call	___	___	___
Buyer of put	___	___	___
Seller of call	___	___	___
Seller of put	___	___	___

Financial Alchemy with Options

Now you can see how the transmutations in Figure 24.1 are actually done. The rows of diagrams in Figure 24.4 take us from one panel of Figure 24.1 to the next.

● **EXAMPLE 24.1 Portfolio Insurance**

The top left diagram in Figure 24.4 corresponds to Figure 24.1(a). First you buy a share of BCE stock. Then you get some downside insurance by buying a put option with an exercise price of $45. The middle diagram in the first row of diagrams shows that the payoff to the put increases dollar-for-dollar as the BCE stock price falls below $45. In the extreme case where the stock is worthless, the put is worth $45. Of course the put turns out worthless if the stock goes up.

So now you own the stock and put together. Add up their payoffs, and you have the top right diagram in Figure 24.4, which matches Figure 24.1(b). This is called a portfolio insurance strategy because the put option provides insurance against decreases in the value of your investment in BCE stock.

We suggested earlier that you would be prepared to pay a fee to a financial alchemist who could transform investment payoffs in this way. You should now be able to check the going rate for alchemists. If you hold BCE stock, it will cost you $1.00, the price of a put option, to ensure your investment in BCE up to February.

● **EXAMPLE 24.2 Profiting from Volatility**

To get to Figure 24.1(c), in which your payoff increases regardless of how BCE stock moves, just buy *two* insurance policies, that is, one more put. The middle row of diagrams in Figure 24.4 shows how this gives the V-shaped payoffs of Figure 24.1.

Of course, there is no free lunch here. While the V-shaped payoff is at least as much as and sometimes greater than the payoff from simply purchasing the

FIGURE 24.4
Each row shows how a BCE shareholder can create the payoffs shown in Figure 24.1.

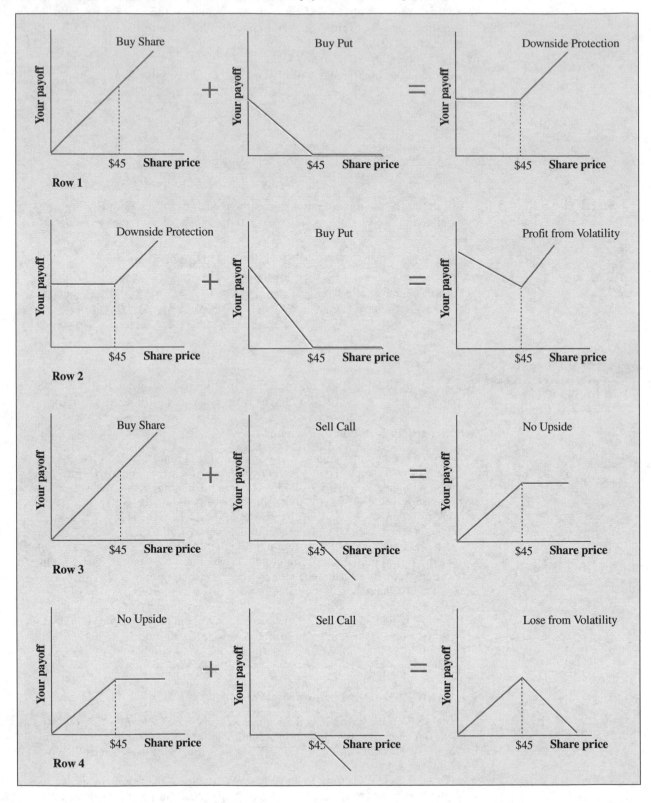

stock, remember that you have to pay more to obtain this attractive profile. To buy the V-shaped payoff, you have to pay for the stock *and* the two put options. The higher total *payoff* might not represent a higher *profit* once you account for the higher original cost of the portfolio.

● EXAMPLE 24.3 Losing from Volatility

The route to Figure 24.1(d), the upside-down V-shaped payoffs, is mapped in the last rows of diagrams in Figure 24.4. First you have to go back to the beginning and buy one share of BCE stock without the insurance policies represented by the puts. This reexposes you to the downside risk of holding BCE shares — see the left-hand diagram in the third row of Figure 24.4. Then you sell away the upside — that is, you sell one call. That gets you to the right-hand diagram in the third row. At this point, your payoff neither increases nor decreases if BCE stock rises.

In order to *lose* from a stock price increase, you have to sell a *second* call. The last row of Figure 24.4 shows how this takes you to the payoffs in Figure 24.1(d).

Therefore, an investment strategy of (1) buying the stock and (2) selling two calls for every stock purchased means that the value of your portfolio will be reduced by *any* movement in the stock price. Notice, however, that this "guaranteed-loss" strategy is not necessarily a bad idea. Remember, you get paid up front when you sell the two calls. If the stock doesn't move very far, the up-front payment may more than cover the loss you incur from the stock price movement.

WHAT DETERMINES OPTION VALUES?

We have seen that February-maturity calls on BCE are trading at $0.20. But we have said nothing about how the market value of options are determined.

....

Upper and Lower Limits on Option Values

We know what an option is worth when it expires. Consider, for example, the option to buy stock at $45. If the stock price is below $45 at the expiration date, the call will be worthless; if the stock price is above $45, the call will be worth the value of the stock minus the $45 exercise price. The relationship is depicted by the heavy line in Figure 24.5.

FIGURE 24.5
Value of a call before its expiration date (dashed line). The value depends on the stock price. The call is always worth more than its value if exercised now (heavy line). It is never worth more than the stock price itself.

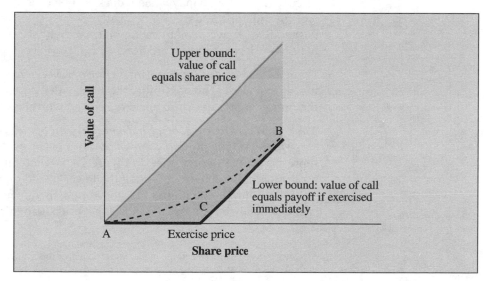

Even before expiration, the price of the option can never remain *below* the heavy line in Figure 24.5. For example if our option were priced at $10 and the stock at $60, it would pay any investor to buy the option, exercise it for an additional $45, and then sell the stock for $60. That would give a "money machine" with a profit of $60 – $55 = $5. The demand for options from investors using this strategy would quickly force the option price up at least to the heavy line in the figure. The heavy line is therefore a *lower* limit on the market price of the option. Thus

Lower limit on value of call option =

the greater of *zero* or (*stock price – exercise price*)

The diagonal line in Figure 24.5, which is the plot of the stock price, is the *upper* limit to the option price. Why? Because the stock itself gives a higher final payoff whatever happens. If when the option expires the stock price ends up above the exercise price, the option is worth the stock price *less* the exercise price. If the stock price ends up below the exercise price, the option is worthless, but the stock's owner still has a valuable security. Thus the extra payoff to holding the stock rather than the option is as follows:

Stock Price at Expiration	Stock Payoff	Option Payoff	Extra Payoff from Holding Stock Rather than Option
Greater than $45	Stock price	Stock price – $45	$45
Less than or equal to $45	Stock price	$0	Stock price

··········· · · · · · · · · · · · · ·
The Determinants of Option Value

The option price must lie between the upper and lower limits in Figure 24.5. In the diagram we have shown this region by the shaded area. In fact, the price will lie on a curved, upward-sloping line like the dashed curve shown in the figure. This line begins its travels where the upper and lower bounds meet (at zero, point A). Then it rises, gradually becoming parallel to the lower bound. This line tells us an important fact about option values: given the exercise price, *the value of a call option increases as stock price increases.*

That should be no surprise. Owners of call options clearly hope for the stock price to rise and are happy when it does. But let us look more carefully at the shape and location of the dashed line. Three points, A, B, and C, are marked on the dashed line. As we explain each point, you will see why the option price has to behave as the dashed line predicts.

Point A. *When the stock is worthless, the option is worthless.* A stock price of zero means that there is no possibility the stock will ever have any future value.[4] If so, the option is sure to expire unexercised and worthless, and it is worthless today.

Point B. *When the stock price becomes very high, the option price approaches the stock price less the present value of the exercise price.* Notice that the dashed line representing the option price in Figure 24.5 eventually becomes parallel to the ascending heavy line representing the lower bound on the option price. The reason is as follows. The higher the stock price, the greater the odds that the option will eventually be exercised. If the stock price is high enough, exercise becomes

---

[4] If a stock *can* be worth something in the future, then investors will pay *something* for it today, although possibly a very small amount.

a virtual certainty; the probability that the stock price will fall below the exercise price before the option expires becomes trivial.

If you own an option that you *know* will be exchanged for a share of stock, you effectively own the stock now. The only difference is that you don't have to pay for the stock (by handing over the exercise price) until later, when formal exercise occurs. In these circumstances, buying the call is equivalent to buying the stock now with deferred payment and delivery. The value of the call is therefore equal to the stock price less the present value of the exercise price.[5]

This brings us to another important point about options. Investors who acquire stock by way of a call option are buying on "installment credit." They pay the purchase price of the option today, but they do not pay the exercise price until they actually exercise the option. The delay in payment is particularly valuable if interest rates are high and the option has a long maturity. Thus *the value of a call option increases with both the rate of interest and the time to expiration.*

SELF-TEST 24.2

> How would the value of a put option be affected by an increase in the exercise price? Explain. Check your answer by looking at the price of put options in the newspaper.

Point C. *The option price always exceeds its minimum value* (except when stock price is zero). We have seen that the dashed and heavy lines in Figure 24.5 coincide when stock price is zero (point A), but elsewhere the lines diverge; that is, the option price must exceed the minimum value given by the heavy line. You can see why by examining point C.

At point C, the stock price exactly equals the exercise price. The option therefore would be worthless if it expired today. However, suppose that the option will not expire until 3 months hence. Of course we do not know what the stock price will be at the expiration date. There is roughly a 50 percent chance that it will be higher than the exercise price, and a 50 percent chance that it will be lower. The possible payoffs to the option are therefore:

Outcome	Payoff
Stock price rises (50 percent probability)	Stock price – exercise price (option is exercised)
Stock price falls (50 percent probability)	Zero (option expires worthless)

If there is some chance of a positive payoff, and if the worst payoff is zero, then the option must be valuable. That means the option price at point C exceeds its lower bound, which at point C is zero. In general, the option price will exceed the lower bound as long as there is time left before expiration.

One of the most important determinants of the *height* of the dashed curve (that is, of the difference between actual and lower-bound value) is the likelihood of substantial movements in the stock price. An option on a stock whose price is unlikely to change by more than 1 or 2 percent is not worth much; an option on a stock whose price may halve or double is very valuable.

---

[5] We assume here that the stock pays no dividends until after the option matures. If dividends were paid, you *would* care about when you get to own the stock because the option holder misses out on any dividends.

For example, suppose that a call option has an exercise price of $45 and the stock price will be either $35 or $55 when the option expires. The possible pay-offs to the option are as follows:

Stock price at expiration	$35	$55
Call value at expiration	0	$10

Now suppose that the value of the stock when the option expires can be $25 or $65. The *average* of the possible stock prices is the same as before, but the volatility is greater. In this case the payoffs to the call are

Stock price at expiration	$25	$65
Call value at expiration	0	$20

A comparison of the two cases highlights the valuable asymmetry that options offer. If the stock price turns out to be below the exercise price when the option expires, the option is valueless regardless of whether the shortfall is a cent or a dollar. However, the option holder reaps all the benefits of stock price advances. Thus in our example the option is worth only $10 if the stock price reaches $55, but it is worth $20 if the stock price rises to $65. Therefore, volatility helps the option holder.

SELF-TEST 24.3

Rework our numerical example for a put option with an exercise price of $45. Show that put options also are more valuable when the stock price is more volatile.

The probability of large stock price changes during the remaining life of an option depends on two things: (1) the variability of the stock price *per unit of time*, and (2) the length of time until the option expires. Other things equal, you would like to hold an option on a volatile stock. Given volatility, you would like to hold an option with a long life ahead of it, since that longer life means that there is more opportunity for the stock price to change. Thus the value of an option increases *with both the variability of the share price and the time to expiration.*

It's a rare person who can keep all these properties straight at first reading. Therefore, we have summed them up in Table 24.3.

TABLE 24.3

What the price of a call option depends on

If the following variables *increase*, . . .	. . . the value of the call option will
stock price	increase
exercise price	decrease
interest rate	increase
time to expiration	increase
volatility of stock price	increase

An Option-Valuation Model

If you want to value an option, you need to go beyond the qualitative statements of Table 24.3; you need an exact option-valuation model — a formula that you can plug numbers into and come up with a figure for option value.

Valuing complex options is a high-tech business and well beyond the scope of this book. Our aim here is not to make you into instant option whizzes, but we can illustrate the basics of option valuation by walking you through a simple example. It turns out that the trick to option valuation is to find a combination of borrowing and an investment in the stock that exactly replicates the option.

Imagine that it is January and you are contemplating the purchase of a call option on BCE stock. The call has a February exercise date and an exercise price of $45. BCE's stock price is currently $44, so the option will be valueless unless the stock price appreciates by at least $1 over the next month. The outlook for BCE stock is uncertain and all you know is that at the end of the month it will be either $39 or $48. Finally, we assume that the rate of interest on a bank loan is 12 percent a year, or about 1 percent per month. Here is the outlook for three alternative investments:

BCE Stock		Call Option		Bank Loan	
January	**February**	**January**	**February**	**January**	**February**
$44 < $39 / $48		? < $0 / $3		$100 < $101 / $101	

The first investment is BCE stock. Its current price is $44 but the price could leap to $48 or plummet to $39. The second investment is the call option. When the call expires in February, the option will be valueless if the stock price falls to $39 and it will be worth $48 − $45 = $3 if the stock price rises to $48. We don't know (yet) how much the call is worth today, so for the time being we put a question mark against the January value. Our third investment is a bank loan at an interest rate of 1 percent per month. The payoff on a $100 bank loan is $101 no matter what happens to the price of BCE stock.

Consider now two investment strategies. Strategy A is to buy three call options. Strategy B is to buy one BCE share and to borrow the present value of $39 from the bank. Table 24.4 shows the possible payoffs from the two strategies. Notice that when you borrow from the bank, you receive a *positive* cash flow now but have a *negative* flow when the loan is repaid in February.

TABLE 24.4

It is possible to replicate the payoffs from BCE call options by borrowing to invest in BCE

	Cash Flow in January	Payoff in February if Stock Equals $39	Payoff in February if Stock Equals $48
Strategy A			
Buy three calls	?	+ 0	+ 9
Strategy B			
Buy one share	−$44	+$39	+48
Borrow PV($39)	+ 38.61	− 39	−39
	−$ 5.39	$ 0	+ 9

You can see that *regardless of whether the stock price falls to $39 or rises to $48*, the payoffs from the two strategies are identical. To put it another way, you can exactly replicate an investment in call options by a combination of a bank loan and an investment in the stock.[6] If two investments give the same payoffs in all

---

[6] The only tricky part in valuing the BCE option was to work out the number of shares that were needed to replicate one option. Fortunately, there is a simple formula that says the number of shares needed is equal to

$$\frac{\text{Spread of possible option prices}}{\text{Spread of possible stock prices}} = \frac{\$3 - \$0}{\$48 - \$39} = \frac{1}{3}$$

To replicate a call option, you need to buy .333 share of stock. To replicate 3 calls, you need to buy .33 × 3 = 1 share of stock.

circumstances, then their value must be the same today. In other words, the cost of buying three call options must be exactly the same as borrowing $38.61 from the bank and buying one BCE share:

$$\text{Price of 3 calls} = \$44.00 - \$38.61$$

$$\text{Price of 1 call} = \frac{\$44.00 - \$38.61}{3} = \$1.80$$

Presto! You have just valued a call option.

Before you let success go to your head, we should warn you that options encountered in practice are likely to be much more complex than our BCE example. For instance, the share price generally takes on a large number of possible future values rather than just the two values in our example. However, in 1973 Fischer Black and Myron Scholes came up with a formula which showed that you could still replicate an option by a series of investments in the stock partly financed by borrowing, as in our simple example. The Black-Scholes formula (or some variant) is regularly used by option traders, investment bankers, and financial managers to value a wide variety of options.

SELF-TEST 24.4

Suppose that the price of Seagram stock is $40 in January and it could either double to $80 or halve to $20 by February. Show that the following two strategies have exactly the same payoffs regardless of whether the stock price rises or falls. (a) Strategy A: Buy three call options with an exercise price of $40; (b) Strategy B: Buy two shares and borrow the present value of $40. What is your cash outflow today if you follow strategy B? What does this tell you about the value of three call options? Continue to assume that the interest rate is 1 percent per month.

24.3 SPOTTING THE OPTION

In our discussion so far we may have given you the impression that financial managers are concerned only with traded options to buy or sell shares. But once you have learned to recognize the different kinds of options, you will find that they are everywhere. Unfortunately, they rarely come with a large label attached. Often the trickiest part of the problem is to identify the option.

We will start by looking briefly at options on real assets and then turn to options on financial assets. You should find that you have already encountered many of these options in earlier chapters.

Options on Real Assets

In Chapter 8 we pointed out that in a capital budgeting analysis it is important to recognize that the projects that you accept today may affect the opportunities you have tomorrow.[7] Today's capital budgeting decisions need to recognize these future opportunities. We looked in Chapter 8 at several ways that companies may build future flexibility into a project. Let us review briefly two of the more important **real options.**

real options: Implicit options on real assets.

The Option to Expand. Many capital investment proposals include an option to buy additional equipment in the future. For instance, a drug company may invest in a patent that allows it to exploit a new technology, an airline may acquire an

---

[7] See Section 8.3.

option to buy a new aircraft, or a retailer may purchase adjoining land that has no immediate value but offers an opportunity to expand at a later date.

Here is another disguised option that might arise in a capital budgeting analysis. You are considering the purchase of a tract of desert land that is known to contain gold deposits. Unfortunately, the cost of extraction is higher than the current price of gold. Does that mean the land is almost worthless? Not at all. You are not obliged to mine the gold, but ownership of the land gives you the *option* to do so. Of course, if you know that the gold price will remain below the extraction cost, then the option is worthless. But if there is uncertainty about future gold prices, you could be lucky and make a killing.

Buying the mine gives you an option to extract the gold. The exercise price of that option is the cost of extraction. In effect, you have a call option to acquire gold for the extraction cost. If there is a chance that gold prices will increase enough to make extraction profitable, the option will have value and might justify the cost of the option, which is the purchase price of the land.

The Option to Abandon. Suppose that you need a new plant ready to produce turbo-encabulators in 3 years. You have a choice of designs. If design A is chosen, construction must begin immediately. Design B is more expensive but you can wait a year before breaking ground.

If you know with certainty that the plant will be needed, you should opt for design A. But suppose that there is some possibility that demand for turbo-encabulators will fall off and that in a year's time you will decide the plant is not required. Then design B may be preferable because it gives you the option to bail out at low cost any time during the next 12 months.

You can think of the option to abandon as a put option. The exercise price of the put is the amount that you could recover if you abandon the project. The abandonment option makes design B more attractive by limiting the downside exposure; the worst outcome is that you receive the project's salvage value. The more uncertain is the need for the new plant, the more valuable is the downside protection offered by the abandonment option. As always, options are more valuable when the value of the underlying asset is more volatile.

It is also possible that, once built, design B can be converted readily into producing retro-chrysalids, while design A has no alternative uses. Again, the extra flexibility provided by design B may tip the balance in its favour.

SELF-TEST 24.5

A real estate developer buys 70 hectares of land in a rural area, planning to build a subdivision on the land if and when the population from the city begins to expand into the area. If population growth is less than anticipated, the developer believes that the land can be sold to a country club that would build a golf course on the property.

a. In what way does the possibility of sale to the country club provide a put option to the developer?

b. What is the exercise price of the option? The asset value?

c. How does the golf course option increase the NPV of the land project to the developer?

Options on Financial Assets

When companies issue securities, they often include an option in the package. In fact, we will explain shortly that, whenever a company borrows, it creates an option. Here are a few examples of the options that are associated with new financing.

warrant: Right to buy shares from a company at a stipulated price before a set date.

Warrants. We saw in Chapter 13 that a company issuing a bond or preferred share will occasionally add some **warrants** as a "sweetener." A warrant is a long-term call option on the company's stock. Unlike the BCE option that we considered earlier, a warrant is issued by the company. The company sells the call; the investor buys it.

In 1990 BCE raised over $400 million by selling packages of preferred shares and warrants. Each warrant gave an investor the right to buy one share of BCE stock at $45.75 any time within the next 5 years. Since the price of BCE stock in 1990 was $38, investors in the warrants were betting that the stock price would rise at least 20 percent above the initial share price.[8]

Warrants are valuable to investors. Therefore, they are prepared to pay a higher price for a package of bonds and warrants than for the bond on its own. Managers sometimes look with delight at the price that they have received for the package and forget that in return the company has incurred a liability to sell its share to the warrant holders at what with hindsight may turn out to be a low price.

convertible bonds: Bond that the holder may exchange for a specified number of shares.

Convertible Bonds. The **convertible bond** is a close relative of the bond-warrant package. It allows the bondholder to exchange the bond for a given number of shares of common stock. Therefore, it is a package of a straight bond with a call option. The exercise price of the call option is the value of the "straight bond" (that is, a bond that is not convertible). If the value of the stock exceeds the value of the straight bond, it will be profitable to convert.

Here is an example of a convertible bond. In 1986 PWA Corp. issued $250 million of 7 7/8% convertible debentures due in 1996. Each bond had a face value of $1000 and could be converted at any time before maturity into 41.66 shares of PWA common stock. In other words, the owner had a 10-year option to return the bond to PWA and receive 41.66 shares of PWA stock in exchange. The number of shares that are received for each bond is called the bond's conversion ratio. The *conversion ratio* of the PWA bond was 41.66.

In order to receive 41.66 shares of PWA stock you had to surrender bonds with a face value of $1000. Therefore, in order to receive *one* share, you had to surrender a face amount of 1000/41.66 = $24.00. This figure is called the *conversion price*. Anybody who bought the bond at $1000 in order to convert into 41.66 shares paid the equivalent of $24.00 per share.

The owner of a convertible bond owns a bond and a call option on the firm's stock. So does the owner of a package of a bond and a warrant. However, there are differences, the most important being that a convertible bond owner must give up the bond to exercise the option. The owner of a package of bonds and warrants exercises the warrants for cash and keeps the bond.

The value of a convertible bond depends on its *bond value* and its *conversion value*. The bond value is what the bond would sell for if it could *not* be converted into stock. The conversion value is what the bond would be worth if it were converted immediately.

Since the owner of the convertible always has the option *not* to convert, bond value establishes a lower bound, or *floor*, to the price of a convertible. Of course, this floor is not completely flat. If the firm falls on hard times, the bond may not be worth much. In the extreme case where the firm becomes worthless, the bond is also worthless.

---

[8] In this case the bet did not pay off. The warrants expired on April 28, 1995 when the stock price was $42.50.

Conversion value is the value of the convertible bond if it were converted immediately. For example, the PWA convertible could be exchanged for 41.66 shares. Thus if PWA's share price were $24, the conversion value would be its face value: $41.66 \times \$24 = \$1,000$. Unfortunately, PWA did fall on hard times and its shares have been trading for less than $1.

A convertible can never sell for *less* than its conversion value. If it did, smart investors would buy the convertible, exchange it for stock, and sell the stock. Their profit would be the difference between the conversion value and the price of the convertible.

This means that there are *two* lower bounds to the price of any convertible: its bond value and its conversion value. When the firm does well, conversion value exceeds bond value; the investor would choose to convert if forced to make an immediate choice. Bond value exceeds conversion value when the firm does poorly. In these circumstances the investor would hold on to the bonds if forced to choose.

Convertible holders do not have to make a now-or-never choice for or against conversion. They can wait and then, with the benefit of hindsight, take whatever course turns out to give them the highest payoff. Thus a convertible is always worth *more* than its bond value and its conversion value (except when time runs out at the bond's maturity).

We stated earlier that it is useful to think of a convertible bond as a package of a straight bond and an option to buy the common stock in exchange for the straight bond. The value of this call option is equal to the difference between the convertible's selling price and its bond value.

callable bond: Bond that may be repurchased by firm before maturity at specified call price.

Callable Bonds. Unlike warrants and convertibles, which give the *investor* an option, a **callable bond** gives an option to the *company*. The company that issues a callable bond has an option to buy the bond back at the stated exercise price. Therefore, you can think of a callable bond as a *package* of a straight bond (a bond that is not callable) and a call option held by the issuer.

The option to call the bond is obviously attractive to the issuer. If interest rates decline and bond prices rise, the company has the opportunity to repurchase the bond below its true value. Therefore, the option to call the bond puts a ceiling on the bond price.

Of course, when the company issues a callable bond, investors are aware of this ceiling on the bond price and will be prepared to pay less for a callable bond than for a straight bond. The difference between the value of a straight bond and a callable bond is the value of the call option that investors have given to the company:

Value of callable bond = value of straight bond – value of the issuer's call option

SELF-TEST 24.6

"Extendable bonds" allow the investor to redeem the bond at par or to allow the bond to remain outstanding until maturity. Suppose a 20-year extendable bond is issued with the investor allowed after 5 years to redeem the bond at par.

a. These bonds are sometimes called put bonds. Why? Who holds an implicit put option?

b. On what asset is the option written? (What asset do the option holders have the right to sell?)

c. What is the exercise price of the option?

d. In what circumstances will the option be exercised?

The Difference between Safe and Risky Bonds

The option provided by convertible bonds and callable bonds is relatively easy to spot. But we will now show you that whenever the company borrows it creates an option. This is because the borrower is not compelled to repay the debt at maturity; it has the option to walk away from its obligation.

In Chapter 15 we discussed the plight of Circular File Company, which borrowed $50 per share. Unfortunately the firm has fallen on hard times and the market value of its assets is now only $30. Circular's bond and stock prices have fallen to $25 and $5, respectively. Circular's *market*-value balance sheet is now:

MARKET-VALUE BALANCE SHEET
FOR CIRCULAR FILE COMPANY

Asset value	$30	Bonds	$25
		Stock	5
	$30	Firm value	$30

If Circular's debt were due and payable now, the firm could not repay the $50 it originally borrowed. It would default: the bondholders would take over the company and receive assets worth $30, leaving the shareholders with nothing. The reason Circular stock is worth $5 is that the debt is *not* due now but rather is due a year from now. A stroke of good fortune could increase firm value enough to pay off the bondholders in full, with something left over for the stockholders. If not, the firm will choose to default on the loan and turn the company over to its creditors, the bondholders.

Think of it this way. The shareholders have a choice. They can either pay off the debt at maturity or they can declare bankruptcy. In the latter case, the shareholders hand over the firm's assets to the bondholders and are no longer liable for the debt.

In effect shareholders have the *option* to sell the firm's assets to the bondholders in exchange for the amount of the debt. Of course they will exercise this option only if the assets are worth less than the face value of the debt.

Suppose that the company did not have unlimited liability. In this case the shareholders would not have the option to walk away from their debt. They would be obliged to repay it come hell or high water. Such debt would be effectively risk-free. The difference between holding safe and risky debt is that with risky debt the bondholders have given shareholders the option to escape from the debt by handing over the firm's assets. Thus

Value of risky debt = value of safe debt – value of put option to sell the firm's assets for the face value of the debt

We can sum up by presenting Circular's balance sheet in terms of the value of its assets, the present value of a sure-fire $50 payment, and the value of the shareholders' option to sell the asset to the bondholders:

MARKET-VALUE BALANCE SHEET FOR CIRCULAR FILE COMPANY

Asset value	$30	Bond value = present value of promised payment – value of put	$25
		Stock value = asset value – present value of promised payment + value of put	5
	$30	Firm value = asset value	$30

In the case of Circular File there is a good chance that the shareholders will exercise their option to sell the firm's assets to the bondholder. At the other extreme, Imperial Oil's assets are worth substantially more than the face value of its debt. Default on Imperial Oil bonds is possible but extremely unlikely. The value of Imperial's option to default is very low and the bonds sell for only a little less than comparable Canadian government bonds.

SELF-TEST 24.7   What will happen to the value of Circular shareholders' option if the volatility of the assets increases? (Think back to Self-Test 24.3.) What will happen to the value of the bonds?

SUMMARY

1. There are two basic types of option. A call option is the right to buy an asset at a specific exercise price on or before the exercise date. A put is the right to sell an asset at a specific exercise price on or before the exercise date.

2. The value of a call option depends on the following considerations:

   - To exercise the option you must pay the exercise price. Other things equal, the less you are obliged to pay, the better. Therefore, the value of the option is higher when the exercise price is low relative to the stock price.
   - Investors who buy the stock by way of a call option are buying on installment credit. They pay the purchase price of the option today but they do not pay the exercise price until they exercise the option. The higher the rate of interest and the longer the time to expiration, the more this "free credit" is worth.
   - No matter how far the stock price falls, the owner of the call cannot lose more than the price of the call. On the other hand, the more the stock price rises above the exercise price, the greater the profit on the call. Therefore, the option holder does not lose from increased variability if things go wrong, but gains if they go right. The value of the option increases with the variability of stock returns. Of course the longer the time to the final exercise date, the more opportunity there is for the stock price to vary.

3. The importance of building flexibility into investment projects (discussed in Chapter 8) can be reformulated in the language of options. For example, many capital investments provide the flexibility to expand capacity in the future if demand turns out to be unusually buoyant. They are in effect providing the firm with a call option on the extra capacity. Firms also think about alternative uses for their assets if things go wrong. The option to abandon a project is a put option; the put's exercise price is the value of the project's assets if shifted to an alternative use.

4. Many of the securities that firms issue contain an option. For example, warrants are nothing but a long-term call option issued by the firm. Convertible bonds give the investor the option to buy the firm's stock in exchange for the value of the underlying bond. Unlike warrants and convertibles, which give an option to the investor, callable bonds give the option to the issuing firm. If interest rates decline and the value of the underlying bond rises, the firm can buy the bonds back at a specified exercise price.

5. Whenever a company borrows, it acquires the option to default. This is equivalent to an option to sell the company's assets to the bondholders for the face value of the debt. The difference between the value of a safe government bond and a risky company bond is the value of this put option.

KEY TERMS

call option	**real options**	**convertible bond**
put option	**warrant**	**callable bond**

SUGGESTED READINGS

The classic articles on option valuation are

F. Black and M. Scholes. "The Pricing of Options and Corporate Liabilities," *Journal of Political Economy* 81 (May–June 1973):637–654.

R. C. Merton. "Theory of Rational Option Pricing," *Bell Journal of Economics and Management Science* 4 (Spring 1973):141–183.

There are a number of good texts on option valuation, including

J. Hull. *Options, Futures and Other Derivative Securities*, 2d ed. Englewood Cliffs, N.J.: Prentice-Hall, 1993.

R. Jarrow and A. Rudd. *Option Pricing*. Homewood, Ill.: Dow Jones-Irwin, 1983.

A good introduction to the importance of options in capital investment strategy is

W. C. Kester. "Today's Options for Tomorrow's Growth," *Harvard Business Review* 62 (March–April 1984):153–160.

PROBLEMS

1. Fill in the blanks by choosing the appropriate terms from the following list: *call, debtholders, exercise, face value of the debt, put, transfer.*

   A _____ option gives its owner the opportunity to buy a stock at a specific price, which is generally called the _____ price. A _____ option gives its owner the opportunity to sell stock at a specified _____ price.
   Corporate debt effectively gives the stockholders an option. Instead of paying off the debt, they can _____ the firm's assets to the _____ .
   Thus the option to default is equivalent to a _____ option. The exercise price is the _____ .

2. Note Figure 24.6(a) and 24.6(b). Match each figure with one of the following positions:
   a. Call buyer
   b. Call seller
   c. Put buyer
   d. Put seller

3. "The buyer of a call and the seller of a put both hope that the stock price will rise. Therefore the two positions are identical." Is the speaker correct? Illustrate with a simple example.

4. Suppose that you hold a share of stock and a put option on that share with an exercise price of $100. What is the payoff when the option expires if

FIGURE 24.6
See problem 2.

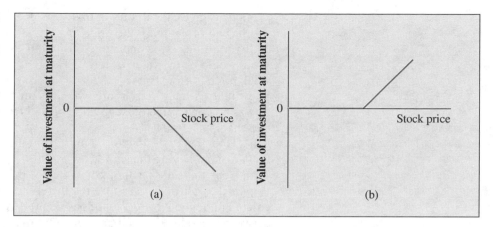

a. the stock price is below $100?
b. the stock price is above $100?

5. Mixing options and securities can often create interesting payoffs. For each of the following combinations show what the payoff would be when the option expires if (i) stock price is below the exercise price, and (ii) stock price is above the exercise price. Assume that each option has the same exercise price and date.
   a. Buy a call and invest the present value of the exercise price in a bank deposit.
   b. Buy a share and a put option on the share.
   c. Buy a share, buy a put option on the share, and sell a call option on the share.
   d. Buy a call option and a put option on the share.

6. What is the lower bound to the price of a call option? What is the upper bound?

7. What is a call option worth if
   a. the stock price is zero?
   b. the stock price is extremely high relative to the exercise price?

8. How does the price of a *put* option respond to the following changes, other things equal? Does the put price go up or down? (Assume the option is an American put that can be exercised at any time at or before the exercise date.)
   a. Stock price increases.
   b. Exercise price is increased.
   c. Risk-free interest rate increases.
   d. Expiration date of the option is extended.
   e. Volatility of the stock price falls.
   f. Time passes, so the option's expiration date comes closer.

9. As manager of United Bedstead you own substantial executive stock options. These options entitle you to buy the firm's shares during the next 5 years at a price of $100 a share. The plant manager has just outlined two alternative proposals to reequip the plant. Both proposals have the same net present value but one is substantially riskier than the other. At first you are undecided which to choose but then you remember your stock options. How might these influence your choice?

10. Look again at the BCE call option that we valued in Section 24.2. Suppose that by the end of February the price of BCE stock could rise to $65 or fall to $25. Everything else is unchanged from our example.
    a. What would be the value of the BCE call at the end of February if the stock price is $65? If it is $25?
    b. Show that a strategy of buying two calls provides exactly the same payoffs as borrowing the present value of $25 from the bank and buying one share.
    c. What is the net cash flow in January from the policy of borrowing PV($25) and buying the share?
    d. What does this tell you about the value of the call option?
    e. Why is the value of the call option different from the value that we calculated in Section 24.2? What does this tell you about the relationship between the value of a call and the volatility of the share price?

11. Look once more at the BCE call option that we valued in Section 24.2. Suppose (just suppose) that the interest rate on bank loans is zero. Recalculate the value of the BCE call option. What does this tell you about the relationship between interest rates and the value of a call?

12. Fill in the blanks:
    a. An oil company acquires mining rights to a silver deposit. It is not obliged to mine the silver, however. The company has effectively acquired a _____ option, where the exercise price is the cost of opening the mine.
    b. Some preferred shareholders have the right to redeem their shares at par value after a specified date. (If they hand over their shares, the firm sends them a cheque equal to the shares' par value.) These shareholders have a _____ option.
    c. An investor who buys stock in a levered firm acquires a _____ option on the firm's assets.
    d. A firm buys a standard machine with a ready secondhand market. The secondhand market gives the firm a _____ option.

13. What is the option in each of the following cases. Is it a call or a put?
    a. Northern Telecom commits to production of digital switching equipment specifically designed for the European market. The project has a negative NPV, but it is justified by the need for a strong market position in the rapidly growing, and potentially very profitable, market.
    b. Northern Telecom vetoes a fully integrated automated production line for the new digital switches. It will rely on standard, less expensive equipment even though the automated production line would be more efficient overall, according to a discounted-cash-flow calculation.

14. Describe each of the following situations in the language of options.
    a. Drilling rights to undeveloped heavy crude oil in Alberta. Development and production of the oil now is a negative-NPV endeavour. The break-even price is $32 per barrel, versus a spot price of $20. However, the decision to develop can be put off for up to 5 years.
    b. A restaurant producing net cash flows, after all out-of-pocket expenses, of $700,000 per year. There is no upward or downward trend in the cash flows, but they fluctuate. The real estate occupied by the restaurant is owned, and it could be sold for $5 million.

15. The price support system for various agricultural products allows farmers to sell their crops to the government for a specified "support price." What kind of option has the government given to the farmers? What is the exercise price?

16. Some investment management contracts give the portfolio manager a bonus proportional to the amount by which a portfolio return exceeds a specified threshold.
    a. In what way is this an implicit call option on the portfolio?
    b. Can you think of a way in which such contracts can lead to incentive problems? For example, what happens to the value of the prospective bonus if the manager invests in high-volatility stocks?

17. How would the value of Circular File common stock (see Section 24.3) change if
    a. the value of the firm's assets increased?
    b. the maturity of its debt were extended?
    c. the assets became safer (less volatile)?
    d. the risk-free rate of interest increased (the value of the firm's assets held constant)?

18. The Rank and File Company is considering a stock issue to raise $50 million. An underwriter offers to guarantee the success of the issue by buying any unwanted stock at the $25 issue price. The underwriter's fee is $2 million.
    a. What kind of option does Rank and File acquire if it accepts the underwriter's offer?
    b. What determines the value of the option?

19. a. Some banks have offered their customers an unusual type of time deposit. The deposit does not pay any interest if the market falls, but instead the depositor receives a proportion of any rise in the TSE's Index. What implicit option do the investors hold? How should the bank invest the money in order to protect itself against the risk of offering this deposit?
    b. You can also make a deposit with a bank that does not pay interest if the market index rises but that makes an increasingly large payment as the market index falls. How should the bank protect itself against the risk of offering this deposit?

20. The CDIC insures bank deposits. If a bank's assets are insufficient to pay off all depositors, the CDIC will contribute enough money to ensure that all depositors can be paid off in full. (We ignore the $60,000 maximum coverage on each account.) In what way is this guarantee of deposits the provision of a put option by the CDIC? *Hint*: Write out the funds the CDIC will have to contribute when bank assets are less than deposits owed to depositors. What is the exercise price of the put option?

21. a. Circular File stock is selling for $25 a share. You see that call options on the stock with exercise price of $20 are selling at $3. What should you do? What will happen to the option price as investors identify this opportunity?
    b. Now you observe that put options on Circular File with exercise price $30 are selling for $4. What should you do?

22. A 10-year maturity convertible bond with a 6 percent coupon on a company with a bond rating of A++ is selling for $1050. Each bond can be exchanged for 20 shares, and the stock price currently is $50 per share. Other A++-rated bonds with the same maturity would sell at a yield to maturity of 8 percent. What is the value of the implicit call option on the bond? Why is the bond selling for more than the value of the shares it can be converted into?

SOLUTIONS TO SELF-TEST QUESTIONS

24.1

| | Stock Price | | |
	$30	**$45**	**$50**
Buy call	0	0	5
Buy put	15	0	0
Write call	0	0	–5
Write put	–15	0	0

24.2 The value of a put option is higher when the exercise price is higher. You would be willing to pay more for the right to sell a stock at a high price than the right to sell it at a low price.

24.3 First consider the payoff to the put holder in the lower volatility scenario:

Stock price	$35	$55
Put value	$10	0

In the higher volatility scenario, the value of the stock can be $25 or $65. Now the payoff to the put is

Stock price	$25	$65
Put value	$20	0

The expected value of the payoff of the put doubles.

24.4 The payoffs are as follows:

| | Cash flow in January | Payoff in February if Stock Price Equals | |
		$20	**$80**
Strategy A			
Buy three calls	?	$ 0	+$120
Strategy B			
Buy two shares	–$80	+$40	+$160
Borrow PV($40)	– 39.60	– 40	– 40
	–$40.40	$ 0	+$120

Note: PV($40) at an interest rate of 1 percent for 1 month is 40/1.01 = $39.60.

The net cash outflow in January from strategy B is $40.40. Since the three calls offer the same payoffs in the future, they also must be worth $40.40. One call is worth 40.40/3 = $13.47.

24.5

a. The developer has the option to sell the potential housing project to the country club. This abandonment option is like a put that guarantees a minimum payoff from the investment.

b. The exercise price of the option is the price at which it can be sold to the country club. The asset value is the present value of the project if maintained as a housing development. If this value is less than the value as a golf course, the project will be sold.

c. The abandonment option increases NPV by placing a lower bound on the possible payoffs from the project.

24.6

a, b. In 5 years, the bond will be a 15-year maturity bond. The bondholder can sell the bond back to the firm at par value. The bondholder therefore has a put option to sell a 15-year bond for par value even if interest rates have risen and the bond would otherwise sell below par.

c. The exercise price is the par value of the bond.

d. The bondholder will extend the loan if interest rates decrease.

24.7 When the asset is more volatile, the put option is more valuable. Therefore the equityholders (who own the option) benefit. Since the equity is worth more, and the value of the firm's assets are unchanged, the bonds must be worth less. The higher volatility makes the option to default more valuable, which hurts the bondholders.

TWENTY-FIVE

Risk Management

We often assume that risk is beyond our control. A business is exposed to unpredictable changes in raw material costs, tax rates, technology, and a long list of other variables. There's nothing the manager can do about it.

This is not wholly true. To some extent a manager can *select* the risks of an asset or business. For example, in the last chapter we saw that companies can consciously affect the risk of an investment by building in flexibility. A company that reduces the cost of bailing out of a project by using standardized equipment is taking less risk than a similar firm that uses specialized equipment with no alternative uses. In this case the option to resell the equipment serves as an insurance policy.

Sometimes, rather than building flexibility into the project, companies accept the risk but then use financial instruments to offset it. This practice of taking offsetting risks is known as *hedging*. In this chapter we will explain how hedging works and we will describe some of the specialized financial instruments that have been devised to help manage risk. These instruments include options, futures, forwards, and swaps. They are essentially side bets on the prices of commodities or financial assets. For this reason they are often known collectively as *derivative instruments* (or *derivatives* for short)[1].

After reading this chapter you should be able to

- Understand why companies hedge to reduce risk.
- Use options, futures, and forward contracts to devise simple hedging strategies.
- Explain how companies can use swaps to change the risk of securities that they have issued.

25.1 WHY HEDGE?

In this chapter we will explain *how* companies use derivatives to hedge the risks of their business. But first we should give some of the reasons *why* they do it.

Like insurance, hedging is seldom free. Most businesses hedge to reduce risk, not to make money. Why then bother to hedge? For one thing, reducing the risk makes financial planning easier and reduces the odds of an embarrassing shortfall. A shortfall might mean only an unexpected trip to the bank, but in extreme cases it could trigger bankruptcy. Why not reduce the odds of these awkward outcomes with a hedge?

In some cases hedging also makes it easier to decide whether an operating manager deserves a stern lecture or a pat on the back. Suppose that your export division shows a 50 percent decline in profits when the dollar unexpectedly strengthens against other currencies. How much of that decrease is due to the exchange rate shift and how much to poor management? If the company had protected itself against the effect of exchange rate changes, it's probably bad management. If it wasn't, you have to make a judgment with hindsight, probably by asking, "What would profits have been *if* the firm had hedged against exchange rate movements?"

---

[1] "Side bet" conjures up an image of wicked speculators. Derivative instruments attract their share of speculators, some of whom may be wicked, but they are also used by sober and prudent business people who simply want to reduce risk.

Finance in Action

Developers and Derivatives

Because big losses make juicy headlines, newspaper readers from time to time see stories about huge damages resulting from speculation in financial derivatives. And there have been some notable setbacks. Between the three of them, Procter & Gamble, Orange County California, and German industrial conglomerate Metalgesellschaft lost over $2.5 billion U.S. Such facts can excite even those who don't have the foggiest idea of what a derivative is and why prudent business managers may find them useful or even essential.

Without the benefit of splashy news stories, hundreds of businesses in local communities are using derivatives to make their investments less risky. Consider, for example, the situation faced by a developer of new residential houses during the fall of 1994. Political uncertainties created a major "downside" risk for the developer. In normal circumstances, the developer could count on borrowing funds at normal short-term rates, and on being able to sell the houses within a few months of their completion. But the progress of the Quebec separation referendum, and/or concern about inadequate government deficit-control efforts could easily have led to an interest rate "spike" — and a period of turmoil during which the completed houses might become difficult to sell. For the developer, this unlikely but disastrous outcome would have meant paying interest on a $20 million loan at who knows what interest rate for perhaps more than a year. Obviously the existence of this risk would make it more difficult to justify the project within the firm and to lenders.

James MacKinnon, Scotiabank's Assistant General Manager for Derivative Products, commented on the situation: "The client wasn't interested in an interest rate swap, because there was no way of knowing how much time would go by between construction and sale of a house. They wanted to borrow short term, using a rate that floated up and down with prime, but were looking for something like an insurance policy; something that would protect them if the prime went far higher than expected. Scotiabank put together a derivative product that provided this insurance. Such a product is commonly referred to as an interest rate "cap." For a one-time payment of $116,000 the developers were able to effectively protect themselves from interest rates going above $10\frac{1}{2}$ percent. This allowed them to generate some "worst case" projections based on guaranteed borrowing costs, and to ensure that the firm would be able to continue to operate, even if the referendum results caused considerable turmoil in financial markets."

Purchase of this derivative allowed the developers to begin construction without betting the company.

Said MacKinnon "Given conditions in May 1995, the developer seems unlikely to collect on their 'insurance policy,' but there were some real benefits to them of being able to proceed with the project last fall, instead of waiting for the political uncertainties to be resolved."

Source: James MacKinnon, interview with Guus Saaltink, May 1995.

Finally, hedging extraneous events can help focus the operating manager's attention. We know we shouldn't worry about events outside our control, but most of us do anyway. It's naive to expect the manager of the export division not to worry about exchange rate movements if his bottom line and bonus depend on them. The time spent worrying could be better spent if the company hedged itself against such movements.

25.2 REDUCING RISK WITH OPTIONS

In the last chapter we introduced you to put and call options. Managers regularly buy options on currencies, interest rates, and commodities to limit their downside risk. Many of these options are traded on options exchanges, but often they are simply private deals between the corporation and a bank.

Petrochemical Parfum, Inc., is concerned about potential increases in the price of heavy crude oil, which is one of its major inputs. To protect itself against such increases Petrochemical buys 6-month options to purchase 1000 barrels of crude oil at an exercise price of $20. These options might cost $.50 per barrel.

If the price of crude is above the $20 exercise price when the options expire, Petrochemical will exercise the options and will receive the difference between the oil price and the exercise price. If the oil price falls below the exercise price, the options will expire worthless. The overall payments will therefore be as follows:

	Oil Price, Dollars per Barrel		
	$18	**$20**	**$22**
Cost of 1000 barrels	$18,000	$20,000	$22,000
− Payoff on call option	0	0	2,000
Net payments	$18,000	$20,000	$20,000

You can see that by buying options Petrochemical protects itself against increases in the oil price while continuing to benefit from oil price decreases. If prices fall, it can discard its call option and buy its oil at the market price. If oil prices rise, however, it can exercise its call option to purchase oil for $20 a barrel. Therefore, options create an attractive asymmetry. Of course, this asymmetry comes at a price — the $500 cost of the options.

Consider now the problem of Onnex, Inc., which supplies Petrochemical with crude oil. Its problem is the mirror image of Petrochemical's; it loses when oil prices fall and gains when oil prices rise.

Onnex wants to lock in a minimum price of oil but still benefit from rising oil prices. It can do so by purchasing *put* options that give it the right to *sell* oil at an exercise price of $20 per barrel. If oil prices fall, it will exercise the put. If they rise, it will discard the put and sell oil at the market price:

	Oil Price, Dollars per Barrel		
	$18	**$20**	**$22**
Cost of 1000 barrels	$18,000	$20,000	$22,000
− Payoff on call option	2,000	0	0
Net payments	$20,000	$20,000	$22,000

If oil prices rise, Onnex reaps the benefit. But if oil prices fall below $20 a barrel, the profit on the put option exactly offsets the revenue shortfall. As a result,

Onnex realizes net revenues of at least $20 a barrel, which is the exercise price of the put option. Once again you don't get something for nothing. The price that Onnex pays for insuring itself against a fall in the price of oil is the cost of the put option.

Notice that both Petrochemical and Onnex use options to insure against an adverse move in oil prices. But the options do not remove all uncertainty. For example, Onnex may be able to sell oil for much more than the exercise price of the option.

SELF-TEST 25.1

Suppose that a pension fund is invested in a diversified portfolio of shares in Canadian companies. How can it use options to insure that the value of its portfolio does not fall by more than 10 percent? *Hint*: You might find it helpful to look in the financial pages of a newspaper to see the menu of options.

25.3   FUTURES CONTRACTS

futures contract: Exchange-traded forward contract with gains or losses realized daily.

In Chapter 13 we introduced you to the example of a wheat farmer who is worried about the price that he will receive for his crop. We described how he can reduce this uncertainty by selling wheat *futures*. In this case he agrees to deliver so many bushels of wheat in (say) September at a price that is set today. Do not confuse this *futures contract* with an option, where the holder has a *choice* whether or not to make delivery; the farmer's **futures contract** is a binding promise to deliver wheat.

A miller is in the opposite position. She needs to *buy* wheat after the harvest. If she would like to fix the price of this wheat ahead of time, she can do so by *buying* wheat futures. In other words, she agrees to take delivery of wheat in the future at a price that is fixed today. The miller also does not have an option; if she still holds the futures contract when it matures, she is obliged to take delivery.

Both the farmer and the miller have less risk than before. The farmer has hedged (that is, offset) risk by selling wheat futures; the miller has hedged risk by buying wheat futures.[2]

The price of wheat for immediate delivery is known as the *spot price*. When the farmer sells wheat futures, the price that he agrees to take for his wheat may be very different from the spot price. But the future eventually becomes the present. As the date for delivery approaches, the futures contract becomes more and more like a spot contract and the price of the futures contract approaches the spot price.

The farmer may decide to wait until the futures contract matures and then deliver wheat to the buyer. But in practice such delivery is rare, for it is more convenient for the farmer to buy back the wheat futures just before maturity.[3]

For example, suppose that the farmer originally sold 20 tonnes of October wheat futures at a price of $136.70 per tonne. In October, when the futures contract matures, the price of wheat is only $130.00 per tonne. The farmer buys back the wheat futures at $130.00 per tonne just before maturity, giving him a profit of $6.70 per tonne on the sale and subsequent repurchase. At the same time he sells his wheat at the spot price of $130.00 a bushel. His total receipts are therefore $136.70 per tonne:

---

[2] Neither has eliminated all risk. For example, the farmer still has quantity risk. He does not know for sure how many bushels of wheat he will produce.

[3] In the case of some of the financial futures described later, you *cannot* deliver the asset. At maturity the buyer simply receives (or pays) the difference between the spot price and the price at which he or she has agreed to purchase the asset.

Profit on sale and repurchase of futures	$ 6.70
Sale of wheat at the September spot price	130.00
Total receipts	$136.70

You can see that the futures contract has allowed the farmer to lock in a price of $136.70 a bushel.

The Mechanics of Futures Trading

Futures contracts are bought and sold on organized futures exchanges such as the Toronto Futures Exchange, the Montreal Exchange and the Winnipeg Commodity Exchange. But the largest of these futures exchanges is the Chicago Board of Trade, which traded 179 million futures contracts in 1993.

Table 25.1 shows the price of wheat futures at the Winnipeg Commodity Exchange in February 1995. Notice that there is a choice of possible delivery dates. If, for example, you were to sell wheat for delivery in May before the main harvest, you would get a higher price than by selling October futures.

TABLE 25.1
The price of wheat futures at the Winnipeg Commodity Exchange

Delivery Date	$ per tonne
March	153.8
May	151.3
July	150.1
October	136.7
December	136.7

The miller would not be prepared to buy futures contracts if the farmer were free to deliver half-rotten wheat to a leaky barn at the end of the cart track. Futures trading is possible only because the contracts are highly standardized. For example, in the case of wheat futures, each contract calls for the delivery of 20 tonnes of wheat of a specified quality at a warehouse in Thunder Bay.

When you buy or sell a futures contract, the price is fixed today, but payment is not made until later. However, you will be asked to put up some cash as *margin* to demonstrate that you are able to honour your side of the bargain.

In addition, futures contracts are *marked to market*. This means that each day any profits or losses on the contract are calculated; you pay the exchange any losses and receive any profits. For example, our farmer agreed to deliver 20 tonnes of wheat at $136.70 a bushel. Suppose that the next day the price of wheat futures increases to $145.00 a tonne. The farmer now has a loss on his sale of $20 \times $8.30 = $166 and must pay this sum to the exchange. You can think of the farmer as buying back his futures position each day and then opening up a new position. Thus after the first day the farmer has realized a loss on his trade of $8.30 a tonne and now has an obligation to deliver wheat for $145.00 a tonne.

Of course our miller is in the opposite position. The rise in the futures price leaves her with a *profit* of $8.30 per tonne. The exchange will therefore pay her this profit. In effect the miller sells her futures position at a profit and opens a new contract to take delivery at $145.00 a tonne.

SELF-TEST 25.2

Suppose that 2 days after taking out the futures contracts the price of October wheat increases to $165 per tonne. What additional payments will be made by or to the farmer and the miller? What will be their remaining obligation at the end of this second day?

....
Commodity and Financial Futures

We have shown how the farmer and the miller can both use wheat futures to hedge their risk. One may also trade futures in a wide variety of other commodities, such as sugar, soybean oil, pork bellies, orange juice, crude oil, and copper.

Commodity prices can bounce up and down like a bungee jumper. For example, raw sugar prices rose from about 4 cents a pound in 1986 to touch 15 cents in 1990 before falling to 8 cents a year later. For a large buyer of sugar, such as Hershey, these price fluctuations could knock the company badly off course. Hershey therefore reduces its exposure to movements in sugar and cocoa prices by hedging with commodity futures.

For many firms, the wide fluctuations in interest rates and exchange rates have become at least as important a source of risk as changes in commodity prices. You can use *financial futures* to hedge against these risks. Financial futures are similar to commodity futures but, instead of placing an order to buy or sell a commodity at a future date, you place an order to buy or sell a financial asset at a future date. You can use financial futures to protect yourself against fluctuations in short- and long-term interest rates, exchange rates, and the level of share prices.

Financial futures have been a remarkable success. They were invented in 1972; within a few years, trading in financial futures significantly exceeded trading in commodity futures. Table 25.2 lists some of the more popular financial futures contracts.

TABLE 25.2
Some financial futures contracts

Future	Principal Exchange
Canadian government bonds	Montreal Exchange
U.S. Treasury bonds	Chicago Board of Trade
Canadian bankers' acceptances	Montreal Exchange
Toronto Stock Exchange 35	Toronto Futures Exchange
Deutschemark	International Monetary Market (at the Chicago Mercantile Exchange)
Yen	International Monetary Market

SELF-TEST 25.3
....

You plan to issue long-term bonds in 9 months but are worried that interest rates may have increased in the meantime. How could you use financial futures to protect yourself against a general rise in interest rates?

....
Hedging and Speculation

Our examples of the farmer and the miller showed how futures are used to reduce business risk. If spot prices fall by harvest time, the farmer receives a lower price for his crop, but this fall in the value of the crop is offset by the gain on his futures position. Conversely, if spot prices rise, the farmer's crop is worth more, but he has an offsetting loss on his futures.

If you were to copy the farmer and sell wheat futures without an offsetting holding of wheat, you would not be *reducing* risk; you would be *speculating*. A successful futures market needs speculators who are prepared to take on risk and provide the farmer and the miller with the insurance they need. For example, if an excess of farmers wished to sell wheat futures, the price of futures would be forced down until enough speculators were tempted to buy in the hope of a profit. If there is a surplus of millers wishing to buy wheat futures, the reverse will happen. The price of wheat futures will be forced up until speculators are drawn in to sell.

Speculation may be necessary to a thriving futures market but it can get companies into serious trouble. For example, the German metals and oil trading company Metallgesellschaft agreed to deliver oil to customers in the future at a fixed

Finance in Action

Punting for Fun and Profit

PARIS — Imagine a perfect market: one with no insider trading, an uninterrupted flow of information, and minimal transaction costs. Then guess which real market fits the bill. Oil? Gold? Currencies? Wrong. The answer is rugby. And just to prove the point, during the recent rugby World Cup, Société Générale ran a special derivatives market for those who wanted to bet on the semi-final between Australia and New Zealand.

For the 30 punters who turned up to play, the aim of the game was to buy and sell both futures and options via open outcry in reaction to "market movement" like a dropped goal or a scrum (on the pitch rather than on the trading floor, though it was often hard to tell the difference). Bank staff who work at MATIF, France's futures exchange, and MONEP, the traded-options exchange, made markets in options and futures on the likely outcome. The contract was defined as New Zealand's score minus Australia's

plus 100. Thus Australia's 12–6 win over New Zealand translated into a closing price of 94.

At kick-off, market sentiment clearly favoured the All Blacks as the spot price hovered around 105. Bulls sure of a New Zealand victory pushed the price up to 106 in the first few minutes of the game by buying calls and selling puts. But then Australia's David Campese scored a try, and more swung into buying puts and selling futures. The most clued-up players were also using straddles and strangles, which happen to be trading strategies as well as rugby tactics.

The winner, in the end, was a contrarian who had gone long on Australia from the start. His prize? A round-trip to Tokyo or New York courtesy of Air France. As this was, after all, a marketing gimmick, Société Générale is now thinking of repeating it in America, perhaps on a fast-moving game like basketball. Is there such a thing in futures markets as a full-court press?

Source: The Economist, November 23, 1991, p. 86. © 1991 The Economist Newspaper Group Inc. Reprinted with permission. Further reproduction prohibited.

price. Since the company would later need to buy this oil in the market, it stood to take a large loss if oil prices rose. The firm's policy was to hedge this risk by buying oil futures, but someone decided that speculation was more fun. In January 1993 Metallgesellschaft reported that it had lost $470 million through trading in oil futures, with a possible $900 million of further losses.

25.4   FORWARD CONTRACTS

forward contract: Agreement to buy or sell an asset in the future at an agreed price.

Each day billions of dollars of futures contracts are bought and sold. We have seen that this liquidity is possible only because futures contracts are standardized and mature on a limited number of dates each year. But if the terms of futures contracts do not suit your particular needs, you may be able to buy or sell a **forward contract.**

Forward contracts are simply made-to-measure futures contracts.[4] For example, suppose that you know that you will need to pay out yen in 3 months' time. You can fix today the price that you will pay for the yen by arranging with your bank to buy yen forward. At the end of the 3 months, you pay the agreed sum and take delivery of the yen.

The most active trade in forwards is in foreign currencies, but in recent years companies have increasingly entered into forward agreements that allow them to fix in advance the interest rate at which they borrow or lend.

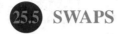 **SWAPS**

swap: Arrangement between two traders to exchange a series of future payments on different terms.

Suppose that the Possum Company wishes to borrow deutschemarks (DM) to help finance its European operations. Since Possum is better known in Canada , the financial manager believes that the company can obtain more attractive terms on a dollar loan than on a deutschemark loan. Therefore, the company borrows $10 million for 5 years at 5 percent in Canada. At the same time Possum arranges with a bank to trade its future dollar liability for deutschemarks. Under this arrangement the bank agrees to pay Possum sufficient dollars to service its dollar loan and in exchange Possum agrees to make a series of annual payments in deutschemarks to the bank. This arrangement is known as a currency **swap**.

Possum's cash flows are set out in Table 25.3. Line 1 shows that when Possum takes out its dollar loan, it promises to pay annual interest of $.5 million and to repay the $10 million that it has borrowed. Lines 2a and 2b show the cash flows from the swap, assuming that the spot exchange rate for the deutschemark is $1 = DM2. Possum hands over to the bank the $10 million that it borrowed and receives in exchange 2 × $10 million = DM 20 million. In each of the next 4 years the bank pays Possum $.5 million, which it uses to pay the annual interest on its loan. In Year 5 the bank pays Possum $10.5 million, which covers both the final year's interest and the repayment of the loan. In return for these future dollar receipts, Possum agrees to pay the bank DM 1.2 million in each of the next 4 years and DM 21.2 million in Year 5.

TABLE 25.3

Cash flows from Possum's dollar loan and currency swap (figures in millions)

		Year 0		Years 1 – 4		Year 5	
		$	DM	$	DM	$	DM
1.	Issue dollar loan	+10		– .5		–10.5	
2.	Arrange currency swap						
	a. Possum receives $	–10		+ .5		+10.5	
	b. Possum pays DM	—	+20	—	–1.2	—	–21.2
3.	Net cash flow	0	+20	0	–1.2	0	–21.2

The combined effect of Possum's two steps (line 3) is to convert its 5 percent dollar loan into a 6 percent deutschemark loan. The device that makes this possible is the currency swap.

Swaps are not limited to future exchanges of currency. For example, firms often swap fixed-interest-rate loans for floating-rate loans, whose interest payments go up and down with the general level of interest rates. It is even possible to swap commodities. You don't need to deliver the commodities; you just settle up any differences in their value.

---

[4] One difference between forward and futures contracts is that forward contracts are not marked to market. Thus with a forward contract you settle up any profits or losses when the contract matures.

Like futures and options, swaps are one of the great success stories in finance. About three-quarters of firms borrowing in the international bond market follow Possum's example and enter into a swap. Worldwide, the outstanding value of currency and interest rate swaps is estimated to have grown by 40 percent in 1994 to more than $4 trillion.

SELF-TEST 25.4   Suppose that the exchange rate is $1 = DM3 and that German interest rates are 8 percent. Recalculate the deutschemark cash flows that the bank would agree to (line 2b of Table 25.3) and Possum's net cash flows (line 3).

25.6   SUMMARY

1. Fluctuations in commodity prices, interest rates, or exchange rates can make planning difficult and can throw companies badly off course. Financial managers therefore look for opportunities to manage these risks, and a number of specialized instruments have been invented to help them. These are collectively known as *derivative instruments*.

2. In the last chapter we introduced you to put and call options. Options are often used by firms to limit their downside risk. For example, if you own an asset and have the option to sell it at the current price, then you have effectively insured yourself against loss.

3. Futures contracts are agreements made today to buy or sell an asset in the future. The price is fixed today, but the final payment does not occur until the delivery date. Futures contracts are highly standardized and are traded on organized exchanges. Commodity futures allow firms to fix the future price that they pay for a wide range of agricultural commodities, metals, and oil. Financial futures help firms to protect themselves against unforeseen movements in interest rates, exchange rates, and stock prices.

4. Forward contracts are equivalent to tailor-made futures contracts. For example, firms often enter into forward agreements with a bank to buy or sell foreign exchange or to fix the interest rate on a loan to be made in the future.

5. Swaps allow firms to exchange one series of future payments for another. For example, the firm might agree to make a series of regular payments in one currency in return for receiving a series of payments in another currency.

KEY TERMS

futures contract   **forward contract**   **swap**

SUGGESTED READINGS

There are several useful books devoted to risk management using futures and options. They include

D. Duffie. *Futures Markets*. Englewood Cliffs, N.J.: Prentice-Hall, 1989.

S. Figlewski, K. John, and J. Merrick. *Hedging with Financial Futures for Institutional Investors: From Theory to Practice*. Cambridge, Mass.: Ballinger, 1986.

C. W. Smith, C. H. Smithson, and D. S. Wilford. *Managing Financial Risk*. New York: Harper & Row, 1990.

PROBLEMS

1. Large businesses spend millions of dollars annually on insurance. Why? Should they insure against all risks or does insurance make more sense for some risks than others?

2. a.   An investor currently holding $1 million in long-term Canada bonds becomes concerned about increasing volatility in interest rates. She decides to hedge her risk using government bond futures contracts. Should she buy or sell such contracts?

   b.   The treasurer of a corporation that will be issuing bonds in 3 months also is concerned about interest rate volatility and wants to lock in the price at which he could sell 8 percent coupon bonds. How would he use government bond futures contracts to hedge his firm's position?

3. A gold mining firm is concerned about short-term volatility in its revenues. Gold currently sells for $300 an ounce, but the price is extremely volatile and could fall as low as $280 or rise as high as $320 in the next month. The company will bring 1000 ounces to the market next month.

   a.   What will be total revenues if the firm remains unhedged for gold prices of $280, $300, and $320 an ounce?

   b.   The futures price of gold for 1-month-ahead delivery is $301. What will be the firm's total revenues at each gold price if the firm enters a 1-month futures contract to deliver 1000 ounces of gold?

   c.   What will total revenues be if the firm buys a 1-month put option to sell gold for $300 an ounce? The puts cost $2 per ounce.

4. A large dental lab plans to purchase 1000 ounces of gold in 1 month. Assume again that gold prices can be $280, $300, or $320 an ounce.

   a.   What will total expenses be if the firm purchases call options on 1000 ounces of gold with an exercise price of $300 an ounce? The options cost $3 per ounce.

   b.   What will total expenses be if the firm purchases call options on 1000 ounces of gold with an exercise price of $295 an ounce? These options cost $7 per ounce.

5. What is a currency swap? An interest rate swap? Give one example of how each might be used.

6. Firms A and B face the following borrowing rates for a 5-year fixed-rate debt issue in Canadian dollars or Swiss francs:

	Canadian dollars	Swiss francs
Firm A	10%	7%
Firm B	8%	6%

   Suppose that A wishes to borrow Canadian dollars and B wishes to borrow Swiss francs. Show how a swap could be used to reduce the borrowing costs of each company. Assume a spot exchange rate of 2 Swiss francs to the dollar.

7. Assume that the 1-year interest rate is 10 percent and the 2-year interest rate is 12 percent. You approach a bank and ask what rate the bank will promise to make a 1-year loan in 12 months' time. The bank offers to make

a forward commitment to lend to you at 15 percent. Would you accept the offer? Can you think of a simple, cheaper alternative?

8. Your firm has just tendered for a contract in Japan. You won't know for 3 months whether you get the contract but if you do, you will receive a payment of ¥10 million 1 year from now. You are worried that if the yen declines in value, the dollar value of this payment will be less than you expect and the project could even show a loss. Discuss the possible ways that you could protect the firm against a decline in the value of the yen. Illustrate the possible outcomes if you do get the contract and if you don't.

9. Show how Petrochemical Parfum can also use futures contracts to protect itself against a rise in the price of crude oil. Show how the payoffs would vary if the oil price is $18, $20, or $22 a barrel. What are the advantages and disadvantages for Petrochemical of using futures rather than options to reduce risk? Repeat the exercise for Onnex.

10. What other commodity futures are traded on futures exchanges? Who do you think could usefully reduce risk by buying each of these contracts? Who do you think might wish to sell each contract?

11. "The farmer does not avoid risk by selling wheat futures. If wheat prices stay above $140 a tonne, then he will actually have lost by selling wheat futures at $140." Is this a fair comment?

12. Suppose that in the 5 days following the farmer's sale of October wheat futures the price of the futures is

Day	1	2	3	4	5
Price	$140	$145	$135	$137	$135

At the end of Day 5 the farmer decides to quit wheat farming and buys back his futures contract. What payments are made between the farmer and the exchange on each day? What is the total payment over the 5 days? Would the total payment be any different if the contract was not marked to market?

13. Look in *The Globe and Mail* at the prices of gold futures quoted on the New York Commodity Exchange. What is the date of the most distant contract? Suppose that you buy 100 ounces of gold futures for this date? When do you receive the gold? When do you pay for it? Is the futures price higher or lower than the current spot price? Can you suggest why?

14. We saw in Chapter 23 that when the deutschemark strengthened in 1991 and 1992, German luxury car manufacturers found it increasingly difficult to compete in the North American market. How could they have hedged themselves against this risk? Would a company that was hedged have been in a better position to compete? Explain why or why not.

15. What do you think are advantages of holding futures rather than the underlying commodity? What do you think are the disadvantages?

SOLUTIONS TO SELF-TEST QUESTIONS

25.1 It can buy a put option on a stock market index with an exercise price 10 percent below the current level of the index. If stock prices fall by more than 10 percent, the fund will exercise its option and the profit on the option will approximately offset the losses on the underlying stocks. Notice that when you exercise an option on a market index, it is impossible to *deliver* the index; instead you simply receive the profit on your option.

25.2   The farmer has a further loss of $20 per tonne ($165 – $145) and will be required to pay this amount to the exchange. The miller has a further profit of $20 per tonne and will receive this from the exchange. The farmer is now committed to delivering wheat in October for $165 a bushel and the miller is committed to paying $165 a bushel.

25.3   You sell long-term bond futures with a delivery date of 9 months. Suppose, for example, that you agree to deliver long-term bonds in 9 months at a price of 100. If interest rates fall, the price of the bond futures will rise to (say) 105. (Remember that when interest rates fall, bond prices rise.) In this case the profit that you make on your bond futures offsets the lower price that the firm is likely to receive on the sale of its own bonds. Conversely, if interest rates fall, the company will make a loss on its futures position but will receive a higher price for its own bonds.

25.4   The following table shows revised cash flows from Possum's dollar loan and currency swap (figures in millions):

		Year 0		Years 1 – 4		Year 5	
		$	**DM**	**$**	**DM**	**$**	**DM**
1.	Issue dollar loan	+10		– .5		–10.5	
2.	Arrange currency swap						
	a. Possum receives $	–10		+ .5		+10.5	
	b. Possum pays DM		+30		–2.4		–32.4
3.	Net cash flow	0	+30	0	–2.4	0	–32.4

Notice that in exchange for $10 million today the bank is now prepared to pay over DM 30 million. Since the German interest rate is now 8 percent, the bank will expect to earn .08 × 30 = DM2.4 million interest on its deutschemark outlay.

APPENDIX

Present Value Tables

Appendix Table 1 Discount factors: Present value of $1 to be received after t years $= \dfrac{1}{(1 + r)^t}$

t	1%	2%	3%	4%	5%	6%	7%	8%	9%	10%	11%	12%	13%	14%	15%
								Interest rate r							
1	.990	.980	.971	.962	.952	.943	.935	.926	.917	.909	.901	.893	.885	.877	.870
2	.980	.961	.943	.925	.907	.890	.873	.857	.842	.826	.812	.797	.783	.769	.756
3	.971	.942	.915	.889	.864	.840	.816	.794	.772	.751	.731	.712	.693	.675	.658
4	.961	.924	.888	.855	.823	.792	.763	.735	.708	.683	.659	.636	.613	.592	.572
5	.951	.906	.863	.822	.784	.747	.713	.681	.650	.621	.593	.567	.543	.519	.497
6	.942	.888	.837	.790	.746	.705	.666	.630	.596	.564	.535	.507	.480	.456	.432
7	.933	.871	.813	.760	.711	.665	.623	.583	.547	.513	.482	.452	.425	.400	.376
8	.923	.853	.789	.731	.677	.627	.582	.540	.502	.467	.434	.404	.376	.351	.327
9	.914	.837	.766	.703	.645	.592	.544	.500	.460	.424	.391	.361	.333	.308	.284
10	.905	.820	.744	.676	.614	.558	.508	.463	.422	.386	.352	.322	.295	.270	.247
11	.896	.804	.722	.650	.585	.527	.475	.429	.388	.350	.317	.287	.261	.237	.215
12	.887	.788	.701	.625	.557	.497	.444	.397	.356	.319	.286	.257	.229	.208	.187
13	.879	.773	.681	.601	.530	.469	.415	.368	.326	.290	.258	.229	.204	.182	.163
14	.870	.758	.661	.577	.505	.442	.388	.340	.299	.263	.232	.205	.181	.160	.141
15	.861	.743	.642	.555	.481	.417	.362	.315	.275	.239	.209	.183	.160	.140	.123
16	.853	.728	.623	.534	.458	.394	.339	.292	.252	.218	.188	.163	.141	.123	.107
17	.844	.714	.605	.513	.436	.371	.317	.270	.231	.198	.170	.146	.125	.108	.093
18	.836	.700	.587	.494	.416	.350	.296	.250	.212	.180	.153	.130	.111	.095	.081
19	.828	.686	.570	.475	.396	.331	.277	.232	.194	.164	.138	.116	.098	.083	.070
20	.820	.673	.554	.456	.377	.312	.258	.215	.178	.149	.124	.104	.087	.073	.061
21	.811	.660	.538	.439	.359	.294	.242	.199	.164	.135	.112	.093	.077	.064	.053
22	.803	.647	.522	.422	.342	.278	.226	.184	.150	.123	.101	.083	.068	.056	.046
23	.795	.634	.507	.406	.326	.262	.211	.170	.138	.112	.091	.074	.060	.049	.040
24	.788	.622	.492	.390	.310	.247	.197	.158	.126	.102	.082	.066	.053	.043	.035
25	.780	.610	.478	.375	.295	.233	.184	.146	.116	.092	.074	.059	.047	.038	.030
26	.772	.598	.464	.361	.281	.220	.172	.135	.106	.084	.066	.053	.042	.033	.026
27	.764	.586	.450	.347	.268	.207	.161	.125	.098	.076	.060	.047	.037	.029	.023
28	.757	.574	.437	.333	.255	.196	.150	.116	.090	.069	.054	.042	.033	.026	.020
29	.749	.563	.424	.321	.243	.185	.141	.107	.082	.063	.048	.037	.029	.022	.017
30	.742	.552	.412	.308	.231	.174	.131	.099	.075	.057	.044	.033	.026	.020	.015

E.g.: If the interest rate is 10% per year, the present value of $1 to be received at the end of year 5 is $0.621.

						Interest rate r									
16%	17%	18%	19%	20%	21%	22%	23%	24%	25%	26%	27%	28%	29%	30%	t
.862	.855	.847	.840	.833	.826	.820	.813	.806	.800	.794	.787	.781	.775	.769	1
.743	.731	.718	.706	.694	.683	.672	.661	.650	.640	.630	.620	.610	.601	.592	2
.641	.624	.609	.593	.579	.564	.551	.537	.524	.512	.500	.488	.477	.466	.455	3
.552	.534	.516	.499	.482	.467	.451	.437	.423	.410	.397	.384	.373	.361	.350	4
.476	.456	.437	.419	.402	.386	.370	.355	.341	.328	.315	.303	.291	.280	.269	5
.410	.390	.370	.352	.335	.319	.303	.289	.275	.262	.250	.238	.227	.217	.207	6
.354	.333	.314	.296	.279	.263	.249	.235	.222	.210	.198	.188	.178	.168	.159	7
.305	.285	.266	.249	.233	.218	.204	.191	.179	.168	.157	.148	.139	.130	.123	8
.263	.243	.225	.209	.194	.180	.167	.155	.144	.134	.125	.116	.108	.101	.094	9
.227	.208	.191	.176	.162	.149	.137	.126	.116	.107	.099	.092	.085	.078	.073	10
.195	.178	.162	.148	.135	.123	.112	.103	.094	.086	.079	.072	.066	.061	.056	11
.168	.152	.137	.124	.112	.102	.092	.083	.076	.069	.062	.057	.052	.047	.043	12
.145	.130	.116	.104	.093	.084	.075	.068	.061	.055	.050	.045	.040	.037	.033	13
.125	.111	.099	.088	.078	.069	.062	.055	.049	.044	.039	.035	.032	.028	.025	14
.108	.095	.084	.074	.065	.057	.051	.045	.040	.035	.031	.028	.025	.022	.020	15
.093	.081	.071	.062	.054	.047	.042	.036	.032	.028	.025	.022	.019	.017	.015	16
.080	.069	.060	.052	.045	.039	.034	.030	.026	.023	.020	.017	.015	.013	.012	17
.069	.059	.051	.044	.038	.032	.028	.024	.021	.018	.016	.014	.012	.010	.009	18
.060	.051	.043	.037	.031	.027	.023	.020	.017	.014	.012	.011	.009	.008	.007	19
.051	.043	.037	.031	.026	.022	.019	.016	.014	.012	.010	.008	.007	.006	.005	20
.044	.037	.031	.026	.022	.018	.015	.013	.011	.009	.008	.007	.006	.005	.004	21
.038	.032	.026	.022	.018	.015	.013	.011	.009	.007	.006	.005	.004	.004	.003	22
.033	.027	.022	.018	.015	.012	.010	.009	.007	.006	.005	.004	.003	.003	.002	23
.028	.023	.019	.015	.013	.010	.008	.007	.006	.005	.004	.003	.003	.002	.002	24
.024	.020	.016	.013	.010	.009	.007	.006	.005	.004	.003	.003	.002	.002	.001	25
.021	.017	.014	.011	.009	.007	.006	.005	.004	.003	.002	.002	.002	.001	.001	26
.018	.014	.011	.009	.007	.006	.005	.004	.003	.002	.002	.002	.001	.001	.001	27
.016	.012	.010	.008	.006	.005	.004	.003	.002	.002	.002	.001	.001	.001	.001	28
.014	.011	.008	.006	.005	.004	.003	.002	.002	.002	.001	.001	.001	.001	.000	29
.012	.009	.007	.005	.004	.003	.003	.002	.002	.001	.001	.001	.001	.000	.000	30

Appendix Table 2 Accumulation factors: Future value of $1 by the end of *t* years = $(1 + r)^t$

t	1%	2%	3%	4%	5%	6%	7%	8%	9%	10%	11%	12%	13%	14%	15%
1	1.010	1.020	1.030	1.040	1.050	1.060	1.070	1.080	1.090	1.100	1.110	1.120	1.130	1.140	1.150
2	1.020	1.040	1.061	1.082	1.102	1.124	1.145	1.166	1.188	1.210	1.232	1.254	1.277	1.300	1.322
3	1.030	1.061	1.093	1.125	1.158	1.191	1.225	1.260	1.295	1.331	1.368	1.405	1.443	1.482	1.521
4	1.041	1.082	1.126	1.170	1.216	1.262	1.311	1.360	1.412	1.464	1.518	1.574	1.630	1.689	1.749
5	1.051	1.104	1.159	1.217	1.276	1.338	1.403	1.469	1.539	1.611	1.685	1.762	1.842	1.925	2.011
6	1.062	1.126	1.194	1.265	1.340	1.419	1.501	1.587	1.677	1.772	1.870	1.974	2.082	2.195	2.313
7	1.072	1.149	1.230	1.316	1.407	1.504	1.606	1.714	1.828	1.949	2.076	2.211	2.353	2.502	2.660
8	1.083	1.172	1.267	1.369	1.477	1.594	1.718	1.851	1.993	2.144	2.305	2.476	2.658	2.853	3.059
9	1.094	1.195	1.305	1.423	1.551	1.689	1.838	1.999	2.172	2.358	2.558	2.773	3.004	3.252	3.518
10	1.105	1.219	1.344	1.480	1.629	1.791	1.967	2.159	2.367	2.594	2.839	3.106	3.395	3.707	4.046
11	1.116	1.243	1.384	1.539	1.710	1.898	2.105	2.332	2.580	2.853	3.152	3.479	3.836	4.226	4.652
12	1.127	1.268	1.426	1.601	1.796	2.012	2.252	2.518	2.813	3.138	3.498	3.896	4.335	4.818	5.350
13	1.138	1.294	1.469	1.665	1.886	2.133	2.410	2.720	3.066	3.452	3.883	4.363	4.898	5.492	6.153
14	1.149	1.319	1.513	1.732	1.980	2.261	2.579	2.937	3.342	3.797	4.310	4.887	5.535	6.261	7.076
15	1.161	1.346	1.558	1.801	2.079	2.397	2.759	3.172	3.642	4.177	4.785	5.474	6.254	7.138	8.137
16	1.173	1.373	1.605	1.873	2.183	2.540	2.952	3.426	3.970	4.595	5.311	6.130	7.067	8.137	9.358
17	1.184	1.400	1.653	1.948	2.292	2.693	3.159	3.700	4.328	5.054	5.895	6.866	7.986	9.276	10.76
18	1.196	1.428	1.702	2.026	2.407	2.854	3.380	3.996	4.717	5.560	6.544	7.690	9.024	10.58	12.38
19	1.208	1.457	1.754	2.107	2.527	3.026	3.617	4.316	5.142	6.116	7.263	8.613	10.20	12.06	14.23
20	1.220	1.486	1.806	2.191	2.653	3.207	3.870	4.661	5.604	6.727	8.062	9.646	11.52	13.74	16.37
21	1.232	1.516	1.860	2.279	2.786	3.400	4.141	5.034	6.109	7.400	8.949	10.80	13.02	15.67	18.82
22	1.245	1.546	1.916	2.370	2.925	3.604	4.430	5.437	6.659	8.140	9.934	12.10	14.71	17.86	21.64
23	1.257	1.577	1.974	2.465	3.072	3.820	4.741	5.871	7.258	8.954	11.03	13.55	16.63	20.36	24.89
24	1.270	1.608	2.033	2.563	3.225	4.049	5.072	6.341	7.911	9.850	12.24	15.18	18.79	23.21	28.63
25	1.282	1.641	2.094	2.666	3.386	4.292	5.427	6.848	8.623	10.83	13.59	17.00	21.23	26.46	32.92
26	1.295	1.673	2.157	2.772	3.556	4.549	5.807	7.396	9.399	11.92	15.08	19.04	23.99	30.17	37.86
27	1.308	1.707	2.221	2.883	3.733	4.822	6.214	7.988	10.25	13.11	16.74	21.32	27.11	34.39	43.54
28	1.321	1.741	2.288	2.999	3.920	5.112	6.649	8.627	11.17	14.42	18.58	23.88	30.63	39.20	50.07
29	1.335	1.776	2.357	3.119	4.116	5.418	7.114	9.317	12.17	15.86	20.62	26.75	34.62	44.69	57.58
30	1.348	1.811	2.427	3.243	4.322	5.743	7.612	10.06	13.27	17.45	22.89	29.96	39.12	50.95	66.21

E.g.: If the interest rate is 10% per year, an investment of $1 today will be worth $1.611 at the end of year 5.

							Interest rate r								
16%	17%	18%	19%	20%	21%	22%	23%	24%	25%	26%	27%	28%	29%	30%	t
1.160	1.170	1.180	1.190	1.200	1.210	1.220	1.230	1.240	1.250	1.260	1.270	1.280	1.290	1.300	1
1.346	1.369	1.392	1.416	1.440	1.464	1.488	1.513	1.538	1.562	1.588	1.613	1.638	1.664	1.690	2
1.561	1.602	1.643	1.685	1.728	1.772	1.816	1.861	1.907	1.953	2.000	2.048	2.097	2.147	2.197	3
1.811	1.874	1.939	2.005	2.074	2.144	2.215	2.289	2.364	2.441	2.520	2.601	2.684	2.769	2.856	4
2.100	2.192	2.288	2.386	2.488	2.594	2.703	2.815	2.932	3.052	3.176	3.304	3.436	3.572	3.713	5
2.436	2.565	2.700	2.840	2.986	3.138	3.297	3.463	3.635	3.815	4.002	4.196	4.398	4.608	4.827	6
2.826	3.001	3.185	3.379	3.583	3.797	4.023	4.259	4.508	4.768	5.042	5.329	5.629	5.945	6.275	7
3.278	3.511	3.759	4.021	4.300	4.595	4.908	5.239	5.590	5.960	6.353	6.768	7.206	7.669	8.157	8
3.803	4.108	4.435	4.785	5.160	5.560	5.987	6.444	6.931	7.451	8.005	8.595	9.223	9.893	10.60	9
4.411	4.807	5.234	5.695	6.192	6.727	7.305	7.926	8.594	9.313	10.09	10.92	11.81	12.76	13.79	10
5.117	5.624	6.176	6.777	7.430	8.140	8.912	9.749	10.66	11.64	12.71	13.86	15.11	16.46	17.92	11
5.936	6.580	7.288	8.064	8.916	9.850	10.87	11.99	13.21	14.55	16.01	17.61	19.34	21.24	23.30	12
6.886	7.699	8.599	9.596	10.70	11.92	13.26	14.75	16.39	18.19	20.18	22.36	24.76	27.39	30.29	13
7.988	9.007	10.15	11.42	12.84	14.42	16.18	18.14	20.32	22.74	25.42	28.40	31.69	35.34	39.37	14
9.266	10.54	11.97	13.59	15.41	17.45	19.74	22.31	25.20	28.42	32.03	36.06	40.56	45.59	51.19	15
10.75	12.33	14.13	16.17	18.49	21.11	24.09	27.45	31.24	35.53	40.36	45.80	51.92	58.81	66.54	16
12.47	14.43	16.67	19.24	22.19	25.55	29.38	33.76	38.74	44.41	50.85	58.17	66.46	75.86	86.50	17
14.46	16.88	19.67	22.90	26.62	30.91	35.85	41.52	48.04	55.51	64.07	73.87	85.07	97.86	112.5	18
16.78	19.75	23.21	27.25	31.95	37.40	43.74	51.07	59.57	69.39	80.73	93.81	108.9	126.2	146.2	19
19.46	23.11	27.39	32.43	38.34	45.26	53.36	62.82	73.86	86.74	101.7	119.1	139.4	162.9	190.0	20
22.57	27.03	32.32	38.59	46.01	54.76	65.10	77.27	91.59	108.4	128.2	151.3	178.4	210.1	247.1	21
26.19	31.63	38.14	45.92	55.21	66.26	79.42	95.04	113.6	135.5	161.5	192.2	228.4	271.0	321.2	22
30.38	37.01	45.01	54.65	66.25	80.18	96.89	116.9	140.8	169.4	203.5	244.1	292.3	349.6	417.5	23
35.24	43.30	53.11	65.03	79.50	97.02	118.2	143.8	174.6	211.8	256.4	309.9	374.1	451.0	542.8	24
40.87	50.66	62.67	77.39	95.40	117.4	144.2	176.9	216.5	264.7	323.0	393.6	478.9	581.8	705.6	25
47.41	59.27	73.95	92.09	114.5	142.0	175.9	217.5	268.5	330.9	407.0	499.9	613.0	750.5	917.3	26
55.00	69.35	87.26	109.6	137.4	171.9	214.6	267.6	333.0	413.6	512.9	634.9	784.6	968.1	1193	27
63.80	81.13	103.0	130.4	164.8	208.0	261.9	329.1	412.9	517.0	646.2	806.3	1004	1249	1550	28
74.01	94.93	121.5	155.2	197.8	251.6	319.5	404.8	512.0	646.2	814.2	1024	1286	1611	2015	29
85.85	111.1	143.4	184.7	237.4	304.5	389.8	497.9	634.8	807.8	1026	1301	1646	2078	2620	30

Appendix Table 3 Annuity table: Present value of $1 *per year* for each of t years $= \dfrac{1}{r} - \dfrac{1}{r(1+r)^t}$

	Interest rate r														
t	1%	2%	3%	4%	5%	6%	7%	8%	9%	10%	11%	12%	13%	14%	15%
1	.990	.980	.971	.962	.952	.943	.935	.926	.917	.909	.901	.893	.885	.877	.870
2	1.970	1.942	1.913	1.886	1.859	1.833	1.808	1.783	1.759	1.736	1.713	1.690	1.668	1.647	1.626
3	2.941	2.884	2.829	2.775	2.723	2.673	2.624	2.577	2.531	2.487	2.444	2.402	2.361	2.322	2.283
4	3.902	3.808	3.717	3.630	3.546	3.465	3.387	3.312	3.240	3.170	3.102	3.037	2.974	2.914	2.855
5	4.853	4.713	4.580	4.452	4.329	4.212	4.100	3.993	3.890	3.791	3.696	3.605	3.517	3.433	3.352
6	5.795	5.601	5.417	5.242	5.076	4.917	4.767	4.623	4.486	4.355	4.231	4.111	3.998	3.889	3.784
7	6.728	6.472	6.230	6.002	5.786	5.582	5.389	5.206	5.033	4.868	4.712	4.564	4.423	4.288	4.160
8	7.652	7.325	7.020	6.733	6.463	6.210	5.971	5.747	5.535	5.335	5.146	4.968	4.799	4.639	4.487
9	8.566	8.162	7.786	7.435	7.108	6.802	6.515	6.247	5.995	5.759	5.537	5.328	5.132	4.946	4.772
10	9.471	8.983	8.530	8.111	7.722	7.360	7.024	6.710	6.418	6.145	5.889	5.650	5.426	5.216	5.019
11	10.37	9.787	9.253	8.760	8.306	7.887	7.499	7.139	6.805	6.495	6.207	5.938	5.687	5.453	5.234
12	11.26	10.58	9.954	9.385	8.863	8.384	7.943	7.536	7.161	6.814	6.492	6.194	5.918	5.660	5.421
13	12.13	11.35	10.63	9.986	9.394	8.853	8.358	7.904	7.487	7.103	6.750	6.424	6.122	5.842	5.583
14	13.00	12.11	11.30	10.56	9.899	9.295	8.745	8.244	7.786	7.367	6.982	6.628	6.302	6.002	5.724
15	13.87	12.85	11.94	11.12	10.38	9.712	9.108	8.559	8.061	7.606	7.191	6.811	6.462	6.142	5.847
16	14.72	13.58	12.56	11.65	10.84	10.11	9.447	8.851	8.313	7.824	7.379	6.974	6.604	6.265	5.954
17	15.56	14.29	13.17	12.17	11.27	10.48	9.763	9.122	8.544	8.022	7.549	7.120	6.729	6.373	6.047
18	16.40	14.99	13.75	12.66	11.69	10.83	10.06	9.372	8.756	8.201	7.702	7.250	6.840	6.467	6.128
19	17.23	15.68	14.32	13.13	12.09	11.16	10.34	9.604	8.950	8.365	7.839	7.366	6.938	6.550	6.198
20	18.05	16.35	14.88	13.59	12.46	11.47	10.59	9.818	9.129	8.514	7.963	7.469	7.025	6.623	6.259
21	18.86	17.01	15.42	14.03	12.82	11.76	10.84	10.02	9.292	8.649	8.075	7.562	7.102	6.687	6.312
22	19.66	17.66	15.94	14.45	13.16	12.04	11.06	10.20	9.442	8.772	8.176	7.645	7.170	6.743	6.359
23	20.46	18.29	16.44	14.86	13.49	12.30	11.27	10.37	9.580	8.883	8.266	7.718	7.230	6.792	6.399
24	21.24	18.91	16.94	15.25	13.80	12.55	11.47	10.53	9.707	8.985	8.348	7.784	7.283	6.835	6.434
25	22.02	19.52	17.41	15.62	14.09	12.78	11.65	10.67	9.823	9.077	8.422	7.843	7.330	6.873	6.464
26	22.80	20.12	17.88	15.98	14.38	13.00	11.83	10.81	9.929	9.161	8.488	7.896	7.372	6.906	6.491
27	23.56	20.71	18.33	16.33	14.64	13.21	11.99	10.94	10.03	9.237	8.548	7.943	7.409	6.935	6.514
28	24.32	21.28	18.76	16.66	14.90	13.41	12.14	11.05	10.12	9.307	8.602	7.984	7.441	6.961	6.534
29	25.07	21.84	19.19	16.98	15.14	13.59	12.28	11.16	10.20	9.370	8.650	8.022	7.470	6.983	6.551
30	25.81	22.40	19.60	17.29	15.37	13.76	12.41	11.26	10.27	9.427	8.694	8.055	7.496	7.003	6.566

E.g.: If the interest rate is 10% per year, the present value of $1 to be received at the end of each of the next 5 years is $3.791.

							Interest rate *r*								
16%	17%	18%	19%	20%	21%	22%	23%	24%	25%	26%	27%	28%	29%	30%	*t*
.862	.855	.847	.840	.833	.826	.820	.813	.806	.800	.794	.787	.781	.775	.769	1
1.605	1.585	1.566	1.547	1.528	1.509	1.492	1.474	1.457	1.440	1.424	1.407	1.392	1.376	1.361	2
2.246	2.210	2.174	2.140	2.106	2.074	2.042	2.011	1.981	1.952	1.923	1.896	1.868	1.842	1.816	3
2.798	2.743	2.690	2.639	2.589	2.540	2.494	2.448	2.404	2.362	2.320	2.280	2.241	2.203	2.166	4
3.274	3.199	3.127	3.058	2.991	2.926	2.864	2.803	2.745	2.689	2.635	2.583	2.532	2.483	2.436	5
3.685	3.589	3.498	3.410	3.326	3.245	3.167	3.092	3.020	2.951	2.885	2.821	2.759	2.700	2.643	6
4.039	3.922	3.812	3.706	3.605	3.508	3.416	3.327	3.242	3.161	3.083	3.009	2.937	2.868	2.802	7
4.344	4.207	4.078	3.954	3.837	3.726	3.619	3.518	3.421	3.329	3.241	3.156	3.076	2.999	2.925	8
4.607	4.451	4.303	4.163	4.031	3.905	3.786	3.673	3.566	3.463	3.366	3.273	3.184	3.100	3.019	9
4.833	4.659	4.494	4.339	4.192	4.054	3.923	3.799	3.682	3.571	3.465	3.364	3.269	3.178	3.092	10
5.029	4.836	4.656	4.486	4.327	4.177	4.035	3.902	3.776	3.656	3.543	3.437	3.335	3.239	3.147	11
5.197	4.988	4.793	4.611	4.439	4.278	4.127	3.985	3.851	3.725	3.606	3.493	3.387	3.286	3.190	12
5.342	5.118	4.910	4.715	4.533	4.362	4.203	4.053	3.912	3.780	3.656	3.538	3.427	3.322	3.223	13
5.468	5.229	5.008	4.802	4.611	4.432	4.265	4.108	3.962	3.824	3.695	3.573	3.459	3.351	3.249	14
5.575	5.324	5.092	4.876	4.675	4.489	4.315	4.153	4.001	3.859	3.726	3.601	3.483	3.373	3.268	15
5.668	5.405	5.162	4.938	4.730	4.536	4.357	4.189	4.033	3.887	3.751	3.623	3.503	3.390	3.283	16
5.749	5.475	5.222	4.990	4.775	4.576	4.391	4.219	4.059	3.910	3.771	3.640	3.518	3.403	3.295	17
5.818	5.534	5.273	5.033	4.812	4.608	4.419	4.243	4.080	3.928	3.786	3.654	3.529	3.413	3.304	18
5.877	5.584	5.316	5.070	4.843	4.635	4.442	4.263	4.097	3.942	3.799	3.664	3.539	3.421	3.311	19
5.929	5.628	5.353	5.101	4.870	4.657	4.460	4.279	4.110	3.954	3.808	3.673	3.546	3.427	3.316	20
5.973	5.665	5.384	5.127	4.891	4.675	4.476	4.292	4.121	3.963	3.816	3.679	3.551	3.432	3.320	21
6.011	5.696	5.410	5.149	4.909	4.690	4.488	4.302	4.130	3.970	3.822	3.684	3.556	3.436	3.323	22
6.044	5.723	5.432	5.167	4.925	4.703	4.499	4.311	4.137	3.976	3.827	3.689	3.559	3.438	3.325	23
6.073	5.746	5.451	5.182	4.937	4.713	4.507	4.318	4.143	3.981	3.831	3.692	3.562	3.441	3.327	24
6.097	5.766	5.467	5.195	4.948	4.721	4.514	4.323	4.147	3.985	3.834	3.694	3.564	3.442	3.329	25
6.118	5.783	5.480	5.206	4.956	4.728	4.520	4.328	4.151	3.988	3.837	3.696	3.566	3.444	3.330	26
6.136	5.798	5.492	5.215	4.964	4.734	4.524	4.332	4.154	3.990	3.839	3.698	3.567	3.445	3.331	27
6.152	5.810	5.502	5.223	4.970	4.739	4.528	4.335	4.157	3.992	3.840	3.699	3.568	3.446	3.331	28
6.166	5.820	5.510	5.229	4.975	4.743	4.531	4.337	4.159	3.994	3.841	3.700	3.569	3.446	3.332	29
6.177	5.820	5.517	5.235	4.979	4.746	4.534	4.339	4.160	3.995	3.842	3.701	3.569	3.447	3.332	30

Appendix Table 4 Values of e^{rt}: Future value of $1 invested at a
continuously compounded rate r for t years

rt	.00	.01	.02	.03	.04	.05	.06	.07	.08	.09
.00	1.000	1.010	1.020	1.030	1.041	1.051	1.062	1.073	1.083	1.094
.10	1.105	1.116	1.127	1.139	1.150	1.162	1.174	1.185	1.197	1.209
.20	1.221	1.234	1.246	1.259	1.271	1.284	1.297	1.310	1.323	1.336
.30	1.350	1.363	1.377	1.391	1.405	1.419	1.433	1.448	1.462	1.477
.40	1.492	1.507	1.522	1.537	1.553	1.568	1.584	1.600	1.616	1.632
.50	1.649	1.665	1.682	1.699	1.716	1.733	1.751	1.768	1.786	1.804
.60	1.822	1.840	1.859	1.878	1.896	1.916	1.935	1.954	1.974	1.994
.70	2.014	2.034	2.054	2.075	2.096	2.117	2.138	2.160	2.181	2.203
.80	2.226	2.248	2.270	2.293	2.316	2.340	2.363	2.387	2.411	2.435
.90	2.460	2.484	2.509	2.535	2.560	2.586	2.612	2.638	2.664	2.691
1.00	2.718	2.746	2.773	2.801	2.829	2.858	2.886	2.915	2.945	2.974
1.10	3.004	3.034	3.065	3.096	3.127	3.158	3.190	3.222	3.254	3.287
1.20	3.320	3.353	3.387	3.421	3.456	3.490	3.525	3.561	3.597	3.633
1.30	3.669	3.706	3.743	3.781	3.819	3.857	3.896	3.935	3.975	4.015
1.40	4.055	4.096	4.137	4.179	4.221	4.263	4.306	4.349	4.393	4.437
1.50	4.482	4.527	4.572	4.618	4.665	4.711	4.759	4.807	4.855	4.904
1.60	4.953	5.003	5.053	5.104	5.155	5.207	5.259	5.312	5.366	5.419
1.70	5.474	5.529	5.585	5.641	5.697	5.755	5.812	5.871	5.930	5.989
1.80	6.050	6.110	6.172	6.234	6.297	6.360	6.424	6.488	6.554	6.619
1.90	6.686	6.753	6.821	6.890	6.959	7.029	7.099	7.171	7.243	7.316
2.00	7.389	7.463	7.538	7.614	7.691	7.768	7.846	7.925	8.004	8.085
2.10	8.166	8.248	8.331	8.415	8.499	8.585	8.671	8.758	8.846	8.935
2.20	9.025	9.116	9.207	9.300	9.393	9.488	9.583	9.679	9.777	9.875
2.30	9.974	10.07	10.18	10.28	10.38	10.49	10.59	10.70	10.80	10.91
2.40	11.02	11.13	11.25	11.36	11.47	11.59	11.70	11.82	11.94	12.06
2.50	12.18	12.30	12.43	12.55	12.68	12.81	12.94	13.07	13.20	13.33
2.60	13.46	13.60	13.74	13.87	14.01	14.15	14.30	14.44	14.59	14.73
2.70	14.88	15.03	15.18	15.33	15.49	15.64	15.80	15.96	16.12	16.28
2.80	16.44	16.61	16.78	16.95	17.12	17.29	17.46	17.64	17.81	17.99
2.90	18.17	18.36	18.54	18.73	18.92	19.11	19.30	19.49	19.69	19.89

E.g.: If the continuously compounded interest rate is 10% per year, an investment
of $1 today will be worth $1.105 by the end of year 1, $1.162 by the end of
year 1.5, and $1.221 by the end of year 2.

r t	.00	.01	.02	.03	.04	.05	.06	.07	.08	.09
3.00	20.09	20.29	20.49	20.70	20.91	21.12	21.33	21.54	21.76	21.98
3.10	22.20	22.42	22.65	22.87	23.10	23.34	23.57	23.81	24.05	24.29
3.20	24.53	24.78	25.03	25.28	25.53	25.79	26.05	26.31	26.58	26.84
3.30	27.11	27.39	27.66	27.94	28.22	28.50	28.79	29.08	29.37	29.67
3.40	29.96	30.27	30.57	30.88	31.19	31.50	31.82	32.14	32.46	32.79
3.50	33.12	33.45	33.78	34.12	34.47	34.81	35.16	35.52	35.87	36.23
3.60	36.60	36.97	37.34	37.71	38.09	38.47	38.86	39.25	39.65	40.04
3.70	40.45	40.85	41.26	41.68	42.10	42.52	42.95	43.38	43.82	44.26
3.80	44.70	45.15	45.60	46.06	46.53	46.99	47.47	47.94	48.42	48.91
3.90	49.40	49.90	50.40	50.91	51.42	51.94	52.46	52.98	53.52	54.05
4.00	54.60	55.15	55.70	56.26	56.83	57.40	57.97	58.56	59.15	59.74
4.10	60.34	60.95	61.56	62.18	62.80	63.43	64.07	64.72	65.37	66.02
4.20	66.69	67.36	68.03	68.72	69.41	70.11	70.81	71.52	72.24	72.97
4.30	73.70	74.44	75.19	75.94	76.71	77.48	78.26	79.04	79.84	80.64
4.40	81.45	82.27	83.10	83.93	84.77	85.63	86.49	87.36	88.23	89.12
4.50	90.02	90.92	91.84	92.76	93.69	94.63	95.58	96.54	97.51	98.49
4.60	99.48	100.5	101.5	102.5	103.5	104.6	105.6	106.7	107.8	108.9
4.70	109.9	111.1	112.2	113.3	114.4	115.6	116.7	117.9	119.1	120.3
4.80	121.5	122.7	124.0	125.2	126.5	127.7	129.0	130.3	131.6	133.0
4.90	134.3	135.6	137.0	138.4	139.8	141.2	142.6	144.0	145.5	146.9
5.00	148.4	149.9	151.4	152.9	154.5	156.0	157.6	159.2	160.8	162.4
5.10	164.0	165.7	167.3	169.0	170.7	172.4	174.2	175.9	177.7	179.5
5.20	181.3	183.1	184.9	186.8	188.7	190.6	192.5	194.4	196.4	198.3
5.30	200.3	202.4	204.4	206.4	208.5	210.6	212.7	214.9	217.0	219.2
5.40	221.4	223.6	225.9	228.1	230.4	232.8	235.1	237.5	239.8	242.3
5.50	244.7	247.2	249.6	252.1	254.7	257.2	259.8	262.4	265.1	267.7
5.60	270.4	273.1	275.9	278.7	281.5	284.3	287.1	290.0	292.9	295.9
5.70	298.9	301.9	304.9	308.0	311.1	314.2	317.3	320.5	323.8	327.0
5.80	330.3	333.6	337.0	340.4	343.8	347.2	350.7	354.2	357.8	361.4
5.90	365.0	368.7	372.4	376.2	379.9	383.8	387.6	391.5	395.4	399.4

Appendix Table 5 Continuous annuity table: Present value of $1 per year received in a continuous stream for each of t years discounted at an *annually compounded* rate r is $\dfrac{1}{\ln(1+r)}\left(1-\dfrac{1}{(1+r)^t}\right)$

	Interest rate r														
t	1%	2%	3%	4%	5%	6%	7%	8%	9%	10%	11%	12%	13%	14%	15%
1	.995	.990	.985	.981	.976	.971	.967	.962	.958	.954	.950	.945	.941	.937	.933
2	1.980	1.961	1.942	1.924	1.906	1.888	1.871	1.854	1.837	1.821	1.805	1.790	1.774	1.759	1.745
3	2.956	2.913	2.871	2.830	2.791	2.752	2.715	2.679	2.644	2.609	2.576	2.543	2.512	2.481	2.450
4	3.921	3.846	3.773	3.702	3.634	3.568	3.504	3.443	3.383	3.326	3.270	3.216	3.164	3.113	3.064
5	4.878	4.760	4.648	4.540	4.437	4.338	4.242	4.150	4.062	3.977	3.896	3.817	3.741	3.668	3.598
6	5.824	5.657	5.498	5.346	5.202	5.063	4.931	4.805	4.685	4.570	4.459	4.353	4.252	4.155	4.062
7	6.762	6.536	6.323	6.121	5.930	5.748	5.576	5.412	5.256	5.108	4.967	4.832	4.704	4.582	4.465
8	7.690	7.398	7.124	6.867	6.623	6.394	6.178	5.974	5.780	5.597	5.424	5.260	5.104	4.956	4.816
9	8.609	8.244	7.902	7.583	7.284	7.004	6.741	6.494	6.261	6.042	5.836	5.642	5.458	5.285	5.121
10	9.519	9.072	8.658	8.272	7.913	7.579	7.267	6.975	6.702	6.447	6.208	5.983	5.772	5.573	5.386
11	10.42	9.884	9.391	8.935	8.512	8.121	7.758	7.421	7.107	6.815	6.542	6.287	6.049	5.826	5.617
12	11.31	10.68	10.10	9.572	9.083	8.633	8.218	7.834	7.478	7.149	6.843	6.559	6.294	6.048	5.818
13	12.19	11.46	10.79	10.18	9.627	9.116	8.647	8.216	7.819	7.453	7.115	6.802	6.512	6.242	5.992
14	13.07	12.23	11.46	10.77	10.14	9.571	9.048	8.570	8.131	7.729	7.359	7.018	6.704	6.413	6.144
15	13.93	12.98	12.12	11.34	10.64	10.00	9.423	8.897	8.418	7.980	7.579	7.212	6.874	6.563	6.276
16	14.79	13.71	12.75	11.88	11.11	10.41	9.774	9.201	8.681	8.209	7.778	7.385	7.024	6.694	6.390
17	15.64	14.43	13.36	12.41	11.55	10.79	10.10	9.482	8.923	8.416	7.957	7.539	7.158	6.809	6.490
18	16.48	15.14	13.96	12.91	11.98	11.15	10.41	9.742	9.144	8.605	8.118	7.676	7.275	6.910	6.577
19	17.31	15.83	14.54	13.39	12.38	11.49	10.69	9.983	9.347	8.777	8.263	7.799	7.380	6.999	6.652
20	18.14	16.51	15.10	13.86	12.77	11.81	10.96	10.21	9.533	8.932	8.394	7.909	7.472	7.077	6.718
21	18.95	17.18	15.65	14.31	13.14	12.11	11.21	10.41	9.704	9.074	8.511	8.007	7.554	7.145	6.775
22	19.76	17.83	16.17	14.74	13.49	12.40	11.44	10.60	9.861	9.203	8.618	8.095	7.626	7.205	6.824
23	20.56	18.47	16.69	15.15	13.82	12.67	11.66	10.78	10.01	9.320	8.713	8.173	7.690	7.257	6.868
24	21.35	19.10	17.19	15.55	14.14	12.92	11.87	10.94	10.14	9.427	8.799	8.243	7.747	7.303	6.905
25	22.13	19.72	17.67	15.93	14.44	13.16	12.06	11.10	10.26	9.524	8.877	8.305	7.797	7.344	6.938
26	22.91	20.32	18.14	16.30	14.73	13.39	12.24	11.24	10.37	9.612	8.947	8.360	7.841	7.379	6.966
27	23.68	20.91	18.60	16.65	15.01	13.60	12.40	11.37	10.47	9.692	9.010	8.410	7.880	7.410	6.991
28	24.44	21.49	19.04	16.99	15.27	13.80	12.56	11.49	10.56	9.765	9.066	8.454	7.915	7.437	7.012
29	25.19	22.06	19.47	17.32	15.52	13.99	12.70	11.60	10.65	9.831	9.118	8.494	7.946	7.461	7.031
30	25.94	22.62	19.89	17.64	15.75	14.17	12.84	11.70	10.73	9.891	9.164	8.529	7.973	7.482	7.047

E.g.: If the interest rate is 10% per year, a continuous cash flow of $1 per year for each of 5 years is worth $3.977. A continuous flow of $1 in year 5 only is worth 3.977 − 3.326 = $0.651.

						Interest rate *r*									
16%	17%	18%	19%	20%	21%	22%	23%	24%	25%	26%	27%	28%	29%	30%	*t*
.929	.925	.922	.918	.914	.910	.907	.903	.900	.896	.893	.889	.886	.883	.880	1
1.730	1.716	1.703	1.689	1.676	1.663	1.650	1.638	1.625	1.613	1.601	1.590	1.578	1.567	1.556	2
2.421	2.392	2.365	2.337	2.311	2.285	2.259	2.235	2.211	2.187	2.164	2.141	2.119	2.098	2.077	3
3.016	2.970	2.925	2.882	2.840	2.799	2.759	2.720	2.682	2.646	2.610	2.576	2.542	2.509	2.477	4
3.530	3.464	3.401	3.340	3.281	3.223	3.168	3.115	3.063	3.013	2.964	2.917	2.872	2.828	2.785	5
3.972	3.886	3.804	3.724	3.648	3.574	3.504	3.436	3.370	3.307	3.246	3.187	3.130	3.075	3.022	6
4.354	4.247	4.145	4.048	3.954	3.865	3.779	3.696	3.617	3.542	3.469	3.399	3.331	3.266	3.204	7
4.682	4.555	4.434	4.319	4.209	4.104	4.004	3.909	3.817	3.730	3.646	3.566	3.489	3.415	3.344	8
4.966	4.819	4.680	4.547	4.422	4.302	4.189	4.081	3.978	3.880	3.786	3.697	3.612	3.530	3.452	9
5.210	5.044	4.887	4.739	4.599	4.466	4.340	4.221	4.108	4.000	3.898	3.801	3.708	3.619	3.535	10
5.421	5.237	5.063	4.900	4.747	4.602	4.465	4.335	4.213	4.096	3.986	3.882	3.783	3.689	3.599	11
5.603	5.401	5.213	5.036	4.870	4.713	4.566	4.428	4.297	4.173	4.057	3.946	3.841	3.742	3.648	12
5.759	5.542	5.339	5.150	4.972	4.806	4.650	4.503	4.365	4.235	4.112	3.997	3.887	3.784	3.686	13
5.894	5.662	5.446	5.245	5.058	4.882	4.718	4.564	4.420	4.284	4.157	4.036	3.923	3.816	3.715	14
6.010	5.765	5.537	5.326	5.129	4.945	4.774	4.614	4.464	4.324	4.192	4.068	3.951	3.841	3.737	15
6.111	5.853	5.614	5.393	5.188	4.998	4.820	4.655	4.500	4.355	4.220	4.092	3.973	3.860	3.754	16
6.197	5.928	5.679	5.450	5.238	5.041	4.858	4.687	4.529	4.381	4.242	4.112	3.990	3.875	3.767	17
6.272	5.992	5.735	5.498	5.279	5.076	4.889	4.714	4.552	4.401	4.259	4.127	4.003	3.887	3.778	18
6.336	6.047	5.782	5.538	5.313	5.106	4.914	4.736	4.571	4.417	4.273	4.139	4.014	3.896	3.785	19
6.391	6.094	5.821	5.571	5.342	5.130	4.935	4.754	4.586	4.430	4.284	4.149	4.022	3.903	3.791	20
6.439	6.134	5.855	5.600	5.366	5.150	4.952	4.768	4.598	4.440	4.293	4.156	4.028	3.908	3.796	21
6.480	6.168	5.883	5.623	5.385	5.167	4.966	4.780	4.608	4.448	4.300	4.162	4.033	3.913	3.800	22
6.516	6.197	5.908	5.643	5.402	5.181	4.977	4.789	4.616	4.455	4.306	4.167	4.037	3.916	3.802	23
6.546	6.222	5.928	5.660	5.416	5.192	4.986	4.797	4.622	4.460	4.310	4.170	4.040	3.918	3.804	24
6.573	6.244	5.945	5.674	5.427	5.201	4.994	4.803	4.627	4.464	4.314	4.173	4.042	3.920	3.806	25
6.596	6.262	5.960	5.686	5.437	5.209	5.000	4.808	4.631	4.468	4.316	4.175	4.044	3.922	3.807	26
6.615	6.277	5.973	5.696	5.445	5.216	5.005	4.813	4.635	4.471	4.318	4.177	4.046	3.923	3.808	27
6.632	6.291	5.983	5.705	5.452	5.221	5.010	4.816	4.637	4.473	4.320	4.179	4.047	3.924	3.809	28
6.647	6.302	5.992	5.712	5.457	5.225	5.013	4.819	4.640	4.474	4.322	4.180	4.048	3.925	3.810	29
6.659	6.312	6.000	5.718	5.462	5.229	5.016	4.821	4.641	4.476	4.323	4.181	4.048	3.925	3.810	30

Glossary

additional paid-in capital: Difference between issue price and par value of stock. Also called capital surplus.

agency problem: Conflict of interest between the firm's owners and managers.

aging schedule: Classification of accounts receivable by time outstanding.

annual percentage rate (APR): Interest rate that is annualized using simple interest.

annuity: Equally spaced level stream of cash flows.

annuity factor: Present value of a $1 annuity.

articles of incorporation: A legal document outlining the nature of the firm's business and the characteristics of its shares and the rights of its shareholders.

asset beta: Market risk of the firm's projects.

asset classes: Each depreciable asset is assigned to an asset class for tax purposes. The definition as well as the maximum allowable depreciation rate for each category is set by Revenue Canada.

authorized share capital: Maximum number of shares that the company is permitted to issue, as specified in the firm's articles of incorporation.

availability float: Cheques already deposited that have not yet been cleared.

average tax rate: Total taxes owed divided by total taxable income.

balance sheet: Financial statement that shows the value of the firm's assets and liabilities at a particular time.

balancing item: Variable that adjusts to maintain the consistency of a financial plan. Also called *plug*.

banker's acceptance: Short-term unsecured notes issued by a firm and guaranteed by a bank.

bankruptcy: The reorganization or liquidation of a firm that cannot pay its debts.

beta: Sensitivity of a stock's return to the return on the market portfolio.

bond: Security that obligates the issuer to make specified payments to the bondholder.

book rate of return: Average income divided by average book value over project life. Also called accounting rate of return.

book value: Net worth of the firm according to the balance sheet.

break-even analysis: Analysis of the level of sales at which the company breaks even.

call option: Right to buy an asset at a specified exercise price on or before the exercise date.

callable bond: Bond that may be repurchased by firm before maturity at specified call price.

capital asset pricing model (CAPM): Theory of the relationship between risk and return which states that the expected risk premium on any security equals its beta times the market risk premium.

capital budget: List of planned investment projects.

capital budgeting decision: Decision as to which real assets the firm should acquire.

capital cost allowance: The depreciation charge against taxable income allowed by Revenue Canada.

capital gain (loss): The amount by which the selling price of an asset exceeds (is less than) the price at which the asset was bought.

capital markets: Markets for long-term financing.

capital rationing: Limit set on the amount of funds available for investment.

capital structure: Firm's mix of long-term financing.

carrying costs: Costs of maintaining current assets, including opportunity cost of capital.

cash conversion cycle: Period between firm's payment for materials and collection on its sales.

cash dividend: Payment of cash by the firm to its shareholders.

CCA tax shield or depreciation tax shield: Reduction in taxes attributable to the capital cost allowance.

chief financial officer (CFO): Officer who oversees the treasurer and controller and sets overall financial strategy.

collection policy: Procedures to collect and monitor receivables.

commercial paper: Short-term unsecured notes issued by firms.

common stock: Ownership shares in a publicly held corporation.

common-size balance sheet: Balance sheet that presents items as a percentage of total assets.

company cost of capital: Expected rate of return demanded by investors in a company, determined by the average risk of the company's assets and operations.

compound interest: Interest earned on interest.

concentration banking: System whereby customers make payments to a regional collection centre that transfers funds to a principal account.

constant-growth dividend discount model: Version of the dividend discount model in which dividends grow at a constant rate. Also called the Gordon growth model.

controller: Officer responsible for budgeting, accounting, and auditing.

convertible bond: Bond that the holder may exchange for a specified amount of another security.

corporation: A business owned by stockholders who have limited liability.

correlation coefficient: Measure of the closeness of the relationship between two variables.

costs of financial distress: Costs arising from bankruptcy or distorted business decisions before bankruptcy.

coupon: The interest payments paid to the bondholder.

coupon rate: Annual interest payment as a percentage of face value.

credit analysis: Procedure to determine the likelihood a customer will pay its bills.

credit policy: Standards set to determine the amount and nature of credit to extend to customers.

cumulative voting: Voting system in which all the votes one shareholder is allowed to cast can be cast for one candidate for the board of directors.

current yield: Annual coupon payments divided by current price.

decision tree: Diagram of alternative sequential decisions and possible outcomes.

default premium: Difference in promised yields between a default-free bond and a riskier bond.

degree of operating leverage (DOL): Percentage change in profits given a 1 percent change in sales.

discount factor: Present value of a $1 future payment.

discount rate: Interest rate used to compute present values of future cash flows.

diversification: Strategy designed to reduce risk by spreading the portfolio across many investments.

dividend discount model: Computation of today's stock price which states that share value equals the present value of all expected future dividends.

dividend payout ratio: Percentage of earnings paid out as dividends.

dividend tax credit: A credit given by Revenue Canada to any individual receiving dividends from a Canadian company. The credit reflects part of the taxes already paid by the company on the dividend.

dividends: Periodic cash distributions from the firm to its shareholders.

Dow Jones Industrial Average: Index of the investment performance of a portfolio of 30 U.S. "blue-chip" stocks.

Du Pont System: Group of relationships that breaks down ROE and ROA into component ratios.

economic order quantity: Order size that minimizes total inventory costs.

effective annual interest rate: The rate of interest that would apply if interest was compounded once per year.

efficient capital markets: Financial markets in which security prices reflect all relevant information about asset values available.

equivalent annual cost: The cost per period with the same present value as the cost of buying and operating a machine.

eurobond: Bond that is marketed internationally, typically outside the country in whose currency the bond is denominated.

eurocurrency: Money deposited in financial institutions outside the currency's home country. For example, euroCanadian dollars are Canadian dollars held outside of Canada.

eurodollars deposits: Dollars held on deposit in a bank outside of Canada.

exchange rate: Amount of one currency needed to purchase one unit of another.

ex-dividend date: Date that determines whether a stockholder is entitled to a dividend payment; anyone holding stock before this date is entitled to a dividend.

face value: Payment at the maturity of the bond. Also called par value or maturity value.

financial assets: Claims to the income generated by real assets. Also called *securities*.

financial leverage: Increase in the variability of shareholder returns that comes from the use of debt.

financial markets: Markets in which financial assets are traded.

financial risk: Risk to shareholders resulting from the use of debt.

financing decision: Decision as to how to raise the money to pay for a firm's investments in real assets.

fixed costs: Costs incurred regardless of the level of output.

floating-rate preferred: Preferred stock paying dividends that vary with short-term interest rates.

foreign bond: Bond that is marketed outside the country of the borrower and inside the country in whose currency it is denominated.

forward contract: Nontradeable contract to buy or sell an asset in the future at an agreed price.

forward exchange rate: Exchange rate for a forward transaction.

fundamental analysts: Analysts who attempt to find under- or overvalued securities by analyzing fundamental information, such as earnings, asset values, and business prospects.

future value: Amount to which an investment will grow after earning interest.

futures contract: Tradable contract to buy or sell an asset in the future at an agreed price.

general cash offer: Sale of securities open to all investors by an already-public company.

generally accepted accounting principles (GAAP): Procedures for preparing financial statements.

income statement: Financial statement that shows the revenues, expenses, and net income of a firm over a period of time.

inflation: Rate at which prices as a whole are increasing.

initial public offering (IPO): First offering of stock to the general public.

interest rate parity: Theory that forward premium equals interest rate differential.

interest tax shield: Tax savings resulting from deductibility of interest payments.

internal growth rate: Maximum rate of growth without external financing.

internal rate of return (IRR): Discount rate at which project NPV = 0.

internally generated funds: Cash reinvested in the firm; depreciation plus earnings not paid out as dividends.

international Fisher effect: Theory that real interest rates in all countries should be equal, with differences in nominal rates reflecting differences in expected inflation.

investment grade: Bonds rated B++ or above by the Canadian Bond Rating Service or BBB or above by the Dominion Bond Rating Service.

issued shares: Shares that have been issued by the company.

junk bond: Bond with a rating of B+ or below by the Canadian Bond Rating

Service (BB or below by the Dominion Bond Rating Service).

law of one price: Theory that prices of goods in all countries should be equal when translated to a common currency.

lease: Long-term rental agreement.

leveraged buy-out (LBO): Acquisition of the firm by a private group using substantial borrowed funds.

limited liability: The owners of the corporation are not personally responsible for its obligations.

line of credit: Agreement by a bank that a company may borrow at any time up to an established limit.

liquidation: Sale of bankrupt firm's assets.

liquidation value: Net proceeds that would be realized by selling the firm's assets and paying off its creditors.

liquidity: Ability of an asset to be converted to cash quickly at low cost.

lock-box system: System whereby customers send payments to a post office box and a local bank collects and processes cheques.

long-term debt: Debt with more than 1 year remaining to maturity.

majority voting: Voting system in which each director is voted on separately.

management buy-out (MBO): Acquisition of the firm by its own management in a leveraged buy-out.

marginal tax rate: Additional taxes owed per dollar of additional income.

market index: Measure of the investment performance of the overall market.

market portfolio: Portfolio of all assets in the economy. In practice a broad stock market index, such as the TSE 300 is used to represent the market.

market risk: Economy-wide (macroeconomic) sources of risk that affect the overall stock market. Also called *systematic risk.*

market risk premium: Risk premium of market portfolio. Difference between market return and return on risk-free Treasury bills.

market-value balance sheet: Financial statement that uses the market value of all assets and liabilities.

maturity premium: Extra average return from investing in long- versus short-term Treasury securities.

merger: Combination of two firms into one, with the acquirer assuming assets and liabilities of the target firm.

MM dividend-irrelevance proposition: Theory that under ideal conditions, the value of the firm is unaffected by dividend policy.

MM's Proposition I (debt irrelevance proposition): The value of a firm is unaffected by its capital structure.

MM's Proposition II: The required rate of return on equity increases as the firm's debt-equity ratio increases.

money market: Market for short-term financial assets.

multiple voting shares: Common shares with more than one vote per share. Multiple voting shares are always found in companies with subordinate voting shares.

mutually exclusive projects: Two or more projects that cannot be pursued simultaneously.

net float: Difference between payment and availability float.

net present value (NPV): Present value of project cash flows minus initial investment.

net working capital: Current assets minus current liabilities. Often called working capital.

net worth: Book value of common stockholders' equity plus preferred stock.

nominal interest rate: Rate at which money invested grows.

non-voting shares: Restricted shares that do not entitle shareholders the right to vote for the board of directors.

off-balance sheet items: Assets and liabilities that are not shown on the balance sheet but nonetheless have genuine financial consequences for the firm, such as short-term leases and swaps.

open account: Agreement whereby sales are made with no formal debt contract.

operating leverage: Degree to which costs are fixed.

operating risk, business risk: Risk in total income of the firm.

opportunity cost: Benefit or cash flow forgone as a result of an action.

opportunity cost of capital: Expected rate of return given up by investing in a project.

option: The right to buy or sell an asset in the future at a stipulated price.

outstanding shares: Shares that have been issued by the company and are held by investors.

par value: Value of security shown on certificate.

partnership: A business owned by two or more persons who are personally responsible for all its liabilities.

payback period: Time until cash flows recover the initial investment of the project.

payment float: Cheques written by a company that have not yet cleared.

payout ratio: Fraction of earnings paid out as dividends.

pecking order theory: Theory stating that firms prefer to issue debt rather than equity if internal finance is insufficient.

percentage of sales model: Planning model in which sales forecasts are the driving variables and other variables are proportional to sales.

perpetuity: Stream of level cash payments that never ends.

planning horizon: Time horizon corresponding to a financial plan.

plowback ratio: Fraction of earnings retained by the firm.

poison pill: Measure taken by a target firm to avoid acquisition; for example, the right for existing shareholders to buy additional shares at an attractive price if a bidder acquires a large holding.

POP System: A procedure that allows qualifying firms to file a short-form version of a prospectus with Ontario Securities Commission to speed up the issuing process.

preferred stock: Stock that takes priority over common stock in regard to dividends.

present value (PV): Value today of a future cash flow.

present value of growth opportunities (PVGO): Net present value of a firm's future investments.

price-earnings (P/E) multiple: Ratio of stock price to earnings per share.

primary market: Market for the sale of new securities by corporations.

prime rate: Interest rate at which banks lend to most favoured customers.

private placement: Sale of securities to a limited number of investors without a public offering.

pro formas: Projected or forecast financial statements.

profitability index: Ratio of present value to initial investment.

project cost of capital: Minimum acceptable expected rate of return on a project given its risk.

prospectus: Formal summary that provides information on an issue of securities.

protective covenant: Restriction on a firm to protect bondholders.

proxy contest: Takeover attempt in which outsiders compete with management for shareholders' votes. Also called *proxy fight.*

purchasing power parity (PPP): Theory that the cost of living in different countries is equal, and exchange rates adjust to offset inflation differentials across countries.

pure play approach: Estimating project cost of capital using the cost of capital of another company involved exclusively in the same type of project.

put option: Right to sell an asset at a specified exercise price on or before the exercise date.

random walk: Security prices change randomly, with no predictable trends or patterns.

rate of return: Earnings per period per dollar invested.

real asset: Asset used to produce goods and services.

real interest rate: Rate at which the purchasing power of an investment increases.

real options: Implicit options on real assets.

real value of $1: Purchasing power-adjusted value of a dollar.

recaptured depreciation: When the sale of an asset would result in an as-

set class with a negative balance, the amount of the negative balance is referred to as recaptured depreciation and is included in taxable income.

reorganization: Restructuring of financial claims on failing firm to allow it to keep operating.

restricted shares: Common shares that do not have voting rights equal to another class of common shares issued by the firm.

restricted voting shares: Restricted shares that have special limitations on voting rights of shareholders. For example, only Canadian shareholders may be entitled to vote or each shareholder may have a maximum number of votes, regardless of the number of shares owned.

restructuring: Process of changing the firm's capital structure without changing its assets.

retained earnings: Earnings not paid out as dividends.

rights issue: Issue of securities offered only to current stockholders.

risk premium: Expected return in excess of risk-free return as compensation for risk.

scenario analysis: Project analysis given a particular combination of assumptions.

secondary market: Market in which already-issued securities are traded among investors.

secured debt: Debt that has first claim on specified collateral in the event of default.

security market line: Relationship between expected return and beta.

semi-strong-form efficiency: Situation in which market prices reflect all publicly available information.

sensitivity analysis: Analysis of the effects of changes in sales, costs, and so on, on project profitability.

shark repellent: Amendments to a company charter made to forestall take-over attempts.

shortage costs: Costs incurred from shortages in current assets.

simple interest: Interest earned only on the original investment; no interest is earned on interest.

sinking fund: Fund established to retire debt before maturity.

sole proprietor: The sole owner of a business that has no partners and no shareholders.

spot exchange rate: Exchange rate for an immediate transaction.

spread: Difference between public offer price and price paid by underwriter.

stakeholder: Anyone with a financial interest in the firm.

Standard and Poor's Composite Index: Index of the investment performance of a portfolio of 500 large U.S. stocks. Also called the *S&P 500.*

standard deviation: Square root of variance. Another measure of volatility.

statement of cash flows: Financial statement that shows the firm's cash receipts and cash payments over a period of time.

stock dividend: Distribution of additional shares to a firm's stockholders.

stock repurchase: Firm buys back stock from its shareholders.

stock split: Issue of additional shares to firm's stockholders.

straight-line depreciation: Depreciation method in which a constant proportion of the cost is depreciated each year over the accounting life.

strong-form efficiency: Situation in which prices rapidly reflect all information that could in principle be used to determine true value.

subordinate voting shares: Restricted shares that have fewer votes per share than another class of common shares.

subordinated debt: Debt that may be repaid in bankruptcy only after senior debt is paid.

subscription price: Price to be paid per share in a rights offering.

sustainable growth rate: Steady rate at which a firm can grow without changing leverage; plowback ratio × return on equity.

swap: Agreement between two firms to exchange a series of future payments on different terms.

technical analysts: Analysts who attempt to find patterns in security price movements.

tender offer: Takeover attempt in which outsiders directly offer to buy the stock of the firm's shareholders.

term structure of interest rates: Relationship between time to maturity and yield to maturity.

terminal loss: When the last asset in an asset class is sold and the asset class has a positive balance, the balance is treated as a loss for tax purposes and referred to as a terminal loss. Recognizing a terminal loss will result in the UCC being set to zero.

terms of sale: Credit and discount terms offered on a sale.

Toronto Stock Exchange (TSE) 300 Composite Index: Index of the investment performance of a portfolio of 300 major stocks listed on the Toronto Stock Exchange. Also called the *TSE 300.*

Toronto Stock Exchange (TSE) 300 Total Return Index: Index based on the prices plus the dividends paid by the 300 stocks in the TSE 300 Composite Index.

trade-off theory: Theory that capital structure is based on a trade-off between tax savings and distress costs of debt.

treasurer: Manager responsible for financing, cash management, and relationships with financial markets and institutions.

undepreciated capital cost (UCC): The amount of an asset class that has not been depreciated for tax purposes.

underpricing: Issuing securities whose offering price is set below true value of the security.

underwriter: Firm that buys an issue of securities from a company and resells it to the public.

unique risk: Risk factors affecting only that firm. Also called diversifiable risk.

variable cost: Costs that rise with the level of output.

variance: Average value of squared deviations from mean. A measure of volatility.

venture capital: Money invested to finance a new firm.

warrant: Right to buy shares from a company at a stipulated price before a set date.

weak-form efficiency: Situation in which market prices rapidly reflect all information contained in the history of past prices.

weighted-average cost of capital (WACC): Expected rate of return on a portfolio of all the firm's securities.

white knight: Friendly potential acquirer sought by a target company threatened by an unwelcome suitor.

workout: Informal arrangement between debtor and creditor establishing steps debtor may take to avoid declaring bankruptcy.

yield curve: Graph of the term structure.

yield to maturity: Interest rate for which the present value of the bond's payments equals the price.

Index

— — — — — — — — — — cut here — — — — — — — — — —

STUDENT REPLY CARD

In order to improve future editions, we are seeking your comments on
Fundamentals of Corporate Finance, First Canadian Edition,
by Giammarino, Maynes, Brealey, Myers, and Marcus. After you have read this
text, please answer the following questions and return this form via Business Reply
Mail. *Your opinions matter! Thank you in advance for your feedback!*

Name of your college or university: _____

Major program of study: _____

Course title: _____

Were you required to buy this book? ——— yes ——— no

Did you buy this book new or used? ——— new ——— used ($ ———)

Do you plan to keep or sell this book? ——— keep ——— sell

Is the order of topic coverage consistent with what was taught in your course?

cut here

— — — — — — — — — fold here — — — — — — — — — —

Are there chapters or sections of this text that were not assigned for your course?
Please specify:

Were there topics covered in your course that are not included in this text?
Please specify:

What did you like most about this text?

What did you like least?

If you would like to say more, we'd love to hear from you. Please write to us at the
address shown on the reverse of this card.

— — — — — — — — — — — — — — — — cut here — — — — — — — — — —

— — — — — — — — — — — — — — fold here — — — — — — — —

Postage will be paid by

MAIL ⮚ POSTE

Canada Post Corporation / Société canadienne des postes

Postage paid
if mailed in Canada

Port payé
si posté au Canada

**Business
Reply**

**Réponse
d'affaires**

0183560299   01

cut here

0183560299-L1N9B6-BR01

Attn.: Sponsoring Editor
College Division

MCGRAW-HILL RYERSON LIMITED
300 WATER ST
WHITBY ON   L1N 9Z9